PERSONALITY

PERSONALITY

A Biosocial Approach
to Origins and Structure

BY

GARDNER MURPHY

BASIC BOOKS, INC., PUBLISHERS

New York   London

For L O I S

Personality Revisited

IN 1947 I made an effort to put into ordered form the ideas about personality that I had thought out and shared with others, especially with my wife, Lois, for a good many years.

This book is not based, as are many books about personality, on clinical data. I had no competence in the matter of making a clinical book, and I may as well deal first of all with this question of the clinical versus the general or "normal" or everyday, functional view of personality.

It seems to me that owing to quite evident historical forces—some of them socio-economic, some of them broadly intellectual and cultural—personality was first seriously investigated by clinicians. I have in mind the great European physicians of the eighteenth and early nineteenth centuries—people like Itard, Maudsley, Ribot—and, later, Sigmund Freud and his collaborators, followers, and competitors, who developed, with varying success, modes of systematic description and interpretation of personality based largely upon clinical observations. They accomplished a remarkable work indeed.

But I think of the parallel to the task of building a bridge. Suppose that the art of bridge-building were not very well developed, and that engineers were known mainly as men who mended broken bridges, who shored up defective spans, who marked necessary detours near abutments, and who wrote systematic—even brilliant—treatises on how bridges can fail to serve their functions. It seems that the presence of a great deal of recognizable psychopathology in our society during the nineteenth century, and the availability of very little sound and systematic psychology, forced the systematists to become engineers and forced many who were not systematic at all to try to develop engineering and systematic bridge theory at the same time. I agree that there is need for a large number of experienced clinicians working on personality material. I suspect that today they outnumber the systematic non-clinical students of personality by at least a hundred to one. I don't know whether this is good or bad. Perhaps, however, an effort toward achieving a balance is appropriate when the long-range development of personality theory and the various applied forms of personality practice are concerned. At any rate, I have tried to use *every* kind of psychological data that exist.

Another question arises: If we are not primarily clinicians, do we not have to agree that *normal child development* offers the sole basis for personality study? Child development began to come into its innings after the First World War, especially through the development of behavior studies in childhood with the aid of large private foundations, and of university nursery schools and departments of child development. I am afraid that the behavior theory which they promulgated as a system of scientific facts was itself extraordinarily thin and naïve, and offered very little knowledge of human conditions and human potentials. Moreover, these efforts, after the First World War, and continuing to today, inevitably began to be soaked and saturated in clinical material, or to be referred vaguely to general dynamic principles which are supposed to have emerged somewhere by direct observation, though no specification of the clinical tools through which they were observed is vouchsafed to the reader. The result, I feel, is that child development, a potentially valuable source of information about basic personality structure, growth, functioning, and meaning, is not really in a position today to provide all that systematic theory requires. There are many other kinds of necessary information: from genetics, from learning theory, from physiology, from neuropsychology, from phenomenology, and from the world of the arts.

Objection might well be raised: It may be maintained that cultural anthropology, so brilliantly developed in this century, especially by British and American students of "personality and culture," has given us a broad functional picture of personality, replacing essentially what psychology, as psychology, could offer. Here again, I cannot agree that any one method is all-sufficient. It seems to me that the wisest and most mature of the cultural anthropologies, as expressed for example in the work of Boas, Benedict, and Mead, has represented biological individuality and the individual dynamics of growth as both a constant foil and a constant aid to the study of cultural predispositions and cultural shapings of personality growth. Indeed I have, though without benefit of anthropological field training, felt myself into this way of integrated thinking for a very long time, and I have attempted to do justice to it toward the end of the present volume.

Such a book as this is likely to be called "eclectic." The word means two very different things: (1) the juxtaposition of fragments from different systems, effecting a loose federation of essentially unrelated ideas; (2) the organization of a coherent theoretical system into which observations from different viewpoints can be integrated. It is in the second sense that I respect and try to accept this conception.

These few words, then, by way of retrospective explanation of a book which aspires to develop a system, and tries to utilize clinical and cross-cultural approaches, but does not in any sense repudiate the responsibility of psychology for systematic personality theory as we move on into the last third of the twentieth century. To try to bring it up to date, however, would completely, fundamentally, and absolutely alter the book. There are, in the years which I hope are still remaining for me, many tasks to which I feel a heavy commitment. I do not really feel that rewriting this book is warranted. Joint authorship in the development of these ideas with other good friends who share my way of thinking is indeed in the cards. There are two such books that will appear, I hope, within the next few years. But they are not, in any sense, new editions of this book on personality, and, in my own judgment, it would be unwise for me to attempt a new edition. The book belongs in the stream of time just where it is; and I do not think it should be superseded by a junior edition of itself.

Topeka, Kansas　　　　　　　　　　　　　　　　　　GARDNER MURPHY
January 30, 1966

Foreword

TO WRITE about personality in such a way as to help in clarifying the little that we know and to show its possible relations to the vast and confused domain that we do not yet understand—this is my aim. Not much, I believe, is known about man; and what is known relates mostly to Homo sapiens as a species, not to persons as known to others and to themselves. But to ask questions in the midst of our confusion may focus the effort to explore. The best way to attempt the exploration, perhaps, is to write in terms of the foci of present research, expanding fanwise, through hypotheses, into realms of inarticulate groping.

This will mean that in reference to every problem there may be found, at least ideally, four stages of analysis: *first*, principles established with certainty or already reasonably dependable; *second*, the systematic implications, or theories, that arise fairly directly from a perspective upon a number of these principles; *third*, the research hypotheses that are dictated directly by the first two classes of material; *fourth*, speculations suggesting a few of the unlimited possibilities which might conceivably at some time prove to articulate with present knowledge. Of course in practice each of the four approaches merges into the adjacent ones. Though all are essential to the present purpose, the emphasis is upon research questions, that is, upon the third and fourth stages of analysis.

No one person's evaluation of present data and systematic theories is of great value. But the psychology of personality is spreading in all directions, and no one can make it stand still to be assessed. One thing that might practically be done is to formulate problems in terms of types of significant and manageable research tasks that lie just beyond present thresholds. When that is done, and one raises his head to look considerably beyond the threshold, he may shield his eyes from the glare of outdoors and look at the horizon. No two of us will agree as to what is closest to the threshold, nor of course upon the fertility of the soil just beyond. Least of all shall we agree as to what the horizon is; there is too much mist and dust to see clearly. But with dirt on our hands from digging into present problems we may perhaps be more sure that there is good soil all the way from here to there, and that an effort to see both near and far may make a difference in choosing the way.

This book, then, if at all successful in its aim, will be not so much a safe-deposit vault for jealously guarded facts as a companion for the investigator who likes to see problems defined in terms of directions in which they might lead; an explorer's kit, containing, to be sure, some standard tools, and also some maps. Some of the maps are sober, some eccentric, no doubt; but all are drawn in the belief that any map of a far country encourages more travel than an architect's finished representation of the doorway as it is here and now.

Throughout the volume the approach to personality is made chiefly in terms of origins and modes of development on the one hand, interrelations or structural problems on the other. It has not been possible to do justice to the quantitative problems revealed by psychometrics, by factor analysis, by ratings, and by questionnaires, or to personality tests or therapeutic and educational problems. The literature in all these fields is huge, and an attempt to summarize it would be outside the manageable compass of such a book as this, already too large. A glance at Rapaport's two-volume *Diagnostic Psychological Testing* may give the reader one sample of the rich clinical findings discovered by systematic research, and such a volume as Tomkins' *Contemporary Psychopathology* will show at a glance why present-day psychiatric research lends itself poorly to compression and simple exposition. In particular, the literature of psychoanalysis is already overwhelming; it is considered here only as it articulates with the author's somewhat simpler conceptions. It is hoped that some of the present chapters will, by raising questions, whet the reader's appetite for a hearty feast upon the clinical and therapeutic literature. But lest the reader waste time upon what he does not want, it must be emphasized that this is *not* a book on diagnosis or therapy of personality problems, or upon any type of clinical approach. It is simply an attempt at evaluation of data on how personality grows.

To avoid the constant use of footnotes or reference numbers, the sources are noted on pages 929 ff., referring to the text by page, paragraph, and line. Definitions of technical terms appear in a glossary combined with the index.

I should not have ventured to publish a book extending so far beyond my own area of experience without calling for the aid of friends competent to give a critical reading, to remove errors, and to offer constructive suggestions. This generous help has been given me by Gordon W. Allport, Gregory Bateson, Ernest R. Hilgard, Margaret Mead, Bela Mittelmann, Ruth Munroe, David Rapaport, Saul Rosenzweig, and L. Joseph Stone. Miss Dorothy A. Buck and Mr. Morton Leeds gave invaluable help with the preparation of the bibliography.

This is an attempt to formulate hypotheses which my wife and I have studied, applied, and redefined in teaching, and in research with children and young adults, for some fifteen years. It is, in no mere rhetorical sense, hers as much as mine.

G. M.

City College,
New York,
January, 1947

Acknowledgments

Thanks are due the following publishers for permission to use the materials indicated:

The American Journal of Orthopsychiatry: The case study in Chapter 29. Copyright 1944, American Orthopsychiatric Association.

Charles Scribner's Sons: The quotations from Robert Louis Stevenson's "A Chapter on Dreams," from *Across the Plains and*

Other Essays, in Chapter 17. Copyright 1892, 1905, by Charles Scribner's Sons; copyright 1920 by Lloyd Osbourne.

The Duke University Press and *Character and Personality* (Vol. 13, No. 1, 1944): The case study in Chapter 28.

The Journal Press: E. L. Horowitz's method and case material on the "spatial localization of the self" in Chapter 20. Copyright 1935 by Clark University.

The Stanford University Press and the *Applied Psychology Monographs:* The account of Ruth L. Munroe's Inspection Technique, and her findings, in Chapter 28. Copyright 1945 by the Board of Trustees of the Leland Stanford Junior University.

Contents

[*xiii*]

CONTENTS

PERSONALITY

1. The Approach

THERE are two current uses of the term "personality," which involve basic differences in point of view and method. In the commoner usage the term embraces the sphere of *individual differences*, or such of these differences as are relatively persistent, or such of them as are affective and volitional as distinct from intellectual. Thus a psychology of personality deals with all the individual aspects of a given human organism except for certain expressly excluded ones. It is a catalogue of certain human variabilities. The second usage embraces the thing which all personalities, *as such*, possess—the thing that marks off a personality from all other objects, such as a tree or a triangle. From this vantage point one tries to discover the nature of personality in general, as he might try to discover the nature of trees in general. This double usage of the term is natural and inevitable, because we are interested both in man in general and in the individual man for his own sake. But an author must say what he means; and if he writes a book about two subjects at once, bracketed under a common term, he must "show cause."

Both of these conceptions of personality have to be used, but in every discussion of personality it makes a considerable difference where the interest lies. In the present volume the emphasis is upon the general rather than upon the particular; we are more interested in formulating a working conception of personality than in endeavoring to define in detail the infinite variability of personalities. It is hard to see what serious purpose could be served by attempting a catalogue of all the individual differences in all the traits known to psychology—a manual of human diversities. Inventories of definable traits and full descriptions of the ways of studying and measuring them have already given place, as the literature has piled up, to more specifically defined trait areas; there are compact summaries of childhood social traits, of

[1]

vocationally significant traits in the adolescent, of methods of identifying and measuring adult socio-economic attitudes.

But there is another reason for preferring the general to the particular. The man who tells you about the peculiarities of a radio must think and talk in terms proceeding from the general properties of radios; it is out of the general consideration of radio construction that the meaning of a particular emerges. Personality traits, in inventories or elsewhere, presuppose a working conception as to what traits are and, a fortiori, a working conception as to what a personality is. For the present writer at least, it is compellingly necessary to keep the focus on the central problem of defining the nature of personality, drawing upon the data which clarify a working conception and allowing the particulars, the individual forms of response, in traits or in their mode of interrelation, to gather about the focus, just as an individual who is studying internal combustion engines or architectural form finds the specific engine and the specific cathedral more interesting and more meaningful when the general philosophy of the total construction precedes the analysis of particulars. Methods which, like the case study or the biography or psychoanalysis, seek to understand the organized totality of a person are presumably richer in their perception of their problem when they are fortified by a broad and clear conception of the laws governing such totalities.

But if one is thinking of personality in general, is he not simply thinking of man in general? If one wishes to talk about man as man, man in the abstract, are there not already enough disciplines concerned with him? And is not general psychology itself, with its principles relating to perception, motivation, learning, thinking, sufficient to the theme? The answer will be in the affirmative if this general psychology includes and emphasizes the interrelations, the organic wholeness of all these functions, and, in particular, the awareness of self and of individuality which is one of the central facts about being human. The use of the principles of general psychology in such a view of the whole individual would constitute, I believe, a *general psychology of personality* which deals with the universal fact of organization, and awareness of such organization and individuality, the sense of personal identity, continuity, distinctiveness, responsibility. This sense of personal identity will of course vary from man to man, but we are at the moment concerned solely with the legitimacy of a general inquiry into a general phenomenon.

Beneath all the limitless complexity of personal acts there is the general organic substratum, the system of organic potentialities—in short, the organism. This is approachable from many vantage points, by many techniques. When one combines several, and tries to see the whole organism at once, he may, if he wishes, say that he is studying personality. The organism the biologist studies and the personality the psychologist studies would be the same thing, except that the psychologist would tend to emphasize more complex functions, and more expressly indicate his desire to see all interrelations within the organism at once, as well as the hierarchy of laws governing those interrelations. Psychology of personality would then be that particular kind of general psychology that emphasizes totality and the organic systematic relations which obtain within it.

Three Levels of Complexity

At least three levels of complexity must be considered when confronting personality problems. Personality may be conceived, first, as an object or an event in a larger context—a dot on a chart, a billiard ball on a table. It is identifiable, strictly localized in time-space, and homogeneous. Its internal structure need not be considered. This view is useful in many sociological and some psychological problems, especially those of a statistical character. For example, just as we may compare large dots with small dots, or red balls with white, we may compare adults with children, men with women, Chinese with Japanese.

At a second level of complexity, personality may be likened to a chrysalis. It is again identifiable and strictly bounded, but it has internal structure. It is no longer homogeneous; it is organized. One chrysalis differs from another not only in size, weight, and color, as in the first-level analysis, but in the character of its constituent parts and of their interrelations. This second level requires patient and penetrating consideration of the nature of the internal structure from one such chrysalis to another, and of problems of types, or classes of organization. This approach is currently being used more and more, with great improvement in prediction and control.

At the third level of analysis, however, the chrysalis is an unsatisfactory model. It is encapsulated and it stays put. When you find one in the woods you may wonder whether there is still life in it. Something may have snuffed out its capacity to yield a butterfly. This something indicates that encapsulated though it was, it was not really self-contained. It could live only as long as a delicate relation obtained between its own structure and the outer structure of its habitat. The inner structure was supported and partly guided in its development by a field of external relations.[1]

If this is true even of a chrysalis, it is much more compellingly true of the butterfly or the mouse or the man. Here there is even less encapsulation. The world of atmosphere, food, light, gravitation flows into the defenseless organism. The organism exists because outer changes and inner adjustments are nicely attuned, because in the broad sense of the evolutionist the organism evolved only so far as it maintained itself in intimate unity with the environment at each stage of its development—literally as a node in a physical field, defined, limited, governed by the field relations. The organism has *a practical boundary* for some purposes— for example, the skin and mucous membranes. From other standpoints, however, the skin makes by no means an absolute barrier. The air we breathe is "within us" not when it passes valve-like barriers, but by degrees as it passes through nostrils, bronchi, the red blood cells and, with chemical reshuffling, back through veins and breath to the windowpane or to the people around us. To find a sharp barrier between self and non-self is a nice metaphysical task. If this is true of the simplest facts of biological existence, it is hard to see how people can be considered solely from the point of view of internal structure, of the personality that lies within the skin.

---

[1] Greek philosophy made use of the three methods of interpretation suggested here; they are too obvious to have been overlooked by such analytical minds as Democritus, Plato, and Aristotle, to whom, in the order named, the three present approaches could quite properly be ascribed.

If biology is right in considering the organism not as an encapsulated unit but as a node, an organizing point in a field, there is a level of analysis at which the man-world relation, the organism-environment field, may be studied.

Such a view may, if we wish, be called a *field* view, if we note that fields studied by biology are in a state of perpetual *redefinition*. Inner and outer structures are unstable; indeed, in the chemistry of nutrition and respiration there are structures which are neither outer nor inner, but lie in a zone where the two flow together or apart, moment by moment. The perpetually resulting changes mean that the time dimension is as essential to biology as it is to physics. The word "field" may remind us of the surveyor, and the maps used to portray a field are, after all, just maps; but world and self flow into one another. The boundary is often vague or non-existent, but the flow is always *directed* to some extent by the relations between the outer and inner structures.

No single word is likely to serve perfectly for this conception. The word "field" will perhaps serve if we expressly state that it is used as it is in physics; an electromagnetic field, for example, permits no strict demarcation of a boundary and may change continually as a result of varying currents.

All three conceptions of personality just indicated will need to be used. In discussing the simplest relations of age to behavior, the first will often suffice. In discussing the interaction of conflicting motives, the second will often be adequate; at least, it will suffice when we are gathering data about events within the organism (strictly, within the skin). When the thing we recognize as personality in our daily doings confronts us, we shall find ourselves pushing forward to the third level of analysis, knowing that in doing so we are abandoning simplicity, courting trouble, and raising far more questions than we can solve.

It has become accepted doctrine that we must attempt to study the whole man. Actually we cannot study even a whole tree or a whole guinea pig. But it is a whole tree and a whole guinea pig that have survived and evolved, and we must make the attempt. When it comes to studying the whole man, we are confronted by three ways in which he refuses to cooperate. First, his traits do not seem intelligible in their own right; they express something complicated going on inside. This is what has driven us from the first level to the second, namely, the study of inner structure. Second, some of the phases of this inner structure are hidden, pocketed off, oriented with respect to some long-past situation which man had to confront; the students of conditioning and of psychoanalysis tell us we need to reconstruct the man historically after the manner of the archeologist. Often there is only a fragment, and the reconstruction fails or is incomplete. Third, the man is reacting to something in the present that we do not understand. We have, if you like, the response but not the stimulating situation, and we are driven into an arduous and often futile search for what the environmental structure means to him, so that the field relations will be clear.

But let us suppose that we succeed at all three levels. We discover events relating to the whole man as he is and as he changes. Since whole personalities in their interrelations make a society, we have, if our logic is sound, made a first approach to a theory of interpersonal relations, a theory of society. Man is a creature that responds to other men in as full a sense as he responds to oxygen or gravity; he is as fully anthropotropic as geotropic. Man as man is in some degree social; the inner-outer structure which is the product of a particular organism-culture interaction gives at the same time the first law of cultural reaction, the key to the cultural nexus itself. If all the man and all of the culture—its geographic, economic, institutional patterns—are held in view at once, personality study becomes a biosocial, not only a biological investigation. In these terms, the social is simply the biological pattern that embraces interorganism events.

But man is not only one with his immediate physical environment in the sense that he is enmeshed within it, and in the same sense enmeshed within his social environment. He is part of a still larger context, as an aspect not only of a community but of a cosmos. This is the cosmos which has, as one of its limitless propensities, the propensity of producing man. Man is the kind of creature that can love not only his fellow man, but the trees and rocks, sands and oceans of his Mother Earth, and the sun and stars beyond. Because, as man has wondered at the beauty of the world and striven with tubes and numbers to fathom it all, personality is actualized not only through his being drawn to other men but through his being drawn, as artist, to patterns of color and tone or, as scientist, to schemata in time and space. Such patterns are sought, seized, appropriated, lived for. Personality is social, but it is more. It is a drop of the cosmos, and its surface tensions bespeak only a fragile and indefinite barrier that marks a region of relative structuring, relative independence. This structuring and independence can exist only because they are relative, that is, because of the confluence of the self and the nonself. As the musician melts into and identifies with his beloved instrument, the Hopi Indian on the rim melts into his Grand Canyon.

Man is, then, a nodal region, an organized field within a larger field, a region of perpetual interaction, a reciprocity of outgoing and incoming energies. We shall need, from time to time, sharp definition of our terms, and visual schemata with which to show their relations to other terms. The three conceptions of personality may now be put into definitions and portrayed in such visual schemata.

1. A personality is a distinguishable individual, definable in terms of a qualitative and quantitative differentiation from other such individuals.

A, B, C, and D are individuals; their interrelations, their manifest external likenesses and differences, may be studied without reference to their internal organization, which need not even be portrayed.

2. A personality is a structured whole, definable in terms of its own distinctive structural attributes.

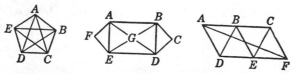

The letters constitute parts or attributes, such as the different organs of the body, which stand in specific interrelations.

3. A personality is a structured organism-environment field, each aspect of which stands in dynamic relation to each other aspect. There is organization within the organism and organization within the environment, but it is the cross organization of the two that is investigated in personality research.

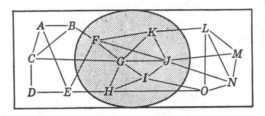

All the functional relations within the shaded area,
and between the shaded and unshaded areas, constitute
personality. The shaded area is the organism.

These three schemata are presented as if the organism were static, "frozen," at a moment of time. Considered developmentally and dynamically in the time dimension, the first would imply gradual qualitative or quantitative change (e.g., change in size or shape); the second would involve a reshuffling of inner relations (e.g., change in relative activity of parts, or inner equilibrium); the third would mean a reordering of inner-outer relations conjointly with a reordering of inner structure (e.g., the biosocial process by which personality adjustments at puberty involve simultaneous alterations of social demands upon the individual and of inner endocrine balance, so that the "changed personality" both reflects a biological change and is determined by a larger field).

To illustrate the three standpoints: We may say from the first standpoint that each two-year-old has his own patterns of language; from the second, that these language patterns, though "acquired" from his environment, express his own inner pattern of needs and bodily dispositions; from the third, that both his own unique inner organization and his own unique personal environment are in intimate, fluid reciprocity; that just as his language reflects his whole organic system, it reflects the response of the system that envelops and engulfs it, and the outflowing response by which this system pervades and engulfs many aspects of the enveloping environment.

All three points of view have their regions of adequacy. All three, for example, take account of the reality of individual differences, and of both temporary and permanent forms of uniqueness. But in relation to developmental problems such as those just mentioned, the second has an advantage over the first, because the dynamics of change become clearer when attention is directed to the reordering of parts. The third view, moreover, has a considerable advantage over the second, because the uniqueness of the individual is seen to lie in his peculiar capacity for interaction with his environment, the peculiar field properties which, during growth, express his potential in relation to his specific environmental situation, a situation which would draw out and express different reaction tendencies in any other organism. It is the interaction of the two that is available for study, and nothing psychological can be observed except in such an interaction field.

Consequently, though the first two points of view will at times be sufficient, our preference for the third must be clearly indicated at the outset. We shall, in this way, attempt for personality study a point of view that has long been commonplace in the biological sciences, a view which emphasizes the full reciprocity of inner and outer events. This outer-inner reciprocity means that the *life process* is itself a matter of world as much as organism. The organism is structurally definable for some purposes in terms of a spatially localized capsule, but its *life functions* are organized in terms of an adaptation polarity which gives the environment pole the same relation of absolute necessity to the process, the field, as that held by the organism pole.

THE BIAS OF OUR CULTURE REGARDING PERSONALITY

Though this last principle is so central in biology, and though general psychology based upon biological conceptions has necessarily adopted it, it seems to have been given only scant attention in our studies of individual persons. These are conceived as self-contained objects of contemplation; pressed flowers, or gems, interesting or beautiful or instructive in themselves.

The reasons for this disparity of approach are clear and intelligible. First, there is and always has been, at least from Plato's time, a profound esthetic satisfaction in the contemplation of an ordered and self-contained unity. Persons are even more interesting and beautiful than gems. Gems that flowed out into the jewel case would be a nuisance and a mess; persons that insist on flowing into the environment are an abomination; they confuse the eye and muddy the soul. The encysted person must be idealized because he is so obviously ideal— that is, in Plato's sense, the *real* person. For the Platonist, the fluctuations, the fuzzy boundaries characterize only the *apparent* person.

The other reason is the moralistic. People can be relied on if their boundaries are definite and fixed; you know where to put them; you know they will stay put. Above all, they can be held responsible. A society made up of persons of this sort can manage itself and—still more important for philosophers as kings, or just ordinary kings (civil, economic, or moral)—can be conveniently managed from above. For them it would be ideal if all men were alike; but even failing likeness, all men, statesmen and chamberlains as well as vassals and thralls, can be handled if they can be regarded as constants. People *ought* to be tightly organized within, sharply separable from one another and from their world, because, like checkers, robots, or at least beautiful flowers in the garden of the Lord, you always know where they can be found. No post-Platonic Greek but Epicurus would ever have thought of personality as a flux; no Englishman but Hobbes would ever have thought of it as a phase of reciprocal motion between objects. Both, of course, were heartily despised for their effrontery, their evident lack of fine feeling, of moral responsibility.

Psychological conceptions are regularly guided in some measure by esthetic, moralistic, and other normative attitudes. Personalities differ in value, but personality in general is "good." There are clear cultural-historical reasons for these attitudes. But there is one especially cogent reason for the development of what might be called an adoring attitude, a certain preciosity toward personality. In feudal times the lord and knight had personality, but not the villein or the thrall. The breakup of feudalism and rigid class structure, the Commercial Revolution, tended to put the individual, regardless of birth, on his own. He got ahead because of himself, because of his personality. With the collapse of class lines, individual artisans and merchants achieved personalities; Shakespeare and Molière are full of them. Again, in our pioneer days, frontiersmen were supposedly alike in their situation, their predicament, and their opportunity, but different as personalities; from their individualism arose a Daniel Boone, an Andrew Jackson, an Abraham Lincoln. It was evident to any member of such a world that personality was the most valuable thing on earth; that since individualism set the stage, the individual was the actor. For the pioneer, everybody had, or morally ought to have, a distinct personality. As settled living developed behind the frontier, in the "Flowering of New England," the fully achieved and vastly enriched conception of the individual personality appeared, as in Holmes or Emerson; the feeling for humanity flowered into a reverent and absorbing idealization of the individual.

That much of our present existence under industrialism is vague or impersonal, that much is drab and shoddy, that much is chaotic and nondescript, are data not usable in the picture. The picture, like any work of art or science, is a selection, an organization for a purpose. From the welter of confusion in which personal traits often blur into intangibles, everything that has coherence which the scientist or artist can grasp is precious. This is the aspect of personality that we love and about which we wish to read.

Here and elsewhere I hope only to describe, not to sit in judgment. All these tendencies are natural and intelligible. So also are the counter-tendencies which arise in such eras of confusion and disillusionment: the pictures of robots, "hairy apes." The counter-tendencies are themselves only facets of the truth, and any appreciation of or protest against these tendencies is merely another tendency to be put into its own perspective. But there is no danger that anyone will succeed in this century in getting the perspective completely right or, indeed, in defining clearly what personality is.

[11]

PERSONALITY

If personality is half as complex as this suggests, it may be viewed in all sorts of ways and from all sorts of vantage points. There are perennial counter-views as to what it is: a primordial stuff; a pattern of accidentally imposed conditionings; an achieved inner structure; a cultural mold. Here, then, is much quarreling. But I have no stomach for these controversies. These views have all arisen in genuine efforts to seize the thing and to articulate what is seen. They are like the arguments of music lovers whether Beethoven is classical or romantic, German or universal. Personality is a biological conception and a cultural-science conception, a sum and a fusion, a laboratory datum and a next-door neighbor. You will see in it what you are trained to see, and in some measure all the things that are seen are really seen, not hallucinated. The views differ in value and in range of utility, but in general there are not too many but too few. Considering how little is known, it is sad that there are only eight or ten coherent living views of personality that are widely shared by psychologists; and of these, two or three (Janet, Ward, McDougall) are almost moribund. Not that they have been outlived; they have been lost in the whirlwind of excitement about other more complicated and in some ways more exciting doctrines, the teachings of behaviorism, Gestalt, Freud, Jung, and Adler. There might well be more boldness in ordering the data of laboratory and clinic to freshly conceived schemata of structure.

Eclecticism, of course, is no substitute for such boldness. The particles wrenched from varying systems cannot be made to cohere. Each particle has "membership character" in a system and there is no help for it. The nineteenth- and twentieth-century concepts of personality may, however, be used in a very different way. All of them may, if required, be recast, along with still other conceptions, in a new unity; the diverse views may be rephrased and simultaneously used. Anyone may reexamine the experimental and clinical evidence of today and attempt his own unified conception. When it fails, another may improve it through reconstruction or by making still another fresh effort at systematic completeness and unity. Our own effort is toward the systematic; it aims at consistency rather than confusion; it prefers the systematized delusions of paranoia to the confused delusions of hebephrenia.

Science, Art, and Engineering

Somehow or other the idea has fastened itself upon us that the three enterprises known as science, art, and engineering are utterly distinct. One may serve as a back door to another, but the door marks their independence as well as their continuity. The novelist, we learn, provides the psychologist with valuable data, but his task as an artist is not the task of the scientist. The therapist may gather valuable data about psychopathology, but his work is directed to the healing of the individual, not to the generalizing method of science.

That these distinctions are at times serviceable need not be denied. In everyday psychology, however, considerable stultification has arisen from their status as fetishes. The passionate love of the beauty of crystals, the contemplation of their order, internal structure, interrelations, has played a large part in the development of mineralogy; the same symmetry may satisfy an esthetic need and a generalizing need. The psychologist himself has done much to show how hard it is to drive knife blades between different human needs and to trace each of them to a biologically simple germ. The botanist seeking Cypripedium and the field naturalist in quest of turtle eggs are not ashamed of their love, not apologetic for the "mixed motives" in their quest.

Psychologists seem half the time to be afraid that their attitudes toward human beings may be construed in esthetic terms rather than in terms of scientific contemplation, the ordering of events for the one purpose being conceived to be independent of the ordering of events for the other purpose. It is the writer's bias that where order and complexity are the rule the artist's view is a valuable and at times indispensable aid. Broadly speaking, one of the chief guides in looking at a personality is *appreciation*, just as one appreciates a maple leaf or the Pleiades. This may at times be carried so far as to interfere with science, as we shall try to show in Chapter 27; but by far the larger danger is that it will not be carried far enough.

As for the separation of human engineering (as in therapy, education, or industrial counseling) from the scientific enterprise, it is the task of all such labor to form valid generalizations, sometimes for the individual, sometimes for the group. Our customary refusal to give a certificate of election to scientific status is usually based on the alleged narrowness of these aims; science deals with the absolutely universal, that which has, in Lewin's fine phrase, "exceptionless validity." But we should, I think, lop off not only the ears, but most of the living members of contemporary psychology, and indeed of most of the contemporary life sciences, if we applied any such absolute rule. If therapy, or education, or other engineering enterprises find any principles, coherences among data, as part of their task of controlling their material, the psychologist will put himself in a precarious condition by refusing to attend. It is largely by using, as capital, all that we have, that we have been able to build a psychology of sufficient value to engage the interest of serious people.

Our effort, then, will be to look at individual persons under all the lights and through all the glasses that we can find. It is only when the artist has sought to appreciate and the engineer has sought to guide that we shall dare say that the data for a psychology of personality have been gathered. The aim of the volume is a generalizing aim to a greater degree than it is an applying or appreciating aim. But personality study is an art and an engineering enterprise as well as a science, and at the present stage in its development the three often flow together and refuse to be separated.

The data to be used in such an enterprise are of every conceivable sort: experimental, biographical, clinical; gleanings from anthropological and sociological field studies; oddments from general biology and general sociology, as well as general psychology; educational experience; artistic perception of meanings; impressions of an individual observer of an individual subject; tables of statistical findings from large groups. In view of the general plan of the book, data will be employed whenever they help in any way to round out a systematic view, to develop a useful hypothesis, or to show the way toward verification. Many will therefore be examined which in a compact manual of certainties would not be worth a sentence.

THE APPROACH

The obligation is therefore assumed by the writer to indicate as well as he can their approximate status on the continuum between fact and conjecture, first, by flatly naming types of evidence when needed; second, by freely using "probably," "perhaps," "conceivably," etc.; third and most important, by documenting clearly. The reader necessarily assumes at the same time the obligation to read in a spirit of exploration, curiosity, tentativeness, and to ride the material and the author with the taut reins of skepticism rather than at a gallop.

METHODS

The value of the data depends, of course, a good deal upon the *methods* by which they have been derived. We have as major research tools (1) the genetic methods (the cross-sectional comparison of groups at different developmental levels, and the longitudinal-biographical study of individuals); (2) the comparative methods (the phylogenetic and the anthropological-sociological); and (3) the experimental method. We might add the statistical method, but with the development of statistical procedures for the study of small groups, it now seems reasonable to regard statistical methods as tools to accompany all the other methods whenever the data assume quantitative form and suggest the possibility of functional dependencies. Our first methodological problem has to do with the kinds of uses to which we may put the genetic, the comparative, and the experimental methods.

The genetic method has long been used in biology and a great deal may be learned about its general values and limitations. The gardeners' and stockbreeders' data on the lineage of observable traits, the effects of crossing and of inbreeding, give a general conception of the continuities traceable to heredity and of the possibilities of augmenting trends which are present only to a small degree. The experiments of Mendel on crossing, and of Weismann on the continuity of the germ plasm, offer a broad framework in which new manifestations embodying structures and functions are traced to recombinations of elements. The role of "sports," or *mutations*, known to gardeners and stockbreeders, clarifies the meaning of sudden devia-

[15]

tions. But it is chiefly the experimental manipulation of mutants that indicates the dynamics (dominance, etc.) of such mutations; in recent years the experimental production of mutations by x-rays has helped in giving a rational view of their mechanics. Again, comparative embryology had for decades shown many formal principles of development; but it has been *experimental interference* by means of excision, isolation, grafts, and transplants, rather than the "normal" (that is, left to its own devices) that has given us our chief understanding of the *modus operandi* of growth, differentiation, and integration.

Protest sometimes arises against such interference with the normal. Yet it is by controlling the variables that appear in the natural situation that their interaction in the usual or normal situation is understood. It becomes meaningless to say that such procedures destroy the integrity of life or falsify the life picture. All the understanding we have of the dynamics of integration has come from such union of analytic and synthetic procedures. The danger of oversimplification is indeed great, but probably not so great for the genuine experimenter as for him who confines himself to the products of nature's blind and confused experiments. What is properly meant by such protests is usually that an overgeneralization from the necessarily artificial (because planned) situations to the more complex situations of daily life may be unwarranted. This is, however, less likely to occur if definite variables are held in mind so that the life situation is regarded not merely globally, but in terms of factors not presented in the experiment.

The experimental method, as known to science, never stops with analysis; it is always necessary to work slowly from the simple to the complex, verifying hypotheses by fulfillment of prediction until the original whole can be experimentally reconstituted. Thus Helmholtz, resolving tone quality into a pattern of overtones, was not content with his analytic findings, but actually reproduced with resonators the tone quality of organ and violin.

The data from genetic and comparative method are the first raw material, the thunderstorms and rainbows from which, for three hundred years, the conceptual system of physics and chemistry has been derived. Even the physical data were much too complex to yield a scientific understanding without isolation and measurement. When the point is made that the phenomena of personality are still more complex and therefore not amenable to experimental study, the logic seems perfectly inverted; it is the very complexity of these data that makes the thoughtful student despair of genuine validation of hypotheses without the control of variables, and therefore of interrelations, which the experimental method entails.

But this does not mean that the full-fledged experimental method is ready, or can be instantly improvised, whenever a hypothesis about the dynamics of cultural phenomena is suggested. In the physical sciences, experimentation has proved a long path, with pitfalls and the loss of the way at every turning. The first hypotheses are usually so bad that they suggest experiments which lead either nowhere or to confusion. The discipline of new and unexpected data, and the further thought they stimulate, offer new hypotheses for old which are a shade better, partly by the accumulation of ordered masses of data placed in recognizable classes through nothing more than sheer resemblance, partly by verification of hypotheses which relate to the reasons for their coherence, partly by deductive steps which bring one principle into alignment with another. A broader generalization is achieved, tested, and used as a landmark for the mapping of the next exploratory steps.

It is likely that most of the steps taken in personality research are, like those taken in the physical sciences two hundred years ago, not much better than blind gropings from poor hypotheses, but still the ancestors of a more noble strain of hypotheses which our great-grand-children may rework. The question is not primarily one of precision as such, for quantification with poor hypotheses does not make them into good ones. To be good, they have to make use of all the experience available from every source. For this reason the experimental method is not the sovereign lawgiver but the abject slave of the observational methods which precede and accompany it. Yet *when it is available* and *when it has something clearly pertinent to say,* its clarity and eloquence are such that we shall have to allow it the seat of honor.

PERSONALITY

THE STAIRCASE OF PERSONALITY STUDY

In view of the difficulty of the task confronting us, it will be necessary to order our conceptions on a scale from the simplest to the most complex, to introduce one conception at a time and to look at it for a while before turning to another. Or we may schematize the steps that we shall take in terms of a staircase. Each step stands in a necessary position which can be reached only when other steps have been traversed, and must be passed before those beyond can be undertaken. These are the steps of the staircase we shall use in this book, ordering the data as we proceed from each level to the next.

1. The opening chapters will consider personality as a biological system, an organic matrix, from which, through outer and inner pressures, evolves the socially known individual. Here we shall use the conception of heredity-environment as a single developmental fact, the conception of biological individuality, the conception of inner structure, the conception of interorganism response. Personality traits are, from this point of view, simply biological dispositions; the interrelation of these dispositions constitutes personality. Our chief sources of information in this analysis, to which Chapters 1 to 7 are devoted, are genetics, embryology, physiology, and comparative psychology.

2. When the conception of the organic system seems developed with reasonable clarity, we shall turn to the study of responses arising through the interaction of the individual constitution and a specific environment—the problem of learning. Such responses are occasioned by the circumstances of the life history; behavior is conditioned both to outer and to inner stimuli, the inner system including the system of symbols. The resulting personality traits will be studied in their dependence upon the individual history and arranged in a hierarchical system, as growth and experience daily complicate the behavior patterns and lead into complex integrations as well as into conflict. Our chief sources of information here will be genetic and experimental psychology. The analysis of the acquisition of such a behavior system will be worked out in Chapters 8 to 13.

3. Along with the behavior modifications of the organic system,

we encounter the development of a world of perception and thought. This is a more complex world, perhaps; at any rate, it is harder to study. The developing system comprises not only muscular and glandular patterns, but patterns of cognitive and affective responses. The structure of the individual personality comprises the structure of one's sense perceptions, imagery, feeling, and the complex activities of imagination and thought. Here our data come partly from experimental psychology, but largely from the observations and inferences of the clinic, and from life histories. Just as the organic system had to be considered before the behavior system, which results from learning, so the behavior system is presupposed and included in this more complex world of the cognitive-affective system; an effort is made to show that in this extension of the system the fundamental principles already worked out remain essentially unaltered. The personality system described in Chapters 14 to 19 aims to comprise a study of all such central processes, from the simplest percept to the most complex creative construction, with a place for individuality at every point.

4. But major steps remain to be taken. The organism perceives, thinks about, and responds to itself. The study of the resulting functions of self or ego presupposes an understanding of the earlier steps, but it presents problems of its own. Sources of information about the self include genetic observations, experiments, clinical interviews or interrogations, and in particular, the psychoanalytic methods. The search for the dynamics of selfhood reflects the special genius of Freud. The Freudian conception of the self proceeds from, and is a much needed extension of, the cognitive-affective psychology just mentioned. The notion of a self struggling against tendencies of which it is unaware, or only partially aware, leads into the theory of unconscious dynamics and into a system of principles defining the relation of self and non-self; it helps therefore to extend and enrich the theory of integration and of conflict. But since this conception utilizes the biological approach and the facts of learning and perceiving, the ultimate dynamics appear to be closely related to those which appear at the behavior and the conscious levels; the main working principles seem to be supported rather than rejected. There will be

no place for a debate between psychoanalytic and other psychologies; rather, the aim is to see where the psychoanalytic contributes and enriches the system already sketched in simpler terms. But individual differences in the structure of selfhood and in the form of integration will call for attention.

Since the main outlines of this "depth" psychology, as developed here, are simplifications of Freudian doctrine in a form compatible with the systematic outlook already developed, there will be no need for extensive comparisons of Freud, Jung, and Adler. Instead, our question will concern what Jung and Adler have contributed to the understanding of the organic-behavorial-cognitive-unconscious system developed up to this point. The typology developed by Jung proves on inspection to offer some valuable hypotheses about individual differences which derive from unconscious dynamics. Adler's contributions are considered (as the Freudians first considered them) valuable studies of the nature and functions of the ego, which, if examined empirically, involve little with which clinical or experimental observation can quarrel. The study of the self and its dynamics extends from Chapter 20 to Chapter 25.

5. Unconscious dynamics, the enhancement and defense of the self, necessarily call our attention to conflict, disunity. But personality also achieves a kind of genuine unity or wholeness. This conception has led to the amassing of much experimental evidence on the interrelations of traits and on the recognizability of whole personality patterns. From this point of view, traits are not individual *parts*, but *aspects* of a totality. Each trait has "membership character" (to use the language of Gestalt psychology) which places it in a contextual system. From this approach, personality dynamics may be considered to involve not merely the conflict or summation of separate tendencies, but functional modes of organization. Such a view appears to be a necessary derivative from the implications of the preceding views. Our data here come chiefly from experimental psychology. The wholeness of personality is considered in Chapters 26 to 31.

6. Wholeness, however, does not stop with the skin. We have already seen that the individual-environment relation involves larger fields, the organism being an aspect of such a field. Each individual is a

member of a community; is guided, inhibited, molded, structured by the life of the community; each personality is a reflection of a developmental history in a specific cultural whole. This is often called a social science view. Wholeness of culture and wholeness of organic response are conjointly stressed.

From this social science view two others develop. The first of these is that personality at a given time is a reflection and an epitome of specific cultural requirements. This we shall call *situationism*. The other, which is as much concerned with the capacity of the organism to select from the situation as with the capacity of the situation to select from the dispositions of the organism, might well be called simply the personality-and-culture view. But since this type of mutual selection between organism and environment involves the necessity of regarding the barrier between individual and environment as indefinite and unstable, and requires the consideration of an organism-environment field whose properties are studied as field properties, the approach will be called *field theory*. Personality is considered here as a flowing continuum of organism-environment events. The general nature of these events, and the problem of individuality in their history, are considered jointly. This is the most inclusive integration of data which we shall attempt. It is not the last word, though it is this book's last word, on our problem of personality. Throughout its presentation of the "social science" and "field" points of view, suggestions about the present characteristics of personality in the American scene will be hazarded. These approaches comprise Chapters 32–41.

In attempting this type of architectural structure I have followed wherever possible a method successfully used by Paul Weiss in his *Principles of Development*, namely, the raising, at each major point in the analysis, of a *critical question*, and the presentation of a clear and compact piece of research which gives a provisional answer to this question. The reader thus becomes as fully aware of the exploratory character, the spirit of uncertainty and tentativeness, of the work as the author is.[2]

---

[2] The list of references appears on p. 29. In each case the citation is given by page, paragraph and line.

Even in a book committed to theoretical analysis rather than to biographical portrayals of personality, it is well to begin with a concrete problem. Because William James is well known and deeply loved, his life history will set us on our way. At every point our hope is to ask relevant psychological questions—questions with which such a book as this ought to be concerned—and in this way help to make clear what sort of thing personality study is.

Believing that it is perfectly true that a man's biography begins with his grandfather (or better, all four grandparents), we have to take account of the high level of steadiness and success shown in many of James' immediate ancestry, and in particular, in the robust and competent "William of Albany," a pillar of society, whose religious orthodoxy and firm authority are background against which to view the restless heterodoxy of his children, notably of his son Henry, William James' father. Just how might the hard-driving energies of the successful grandfather—both as regards heredity and as regards home atmosphere—be related to the lifelong *quest*, the unceasing explorations into the intangible which characterized the father, and to William James' own intense, strenuous, nervously sthenic struggle with the ultimates of mind, heart, and universe? Tenderness and liberality toward his children were alike features of all three: grandfather, father, and son. Catherine Barber, third wife of "William of Albany" and William James' grandmother, is described by her son Henry as "the most democratic person by temperament I ever knew," and appears also to have been a woman of solid good sense and practical judgment. But most of the eleven children of the Albany patriarch went through their patrimony like water through a sieve; their lives offered "amusing flashes of light and occasional dark moments of tragedy." To Henry, the father, a passionate boyhood lover of the streams and fields, the world of nature, the amputation of a leg had brought what others might call tragedy; yet in all the story of his career it is eager, exuberant love of life and the search for its meaning that impel him.

We know little of the other grandfather and grandmother, except that they were apparently people of substance and ability. Henry

James' wife, William James' mother, gave whole-souled devotion, simple, warm, absolute devotion to her husband and her children, and William James' son believes one might well "look to her in trying to account for the unusual receptivity of mind and aesthetic sensibility that marked her two elder sons." And as Perry makes clear in his *Thought and Character of William James*, their children's gentle doubts about "father's ideas" were only foam on the deep sea of family solidarity, the warm togetherness of a family whose members lived for one another. Having no "job" to hold, enabled by the family inheritance to pursue philosophical and theological questions, and literature, art, music, conversation, and all the amenities of dignified leisure, Henry James could provide for his children a rich world of intellectual interests, and European travel and schooling. William was "early blessed with an effortless and confirmed cosmopolitanism of consciousness." The one apparent shortcoming of such an education —its constant change of direction year by year—seems in the sequel a feature which probably added much directly and indirectly to the versatility, the complexity, the unfinished quality, the "pluralism" of William James' work, and to some degree also of the work of his brother, Henry James the novelist. Whatever the limitations of William James' formal schooling, there was much intensity of new experience along the way. A microscope given him by his father at fifteen was one of the great events of his life, and we find him getting an anatomy text and studying skeletons in the Geneva Museum. Sketching and painting, to which he had always given himself freely, became his main preoccupation in his late teens; he would try being a painter and see if he succeeded.

Already a number of questions have arisen about what heredity can do and what it cannot do; about the early formation of tastes, values, attitudes toward life; about the role of identification with a loving tolerant father and with a brilliantly perceptive brother. As William James enters Harvard several additional questions arise: Whence the unbearable fatigue and physical inadequacy that attract his instructor's notice in chemistry, and that disqualify him for military service; whence the eye trouble, indigestion, backaches, nervousness?

Are these, in the jargon of today, partly psychosomatic expressions of an unconscious struggle; do they have a hereditary aspect? Or more likely, are they a unique personal expression of something for which heredity provided a base; to which the many changes of place, food, physical and social atmosphere offer a clue; and to which the sheer intensity of his intellectual and emotional concentration offers a psychosomatic approach? The range of his response to life is measured by his desire to be a painter, by his pursuit of a medical degree through thick and thin, by his luxuriating in German philosophy, by his English friendships. In such a range of intense response, could the fragile organism be simply paying the price?

Despite the continued fatigue and the backaches that drove him to the Moravian mudbath when he essayed to study in Germany, he clung doggedly to his maturing purposes: the understanding of body and mind through medicine, experimental psychology, the new French psychiatry, psychical research, the evolutionary principle, the new humanistic, empirical, relativistic philosophies. His letters tell constantly of time "wasted" in illness, but the record of what he read and wrote sounds more like that of an iron man than that of an invalid. Could he be repressing the most elementary and primitive in human nature; could he be sublimating? Or could he be compensating for a physical inferiority? How can we evaluate the areas of applicability of such concepts as these? How far may we rely on the expansion and integration of personal taste and values already mentioned?

Of two things we may be very sure: as an American who loved new things, the changing and the creative, he exulted in the strenuous, the heroic, rather than in the safe and sane; and he found in the philosophy of spontaneity, genuine creativeness, a basis for hope that he could make himself sound and well. He had integrated the evolutionary and the progressive with the healing touch of personal freedom. Granting, as he himself did, that each man builds a philosophy out of his own cravings, is there anything more specific that a psychology of personality can say about this organization of the whole world view in terms of a personal demand upon life? Tremendous self-discipline he always retained; he was no dilettante whose tastes changed with the weather. His attacks on formalism, absolutism, the "thin" in philosophy are documented with relentless citations of the absurdities of his opponents' case; and in the prosecution of a large and tough assignment, like the series of chapters on perception in the *Principles of Psychology*, one comes to grips with those huge masses of technical material which show how far he has moved from William James the painter.

Two great events helped to turn the physician and philosopher to the path his genius craved: his marriage to a congenial and understanding woman who knew how to give him security, and his appointment by President Eliot to lecture and give demonstrations to Harvard students in physiology, later in all sorts of psychological and philosophical fields. How much of all that he became was an experience of this specific relation of man and environment; how do the America, the Harvard, the late nineteenth century, the Alice Gibbens, the children she bore him, the fame which his books brought him integrate in making the man we know? It is of extraordinary interest to see how long the process took. James was forty-eight when the *Principles of Psychology* appeared; for ten years thereafter much of his published work consisted of short articles and lectures, many of which were addressed to the preacher, the classroom teacher, the general reader, rather than primarily to the technically trained philosopher or psychologist. As he sought, at the age of fifty-seven, to escape to Europe for a rest, he collapsed, and for a year he lay an invalid; then with returning strength came the tremendous *Varieties of Religious Experience*, and then there followed despite recurring illness, through the remaining years (he was in his sixties, and died at sixty-eight), the *Pragmatism*, the *Meaning of Truth*, *A Pluralistic Universe*, and several books which appeared posthumously.

Such facts as these make one wonder whether any cross-section of individual life at a point in time can ever tell what personality is; whether it does not rather behoove us to emphasize the time dimension, the changing, growing, self-renewing processes of personality evolution, of release of personality in a new way in each situation. For what came forth from James in each decade, each year of his life, came from all that he had been before, and from the new situation as advancing years brought a sense of what remained to be done.

Can such ideas as these, so simple, so obvious, so transparent, be actually put to work in a systematic essay on personality? Can we learn how to focus and integrate all that is known about heredity so as to use it wisely, with vision and with restraint, in approaching the individual? Can today's clinical and biographical approach to individual growth serve to gather and to interpret the data on the learning process, the formation of tastes and of values, the molding of the personal outlook in childhood? Can the social sciences take hold of the problem of the interaction of the growing individual with his cultural environment, and make clear in what sense the fulfillment of the individual himself is, at the same time, a realization of the meanings implicit in the social order? About all these matters we know, even in the case of so rich and well documented a record as that of William James, very little. Can we do better with those who are coming to maturity today? In short, can the threads from biology, from clinical experience, from the social sciences, be brought together in defining how personality grows? At least, we can try.

Part One

ORGANIC FOUNDATIONS

2. The Organism

FROM time to time in the world process objects are formed by accretion, or mixture, or chemical reaction. Sometimes they are rather stable, and endure; sometimes they disintegrate, or change progressively into other objects. Among the complex and relatively stable objects are some which not only grow but repair their losses and generate more objects of their kind. These are called *living* objects; the simplest are single cells. They live by assimilating material from the world outside, and by chemical reaction with outside matter. Such new matter is not merely added to, it is organized within, the living structure.

Sometimes these living objects divide to form two such living objects. Sometimes these two new objects cling together, and when each of these two divides, the four cling together; the process may continue until a very complicated structure appears. This complexity depends not merely on the number and diversity of cells, but on their interrelatedness. Every cell is part of the environment of every other cell, and the system as a whole maintains itself as it grows. Some cells in this complex structure—the "germ cells"—can survive and generate a new complex structure of the same general type. Within the germ cells are rod-like bodies, *chromosomes*, along which are ranged the *genes*, the tiny carriers of hereditary traits.

The clues to this process appear to lie, first, in the ceaseless flux and change of inorganic nature, and the occasional realization of favorable conditions for the formation of living particles; second, in the tendency of individuals of each new generation, though resembling their parents, to vary somewhat from one another (partly through slight fortuitous recombinations of the chemical tendencies received from the parents, partly through sudden and dramatic chemical alterations—mutations—in the germ cells); third, in the suitability of *some* but not all, of the resulting individuals of each generation to carry on with the environment the kind of interaction called life.

It follows that, though the environment may change, there will be in each generation *some* organisms which can live until the reproduction age; and that as members of a type wander into different environments, some will survive in one kind of environment, others will be able to survive only in a very different environment, so that out of nature's prodigality a few will be found here and there, carrying on the life process in terms which each environment permits. There will be many species of creatures, each clinging to its own world. Within each species, however, there are always differences—differences not only in specific traits, but in the interrelations of these traits, the structure of the whole individual. Each such individual moves in its own environment, necessarily not quite identical with that of another. As the fledgling chickadees make their way to the windowsills, it is obvious that each is different from the rest; and each has found its favorite window, and approaches it in its own way.

These are, then, primitive individual personalities, defined first in terms of the species-environment relation, second in terms of the individual-environment relation realized in their own specific case. Their existence is rooted in two things: first, the world which has chosen them and constantly maintained them by flowing into them and allowing them to flow into it; second, the continuity of the stream of heredity, reaching back to the remotest beginnings of life, which has itself at all times maintained some degree of isolation while maintaining its own give-and-take with the changing environments. The individual organism can no more be considered an isolated object than it can be considered homogeneous with the environment, for either its complete isolation or, on the other hand, the loss of its boundaries would equally signify its obliteration. It is a region of relatively high structuring in a field of complex and ever-changing relations.

The nature of the inner structure needs closer attention. First of all, it is chemical. The particles visible within an individual cell are seen to change, and the chemist's methods show that they change in accordance with general chemical principles. The laws of the organism relate first, then, to chemical compounds within the body, the chemical reactions between them, and the chemical reactions with the outer world. *Structure* is first of all a name for a system of chemical reactions which define the life of the organism, a system involving relations between both simultaneous and successive reactions, such that the organism is continually in touch with its environment yet is neither inundated by it nor encapsulated from it. This system, however, does more than *preserve* life; it provides for change and growth, for a sequence of related changes as well as the preservation of life from moment to moment. Part of this systematic change is provided by specific enzymes which facilitate, over a long period, a specific kind of reaction, the influence of which is to guarantee growth at a certain pace; but still other enzymes must keep pace, so that the growing totality is still in balance. The conception of system is important, for if the reactions were chaotic or independent, the organism could not exist. Life was achieved in the first place because one reaction led to another which led to a third, etc., in such a way as to keep the fires burning; accretion and juxtaposition alone would never have given life. It was through system, through inner organization, that the integrity of the individual was maintained despite the fluid inter-action with the world. The first definition of personality is therefore in terms of a biochemical system. Every individual is an almost infinitely complex pattern of biochemical tendencies. There is much more to enter into the definition; but this is the first foundation principle.

The chemical system of an individual member of a species differs somewhat, however, from that of another individual. This is conspicuously true in a starfish, even more so in a kitten. Such biochemical individuality is recognizable even in the embryo, and clearly in the newborn; and upon this early individuality are impressed still further individualities due to the vicissitudes of the individual life process, the individual organism-environment interactions.

The life process can occur only within rather narrow limits of temperature and oxygen concentration, and of alkalinity-acidity. There are in fact a very large number of specific limiting conditions which must be realized if life is to go on. Consequently, within the tenuous capsule of the living, a much higher degree of constancy is maintained than in the world outside. In particular, the nervous system can carry on its functions only under very specific determining and limiting conditions. This was vividly brought out in Claude Bernard's masterly phrase, the "constancy of the inner environment." Thanks to the labors of biochemists and physiologists, two types of advance have been made in recent years with reference to this principle: First, its general relation to the physiology of normal tissues has been more sharply defined; and second, the types of constancy which are requisite have been more fully specified. For Cannon the principle of inner constancy is formulated under the term *homeostasis*, meaning the "maintenance of stability."

The principle is of such evident importance to personality study that we find writers like Guthrie insisting that action occurs only when there is a threat to this inner stability, and writers like Raup who maintain that life consists essentially of efforts to restore this stability or complacency. Yet in the ebb and flow of life processes there must be as much digression from homeostasis as there is return to it, as much exploration as there is homecoming, as much "extravagance" as there is thrift. In fact, homeostasis is a useful concept not merely in showing the safety-maintaining systems of the body, but in suggesting that against a background of relatively constant factors there are factors which permit wide variability, "trial and error" in the execution of activities in contact with the outer world. Homeostasis means, moreover, more than relative constancy of separate features such as hydrogen-ion concentration or temperature. It appears to be very intimately related to the maintenance of the relative constancy of *interrelations*, such that variation in one aspect of the balanced living system induces compensating changes in other aspects, thus maintaining the integrity of the system.

But does *the system as a system* actually have this capacity to resist destruction, to preserve itself intact? Yes; this was classically demonstrated by Wilson's experiment on the tendency of living matter to preserve its form. He reduced a sponge to a pulp, squeezed and rolled

it flat, and centrifuged it so that no trace of the creature's original outline remained. He then allowed the material to stand overnight.
Slowly and in orderly fashion the material reconstituted itself into the
organized sponge which it had been before. It is hardly necessary to
refer here to a disembodied life goal or entelechy. The particles themselves demand one another in specific chemical and spatial relations.
As far as we know, this maintenance of relations is of the essence of
life, and therefore of personality. There are of course limits to the
capacity for self-maintenance and self-restoration, but it is worth
while to stress that homeostasis is not merely the maintenance of
constancy in a single phase of inner existence; it implies the maintenance of the structural wholeness of the living individual.

It is this maintenance of the balanced individual system that can be
put forward as the key to Kurt Goldstein's labors over a quarter of a
century. In his studies of men who suffered brain injuries in the First
World War, he was able to show that local damage, if limited, tends
to be functionally ignored both by the subject and by those about him.
Thus a small blind or distorting area in the field of vision is compen-
sated for by systematic shifts such that well-ordered total vision
remains. Even in gross brain injury, the individual finds a method of
maintaining his integrity by avoiding "catastrophic" situations. He is
to some degree crippled, yet preserves his balance by thrusting the
threatening element away, so that his life exists at a simpler yet still
highly ordered systematic level of living. Furthermore, Goldstein's
data indicate that normal interaction with the environment involves
the establishment of a balance between stresses within the tissue
system. A powerful stimulus acting on one part of the organism leads
to the diffusion of tension and therefore to an equalization process.
Under certain conditions of breakdown, however, the threat is too
great; the full impact of the alien stimulus cannot be received without
catastrophe. The consequence is either the development of a functional
split, such that the shock stimulus cannot get through to damage the
main life system of the individual, or the development within him of
safety-maintaining devices by which he avoids the shock situation. All
of these concepts reemphasize the systematic integrity of the normal

individual and the fact that even under gross impairment what happens is not the deletion of parts but the reconstituting of the individual at a new level.

Considerations such as these have raised in a new way questions about the definition of life, questions that are as old as the difference of opinion between Aristotle and his predecessor Democritus. The trouble with the atomism of Democritus lay not in the atoms themselves but in the neglect to consider those formal and systematic interrelations upon which their effectiveness as atoms depended—the presence, in highly organized matter, of organized patterns which are themselves more enduring than the individual particles which enter into them, just as a vortex (such as a cyclone) may maintain itself though old particles are dropping out and new ones being added constantly. (We are here not raising questions as to the difference between organization in the inorganic and in the organic worlds, but simply noting as an empirical generalization that life cannot be studied at all except in terms of organizational constants of this type, like those that appeared in the sponge or in the wounded man.)

Now if this be granted, the evolutionary significance of a tissue system may be largely independent of the particular particles of matter involved. During long eons of adaptation to different environments, wings may, for example, arise out of different organs, yet functionally achieve the same role. For the surviving organism, the important thing is that the function be performed, not *the organs through which* it is performed. Tissues will in time appear that permit the function necessary to the species to be carried out. The function is consequently not "explained by" the tissues. The tissues are chronologically and logically "explained by" the functions that must be performed if there is to be a living creature for us to talk about.

This was the point upon which nineteenth-century naïve materialism came to grief. The issue is not whether life involves physical and chemical principles similar to those found elsewhere; this is hardly worth arguing about. The real issue is whether the physical and chemical principles operating in their customary way accidentally produced life and the specific expressions of life under various environments, or whether the functional necessities and continuities of nature were such as to call upon specific chemical reagents and physical forces, pulling them into the ongoing system.

The point is well made by C. D. Broad in his distinction between "substantive" and "emergent" vitalism. Few are inclined today to believe in substantive vitalism, the presence of a life substance or life principle independent of tissue behavior; but there is good reason to believe in emergent vitalism, the genuineness of principles or functions characterizing the life process but existing at no simpler level of organization. In this fashion, the organized living system makes use of one or another physical principle in the world outside, draws upon it, and exploits it. To explain personality from within, i.e., atomistically, step by step in terms of tissue changes, would be like saying that a man is five feet nine because he must fit clothes which are made to that specification. As the clothes are chosen and shaped to the individual, the functions of life (growth, repair, reproduction, and all the complex processes which mediate them) draw "clothing," as it were, from the physical and chemical forces outside, so of course they "fit."

This general principle was of course long ago recognized by evolutionists. They noted, however, an important apparent exception in the form of another principle known as orthogenesis, the tendency of living matter during evolution to move continuously in a given direction (through cumulative mutations, cf. page 29), whether this happens to serve a survival purpose or not. It was noted, for example, that the long canine tooth of the sabre-toothed tiger seemed to be getting too long to be useful. Contemporary paleontologists reject this example, and are skeptical of the general principle of a direction in evolution, aside from the requirements of adaptation. But *long time trends*, having an environmental origin, e.g., the successive impacts of cosmic rays, and a corresponding internal origin, e.g., the tendencies of some unstable molecules to break up in response to cosmic rays, seem nevertheless to need to be fitted into the picture.

It is quite likely that the tendency to extreme individuality among living tissues expresses one of these orthogenetic principles. Organisms need to vary, of course, if diversity is to exist so as to permit a rapid selection of the most fit. But the variation has admittedly become extreme in many higher forms, to a point where natural packs and flocks fail to maintain a biologically necessary unity of action, large numbers of individuals being unable to follow the modal tendency of the group. And even under conditions of stockbreeding, intended to reduce the variability in certain traits, an endless selective process is required. The tendency toward complexity is then probably an orthogenetic principle inherent in the ultimate biochemistry of life, and such complexity would be expected to give an extravagant degree of individuality, i.e., more variability than natural selection calls for.

Throughout all this discussion the chemical rather than the anatomical aspects of life have been stressed. Still, they have probably not been stressed enough. For a long period, psychology suffered from an emphasis upon the supposed primacy of the anatomical and physiological properties of nerve cells and muscles. The studies of physiologists and zoologists have made clear over the last half century that the existence of life is first of all a chemical fact, that the development of tissues depends first of all upon chemical laws, that recognizable fixed chemical structures appear only when the chemical problems have been solved, and that the structures and their interrelations are basically chemical systems. Nature, of course, ignores our overnice distinction between the physical and the chemical. What is meant is simply that the molecular and chemical processes require concentrated study if the molar physical processes are to be understood.

It is necessary, then, in personality study, to stress the maintenance of a stable complex individual system; this is a homeostatic problem and a broader biochemical problem. Secondarily arises another chemical problem, the interindividual variability in the chemical systems of life and the intra-individual variabilities day by day as the personality process changes. When this chemical context has been well defined, problems of anatomical, physical, behavioral response will yield more readily to analysis.

THE ORGANISM

THE ORGANISM-ENVIRONMENT RELATION

The organism-environment interactions are both local and general; often there are several different local interactions, each of which must occur concurrently with the rest, so that the general reaction is a complex integrated whole. This requires that the environmental field itself be capable of several related interactions with the organism, and points to the fact that the reciprocity of outer and inner is itself an organized event. The life process is not simply a series of events within the organism, but a field of events in which inner and outer processes constitute a complex totality. The potentialities of life, as in the spore of a fern, can conveniently be conceived as packed within a particle, but the life process itself is not so narrowly localized. A man's life, too, is not within his body, nor is his personality. Potentialities, yes; if we mean by personality the potentiality of individual achievement or social reaction, they are there. The potentialities also exist in an environment which liberally interacts with the potentialities within the man. The actual event, the personal life history, is an inner-outer reciprocity, as is all life; personality as we know it is not within the skin, but coextensive with the individual life process, the sequences of liberated potentialities. We know in fact only an infinitesimal fraction of the potentialities within the skin; their status is indeterminate. The more we can find out, the better. But personality study should not be defined in terms of what lies within the skin until we can describe these potentialities adequately. The life processes which we *can* observe are rewarding objects of study. It is likely, in fact, that it is chiefly through these that such knowledge as we shall ever have about human potentialities will be achieved.

Biochemical systems or fields need first to be defined at given points in time; but it is of their nature to exhibit a time dimension, just as they exhibit three space dimensions. Fields—distributions of energy in space and time—are forever in flux. The most important thing to know about a field may frequently be its direction of change, a direction which can be understood in terms of its own "orthogenesis" and its relation to still larger fields which make up its context.

Spemann and Weiss have shown that to refer here to fields is no meta-phorical manner of speaking; the embryonic field, the distribution of energy in maternal and embryonic bodies, is a field in just as definite a sense as is any electromagnetic field. If this is true where the living organism in relation to its living environment is most fully under-stood, it is likely to be the case also as tissue systems become more complex and as their dependence upon other distant tissue systems after birth becomes more complex. This is enough to say at the moment regarding the field orientation of our present treatment. The whole book will aim to show, step by step, the validity and practical importance of a field definition.

Fields, however, are not homogeneous. The simplest electro-magnetic field as used in a telephone circuit reminds us that energy is more concentrated at one place than another, that the external bound-aries of the field need not make a circle or sphere, that the structure of the field may be both spatially and dynamically very complex, with *nodal points*, regions of high and low energy concentration, constitut-ing points of special interest in the systematic whole. The same is clearly true in the embryo, and in any experimentally analyzed tissue system within the adult, such as the heart. There are regions of maxi-mum activity from which gradients—gradual physicochemical transi-tions—lead to regions of lesser activity. A suitable analogy at a simple level is the weather bureau charts indicating "highs" and "lows" with intervening pressure areas, the whole moving and shift-ing, both in more or less straight lines in one direction and simulta-neously through rotation. The organic system, then, though it is a tension system, is not a single indivisible uniform total; it is rather a complex system of interdependent aspects, with complex yet shifting structural relations, and with nodal regions which, if not more impor-tant, are at least more interesting than others, as regions of greatest energy concentration and clearest functional meaning.

There need be nothing vague about the matter of interdepend-ence; the reasons for it are often clear. One type of interdependence is exemplified in the selective affinities of various chemical reagents for one another; for example, in the tendency of toxins manufactured within the body, or introduced into it, to react most intensely with particular groups of cells and to have slight or no effect upon others. Just as the histologist's stain picks out certain tissues, so the chemical gradients involve not the haphazard but the selective extension of chemical influences in certain directions rather than in others. The same is true of gradients of muscular tension which spread because of neural communication elements and reach some regions more easily than others. There is, indeed, much evidence to show that part of the synchronization of muscles is biochemical, part neural. In the broadest sense, then, communication systems within the organism are lines of transmission of energy, following either anatomical paths such as are provided by nerves, or functional lines defined by selective affinities. Interdependence and intercommunication are questions of directed flow within the organic system. They are, in other words, organized at the very start, in the sense that many types of intercommunication are constantly going on, each tissue being the recipient of many kinds of messages and serving in some degree, as a result of its own metabolism or excitation, to initiate such impulses to many other cells.

ORGANIZATION

This leads us to a preliminary definition of the term "organization," a term which will be constantly used in relation to every aspect of personality development. Organization involves, first of all, the transmission of energy from one region to another; second, the simultaneous passage of energies in various directions in an interdependent fashion as described above; third, the consequent adjustment of one part to another, the constant regularizing effect of tissues upon one another, of which homeostasis or the maintenance of constancy is one aspect. Finally, organization involves not only interstimulation of parts but response of the separate parts of the whole system to outer stimulating forces. As L. J. Henderson has shown in his nomogram of the blood, the structure of life is no mere question of the interdependence of all that lies within the body; it is a question of the balance, the interstimulation which goes on between outer and inner forces. As oxygen comes into the lungs and the organism maintains itself by using it at a certain rate, there is no real problem as to when and where the gas becomes part of the living system. If as the oxygen goes down the respiratory passages it is still technically outside the body, what shall we say about the oxygen which is being carried by the red blood cells, or indeed about the oxygen within the individual cells served by the capillaries? The life process is merely focused in the organism; it involves a field extending beyond the body. Organization embraces the entire organism-environment relation, of which the organism is the nodal point but not the complete functioning system.

One more factor, however, remains to be included when the term organization is used. Not only do the tissue systems maintain their homeostatic balance and swing back to a poised normality after an upset; they also undergo systematic progressive change. Organization, then, applies to the temporal dimension as well as to the spatial. Individual growth is organized not merely in the sense that the parts change in an orderly way; since each part is an aspect of a system, the system as a whole changes according to a unified dynamic. Just as lengthening of shadows on a rugged mountainside involves more than the lengthening of individual lines, the growth of any living form involves a progressive alteration of relations in which, despite all change, fundamental unities remain, and in which, despite all fundamental unities, a progressive alteration occurs in the structure of the system. Thus, for example, a study of human aging in terms of decade-by-decade changes in visual acuity is not a study of changes in the eye alone; it is part of a more comprehensive study in which the relation of visual acuity to total functioning efficiency is seen as an aspect of the basic reorganization of human powers throughout the life span.

The entire evolutionary process appears to depend upon the capacity for maintaining basic stability and integrity within the organic system while adding a new feature which establishes a new direction. Thus mutations—sudden appearance of genes within the germ cell, giving rise to radical new body characteristics—initiate new species structurally and functionally different from their progenitors, and over vast periods of time are responsible for progeny that might never be classified as descendants of their ancestors were not the fossil remains convincing. The process of successful mutation involves the maintenance of life and of most of the essentials of a given form of organization, while at the same time it suddenly adds a completely new characteristic. Whatever may be attributed to the reshufflings of the chromosomes that are responsible for the endless diversities within a species, it is clear that most of the great steps which nature takes by way of initiating new forms of life occur because, upon a base of extreme stability, amazing diversity in new additions is permitted.[1]

Many of the forms which arise through mutation do not survive as well as their parents; indeed, the mutation may be so maladaptive as to be lethal, and with it the bold experiment ends. Often, however, the mutation gives rise to an organism that fits into a niche in the environment which is not already overcrowded with organisms adapted to it. The niches or holes in the environment—capacity to use types of food not already monopolized or to make use of habitats in air, earth, or water not already preempted—permit the newcomer to find, as it were, a place prepared. It is the environment that determines which trend among the countless mutations can be realized in a new species. Both the intrinsic tendencies of living matter and the invitations given by the environing world of nature determine in what direction life will move.

Huxley's "barrel analogy" serves well to exemplify the point. Let a man fill a barrel with apples; it is full to the brim. He now has the task of filling it with pebbles; the interstices permit him to shovel enormous quantities into the already "filled" barrel. Let it next be filled with sand; there is plenty of room. When this has been done, there is still room for water. The interdependence of living forms needing one another, parasitic upon one another, helping one another, constitutes a continuous pressure of prolific life upon the vacant spaces,

---

[1] There is much evidence to suggest that mutations are direct expressions of the quantum principle of physics: the protein molecule is reconstructed when sufficient energy impinges upon it.

the interstices which physical nature and the existing forms of life present.

Almost all the behavioral complexities with which psychologists must deal are basically features of this principle. The primate stock is not, as such, any better stock in survival terms than were earlier existing forms; but the arboreal environment permitted the expansion of a race which had both the physical ability and the wit. The various succeeding forms of anthropoid apes and of primitive man appear to exemplify the barrel analogy well, in the sense that there was always a place for more wit than was already at hand.

There was also a place for huge *individual differences*. In all the higher forms, mutation can function not only to initiate new species, but to initiate traits which lead to the diversification of types within the species. This diversification, together with the endless chromosome reshufflings already mentioned, means literally that personality, a very complex , highly individualized, highly organized sort of thing, was demanded by nature—demanded in the sense that there was a gap waiting for it, and that when, as a result of mutation and recombination, steps led more and more toward filling the gap, they were "selected" rather than "eliminated."

A formulation used by Selig Hecht seems to be profoundly insightful in this connection, though he used it in relation to a different problem: The organism does not adapt itself to the environment; the environment adapts the organism to itself. The kind of thing that man is, and the kinds of thing that individual men are, are both products of a "necessity"—a physical, spatial, dynamic necessity which demands the filling of the gap in the same sense that a vacuum demands the air which will fill it.

The barrel analogy is also useful in reinforcing the point which we shall have to make constantly regarding discontinuity. Species are discontinuous; they are forms distinct enough so that two species, when crossed, cannot produce fertile offspring. Mutations introduce discontinuities; and species, when once defined, maintain themselves independently for vast periods of time. Even within species, as we have seen, there are some mutations that produce important discontinuities. There are also the discontinuities which result whenever the middle of a distribution is eliminated in the competition with some similar form of life, leaving only the extremes.

But the concept of discontinuity usually relates not to discontinuity in a single trait measured on a linear scale, but to basic differences in structural organization. A bird with a new type of wings produced by mutation can fly only if the wings are related in a specific way to its size, shape, and weight; what survives is a new *interrelation* of parts. Even a very primitive type of "personality" or "organismic structure" reveals basic gaps between viable types of organization, on both sides of which stand fundamentally different systems of interrelationship. So far as one man's inheritance includes genes which another man's inheritance lacks, and so far as the structural possibilities associated with different genes are necessarily discontinuous, there are true discontinuities between all men.

UNIQUENESS

This matter of discontinuity—the distinctiveness of the individual—leads to a final broad philosophical problem that has to be faced, and the sooner the better. As G. W. Allport has eloquently shown, personality is unique. Much of the best work of today is centered in this sound and important principle. So, too, it is clear from biology that every individual is unique; not only every tree, but every leaf. Microscopy and mathematics have demonstrated that every snowflake is unique. Every geological formation, every village street, is unique. The uniqueness seems to the present writer to lie not in the constituents but in the modes of interrelation, the organization of the constituents. It is from this general fact of uniqueness of the particular that science, with its disentangling, measuring, conceptualizing method, has proceeded; from such a method has arisen a science of crystals, a science of botany. Why not a general science of the psychology of personality, that is, a science dealing not only with particulars but with laws of organization, the general principles governing the interrelations of the constituent parts? Such a science would be concerned with organization, with architectonics, exactly as crystallography or botany are; it would be interested not only in the individuality of each human being, but in all the reasons for each individual variation in parts or structures, just as the botanist is interested not only in Mendel's laws or in osmotic pressure, but in the way in which they reflect themselves in endlessly diverse fashion when one complete plant is compared with another. There are laws of an extremely general sort that govern all plants; as we move away from such generalization, we find other, more particular laws governing only certain species; and at the end of such a continuum there are very specific principles that govern only one class of event—say the respiratory process of an aspen leaf at sea-level atmospheric pressure. Such laws are presumably uniformities in nature, but uniformities which sometimes have significance for all life processes in all living things, at other times for some processes in some living things, at still other times for a single event in a single living thing.

There may have been just once in cosmic history a whale like Moby Dick. The response of that leviathan would necessarily be an expression of all the physicochemical laws in their specific application to that special case. So, too, there has been in cosmic history just one Confucius, one Jeanne d'Arc, and one you. But your uniqueness does not exempt you from any of the forms and norms of the generalizing method of science. As end results we are indeed unique; but as evolutionary products, and processes, we all express the same cosmic principles. At least, this is the frame of reference within which the present treatment proceeds.

3. Heredity and Individual Growth

JUST as it has been the habit of the Calvinist to accept the Biblical miracles while insisting that the age of miracles has ceased, so it has been the habit of our era to start from evolutionary principles and yet to regard man, just as he is, as the fine fulfillment of a cosmic process, the apex of destiny. The self-containedness and the value of personality are such evident realities that the *incompleteness*, the *indeterminateness*, the *becomingness* of personality have been almost ignored. The potentialities from which personality springs change with each generation.

For at least three types of evolutionary process are going on today. First there are endless recombinations of germinal tendencies through crossings, the disappearance of old types, the creation of new ones. It is easy for the biologist to watch this process in large-scale racial mixture and in the mixture of contrasting stocks within a race. It is only here and there, as in studies of homogamy (the tendency of like to mate with like), that the psychologist has taken hold of the problem. If individual response, individual organization, depend in any degree upon the stuff one is made of, the shuffling and recombination of genes entail the same biological necessity for new chemical and neural results as for new results in skin or bone; new gene groupings mean new personality potentialities.

Second, the differential birth rates are already yielding striking data on selective factors. We have to do not only with reshufflings but with shufflings out and shufflings in, the weakening or disappearance of some strains and the strengthening of others, in accordance both with the ancient laws of survival and with the more salient modern laws of struggle for standards of living, social ascendancy, political power. Such results are almost infinitely complex, and the degree of their significance is necessarily a matter of inference from the biology of the individual rather than a matter of laboratory demonstration. The tragedy of the situation lies not in the hopelessness of the problem but in the vapid propaganda of the racialists, who have proceeded (with no genuine evidence) to identify the problems of human biological individuality with the problems of national or racial ascendancy. This, in an era of progress in the cultural sciences, has resulted in a general disgust, on the part of psychologists, with the biological approaches to individuality; the individual baby has been thrown out with the racialist bath.

Third, the cultural forces themselves redefine the significance of biological traits. The same biological dispositions that result in rage, courage, or persistence at a level of hunting or individual or group combat may, in an industrial society, result in indiscriminate savagery or the butting of one's head against the impersonal wall of a frustrating social institution. The consequence is that the biological selection goes on in different terms today from those in which the traits were originally developed, with the probable result that different kinds of men are tending to appear in different subcultural areas, in different social classes. It is an axiom of the stockbreeder that one generation gives only a starter, an intimation; but in a hundred years the domestic strains of swine, cattle, and poultry have been enormously altered, rendered stronger, hardier, more resistant to disease, different strains being developed for different requirements. Tryon needed only a few generations to get non-overlapping "bright" and "dull" strains of rats (in a maze problem) through inbreeding; Hall needed only a few to get well-defined bold and timid rats.

As always, of course, it is the individual that is selected and bred with another selected individual. But with human genetics we have scarcely made a beginning; we are still forced to use animal analogies. A humanity saddled with the most chauvinistic conceptions of racial or national superiority and a humanity suffering from the conviction that cultural situations may indiscriminately make anything out of any human material have, between them, lost the significance of individual protoplasm. When the individual appears he may be obeyed, believed, worshiped; but it would be sacrilege to inquire as to his origin. In the fashion of Carlyle, or Alger, we hail the individual who climbs through the muck and stands forth in glory; but as to studying how such people achieve existence in the first place, such an attempt would be an affront to the inscrutable ways of nature!

In the meantime, for our own infinitesimal project this situation has a clear result: since most of the inquiries about the facts of personality have been made in terms of the learning process, we must, whenever we emphasize established principles, place emphasis upon cultural dynamics. But wherever we have biological information we shall use it, and in using information from the social sciences we shall try to relate the data to the biological individuality of the persons involved. For just as there is no biological process which is today completely independent of the social conditions of life, so there is no social science process except in and between the individual tissues of persons. Human evolution, then, as it goes on, yielding new biotypes, new personal potentialities, not only reflects but in subtle and obscure fashion plays a part in guiding the more dramatic and obvious changes in social forms.

This is the thought that prompted Clarence Day in *This Simian World*. Let us ask ourselves, says Day, what civilization would be like if the great cats—the lions, leopards, jaguars—had invented it; if the great overreaching cerebral hemispheres had been superimposed upon the carnivorous ferocity of William Blake's *Tiger*. Civilization could be sublime in the manner of Assyrian art, gentle in the manner of kittens' play, but culture would express feline rather than simian needs. What, for example, shall we say about the right of free speech? Watch the simians in the field, forest, or zoo, as they chatter. For the great cats, the right of free speech would yield to the right of personal combat. To this "simian world," chatter is so important that we assemble in vast buildings the collections of canned or bottled chatter which the ages have accumulated. Or turn, as did Swift, to a civilization built by the equines. What are the loyalties, the securities which this herd-minded, this intensely social race would demand? Can one believe, any more than could Gulliver, that the equines would be capable of the chicaneries and brutalities of which the simians are perennially guilty?

We might gently remind Day that the simians are of many sorts. Gibbons differ from gorillas, and Heidelberg men probably differed from the presumptive Cro-Magnon ancestors of today's Europeans. But there is a common fund of drive, of nervous exploratory activity, of easy fear and rage, of persistence, devotion, and brutality which lies deep in the tissues. Personality is ultimately made out of simian stuff and action. As Swift saw, our resentment at such a generalization as this is due not merely to dislike of the sights, sounds, and smells of the zoo, but to the recognition that, though a little lower than the angels, men are also in many respects only a little higher than their arboreal relatives.

We are speaking now, of course, of very raw impulse. Mankind puts an incredible amount of effort into shaping this mass of impulse into integrated and symbolic activities adapted to fantastically complicated social requirements. Everyone born into this world, however, begins with a set of tissues which goes back far beyond the ice age in their primordial demands, their basic insistences, their raw impressions as to what life is about. To forget the stuff of which man the organism is built may facilitate the construction of ideal patterns —in both senses of the term—but adjustment to these patterns may involve tensions or, often enough, biological contradictions.

This does not in any sense mean that society needs to be more apish, more feral than it is. Rather, the argument is that the highest of which man has dreamed is itself ultimately an expression of the kind of tissues of which he is made up. Indeed, we should go much further. We shall try to show in later chapters that organized society has overlooked much of the gentleness, tenderness, sensitivity, and sympathy which are actually the birthright of simian stock. But our chief concern here is to make sure that attention is given to humankind as a species; for whatever we shall have to say about individuality, the traits which enter into it are derivatives of human biology and continuing human evolution.

HEREDITY AND INDIVIDUAL GROWTH

THE MECHANISM OF HEREDITY

We must now study more closely the mechanism of heredity that was briefly considered on pages 29 ff. In all the many-celled forms of life, some cells have achieved specialized functions which involve the loss of their primitive capacity to yield new life forms; the task of carrying on the stock is the property of a restricted group of cells, the germ cells. Body cells and germ cells are distinct. The germ cells are nourished and protected, but, so far as is known, not greatly influenced by the vicissitudes affecting the life of the body. They are capable of transmitting the ancestral traits from generation to generation regardless of crafts acquired, languages spoken, prejudices cultivated by the people who carry them.

Germ cells, however, play their role in the changing, as well as in the continuing, of life. Preparatory to the reproduction process, in which a germ from the father and a germ from the mother unite, each germ cell has undergone a process which throws out half of its germinal potentialities. This "reduction division" yields two gametes, each of which has half the number of chromosomes which the germ cell had before; thus, in man, there are 24 instead of 48. When the fusion of male and female germ cells occurs, the original number, 48, is reconstituted by sheer addition. This process means, however, that of the total 96 available chromosomes in the two parents, there can never actually be more than 48 in the new individual; and which ones they are, so long as there are 24 from each parent, is determined by such infinite biochemical complexities that we have to treat them as occurring at random. Two children with the same parents may be very much alike or they may be very different indeed, depending on similarity or difference in the germinal constitution which they have received; the striking difference between two such children thus occurs not in *spite* of heredity but *because* of it. Around a common core of biological similarities in any stock there are the endless individualities traceable to unique combinations of genes. (New genes—mutations—also appear; although they are studied in the fruit fly as soon as they appear, their role in man is practically unknown.)

Another problem relating to gene structure that has taken on importance recently is the likelihood that groups of genes located on the same chromosome, linked together and remaining linked through the formation of the new individual, may be traceable in the individual constitution. Burks succeeded in identifying, through life history data and direct clinical examination, the linkage of certain hair colors with certain tooth conditions such that the members of a family who have this hair color have the same peculiar tooth structure. With techniques established through these somatic studies, she laid a foundation for investigating the linkage of psychological peculiarities with physical peculiarities. The incidence of the manic-depressive psychosis, she suspected, may in some families be linked with identifiable idiosyncrasies of the teeth. As always in such studies, one abstracts a relation from a maze of particulars. Patient care and mental hygiene may help the person with a germinal weakness, just as dental care and orthodontia can. But the importance of such linkage lies not in the fact that anomalies become more controllable, but in the great likelihood that functional unities, genuine elements in personality structure, will be revealed. Whatever clings consistently together with a somatic trait, or stems from a common origin with it, has a chance of being "elemental." Since distinct personality features are scarcely likely to be the direct results of such characteristics as nonerupted teeth, and since, nevertheless, the two characteristics cling together from one generation to the next, it is likely that the specified psychological trait has a simple genetic structure. Again we say that this structure is ultimately a biochemical disposition; it is realized only in the process of growth and interaction with the environment; and if it is pathological, therapy may remove it. The fact that a man shaves, although making the face as smooth as one pleases, does not affect the situation confronting one's adolescent sons; the germinal dispositions go on generation after generation.

Of all the verbal quagmires into which man has fallen in his attempt to tell what he is, none has caused more damage than the uncritical use of the opposing terms "heredity" and "environment." Our folklore is saturated with the belief that we inherit certain full-fledged traits and that we acquire other traits by virtue of environmental forces. For three-quarters of a century the literature on "nature and nurture" seemed to support such a belief, and authorities are still quoted to show that some traits are truly hereditary, others truly acquired. The toughness of this form of thinking, its resistance to evidence, is shown by the fact that modern geneticists, embryologists, comparative psychologists, and students of the infant and small child, though perfectly aware of the fallacies in this type of language, find themselves forced, if they are to make contact with their readers or hearers, to employ these question-begging terms.

But if the organism is a tissue system undergoing changes partly because of its own dynamics, partly because of interaction with the outer world, it is "acquiring" new characteristics all the time, never by accretion but always by modification of what it is. No organism differently *constituted* could acquire in the same way or acquire the same tendencies. What is acquired is just as completely an expression of the inherited make-up of the organism as it is an expression of the outer forces. Nothing meaningful can be said about our acquisition of tendencies, or about the effects of the environment, except in terms of a specific knowledge of the dispositions of the living system. New tendencies, habits, traits are not acquired, plastered on, or stuck on as one affixes a postage stamp to a letter. The organism grows into new phases of behavior, under one form of pressure or another, as long as life continues. Similarly, to use the term "acquired traits" is to talk redundantly, for all traits are acquired by some kind of reaction with environmental forces. There was a time when any given trait was not there; and if one speaks precisely, no trait that is there will remain long in its present apparent form. As Heraclitus said, no man can step twice into the same river; it is a different man, a different river. The way a man talks, or even his attitude toward himself, basic as it may be, is a function both of past tissue changes and of present environing pressures.

If it is true that nothing is acquired in the popular sense, it is equally true that nothing is inherited. As a result of very complex interactions—each of two cells merging its field dynamics with that of the other cell—a new life system involving its own field relationships is established; in it some features of each of the two earlier life systems are still recognizable, but it has a large number of new dispositions which never existed before in any creature on the face of the earth. Hence even the near-identities between the offspring and the parent are not instances of heredity in the popular sense. Since it is not the bodily characteristics of the parents that are transmitted, but only the germinal dispositions, and since organisms show wide differences from their parents in bodily characteristics, the word heredity refers at best to the continuity of certain dispositions from one generation to the next. Even in this sense, however, the term causes a great deal of trouble because dispositions as such cannot be observed. It is the dispositions *as realized*, as fulfilled by certain environing circumstances, that we can study. There develops the paradox that heredity is known only by the liberation of the hereditary potentials *through specific environmental forces;* and what is liberated is as much a function of the environing pressures as it is of the latent or potential dispositions.

In the life process, whether studied in embryology or later, nature is not made up, mosaic fashion, of hereditary and environmental elements. The terms heredity and environment serve no purpose for referring to methods of classifying types of behavior, and they can profoundly damage the whole effort in personality study. What they really denote, if carefully studied, is a dual function; the two always occur together and are separated only for conceptual convenience, as we might, for convenience, define two interacting chemical reagents as if one were the agent and the other the substance acted upon.

Defining the environmental pressures as those observed by the physical sciences in terms of light, temperature, acidity, etc., we shall reserve the term heredity for the dispositions of the organism which allow these physical forces to produce greater or lesser changes in it or to manifest this or that type of qualitative variation in its response pattern. Heredity, then, will be the system of predispositions, throughout the life history of the individual organism, which, when different organisms are compared, is responsible for the varying effects of known environmental pressures. In this sense, a birch tree and a man differ in heredity in that they chronically react differently to sunlight and water; and so far as two human beings in the same sense chronically (from the germ cell on) react differently to sunlight and water, for example, they are different in heredity. Genes and chromosomes are neither a miniature of the later adult life form nor a prophecy of what it is to be. They are simply keys to potentials for differential responses which will ultimately appear under environmental pressure.

The meaning of heredity becomes clear, then, as the prenatal environment induces more and more specificity in a growing mass which accepts increasing specificity as it accepts oxygen or water. This increase of specificity involves the gradual freeing of each tissue, step by step, from the intimate interdependence which at first characterizes its relations with other tissues. Inherited dispositions become clearer and clearer as more and more of the particularized make-up of the individual, its way of interacting with the environment, becomes evident. The degree of independence of each tissue from other tissues—the degree to which it carries out its own task without submitting to the control of environing tissues—is largely a question of its *maturity*, as demonstrated in the work of experimental embryologists. Tissues that are grafted very early in embryonic development, say in the period of gastrulation, take on in rather complete detail not only the functional role but the anatomical form which their position requires. Cells which when left to their own devices in saline solution become skin or hair cells may, when grafted in a region destined to become an eye, become typical cells of the eye structure. Let this transplantation be done a little later, and a considerable number of cells will fail to yield to this environing pressure. If it is attempted later still, none of the cells will thus yield. In the process of achieving maturity, each cell has become more refractory to influences from without, except those it accepts in terms of its own basic rhythm. If belly ectoderm from the newt is grafted over the head region of the young axolotl early enough, it takes on the form of the little rods or "balancers" which, in newt organization, characterize the head surfaces, despite the fact that the axolotl itself develops no such head decorations. "The cells have reacted to the lateral head field of the *axolotl* to the best of their *newt* knowledge, according to which a balancer is the proper thing to form on the side of the head." (Weiss.) Within certain limits, a cell, *if young enough*, does what the environment tells it to do. There is, perhaps, no more universal generalization about organismic development than the generalization that the younger the organism, the less specific its identity, the more plastic its modalities.

All this illustrates the gradual transformation of any tissue or tissue system into something else; at no point is anything ever "added" to the organism; no "acquired" traits are affixed to it. The genes establish inexorable limits, but what will be done with their potential depends on growth circumstances. Environing pressures do what they can do because tissue potentialities await them; the latter, however, are nothing but potentialities, have no clear destiny of their own. There are many things which a given tissue cannot become, but there is no one thing which it is inexorably destined to become.

These principles are illustrated in the development of bone and sinew. Stature and body structure clearly express individual gene patterns that are guided by specific nutritive and climatic forces. For example, Shapiro's studies of Japanese who were born and reared in Japan, of Japanese who migrated early in life to Hawaii, and of individuals of Japanese descent who were born in the United States, showed the thorax to have three characteristic forms, each expressing specific conditions of climate and nutrition which bring to reality the primitive vague potentialities of the ancestral body structure.

In the same vein are the data on blood pressure and basal metabolic rate among whites and Orientals. Blood pressure and basal metabolic rate are characteristically higher in whites than in Orientals. But the white man in China, long habituated to the tempo of Chinese life, has a lower blood pressure and basal metabolism than whites in the Occident, whereas Chinese who have become adapted to the occidental tempo of life are in these respects more like occidentals than like the Chinese of China.

It must be noted in the comparisons just made that *individual differences* still remain within each of the contrasting groups. We never find ourselves obliterating these differences or reducing all humanity to a common pulp. There is a profound response to changed environing conditions—by and large, the earlier the influence the more profound its effects—but we never find infinite plasticity, the complete emptying of individuality into the great sink of a cosmic process. The developmental process that underlies all organismic structuring is a process within specific individual tissues which can be molded into superficially identical forms, but only with varying degrees of reluctance. Traits display varying degrees of modifiability, depending partly upon which traits are involved, partly upon the severity of the environmental pressure, and partly upon the life period during which the pressure is applied. There is always individuality, even in the most extreme environmental pressure, just as there is always a basic humanity appearing through all the individualization which human stuff possesses, in whatever cultural arrangements men may contrive.

These individual differences call at times for a statistical evaluation in which it is legitimate and important to separate (for purposes of abstraction) the contributions of nature and nurture. There is a large difference between the method most suitable for approaching the individual and the method most suitable for reaching a quantitative generalization about the roles of nature and nurture in a given population. It is true that in every individual case nature-nurture is a single indivisible whole; if we describe an individual, making no comparison with other individuals but simply following the chromosome pattern and the embryonic growth, there is nothing hereditary in the organism, and nothing attributable to environment. Since, however, many creatures come from the same stock—indeed, identical twins come from the same germ cell—there is an advantage in abstracting from the field the aspect which we may call genetic similarity. Similarly, since many organisms of different stock may be exposed to essentially the same temperatures, pressures, or hydrogen-ion concentrations, we may abstract from many life histories the aspect of environmental uniformity. We may then suitably set up statistical evaluations of the concrete effects of allowing the stock to vary to such and such a degree in any given case, or allowing the environment to vary to such and such a degree. We may say, for example, that with a given group of cases the stock variations produce offspring which in a given environment differ from one another in length by so many inches. Or we may say that members of the same stock (within specified limits) who are subjected to such and such widely varying temperatures have such and such variations in length of body.

No such statistical statement is ever a quantitative generalization regarding the relative importance of nature and nurture. There is no such thing as a trait that is primarily hereditary or a trait that is primarily environmental; every trait is completely and absolutely a hereditary tendency brought to its fulfillment by a specific environmental pressure. But the *variability from person to person* in respect to each trait within any sample of people under any sample of conditions can always be treated with respect to the question: How is the variability of individuals related to the variability of stock and of environment? Some stocks are empirically widely variable; others, especially as a result of inbreeding, are relatively invariable. When subjected to roughly uniform environmental forces, there are inevitably wider individual differences in the former than in the latter; and though in the case of the isolated individual we need apply no statistics, we may appropriately attribute the wide variability of the observed members of the first group to the stock variability. In the same way, two roughly equated samples from the same stock may be exposed to two environments, the first narrow, rigid, and homogeneous, the second wide, flexible, and heterogeneous. The observed members of the second group will display a variability in accordance with the range of environmental excitations. Combining the two principles, whenever we have known and measurable variabilities of stock and known and measurable variabilities in environmental pressures, we can calculate the approximate relative contributions made by the two types of factors to the observed variability of developing individuals. For our purposes—namely, the discussion of individual personality with relatively little statistical generalization—the concept of the unity of the specific individual nature-nurture field is as important as the question of degrees of dependence upon stock variation or upon environment variation.

Since this is so, and since the heredity of the individual is a constant, whereas the environment is a variable, our task includes the study of individual continuity through the growth process, showing the ways in which the primordial potentialities of the individual develop as a result of the interaction of the potentials with a constantly changing and expanding environing field. At every point in the expansion of the individual, new hereditary potentialities arise; but at every point in this expansion, what is realized in action is not heredity alone but the field relationships which potentialities exhibit when liberated and focused by the specific requirements of the world.

MULTI-FACTOR DETERMINATION

Up to this point we have been content to think of one hereditary factor, one gene, at a time. For the great majority of functional characteristics, however, it is clear that the number of contributing genes is many. R. C. Tryon (page 46), breeding rats for their "brightness" or "dullness" in learning a specific maze, found that many genes were at work. The same evidence for multi-gene determination appears in Hall's studies of the inheritance of temperaments (page 46). It is generally agreed that the traits of temperament which differentiate various breeds and families of dogs are not reducible to single genes. Temperamental differences appear in puppyhood and are stable and dependable enough to be of great commercial importance. But they do not seem so very different from the variations in temperament found by Ruth Washburn in a group of forty infants whom she studied month by month through the first year of life and who maintained their characteristic jolly, somber, or expressionless temperaments in an experimental situation. Nor are these month-to-month continuities so very different from the continuities through the first two years reported by Shirley in her study of the personalities of twenty-five children in conjunction with studies of their motor and intellectual growth (cf. page 69). Likewise suggestive of multi-factor inheritance, rather than of single genes, are the data of Jost and Sontag, showing that in vasomotor persistence, heart and respiration period, and other autonomically controlled processes, the resemblance of identical twins is greater than that of sibs, and of sibs greater than that of random pairs, but with some overlapping of groups.

So, though it is more convenient to think of single genes, the fact seems to be that every one of the traits we are dealing with involves continuities, with an unbroken sweep from one extreme to another; and this means not a single gene, acting on an all-or-none basis, but a multiplicity of genes. The evidence today converges to indicate on the one hand the enormous importance of heredity, and on the other hand its operation through highly complex syndromes in which, in spite of the present experimental and mathematical skill, very few single-gene factors related to personality have been found.

The complexity is such that at times we may be tempted to abandon analysis and argue for the global or non-atomic character of such functional attributes. But this would defeat our purpose. That exquisite global unity to which Goldstein refers has been achieved empirically by nature by the atomic method, i.e., by the development of discontinuous and isolable genes. The resolving power of a telescope may be insufficient to reveal a double star, and the resolving power of psychological methods may be insufficient to reveal the components in a complex pattern; but as the technique improves, the specification of components becomes more exact. Whether we are actually dealing with a homogeneous or global process or with one which merely *seems* global (because the resolving power of our methods is inadequate) is always an empirical question to be prejudged not in terms of esthetic simplicity but in terms of available knowledge regarding dynamics. In the case of heredity and many aspects of early embryology we do know by transplanting or excising tissues what the atomic influences are and how they work.

There are, indeed, countless instances in which atoms neutralize or stabilize one another and other instances in which they facilitate, arithmetically or otherwise, one another's effects. For practical purposes we are frequently more concerned with the dynamic pattern of interaction than with the identification of the components, and fortunately the discovery of types of equilibrium is often possible without a full understanding of the forces which are counterpoised one to another. An example is the conception of biotypes developed by the Italian school of anthropology over half a century ago, and by Kretschmer and by Sheldon and his collaborators in recent years (page 149). It is quite possible that there exist fundamental and discontinuous types of bodily and psychological organization, *pure types* which, like pure chemicals, constitute theoretical clues to all the empirical confusion due to impurities or overlappings (page 740). But however successful these typological methods may ultimately be, the fact is that the individual remains salient and unyielding within the type, that he appears all over the type, or between types, or where types overlap. In contrast with the enormous effort required to convince one's colleague that there are any types at all—types which at best hold only in a broadly general and abstract sense—one is thrown hour by hour into contact with individuality which makes even a primary classification into types very difficult, and then calls for a long specification of subtypes, overlaps, impurities, and complications. We are closing no doors upon types; we are merely noting that the very fact of multi-gene determination and the confusion and crisscrossing that threaten or trip up every venture toward typing, still leave us primarily with the problem of complex individuality, which necessitates empirically as many types as there are persons.

The complexity is almost frightening. The more exact knowledge of hereditary resemblance which has come to us from the study of identical twins, of ordinary siblings, of the Dionne quintuplets, and of other dramatic experiments of nature, has indicated that where we know the most the problems of psychological heredity are the most baffling. Thus identical twins reared apart may properly be regarded as "temperamentally" alike but "socially" much less alike. Yet the two terms clearly overlap to a large extent; and on the critical question as to how much temperamental similarity there is, and the degree to which it influences social adjustment, we still struggle with vague and unsatisfactory data. If there were simple discontinuities, simple all-or-none traits, the problem would be relatively straightforward. The "quints" have taught us the lesson well. Though according to all professional testimony this sistership of five is uni-ovular, all sharing the same heredity, and though they were for a long time brought up in an extraordinarily uniform fashion, they early displayed very different personalities. One may fall back here upon hypotheses regarding uterine position and accidental favoritism on the part of the nurses, and develop interesting theories about the sisters' inter-stimulation in their own little world. The one empirical fact of which we can really be sure is that neither the genetic nor the environmental forces were as simple and homogeneous as they looked. A multiplicity of factors is clearly at work both in the genetic and in the environmental spheres.

As Bichat suggested long ago, tissue needs are older, more fundamental, than the structure of the neural communication systems. In the progressive differentiation and elaboration which make up so much of the subject matter of *growth*, the biochemical has the lion's share, and the biochemist consequently has the lion's share of the research tools and of the data for this enterprise. To understand *growth*, as to understand *life*, one studies the chemistry of crystals and of colloids; the chemistry of food and nutrition; the chemical nature of enzymes, of metabolism, and of self-repair; the chemistry and physiology of emerging tissues and tissue systems, and of *differential* growth in different regions; and behind all these, the chemical balances and reciprocities that express themselves as the organism becomes larger and its parts become recognizably distinct. The nervous system appears slowly, and for a long time holds a subordinate position. Its properties depend partly on the prevailing chemistry of non-neural organs; it takes over a regulatory function only slowly, and under conditions of responsibility shared throughout by the biochemical system. We do not mean to labor the obvious fact that the nervous system is itself a chemical system and its transmission of impulses a chemical process; rather, we mean that completely non-neural biochemistry never withdraws altogether into the background to give the nervous system an entirely free hand in those complex regulatory processes to which the spectator gives the name "personality."

The biochemical system may well prove to be carrying another responsibility; it may be playing a larger role than we thought in the early development of the central nervous system. It was customary not long ago to trace the individual differences in nervous systems directly to combinations of certain genes which in themselves were the specific determiners of a good or poor neural product. If the brain was good, this was because the genes producing the brain were good. The issue has been complicated, however, by the discovery of genes which by playing a role in the development of the biochemical system affect the growing nerve cells. Thus Jervis, noting that individuals with a rare but very definite type of mental defect regularly show phenylpyruvic acid in the urine, demonstrated that this specific *type* of mental defect (not mental defect in general) is a simple Mendelian dominant. (A simple Mendelian trait is one due to a single gene; a trait is dominant if it appears when the gene for it is received from one parent despite the fact that a gene for another trait, incompatible with the first, is received from the other parent.) He traced the family trees of some 1700 individuals, and found that the phenylpyruvic trait appeared in the required Mendelian proportions. If, moreover, there are seven children in a family, four of whom have this type of mental defect, the other three being normal, the four will show phenylpyruvic acid in the urine, the other three will not. Now obviously phenyl-pyruvic acid is not the "clue to intelligence." It is an intermediary product of metabolism, and apparently is so highly toxic that it damages the growing nerve cells. In short, it is not "the genes for neural growth" that are wanting in the individual; it is the genes for a biochemical trait that are at fault. If it be asked whether the whole situation is not environmental, emphasis must be placed on the nature of the initial finding. The biochemical difficulty is Mendelian; it appears in some of the children in a family but not in others; and it cripples mentally those whom it strikes. We may combine two general hypotheses: Instead of the older procedure of endeavoring to show that individual human traits are simple Mendelian characters, we must be prepared to recognize today that each trait may be either single-gene- or multi-gene-determined, with the probabilities in the latter direction, and that each trait may be either a *direct* or an *indirect* reflection of a gene situation, again with the probabilities in the latter direction.

The process of differentiation in the growing individual must in the first instance be largely chemical, involving the normal metabolic processes and the continuous action of enzymes. Areas which appear to be biochemically homogeneous undergo progressive differentiation into biochemically distinct regions. Spatial, thermal, and gravitational factors exert different influences in different regions, but they do not explain the form which the differentiation process reveals. For even a high degree of unity in these spatial, gravitational, and thermal factors from one species to another within a genus still permits the emergence of striking differences in species which are known to be due to distinct differences of genetic structure, and the chemical modification of early growth shows clearly that the chemical properties of cells set limits upon the properties of organs which may appear and the time of their appearance.

MATURATION

In studying the emergence of organs, we find ourselves confronted by Herbert Spencer's conception of *differentiation from a homogeneous matrix.* The homogeneity is far from absolute, and reciprocal relations are present both between the somewhat heterogeneous elements in the matrix and between them and the somewhat heterogeneous forces surrounding the organism. Spencer's formulation is nevertheless sound in the broad sense that all growth involves a progressive sharpening or accentuation of those differences which at first appear slight or blurred. When contrasted, for example, with "pre-formism," which holds that all the parts must be present in the germ if they are to appear in the adult, the relative correctness of the Spencerian view becomes evident. By maturation we shall mean simply this progressive differentiation from the non-specific to the specific.

In the same general sense, the relative correctness of Haeckel's biogenetic law must be admitted, to the effect that as the organism grows it passes through phases similar to phases in the evolutionary history of the species. The human individual not only betrays his aquatic ancestry in the early months of prenatal life; but resembles his mammalian brethren in form and function until about half the gestation period is over; he does not take on the characteristically human traits until the time of birth approaches. To show that there are many omissions, modifications, and transpositions is appropriate if one is in danger of foolhardy generalization; but for general orientation purposes it is important to remember that human individuality has its richness, its distinctiveness, largely because it is superposed, as a very complex end result, upon a developmental continuity.

In terms of the often-quoted researches of Coghill, development arises from "individuation within the total mass" rather than from accretion of originally distinct particles. The experiments of Kuo with chick embryos and of Avery with prematurely delivered guinea pigs tend to support this hypothesis, for the reflex arc appears not at the beginning but as individuation takes place. Similarly, studies of infants removed through Caesarean section permitted Minkowski to show that the mass movements of the early months are replaced only slowly by the specific localized reflex units of the later months. The process of birth leaves this slowly emerging individuation trend unaffected. The infant at birth is still developing, not only in the sense of growing larger, but in the sense of unfolding, exhibiting day by day new functional units which have become individuated, as Gesell has shown, in terms of the actual number of days of individual existence since conception. McGraw has described in detail the process of locomotor development; Shirley, following Charlotte Bühler's early observations, presented a "maturation sequence" of patterns appearing in roughly the same order from one infant to another.

It becomes probable that practically all the phenomena of the maturation sequence ordinarily studied are dependent upon differentiation within the central nervous system traceable to the functional ripening of connector systems, the action of the lower systems of the brain stem and cord being much more uniform and predictable than that of the higher centers. The result is that action systems can be watched in their development, their integrated form observed more easily and clearly than is the case with the communication systems which require the control of higher centers.

But this does not mean that the whole process of maturation from the general to the specific, from the diffuse to the well ordered, results from an inevitable clockwork resident in the genes or tissues of the embryo; it depends upon interaction of embryo and uterine environment. Some of it indeed may result from the movements of the mother and of the fetus itself, and some of it may result from intra-uterine learning. Muscular movements elicited upon specific stimulation from newly formed organs must certainly work jointly with a maturation process dependent upon anabolic and katabolic processes, and growth and exercise occur together. Diffuse responses will be replaced more and more by specific responses, partly because elements in the chaos are being dropped out and others fixated. After birth, also, as well as before, interaction with the environment contributes to maturation.

The same logic applies to the maturation of motives or needs. Since need patterns depend upon both the emergence of organs and the emergence of more and more specific connector systems, there are, by the time of birth, highly complex need patterns or systems of interrelations between needs; but there is far less complexity than we should expect to find at a year or two after birth. The organism at birth is not only functionally incomplete in the sense of helplessness and dependence; it is incomplete with respect to its behavior potentialities just as clearly as it is with respect to its teeth or skull or skeletal structure. No specification of human motives or human behavior based upon the neonate as a model is any more serviceable than the specification of human dentition based on jaw and tooth structure at the time

of birth; motives, as much as teeth, are a function of developmental
level.

We are again dealing with the principle of organism-environment
interaction. There exists in the neonate a system of chemical potentialities which under certain nutritional and cultural conditions will
permit the emergence of "human nature," a human nature which will
vary somewhat from clime to clime as nutritional and cultural conditions permit. In general, wide extremes of nutrition will be required
to produce large differences in motor structure, and the same is true
for cultural extremes. But cultural conditions *do* vary through fantastic extremes, and the realized human nature of the adult does
present profoundly varying patterns (Chapters 32–37). To speak of a
single human nature running through all historical and present cultural conditions could mean only a potential human nature—a human
nature independent of cultural and developmental conditions—which
from the present point of view is as meaningless as a human nature
independent of all specifiable conditions of nutrition, climate, or
exercise.

The order in which traits appear is definitely not a question of
heredity alone. Anderson points out that the order of development
of response patterns—"the maturation sequence," as Shirley defines it
—depends partly on interaction with the environment. The child
must stand before he can walk; he must be able to fixate visually
before he can reach for a dangling object. Anderson believes that
all through the list of maturing responses, structure and function at a
given level, and the type of environment in which they permit the
child to function, set the stage and determine what must mature next.
We are dealing with no foreordained destiny, but with functional
necessities.

The view adopted here makes use of Anderson's suggestion but
goes considerably further in defining the conditions which permit
maturation. Not only practice in the more obvious sense, but the
very structural and functional conditions of growth itself, force at
every point the evolution of succeeding possibilities. There is no
reason to insist that formal opportunities for practice are of any more

importance than opportunities offered by the basic biochemical and neural conditions of life. The maturation sequence is indeed no clockwork system; it shows the variability which we should expect in view of the plastic character, the dynamic equilibrium, which characterizes life itself. Broadly, however, the maturation stages must depend in part upon exercise, because exercise is part of the process by which regions are more intimately interconnected. There would be no more meaning, from the present point of view, in insisting on a foreordained evolution from the genes alone, than there would be in insisting on a foreordained pattern of exercise imposed on the child. Moreover, the effect of practice is likely to depend largely on biological readiness, and practice itself is likely to do its work as an aspect of a system, not as an isolated agent.

Dennis has indeed shown that development can go on without social stimulation; even the Hopi child, after months on a cradle-board, is ready to walk when the occasion comes. Yet during hours when he is not on the cradle board, there is "practice" of a sort. Quantitative studies of similar functions in animals, such as Shepard and Breed's studies of pecking in chicks and Fromme's studies of swimming in tadpoles, suggest that the maturation pattern is quantitatively different in practiced and in unpracticed organisms; why the maturation phenomena in man should be *entirely* determined by inner factors is not at all evident.

But however and whenever it occurs, differentiation sets the stage for a later process, that of integration. As Herbert Spencer first pointed out and as Heinz Werner has documented so fully, the growth process necessarily entails three developmental levels: (1) *a level of global, undifferentiated mass activity*; (2) *a level of differentiated parts, each acting more or less autonomously*; (3) *a level of integrated action based upon interdependence of the parts*. (The phrasing, not the idea, is the writer's.) When there are specific parts, there can be interaction; they can constitute a pattern. This third and highest level of functioning can occur only when the two other levels—the global and the differentiated—have preceded. These levels will appear whether we are dealing with growth, with learning, or with the typical interaction of the two. We shall have occasion to refer frequently to these three levels of development.

In the light of the conception of levels, the statement that the organism reacts "as a whole" has a different meaning at each stage of development. *Diffuse* wholeness at the first level of development is different from the more and more *differentiated* wholeness exhibited at the second level in the maturation phenomena, and differs again from the *integrated* wholeness which appears when the differentiated functions achieve a stable, articulated interdependence.

Yet with reference to all organismic philosophies which stress totality, emphasis needs to be placed upon the continuum that exists between levels one and two, i.e., between pure undifferentiatedness at the one theoretical extreme and absolute sharpness of differentiation at the other, and likewise on the continuum between the second level, complete differentiation, and the third level, complete integration. These extreme or pure cases are seldom completely realized in fact, but enormous variations exist which can be ranged between the extremes. The principle of increasing specificity is a needed one, but it has to do with the *relative* distinguishability of components which are never merged in an absolute Spencerian homogeneity, but are also never arrayed like separate notices on the bulletin board to be put up and taken down as complete units.

The steps in differentiation and integration are, moreover, sometimes reversible. Differentiation may be lost in disease or even in frustration (cf. page 145), so that global, stage-one conditions recur. So, too, integration may be lost, permitting reestablishment of the second, differentiated stage, whether in absent-minded and other "dissociated" states of daily life or in such experiments as those of Girden and Culler (page 325), who by means of drugs have separated the dog's habit system into two subsystems. Though movement from general to specific is the rule, embryology shows some regressions, some instances of return to the more general response, just as the child or adult may pass from a condition of sharp checkerboard differentiation to the most delicious relaxed dissolution or the most frenzied "decerebrate" chaos. The three stages in development characteristically appear in the order named, but a step back and then forward again is frequently observed. And alongside the differentiated and the integrated, some of the original undifferentiated survives. Not only is it especially likely to emerge when the later-derived structures are weakened; it is present all the time as an energy source closely related to activity level, to outgoingness and creativeness. Moreover, the homogeneity, the fluidity of the system is never the absolute fluidity of a theoretical thermo-dynamic system, with evenness of spread in all directions; and the capacity for cleavage and for integration depends both upon the developmental level and upon the individual constitution. This last principle, the principle of individuality, is involved in the psychiatric analysis of dissociation, in the experimental study of "cleavage capacity," in the ability to do two things at once, and in the Rorschach emphasis upon "integrating power."

There is good reason why the very principle of compounding should necessitate recognition of the principle of fluidity. The energies concentrated in the various parts of the body—tensions we may call them—spread like ripples and make contact with one another; a general *tension level* thus tends to be established. But the tension never spreads with absolute evenness, and hence various tension levels are present at a given time within the organism. In consequence, the integration of tensions within the structure is no mere joint resultant of many localized tensions active at a given time. Rather, it is an expression of the functional dominance of some regions over others, all contributing, however, to the behavior pattern.

At the cross section of a moment in time, one may speak of the integration of all tensions in a momentary *tension pattern*. The time dimension must be included, because a tension is not only a state, it is also a temporal process. Moreover, the developmental level of the individual partially determines the ease with which local tension will spread (the rigidity or fluidity of boundaries, as Lewin would say). In the simpler functions, the younger the child, the greater the plasticity. Some kinds of flexibility increase, to be sure, with age; two- to four-year-olds may be very rigid—because anxious—in situations where six-year-olds show flexibility. But in general both growth and learning build structure to replace fluidity. Thus the child's capacity for abrupt changes in mood and interest reflects the lack of those sharply differentiated objectives which hold the adult at a task for hours.

Children betray their individuality partly in the tempo of their maturation; and when we turn to the more complex phenomena, individuality is so striking that many have despaired of tracing it to "lawful" principles. Shirley's data, however, permit us to view individuality in the broad, dynamic interrelations between the different aspects of behavior, differences which we should not hesitate to call differences in "temperament." For example, the proclivity to do things "other than those demanded by the test situation"—a trait which among infants we might call either "negativism" or "ingenuity" —is remarkably consistent month by month.

There is, moreover, maturation not only of reflex and of cerebral patterns, but of biochemical patterns, as in the endocrines—specifically, sexual maturation phenomena in almost complete independence of what is going on in the central nervous system (cf. page 101). With the acceleration of activity of the anterior pituitary there comes not only accelerated body growth but a shift in the physiological system that spells sexual differentiation and sexual maturing; parallel to these physiological changes occur psychological changes. Moreover, as the physiologically maturing pattern takes a characteristic individualized form in each person, the psychological puberty changes reflect an individuality that appears in every clinical approach, whether by questionnaire, Rorschach test, or response to interview.

But changes in behavior with age arise also from other principles besides maturation. Any specific developmental process may be of any one of three types (though they may be combined in actuality, they require sharp differentiation at the theoretical level): (1) We may be dealing with true maturation, a matter of the establishment of new functional relations within the body, as just described. (2) New behavior may result from sheer change in body proportions; e.g., the size or weight of the child may permit new postural responses, no new nervous elements being added. (3) The same organism confronting a series of different situations must pass through a sequence of behavior elicited by the various types of stimulation, the infant's behavior depending to some extent upon the fact that different aspects of the environment act upon children of different ages.

With respect to this last point the Spencer formulation—and, as far as we are aware, every modern formulation of maturation theory— is defective in the light of present physical and biological knowledge. The differentiated fields are properties not simply of organisms, but of organism-environment relations. It is not within the encapsulated individual that the process of cleavage and integration appears; it is within the larger context of the life process, involving a reciprocity of outer and inner influences. As selection between outer and inner worlds goes on, the differentiated products appear, deriving their qualities as much from the nature of the outer world as from the nature of the inner. This has important implications for the study of those individual differences in development which concern the student of personality. As each new trait or aspect of the individual becomes manifest, it becomes a trait or aspect not of tissue systems only but of field forces. The individual differences between persons are in the first instance, as well as in the last, attributes of the prenatal or postnatal biochemical or social field.

The continuity *in time* is a field continuity as well. As soon as emphasis is placed upon the time dimension and the organism is seen to be in ebb and flow with its environment, both locally and generally, and to be pursuing cycles of interaction (as in the respiratory and locomotor process), attention swings to the life span as a whole. Here there appear not only the general problems of growth, of adaptation, of characteristic phases of living at different epochs in personal existence, but also the very specific problems of the individual idiosyncrasy in growing, in adapting, in realizing the specific modes of living which are peculiar, in each phase, to an individual person. The field naturalist and the biometrist have long dealt with general laws of individual growth and decline in living things; the data are ready for us. But the biographer, and in recent years the clinician, have ordered for us in chronological terms the material of many an *individual life*; these data are likewise ready. The latter groups of data reveal and particularize the general dynamics of life changes rather than transcending them; personality is revealed more through its cycles and trends than through its cross section, more through its continuities and discontinuities, through change in its tissues and in its outer world, than through any inventory of the traits of the moment, however subtle. This fact, though ignored in most of the profile methods of assaying the individual, is involved in the history-taking and the assessment of personal outlook that appears in every systematic interview or character sketch.

4. The Individual Constitution

AS A result of the factors discussed in Chapter 3, individual "constitutions" differ, the organic make-up reflecting heredity-environment interactions. They differ spectacularly in size, proportion, strength, resistance to disease. They differ also with respect to receptors, striped and unstriped muscles, biochemical systems, and the autonomic, central, and peripheral nervous systems. Their differences need to be seen not only in terms of the normal and pathological, but in terms of gradations within the accepted range of the normal. Most of these types of variation are already the subject of study by the biological sciences, and many of them have already been studied in relation to behavior syndromes, both local and general, temporary and permanent.

Most of these differences have not greatly interested a psychology concerned with generalizations based on averages. Traditionally, for example, we have studied the *general* functions of the retina. When "exceptions" were found we spoke of "color blindness," usually of two or three sharply distinct types. Modern method reveals many forms and gradations of "color weakness," and necessarily many modes of interrelation of the constitutional dispositions. Where, as in this instance, we have looked for differences, they have appeared in abundance. It may be worth while to consider, both at the factual level and at the level of hypothesis construction, the individual differences in constitutional make-up which participate in the process of personality development.

Nothing could be more futile today than to assume that the individual constitution is a simple algebraic sum of such constitutional dispositions. The distance runner is no sum of leg muscles, oxygen utilization, and "nerve," nor is the musician the sum of tone enjoyment, rhythm perception, and manual dexterity. Human traits, moreover, are responses not to outer stimulation alone; they are simultaneously responses to inner stimulation, which in turn depends upon an uninterrupted inner flow of energies, permitting an energy distribution that is unique for each organism. Each central nervous system responds in its own way to ongoing muscular activity in the arms or legs, just as the arms and legs respond differently to impulses from different central nervous systems. When the complexity of these inner stimulation circuits is grasped, there will be less danger of directly assigning a given functional significance to each organic characteristic. This never justifies the statement that organic characteristics are unimportant; but, being organic, they speak an organic language and refuse to make themselves understood through any other medium.

Since they are organic, they involve a continuous reciprocity of inner and outer forces. Even the most distinctive hereditary disposition, such as brown eye color, depends in some measure on growth factors (it changes during growth); and the more fluid functional characteristics, like timidity, must be constantly watched with reference to a subtle but unceasing process of environmental molding. There is no room, *ever*, for special pleading for heredity any more than for environment. The task of the present chapter, however, is to define biological attributes as they are observed in the growing or the adult individual, and in this the description of attributes is primary, the nature-nurture question secondary. It will not be enough to ask whether Johnny and Jimmy, twin sons of a New York taxi driver, are alike. We must ask in what ways they are alike. Moreover, temperamental differences appear early which are as striking as the morphological similarities between the twins. One is more self-assured, the other shy. This contrast shows why, if we are to speak of personality development as a whole, we must first itemize the various attributes of the functioning individual and consider the constitutional aspect of each attribute.

Sensory and Affective Qualities

One may begin with receptor functions and their attributes. Do children differ in their thresholds for sensory stimulation? They very emphatically do. Individual differences in taste, smell, and pain sensitivity appear soon after birth, and differences in auditory sensitivity likewise appear early. Differences in visual and tactual functions are hard to test at birth but appear within the first six months. Other quantitative attributes in the sensory functions are the latencies or time lags—the periods during which stimulation must continue in order to elicit response—and correspondingly the length of the afterdischarge, the period during which activity continues after the stimulus has ceased to act.

The affective aspects of these sensory responses are of special importance. Some children turn toward lights, sounds, or touches more actively than others. Color preferences are distinct in early infancy. There is enough uniformity over the globe to suggest a broad biological basis for the main trends—a liking for sweet tastes, colors, rhythms, and a dislike for bitter tastes, cold, loud voices; enough variation between culture groups to suggest the influence of cultural emphasis; and enough individual differences between children in the same family to suggest an individual genetic factor. Small infants differ considerably in the kinds of sounds to which they make positive orientations, and very strikingly in their interest in sound in general. Recent work with the projective methods (cf. page 701), in which children use clay, paste, cold cream, etc., to dabble, mess, create with as they like, reveals huge individual differences in tactual interest, ranging from the inactive and bored to the delighted gush-gushers who love nothing more than to touch richly, as another might see or hear richly. Individual kinesthetic differences are suggested by a comparison of active and passive, rhythmical and non-rhythmical, fine-muscle and large-muscle users, activity-streamers and stop-and-goers.

All such differences as these in the sensory-affective patterns are present in infants as well as adults, and demonstrable in free and in experimental situations. The attempt to derive any or all of them from indirect or hidden sources, as in the psychoanalytic method, is always legitimate, but must accept the burden of proof. The kinds of differences we have described are found among the mammalian young of many species, and develop smoothly without any need for the gross intervention of teaching. Our hypothesis, then, is that individuality is reflected very early in sensory spheres of interest, in selective response to the world of sensory stimulation. Sensory interests are rooted in individual factors, as are other behavior dispositions.

Beyond the question of sheer affective response to simple stimulation there is the question of the length of time required by a stimulus before it brings its result—the "warming up"—and the length of time before the new stimulus loses its value, as brought out in Cushing's demonstration of the differences shown by little children in the time given to each new toy. We have, then, throughout the material on infants' free play, many suggestions that receptor functions and the associated affective responses serve as initial clues to the direction in which personal idiosyncrasy is likely to move.

EFFECTOR QUALITIES

Constitutional factors expressed in the effector system are even more obvious. Individual differences in striped-muscle activity appear, for example, in the records of arm and leg activity made by movement tracings. In regard to the activity of unstriped muscles, good examples of early individual differences appear in the circulatory and gastro-intestinal responses to noise. (It is not yet possible to say in what degree all this depends on the muscles directly and in what degree it depends on the nervous control of muscles.) In the functioning of the duct glands, huge individual variability is to be expected; this is shown by the fact that galvanometric work requires very careful study of personal idiosyncrasy in the activity of the sweat glands, and that some conditioning experiments require a long initial period to ascertain the subject's salivary secretory level.

The differences are equally striking and of much greater importance in the case of the ductless or endocrine glands. Here the endocrines will be briefly considered in relation to constitutional differences. Their role in motivation will be considered in the next chapter. Individual differences in thyroid output as measured by the basal metabolic rate, though somewhat controllable medically are to some extent resistant to outside interference, a fact that fits well with Stockard's suggestions as to the heredity of endocrine patterns. The parathyroids, as gauged by calcium metabolism, differ much from person to person, thyroid and parathyroids together appearing to play a role in the maintenance of emotional tone. (Either thyroid excess or parathyroid deficiency seems to predispose to emotional instability, especially in the direction of apprehensiveness; but cf. page 98.) The anterior and posterior lobes of the pituitary are both involved in metabolic processes. There appear to be marked individual differences in the anterior pituitary, which is sometimes regarded as a sort of "master gland" or general regulating device for growth in general and for sexual maturation in particular. Finally, the gonads, stimulated in growth partly by the accelerated activity of the anterior pituitary and partly by other interacting mechanisms, help to determine the wide differences in sexual maturation and in thresholds for both inner and outer sexual stimulation; these individual differences are so great as to make some normal children at sixteen no more advanced sexually than others are at nine.

It has become clear, however, from the many recent studies of sexual development that no single factor determines the process of maturing, and that no single expression of sexual maturity correlates perfectly with any other. The primary and the various secondary sex characteristics of each individual do not appear all at once; often their appearance is strung along over a period of several years. Thus the boy whose voice changes early may be the boy whose facial hair appears rather late. Both sexes have both masculine and feminine hormones, the main differences being quantitative or a matter of endocrine balance. But to say that the process is complex does not mean that it is unimportant, or that it is so dominated by social factors as to be properly negligible. Transplantation of sex glands from one animal to another indicates clearly that both sexual and general maturation depend in large measure upon this one specific factor; for example, after endocrine changes, male rats build nests and care for the young. The study of personality changes in man in adolescence and in the period of sexual aging, and the clinical estimate of individual gonad endowment, have tended to confirm and reemphasize the importance of the hormone factor in such psychological variables as sex interest, social aggressiveness, energy, warmth, tenderness, protective attitudes toward children—characteristics which stem partly from the endocrine basis shared by the two sexes and partly from factors more specifically male or more specifically female. As we shall later see, variations in the definition of sex roles from one culture to another may in considerable measure redefine the attitudes of males and females, though it is not clear that they overrule the general biological dispositions. Directly pertinent, however, to the present argument is the fact that the cultural environment may alter the rate of sexual maturation, as shown in Franzblau's study of Danish and Italian girls in European and American habitats (page 100). The *degree* of this modifiability of the endocrine system by environmental pressure is unknown; but from her data and from other studies it appears likely that such factors act to accelerate or retard endocrine and other growth processes, though not to obliterate or basically to recast them.

Within the normal person and aside from "clinical types" there appear to be at least three ways in which the endocrine system may be related to personality syndromes: (1) The endocrine products in the blood stream may lower the thresholds for reaction patterns of both unstriped and striped muscles, predisposing both to affective and behavioral sensitiveness of individuals to the behavior of other persons. (2) When the threshold has been reached, the endocrine products may intensify unstriped- or striped-muscle patterns, or cause them to continue longer. (3) The endocrines may serve as balancing factors, facilitating or inhibiting the processes already at work in visceral or skeletal organs, and coordinating such activities.

When the issue is stated in this way, it becomes clear that in an interacting whole any one organ may be said to be "coordinating" the other organs. The striped muscles serve to coordinate the unstriped, and vice versa, and either or both may serve to coordinate endocrine influences. There are consequently two-way relations between endocrine patterns of activity and other patterns with which the observer is more directly in contact. In the textbooks of a quarter century ago it was customary to define the properties of the endocrine system and to interpret the behavior of clinical cases on the assumption that the clinical picture was simply the *result* of a disordered endocrine balance. But it has become more and more clear that patterns of adjustment involving the nervous system have a powerful and continuous influence upon the endocrine balance. Instead of saying, as once we did, that hyperthyroidism produces apprehensiveness, we now add that prolonged apprehensiveness may give rise to hyperthyroidism. This whole problem will be more fully considered in the next chapter. Similarly we look for psychogenic, i.e., primarily cerebral or symbolic patterns as clues to both simple and complex endocrine disturbances. And instead of saying that such and such applies only in the exceptional or clinical case, we have come to see that we are dealing with broad questions of physiology which transcend our convenient distinction between "normal" and "abnormal."

The term "psychosomatics" properly includes all the above-mentioned relationships, and more besides. (Although it is often limited to instances in which a psychological disturbance expresses itself in a physical disturbance, there seem to be no sound reasons for this limitation.) Psychosomatic medicine has shown how personality difficulties may express themselves in disease or in deviation from normal physiological functioning. The effects of chronic emotional excitation may appear in temporarily or chronically disturbed functioning which in time manifestly affects the physiological system and eventually may produce visible damage to tissue. Gastric disorders of a chemical and physiological type, eventuating in ulceration, may result from the tensions of chronic anxiety.

Normal physiology and psychology appear to be neglected by psychosomatic medicine (it is the *pathology* that is interesting to the physician). The discipline is, despite exceptions, still at the stage which is represented by regarding high blood pressure as pathology. On this basis one either has high blood pressure or he has not. If he has, this is a psychosomatic problem; if not, there is held to be no problem, no general implication of blood pressure for psychology. But, as Margaret Mead has pointed out, the cross-cultural study of personality will never be adequate as long as students of psycho-somatics think chiefly in terms of those marked deviations from the normal which give rise to gross clinical syndromes such as allergies and hypertensions. Within the normal range of personality in all cultures, stresses are at work which tend toward the production of hypertensions, allergies, and the rest; and the general, continuous load or strain upon the organism involved in the primary adjustment to the culture must be understood if the secondary load or strain of a specific environmental demand is to be appraised. In the same way, the satisfactions, the positive fulfillments, have profound psychosomatic consequences.

As with the endocrines, so with other biochemical systems like those of intermediary metabolism, we seem to have an initial genetic bias of the individual (as shown for example in ease or difficulty of blood clotting), but we find considerable month-by-month variability, controllable partly through diet (e.g., vitamin K) and partly through the general regimen and mental hygiene. We know less here, however, than we do regarding endocrine balance. Hammett's demonstration that emotional instability in clinical cases correlates substantially with instability in the products of intermediary metabolism still leaves us uncertain as to causal relations; for just as the cultural pressures may influence endocrine development, so the very factors that make the individual patient emotionally unstable may lead to disturbed biochemical activity. The ability to incur an "oxygen debt," i.e., to work for a time without the needed oxygen supply and still keep the tissues going, has been shown by A. V. Hill to reflect some of the deeply ingrained biochemical idiosyncrasies of the person; but even here the habits of breathing play a part and these at times reflect early emotional experience—for example, chronic (though often unconscious) fear states.

A word or two on terminology. It might possibly be helpful at this point to suggest that the term "temperament" be used to define such predispositions to one or another type of affective (or behavioral) response. But the term is in use in many senses. It seems best to make sparing use of it (and of the term "character" for the same reason).

PERSONALITY

THE CENTRAL AND AUTONOMIC NERVOUS SYSTEMS

The evidence regarding individual constitutional attributes of the central nervous system is of four types. We have first the histological data, which indicate that development of the various parts of the cerebral cortex follows distinct individual patterns, resulting in different rates and types of functional maturation; second, the data from gross and microscopic anatomy, which show in the lower grades of mental defect more and more inadequacy in both the number and the quality of nerve cells, leading to the presumption that at higher levels, where the microscope serves us less well, there may be corresponding differences in cell adequacy; third, animal pedigree data suggesting indirectly a wide variability in brains that is due to genetic factors; and fourth, direct pedigree and correlational studies of human beings, involving comparisons of identical twins, siblings, first cousins, etc., and including parent-child and grandparent-grandchild resemblance. All four types of evidence may be said to point in the same direction; although largely indirect, the evidence indicates a fair case for the inheritance of more or less superior or inferior adjustment capacities as mediated through the central nervous system.

But we cannot stop with a consideration of the "functional adequacy" of the central nervous system. There are many other important properties at which we must glance. Qualitative variability of various parts of the cortex may well be responsible for differences in the richness of sensory experiences in the various fields. For example, visual eidetic imagery—imagery that persists, almost like a copy of the original (cf. page 392)—may well depend to some degree upon constitutional attributes of the visual centers or upon their special susceptibility to thyroid, parathyroid, or other endocrine influences. The latent time for excitation and the period of after-discharge, as well as the sheer intensity of cortical response, may be important in relation to the capacity to become interested and to sustain interest in mental tasks. The sense organs and the midbrain (through which many sensory impulses pass) play a part in the sensory interests noted above (page 73); and in view of the apparent relation of some of these interests to intellectual levels and of the fact that they are weak in the lowest mental defectives, it is likely that the cerebral cortex also contributes. But there are many instances in which the cortex appears to be not simply a contributor to but the chief seat of sensory interests. Prolonged positive responses to sensory stimulation, as when a person keeps himself oriented in such a way as to secure all the stimulation he can, depend largely on cortical factors. Individual differences in such perseverative tendencies have been found to be very great in three-year-olds as well as in adults. The maintenance of set for an absent object, as in the delayed-reaction experiment, enters into these tendencies; and many of the more complex esthetic responses, as well as delight in ordering and structuring the confused world of the senses (as in philosophy and science), call for a cortical contribution. There may also be in the cortex a constitutional capacity to withstand nervous strain, a factor responsible for the maintenance of integrated behavior under severe stress in some persons but not in others (cf. page 316).

The evidence regarding constitutional factors in relation to the autonomic nervous system is of the same general type, but less clear cut. While to some observers such animal-breeding experiments as those of Hall (page 46) will be especially impressive, to others the direct evidence of individual differences in human autonomic stability will appear more cogent. In conjunction with the Washburn and Shirley material on continuity of individual temperament (page 57) must be stressed the data on autonomic stability in adults—such as the findings of G. L. Freeman—which indicate great individual differences in the point at which one "cracks up" under severe strain.

Relevant also is the McFarland-Huddleson study of differences in circulatory adequacy under conditions of slight physiological stress (page 137). Considerable evidence is of course available regarding individual differences in pulse and blood pressure. Since these responses are under autonomic and endocrine control, much attention has recently been given to a broad typology which classifies persons as prone to sympathetic or to parasympathetic dominance or, in more modern terms, to adrenergic or to cholinergic dominance.[1] This typology has the defect common to most typologies, in that

---

[1] The sympathetic system liberates adrenin; the parasympathetic, acetylcholine.

most people fall "in between" the types. It would be safer to say simply that the outlines of the present research suggest that autonomic stability is related both to genetic and to early environing factors, and that the biochemical and autonomic elements are, as usual, profoundly involved in each other's function.

One form of typology involving response to stress does, however, seem of rather unusual helpfulness: the suggestion that even in early infancy some individuals may be classified as tending to express stress reactions either outwardly or inwardly, but not both. H. E. Jones was able to show that a mildly disturbing stimulus produced in infants either striped-muscle behavior or galvanic—i.e., visceral—responses; one tended to preclude the other. The data suggest that the activation of one system takes care of the discharge, so that the other system is not involved. In the same vein, Macfarlane's material suggests that "internalizing" infants—i.e., those who show their difficulties by circulatory, gastrointestinal, and other types of upset—are often relatively free of behavior difficulties of an overt type, and that those inclined to an overt expression of response are more likely to be free of inner disturbance. This is as good a hypothesis for a constitutional typology as we have, though the problem will doubtless be restated many times before a really workable typology is found.

Interorgan Generalities

We have noted constitutional differences in all the tissue systems upon which personality chiefly depends, namely, the receptors, the effectors (including striped and unstriped muscles, duct and ductless glands), and the central and autonomic nervous systems. Over and above these specific contributions of specific tissue systems, with their thresholds, latencies, periodicities, and after-discharges, as well as their qualitative variations, we must stress what might be called "interorgan generalities" of function. There appear in the embryo, for example, pacemaking or time-determining factors which predetermine the qualities of all the cells of the body and which, so to speak, make all the cells more alike than they would otherwise be. There are also structured or patterned interrelations that depend upon the dominance of one system over another or on the facilitating or inhibiting effects of the various components upon one another. There are, then, properties of systems as well as properties of individual tissue groups. Some of these, such as colloidal dispersity and tissue irritability, are doubtless general biochemical properties of the organism, and share in the regulation of the influences which tissues may exert upon one another. As soon as the nervous system appears, it may serve to some degree as master builder in relation to certain types of structural properties. As a result of these general factors, we should expect to find a specific personal constant, or quale, of the organism which is not necessarily the quale of any individual tissue; it might express itself through its influence upon such attributes as thresholds, latencies, and maximal and minimal capacities for response.

An example of a quale may be the disposition of some individuals toward functional cleavage or dissociation, the capacity to carry on at once two highly integrated activities under conditions which would require of most people an alternation of attention. This may constitute an all-or-none difference between persons, or, more likely, there may be a gradation from one extreme to the other. Such a personal constant is suggested by the fact that under hypnosis there are wide individual differences in the degree to which a given pair of behavior systems interfere with each other. Correspondingly, we should expect to find characteristic forms of integration, modes of interrelation between functioning parts. The plasticity or rigidity of the individual may lie in the lability of individual tissue systems.

It is likely, of course, that some of the generic properties of developed organisms are less generic than they seem; in their genesis they may be attributable to dominant groups of cells which act as pacemakers or lawmakers for the system. We might call these "nodal" points, points from which the most complex and pervasive influences emanate. The clinician finds, when the system as a whole behaves badly, that there are nodal points of stress from which other stresses flow. Whether he thinks biochemically or psychoanalytically, he looks for "the trouble" or the "root of the difficulty" and regards the architecture of the whole sick personality as deriving from faulty placement of an individual stone. But this local or nodal emphasis is by no means always warranted. Whatever one's theory regarding architecture, one must accept the basic fact that the interrelations of tissues underlie personality and that no tissue alone can determine any trait in a direct manner. Just as we saw that somatic traits derive from the interaction of many genes, so we shall find that individual personality traits, however simple and measurable they may be, are surface indicators of dynamic interrelations of very high complexity. In other words, we shall find that the clue to personality usually lies not in the establishment of independent foci or centers of "motive" or "trait," but in the adjustment of parts to one another or to outer environing pressures, and of the whole inner system to the whole outer system of stresses. What would otherwise remain vague in such a conception is fortunately removed by the present-day possibilities of measuring these interrelations of parts. In modern endocrinology, for example, we have a few direct methods of determining the influence of a single endocrine organ upon the activity of two or three others. Similarly in Henderson's nomogram of the blood (page 39) we have a precise formulation of the interrelations of six variables which express the oxygen-carrying activity of red blood cells. We may well extend our efforts to define such measures of interrelation.

Up to this point, we have been concerned with cross sections in time, with states of balance, or at best with momentary vectors that indicate the reinforcement or inhibition of impulses. But personality is a continuity, a continuity determined partly by inner forces, partly by impulsions from without, but maintaining a recognizable individuality, a constancy or recurrence of patterned tendencies such as permits the recognition of identity. This continuity would be a necessary postulate in relation to all those "dependable" characteristics of which one speaks, such as the "capacity of the individual for adjustment" or the ability to "take" what life presents. Not only must the stability be sufficient to permit carry-over from the test situation to a specific life predicament occurring a week or a month later; it must be sufficient to permit an over-all personality description in terms of a basic and continuing disposition.

Here, however, we confront a final paradox. Nothing is more certain than discontinuities, unpredictabilities in relation to new and different situations. Even the chemist, with his fine control of his data, no longer speaks of the fixed attributes of Mendeleev's 92 elements, for he knows that at very high temperatures there are hundreds of elements whose properties are unforeseen in classical atomic theory. The human personality can never be so defined as to permit precise prediction in new situations, not because of any necessary arbitrariness of behavior, but because the properties of the new situation have never been brought into relation with the properties of the organism. If the situation is really new, new valences will be called for, untapped possibilities released, earlier assumed adequacies found inadequate. The individual is capable of a stable equilibrium at one point or in a broad area; but let the situation push upon him in a new way and he may move abruptly to a new and very different equilibrium. If one pushes a chair backwards a few inches, pivoting it upon the rear legs, he can remove his hand and the chair will fall forward to resume the old equilibrium; but let him pass by a hair's breadth beyond a given point, and the old equilibrium cannot be regained. The chair falls backward to the floor, to come to rest in a completely new position and with no tendency to return to the old. Catastrophic situations, or indeed *new* situations of any sort, lead to responses showing that however deep the continuities within the person may be, new centers of equilibrium exist; a new relation with the environment may be established. Much depends, of course, upon the individual's age and experience, his achieved stability. It may take a major cataclysm, or only a persistent annoyance, to cause a crack-up; similarly, *any* redirection of the whole person depends both on inner stability and on the force of the hammer blow directed against it.

5. The Elementary Biology of Motivation

AS THE story unfolds, it will become evident that this whole volume is about motivation; every aspect of personality is conceived in terms of the molding, the complication, the interpenetration, the concealment, the indirect expression of motives. In this chapter a first crude oversimplified picture of motives will be presented, with emphasis upon the raw materials given by biology.

The newborn are as recognizably distinct in their demands upon life as in the structure of their bodies. In their waking minutes and in their sleeping hours, their restlessness takes *individual* form; their protests and their fulfillments differ in intensity and in form from infant to infant. Helpless as they may be, they are not inert; like all living things, they are energy systems, patterned bundles of motivation. In surveying the individual constitution, attention has been given to the individual tissue systems of the newborn; but if the story is to be carried further, a closer view must be taken of the sources of their activity, the dynamic substrate from which proceed their smiles, their cries, their squirmings, their first vague exploratory turnings of head and trunk.

The system of human energies will, then, be considered in the relatively simple form present in early childhood, before the complications of the learning process have become excessive. In Chapters 8–13 we shall see these energy systems undergoing transformation through the process of learning; and later (especially in Chapters 26–35) we shall examine the more complex form of motivation dynamics which typically characterizes the adult in our western culture.

According to one conception which goes back at least as far as Democritus, the inner make-up of man is a delicate machine carrying out acts determined by outer energies. The arrangements are "mechanisms," i.e., they contain no energy sources. They utilize and direct energies, as all machines do, but they stand still when not in use, and there must be action from without to initiate movement within. Descartes' conception of the reflex and the title of La Mettrie's essay, *L'Homme machine*, precisely defined such a view, and the past two centuries have applied it in exquisite detail.

Despite the popularity of analogies based on human contrivances which work because of energies acting upon them, it is a rather remarkable fact that modern psychologists, with almost absolute unanimity, place the initiation of many activities on a different basis. There are conceived to be *motors* here and there within the body, each delivering energy to appropriate muscles and glands. As Dashiell puts it, "Tissue needs are the sources of drives." Motives are assigned to regions of high tension, or unstable equilibrium, within the body. Action patterns which are motivated are conceived to differ sharply from those of a reflex type. In animal studies we keep the motivation constant, then discover the laws of forming connections. Or we may invert the relation, keeping the stimuli to reflex action constant in order to discover the variations due to motivation. To La Mettrie this distinction would be a trifle odd.

Of course this second conception is no less "mechanistic," in the final philosophical sense, than the first. Many psychologists would swear by mechanism as a philosophy more confidently than by any specific empirical principle yielded by their science. But in experimental practice the habit of looking first for the motivation, then for the mechanism, has suggested the presence of a number of sensitive spots or motivation regions, as contrasted with the reflex pathways which are utilized when an external stimulus, an incentive, initiates the action through these preformed pathways. Many of these sensitive spots have been experimentally studied as basis for the visceral drives.

TENSION GRADIENTS

As we learn to look more closely, however, we find sensitiveness *everywhere*; the evidence is against any sharp distinction between regions which are seats of impulsions and other regions which merely receive and transmit these impulsions. All tissues are rather unstable. All points in the body are at all times the site of chemical reaction, of energy changes, that pass, gradient-wise, in many directions. The nervous system is no mere connection system; it is itself the site of many tensions. Adrian tells us that the brain, even under deep ether anesthesia and pocketed off from the viscera and muscles, shows its own continuous discharges. Molecular instability is a feature of nerve cells, just as it is of muscles and glands. Thus every cell in the body is an initiator of motivation; there are no sharply defined "motive spots," there are simply *degrees* of motivation—tension gradients— throughout the living system.

Motivation, moreover, never "starts" or "stops." There are rapid or slow rises in tension level, and rapid or slow transmissions of the tension. The level in a given region is a function of local chemical reaction and depends on food, temperature, the blood stream, and much besides. But the essential fact about motivation seems to be the state of continuous instability or restlessness, and the consequent interstimulation which characterizes all living systems. If energy changes resulting from inner and outer impulses converging upon a given region pass slowly or swiftly from one region to another, a time comes when a *manifest* change with reference to the environment forces our attention upon a given muscle group; then, as we look back, a "motive" for the act is artificially designated. But in reality the cycle of internal stimulation goes on ceaselessly; life processes know nothing of either the sharp temporal or the sharp spatial distinctions which the mechanical approach has imposed. If La Mettrie had thought more in chemical, less in mechanical terms, less of springs and pulleys and more of fire and respiration, he would have prophesied better regarding the structure of the biology that was destined to develop.

Life is a complex cycle of such ceaseless "inner-outer adjustments." This conception of Herbert Spencer's is certainly closer to the contemporary habit of thought regarding the analysis of personality than is any formulation of the era of Descartes and Newton. The best present approximation seems to be that there is some instability, and therefore some motivation, everywhere; that this instability tends to propagate itself to other regions; that other stimulation complicates the inner propagation of tensions and redirects it—in short, that outer-inner stimulations everywhere at work are the joint determiners of "motivated" and of "reflex" acts. Our first hypothesis, then, is that all activity is traceable to tension, that tension is "need" for acting, and that tension, need, and motive are one and the same. The term "tension" is used as in physics. There are tensions of many sorts: e.g., mechanical tensions, as of a muscle; chemical tensions; the surface tensions of individual cells. The living body is a complex system of interrelated tensions, partially discharging, partly blocked from discharge, but in some sort of intercommunication with one another.

If this modern biological view is essentially sound, it does curious things to the catalogues of motives which in one form or another still beset us. But it is hard to tell whether we are more misled by the crisp itemizations which used to be presented as keys to the "fundamental" human motives, or by those pseudo-modest lists which define four or five obvious visceral drives and then summarize all the other life energies under the term "socially acquired drives" or some other convenient abstraction, implying that motivation is forced into the organism from without, like air into a football. The squirming infant whose eyes haltingly follow the light and whose smiles and whimpers punctuate the uninterrupted sentence of his waking activity, is motivated; the old man by the fireside who quietly dozes and dreams of his boyhood is motivated, too. There is nothing in the life of the organism to suggest that the vital organs are either more or less important than are other tissues with references to this uninterrupted activity stream.

The term *motivation*, then, does not define a box that contains a few distinct tools for our use, but the abstraction of one of the properties of the living process—its instability, push, or, as Bergson liked to call it, *élan*. Even if we could find where the push "starts" we should find other pushes cooperating (the summation of stimuli) in a complex nexus of pushes, and cooperating through a process of *fusion* rather than one of mechanical addition. As Sherrington said of the reflexes, the motives are "convenient abstractions." Or we might agree with contemporary neurology in saying that all too often they are *inconvenient* abstractions.

But we certainly do have to abstract from the process of living. Though motivation is complex, we must utilize one or the other of two ways of classifying the phenomena of motivation: one in terms of the recognition of external behavior to which motives give rise, the other in terms of their specific inner character, i.e., the types of tissue situation most directly and obviously involved. The former procedure is represented by references to "food-seeking behavior" and "flight"; we assess the degree of motivation in relation to the amount it accomplishes. The latter procedure is exemplified by reference to hunger or to fear; we go beyond the outer evidence and closely examine the tissue changes which we have learned to suspect. The former method, when relied on exclusively, becomes less and less useful to psychologists, for the good reason that external conduct often gives scant understanding as to what is going on inside. The only procedure open to us today is to attempt, despite the difficulties, a classification of the sources of inner instability.

In view of the foregoing, it must be emphasized that no single act can point directly to a source in some one local and circumscribed tissue situation. The term refers to interrelated and interdependent energy systems; acts are, one and all, terminal expressions of complex dynamic interrelations and sequences. It is, however, practical to do some abstracting and list the regions of inner tension, recognizing their characteristic lines of communication from one to another, and their characteristic syndromes or excitation patterns. Indeed, such a list is necessary if the interaction of inner forces with one another and with outer forces is to be considered in terms of processes of development and learning. Yet our list must be understood to include not sharply separated and independent motives, but generalized tissue situations from which, through a very complex process, the dynamics of the individual personality can be seen to emerge.

First of all we must consider the disturbances of chemical equilibrium. As we have seen (page 32), life depends upon the relative constancy of the inner environment. The nervous system lives in its own environment, much of which, being within the skin, we ordinarily fail to think of as belonging to environment rather than self. Every cell, however, is a part of the environment of every other cell. The cells within the body require relative constancies of several types, the nervous system being especially exacting with reference to the constancy of chemical state and temperature in which it must carry on its work. There is an optimal environment from which relatively slight variations produce malfunction or even death. Deviations from this balance, this homeostatic condition, may occur when one is "doing nothing" (the hunger state may develop during a long deep sleep), or they may develop rapidly in the striped muscles and blood stream as a result of meeting specific environmental demands.

The more obvious "needs" of the organism are the results of disequilibrium due either to the depletion of substances required for the homeostatic condition ("deficit stimuli") or to the taking into the body, or the manufacturing within the tissues, of substances which cannot be handled without further chemical or other readjustments by the body. Many of the more obvious needs are of the first type; they are deficit conditions, such as shortages of oxygen, water, and food. Some of these conditions permit exact specification; for example, in the experienced organism, the need for specific foods results in behavior adjustments which in the long run correct the deficit. Not only do herds follow the long trail to the salt lick; periods of calcium shortage find them wandering far afield until they discover the necessary bone deposits, and when the shortage of phosphorus is extreme it is the bones rich in this substance that are most vigorously sought. The process is at first usually blind; the essential fact is that the ill-balanced inner condition results in the activation of many systems, including the locomotor system; and there is no terminal state, no living down or outgrowing the condition, except through the restoration of the balance.

PERSONALITY

THE INTERDEPENDENCE OF OUTER
AND INNER PRESSURES

The term *tropism* is used for a forced movement imposed upon a living creature by directing upon it certain energies. Thus the moth, or even the baby rat, follows a beautifully definite curve of orientation toward a source of light. It is necessary only to know the distance of the organism from the light, the amount of light reaching each of the eyes, and (roughly) the process by which muscular activity is initiated and sustained. The tropism is therefore a relatively simply physico-chemical concept for translating the problem of motivation into the problem of external control of the inner patterns of life.

This concept has been exceedingly useful. Its chief modern exponent, Jacques Loeb, organized his data to show that the line of march of the energies impinging upon the organism proceeds within the internal organization of the creature; that the fresh sources of stimulation must articulate with the energy dispositions already at work; and that the way in which the organism utilizes these new energies will depend on its state at the time. The concept of the tropism has some value even when one simply attributes the behavior to the environmental forces lying beyond the creature's outer surface, contenting himself with the safe prediction of behavior when the variability in inner condition can be ignored. But the more complex the organism, the more difficult it has proved to be to ignore what we might call the pattern of its own inner tropisms, its own homeostatic system, and its own propagation of tensions from one region to another.

It is convenient to set up the tropism as a limiting case, an extreme, a single pole useful in defining a continuum. The tropism concept can be used when the inner variability of the organism is so slight that prediction can be made on the sole basis of knowledge about the physical energies acting from without. The other extreme, the antithetical pole, represents those instances in which the demands of the inner environment are so imperious that no external energy produces observable variation in behavior pattern, except along lines specifically made ready by the inner need; the organism is focused completely on a single need, utilizing all the behavior mechanisms that are sensitive to this specific type of inner turmoil. Neither pole, of course, represents a real human situation; the energies from the external source are fed into and incorporated within the system at work at any given time. Strictly, then, there is no reflex behavior, in Descartes' sense; there is always interdependence of excitation arising from within and from without. We shall later find, nevertheless, some almost reflexive reactions and some almost completely autonomous reactions in which outer stimulation is relatively ineffectual.

The principle of interdependence between tissue systems, and between the whole living system and the environment, developed in the preceding and the present chapter, may be illustrated by refer-

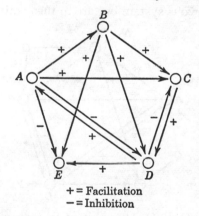

+ = Facilitation
− = Inhibition

A, B, C, D, E *are endocrine organs, each of which influences all the others.*

ence to the influence of the endocrine glands upon behavior. Let the accompanying figure represent the endocrine system of some imaginary mammal. The glands that influence one another through the blood stream have more interrelations than can be shown; but the salient effects of one upon another are indicated by arrows, facilitating effects being marked plus, inhibiting effects minus. The arrows indicate effects, not the sheer transportation of substance. Even in so simple a schema it is clear that rarely if ever is a behavior tendency the work of a single endocrine organ. The chemistry of the blood stream may sensitize the sex reflexes, lower their thresholds; but the degree of such sensitization can never reflect the influence of sex secretions alone. The activity of *A* means activity of *B* and *C*, and conjoint reduction of activity of *D* and *E*. And these are only the most obvious implications; for *B*, *C*, *D*, and *E* not only affect the blood stream, but through the indicated system of arrows affect each other in a pattern of complexity limited only by the investigator's interest. If he resorts to gland feeding or to surgery, he alters the whole endocrine balance; his situation is baffling enough even with the most extreme simplification he can achieve.

Yet with recognition of all this the picture still remains ridiculously abstract. The endocrines not only play their part in regulating the functions of the nervous system but are in turn activated by the nerv-

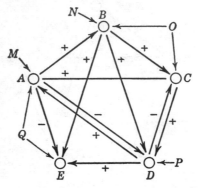

M, N, O, P, Q, *other parts of the body, respond to energies coming from outside the organism and influence the endocrine system.*

ous system. And they are affected by conditions of nutrition and health, and by many other conditions of the organism. These additional relations are suggested by the arrows *M*, *N*, *O*, *P*, and *Q* in the figure above, serving merely to suggest how far the endocrine system is from genuine autonomy. To say, then, that this or that trait stems from this or that endocrine function is an abstraction of such a type as to be useful only when a great deal of valid evidence shows clearly the virtual irrelevance of other contributing functions; and such cases are rare. But to say that for such reasons the endocrine system is unimportant for normal personality is to misconceive the problem in equally serious fashion. Most current efforts to find one-to-one relations between an endocrine function and a personality trait have perhaps failed because they have not looked for the clue where nature provides it. Whether endocrine functions are or are not significant is a different question, an open question except so far as research can be found in which endocrines and personality are regarded in terms of the complex structure that each possesses.

Not so many years ago it was considered probable that the biochemical system constituted simply a supplement, a support to the nervous system. In the fall of 1916 the writer entered in his notes on G. H. Parker's course on "The Structure and Function of Central Nervous Organs" the lecturer's opinion that the nervous system is "one of the most interesting things in nature, partly in its own right, partly because it is the basis of personality." Cannon's emphasis on the adrenals was new and exciting, but the adrenals were characteristically conceived as simply reinforcing the effects already guaranteed by the sympathetic system, which in turn responded to the central nervous system. Physiological psychology had so long been centered in the central nervous system that even the divisions of the autonomic were mentioned only for completeness or courtesy.

The picture has strangely transformed itself in the past quarter century. Parker himself has done much to show how the ancient biochemical needs and systems gave rise not only to effector systems which served them, but to an "elementary nervous system" which supplemented and facilitated the biochemical; just as the biochemical was there before the elementary system, so the latter was there before the central nervous system refined and complicated the process. The last few years have carried us much further. Today we learn that biochemical functions initiate, guide, inhibit nervous functions at almost every step; often, as in the liberation of adrenin, it is found that the nervous system abets and supplements an already existing biochemical response. The liberation of acetylcholine—sometimes in response to neural stimulation, sometimes without it—is responsible for muscular contractions for which the parasympathetic system was long held directly responsible. What the parasympathetic is now seen to do in many organic upheavals is, among other things, to participate in causing the liberation of acetylcholine, which activates characteristic "expression of the emotions." The experimental physiologist has therefore undertaken to simplify the picture; he has short-cut the process, severed the parasympathetic, frightened the animal, and directly examined the resulting muscular changes which reveal biochemical control more directly. Thus in the facial muscles of the monkey direct expression of fright can be examined, just as in the iris muscles of the cat direct expression of the same general response is examined. The reason for the difference in muscles lies in the fact that in the monkey the acetylcholine response is more evident, the adrenin response less evident, than in the cat. In studies of man it is likely that within the next few years we shall see as much experimental literature on the adrenin-acetylcholine balance as we saw a few years ago on the sympathetic-parasympathetic balance.

It must be heavily underscored that during the same era of the last twenty-five years, partly for experimental reasons and partly as a result of improved statistical sophistication, research has regularly made use of groups of experimental animals subjected to a uniform situation and has become interested in the *individual differences* among them. From the older rather Platonic standpoint, the results have often been shocking; from the newer point of view, even more confirmatory than was expected. Often the characteristic biochemical response is slight in one animal or even fails to be detected at all, whereas in another animal of the same species it is overwhelming. This is true not only of the magnitude of response, but of latent time and especially of continuance of the response beyond the time of stimulation. We should expect something of the sort, because each of the endocrine organs of a mammalian species varies so greatly from one individual to another, even in so simple a matter as mass, both in the adult and at each age level. In explaining individuality, genetic considerations come to the fore; the endocrine organs are present very early in fetal life and reflect family strains so clearly that systematic animal-breeding for the study of genetic relations is already well under way.

Many of the general principles relating to the influence of the endocrines upon personality structure are illustrated by the thyroid. It is worth while to proceed from the clinical study of extremes to the experimental study of average individuals. The classical picture of extreme hyperthyroidism is seen in Graves' disease. Since a major function of the thyroid is the regulation of the rate at which the body fuel is burned—the lowest oxidative rate, or basal metabolic rate, of the individual—the diagnosis rests not only upon grosser evidences of thyroid hyperactivity but upon determination of an extreme rate of oxidation. Directly or indirectly related to the same imbalance are rapid pulse and respiration, sweating, and emaciation. The classical psychological picture in Graves' disease is one of extreme hyperactivity, nervousness, general restlessness, a condition of general and unremitting stress. The opposite picture, in cases of hypothyroidism (called cretinism when congenital, myxedema when appearing for the first time in maturity), yields the expected low pulse and respiratory rate, and many indices of retarded tempo of activity.

Here, however, the beautiful symmetry of the expected relation begins to fail. Hypothyroid patients are often nervous and restless, as are hyperthyroid patients. Torpor, poise, or serenity may be found in individual cases, but the general run of clinical descriptions fails to yield a *psychological* antithesis to the condition found in Graves' disease. Maybe there is something wrong with the way in which the relation of glands to personality has been stated.

An investigation by John Levy is instructive. A group of problem children characterized by hyperactivity was compared in terms of basal metabolic rate with a group characterized by hypoactivity. The first group showed on the average a *lower* basal metabolism than the second. The groups were small and a repetition was obviously necessary. But in the meantime such data as these will constitute a disturbing paradox only if one forgets the everyday adjustments of normal persons. The excited over-responsive individual may try to slow down, to take it easy; the chronically tired and strained person may learn, consciously or unconsciously, to spend his energy thriftily, to avoid waste and excitement. So, too, the person long cooped up,, who is suffering from insufficient activity, feels better when he can begin to take exercise, and he will tend to an activity level which is high not in spite of but because of a rather low metabolic rate. If one wishes, this may all be called "compensatory"; or it may be schematized as the end result of trials and errors, and with reference to a way of living that gives more satisfaction. It remains true that in general there is a positive relation between thyroid and general activity; the glandular situation yields its results not in a simple and obvious way, like an organist's pulling a stop to get a given tone quality, but through a devious, complex route.[1]

In the usual schematizations of the roles of the endocrines, emphasis has been placed upon their effects upon nervous functions. Clinically, however, effects in the reverse direction have long been obvious. As Levy's study suggests, the nervous system can activate, and can therefore derange the endocrines. It is a common finding that a fright, a nervous shock, leaves an individual with a hyperthyroid condition. A neurochemical cycle is involved. We are dealing with no one-way street from glands to external traits; excess thyroid activity may lead to apprehensiveness, but it may also arise from it.

A modern approach to the problem appears in a study of sixty cases of Graves' disease, in fifty-four of which a history of apprehensiveness *preceded* the onset of clinical signs of hyperthyroidism. The cerebral and autonomic systems were both involved, and the involvement was scarcely attributable to a thyroid condition. Here very complex interactions indeed are involved. It will be recalled that in

---

[1] There may possibly be something of the same sort in Steinberg's demonstration that a group of adolescent girls achieved speed in psychological tests not in direct relation but —so far as the data went, for the findings were not cleancut—in inverse relation to their basal metabolic rates. The correlation, however, was only three times its probable error when the effects of age were held constant. If not a chance finding, the conclusion would be that the girls tended to work faster when the tissue tempo was slower. The study differs essentially from Levy's in that we are dealing here not with spontaneous speed in the general activity level but with approximately the *maximum* speed attainable by the individual in a rather uniform test situation. Whether our "compensatory" functions could operate here in the same fashion as that shown by the overwrought man's spontaneous slowing down can hardly be determined.

the discussion of tropisms, the point was urged that inner systems can be understood only in terms of the dynamics of inner-outer relations. We seem, correspondingly, to have found empirical evidence that our picture of the endocrine system (as of every organic system) must be so drawn as to emphasize forces outside the system, traceable in large measure to forces outside the skin, that control in a patterned fashion the patterned functions of the system.

All this may likewise be illustrated in the relation between *gonad development* and sexual-social maturation. Individual differences in the changes at puberty are generally large in mammals, particularly so in man. Though the mean menarche age for American girls is in the neighborhood of thirteen years, about a sixth pass the critical point before twelve, and another sixth not till after fourteen. The "corresponding" mean age for boys is about fourteen and a half, with comparable variability. The single criteria of menarche and germ-cell ripening are sufficient to show that there are personality changes directly associated with the process, for, after elaborately controlling disturbing factors, Stone and Barker demonstrated that the post-menarchical status as such is in some degree associated with greater interest in boys and in feminine status; consequently, girls of the same *age* may differ in their tendency to cling to girlhood or to press toward womanhood.

But these endocrine functions prove to be very complex. The pattern of sexual maturation, initiated largely by the anterior pituitary, involves many endocrine and other organs. It is increasingly clear that puberty, like all other phases of development, is a process in which no single indicator describes the physiological picture; the bone, skin, and vascular system, as well as the more obvious secondary sex characteristics, must be considered, though the changes are to some degree interlocked. And there are not only multiple causes, but multiple *expressions* of the process. The boy may develop a deep voice but scant facial hair; in the same way, he may develop some psychological aspects of "masculinity" but remain childlike in others: or the psychological syndrome, directly dependent on inner mechanisms that do not overlap perfectly with those reflected in somatic growth, may as a whole lag behind them. For the girl who is physiologically more mature than she is psychologically, the situation is confusing at best, and at worst sheer chaos; to be puzzled, amused, or disturbed by boys, or all three at once, is "unacceptable" adolescent behavior unless boys are at the same time *interesting* to her.

Moreover, environmental factors profoundly affect the puberty pattern, so that even the apparent differences between races in rate of maturing must be seen against the background of climatic, cultural, and other factors. The average menarche age of Nordic girls in Denmark is about fourteen, while among girls of Danish stock in the United States, according to Franzblau, it is more than six months less. Climate and diet hardly explain this. Indeed, our tendency to derive behavior from the biochemical system must be tempered by noting the continuous and often marked effects of the behavior world, the cultural world, upon the biochemical system. Indeed, just as we have seen thyroid activity both causing behavior responses and in turn being caused by them, it seems probable that the same is true of the gonads. The ages of menarche and of menopause in various cultural areas reflect not only the stock but the way of life, the cultural and ecological situation of the individual; so, too, individual sex interest and sex attitude probably operate through the autonomic system to affect sex maturing.

Moreover, the effects of puberty are to "classify" one socially, and one responds to his classification. In the California Adolescence Study there were a handful of late-maturing boys who constituted an unhappy, maladjusted group. Not only were their interests somewhat marked off from those of the majority, but they were aware of their peculiar status, bewildered to see the group moving from them; they were shy, irritable, or confused. In such instances the role of the endocrines can never be simply a direct one; in a society such as ours, to be fully masculine or fully feminine is essential to status. But the problem does not concern merely a few exceptional unfortunates. Every man is more obviously "masculine" in some respects than in others, every woman more "feminine" in some respects than in others. Each individual is necessarily concerned to develop, maintain, and exhibit enough of the available standard traits to win full status as a genuine and complete member of his sex group. Personality reflects not only the endocrine balance but the socially ordered responses to this balance.

In discussing the behavior which results from tensions, we have been content, up to this point, to say that inner disequilibrium leads to general restlessness. The restlessness, however, is never completely diffuse and generalized. Just as the inner disequilibrium is partly local, partly general, so the restlessness, the sensitizing of certain pathways leading to the muscles (the lowering of their thresholds), is partly general, partly local. The result is that beyond the general restlessness appear the specific earmarks betraying the specific character of the disturbance. The specific and local responses include those of striped muscles and of unstriped muscles, of duct glands and of ductless glands. The hungry man, says Carlson, exhibits not only general distress; as a strong stomach contraction occurs, there is a gush of saliva. The hungry infant sucks, though no breast is near. Stone's rats, Craig's doves, show upon sexual maturation not only restlessness in general, but a simultaneous activation of many sexual reflexes. McQueen-Williams' "male" rats that were artificially made into "females" by gland transplantation are tremendously sensitized to nesting material and to baby rats.

In other words, a region of organic disturbance both radiates disturbance through the blood stream to other points and affects the nervous system specifically. Since there is always some tone in living muscles, a chemical disturbance in the blood stream can so alter thresholds as to make a relatively inactive muscle relatively active. The nervous network can throw muscles into action. But not only is there *more* response; there is local movement that, indeed, is often *coordinated* as well.

THE THRESHOLD

Our next step is to attempt a more precise theoretical statement of motivation dynamics, upon which, fortunately, we have clear and direct data. K. S. Lashley, summarizing the work of previous investigators as well as his own, laid down the proposition that a drive consists of a bodily mechanism which lowers the threshold for a *behavior pattern*, i.e., permits the appearance of synergic responses. The drive is an internal stimulating agent; it is not the initiator of behavior (which in any event is never removed from control of some outside stimulation), but it facilitates or inhibits the activation of the system responsible for the behavior. The infant is hungry; pressure of the nipple on his cheek leads to the turning of his head toward the nipple. Hunger continues; now pressure of the nipple on his lips leads to sucking. Hunger continues; now milk in his mouth leads to swallowing. If the organic state of hunger is wanting, all the three thresholds are high, all three responses hard to elicit. It should, however, be borne in mind that since internal and external stimulation are jointly involved, the relation of organic state to external stimulus is simply the relation between cooperating agencies. "Endogenous" and "exogenous" stimuli summate or facilitate one another within the nervous system. The weaker the endogenous factors, the stronger the exogenous factors have to be; the stronger the former are, the weaker the latter may become without ceasing to elicit the action pattern. In other words, drives are relatively localized internal factors that affect thresholds; physiologically they participate in a nexus of mutually facilitating stimulations. Lashley might well have added that all the tissues are sources of, and participate in, the drive pattern.

The Lashley formulation fits well into the classical formulation by Sherrington, who has stressed the distinction between *preparatory responses*—i.e., activities which prepare the organism for contact with a drive-activating stimulus—and *consummatory responses*, which bring the organism into contact with the object and upon completion manifestly remove the drive. Salivation is a preparatory response, digestion a consummatory response. The preparatory response is conceived by Sherrington to be biologically ingrained and to serve its biological function by making more certain and effective the completion of the consummatory response. The simple test as to whether we are dealing with preparatory or consummatory responses is always whether the drive continues or ceases when the response has been completed. On this basis it is proper to stress that the preparatory responses of man are far more variable and betray much more individuality than his consummatory responses, and that cultural arrangements involve much greater modification and elaboration of the preparatory than of the consummatory. If this is true, we should expect to find that personality study is to a considerable degree a study of preparatory responses.

We have, however, already hinted at a complication in connection with the nature of hunger behavior. Any given behavior is the resultant of a tension system rather than of a single tension spot. One is hungry partly in terms of hunger contractions, and partly in terms of attitudes toward food and the situation in which it is to be eaten. Indeed, salivation and gastric contraction are themselves dependent upon a network of bodily relations. Sometimes the preparatory response is intense, the consummatory response weak; a person's mouth waters but he cannot actually stomach food; or like the Roman banqueter he relishes the preparatory responses far more than the consummatory. As Freud has pointed out, preparatory response may, in certain individuals, become almost consummatory; and Woodworth has demonstrated that many an instrumental act may become satisfying in itself.

Drive, in other words, is a collective name for a bodily condition, always composite and more or less unstable. To say that something "puts an end to the drive" means only that it puts an end to a particular localized tension. This statement is sufficient for some purposes. It is sufficient, for example, to say that the satiated dog no longer salivates much. But as the central nervous system becomes more complex through evolution, so that memory keeps action tendencies alive beyond the waning activity of the chief center of physiological intensity, the expression "a drive has been satisfied" means less and less. Although the drive system has been altered by the reduction of an important component, energy flows constantly into new channels; and as a person remembers, what was at first a memory may, a few minutes later, become a center of especially eager motivation. Anticipations, expectancies, appetites, enrich the world of drives, and the life of motivation is as much a matter of *increasing* tensions in such ways as it is a matter of reducing them.

From the foregoing it is clear that the nature of a motive calls for restatement in terms of the relations of the individual's tension system to specific patterns of outer stimulation, i.e., a proneness to respond in one way rather than in another as a consequence of new stimulating factors. Even when a man awakens in the early morning darkness and, before opening his eyes, determines upon a plan of conduct for the day, more than the pattern of activities within the skin is involved. The fact that it is dark and cold and quiet, the fact that the world presses in upon him less vigorously than usual, is a component in the motive pattern. The distinction made in experimental work between incentives and drives (as when hunger is the drive, food the incentive) and the discussion regarding the "externalization of drives" indicate that the tension system of the individual is maintained and guided by both internal and external factors. Sometimes, indeed, the inner tensions may fall so low that a creature without imagination or external stimulation would fail to make much overt reaction; but a "reminder," an external stimulus, without reactivating the inner localized visceral tension, can still start activity again. Motivation or tension is a name for a patterned aspect of the organism-environment relation; and though motives are relatively independent of one another, they are not absolutely so. What chiefly engages the student of personality is the architecture of the motive system.

When an outer stimulus, in cooperation with the inner tension system, leads to an act, we may speak of the outer stimulus as "adequate." Adequacy, then, is relative to the tension system. In other words, *sheer readiness* is the same thing as motivation; it is the inner aspect, whereas the stimulation is the outer aspect, of a behavior situation. Outer energies feed into a structured tension pattern in the organism. "Motivation" is the abstraction that defines the organism–environment situation in which action occurs; and despite broad similarities between men, one man's "motivation," as a structural whole, can never be the duplicate of another's.

6. The Biology of Motive Patterns

THOUGH all human motives appear to express the organic properties just described, it is necessary to turn now to more specific individual problems and attempt to define the classes or types of human motivation, to indicate the nature of individual differences in each kind of motive, and to suggest how motives become interrelated or patterned.

VISCERAL DRIVES

We have taken our examples from the analysis of the hunger drive, which serves as a sort of model for all the *visceral* drives, i.e., those which depend directly on varying visceral conditions. Under the visceral drives we may list hunger; thirst; excretory tensions; oxygen deprivation; vasomotor adjustment needs, arising in response to temperature extremes; sexual tension, deriving initially from gonad and other endocrine tensions; maternal tensions, due in some degree to endocrine and lactation tensions. All these drives are of course profoundly socialized, and all show some degree of periodicity in a form related to habit (e.g., the day's eating cycle). All of them can, of course, facilitate one another, the state of tension being greater when two or more are involved; and they may all fuse, the individual being unable to explain the peculiar quality of his feeling.

Just as some puppies are great eaters and others are mere lickers and tasters, so too in man individual differences in the hunger drive are well marked in the opening months of life. It would be absurd to insist that they are constant throughout his lifetime, but they are constant enough to worry doctors and parents. One child eats like a horse, the next like a canary. It is not all a question of metabolism, either; and it is certainly not a simple question of energy requirements. Some love to stuff; others nibble and run back to their games. So far as this is an abiding trait, it participates in structuring the child's world—and the adult's.

The maternal and the sexual call for special comment. In view of the fact that individual differences in maternal interest are usually large among the young females of a species, it would be reasonable to ask whether this holds for mankind. Noting that some of his patients had always been thrilled by babies—had gone out of their way to be "baby-carriage peekers"—while others had had no interest in them, David Levy made a systematic quantitative comparison between life-long expressions of maternal feeling on the one hand and endocrine data (such as length of menstrual flow) on the other. The positive results strongly suggest a constitutional factor. At the same time the great force of social sentiment regarding motherhood is brought home to the growing girl, its force and its form varying from community to community, from family to family; and it not only reinforces within her the primitive mothering impulses, but brings a wealth of feelings deriving from identification with her feminine role, her eager desire to be a mother and not just a person who is mothered —feelings elaborated from the depths of her being and not just an expression of the narrowly maternal as one might find it in animal societies.

When it comes to the individual elaboration of all the feelings associated with sexuality, not even all of physiology, or of psycho-analysis, or of literature, can do justice to the subtlety of the problem. For erotic feelings in early childhood are manifold and diffuse; they are often slowly consolidated with one another and with other feelings, such as those deriving from the maternal as well as the aggressive, and they are subjected to such a bewildering mass of social reinforcements and inhibitions that they may finally come to involve directly or indirectly almost everything that lies within the personality. They may in some individuals be handled very casually; in our culture, however, such feelings are usually close to the experience of selfhood, and when subjected to tabu, they are rejected as unworthy, so that ego psychology and the psychology of sex are bound to become interwoven, quite aside from the problem of erotic attachment to the self. As if this were not complicated enough, the primitive outgoing responses to other persons, and to animals, to flowers, to sunsets, to a thousand lovely things, may become fused with the erotic (in a form varying with cultural emphasis), so that one has the infinite richness or tenderness of romantic love; or these aesthetic or cosmic cravings may be arbitrarily set in opposition to the erotic, so that one devotes oneself to a "higher," and feels that he must reject a "lower" love. So accustomed are we to this sharp cleavage between complex and overlapping forms of experience that we respond warmly to Bourdillon's words that "The light of the whole world dies when love is done" and to Wilder's suggestion (in *The Bridge of San Luis Rey*) that "love is the meaning of life," though Bourdillon is thinking about the love of man and woman, while this is the one kind of love that Wilder does not allow to fulfill itself.

ACTIVITY DRIVES

We have found that in studying chemical motivation factors we have perforce moved into the sphere of muscle activity. Here we come face to face with the fact that tensions in the muscles are also, in all these same senses, motivators. Tension of a muscle group lowers thresholds for another contraction (as in the familiar reinforcement of knee jerks by gripping the hands). Muscle tone is constantly changing and causing new activity. Perseveration—the tendency of an activity in progress to continue beyond the period of outer stimulation, like the maddening thought that runs in the head—is a motivator of no mean significance. So, too, are the direct and indirect effects of any keyed-up condition (excitement) or any relaxed condition. Thus the muscles both guide and initiate action. The movements of the newborn are dependent alike on outer, on visceral, and on muscular stimulation.

We have suggested that the homeostatic balance is often destroyed by events which are not behavioral events. Thirst, for example, may result from sheer evaporation on a warm day, and a considerable caloric requirement must be met even when lying still. One might consequently be tempted to think of the organism as striving to maintain a sort of inactivity, remaining at rest except in periods of extreme want. Guthrie describes charmingly the homeostasis-seeking group of villagers who have just enough energy to crawl from sun to shade; as the sun slowly moves, they supinely accept an hour or two of coolness before they are goaded again. But it would seem more appropriate to note that in terms of the tension systems which control conduct, the deficits and excesses of inner stimulation (the "too much" and the "too little") both function to cause activity. There are always many imbalances, many forms of restlessness going on. The normal condition is not one of successful escape from activity. Trends toward the reduction of activity and toward the increase of activity are always jointly manifest. The clock is always running down but always being wound up. Even when fatigue, starvation, or illness has forced a violently uncomfortable state of repose upon us, most of the bodily activities go on. The work of the body must be done. Muscular inactivity becomes unbearable; there is a compelling need to do something. At the psychological level something to do, something to occupy one's attention, is compellingly experienced. We seek repose, but we also seek activity. Broadly, the effect of all this may be conveniently summarized by saying that there are not only "visceral needs" but also "activity needs."

It may be worth while to look more closely for the reasons for such activity. Even if a given bodily tissue could carry on its life, its processes of nutrition, oxidation, and self-repair, in complete isolation from all other living tissues, it would maintain an activity level from which there would be daily or hourly variations, and it would therefore permit the notion of relative activity, relative passivity. The instant that any such tissue is considered in relation to its fellows, its activity level is seen to control to some degree the activity level of the rest, and in return to be controlled to some degree by them. The activity level is expressed in an active demand—in the sense of a great readiness to receive—for oxygen, minerals, salts, and a large and complex variety of biochemical agents such as the hormones. All tissues are in this sense active, not only competing with their fellows for a limited supply of needed substances but qualitatively directing the activity and development of other tissues. The student of embryology has long known that one tissue may "rob" another, and the student of muscular exercise has noted the same principle.

But we must go further and stress the qualitative effects which the activity of one tissue has upon the activity of another. We are dealing not simply with robbing, but with the disturbance of the balances required by other tissues, and we are concerned not only with "stimulation" but with organizing capacities. The endocrine glands, for example, act not merely to make other tissues do certain things, but to accelerate some of their many activities in such fashion as to alter the chemical balance and the physiological attributes of other tissues. From this point of view, it will not be sufficient to follow the trail from a deficit in a given region to a visible motor response. It will be necessary to consider the inner shifts which precede or parallel the externally manifested motor pattern. It is not enough to emphasize the system of muscular tensions, for we have learned more and more that the cerebrospinal axis and the peripheral nervous system, the autonomic system and the endocrines, are all parts of one great system mediating the adjustment process; there can be no chemical reaction without its effects on tension in muscle, or tension in the cerebrospinal system.

The term tension is intended literally; the concentration of potential energy under life conditions permits tension reduction. So considered, tension is also characteristic of the nervous system itself. Electrochemical activity goes on constantly in the brain (page 88); the brain cannot stand still any more than the muscles. The brain is no mere telephone switchboard; it is part of the powerhouse. There are, in a literal sense, centrally initiated motive patterns. The nervous system does not wait to be "stimulated"; it is active even under general anesthesia. Activity needs include both striped-muscle factors and cortical factors, factors involving the use of the cerebral equipment.

Although we cannot evaluate the relative intensity of these various kinds of needs, there is one hint that may suggest how subtle the needs of the central nervous system may be. It might be convenient to list the strength, the urgency, the intransigeance of the various tissues in terms of their capacity to force changes in tissues and in external behavior. In view of the current fashion of tracing motives solely to the viscera, it is rather striking from this point of view that although the viscera stand higher in the scale than do the bony and the cartilaginous parts, they are somewhat lower than the muscles and skin, and much lower than the nerve cells. The nerve cells cannot tolerate much by way of toxic effects; the blood is full of buffers which work perpetually for their protection. They can tolerate hardly any water or food shortage; delirium and incoordination appear long before the visceral processes are much affected. And they can tolerate enormously less oxygen deprivation than any other tissues. Thus while in prolonged exposure to "oxygen want" the visual disturbances are traceable both to sense-organ difficulties and to difficulties in the nervous elements in the retina, it is the nervous elements that suffer the most. The cortical needs, then, are not only urgent; they are delicately hinged upon the varying condition of the body and subtly modify all its activity patterns. The point is offered merely as one more suggestion of the artificiality of the current attempt to make the mainsprings of human motivation reside in the unstriped muscles, the glands, the arterial walls, the gastrointestinal tract, or any other visceral structures. These are all of importance, but they are not the only important ones; it would indeed be hard to justify designating them as the most important of all.

The activity needs, probably traceable to tensions both in the nervous system and in the striped and unstriped muscles acting jointly, dominate a large share of the small child's waking hours. Infants may kick when hungry, thirsty, or cold, but they also do a good deal of kicking and rolling, a good deal of wriggling and smiling, when not in any manifest state of visceral need. The little child keeps himself active, knows nothing worse than to have to keep still, just as the adult begins to feel below par when activity is allowed to fall to too low a level. If there is a need to eat, there is in exactly the same sense a need to use all of one's physical machinery. Under the activity needs we should of course include the need to relax and to sleep. And we should also include activity *cycles,* up-and-down swings of the type to which the term "rhythmic" is applied, and symmetrical or balanced activities, such as those involved in the maintenance of posture and in locomotion. There is a physiological continuum from the sheer inability to sit perfectly still to those compelling needs of activity and creativeness to which progressive education gives so much attention.

Activity needs show summation as clearly as do visceral needs, many different centers of tension combining to throw us into overt activity. A given tension level results from the summation of many factors, but there is a center of maximal activity, as in the golfer's arms as he drives, the rest of the muscular system playing an abundant supporting part. In turn, activity drives may facilitate visceral drives, or vice versa. The energies of the happy, excited child— happy whether it be birthday ice cream or the expectation of a prize at school—tend to "spill over" into visceral or into striped-muscle expression. As far as is known, any stimulus whatever tends to raise the tension level; and Jacobson's data suggest that tension anywhere spreads to some extent to other regions.

Individual differences in children are very large with respect to need for striped-muscle exercise, the simpler rhythms of breathing, heart beat, and locomotion, the tendencies to warming up, to perseveration, and to quiescence or the petering-out of activity, and the general cycle of waking and sleeping. All these activity differences have been recorded many times in early infancy, and all the records show large and fairly stable differences among normal infants and children. As two small children wait with their mother for a bus, one plays a continuous push-me pull-you game with her or with the lamppost, the other gazes dreamily at the passing cars; and mostly they run "true to type" through the clinical record. A good many observers believe that infants are more distinguishable in terms of their activity level or activity drive than in any other terms. Indeed, one of the things that most clearly characterizes the individual is his tendency to maintain a given volume or output of behavior. The Ohio State observers noted a high degree of continuity in such output in the first ten days of life, and Shirley found sheer activity level one of the most distinguishing characteristics in the first two years of life. The neuromuscular components in the activity stream—both in its bald quantitative aspects and in its more subtle modifications as involving the spread or the qualitative form of activity—may well be more important for human personality than endocrine or other biochemical clues.

Moreover, the experiments of Schilder and the clinical work of Rado give much striking evidence that this network of unceasing striped-muscle activities may serve as the true core or heart of the self. We shall later (Chapter 20) attempt to describe systematically the components that enter into selfhood; but here it is worth noting that it makes much more sense to trace to the continuous inner struggle of the individual the vaguely conscious or unconscious muscular disposition to keep going somehow, to push, to assert, to maintain whatever one has or is, than it does to attribute it to the cyclical qualities of visceral drives. The real clue to the self, from this point of view, is the sort of thing one sees in the unconscious patient as he struggles back from his ether anesthesia to a normal state, a struggle to breathe, to wake up, to make contact with the world—above all, to keep activity going, to maintain the energy system.

Sensory Drives

Thus far we have taken into account the two main groups of effectors. Under the term visceral we have included the patterns centered in unstriped muscles and glands. Under activity needs we have included the system that involves the central and peripheral nervous systems discharging into the striped muscles. But the story is far from complete. One of the great dangers threatening an adequate personality psychology is the failure to achieve an adequate balance, through neglect of sense perception and other cognitive functions. Personality is as much a *way of becoming sensitive* as it is a way of reacting upon the environment. It is as much a matter of selecting and using outer energies as it is of focusing activity. The little child spends a large part of his time exploring with his senses, pursuing sights and sounds and touches, often carrying the activity forward for a brief period after the sensory stimulation is gone— the beginnings of exploratory behavior. The sense organs and the brain regions with which they are connected stand ready to act and are healthy only when allowed frequent action.

As we saw above (Chapter 4), there are large individual differences in such receptor functions and in the affective responses linked to them. We must now go further and stress that since such affective differences exist we must, if we are to be consistent, say that sensory needs or *sensory drives* differentiate individual infants. This is the implication of the marked individual differences which infants show in their responses to taste stimulation. It is also the basis of the work done by L. J. Stone and L. B. Murphy (page 708) on sensory toys, such as cold cream, dough, and finger paints, in which great differences in delight are shown by children playing with these various tactual and kinesthetic stimuli. These differences appear extremely early; they are like the sensory drives which differentiate one puppy from another. They appear to remain rather stable for individual children, at least during the period of nursery-school observations. There is a prima-facie case, then, for sensory drives cognate in importance with activity and visceral drives, and there is evidence that from the very beginning the intensity of such needs shows a highly individual character. It should be added that many studies of musical prodigies indicate an extremely early sensitiveness to tone that is quickly elaborated by any opportunities afforded for musical training, producing in a few years results which most people cannot achieve even after laborious efforts throughout the entire growth period.

The neglect of sensory drives has been largely due to the effort to place all the real generators of activity in the viscera. But even in studying the visceral drives one keeps bumping into sensory factors of various types. The most pertinent example here is a study by David Katz, or rather a twin pair of experimental studies. In the first experiment, a group of hens eat all the grain they can hold; they are taken to another room where other hens are eating from a large pile, whereupon they immediately start eating again and consume a great deal. In the second experiment they are fed all they will eat of grain that has been artificially colored red; complete satiation is evident. They are then given some of the same grain colored green, and again they proceed to eat a large quantity. Is it hunger that is satisfied in the first instance? It hardly advances our understanding to say that the first behavior is pure hunger behavior and the second pure sensory stimulation. The hens eat as actively in one case as in the other. Sensory stimulation is a major source of activation of tension levels. In fact, if the term "sensory" is used as it should be—to include all the different sensory impulses, including those from the alimentary canal—it is the only source. Féré understood this when in illustrating the principle of dynamogenesis he showed that any flash of color, any touch, any sound increases the force of the grip upon the dynamometer. In all hunger situations there are external as well as internal stimuli; summation of stimuli is always the rule.

It is likely that the principle of the conditioned response (Chapter 9) is of some help here; i.e., the hens have been conditioned to eat because they have eaten in situations where they saw other hens eating. But this again does not advance us far, because conditioning is itself a case of the summation of stimuli (the preparatory facilitating phase shows this), and because stimuli to which the hens have not been specifically conditioned—new grain colors and even revolver shots—increase the intensity of many drive patterns. If this is true, there can easily be complete satiation of an activity, yet immediately thereafter a continuation of the activity when there is an increase in the tension level. And this increase may arise either directly from a local agency acting on the tissues primarily involved, or secondarily through raising tensions elsewhere which are communicated to this primary center. Satiation, then, is always relative; or, to speak more accurately, the question is one of the total field situation, in which the internal dynamics and the quality and quantity of external stimulation must be fully considered. The fields stretch out from the tension center and comprise not only other bodily tissues but all the interacting forces observed within the behavior pattern.[1]

The manner of envisaging the whole problem of the sources of motive has never, perhaps, been described so well as by Diamond, who made clear the misunderstanding of the evolutionary theory which led us to put primitive things at the apex, when actually the evolutionary implications tend to indicate that the more complex structures and functions would never have evolved had they not served a new function different from and sometimes dominant over the more primitive ones. Thus he was able to show that needs for intellectual, esthetic, and other individual and social activities may arise, simply and naturally, from the way in which the human nervous system is constructed and from its interrelations with the rest of the body. From this point of view the music of songbirds, the curiosity and playfulness of chipmunks and kittens, the self-decoration of primates find a phylogenetic place, with science, invention, and art as the natural and necessary products of the sheer process by which complicated functions have led into still more and more complicated functions. The Freudian view that redirected, sublimated sex energies are the source of such activities becomes unnecessary and is seen in its historical perspective as another attempt to Darwinize at a time when Darwinism as a system was conceived to mean the direct derivation of complex processes from simpler ones without recognition of any elements of genuine novelty or any expressions of true emergence. Sexual, aggressive, and other energies may indeed lead to indirect rather than direct expression, and they may be combined with other motives; but the more complex behavior patterns of complex organisms are genuinely functions of their complexity, not merely new revelations of the simpler energies. And when once these complex types of response are possible, they tend to become self-

---

[1] "Intersensory" phenomena appear to be subject to the same principle and to play a similar role in the motive structure. The brightness of a light may increase when a buzzer is sounded; a touch on the hand may seem to involve greater pressure if at the same time a bright light is shown. The field relations of the motive pattern depend upon the energies fed into the organic system. It is quite possible, indeed, that Katz's experiments with the red and green grain express the same principles as the intersensory effects in human vision.

perpetuating through the use of a larger and larger share of the energies available to the organism (cf. page 182).

EMERGENCY RESPONSES

In all the classes of motivation so far considered, we have found the inner tension system prepared, so to speak, to cooperate with outer stimulating conditions; there is a state of readiness. But if we are thrown into a dither by stumbling over a rope or discovering an old letter from an erstwhile loved one, or receiving an unexpected telegram, no "state of readiness" exists. Yet we certainly display "motivation" as we respond. We know no better term to describe this externally aroused state of upheaval than the term "emergency response"; although any term presents difficulties, we shall hope to justify its usage as we develop the story.

From a rough descriptive standpoint motivation may be very crudely divided into two classes of activities, one of which, the "vegetative", serves to maintain the processes of growth, repair, and reproduction, and the other of which (Cannon's "emergency" system) has to do with the mobilization of available resources in a time of direct threat to life itself. Cannon structured the problem very graphically when he assigned the former functions to the parasympathetic (the craniosacral) system, the latter to the sympathetic (cf. page 95).

Cannon's original theory of emotions as emergency upheavals certainly needs to be shaken down a bit, but even so it is surprisingly useful; it is worth the work of refining it. The first major point of criticism is that the vegetative responses themselves show all degrees of stressfulness and, when necessary, involve plenty of sympathetic activity. The hungry man's heart may accelerate when dinner nears; the returning lover scarcely shows the *retardation* of pulse which parasympathetic activity would involve; wild pounding of the heart may appear indiscriminately in a wide variety of conditions, from threat to joyous excitement. It was this feature of Cannon's dichotomy that led to Carlson's classical comment, "Cannon entertains that theory because that theory entertains Cannon."

Despite these and more objections, there is still value in the vegetative-emergency antithesis. Though it draws too sharp a line, some sort of line is necessary if any grouping of phenomena is to be achieved. From the present standpoint the term motive may be used very broadly to include *all* maintenance and extension of life processes, the homeostatic and the continuous motor adjustments to shifting external situations as well as the emergency upheaval states. The term emotion, already used in over fifty senses, may if desired be employed to designate only the emergency responses, notably those of fear and rage. Struggle under pain, suffocation, etc., may be grouped under the fear category if one wishes, and any form of vigorous attack on interfering obstacles may be called rage. Disgust and shame are upheavals due to a threat, too, if the term is stretched. Grief may be regarded as response to an emergency about which nothing can be done. Surprise might be considered a very mild form of startle, and hence of fear. The only purpose of a classification here is to indicate that there is a variety of more or less similar, more or less distinguishable response patterns which overlap physiologically and behaviorally but which, in spite of all difficulties, do constitute a group that no one would confuse with the group of vegetative activities. In general, the distinction lies in the fact that the vegetative activities go on all the time in constant or in cyclical fashion, whereas the emergency group of reactions may appear twenty times a day, or once, or not at all, depending on what happens outside; there may be constant threats or none at all. The patterns are *imposed*; they are not necessary spontaneous expressions of life. This, like all the distinctions in this field, is too sharp; a man climbing Mt. Everest struggles to breathe just as he struggles to climb. When the inner equilibrium of the neurochemical system becomes slowly more and more unstable as a result of the life processes themselves, and inner behavior leads directly to outer behavior, one may speak of visceral drives; when the inner equilibrium is suddenly or forcibly disturbed by external circumstances, such as threats, one may speak of emergency responses. Mixtures and transitions are obvious. The same is true of summer weather and winter weather, but they have to be distinguished.

In all this we are speaking of the source, the locus and character of the inner imbalance, not the external manifestations. A man may struggle to breathe, or, with bitterness hardened into hate, lie quiet to kill. Consequently the individual differences in all the types of motivation conceived here are individual differences in the inner patterns. These can be studied in three ways: (1) directly through pulse, blood pressure, fluoroscopic examination of the stomach, galvanic skin reflex, measures of finger temperature, etc.; (2) indirectly through inference from external behavior patterns, including the verbal and gestural; (3) still more indirectly through the testimony and inferences of observers regarding their own past and present conduct. The writer's bias in favor of the first of these should be clear by now, and perhaps also his conviction that no physiological indicator means a great deal by itself and that converging lines of indirect evidence, correlated if possible with direct evidence, are a great deal better than any single indicator.

One may wish to retain the term emotion in spite of the lack of agreement in its use, for we can hardly dispense with it when we wish to describe the upheaval of the individual when overpowered by some vigorous external stimulus. Certainly the cerebral cortex is involved, and certainly the lower centers, especially in the thalamic region, are profoundly concerned. Certainly also there is abundant discharge both to striped and to unstriped muscles and to duct and to ductless glands. It would be perfectly proper to regard rage or fear as a visceral drive in the sense defined above, if we wished to stress the internal factors which tend to produce generalized bodily tension, many of which make a person vaguely apprehensive or irritable. When we use the word emotion, however, we usually mean to stress something more explosive, a process by which the individual is catapulted into a new and unplanned relation to his environment, not solely as the result of a tension system which existed before he made contact with the new outer stimulus. Considered in such terms as these, involving both cerebral, visceral, and skeletal adjustment, emotions can be equated with emergency reactions. They exhibit the all-or-none principle more clearly than do the other drives, and as a rule have rather clearly definable thresholds which differ sharply from one person to another and from one occasion to another for the same person. Constitutional factors again may be inferred from the data suggested above, at least in reference to fear and rage.

Since, however, we are dealing with elementary reactions abstracted from the total, it is proper to emphasize that there is no sharp distinction between the different emotions; they overlap too much. Nor is there a sharp distinction between emotions and other motives, because there is always some "new outer stimulus" and some "readjustment" to be made. By and large, disgust and shame have more in common with fear and rage than they have with the other groups of responses, if we happen to see fit to stress the suddenness of upheaval and the complexity of response. In all four classes of drives (visceral, activity, sensory, and emotions) there is a synergy of the central nervous system, the autonomic nervous system, and all the various effector systems. Some of the most joyful experiences, like exhilaration and laughter, draw from such wide bodily resources as to involve, more or less, all of the four classes of motives.

In connection with emotion it needs also to be stressed that one learns *how to cope with* one's motives, and that one of the most fundamental and central skills of personality is its means of keeping itself out of certain emotion-rousing situations, notably fear and shame. The degree of success is perhaps the chief factor in the security level of the person. Here, and in so many other aspects of psychology, the laboratory has studied the *fully aroused* response, while the clinic has studied the *means used by the individual to avoid making the response.* Organically, of course, the two are aspects of one system.

In view of the difficulty of differentiating between the emergency patterns at birth (none has been sharply defined experimentally except the "startle pattern"), two lines of evidence must be offered to justify the conception of fear, rage, surprise, and mirth, and perhaps some other patterns, as *recognizably distinct from one another at an advanced maturation level* (cf. page 62), and from the "visceral drives." The first is Goodenough's study indicating that though emotional patterns are not very easily distinguished at birth, they can be differentiated without difficulty at ten months of age; the maturation process involves not an isolated detail, but a complex expressive pattern. The other, likewise a study by Goodenough, indicates, in the case of a girl blind and deaf from birth, that patterns of surprise, anger, joy, and laughter could easily be observed and photographed at ten years of age. It is likely that the mechanism of skeletal-muscle patterning is responsible for this.

Individual differences in such emotional responses among the newborn have been something of a scandal to a psychology chiefly interested in uniformity of response. The startle pattern shows good uniformity of outline from child to child, but varies largely in intensity; and the attempt to study the familiar patterns of "rage," "fear," "love," etc., has in general revealed the fact that stimuli intense enough to pass the threshold of the phlegmatic are positively traumatizing to other people. Some infants begin to smile and laugh much earlier than others; others remain reserved or plaintive month after month (cf. page 57). Wherever we look in the world of motivation, we find big differences; the attempt to iron out individuality by going back to the moment of birth is signally unsuccessful.

But however much we emphasize the functional distinctness of the various individual drives and of the various classes of drives, we must keep constantly in mind that the tension system is a system, that tensions spread through the body, that no one region is ever active without arousing others, and that no drive can ever exist in an otherwise undriven body. There are nodal tension centers, interacting systems at all times. The simplest conceivable formulation would be a figure-ground relationship, such as Goldstein describes, in which relative activity in one region is the figure, relative inactivity elsewhere the ground. Far more frequently we find ourselves confronted by a system of nodes of varying levels of intensity and with networks or communication systems conveying energy to and from these tension centers, the general activity level of the organism (depending upon age, health, etc.) serving as matrix, and the specific responses to specific outer and inner stimuli serving as crystallization points.

From this point of view there is *motive structure*, just as there is perceptual structure. We need not follow Goldstein into that form of holism in which parts cease to exist and the dynamics of the whole permits of no differentiation of discrete elements. Rather, we should feel that the specifications of parts or elements in their complex inter-relations must be clear, if the term whole is itself to convey meaning. If configurations or dynamic structures necessitate the analytical study of relations, they also necessitate clear objectification of what is to be called elemental and what is to be called structural.

The single cell is highly structured. It is structured even in terms of tension gradients; the needs, even of the single cell, are somewhat localized. Growth and differentiation permit, week by week, more and more definite identification of specialized tension regions in the developing body. The degree of specificity exhibited is a function of the embryonic stage, in the strict sense that cellular tissues, trans-planted very early, may grow into almost anything depending on their environment, whereas when transplanted at a later embryonic period they lose this plasticity (cf. page 53).

It follows that the need pattern of interrelations between specific functional regions becomes geometrically more complex with the increase in need areas. There are more needs, and the dynamic inter-relations between them are numerous. This is true not only in the ontogenetic but in the phylogenetic sense. Man has more needs than any other animal,[2] largely because the differentiation process (espe-cially within the nervous system) has proceeded further.

Just as some of the qualities of the bud may be seen in the mature flower, it is important not to think of the achievement of a stage as a renunciation of preceding stages. Thus, for example, the basic tension level of a hyperkinetic system appears in the hyperkinetic qualities of differentiated reflex and of habit. The various components of a habit system share their basic qualities, partly because of com-munication within the system, partly because the components spring from a common matrix.

---

[2] William James wrote "more instincts than any other mammal." The context indicates that he meant something very close to "motives" or "needs."

But because there is differentiation, there are in the same organism recognizably distinct tension levels; e.g., the acquisition of any skilled act involves progressive concentration of the tension in certain muscles, the reduction of tension in others. The resulting *differentiation in tensions* is the process which permits their *integration* in a smoothly flowing activity; the focus of the integration, the figure, shifts in dynamic equilibrium as the act progresses. The figure-ground relations of such integrated acts are seldom absolutely sharp; there is usually a gradient, a tapering-off of tension from center to fringe. There is thus a region of relatively high tension and an adjacent region of lower tension. We are therefore confronted with the question whether the tension drops gradually as one moves outward from a center, or drops quite suddenly at a given point. Superficially, the drop in tension seems to be gradual. Finer measurement, however, usually shows that it involves many all-or-none steps. The characteristic mode of the spread of tension from a given region must then involve an all-or-none mechanism. The passage of impulses over the threshold of a receptor cell and the transmission of nerve impulses from one nerve cell to another are of exactly this sort. The excitation of the sympathetic system is a striking case in point; the last little remark "burns up" the patient listener. This may be called a "quantum manifestation"; the body is full of such manifestations.

For most purposes, the spread of tensions may be regarded as diffuse, and the resulting tension at any given region may be stated in terms of position in a gradient. All-or-none regulation of this sort appears in such manifestations as the sudden maturing of locomotor reflexes, the sudden occurrence of salivation in connection with hunger pangs, and the sudden emergence of sex behavior, as shown in Stone's many experimental studies. The principle of summation, as demonstrated by Sherrington, makes clear the possibility of a gradual approach to a critical point at which the response appears. The response is not necessarily proportional to the stimulation; the stimulation must achieve a certain quantum, after which the response then appears full blown.

Such discontinuity will constantly confront us, for it is upon the discontinuity between two or more differing types of integrated action that the possibility of any real *organization* of personality depends. Since the term "organization" will be used frequently hereafter, a definition of it seems called for at this point, in the light of the case developed thus far. The term organization is used to define the system of interrelations obtaining at a given time between the bodily activities in progress, be these relations spatial, physical, chemical, or what not. The study of organization involves the study of all the dynamic interrelations between processes; and since motives are merely organic processes when looked at from the point of view of degrees of tension, motive structure is simply an abstraction relating to the interrelation of life processes. So far, relations have been viewed at a point in time; often, however, the relational system flows through time. The characteristic cycles, changeabilities, warmings-up, slowings-down, smooth or erratic patterns of change which characterize the individual are as much of the essence of organization as is the system of dispositions at a moment. Briefly, then, organization may be defined as the *spatial and temporal interrelations* of the life process. This is meant to include specific recognition of the reality of the parts rather than a resort to the principle of holism. At the same time it is meant to stress the interdependence of organism and environment. Since some of the temporal and spatial interrelations frequently shift in all-or-none fashion, we find temporal discontinuities, or quantum shifts, at some points in the organized system; but this never involves a complete collapse of all systematic relationships. And with growth (and experience, too, as we shall try to show), such sudden shifts in organization become less and less conspicuous.

In the general summary of the view developed up to this point, motives are not conceived as levers, nor even as fuel supplies; they are *abstractions from an activity continuum,* identifiable only grossly in terms of their locus or their formal effects. They are gradients in the sense that tissue situations may be conceived to be centered at certain points and to melt into other tissue situations at a distance. For all that, the gradients are often sufficiently sharp to permit classification in terms of the region and type of tissue situation *chiefly* involved. The most obvious among them, connected with inner deficits and relations to oxygen, water, and food, may be used as prototypes of visceral motives. The homeostatic or broadly biochemical state is at least an important component of sexual and maternal motivation and of the need for rest and sleep. Activity tendencies in striped and unstriped muscles, reflecting themselves in overt conduct (in stretching, in relaxing, in cramps, in perseverative activity), are cognate with them. Since the phenomena of latency, refractory phase, and hyperexcitability are found in nerve tissue as well as in muscles, and since the muscular and nervous systems are bound in ultimate functional unity, it may be convenient to speak of neuromuscular motivation. This type of motivation differs from the homeostatic or visceral in the sense that homeostatic tension can be most conveniently conceived in terms of instability, especially biochemical instabilities of the blood stream. But the difference is not sharp; the "need" of a tired muscle to relax is doubtless in part biochemical. The biochemical situation acts directly, too, on the nerve cells and muscles, as is familiarly exemplified in the effects of toxins on neural and muscular thresholds and in the unconscious regulation of respiratory movements by the chemistry of the blood. Among the needs of the central nervous system are needs for certain types of stimulation or experience, needs not only for kinesthetic and visceral stimulation, but for stimulation from color, tone, touch, taste, smell. The organism is turned outward; it is gratified by making sensory contact, and it perseverates in, or recurs to, such contact. Finally, though the term need must here be used in an extended sense, induced needs are imposed upon the organism by outer forces which upset it; when these needs develop in stress situations they may be called emotions. In any tissue system, and consequently in any motive system, individual differences are manifest in the early months. It is the development, the differentiation, the integration of these individual motive patterns that constitute the first great biological clue to personality.

actualized before. Throughout the discussion we have tried to stress the interrelations between inner stresses and also their relation to outer stimulation of a complex sort; organism and environment are an interacting field.

From the point of view of the nervous system the distinction between outer and inner—that is, outside and inside the skin—means little. The outer stimuli must go through a series of inner transformations before they become capable of activating the nervous system; and when they have done so, they act in company with the inner stimulations reflected in adjoining tissue changes. When climate, for example, is emphasized as an outer environmental stimulus and conceived to alter the personality structure—as when one asserts that the basic attitudes of the exuberant Vedic peoples were subdued upon their arrival in a much warmer region—the picture is oversimplified. It is the enduring effect of climate as a cooperating agency in the living system that is involved; climate may have done this to a specific group, which had a specific personality structure, but it may not be capable of doing it to all men.

A point of view which recognizes that all tissues are motive centers and that all of them constantly interact with the forces of the environment can, moreover, find no place for the distinction between biologically determined and socially determined motives. There is no conceivable way in which during the developmental process a man (or a society) could remain immune to the systematic modification imposed by a given way of living, or remain detached from the cultural standards and pressures which at every moment determine the form and force of the motive pattern. There is no way in which a biological motive could appear in its pristine form in a context of social events. The hunger, the sleep, the love-making, or the power-craving of a man in western society could in no conceivable sense arise from a primitive, gene-determined disposition, the developing structure of which had remained encapsulated, untouched, free from the reciprocity of social living. In the same way there is no conceivable sense in which the craving for activity, for color and tone, for intense experience, for warmth and affection, could be created out of nothing by a system of cultural rules prevalent outside of the newborn individual. There is no way in which "socially derived" drives could be established and implanted like a graft within the body tissues. Culture can alter, mold, or reorganize drives—or rather, it can permit them one form of development or expression rather than another—but it can hardly "create" them out of nothing.

But there appears to be a difficulty here. Can we not, in a thoroughgoing, literal sense, establish in the organism a number of tissue tensions, drives which it never before possessed? On first thought, it must certainly be conceded that the answer is in the affirmative. Drug addiction is a good example. Civilized man has continued to discover new and exciting ways of acting upon his nervous system by chemical means; the new drugs produced in recent years have given him forms of experience which no man ever experienced previously. He has made frantic attempts, as De Quincey did in the past century, to convey this experience to his fellows. The addictions which are thus established may become the most powerful drives within the individual, dwarfing everything else in comparison. (The biochemical nature of such habit-forming drugs is beginning to be understood; it is clear that in respect to some of them, buffer systems within the blood are established which are responsible for the greater and greater dosage required to circumvent them.) In other words, the tissues may be molded not only so as to "want" more of something which they wanted in the first place, but to want things for which there was no previous want. And if it be argued that these drugs fit neatly into some prearranged, limited number of biological potentialities, the reply is that a continuous stream of new drugs is being discovered and that medical men and lawmakers are perennially busy trying to head off the tendency of their fellowmen to make new addictions out of these new discoveries. There may be a limit to the number of drives that can be created, but the limit is not in sight. If this is true in the biochemical sphere, it is certainly even more obviously and cogently clear in the case of social experience, which constantly creates patterns of needs which never existed before.

Yet what can be created depends upon what is there. There still remains the central fact, that what can become a satisfying drug experience depends on specific tissue dispositions and on specific human learning processes related to the valuation of these experiences. Some of our drugs kill off natives who nevertheless barter soul and body to get them; to others of our drugs they are indifferent. And this is true of *individuals* in every society. New motives thus arise because in reality they are not completely new. It is not true that people can "learn to like anything." Patently they cannot. But they can learn to like a vast array of things which never passed within the purview of primitive man. Civilization consists in large measure of a system of devices for increasing the drives of man, and of both frustrating and satisfying them. In the next few chapters we turn to the ways in which this alchemy is brought about.

7. Organic Traits and Their Measurement

IN THE preceding chapters an approach to the individual organic system was sketched. Before attempting to view more closely the process of learning, by which this organic system develops still more complex interrelations, it may be well to pause here to answer an insistent question: Under what conditions can the individual organic system be analyzed and measured so as to reveal the *organic traits* of the person—his physiological strengths and weaknesses, especially the strengths of his drives; his tendencies to excitement and relaxation; his proneness to one rather than another type of physiological integration? Clearly, if we are to answer this question, we need a working conception of *traits* considered as aspects of the living system, and also a conception of the *relations between traits.*

From the foregoing it would appear that the observation and measurement of human traits from an organic or biological point of view must involve chiefly the direct observation and measurement of individual *tension systems,* or indirectly the observation and measurement of their expression. If so, the conception of personality traits from the organic point of view comprises at least three kinds of dispositions, in accordance with the three developmental levels described above (page 66).

First, at the level of general undifferentiated response, we may look for the characteristic mode of responses of the tissues, taken collectively. Thus the individual's metabolic rate, though depending partly upon a specific organ, the thyroid, is in some respects a *generalized property of his existence* even before the thyroid gland appears; it may manifest itself by influencing thresholds for specific response patterns. Since the classification of traits must, so far as is possible, be in terms of their roots, we must first look for the roots in the *general* dispositions of tissue.

Second, there are traits which depend not globally upon the properties of tissues taken collectively, but upon the properties of specific *kinds* of tissues; they represent the second, differentiating level of development. Thus the central nervous system, though suffering from no injury, may as a totality be inadequate, whereas the autonomic and peripheral systems are adequate. Or, to use another example, the nerve cells throughout the body may have a long or short latent time or when aroused may exhibit a great or slight lag, compared with corresponding nerve cells in other individuals. Such traits as long warming-up time or extreme perseverative tendency may well express the idiosyncrasy of the nervous system (cf. page 69).

Third, traits may arise from a *patterned interstimulation* of various specific differentiated tissues. Here the trait is traceable not to a specific tissue situation, but only to a mode of interdependence among the tissues. A visceral drive may be an expression not of a single local visceral tension but of a system of tensions, the outer behavior being sometimes an additive, sometimes a much more complex expression of an inner tension system. Similarly, stable or chronic personality dispositions may arise from stable tension systems, unstable dispositions from unstable tension systems. Thus lassitude may conceivably be traceable to a neurocirculatory inadequacy; apprehensiveness, to an endocrine involvement. To be sure, it is hard to imagine such systematic idiosyncrasies without some local source or sources; nevertheless, the trait that actually confronts us arises not from the *local* but from the *patterned* situation.

From the organic point of view, personality tendencies of these three types comprise *all* that the organism is, and *all personality traits* are included under one or another of these types. There is therefore no special meaning in asking whether the organic point of view is relevant only to extreme but not to normal cases, or to acquired but not to constitutional responses. Organic responses vary from one person to another and from time to time in the same person, and what is extreme from one point of view is the norm for the purposes of some other comparison. If the psychosomatic approach is sound in looking for psychic manifestations of the organic and for organic manifestations of the psychic, there is no sudden transition to a region in which the organic approach becomes "relevant," no point on a distribution curve in which personality may be "practically conceived" to be an organic system. There are indeed all-or-none responses in tissues, and there are all-or-none traits; but if these particular responses do not occur, or these particular traits do not appear, other traits, with *their* psychosomatic relations, will appear. If extreme hypothyroidism (say a basal metabolic rate of -35) "produces" a trait, slight hypothyroidism (say a basal metabolic rate of -10) also "produces" a trait.

The confusion on this point, resulting in the widespread belief that "within the normal range" tissue changes are irrelevant to personality, arises largely from the failure to note that the functional significance of a tissue situation in terms of its ultimate effects on behavior may be quite different at different points in a distribution. This is true even with respect to the first and second classes of traits mentioned above. For example, the "degree of overt activity" may be greatest when the tissues are at a certain critical point, so that any increase *beyond* that point reduces activity, while increase *up to* that point heightens it. It is even more palpably true of the third class of traits, in which the recognizable trait depends on a network of relations, so that an increase in a local tissue response may either increase, decrease, qualitatively alter, or completely restructure the patterned basis of the trait. All this does not mean that tissues are important only within normal limits; rather, it means that their significance requires intensive empirical research.

And confronted as we are with an organic system which behaves in a certain way because it is so constituted at the time, it does not help us to ask whether the organic point of view is more valid for hereditary conditions, for the after-effects of disease, or for brief "functional disturbances." The organic approach is of course used in different ways, depending on whether the organic situation has been there always (if so, it is usually likely to continue) or only since the time of an injury or disease (if so, the condition and the behavior *may* be removed), or is a momentary situation (if so, the behavior too, so far as it depends on the specific situation, will be momentary). If the organic situation is there, it will make behavior different. Organic situations change continually in some respects with growth, with tissue modification, with reorganization of inner energies in the learning process; but this does not mean that some situations are organic, others "purely functional" or "purely a matter of habit." Functions and habits, too, are organic events occurring in tissues. Like all other organic events, the function and habit depend both on the dispositions of tissues and on the forces acting upon them.

It must instantly be conceded that this is a schema and a promise, not a completed picture. For purposes of method it is important to insist that personality is a coherent, consistent, organic system, not a scattered group of organs with non-organic cross links between.[1] The concept should become clearer and more valuable as we proceed. Whether a unified view of personality could be achieved without it is doubtful. It is true that many personality dispositions are more easily treated at present by placing the emphasis upon other conceptual tools. When these other tools have had their trial, we shall look back (Chapter 26) and restate the organic view in such fashion as to indicate the interrelations between the tools in the unified task of personality study.

From the organic standpoint we have, then, to deal with traits as (1) broad characteristics of tissue response; (2) persistent modes of reaction of individual tissues or organs; or (3) persistent modes of interaction between tissues or organs. All three kinds of traits are useful "constructs" in relation to the complex actualities. They are, however, constructs which, like electrons, may serve a conceptual purpose before anyone sees them, or, like zero and infinity, are useful in the absence of any possibility of perceptual verification. On biological grounds, especially the embryological, they appear to be more comparable to the electron than to the mathematical type of

[1] This is reminiscent of Woodworth's reference in a lecture at Columbia in 1919, to the train of cars held together by "the feelings of amity between the conductor and the engineer."

construct. For many animal strains and for many human clinical types there are, if not *continuous*, at least *intermittent* observations on all three kinds of traits; ratings and experimental behavior observations have already been brought into meaningful relations with all three. The physiological inadequacy of the idiot illustrates the first; the day-by-day instability of intermediary metabolism (Hammett; cf. page 79) is an example of the second; a negative relation between the activity level and the basal metabolic rate (J. Levy; cf. page 97) illustrates the third.

A serviceable example of a trait at the first level is speed of tissue response, as was noted earlier (page 82). The general speed of cellular differentiation characterizes not part but all of the growing individual. A common factor of speed in mental tests was clearly defined by DuBois. The question arises: Is there a connection between physiological speed and speed of intellectual response? Evidently there is, for Rounds found a substantial correlation between speed in the DuBois tests and speed in the Achilles tendon reflex. This is not to close a complicated question, but rather to suggest the value of conceiving speed in generic instead of segmental terms. Incidentally, the word "speed" may lead to misunderstanding, for there is little or no connection between this primitive speed attribute and the "congenial pace" of the individual, molded by cultural and subcultural factors and by varying personal motivations. (Cf. page 630.) In contrast to generalized speed in this sense must be mentioned various specific speeds, such as speed of walking, or talking, or writing (page 630), which are distinctive of the individual; speed in one of these functions is practically independent of speed in others.

GENERALITY AND SPECIFICITY

We find ourselves confronted here with the broad question of generality and specificity of personality traits. Some reaction tendencies are ready to spring forth at the slightest provocation; any stimulus whatever, regardless of quality, can bring them to light. Others are tuned to a single stimulus; the slightest change in its quality means an unresponsive organism. The first is exemplified by Sherrington's strychnine-poisoned dog, aroused by a pinch, a voice, a change of temperature; the second, by the hunter's dog that halts his pursuit when the syllable to which he has been trained is uttered. Neither dog, perhaps, behaves according to the textbook, but as reference points they are recognizable; they incarnate the now classical conception of general and specific personality traits. Let us begin, just for clarity, with ideally general and ideally specific traits.

It might be convenient to think of the general traits in terms of action tendencies so gently poised that any disturbance of the inner-outer balance must reach their low threshold. A trait that is perfectly general is in a sense waiting there in the organism, needing only to be released. It is general in the sense that the structure of individual situations need not be examined, because *any* situation will elicit it. Given the all-or-nothing law, every stimulus provokes the all.

Even in such ideal and abstract terms, one is puzzled by an apparent contradiction. If of necessity there is a threshold to cross, there must be stimuli below that threshold. Consequently there must be situations which will evoke the response and others that will not, by virtue of sheer differences in intensity. Traits are enmeshed in situations at least in the sense that purely quantitative differences in situations produce or fail to produce them. But what does it mean when we say that a situation *as a whole* has greater or lesser intensity? Are we not really referring to salient aspects of the situation and hence of response which is more or less *specific* to *such aspects*?

Upon the heels of this first contradiction, there follows a more serious one. The receptors are necessarily selective; each receptor owes its existence to the evolutionary reduction of thresholds for specific qualities of environmental stimulation; not to sensitiveness in general but to sensitiveness to specific energy relations. Granting that every path *can* lead, as Sherrington says, to every muscle, it is a bit hard to see how all pathways—that is, all threshold sequences in the organism—could ever be equivalent. Granted that strychnine can drive thresholds so low as to make any one of them traversable for a given stimulus, it is hardly likely that a response could be indifferently related to all kinds of stimuli, unless indeed one refers to universal, indiscriminate, total response. And that is exactly what Sherrington is describing. There is, then, just one general trait at this ideal level, and that is the general trait of reacting indiscriminately in a convulsive totality.

Turning to the other ideal pole of the discussion, the ideal of complete specificity, we must conceive a response so attuned to a specific stimulus that nothing else in the universe can evoke it. It must be of exactly the quality and of exactly the intensity defined. But this, once exactly specified, will never occur again; even if it did, it would not be functionally the same to a changed organism. As far as the receptors are concerned, it is hardly likely that they would have evolved for the finely discriminated service rendered to a single, utterly specific stimulus; they must be ready for broad classes of stimuli. The optimal stimulation may indeed be unique enough at a given time, but there are always other stimulations approximately equivalent in quality and intensity, and scarcely distinguishable in effect. A personality trait must at the very least be concerned with a type, a band, an area of possible stimulations.

In defense of specificity, exception may perhaps be taken in terms of those tightly wrought, internally coherent stimulus patterns so distinctive that nothing else under the sun is really like them. The man who is passionately devoted to his church may show no intensity about anything else in life. But such tightness of structure never really completely destroys the identity of the components; there is always *some* resemblance to other components, some transfer of response; and configurations themselves may be structurally similar one to another, and hence elicit transfer. Even the tightly integrated whole that is the known personality of another individual permits transfer by analogy; this is the basis for the childhood acquisition of a general understanding of persons and of affection for them, the basis for childhood morality, for psychoanalytic transference, group membership, and self-understanding. Full specificity in social responses would be as maladaptive as in the simplest contacts with the physical environment. Though ideal generality and ideal specificity thus prove to be unrelated to any real psychological situations, it is nevertheless valuable to approach some personality traits in terms of relative generality, and others in terms of relative specificity. We shall return to this problem when the matter of habit formation has been considered (pages 619 ff.).

The Properties of Tissues and Organs

If the organic point of view is to be serviceable, however, it is of the utmost importance to define traits in terms of the *actual properties of tissues or organs*. Thus emotional instability, though reported clinically in parathyroid defect, is found in many other conditions, and it may appear in cyclical, persistent, or irregularly recurring forms. It is therefore *not* the instability that constitutes the "organic trait," but the *parathyroid defect*. If then we are confronted by the simple fact of instability, we may appeal to many possible organic agencies; the setting-up of a specific construct like parathyroid defect as a "cause" does us no good unless it helps us to search for and find the parathyroid defect. And when we find it, we shall have to ascertain the precise way in which it occasions this behavior. It is never externally observed behavior that constitutes the trait, for the observed behavior is only a starting point, a signboard indicating the direction in which an organic trait may be found. The trait itself is a characteristic of tissues or tissue systems, either a perceived characteristic or a construct which the evidence shows to be useful. In terms of the direction in which our thinking may be effectively ordered, we must be as ready to move from the organ to the behavior as from the behavior to the organ. As long as the organic point of view is strictly applied, a large but not infinite number of organic traits is conceivable, defined in terms of functions of known tissues and of their interrelations. The number of possible outer expressions of organic dispositions is infinite, but the number of organic traits is finite.

An example of the need for extreme caution on this last point is provided by the experiment by McFarland and Huddleson (page 81), showing the functional inadequacy of the circulatory system in neurotics. The results differentiating the three groups are clear; but are the groups characterized by distinctive organic traits? Perhaps; for neuro-circulatory adequacy may be a fundamental biological disposition that serves as a direct clue to psychoneurosis, and if so, such adequacy is in this instance an organic trait. But suppose that the life pattern of the neurotic, with its stresses and anxieties, be conceived as emanating, in certain cases, from the symbolic (cortical) system, undermining the health of the circulatory system; the results would be a *symptom* of cortical disturbance; not, as the definition of organic trait requires, a predisposing condition. In such a problem—and it is typical—we know that there are organic factors, but not how they are patterned. Finally, suppose that some degree of neurocirculatory inadequacy was present before the psychoneurosis appeared, but that the latter has involved a gradual increase in stress, a progressive disturbance of the circulatory system. The present result can not tell us *in what degree* we are dealing with a specific organic predisposing trait of the neurocirculatory system.[2]

The organic tissue system is always exposed to a physical and a cultural environment, and both are forever interacting with it; hence any adequate description of the organic system must place it in its full context. Traits are never "indigenous"; they are always in some measure the responses of specific tissues to specific environmental, usually cultural, stimulation. They are, if one wishes, "biosocial." The term biosocial is used here to indicate that what is biological is at the same time social. Periodic expressions of motivation, as in the

---

[2] Weiss has shown the necessity of working both forward from organic dispositions to their outer expression and backward from expression to disposition. Plumage is in many birds an expression of sex hormones; it would therefore be easy to infer (by the "backward" procedure) that all bird plumage is hormone-controlled. Experiment shows, however, that in some birds—e.g., finches—the sex hormones have nothing whatever to do with plumage; the control mechanism differs in different species. A number of analogues to this in the field of personality determination immediately come to mind. Some masculine or masculoid characteristics, for example, may in certain men be genuinely dependent on endocrine function, necessarily developing rapidly at puberty and waning during involution. But in other men these same characteristics (literally the same, as in comparing the species of birds) may well depend on other biochemical factors or upon factors which are not biochemical at all; the possibility must at least be considered and excluded before any attribution of overt characteristics to organic traits can be made.

hunger cycle, belong to biology; but they belong also to sociology. The biosocial does not constitute a special class of biological events; practically any biological event can be socially controlled to a visibly recognized degree. A cough is purely a biological event if it is due to a cold and is unnoticed by the victim and his associates. It continues to be a biological event that may conveniently be treated as a biosocial event if it spreads through imitation. Turning red is a biological event which may be due to a circulatory disturbance; turning red at an embarrassing remark is a biosocial event. The only thing that can be socialized is a biological process, and in man most biological processes are to some degree socialized. The social is an aspect of the biological, and the biological is usually a potential aspect of the social. When the actualization is evident, we may call the event biosocial.

This usage differs considerably from others which are current. G. W. Allport, for example, uses the term biosocial to indicate a mode of classifying responses in terms of their specific social evaluation by another person; biosocial traits are conceived to have no organized structure within the individual organism. But in our use of the term, no whit of the significance of the biological structure of a trait is lost by its becoming a stimulus pattern for another person, and the other person exhibits his own biological structure in responding as he does.

The Measurement of Organic Traits

The student of personality would like nothing better than to be able to measure organic traits in a systematic and inclusive way, to list all the organic dispositions and measure them methodically. In particular, he would like to explore individual differences in the strength of various drives as fundamental components which are important in the study of personality structure. Organic traits can be measured. But their measurement is subject to very specific limitations. We need here to emphasize certain restrictions which mar, or at least greatly complicate, the process.

As we have seen, the strength of a drive is dependent to a considerable extent on the amount of deprivation involved. Just as the hungriest man may be the one who has gone longest without food, the man most powerfully motivated through any of the tensions described above may be the one whose environment provides the least, relative to the level which the drive characteristically assumes in the individual. A man may be starved for music, famished for prestige, or thrown into almost pathological distress by his failure to obtain the "raise" or the vacation for which he is prepared. From this point of view, the personality is not simply the drive system, but the drive system relative to what the environment offers. Indeed, the environment must be closely scrutinized if we are to be able to assess the degree of satisfaction or frustration with which the individual is actually coping.

There is, for example, the classic argument as to which human drive is strongest. Food, say some; sex, say others; prestige or power, say the more cynical and the more sophisticated. Actually it is largely a question of an environmental shortage relative to the personal organization. The demand for air is not a "strong" drive for most of us most of the time; we make no great effort about it, because we can breathe. But the need for air is certainly stronger than the need for food if we are held under water a few moments. The strongest drive designates what we are most deprived of; deprivation involves both the condition of tissues and the availability of tension reducers.

This leads, then, to the attempt to state quantitatively what we know about the strengths of these various drives; surely an important project, if we are to begin to speak quantitatively regarding the structure of personality. The method usually pursued calls for defining the drives in abstract form and measuring their intensities, as by the amount of punishment which must be administered to prevent a person from moving toward the satisfier of the drive, or the amount of money he will demand to forego the satisfier. The procedure appears sound enough when it is recalled that the satisfier must be fully specified in terms of the specific character which the drives have taken in the individual person.

[140]

Suppose, however, that we wish to measure individual aggressiveness or timidity; not the aggressiveness or timidity stimulated by certain situations, but aggressiveness in general or timidity in general. Suppose we set out to measure reliably individual proneness to rage or fear. We should, of course, find that the various rage situations give no perfect correlations one with another, and that this is true of the various fear situations. By using many rage situations, many fear situations, we should build up highly reliable measures that seek the general factors underlying the specific. As we scanned the data, however, we should find that we had achieved this high reliability, this high consistency of "rage tests" or "fear tests," by making the most of the constancy of the individual relative to the test situations we had prepared, and we should deliberately avoid varying our rage or fear stimuli too much, because of the adverse effect upon our reliabilities (we would throw out items which "correlated too low with the battery"). If successful, we should proceed to measure more and more such general traits. Having made, then, a clear-cut effort to measure personality traits in the abstract—what we might call personality as trait x plus trait y plus trait z—we should find in fact that we had simply measured trait x in *situations of type A*, trait y in *situations of type B*, trait z in *situations of type C*. Or, still more crudely, we should find that we not only had done thus but had also measured all three traits x, y, z, in a common situation of type alpha, perhaps a laboratory setup permitting the expression of all these traits in a paper-and-pencil situation similar for all the measures. E. C. Tolman well formulates the difficulty: Do Chicago rats and California rats inherit and learn in the same way? Do Chicago students and California students yield the same factors when their test scores are analyzed? The trouble is that we cannot measure drives or traits in their abstract form, but only in the form in which they are liberated or expressed in certain defined situations. In other words, the life of motives and traits is an organism-environment kind of life in which we can specify the traits of individuals only when we implicitly assume a constancy or continuity of environment for our measures.

Even so, measurement is decidedly valuable, as we shall see, and usable in two ways: First, when individuals live in roughly the same general environment we can say something meaningful about the use which they make of that environment or about the types of reciprocal selection which organism and environment make from each other. Second, for most practical purposes, the individual stays in more or less the same *general* environment—the same general culture, the same subculture, the same world of symbol and of external compulsives, the same pattern of drive satisfiers and frustrators. And by his very process of living he usually makes the network tighter about himself; his behavior provides that the stimulus world will remain relatively constant for him. In this sense, then, personality measures devised to test the strengths of drives, as defined above, *can* be undertaken. But if the environment in which one man lives is not the environment of another, the test results will have meaning not as comparisons of organisms but only as comparisons of organism-environment patterns, man-world relations. We should, then, expect to find that organic traits can be successfully measured when care is taken to do the measuring in a situation functionally similar to that in which the trait appears. This is indeed the case. An example is G. L. Freeman's successful measurement of response to stress (page 81)—not every conceivable kind of stress, but a clearly defined type, knowledge of which was needed for military reasons.

Organic traits, as we have seen, consist of tissue tensions. Sooner or later the tensions spread in such fashion as to involve the effector processes. This is accomplished largely by the lowering of thresholds for the effector responses, as in the hunger example noted on page 102. But the tension situation usually spreads to other regions before and during its period of influence upon the effectors; thus the hungry man becomes irritable. To speak more ponderously, the sympathetic system is involved through the reduction of thresholds for rage; the man who wants to begin his dinner (or his game) cannot keep still but paces up and down (tensions radiate through many muscle groups). This general fact of the spreading of tension means quite literally that there cannot be unmixed motives. Even in infancy, wants press upon and reinforce one another to some extent, just as they may also inhibit one another; the most imperious one may dull the force of the others when action toward one goal is incompatible with action toward the others. Activity patterns in the service of needs become parts of the larger tension system, so that individual need patterns mark off each man from his fellow.

If this conception of need systems is sound, each full-fledged trait involves qualitative and quantitative aspects of considerable complexity. *Your hunger is different from my hunger*, for it includes considerable irritation but no feeling of anxiety; when I am hungry I experience malaise which verges on fear. You want to walk up and down and talk when you are hungry; I want to hide and speak to no one till after breakfast. We may be alike in the fluoroscopic picture of our stomach behavior, and unlike in other components of the total process. All this, of course, is not offered as an argument against the analysis of traits into their simplest possible components; it is rather an argument for more analytical work. If your hunger differs from mine, your love from my love, the task of disentangling the components and studying their interrelations is complex indeed. Perhaps human cultures and subcultures differ largely in that need patterns are structured in different ways, and personalities largely by virtue of the same principle.

The animal laboratory has shown that the simplest drives upon which research can be done are composites, the elements of which vary in weight, depending upon the circumstances of growth (cf. page 114). The motives of children, specifically their interests, tastes, and enthusiasms, are similarly no mere maturing elements, but clusters or fusions of components, each one of which has developed under conditions of cultural facilitation, molding, or blockage. Even if all that is required of a given component is that it develop at a certain rate, the compound will be qualitatively different in different cultures. The feeling of loving one's mother varies from one community to another (cf. page 842). Affection for her, though never completely obliterated, is weaker, more meager, less complex among some of the more "aggressive" culture groups, whereas it becomes an extraordinarily rich, subtle, and all-pervasive thing among others. Such cultural molding means that the different attributes of the drives must appear in different worlds of experience, and hence it interconnects the drives in different ways, both in simultaneous and in successive patterning. Pride in status and pride in identification with a leader are concrete integrations which are permitted to occur in different forms in different cultures. The pattern of violent defense of one's family as a group, together with violent hostility to every *individual* member of the family, is reasonable and acceptable in many a frontier population, ridiculous in the culture of China.

We are, then, face to face not only with the interlacing of qualitatively varying drives but with the actual *fusion* of drives under conditions which make our customary analytical methods extremely difficult. Just as the student of perception must distinguish between a pattern with recognizable elements (e.g., a circle made of dots) and a blend (e.g., the taste of lemonade) in which the separate sensory qualities are lost, so the student of personality finds that the observed traits of the adult are frequently not *patterns* but rather *blends* or fusions of the original components. This is one of the reasons why the "functional autonomy" of G. W. Allport (cf. page 178), or some principle very much like it, has been so clearly needed. It may be possible to observe the genesis of a compelling value or interest within the individual, but not to sunder it by the current analytical methods. Thus we have come to the same view of interrelations which we reached by another path near the end of Chapter 5. There attention was drawn to the idea that motives are neither spots within the skin nor systems of trunk lines and branch lines connecting them with one another, but abstractions from a flow of activity in which both simultaneous and successive dynamic relations between organism and environment need to be described and interpreted. We have now arrived at the view that organic traits are frequently complex systems of functional relations between tissues and specific environing conditions.

Almost every problem in personality study looks different when this way of thinking is encouraged. Consider, for example, the trait of *aggressiveness* in the light of the current interest in frustration and aggression. Frustration is the blockage of a path to a goal; in our present language tension is kept high, permitted no reduction. From this follows a series of struggling movements more or less directed toward removal of the interference or destruction of the obstacle. If, however, the motive system is itself both complex and fluid, the very failure of tensions to spread is itself frustration; e.g., the excited child must "keep still." We then encounter the problem of the *degree* of frustration, as well as its locus, quality, and form. The tension system that is "frustrated" may initiate a wider tension leading to struggling movements, and these, depending upon the cultural conditions of development, may lead to either diffuse kicking or directed assault. The investigation of the relation of frustration to aggression becomes in large measure an investigation of the locus, the degree, the quality, and the form of the frustration, and similarly of the "aggressive" behavior, the complex inner pattern of tension which may—or, we must add—may not follow. The past and the present relations of organism and environment, not the fixed relations between "frustration" and "aggression," will be involved, and the trait of aggressiveness, as a complex pattern or fusion, may prove to contain ingredients from all three developmental levels described on page 66.

An interpretation of the experiment of Barker, Dembo, and Lewin will serve both to clarify the point and to summarize the present approach. The question here is whether the blockage of impulses produces specific organic results, or whether it yields a variety of responses depending upon the whole situation within and without the organism. Thirty children of nursery-school age were first rated with respect to their "constructiveness." Thus the mere use of a toy telephone as a rattle counted low on the scale, its use to carry on an imaginary conversation counted high; when crayon and paper were provided, scribbling counted low, pretending to write a letter counted high. The week after the preliminary observations of constructiveness, the children were brought to the end of the large playroom and shown a number of fascinating *new* toys with which they wished to play. After a few minutes of play, however, they were led back to the old toys with which they had played before. Under this deprivation and frustration most of them "regressed" in constructiveness; they acted like less mature children. From using the telephone for conversation some regressed to using it as a rattle, etc. The average regression was in the extraordinary amount of seventeen months of mental age, from an average fifty-five-month level as a starting point.

Now what is it that was frustrated? The children's desire for the new toys? At first sight this seems sufficient; some of them pressed their noses against the wire mesh that kept them from these exciting objects. According to the account, however, the children turned away from these new objects, absorbed themselves, for the time being, in the same old telephone, the same old drawing. Is it the interest that was frustrated, or is it the child? That is, broadly speaking, is there a *local* or a *general* increase in tension level? So far, we need only to speak of the organism, and to emphasize that this disorganization in response shows itself in violent, excited activity, in rattling the telephone, scribbling with the pencil, letting off steam. But almost every organ of the body is involved in this petulant expressive pattern. Response has become diffuse, undifferentiated; regression here means loss of differentiation. It appears that the tensions have rapidly spread, that they characterize both the perceptual, the emotional, and the striped-muscle patterns. But we must go further. These disturbed expressive patterns depend upon the specific environment prepared by the experimenter. Had the children been led into the playground, they might well have run faster, kicked the football harder, gone down the slide more courageously, and done many other things which are *less aggressive*, also less *regressive* and *more* "mature," i.e., corresponding to a developmental level which they had not yet reached. One could quite properly set up an experiment in which frustration could be made to increase rather than decrease the "developmental level," and also, by providing new outlets, *reduce* aggressiveness.

The primary thing that Barker, Dembo, and Lewin undertook to show was that *constructiveness*, defined as a rather specific type of adjustment to a rather specific type of environment, undergoes certain measurable changes under certain field conditions. The abstraction "aggression" or "regression" is of little use as a key to the organism; but the conception of a change in field patterns, in which the precise character of the adjustment to the environment is fully specified is of great use. One of the most interesting facts brought out by the experiment is the extent of individual differences; each child reacted in his own way, and eight of them did not regress at all. If frustration and aggression were entities, there should be definable functional relations between them which would hold for all children. The raw data published by these three experimenters show that each child has his own way of being frustrated and of regressing.

It would be valuable if the studies of traits could in general become gradually more fully field-oriented in this sense; if, for example, instead of saying that a man is "artistic" or "interested in music" or "conceited" or "industrious," we could make clear the specific field relations, the forms of dynamic interaction between his tissues and his world. Clearly, we cannot write so large a check today; we do not have enough capital in the form of exact knowledge about tissues. And we have not yet analyzed the role of the learning process in the development of traits (pages 161 and 192). So this is as much as can be said here. This leitmotif will, however, be developed as the data justify it.

Organic Traits in Relation to Gross Anatomy

We must now turn to the various ways in which a study of the parts of the body may give insight into individual traits of personality. First we must take up the classical conception that personality and body form are inextricably linked, a crude but very natural way of looking upon the relation of traits to the bodies of their possessors. The hypothesis is that those having certain body types exhibit certain personality types; body form and personality go together. The cultural demand for such interdependence of body form and personality make-up has been terrific from the time of the Greek "psychognostics" to the present, and there is nothing surprising in the constant exhuming of deceased hypotheses or in the excitement with which new biometric techniques are applied in relation to new psycho-metric techniques. Although psychologists have in the past been violent or scornful in their rejection of such hypotheses, there is in progress today much patient work related to the testing of current hypotheses regarding such relations.

From the point of view of genetics, it is indeed conceivable that some of the genes which are important for the anatomy of the face or hands *might* be linked (in the same chromosome) with genes which are important for neural or biochemical dispositions contributing significantly to personality. They might be linked at one point in a pedigree but not at another. The entire matter is therefore specula-tive, and the question of specific genetic relations between anatomy and personality is an empirical one in which definitive evidence is always required. Burks brought together some evidence which sug-gests that the manic-depressive personality might in some cases arise in genetic linkage with certain simple anatomical traits (cf. page 50).

A larger likelihood exists that the biochemical system, especially the endocrine system, may predispose to a certain physique on the one hand, and to a certain personality on the other, so that the two manifestations of a given endocrine system would be found together. This hypothesis regarding the endocrines is the basis of the work of Kretschmer and his followers, who at first sight appear to have demonstrated a direct tendency of the spindle-shaped man toward schizophrenic habitus, and of the globular man toward emotional cycles of the manic-depressive type. The theory applies not only to full-fledged schizophrenics and manic-depressives, but to all who are schizoid or cycloid in inclination; a typology is set up in which spindle-shaped body form is conceived to go with the introverted tendency of the schizoid, and globular form to go with the extroverted tend-ency of the cycloid. Many dozens of studies have seemed to confirm Kretschmer as far as the full-fledged psychotic groups are concerned; but many dozens have not. Surely it is fair to ask in such a problem that a technique be repeatable, that a result be confirmable by all who patiently and open-mindedly seek it.

But suppose it be granted immediately that Kretschmer's findings may well prove to be broadly correct, as they relate to psychotic groups. The fact remains that schizophrenia is not understood, its biological foundations are almost completely unknown, its relations to various personality deviations are frightfully involved. There is no certainty that the various schizophrenic conditions belong psychologically in one pigeonhole. The assumption that all schizophrenics were introverted personalities prior to their psychosis is almost as fantastic as the generalization that normal introverts are, as such, inclined to schizophrenia. The basic conception of introversion, as we shall try to show in Chapter 25, needs considerable clarification before it can be used at all. And to bring two foggy terms into relation in the hope of gaining light on normal personality structure is hazardous. To establish the relation between body form and normal introvert-extrovert personality trends, or even extreme ones measured on the same continuum with the normal, is an empirical problem upon which only one systematic piece of research appears to have been done. This reasonably exhaustive study of a large population of young adults discovered no relation whatever between the Kretschmer body types and personality.

Sheldon, Stevens, and Tucker, agreed on the inadequacy of the Kretschmer formulation, have recently developed a systematic approach to the measurement of body form and have used this as a clue to personality traits. Referring to the fact that embryonic tissue is classified as ectoderm, mesoderm, or endoderm, and noting that such tissues as the skin, bones, nervous system, viscera, etc., arise from one or another of these tissue types, they have undertaken to define the relative prominence of the three tissue types in the adult individual. One outstandingly valuable point is the sharply defined quantitative method. Each of the three tissue systems is rated on a seven-point scale, from least to greatest development. Thus a man with an average endowment in all three would be 4–4–4. Extreme types take such forms as 7–1–1, the 7 referring to outstanding development of one kind of tissue and each 1 referring to relative underdevelopment of the tissues derived from the other two systems.

Since they show that the ratings are satisfactorily close to the results which strict measurement yields, the question is whether they are closely related to personality measures. Unfortunately, the personality measures are also in the form of ratings; and what is most disturbing is the fact that the ratings of personality can easily be influenced by knowledge of the appropriate body ratings, so that the correlations of the two are hard to interpret. If their biometric methods were used in repeating this study, and if the most reliable personality measures were brought into relation with them, the results might well be very interesting. The published correlations of physical and personality traits are of the order of $+.80$; and even if there has been gross bias in the procedure, it is likely that some important relation is present. But there is no independent confirmatory evidence; at this writing, the question is wide open.

There are, however, three *indirect* ways in which anatomical clues of these or other types are valuable in personality study. The first is the role of anatomical traits in limiting or controlling conduct. An example is a congenital heart lesion, which greatly limits the effort and strenuousness characteristic of childhood and is likely to generate a diffidence in relation to both things and persons. Just as a heart lesion may limit activity, a labile vasomotor disposition may limit adjustment to temperature. The child turns blue when he goes swimming, turns red in the steamer's engine room. Because in medical language such things are "functional" rather than "organic," they are glossed over. The child is told not to be a sissy, not to be sorry for himself. The child with limited oxygen reserve is always last in the foot race, no matter how he strains; he is told that if he had "guts" he could run like the rest. He may, in frantic striving to make the accepted pace, literally develop "guts" in the form of gastric ulcers, mucous colitis, and the rest, expressing in the meantime an anxiety which the cheerful habits of contemporary medicine put down as the "psychogenic" basis for the ultimate "organic" ulceration. Such anxiety does in fact usually follow and is of course in the strictest sense psychogenic with reference to subsequent troubles, i.e., it is a phase in a chain of events, some of which are more conveniently approached in psychological language than are others.

The second way in which physical and personality traits are valuable is the long-time effect of expressive behavior upon the body's appearance, especially the face. The anxious man's tightened fingers and vocal cords, the meeching man's flaccid neck, are often half-consciously used in judging character. It is seldom recognized, however, how profoundly the whole musculature may be molded by the chronic tonus distribution. To watch a man of stormy temperament under ether anesthesia is a profoundly revealing experience. Even in ordinary sleep the face is rather expressionless; under the more profound effects of ether the habitual tonus patterns disappear, the face becoming undifferentiated and impersonal.[3] In death the expression is often gone; the focused energies are dissipated in favor of a "peaceful" artifact. The harried individual may for the first time look serene; the martinet's face may suggest the possibility of tenderness. The habitual expression—or rather, the habitual *range* of expressions—has been activated through a lifetime and is so solidly molded that anesthesia and death alone can soften it.

One can see in the small child how this molding process goes on. Expressive patterns which are frequently elicited do to some extent alter neuromuscular coordination. But the major factor at work is persistent internal stimulation; the individual may, for example, not merely be prone to anxiety in response to immediately disturbing circumstances, but develop chronic anxiety which keeps a chronically anxious expression on his face. Anticipation of or readiness for trouble, as a lifetime habitus, may work more potently upon the features than sheer volume and continuity of externally directed stimulation. The face learns the anxious habits so well that its expression is easily interpreted, no matter what the immediate stimulus may be. And similarly for solemn, or jocose, or affectionate, or hesitant, or domineering faces.

The third of the indirect values in the relations between anatomy and personality is the effects of one's physical appearance upon others.

---

[3] Strictly speaking, two conditions other than those mentioned may approximate the obliteration of facial individuality. (1) In some of the more profound psychiatric disturbances the muscles may lose tone and sag under gravity in such a way that almost complete expressionlessness results. (2) Electric stimulation may activate *all* the elements of facial expression. Cf. G. Dumas, *Nouveau traité de psychologie*, 1933, vol. 3, pp. 136 ff.

Mere size and strength may do a great deal to bludgeon a boy's way into social acceptance, or keep a girl lonely because the boys feel inferior to her. And though handsome is as handsome does, a harelip or a facial blemish, or even flapping ears or knock-knees, may ruin a boy's, and especially a girl's existence. If these malevolent pranks of nature can make life lonely, it is likely that many lesser handicaps do a great deal to fray the cord by which social contact is maintained. To be good-looking, on the other hand, is half the game for girls in our society and in many others. (Standards differ; but the fact that she would be a belle in the Straits Settlements is no great comfort to the Hoosier wallflower.) One's own personality is partly a response to the habitual judgments and attitudes of others. There is, moreover, a tendency to stereotype the possessor of rotundity as good-natured, the possessor of a long jaw as firm-willed, etc.; it is hard not to act as one is expected to act. There is probably no intimate relation between facial structure and character; but if society reacts as if there were, a secondary relation may develop.

On the whole, then, anatomical measures should reasonably be expected to suggest significant clues to personality traits, if the activity sequence of relations is carefully studied in individual cases. Although we should not expect direct one-to-one relations between psychological traits and physiological or anatomical measures, we have glimpsed some complex relationships that promise to prove valuable if we can secure a broad enough perspective to see the personality system in relation to the organic system.

THE PHYSIOLOGICAL APPROACH

While on the whole our gleanings from the anatomical approach are small, those from the physiological approach are large. Personality study in terms of individual physiological constants has proceeded at such leaps and bounds that a manual of practice in this field is clearly needed, and the pathology of physiological function in relation to psychopathology has already yielded thousands of researches. Our concern being chiefly with the normal personality, we shall limit ourselves to a brief survey of some of the standard physiological measures of organic traits in the sense used in this chapter.

We may best begin with measures of visceral activity. Among the measures of endocrine dispositions the basal metabolic rate is still the most useful. The rate at which the body fuel is burned up is measured by ascertaining the oxygen consumption while the subject is breathing in the resting condition at least 14 hours after a meal and after at least a half hour without exertion. Computed in terms of height, weight, age, and sex, the measure indicates rather closely the rate at which the tissues undergo oxidation; this is partly a question of general bodily make-up but to a very considerable degree it concerns thyroid activity. The measure is fairly reliable over a period of a few days, and at the extremes it is closely correlated with clinical signs both of general metabolic disposition and of thyroid activity in particular. Among these signs should be mentioned, in hyperthyroidism, rapid pulse and respiration, loss of weight, protrusion of the eyeballs, and, frequently, restlessness and apprehensiveness; in hypothyroidism, slow pulse and respiration, dry skin, brittle nails. We have already mentioned the difficulty of using the basal metabolic rate as a direct clue to personality (cf. page 98).

The parathyroid activity is gauged roughly in terms of the calcium metabolism, i.e., not the amount of calcium in the blood but the rate at which food calcium is utilized, as in bones and teeth. Clinical indicators of parathyroid insufficiency are excessive striped-muscle tone and emotional instability; the clinical correlates of excess activity are almost entirely unknown.

The biochemical methods of determining sex-gland secretions have improved greatly in the past few years. Several male and several female sex secretions are well known, the hormones forming a complex interacting pattern; each sex has almost the entire array of "male" and "female" endocrines, the two sexes differing chiefly in degree, i.e., in type of balance. The best-known and still standard method of testing for androgens (primary male components) is the "capon-cockscomb" method, in which the rate of growth of comb in an injected capon indicates the amount of the secretion present in a standard urine sample. This suggests the necessarily indirect way in which such assays are made. For coarser and more direct clinical purposes, distribution of hair and of fat, and pitch of voice, still remain primary indices of human sexual differentiation, although many factors other than sex influence these.

Studies of the adrenal glands are in considerable confusion owing to the fact that much which was earlier attributed to the adrenal medulla appears to derive rather from the adrenal cortex. Muscle tone is dependent on the latter to a high degree. Indirect measures of the functioning of the adrenal medulla are found in the pulse and respiration rate, in systolic and diastolic blood pressure, and in the difference between these two, known as pulse pressure. Here, however, we have a system of measures which are less specific for specific endocrine organs than were those mentioned above in connection with the thyroid, parathyroid, and gonads. These measures of the cardiovascular system, while serving to throw some light on adrenal activity, are also indicators of the activity of other endocrine organs. They vary with the presence of bacterial and other toxins in the body, with conditions of diet, exercise, sleep, and of the system as a whole.

It would perhaps be better to speak of these last measures as measures of general cardiovascular adequacy and to bring them into only the most indirect relation with specific endocrine organs. This statement would at least apply to the "Schneider index," a composite measure based upon pulse and blood pressure during and after light exercise; the total obtained indicates the general adequacy of individual adjustment to this mild physiological strain (cf. page 137). The Schneider index is a valuable general measure and definitely has a relation to personality, partly because the endocrines play an important part; partly, perhaps, because a disturbed personality and a disturbed neurocirculatory system are in reality overlapping concepts. While discussing the circulatory system, we should emphasize that Harold Wolff has made use of a method of measuring the radiant energy given off from a small portion of the finger, and, in collaboration with Bela Mittelmann, has shown a striking relation between emotional disturbances and a drop in finger temperature.

The oldest and most widely publicized of the physiological indicators is the galvanic skin reflex, the drop in the body's resistance to a small outside current which occurs during a wide variety of states of upheaval, excitement, and effort, and which is due chiefly to the temporary breakdown of the semi-permeable membranes, particularly those of the sweat glands. This is another complex method that is useful in indicating bodily disturbance, but it does not stand in a one-to-one relation to any simple personality function. To show a consistently small or large galvanic skin reflex in response to a wide variety of situations is an organic trait in the sense defined (and the greatest responses may reveal areas of greatest sensitiveness). Such an organic trait may be a component of many types of outward expression or a constituent of many behavior syndromes.

Other measures of duct-gland activity are useful, especially measures of salivary activity and of the composition of the saliva. The presence of solid matter in the saliva, for example, and its hydrogen-ion concentration appear to be consistently though obscurely related to various syndromes of emotional behavior. The hydrogen-ion concentration of blood and urine is also apparently of some significance—at least it shows disturbances in various marked emotional upheavals; hence it is conceivable that chronic excessive amounts (in the absence of known "organic pathology") may well be related to chronic, though perhaps unconscious, psychic strain. The same can be said of the products of intermediary metabolism (cf. page 79).

Relatively little has been done with *striped-muscle* measures of personality, though in view of the emphasis upon *behavior readiness* in one direction or another they would appear to offer useful clues. Wenger has recently indicated some relations between residual tensions, i.e., average tone of striped muscle, and various dynamic activity tendencies, and likewise between speed of contraction and certain other behavior dispositions. Because of the relative ease of observing the relation between striped-muscle tendencies and behavior patterns, these studies of skeletal musculature may well be among the most important avenues to research on organic traits in the coming years.

Despite the ingenuity that has gone into the preparation of these and literally hundreds of other physiological measures, it should be emphasized that their chief role is in *research*, not in clinical practice. When individual therapy is involved, rough clinical observation is still usually more valuable than these precise physiological indicators, simply because these indicators for the most part measure relatively simple physiological activities whose relations with other activities and with the personality pattern as a whole remain unknown, whereas the rough clinical observations are likely to center on physiological dispositions which are seen in their context in direct relation to abiding and important personality traits.

Organic dispositions of the type described may be *rated*, or they may be *objectively measured* in experimental situations. Ratings based on recurrent observation of such dispositions are likely to show interpersonal agreements in judgments, and consistency over the periods of time in which the dispositions could be expected to endure. Objective determinations are usually more valuable than ratings, both because the situation arousing the response is more fully defined and because the response can register itself rather than having to pass through the verbal symbolic system of the rater before it achieves numerical form. These two advantages are *sometimes* balanced or outweighed by corresponding factors that appear in ratings: first, the fact that a rating incorporates the results of many observations and is consequently more general and more reliable; second, the fact that the verbal symbolic system groups the socially related aspects of response. In the case of the organic constructs, however, it is doubtful whether these two advantages often atone for the limitations of ratings; it is the organic root, not the structured interpretation, that is wanted here; and the organic disposition, if measured at all, should first be fully explored in relation to a known situation, and stated in general terms for other situations only when empirical observations warrant it.

Along with the dozens of organic traits which already throw direct light on behavior there are dozens which are imperfectly understood. There is an organic disposition on the one hand, a related behavior pattern on the other, but a missing link as far as explanation is concerned. It is natural to shy away from these matters as irrational, though it is of course the pursuit of what is not understood that yields the greatest return. An interesting example is afforded by the clear and full report by the Lynns on two extensive experiments, one with normals, one with psychotics. Noting the significance of bodily asymmetries of form and function, they studied the relation between right- and left-handedness and the tendency to predominant use of the right or left side of the face in the involuntary smile (in the first study, ratings of the smile were used; in the second, motion pictures). With large groups and with very substantial correlations the Lynns show that the homolaterals (hand and smile dominance on the same side) tend to ascendance, belligerence, independence, initiative; the heterolaterals to the opposite characteristics. This relation develops slowly during childhood and is full fledged in early adolescence. We are dealing here with some very deep-seated functional pattern, involving both voluntary (hand) and involuntary (smile) response, that takes years to develop and manifests itself in both normal and abnormal personalities. The almost automatic reaction of psychology to such material is to regard it as a "foreign body" which cannot be assimilated. Actually the relation is no more hopelessly obscure than are many of the psychosomatic relations pointed out by psycho-analysis and subsequently studied experimentally (cf. page 315); the very fact that the interrelations are concealed and complex means that they are destined in time to teach us a great deal about the way in which personality is built.

A series of steps will have to be taken before we shall be ready for a more exact statement regarding personality traits and their measurement (page 630). We shall have to consider fully the manner in which the traits become attached to specific stimulus situations and to one another through habit formation. Ultimately it is the profoundly modified, or "habitually ingrained" drives, rather than the drives in their more primitive form, with which the student of personality organization is usually concerned. When the drives are clear, their form of attachment to the outer world defined, and the structure of their interrelations made definite, the organic traits of personality can be measured with huge profit, as we shall strive to show in Chapters 26–29.

Part Two

LEARNING

8. Canalization

NEEDS tend to become more specific in consequence of being satisfied in specific ways. Children all over the world are hungry; their hunger may be satisfied by bread, by ice cream, by peanuts, by raw eggs, by rice, or by whale blubber. Eventually they develop, when hungry, not a demand for food in general, but a demand for what they are used to; in one part of the world peanuts are good food, whale blubber disgusting, and vice versa. So, too, over the face of the earth, children enjoy rhythms; the need is satisfied by different kinds of rhythms, different games, different types of music. Soon they find the ones which they are "used to" natural and satisfying; others seem awkward, difficult, unsatisfying.

If a person is hungry, oriented toward food in general, he may nevertheless be more hungry for bread than for corn, for beef than for mutton. Attitude toward food is general, the valuation of absent food is general; but specific attitudes are defined within the general, and within the specific there are some still more specific, so that one wants not only currant buns but the one with the darkest crust. Tastes have become specific.

The restlessness or muscular distress which in the infant freed of his blankets appears in active writhing soon becomes a regular roll-over or push-and-pull game. Activity has become specific. The muscles develop specifically as differentiated responses appear, and to some extent in relation to specific use; those which have been exercised need still more exercise. The eye, too, tends to turn to the familiar. Novel objects, especially when intense, may disrupt this tendency; but in the roving exploratory movements, periods of fixation and relative stability of adjustment appear. To be sure, satiation occurs sooner or later, and other stimuli break in to upset the balance and redirect the movements; relative convergence, rather than a rigid inflexible pinning of the organism to the object, is the rule. So, too, the lover of Java prints or of Edam cheese turns from his fixation to new objects and returns with new pleasure to the old; moments of absorption, satiation, exploration, recurrent absorption mark the life of all the *acquired tastes.*

This process by which general motives (which are at first rather non-specifically related to a class of stimuli) tend, upon repeated experience, to become more easily satisfied through the action of the specific satisfier than of others of the same general class, has been known so long that it would be impossible to name its discoverer. But good names are a great convenience, and Janet's term *canalization* is a good name for this process. The energies awaiting an outlet break through the barrier at a given spot, are channeled or canalized in the process, and, as the barrier weakens, tend more and more to focus their pressure upon it.

The strength of such canalizations appears to depend first upon the initial selectivity, the preference of the organism; and second, upon frequency of opportunities for specific response. The tone-hungry child may, despite years of deprivation, find his way to music through the force of the original need, but even the run of the people in a German village may come uniformly to love their folk songs and their Schumann through sheer iteration of musical experience.

To investigate canalization experimentally is not difficult. Lukomnik found a variety of esoteric foods with which her subjects were unfamiliar and repeatedly presented small quantities of these foods during a training series; control foods were presented only at the beginning and end of each experimental period. While consistently positive, the data from the ten subjects in her first experiment are not sufficient to achieve statistical significance. The control foods went up in affective rating, not to the same degree, but in such fashion as to make differences between experimental and control foods a little less than absolutely clearcut; i.e., the control foods used at the beginning and end of each session suffered in one respect as genuine controls. In her second experiment with three subjects, however, Lukomnik used a more severe test; these individuals went without food for twenty-four hours before the experiment. These data are statistically significant, indicating a canalization process much more clear cut in the case of the experimental than the control foods.

Rather closely related to this problem are the experiments which indicate the tendency of familiar objects to become better and better liked. Under the term "familiarization" Maslow studied the tendency to prefer stimuli with which one had had earlier experience. On one occasion a series of thirty Russian names for women was divided into two groups of fifteen each. One of the lists was read aloud to a group of student clerical workers every evening for six evenings, the students being asked to write them down, spelling them as well as they could. At the end of the experiment all thirty names were read aloud, and the students were asked to indicate their preference for the names in each pair, one name in each pair being familiar, the other unfamiliar, and also to indicate which was superior in euphony. The familiar terms are better liked and more "euphonious," the critical ratios being respectively 1.9 and 5.0. But it must be stressed that some experiments of this type, especially those utilizing needs which are not very strong, indicate a decline rather than a rise in affective value. There is no intention here of denying the reality of such "habituation"; its exact conditions are not understood.

The experiments just mentioned dealt with adults. It would be well if we had comparable data for early infancy. Pertinent here are the data on the rapidly developing individual differences in response to sensory values in the opening months of life, using stimuli with a wide variety of appeals. Precise measurements are unfortunately lacking; and though infants soon have their favorite toys and games, the more complex the object, the more difficult the demonstration of the principles involved. Thus, for example, the toys obviously possess many appeals besides the simple sensory appeals. In general, however, the picture is fairly consistent; children not only become used to but demand familiar sense qualities, just as they become used to and demand certain types of play and specific companions. That these play preferences are seen among animals, too, is evident in the specific wants as regards playthings shown by caged animals, and the friendship between dogs or horses, which develop on the basis of close and constant satisfying contact. Long ago Evvard showed that swine would stick to their food preferences even when these were nutritionally deficient, and in the many recent experiments of P. T. Young there is a good deal of evidence that familiarity is a factor in the rat's food choices.

We are far from denying the role of constitutional factors in animals or children; on the contrary, we have emphasized them (Chapters 3 and 4). But the fact that we are dealing with canalization rather than with exclusively hereditary wants is well brought out by the attachment of the young animal to its foster parents or to litter mates with which it is reared, and its indifference or hostility to adults or young of its own species when such positive experience with them is lacking (cf. Whitman, page 166), and especially by the progressive development of specific wants in terms of each individual's characteristic mode of finding satisfaction.

Canalization and Conditioning

The mechanism of acquired tastes, wants, values is of the utmost importance. To scrutinize that mechanism closely, we must first ask whether canalization and the "conditioned response" are one and the same thing. The two processes must be critically compared.

It has become traditional to say that motives may be aroused by objects which at first had no capacity to elicit them. The hungry child reacting originally to food by salivating may in time react similarly to the name of the food jointly presented with the food itself. A "substitute stimulus," the name, seems to have acquired the role originally played by the adequate or original stimulus, the food. We have come to think of the dog's salivating to the tuning fork because the tuning fork was presented with, or before, the food.

But how far does the dog's response to the tuning fork resemble his response to the food? It is worth while to note again Sherrington's distinction between preparatory and consummatory responses. The dog salivates (a preparatory response), but he cannot *eat and digest* the tuning fork (a consummatory response); *the tuning fork cannot satisfy, put an end to, the motivation state.* Hunger, the organic state, lowers the thresholds for such preparatory responses as salivation, head-turning, sniffing, etc. Some of these preparatory responses present during the active hunger state occur at the time when the tuning fork and food are presented, and the series of joint stimulations changes the organism so that on a later occasion salivation appears in response to the tuning fork alone. Digestion, however, does not.

This connection between a substitute stimulus and a preparatory response may be broken, extinguished, by failure to continue the association between the two stimuli. The tuning fork alone, not accompanied or followed by food, ultimately loses the capacity to elicit salivation. Thus the connection is "contingent" or "accidental." Many kinds of stimulation could have been paired with the food to elicit the same kind of response, and the extinction of the conditioning is testimony to the "contingency," i.e., the biologically mobile, changeable, reversible aspect of the pattern.

This last point is worth emphasis because of the wide tendency to assert that the difference between an unsocialized organism and a socialized personality consists in conditioning. But let us look more closely at the phenomena of motive satisfaction in canalization, in contrast to conditioning. If the puppy is originally fed meat powder rather than milk-bone or vegetables, he comes in time to differ in a fundamental respect from another dog which has been consistently reared with these other foods. The puppy is "used to" a certain diet, accepts it. Dinner is over when it is eaten, and there is no restlessness, no waiting until the "real food" comes. He has developed an *acquired taste* in the sense that, starting with a background of general non-specific hunger cravings, a specific mode of satisfying them has been standardized or stereotyped or ingrained within him. He becomes a meat-eating, milk-bone-eating, or vegetable-eating puppy. The child becomes a corn-eating, carrot-eating, or rice-eating child. When there is a choice of foods, he goes to the one that is familiar, and often in the training process he shows greater and greater avidity for that particular food. He is "learning to like it."

Whatever object or form of stimulation satisfies a need becomes more and more adequate as a *satisfier*. The very form of the gastric contractions, in animal and man, depends on the food present in the stomach. The puppy eats the unaccustomed food, and the stomach cannot behave in its habitual normal way; thus the *form* of the consummatory response is altered. This is definitely something which he has learned. But it is not the same thing as to say that he is conditioned to one or the other food as he is conditioned to a bell or to a call to his kennel. The conditioning experiment involves a contingent, an adventitious connection not leading to a consummatory response. We noted that the tuning fork activates a preparatory response; indeed, a hungry dog may lick the light bulb that symbolizes food. But this does not put an end to the hunger contractions, he does not develop an acquired taste for light bulbs as a preferred means of satisfying hunger. In canalization we are dealing not merely with a signal that prepares for eating, but with a modification of consummatory behavior, as shown both in the intensity of the visceral manifestations and in the sheer discrimination between familiar and unfamiliar modes of satisfaction.

Moreover, there is a cardinal difference in the history of the two types of behaviors. Conditionings are subject to extinction; canalizations, so far as we know, are not. Whitman's celebrated ringdoves which, reared with carrier pigeons, would mate only with carriers, not with their own species, did not *lose* this tendency; the response was not extinguished. Biographical and psychoanalytic observations of human beings likewise strongly suggest that acquired wants of the type described are not sloughed off, "extinguished," as are conditioned responses. What is once built into the system of wants appears for some reason to stay built in. Nostalgia for one's golden childhood or the wanderer's longing for his home is not obliterated by years of immersion in another world. With delight one greets the doughnuts that mothers used to make, or the tinny old music box that has lain twenty years in the attic. We are far from understanding all of this; but in animals, in children, and in adults we can directly observe something very different from the usual "easy-make, easy-break" of the normal conditioned response. The arctic explorer may be reminded a thousand times of the delights of the temperate zone without any appreciable tendency to lose the preparatory responses, the anticipation set, the longing to return. Men in army camps talk endlessly of their future week-ends at home; the prisoner lives over in fantasy the events of the first week after his expected release. There is no extinction of cravings, despite the endless recurrence of conditioned stimuli which ought, one might think, to yield only extinction in view of the failure of the appropriate satisfactions. Children want their stories in the form in which they have heard them; grownups want their meals, their houses, and their music to be within a rather narrow realm of familiar canalized structure. To avoid "monotony" they may vary within a narrow range; but they could not, even if they would, begin to seek again in the naïve fashion of the child.

Canalization need not be "pleasant." E. B. Holt has suggested that any stimulus which elicits a positive response tends eventually to be sought simply because it is present at the time that the seeking movements occur, so that a person pursues what he has already experienced. He is "fascinated by" or "can't get away from" even something that is horrible or threatening to the self. A special class of avoidance reactions do occur, but avoidance is itself a clumsy and awkward process requiring much tutelage, and it seems to work under a handicap induced by the fact that seeking tendencies coexist with the aversion. It is quite possible that the principle thus defined by Holt, to which he gives the name *adience*, is the basis of the canalization principle; that, without further reason, the little child is caught in a cycle of renewal of activity, such as Freud calls a *repetition compulsion*.

Canalizations can be broken, but apparently, as Holt points out, only by more powerful responses which in their essence block the energies originally established. From this point of view, the canalization could be destroyed only if another more potent behavior tendency could be set up to compete with it so powerfully, so dominantly, as to prevent its physiological expression. Sometimes this does occur (cf. page 304). But canalizations are in general free of interference from one another. The love of Bach does not destroy the love of Shakespeare, nor does the love of raspberry sherbet destroy the love of baseball. There seems to be room for a practically infinite variety of tastes. One may develop many acquired wants within one modality; he may learn to like many kinds of food, many kinds of music. Canalization at one point leaves many other points relatively unaffected. One may learn to like Raphael or Rembrandt, and later, Hokusai, or Sung Dynasty paintings, or Picasso; there is room for them all. When tastes are incompatible, as when a man says that his love of Bach tends to prevent his enjoyment of jazz, the clue appears to lie in secondary habits such as a "fear of being low-brow," just as another man may find his tastes competing because of a "fear of being inconsistent" or a "desire to be at home in all sorts of worlds." Choosing as subjects three men who loved classical music but not "swing," and three others who loved "swing" but not classical music, Krugman found that the sheer experience of listening to the non-preferred music in half-hour periods over eight weeks resulted in building up a new taste in most of his subjects, without weakening the old. In general, it is safe to say that there is room, in the case of human wants, for a very large number of good canalizations, all existing side by side, and not in competition, *unless* the individual is forced to choose among different available satisfiers; here arises the problem of conflict, to be considered later (Chapter 13). Moreover, there appears to be considerable transfer or generalization, since learning to like beer or olives or mysteries carries over to other beer and olives and mysteries; and learning to like one kind of activity (such as athletics) may predispose to a liking for other similar kinds of activity, provided always that there are real similarities of some sort between the original and the new situation. One might like Sung Dynasty paintings, Corot, or Turner, and dislike Velasquez or nineteenth-century portrait painters because one preferred land-scapes, delicate nuances, wide horizons, and disliked the people whose portraits were painted by Velasquez and in the nineteenth century; one might, nevertheless, like Rembrandt portraits because they have the nuances, depth, universality which one felt in the land-scapes mentioned above. Tastes may be multiplied within boundaries defined by needs for rapid tempo, sharp lines, etc., or demand for protection, adventure, or whatever the personal needs are. Canalizations can be *overlaid* or *hidden* if the same sensory complex which satisfies becomes a signal for a negative response; one can block a canalized impulse to drink by telling the gullible freshman that the beer is poisoned. ("Poison" is here a powerful conditioned stimulus.) But when the signal fails and the hoax is discovered, the impulse returns. Fashions and tastes may change; one may ask, "How could I ever have liked that hat?" The question here is perhaps whether new fashions make one ashamed of the antique which one is carrying around. The same sort of ego factor may be responsible for the fact that Puerto Ricans clung to their codfish diet during the war despite the availability of "better" food, and Americans went on demanding far more meat than they needed for their "nutritional requirements."

Not everyone may become catholic in his tastes. When one does, he has, through a broad development of affective response or through the cultivation of insight into the meaning of many different aspects of experience, transcended the narrow channels of his first developmental needs. Many people, moreover, typically give objective value to personal preferences, whether they be for thirteenth-century primitives or for Grant Wood. One derives a sense of status from feeling: "I am one of the rare ones who realize that ——— is the only real art, or music, or literature."

Canalizations, then, are not, so far as we know, subject to extinction, whether by disuse or by displacement by other canalizations. Let one compare, for example, the length of time between extinction to a dinner bell which now means "mail man" rather than "dinner," with the extinction that can be acquired in losing one's interest in corn on the cob or peaches and cream which one in a strange clime has not eaten for many years. It is quite possible that the reason for this lies in the simple fact that the stimulus is by definition satisfying. Every time that the canalized food is eaten, it satisfies. Extinction which is due to the satisfier's failure to satisfy is a contradiction in terms.

Nothing here is intended to imply that children—or adults—have the *same tastes* year after year. New canalizations are constantly being added; some of them will be dominant over the old, and all will, by definition, be related to the active needs of the person at the age at which they are formed. Their number must naturally increase with age. The sole issue worth laboring is whether the old ones die or are merely overlaid—or insufficiently stimulated—and this is important because those which *do* persist are so central to the heart of the personality, so controlling in all its lifelong continuity (cf. Chapter 27).

Whatever its ultimate explanation, the fact is of the utmost importance for any theory of personality wants or any doctrine of human values. It is not the bare wants or any interrelation of wants that makes the adult personality; it is not the adventitious pattern of connections between these inner wants and the conditioning stimuli of daily life. It is to a large degree the system of wants as organized in a directed form toward familiar satisfiers; it is a system of anticipations and preparations for a round of experiences which have compelling value because they are the specific ways in which the diffuse and generalized wants have in the past been converted from tension to satisfaction. The process appears irreversible, as the life process moves forward, consolidating itself into more and more differentiated, firmly constructed patterns. Two of the major clues to personality seem therefore to be the study of the specific ways in which canalized patterns are implanted in children by any society, and the study of the individual differences in content and form which such canalizations may assume in any society.

Such a conception stresses the complexity of what we call a *want*. The hunger contractions could be quieted in many ways. It is not merely the termination of this particular stress, but a variety of experiences of sight, smell, taste, and thermal and tactual contact, that have been woven into the fabric. Hence it is obvious that many complex phenomena of conditioning enter into all such cases.[1] There

---

[1] Canalization may conceivably be a matter of increasing the fixation of a specific response to each of a group of combined stimuli, one of the stimuli originally being

are many substitute stimuli, signals which play their part in activating behavior; in fact, if the distinction between canalization and conditioning is clear, we shall expect to find the two phenomena mingled in most life situations. It is indeed likely that some physiologist of the future may be able to reduce this canalization problem to a formulation differing in no essential from those utilized by the students of conditioning. At the present stage of our inquiry, however, nothing could be more confusing than to describe the slow process of acquiring tastes as if the object for which the taste was developed were itself artificially, contingently related to the need. If the food does not really satisfy, if it has only the relation to the organism that the tuning fork has to the dog's stomach, it will never become a favored food. If the music does not satisfy the child, he will never develop a taste for Bach or Brahms. Conditionings can be established only where there are wants; the artificial conditioning stimuli never become satisfiers, they can only be signals to which some satisfying agency must be tied. The ultimate test of the distinction between conditioning and canalization is whether the stimulus puts into action the consummatory

---

adequate and the others merely facilitating it, until in time each of the constituents can independently evoke the response, and the whole pattern becomes strongly entrenched, overwhelming. Acquired tastes for complicated things like anchovies or James Joyce may then be stronger than tastes for any of the original components. Canalization would involve the consolidation of response to a structural pattern. The point is debatable. An important clue might be given by an investigation to determine whether even the simplest homogeneous stimulation, say with the four primary taste qualities, would produce canalization. It looks today as if it would. It is likely that the preference for sweet over sour, bitter, and salty is slight at first but becomes progressively clearer; eventually the craving for sweet, an ambivalence to salty, and an aversion to sour and bitter are general. If the picture is correct, all this suggests that canalization depends not on the compounding of various psychological elements, but on repetition alone, or at least repetition under conditions leading to organic satisfaction. At any rate, the strengthening of an original response to food of a specific quality is certainly distinct from the strengthening of a response to an arbitrary signal that means food; in the direct observation of infants, most of whose responses are outgoing, or "positive," but which show a progressive increase in specificity, there is an enormous difference between canalizations (direct contact with satisfying objects) and conditionings (contact with signals or preparatory stimuli). If the signal fails, the conditioning begins to weaken, to be extinguished. The canalization does not fail in the same sense. Biochemists assure us that life processes themselves are seldom reversible reactions. Students of neurobiotaxis are sure of progressive trends toward specific stimulus-response relations, but doubt the true loss of this specificity. Another interesting theoretical possibility is that the *drives* which take part in canalization are *composites* (cf. the many components in the "hunger drive") and the canalization involves the separation and recombination of components.

responses, e.g., whether the organism not only salivates but eats and digests the tuning fork, or whatever the stimulus may be.

If the term canalization marked off no specific kind of event but were purely an alternative for such terms as conditioning, positive adaptation, or redintegration, there would be no justification in using it; we have enough terms already. In summary, however, there appears to be (1) a general tendency for motives to move toward greater specificity; (2) evidence that the consummatory responses, not the preparatory alone, are involved; (3) a hint that such responses are not merely connected with new signals but are intrinsically modified; and (4) a strong indication that they are not subject to extinction—the trend is unidirectional.

One may indeed become satiated, surfeited with a satisfier. This is perhaps simply the continuance of an object after it has ceased to be a satisfier, so that it becomes a sheer nuisance. "Overindulgence" in anything may, moreover, produce physical distress, and lead to conditioning away from the object. But it cannot be asserted that these effects are understood—or even fully described.

Progressive Shifts in Preference

It is not suggested that within the realm of hunger satisfiers all are at first *equally good*; in the initial state of demanding food in general, there is no need to insist upon an absolute indifference or neutrality toward different foods. Likely enough, if the hungry infant were presented simultaneously with three "perfectly good foods," he would prefer one or the other, depending upon smells, tastes, mouth contacts, etc., in relation to his own particular wants at the time. It is only necessary to point out that he is sufficiently indifferent, sufficiently neutral, sufficiently plastic to be inducted stage by stage into a state of definite bias in any one of these three (or more) directions determined by his environment.

It is convenient to think of a given organic want as involving susceptibility to a very wide range of stimulation, with an optimal region tapering off in various directions to regions of smaller and smaller susceptibility. If one is only slightly hungry, he may eat candy but, despite their good odor, reject other warm soft foods which the housekeeper offers as a substitute. If he is a little hungrier, he may accept these other foods. If ravenous, he may chew a leather strap or a bit of cloth. We do not claim that there would be equal facility in the canalization process regardless of the object supplied, but only that the normal range of satisfying objects is considerable, and that the canalization phenomenon can appear rather easily at various points in this range, even with objects which are certainly at a considerable distance from the optimum. In other words, the equivalence of stimuli is never absolute; there is always a theoretical optimum for a given response. The farther we draw away from this optimum, the more obvious the difference in the response elicited. But shift in relative position along this continuum is the very function which canalization defines; an object may be moved closer to the optimum by being used as a tension reducer.

If some actual satisfaction of the drive occurs, some degree of canalization or fixation will follow. If there is no satisfaction at all— if, for example, the hungry child chews a blanket and obtains literally nothing to ease his distress—he will, according to the hypothesis, develop no tendency to make *increasing* use of such objects as hunger satisfiers. If, moreover, the difference in satisfaction value between two objects is considerable, a great deal of repetition may be needed to give the inferior satisfier any serious status in competing with the other. A quantitative problem arises regarding the amount of stimulation required from such inferior objects to permit us to equate them with others in a more favored status. The point is nicely illustrated by Craig's studies of doves reared alone. The doves used strips of paper as nest-building material and rapidly consolidated the habit; but when supplied with twigs, they promptly abandoned the paper and refused to use it again. Canalization should be expected to occur with a degree of definiteness determined by the advantage which a stimulus has as a motive satisfier; but if the satisfaction value of the two stimuli is not very dissimilar, the one which is more fre- quently used to satisfy the need should become the one sought and employed. On this basis, we should expect to find wild and domestic animals developing standard or favored food preferences, and human beings in every conceivable form of social organization developing food preferences, shelter preferences, mate preferences, music preferences, activity preferences, etc. The fact that human societies differ so widely in the standardization of foods, mates, art forms, etc., should itself suggest the high degree of plasticity, the great "openness" of the original drives. Nevertheless, the rule holds that the objects in question must satisfy, for the fact of openness does not mean weakness of drive. The drive may be imperious yet be satisfied by the whole range of an enormous variety of socially accepted forms.

In general, there is a great temptation to overdo the concept of equivalence of stimuli. To the little child a wide variety of lullabies or games or strained vegetables may be equivalent; all the members of a given class may be received with approximately the same satisfaction. In such cases we are dealing with true equivalence of stimuli. One suspects, however, in noting such homely illustrations, that quantitative method is needed. What does it really mean to say that the child accepts *all* lullabies with *equal* enthusiasm? All are not presented at the same time; furthermore, comparisons are difficult. The child can indeed become accustomed to a variety of lullabies or games or strained vegetables. But as we look more closely, we begin to suspect that physiological readiness can never be exactly the same for any two types of excitation. Remembering that Craig's doves would shift from paper to twigs but not in the reverse direction, we may draw an analogy here with cultural situations. We may well suspect that all sorts of people adjust to all sorts of cultural situations, but we need not draw the conclusion that they do so "equally easily." The fact that groups of people satisfy their needs in all sorts of different ways is no evidence that the means are really equally satisfying. They may be canalized, but less so than they would be with a more satisfying stimulus. The critical test is the readiness of young individuals to make shifts in one direction or another. When "cultural relativism" is construed to mean that people living under different cultural arrangements are equally satisfied with them, or that the arrangements are, in some broad sense equally good, equally satisfying, we must contest the point, for the reasons just given.

In the same way we must contest the point that some satisfiers are "natural," others "artificial." The distinction between "natural" and "artificial" satisfiers can make a great deal of trouble if we think of the state of nature as giving man what satisfies him most completely, i.e., if we consistently disdain the work of culture in developing new satisfiers. If we think of social arrangements as satisfying the drives less adequately than the natural arrangements do, we shall be puzzled to find men everywhere cooking their food rather than eating it raw, complicating their music rather than making the most of the sounds of sea, wind, and running water. It is the rule, in fact, that wants are satisfied *less than optimally* when nature, unadorned, is the satisfier.

In the presence of two or more competing stimulus patterns, a person moves toward or "selects" the more adequate. But now follows a third stage, the active quest of the preferred. The inner demands, such as hunger contractions and the like, not only set going the restless exploratory behavior characteristic of all these conditions, but activate the organism in a direction characteristically associated with the more adequate among the available satisfiers. Hungry sheep search not simply for food, but for calcium-rich food (cf. page 91). His own calcium need leads the experienced animal toward the region containing bone deposits, and among the various deposits he moves toward those which have given greatest satisfaction. The man, actuated by much more complicated drives, seeks in a fashion that in the light of past experience leads to the T-bone steak, French fried potatoes, and coffee; at the moment they are related more specifically to his wants than any other satisfiers which might confront his nostrils. And he carries such canalizations around with him. A connoisseur pursues a masterpiece through the unlikeliest piles of rococo stuff. The world could be objectively mapped out in terms of interests or directed activities.

This has prompted sociologists at times to regard the entire structuring of personality as derived from the structure of the culture itself —an exaggeration, but worth close study. There is evidence that interests develop through a process of motivated individual living; they generalize not only because culture generalizes them, but because the individual moves by means of generalizing from one interest to a related interest (cf. Chapters 8–10). Transfer is made from one type of Chinese painting to another, so far as individual experience permits it. Hence the biological clue to the discrete patterns of outer activity is needed along with the cultural, whenever individual cases are considered.

Canalization occurs in all the major types of motivation. There are acquired food tastes; there are acquired activity and esthetic tastes; canalization operates in the case of the things and persons most intensely loved, the jokes most appreciated, the tasks most heartily enjoyed. There are emotional patterns more and more definitely fixated for the individual, the "pet peeves" or bêtes noires, the objects most certainly capable of arousing his ire, the compelling individual fears which stand out above all ordinary fears. (There would be a paradox in including the dislikes as well as the likes if our conception of motivation referred to "that which is agreeable." In accordance with our earlier usage, we have tried to think of tension sources as having a universal lawfulness which applies as much to the "need" to fear as to the "need" to eat.)

It is essential to the definition that the canalized motives be still regarded as *motives*, each act reflecting some of the original diffuse quality of the original motive. The hunger for ripe olives is still hunger; the craving for the old familiar faces is still the craving for faces. It is therefore improbable that the present conception can be effectively stretched so as to assimilate to itself any of the theories of general organismic plasticity which posit that practiced activity has an intrinsic tendency to become a drive. Woodworth states expressly that every mechanism may become a drive. But suppose that during a busy week a man reaches every day for a needed reference book on the top shelf and absent-mindedly puts it back in the old spot when finished with it. Does the reaching, as such, become a drive? Automobilists all learn the art of gear shifting as part of the process of driving a car; but do drivers go ceaselessly through gear-shifting motions through sheer love of the process, as they sit waiting in a parked car? As soon as the weather grows warm enough for a child to go bare-footed, his shoelaces are powerless to start the shoelace-tying drive. Mechanisms do not seem to become drives at all. What Woodworth seems to have overlooked is that among the myriad mechanisms associated with myriad drives, many, especially those having to do with sensory qualities and with manipulations, are in themselves satisfying. These canalize quickly. The original purpose which initiated their use is no longer needed; the mechanism has indeed become a drive. But the essential value of a concept lies in the possibilities of predicting from it. There is nothing in the Woodworth schema that tells *which* mechanisms will become drives and which, like the shoelace-tying mechanism, will not. Closer attention to the properties of stimulation and action should guide research to the actual character of primitive satisfiers, spot them in their inception, and ascertain whether, as the present hypothesis demands, it is the satisfaction of these, rather than the conversion of mechanisms into drives, that is involved.

It is likely that canalization goes on faster when there is a choice, a preference, which through contrast marks the preferred direction. Children's play brings rapid canalization of specific toys and games, some being *actually selected* as against others. The canalized value of the familiar world is greater when one places it in contrast with some other world. The mountaineer who has always had his mountains may love them, but nowhere near as much as the person who has been absent from them, in a world of different accents, different values. It may be that distance, or complete absence, is in itself a factor. Research on the canalization process should permit canalization upon objects in the presence of others slightly less appealing, and should test the process both when the canalized object is farther away than the competitor, and when it is out of sight whereas the competitor is still near at hand.

In order to do anything with the problem of motivation along the lines attempted here, it is necessary to regard canalization as dependent on major interests, not on casual bodily activity. Many classes of stimuli are practically indifferent, at least most of the time, for most organisms. Activities controlled by this type of stimulation have no tendency to canalize, but are dropped like hot potatoes when their utility, as means to ends, disappears.

The concept of "functional autonomy," as sketched by G. W. Allport, allows a developed action pattern to move forward, to continue, and to evolve in its own right. Adult motives are "self-sustaining *contemporary* systems, growing out of antecedent systems, but functionally independent of them." A motive may have started with a visceral drive or with anything else, but as an integrated habit system it moves forward even when its roots in the original need are severed. This view has an advantage over Woodworth's in that the *fusion* of motives is clearly stated. But it lacks predictive meaning. Just which of today's action patterns will persist tomorrow? Suppose one spends three hours every day for a week painting the porch. Does it become autonomous? If not, why not? Perhaps because it was simply a means to an end. *If one loves to paint*, he will try to find other things to paint— he may even hope the neighbors will let him paint their fence.

Allport very properly points out that many types of sensory and motor activities used in the prosecution of a means-end activity eventually become adequate satisfiers in their own right. But he too seems to overlook the fact that many of these sensory and motor components are in themselves satisfiers, and can canalize. Indeed, the experiments of Zeigarnik and others, which showed that uncompleted tasks tend to be remembered better than completed ones—and that there are huge individual differences—suggest that some components confronted in executing a task may canalize in different ways and in different degrees with different people. A good deal depends on whether one has been at the task long enough to get warmed up to it (canalize on it), and on the intrinsic properties of the material. After all, we have seen small boys, as well as laboratory subjects, who stop a task at the drop of a hat and reveal no craving to resume it. The natural comment here is that the task was not interesting. But this is exactly the point. It is the nature of the intrinsic motivation, aside from any hope for reward, that we are endeavoring to understand. Some tasks become interesting; others never do. It is this central fact that constitutes the problem. And there is much research to show that if we interrupt an uninteresting task not closely related to *status* (that is, of slight significance to the ego), there is little tendency to remember it.

Allport stresses the fact that it is not the iterative but the cumulatively developing task that releases the capacity to proceed independently of the original drive. This is in a way unfortunate, because it runs counter to his generalization of the law on an earlier page, in which the mere continuation of an activity is given as clue to its achieving autonomy. But the statement that progressive rather than iterative achievements are the supreme exemplification of the principle rings true. This should provoke some thought about the situations in which progressive mastery of a task is involved. A man goes on developing his golf game, his scores being known to his opponents as well as to himself. Does he proceed with the same ardor to develop a skill literally for the sake of developing it, regardless of spectators and regardless of his own sense of worth in achievement? It may be granted that some self-attitudes in normal persons may be completely satisfied in isolation from other people. But to conceive a person developing a complicated task without any pride in it, without any ego at all, is a little dreary. If by definition nothing is gained by it all, it is hard to see what is at work; the windlass winds up forever, though the power will never be used. Allport has wisely stressed ego involvement, *participation*, as of vital significance in motivation. There is much to suggest that self-gratification, or satisfying muscular activity, or both, lurk behind every autonomous act.

Allport's excellent point that there are self-sustaining activities at the physiological level—the circular reflex, the perseverative labor of the scientist—is useful in the analysis. But the circular reflex is a clear case of a conditioned response, and the conditioned response is extinguished when not reinforced; it dies out when its organic motor stops. Even a cramp following a dietetic error, although there is no "motivation" but the persisting circular mechanism, dies out some time because it is fed with no fresh energy, that is, because there is no perpetual motion. Allport admits that these cycles, these cramp-like activities, stop when they are interfered with by new stimuli. But the perseverating scientist or musician is not just perseverating; he is satisfying curiosity, or love of tone, or the activity needs that go with fresh utilization of these loved materials—at least, that is what such people say, and they act as if they knew. There are limitless responses to the objects of nature which do not perseverate, do not build up into anything. There must be value at the root if there is to be value in the leaves. The number of types of roots developed in plant evolution is scant, and the limited types of leaves are organically linked with the types of roots which the plant possesses.

The issue is greatly complicated by the fact that no one could ever list all the possible objects of interest or value. This may make refutation of the Allport hypothesis more difficult, but it seems also to make its verification more difficult. For not only is there the high probability that any complex act contains important ingredients which are original satisfiers of esthetic and activity needs and which tend to become more satisfying as the act proceeds; there is also the high probability that other ingredients not originally satisfying are conditioned, and that, if reinforced often enough through such contact with satisfiers, they can at times function literally in their own right. All this is of special weight, of course, when the activity is deeply colored with the character of selfhood; it is not simply an activity, it is *my own* activity. If I am canalized upon some phase of myself, enjoy watching myself do something, even the spades, pianos, cars, pencils, gadgets that participate in my activity become centers of affection. So, too, when it is not self-contemplation but self-expression that acts as motor.

The argument is offered not as conclusive evidence, but as the reason for uncertainty as to the capacity of ongoing activity as such, and in its own right, to become autonomous. In terms of social consequences the result would be important. Not only musicians and psychologists but structural steel workers, typists, and garbage collectors—everyone, in short—would love their work and want to go on with it after the five-o'clock whistle, and the basic reordering of human institutions would be less imperative.

CANALIZATION

INDIVIDUALITY IN CANALIZATION

We noted earlier that the cultural situation may not only combine but *fuse* diverse drives, so as to produce motives which could occur in no other social situation. If this is true for the cultural group, it is even more clearly true for each individual. Individuals enter the cultural scene with their own motive patterns, their own capacities for growth and canalization, and they very early develop intense and commanding motives which are unique to themselves. The novelist has seen this more clearly than the psychologist. Thompson Seton tells of Yan Yeoman's passionate desire to buy a stuffed owl in a taxidermist's shop; for some months this passion overwhelmed everything else in his existence; he was weak with longing for it. To say that such motives are adventitious, accidental, or the results of conditioning is to say too much and too little. A love of outdoor things, a need to have them close to him, a love of the arts and crafts by which man makes nature closer to himself, the need to have something which was his very own—all these and many other things were pressed together so tightly in Yan's heart that they had lost their identity; he simply had to have that owl. To say that this is a result of conditioning is correct if we mean that a boy who lived too far from the woods or too close to living owls could have developed no such craving. The love of outdoors and the need to have something of his very own were themselves expressions of deep wants that began in their characteristic vague fashion and assumed a more and more specific form as a mélange of conditioning and canalizing factors appeared. The unique outcome, however, is no longer a mosaic of distinguishable pieces. The tragedy that overcame Yan when he tried to buy the owl and could not, would have obliterated the desire if conditioning in the specific sense had been involved. Instead, he became hurt, confused, timid, and self-distrustful as a result of the experience—but he went on wanting the owl.

So, too, Sam Marston's visions of the longed-for Junior Cup were eclipsed countless times by sarcasm and violence from his fellow campers. Prestige was offered him in various other forms, but he did not want them. Even if it be assumed that the prestige need was somehow artificially connected with this special object, which is true as far as it goes, the fact remains that Sam's long dwelling upon the object and the fusion of other wants into the pattern had created so intense a need that no other alternative for satisfying his wants could be found by a friendly director and the counselors; when that particular cup could not be awarded at that particular time, there was no substitute. Illustrations such as these serve only the purpose of suggesting that the end results in the education of motives have reached a level of consolidation, a definiteness of differentiation, which gives them the right to be called "central values." Our richest clinical source of data regarding such values, the study of a group of Harvard students by Murray and Morgan, is full of verbatim quotations suggesting the canalization process. "Our parents, my sister and I have treasured memories of doing things together. Mother and Dad are both very experienced travelers, and we all have intense impressions of strange and fascinating people we have met on our travels."

Not all of these central values, but a great many of them, are highly distinctive of the individual. It is sometimes considered wise, for this very reason, to conclude that a generalized law regarding value structure is not to be found. There seems to be no clear reason for this conclusion; nature is full of such integration and fusion. The individual value is often shared with others up to a certain point. The process of the fusion or integration of values is likewise a universal process. The terminal stages by which values, such as a stuffed owl or an LL.D. or election to Congress, may be organized, are subject to a universal principle. As we suggested above (page 43), the question whether science is capable of handling the problem of such uniqueness is comparable to the question whether science can handle the unique acorn, tornado, or planetary system.

The motion toward uniqueness within the life of the individual is balanced in some cultures by a social counter-flow; many of the developmental processes which drive him to differ from others also drive others to try to be like him. The more different he is, the more striking; the more striking, the more drive-activating. There are specific conditions of aversion or disgust, e.g., with reference to the

deformed or the insane; human beings may shun or deride their fellows and detest imitating them. But though men say they "hate to"
imitate one another even when the conduct is approved, imitate them
they do to a considerable extent. In view of their basic constitutional
differences, it is extraordinary to see the uniformity with which, as
they try to be exceptional, they try to be like some exceptional person
who, for the time, is the standard.

Not only may the group follow the man who at the moment is
"distinguished," that is, marked off from the rest; the distinctiveness
of the individual in question often lies in his completing or living out
a pattern that is only implicit, less fully developed, in others. He is
capable at times of saying in a popular speech what everyone thinks
vaguely and would like to say; even more, he may articulately
formulate a way of feeling, the esthetic resolution of a disturbing
problem as to the relations between norms, styles, modes, social
amenities. Or, like most heroes and heroines, he may be a little more
vividly or intensely what everybody else wants to be, but has neither
the physical make-up nor the skill to be. From this results what one
might call the cultural standardization of a norm which remains half
implicit, a groping demand in a direction never clearly specified, until
the time that an actualization is offered.

The individuality of leaders appears with special vividness in this
connection; the artist, the political or scientific leader has to be not
merely unusual but capable of standing out, of precipitating in
electrifying fashion the implicit demands of the group from which he
springs. And since he is rare, he brings much more to the situation
than this bundle of half-articulate needs actually calls for. He brings
his complete integration of tastes and attitudes, his whole self; and
the group proceeds to integrate its wants, choose him for its idol,
canalize in the fullest sense upon his form and meaning. Granted that
the Union in 1861 needed a powerful, imaginative, indeed a great man,
as leader. Had Abraham Lincoln never been born, there would have
been a President in 1861, and with lesser clay the people would still
have done something in the way of making a hero, as they did with
the distinctly lesser clay of General Grant. But let us suppose that not

Lincoln but some other great man was available. The standardization of American life in the nineteenth century, in terms of a certain home-spun ruggedness, sturdy simplicity, coarse humor, deep tenderness, and magisterial verbal expression, might instead have been made in terms of the very different qualities of a great war President renowned for ingenious planning, subtlety and delicacy of touch, caution and Scottish thrift, irascibility and occasional failure of self-control. Though no Lincoln, he too would have been a hero. The heroic, in other words, could have been made out of other material, provided that two conditions were fulfilled: first, that really exceptional material was at hand, and second, that the need for a great standard and a hero was intense. In various historic epochs heroes have been made, artistic forms established, social conditions accepted in exactly this way. The uniqueness of an individual, the availability of a person who is typical yet exceptional, and the readiness of the group to standardize, regularize, in terms of this individual, give us in fact most of the art forms, ethical standards, and social usages we possess.

Canalization on One's Own Body

Among canalized objects, those that are always present and always acting vividly upon the senses will inevitably have a favored position. This means that the body itself, in all its aspects, is the first great canalization center. The very interrelation of sense organs, by which the activity of each organ is mediated to all the other organs kinesthetically, tactually, or otherwise, means that tensions are constantly being relaxed through one's own bodily activity, just as they are constantly being spread through the pattern of such interstimulation. At first, of course, there is for the individual no "body as a whole." Emerging from the first undifferentiated blur (page 62) there are probably simply moving spots, unstructured sounds, pains, warms and colds, muscular strains and relaxations, all ill defined, fleeting, and confused. They are all, however, interesting; that is, they arouse response, and all to some degree bring satisfaction, release; in particular, what we have called the sensory drives are satisfied by looking and listening, reaching, touching. Activity drives expressed in a need to change the form and direction of movement are interwoven with the sensory drives. The child is manifestly preoccupied with himself a large part of the time, not only in the first months but for a long period thereafter. He is egocentric in Piaget's sense (page 266) that he does not know where self stops and world begins, and he is egocentric in a simpler sense, namely, that the sense organs and activity patterns are acted upon most of the time by a stream of stimulation which arises directly or indirectly from his own activities.

The fact that the visual mechanisms are poorly developed in the opening weeks, convergence and accommodation developing slowly, weights the organism on the side of visceral and kinesthetic pre-occupation. The organ of hearing, as Freud points out, is the only dis-tance receptor that is able to compete. For necessary reasons, there-fore, the individual begins life by being largely "self-centered." This substratum, this fundamental affective anchoring in the qualities of one's own physical existence, need offer no occasion for wonder. It is not, however, simply on the cognitive side that the body image is overpoweringly important; on the affective side, as Schilder has so beautifully shown, the various phases of the body image cannot escape the diffuse but active attention of the child, as the various parts become associated and knit together structurally into a single object—the self—which is slowly differentiated from the outer world. This object can in no way step permanently aside in favor of some other compel-ling object. So far as there is a self at all, it is both the most continu-ously present, and among the most interesting, the most important, the most beloved objects in the world—and loved by each person with all his own personal resources for loving.

Most authors who have struggled with this problem have had to write as if this awareness of self preceded awareness of others. But they have shown, as their discussion develops, that awareness of self and awareness of other persons, such as the mother, go hand in hand. Awareness of self as an entity makes easier a structural perception of the mother as a whole being; and the gradual development of a per-ceptual pattern of the moving, talking, nursing comforter undoubtedly reinforces the evolution of one's self-awareness. Certainly all that we know of the psychology of perception would lead us to suspect transfer of perceptual patterns, transfer of habits of perceiving, so that whatever interest or value the self has, the mother has to some degree; and to whatever extent the mother is a supreme value, to that extent one is such a value to oneself so far as one is like her in face, in voice, in hair, in pigmentation, etc.

But we are moving here into psychoanalytic theory. Indeed, parallel to the inauguration of the concept of canalization by Janet and McDougall, the latter using the term "sentiment," runs Freud's utilization of these concepts, partly under the term *cathexis*, partly under the term *fixation*. The first term refers specifically to the canalization process as we have described it. The love given during the embryonic period to one's own physical self is, after birth, devoted both to this omnipresent self-object and to the gradually emerging form of the mother, who as the most intense satisfier among all the social-personal objects in the surroundings, serves as a huge funnel for the rising tide of affection. But complications ensue. Since the child is growing and is making broader contacts with the world, he develops other wants. At the same time, since he is subject to much social control and blockage, the discovery that he may not love her and possess her as he wishes leads him to give up in some degree as far as his conscious, self-directed activity is concerned. Yet unconsciously a large part of his love remains fixated upon his mother; and this fixation may at times be so deep that the affective dispositions are hardly free to grow and differentiate in the normal way. Fixation, then, is more than canalization. It is a type of canalization which involves a huge segment of the personality, and it may act positively to make the individual unaware of some of his other canalizations; even more important, it may limit some of his contacts with the world, thus preventing canalization upon other objects which would ordinarily be capable of entering into such a role. It therefore interferes with growth. In psychoanalytic language, one fails to pass beyond an early "level of libido development."

In addition, an intense interest in or love for a particular *part* of one's own body, also causing a fixation in the Freudian sense, may interfere with a balanced view of the body as a whole, or, if the part is noticeable or socially unacceptable (as in the case of Cyrano's nose), may become literally a center of a "self-conscious" preoccupied nervous reaction. The fact that a part may become an exaggerated value center may mean that one strives to enhance it; thus Horowitz's subject (page 509) who is devoted to and identified with his right hand tries to enhance the hand, to put it into favorable situations. Similarly, Abraham's mouth-inhibited subjects (page 744), forced to give up nursing before they were ready, become, ever after, mouth-centered individuals to whom talking, singing, smoking, etc., are constant but never quite successful expressions of an early frustrated want.

Self-canalization may become a clue to the entire individual structure of canalizations. If the major object upon which the small child in our culture canalizes is his own physical self, including his visual appearance, the sound of his voice, and the congenial rhythm of his own movements, practically all other canalizations will be directed to some degree by this central fact. "I like it not only because I am used to it, but *because I always was fond of it. It is mine.* It is my own favorite book; my own favorite music; my own way of greeting people or of phrasing my thoughts." If, as we suggested, the canalization process is not subject to extinction, and if, as clinical experience suggests, canalizations upon the self are notoriously refractory to modification, the whole cluster of tastes and values must necessarily be supported by this powerful nuclear structure, even when the peripheral elements are in themselves relatively fragile.

We noted above (page 168) that there is "room for" an almost limitless number of individual canalizations; those already present do not blackball the new candidates. But the instant that the self is brought on the scene, the whole argument changes. If I pride myself on my love of Beethoven, I may turn up my nose at all modern music, the appreciation of which might imply that I was giving up my idol or recognizing that I had missed something (cf. page 168). "I simply am not the kind of person that would like Shostakovich—I am a Beethoven sort of person." Similarly, "Give me a hot dog; I'm not the sort of guy that you find eating pink-tea refreshments." So far as the socialized pattern of the ego makes one system of values incompatible with another, the canalizations can break each other's backs. The apparent waning of canalizations with age seems on this basis to be no true fading, no sheer disuse phenomenon. The adolescent has not merely lost his interest in playing marbles or pinning the tail on the donkey which so delighted him five years earlier; his *picture of himself*, his need to see himself as an almost-grownup is sufficient to block the expression of the more childish tastes. The adolescent or adult may, however, dream childishly; he may, though not "frustrated," nevertheless "regress" to the old canalizations which are still physiologically there but need a field situation (such as a college or an American Legion reunion) to permit their fresh expression. The canalizations are not lost, they are overlaid by new activities; let the crust be removed, free expression granted, and they reappear without the need of new cultivation. The young father has not played with an electric train for twenty years; but when he buys one for Junior's Christmas, there he is on the floor, utterly engrossed in it. Under hypnosis a man may be led back, "regressed," to a childhood level and behave on psychological tests very appropriately for the age indicated.

If these hypotheses are sound, the strength of an individual canalization will depend on the initial strength of the general need from which the canalized need springs, the intensity of the gratification given by the canalized object, the developmental stage, and the frequency of such gratification. From this it would follow that the first great loves of the child will be the persons and things able to yield the most gratification. In cultures in which the mother is with the little child only when called by a cry or other signal of distress, it is the visceral needs that are most satisfied through her; she becomes ancillary to the mouth and stomach or other specific tension region. But in cultures in which she is a steady companion of the child, her face and voice, her touch, the embrace or swinging and rocking, later the games or storytelling which she provides, are satisfiers that weave a broader texture of happiness across most of his hours. The first canalizations are upon specific things so far as the child can discriminate among them; he comes to love mother's face, mother's voice, as sheer sensory canalizations, just as he comes to love his surroundings, over and above the connections between these things and food brought about through conditioning. But he loves her face, her voice, her footsteps long before there is a whole mother. The experiences fuse into a wholeness because they often come together (cf. page 481). In the meantime, however, there is much "transfer" to similar experiences provided by other persons; he comes to love faces in general, voices in general. This is not transfer as seen from the child's point of view; the experiences are cumulative but fresh, not sorted out in terms of their external origins. From these early satisfactions emerge two general bases for prediction as to the roots of later satisfaction: first, one seeks through life the things he learned most to need in childhood; second, if these early satisfiers were bound tightly together so that mother was too completely satisfying, it may not be sufficient that a later associate or lover possess this or that quality—she must "have everything."

Again according to the hypothesis, the part that the father plays in all this depends largely on the amount of time he spends with his child and on the kinds of satisfactions he gives. In some cultures he gives much of himself; in American farm and village life, still characteristically a good deal; in the city, with its businesses and factories, not much, unless he is unemployed and emotionally supple enough to enjoy children. Maids, grandparents, and neighbors are often more important as the child's lovers and as foci of his interest. The individual differences in the importance of brothers and sisters for the little child are too huge to permit any summary here; we shall recur to the problem in discussing order of birth (page 585). As psychoanalysis maintains, brothers and sisters may indeed act as father and mother substitutes respectively. But to the little child father may also be a substitute for mother when she is ill, or to one accustomed to being cared for by his big sister, father may be a big-sister substitute. What the little child needs is contact with an active world as well as food in his stomach and the changing of his diapers; and whoever gives it becomes a nucleus, or first of all a group of nuclei, for satisfaction areas, his life demands.

The home does something else for the early trends of personal growth. It provides not only interesting persons but interesting things to look at, to listen to, or to do. One hears the tinkle of the bottles as the milkman goes his rounds, the grinding of the elevated train wheels, the piping of a distant peanut stand. The city child sent to a camp often complains of the absence of such sounds, is hungry for them. The country child hears the wind in the trees, the distant lowing of cattle, the creaking of the pump, the heavy tread on the kitchen floor; "these became part of that child,"—or, in the less gracious but becomingly authentic words of today, "You can take the boy out of the country but you can't take the country out of the boy." These are the tissues of the first canalizations. They are no more extinguishable than other canalizations. After being "long in city pent," one must have the hills or "go down to the sea again"; after years away, one longs for his old Kentucky home. Ulysses is "a part of all that he has met." Literature is so saturated with the language of a canalized love of the things, as well as the people, of one's individual world that it is harder to avoid than to find examples.

The world that the child loves, then, is largely the familiar world, both familiar persons and familiar things. They are the core of his values, his first real definition of the meaning of life. He can elaborate them, symbolize them, interrelate them, abstract from them, but he cannot live without them. Of course he goes on canalizing, and at a furious tempo—especially during adolescence—but he follows to a considerable degree the general lines established in childhood. He does not often fall in love with people whose skin or hair texture are unrelated to his first experiences; he does not easily slough off his old tastes; he tends rather to add new ones which are derivatives of the old.

Lest it be inferred that emphasis is upon sheer *amount* of familiarity, the fact that *satisfaction* given by an experience is always of cardinal importance should be heavily underscored. A sweet resonant voice may achieve in an hour a cherished quality which a mildly pleasing one can never attain. The orchard odors, the water from the woodland spring, reach their transporting quality at once and hold it forever. The *rate* of the canalization process is likely to reflect the degree of ascendance of one satisfaction over another.

CANALIZATION

Finally, the pull *away from* the familiar, the demand for novelty and adventure, whether rooted in curiosity or challenge or the need to expand and grow, must never be minimized (cf. page 115). It is as fundamental, and its forms are as distinctive, as are the canalization processes. Our concern here has been not to play up one and to play down the other, but to introduce canalization as a major clue to personality development.[2]

---

[2] It is presupposed, throughout this chapter and those that follow, that learning, whatever its form, depends on the relation between needs on the one hand, and, on the other, the constantly varying ("trial-and-error") tendencies which bring the inexperienced organism into contact with one, then another, aspect of the environment. To embark here upon a study of the many factors responsible for these ceaseless shifts in response would commit us to an essay on the whole theory of learning, a task beyond the reach of this volume.

9. Conditioning

MOST learning springs from struggle. The motivated individual strives, blindly or intelligently, to find the means of satisfaction. As he strives, he discovers things and activities that bring him into contact with the source of satisfaction. These things and activities come to elicit, in their own right, part (or sometimes all) of the responses made to the satisfier itself. In this very broad sense the term conditioning will be used. But from the present point of view, conditioning occurs only because motivation is present in the first place.

From one point of view, all personality differences arise from the fact that within a given individual a variety of situations gives rise to a common overt response; they all converge to the same final common path characteristic of that individual. Reduced to its simplest terms, this is a matter of confluence, the converging of many possible energies, on many different occasions, into the same expressive channel. A simplification of this sort may well be extreme, but like other forms of scientific abstraction it may be necessary. It will be well to begin our consideration of the development of the inner world of symbolic living by showing its relation to the simplest mechanisms for this convergence of energies into final common paths. To prevent a possible misunderstanding, it should be noted that this chapter does not attempt a comprehensive theory of the learning process or even of the conditioning process. Rather, it aims simply to emphasize certain aspects of conditioning which seem to help in clarifying a general conception of personality development.

The classical conception of the conditioned response emphasizes the fact that a path ordinarily called into service in response to a given stimulus may come to serve in responding to other types of stimulation as well. The mother's footsteps bring smiling because they have occurred earlier in conjunction with those maternal acts which in themselves arouse smiles. The footsteps are conditioned stimuli, that is, stimuli which would have no power to evoke the smile except through their spatial and temporal connections with the smile-arousing events. Conditioned responses of this general sort have been demonstrated in infants a week or two old, and they are present literally by the hundreds even before the world of visual space is clear enough to permit differentiation between human faces, and even before the auditory world is clear enough to permit any specific differentiation of sounds. As a simple physiological principle, then, it is permissible to say that a given response originally aroused by one or only a few stimuli can in time, as a result of experience, be aroused by a wide range of stimuli, many of which bear no similarity whatever to the original stimulus and are connected with it only by close association with it. Since each individual encounters different patterns of stimulation and acquires different conditioned responses, personality may be conceived to consist in the system of conditionings which distinguishes one man from another. Such conditioned responses may be strengthened by repetition; but if the agency that activated the response is removed, it usually soon disappears. The mother's footsteps coming and going, but no longer reinforced by the acts originally evoking the smiles, lose the capacity to bring out that response. It is the *abiding* pattern of conditioned response with which the study of personality is especially concerned.

Not all reflexes can be conditioned. Garvey found that after hundreds of joint stimulations the Achilles tendon reflex showed no linkage with the substitute stimulus. In general, the mechanically initiated reflexes that depend on simple sensorimotor arcs and have no strong affective components are hard to condition, whereas those of a well-marked affective character are easy. It would be in accordance with our general usage of the terms to say that it is the motivation process (the tension system), not the reflex as such, that undergoes conditioning; conditioning is the arousal of a motivation process by a substitute stimulus because of the establishment of a behavioral relation between the original and the substitute stimulus. The conditioned response is a preparatory or anticipatory response of tissues that are ready for or are undergoing preparation for tension reduction; it is a redirected drive. (There is no meaning in saying that some activities arise from present motives, others out of past association; the habit *is* a specific, established motive pattern acting in the present; cf. page 398.) This is readily seen in Zener's studies of dogs conditioned to food signals. When the signal comes, the dog does not simply salivate; he turns, sniffs, paws about, prances. The external manifestations of readiness are linked only loosely with inner readiness. The motive system is temporarily sensitized to new stimuli; the motives are, in this sense, redirected.

The same thing is evident when responses disappear. When the signal is no longer followed by the satisfier, the behavior relation fades out, but not the inner disposition; if the need continues, new conditioning can quickly be established. "Spontaneous recovery," a mystery to the student of the isolated reflex, is the response when slight new excitations of either outer or inner origin reactivate the expectancy.

Such redirection of drives is involved in all conditioning, both to outer and to inner stimulation. We encounter a good example in Watson's activity stream mentioned in another chapter (page 260). Inner stimulation, whether of striped or unstriped muscle, constitutes a new motor set, a new orientation, a new preparation for action.

At first sight the uniformities in conditioning from person to person are far more striking than the individual differences. All—or nearly all—motorists respond to the uplifted hand of a policeman, and in a rather uniform fashion. Experimental data, however, are required when quantitative questions arise, and fortunately we have considerable exact material on the distribution curves of individual subjects in laboratory conditioning situations. The measures are of three types: number of stimulations required to set up conditioned responses, intensity of the responses established, and number of repetitions required for their extinction. All of them yield well-defined individual differences. Mateer's pioneer study is typical. When children ranging from a few months up to several years of age were conditioned, the contact of a bandage with the face being the conditioned stimulus preceding opening the mouth for a chocolate drop, the number of stimulations was typically twice as large with some children as with other children of the same age.

DOMINANCE AND THE DISAPPEARANCE OF CONDITIONED RESPONSES

Though conditioning is a commonplace, the failure to establish a conditioned response is also a commonplace; and though many conditioned responses persist, many are dropped, inhibited, prevented from occurring. We may look about the room and observe dozens of objects to which we have been conditioned but about which we do little or nothing. We are conditioned to grasp the doorknob, but we can also stare blankly at it; we are conditioned to the light switch, the radio dial, the cigarette case, but we may fail to make the motor responses that are conditioned to them. Perhaps one of the words printed here will start an overt response in the reader. This will depend on a context—for example, whether it is getting dark, whether it is time for a good radio program, whether it is an hour since he finished smoking a cigarette, whether he is at leisure or in a hurry, whether he is negativistic toward such suggestions from another. In other words, every "stimulus" is a phase of a complicated pattern, and what happens depends on the pattern of the pushes and pulls, the total outcome of the various stresses. The word *dominance* will be used in our subsequent discussion in a descriptive sense to designate the specific role of a given conditioned response in relation to other competing *response patterns*, the dominant pattern appearing, the competing patterns failing to do so. (The term might of course be used in a more technical sense, involving a physiological theory as to the reasons for the success of one pattern, the failure of another; but for our purposes nothing would be gained by embracing one physiological theory here as against another. Yet that there are competing response patterns seems a physiological as well as a psychological fact.)

The term dominance refers to the relations obtaining between two or more responses potentially related to a specific stimulus, in the sense that if free of interference from other response tendencies each of these responses could perfectly well be aroused by that specific stimulus. When two or more such responses lie in wait within the individual tissues by virtue of conditionings established earlier, and the stimulus is presented, the result is normally not mutual blockage, or compromise, or alternation, but the appearance of one full-fledged response empirically defined as dominant when it is observed. Blockage, compromise, and alternation do occur, and we shall strive to explain them in Chapter 13; but here our concern is with the usual, the commonplace escape from these difficulties by the normal organism. The principle of dominance involves the resolution of this potential conflict by a process in which one response is dominant over all its competitors.

Schematically, if one has a conditioned response S_2R_1, and if S_2 is then effectively connected with R_3 in such a way as to extinguish S_2R_1, S_2R_3 is *dominant* over S_2R_1.

First phase: The joint stimulation of S_1 (original stimulus) and S_2 (conditioned stimulus) leads to response R_1.

Second phase: S_2 alone elicits R_1.

Third phase: S_3 elicits R_3 in the presence of S_2.

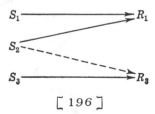

Fourth phase: S_2 no longer elicits R_1; it leads only to R_3.

The classical experiments of M. C. Jones on the elimination of children's fears serve as an excellent example. A child has been frightened by a rabbit—let us say, by its bite. He now fears, by conditioning, the *sight* of the rabbit. Knowing that there is a rough quantitative relation between the nearness of the rabbit and the magnitude of the fear, the experimenter assumes that some other pattern

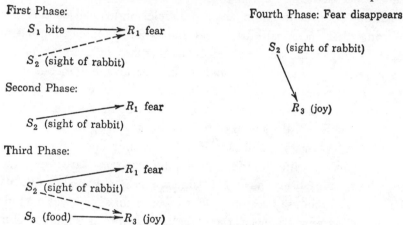

First Phase:

S_1 bite ⟶ R_1 fear

S_2 (sight of rabbit)

Second Phase:

⟶ R_1 fear

S_2 (sight of rabbit)

Third Phase:

⟶ R_1 fear

S_2 (sight of rabbit)

S_3 (food) ⟶ R_3 (joy)

Fourth Phase: **Fear disappears**

S_2 (sight of rabbit)

R_3 (joy)

can become dominant over the fear if the rabbit is *far away* and if this other pattern is made strongly active. Consequently, to remove the fear, he arranges to have the child, when really hungry and when lunch is appetizing, begin eating (a physiologically powerful satisfier) before the rabbit is brought to the door a few feet away. The pattern of active joyful response is so strong that the sight of the rabbit is functionally drawn into the pattern and becomes a substitute stimulus for *joy*. Let the child be insufficiently hungry, the lunch not appetizing enough, or the rabbit too close, and the dominance relations are reversed; the child begins to *fear his food*. This is what happens when children are punished for not eating their vegetables or ridiculed for not liking Shakespeare.

In the process of reconditioning just described, an accident did occur one day—the rabbit bit a child's finger. The result was a return to the original dominance of the negative over the positive response, and the necessity of a long additional learning period.

The complete picture which we have attempted to present involves the *relative strengths of two incompatible tendencies*. It will be noted that fear and joy are physiologically incompatible; for whatever difficulties we encounter in Cannon's theory, it remains true that when fear or rage grips the individual, the *emergency system* rules, and joy is impossible. If responses are *compatible* and can occur simultaneously, there is no problem of dominance.

An objection to the dominance principle might well be raised by insisting that incompatibility, and the whole dominance relation, depend solely on the simple physical fact that two different movements of the body, or of any of its parts, cannot occur simultaneously. Let us put it concretely. Suppose that while a man is driving in slow, heavy traffic near an intersection the policeman's whistle sounds. Depending on the context, the sound of the whistle may be, for the driver, a signal to stop or to go ahead. But one cannot both stop and go. Similarly, in most life situations genuine compromises are impossible, or at best a nuisance. Thus when someone asks me at 8:15 to go to the theater, I must say yes or no, not maybe; but saying yes excludes saying no. It might appear, then, that dominance is simply a name for the fact that a signal cannot call out two responses which are logically incompatible, like going and coming; and since one of these must necessarily be dominant, the name may be held to add nothing.

But dominance is an appropriate term because two primitive and incompatible responses (not involving the development of an inner system of signals) settle their differences not by processes of mutual adjustment and compromise, but by fulfillment of the one, subjugation of the other. The wide importance of the principle derives from the fact that potential conflict of acquired responses is not the exception but the rule. The right hand possesses a thousand skills, but the exercise of one is incompatible with that of the other 999. The fingers, while engaged in shaking hands, clutching a steering wheel, holding a cigarette gently or a pencil firmly, cannot at the same time be activated to play chords on the piano, pull up poison oak, or hold a tennis racket. The speech organs are capable of a still greater number of skills, but the utterance of any given word depends upon a lip-tongue-larynx-respiratory pattern which, at the moment, excludes all the others. Dominance, then, is the universal, the typical relationship between the thousands of conditioned responses within the individual skin; the activation of one conditioned response involves the "inhibition" of countless others. It is common to walk, talk, and gesticulate all at once; there are many other instances of compatible responses located in non-interfering muscle groups. But the more highly integrated the action pattern, the more complete is the exclusion of other potential integrations; there cannot be two apices of the hierarchical pyramid.

The term dominance, as used here, has no meaning unless responses are incompatible. Three experiments on dominance—the first by Erofeeva, the second by Razran, the third by Long—will help to clarify the issue. In Erofeeva's experiment a dog was given an electric shock on the forepaw at the same moment that he was fed meat powder. The animal not only failed to make the normal salivary response to the meat, but became so conditioned that subsequently the meat elicited not salivation, but paw retraction. When, however, the shock was *reduced* and the amount of meat was *increased*, the meat and the electric shock associated with it could both elicit salivation, and paw retraction ceased. The salivation and the paw retraction were aspects of contrasting physiological patterns that appeared in accordance with the principle of dominance. Here we may test the claim that dominance is just a name for the fact that logically exclusive patterns cannot occur together. The question is: Are these responses *logically* incompatible? No. But they may be *physiologically* incompatible, one being an expression of positive activity in the body's vegetative system, the other an expression of the body's defense system, with inhibition of activities in the vegetative system. Dominance appears to be genuinely a question of the tendency of a given physiological tension to lead to one effective functioning system rather than to two conflicting systems.

An experiment by Razran clearly brings out dominance in human conditioning. The *background* for this experiment is the fact that the number of joint stimulations necessary to establish a conditioned response varies not only with the species but with the different members of a species (cf. page 194). In all species below the primates, the number of stimulations required seems to yield an approximately normal distribution. In children up to about the age of three, the same generalization appears to hold. But there are suggestions that among infra-human primates bimodality is to be expected; some individuals condition quickly, others much more slowly. This is also brought out in studies of children over three years of age—generally speaking, children showing negativism. Some condition quickly, others slowly or not at all. In adult human experimentation this is again found. But a sharp distinction in situations must be drawn. When adult reflexes are elicited by mechanical non-human agencies, and their appearance and extent are matters of relative indifference to the subject, as in experiments with eyelid responses, the distribution appears to be normal enough. When, however, the experimenter administers the stimulus in the subject's presence and the response is one over which there is considerable cortical control, bimodality or multi-modality appears.

In the Razran experiment which is relevant to the present issue, the unconditioned stimulus was mint candy on the tongue, the conditioned stimulus a nonsense syllable. After suitable pairing of mint and syllable, we might expect all the subjects to salivate on hearing the syllable. But there are three *kinds of responses* which reliably characterize certain individual subjects throughout the course of the experiment. One group of subjects conditions promptly after the fashion of the Pavlov dogs. The second group fails to condition; the signal causes no significant augmentation of the salivary flow. For a third group, conditioning is in a reverse, or perverse, direction; the signal is followed by a reduction in salivation. It is important to note that the types here are *not types of persons*, but *types of prevailing attitudinal control* during the experiment. One might speculatively attribute the following attitudes to the subjects, verbalizing much that is probably non-verbal: (1) "Oh, that means mint coming." (2) "Mint? So what?" (3) "Why should I condition for you?" Whether or not such temporary attitudes become crystallized into "personality traits" is another question, to which we shall return (page 216). In this experiment attitudes probably operated unconsciously, but there is plenty of experimental evidence that conscious attitudes, systematically set up by the experimenter, also greatly affect the conditioned response.

It is not difficult to schematize the attitudinal control in terms of dominance; an indifferent set, or a flatly negativistic set, is so well established that the new arbitrary connection desired by the experimenter competes unsuccessfully for an effector pathway. Razran has contented himself with emphasizing central factors; we should prefer to go a step further and give these indifferent and negativistic attitudes the status of motor dispositions, motor sets toward the stimulus situation, which have been established earlier in laboratory experience or in relation to the whole syndrome of taking orders or doing what one is expected to do. It is likely, moreover, that any set toward a human situation contains some verbal (and therefore motor) phases, some fleeting or fragmentary inner ordering of symbols (cf. page 253). In this case these dominant dispositions would successfully compete with fresh patterns, exactly as the dominant elements in M. C. Jones' experiments succeeded in uprooting even an established pattern of inferior physiological dominance. Dominance is the name for the *empirical relationship;* the definition is operational. But the *theory of conditioning* offered here is of course just a theory.

In her experiment, Long studied the eyelid response both in relation to an adequate stimulus (sound) and in relation to a conditioned stimulus (light). In order to determine whether the establishment of a conditioned eyelid response would eliminate the original response to the sound, she presented in each instance a flash followed by a sound and obtained a completely negative result—there was never any elimination of the original response. The experiment is definitive in relation to its stated problem; and at the same time it shows that when responses are temporally separated, and thus *in no way incompatible*, they exhibit nothing to suggest the dominance principle.

These three experiments taken together suggest that if stimulation appropriate for two conditioned responses is simultaneously applied, we must first determine whether the pair of responses belongs to one or another of three categories: first, *independent;* second, *synergic;* third, *antagonistic or incompatible.* If the responses are independent, as in the case of responses made by a given muscle group on different occasions, the principle of dominance is utterly irrelevant; and Long's experiment shows clearly that there is no tendency for one response to interfere with, weaken, or in any way inhibit the other. In those instances in which the responses are synergic, the simultaneous presence of S_1 and S_2 will necessarily lead to R_1 and R_2, either in simple conjunction or in reinforced form, each in some fashion enhancing the tendency of the other (as would be expected, on the basis of Sherrington's principle of summation). Third, and all-important for our present purposes, when the two responses are antagonistic, the one which is more powerfully activated will occur; the other will drop out. Indeed, under some circumstances the weaker component will not only disappear but will in its disappearance feed the stronger, so that thereafter the stimulus which originally evoked the weaker response produces an especially powerful response in the stronger component. It is *only* in the case of antagonistic responses that the term dominance will be used here.

We wish, then, to suggest that the principle of dominance is sufficient to explain not only the acquisition but the loss of conditioned responses. In this we borrow from Wendt and other students of inhibition. The principle applies to the constant elimination of incompatible habits, a weeding-out of non-synergic trends. At the same time it facilitates the establishment of compatible simultaneous or closely successive responses to broader situations. Any situation comprising many features to which there are appropriate responses permits the *cross-conditioning process,* the process by which any feature of the total is aroused by any feature of the configuration; and a coordinated or *synergic* act follows. This higher or more complicated act leads in turn to a still higher integration of action patterns, so that a hierarchical structure of conditionings within the individual habit system is possible. If it were not for the principle of dominance, there would be, at each level in the hierarchy, a blockage, or a wild confusion. Antagonistic patterns are rapidly dropped; the child who is learning to write drops the erratic tension of opposed muscle groups and grasps with steady pressure, or, in acquiring a language or a behavior pattern, rapidly drops the antagonistic elements which betray themselves in grimaces and spasms. He drops them so quickly, indeed, that unless there are facetious remarks from a bystander there is no memory of them. Such elements are present, however, at every phase in the establishment of the hierarchical structure. Exactly as in the case of the child's eliminating his fears by the actual process of acquiring a positive response to the rabbit, so the individual's compatible positive conditionings involve the progressive dropping-out of elements which would produce chaos.

It is not asserted that dominance involves the perfect and universal exemplification of an all-or-none principle in behavior. There is much compromise in the process of living; and an action tendency may often be seen *weakening the force of an antagonist*, as when a soiled tablecloth takes the edge off one's appetite, or the zest of excitement mitigates one's fears. But in general the stronger tendency vanquishes the weaker; movement is toward elimination of the weaker antagonist. One comes to ignore the tablecloth if the viands are good, and to forget the joys of excitement if fear becomes abject. Compatibility is relative; compromise occurs, but it is unstable, a sign that the dominant forces are not yet at their zenith.

Finally and more broadly, dominance seems to lie at the very root not only of disappearance of conditioning but of spontaneous recovery, and therefore to permit the recurrence of old attitudes whenever the features essential in the dominance pattern are restored, or whenever features in a previous dominant pattern are lost. The slightest difference in the mannerisms of a frightened stranger may make the difference between his being treated as an arrogant intruder and being accepted as a disturbed soul in need of medical and social help. Social attitudes in general, as we shall try to see later, are not only set up by conditioning; this is only a small part of the story. They are constantly dying and being reborn as a result of the configurations present in the world in which they are relevant, slight alternations in the dominance balance.

Only what is dominant can in turn be integrated into a new pattern, and a new pattern can occur only when it is dominant over other existing or potential patterns. Much that appears new is really new as a hierarchical resultant of a group of dominant responses. Much, however, is simply the reawakening of those earlier dominant responses for which the way has been prepared by the waning of the physiological basis for competing patterns. The business man of fifty who relives with his boy the world of baseball and scouting is returning to an earlier pattern as competing standards of dignified adulthood are allowed to drop out.

TRANSFER AND GENERALIZATION

As soon as they are established, conditionings tend to *transfer*, or *generalize*, on the basis of the similarities between stimulus situations; the child frightened by a furry animal shows fear in response to a muff or to cotton wool. It is worth while to compare the animal laboratory procedure with the everyday procedure in the social training of children. If the dog salivates to the tuning fork at 256 double vibrations per second (because of the earlier joint presentation of meat and the given tone), he will also salivate at 300 or 500. He thus "generalizes." He is now trained to "differentiate" by the experimenter's sounding the fork, say at 500, and *withholding* food, sounding it at 256 and *giving* food, until the salivation is as clearly *lacking* in response to 500 as it is clearly *present* in response to 256. The difference between the two vibration rates is then gradually reduced until the dog no longer makes a differential response. The differentiation may be extremely good; for example, 256 may evoke the full response, whereas 260 fails to elicit any salivation.

CONDITIONING

The child's social generalization and differentiation appear to be of the same type. A wide variety of animals may be called "kitty" on the basis of physical similarities. The child talks of his "kitty" and gets an understanding response, but he cannot do so with the same performance when chipmunks are involved; his misuse of terms brings a condescending smile. Reinforcement, then, occurs only with reference to a certain class of objects which have a certain *socially defined degree of similarity*.

The limits of such generalization are usually much wider than human social arrangements can appropriately encourage; one generalizes until the consequences are no longer satisfying. Generalization goes as far as it is socially allowed to go. But the world is typed or classed by this means under categories that are far indeed from categories of naturalness or obviousness. Thus the classification according to sex which our language enforces on little children is obviously much less important in many situations than the classification according to age; yet the appropriate patterns of conduct toward another two-year-old are to a large degree guided by the social definition of what you can do when you are dealing with another *boy*, as contrasted with situations involving a *girl*. The places where you can play and the places where you can't play are often physically very similar, whereas each class of place as *named* by adults shows extraordinary and bewildering internal differences. Just as the animal may take some time to find the cue, the differentiating mark, that is important in distinguishing the reward from the non-reward situation, so the child, ready at all times to generalize, is constantly on his mettle to discover where the permissive atmosphere stops, where the world of tabu begins, in terms of some similarity in situations obvious enough to the adult but obscure indeed for him. With all these difficulties, however, there is still a process of generalization and a process of enforced differentiation, which permit in time the pigeonholing of the world of experience. Roughly speaking, all the worlds one experiences are worlds to which certain generalized conditioned responses can appropriately be made; the process of habit formation through conditioning is in large part this differentiation process.

·All conditionings, so far as we know, are subject to transfer; transfer appears in every sensory modality and in every motor or visceral response in which the problem has been directly examined. The degree of physical similarity and the degree of psychological similarity sufficient to touch off part or all of the original conditioning have proved to be a complex question, varying with the species, the age and intelligence of the individual, and a number of other factors. It is chiefly important to note that wide variability in stimulus properties is compatible with *complete* transfer of responses, in both animals and man. Conditioning to a given phonetic element such as a word or phrase is not partial but complete, although the word vary in pitch and volume, and with the diverse vocal qualities of individual speech. Melodies, costumes, gestures may be reacted to, despite objectively wide variation, as if they were as uniform as traffic lights. The dinner bell can sound differently on sunny and rainy days, or when sounded by father or mother, but the mouth still waters. A "critical point" can usually be found, however, at which *full* transfer suddenly ceases, as when the dinner bell is faint and confused; and another critical point can be found at which no demonstrable transfer is found, as when the dinner bell does not sound like one *at all*. We appear to be dealing here with discontinuities of a sort to which we shall have to refer many times in discussing the basic ingredients of which human habit structure is composed.

For the most part, we shall be concerned with full or practically full transfer, most of the research material being insufficiently exact to permit us to say how complete the transfer really is. By and large, we shall assume that the earliest social habits are rapidly and widely generalized to broad classes of social stimulation, so that for the little child there is an appropriate reaction to a word, to an irate grownup in masculine attire, to a grinning middle-sized boy, etc. It is this consistency in response to social signals of this sort that gives us the first materials to work with in confronting a new personality. These variables are not necessarily the most important, but they are the most speedily recognized. We may proceed later to a deeper analysis if we have first noted the range and form of the individual's transferred conditioned responses.

These conditionings, however, are apparently not only generalized but intertwined with other conditionings. While the salivary conditioning is occurring, manual and postural conditioning to the food signal is also occurring; if one conditioned response comes to elicit another, we have "cross-conditioning." While salivary conditioning is occurring with respect to the pitch of the tone, it is also occurring with reference to other phases of the situation. Thus, for example, while acquiring a response to tones one can acquire a response to their rhythm, their volume, or their melody in such a way as to make a broad bodily reaction to a broad stimulus situation. From one point of view this is a compound of many conditionings; from another, it is a hierarchical arrangement necessitating the study of structure rather than of individual items. The first point of view must be pursued for a while; for, in origin and everyday form, many of the phenomena of "personality style," or broad disposition to react, can be shown to be rather simple transfers from rather simple situations.

A convenient example of personality style as being *possibly* related to early conditioning is given in Gesell and Thompson's material on the childhood personalities of identical twins. Two little girls, Twin T and Twin C, who had been judged to be "identical" on the basis of a variety of convincing criteria, were used in a series of carefully planned investigations. Twin T, the trained child, was taught when less than a year old to climb stairs and to handle cubes, and, a little later, to use a specific group of words. Twin C was not given this training at the time, but was taught somewhat later to do the same things. Without exception, Twin C, being older when she first attacked a task, learned quickly what it had taken her sister (who had begun earlier) some time to acquire. These twins were followed up in adolescence and were compared not only with respect to simple motor and verbal performances but with respect to personality style in a broad sense. One of them drew with straight lines and produced meager and formal outlines; the other used curved lines and showed a sense of lightness and esthetic enjoyment in the process. In one there was an abundance of detail responses in the Rorschach test; in the other, a strong accent on wholes. One wrote a matter-of-fact account of the school graduation; the other, an imaginative picture reflecting the excitement and joy of the occasion. Some of the many hours of formal training given Twin T in infancy had been spared Twin C. Does the former's constraint have *no* relation to such formal training? The training had not added anything to the skills measured in the earlier experiments, but Twin T had experienced a variety (f forms of constraint that perhaps forced upon her simple, clear, adaptive movements. In perceptual situations, too, there had been drill; the cube test administered for several weeks at about one year of age surely involved a certain amount of tension in actual observation that would normally predispose later toward an accent on form. This interpretation is offered very tentatively and simply as an illustration of an approach. Personality style *might* be regarded as in part a matter of the transfer, even to very complex situations, of responses instilled over a considerable period during infancy.

Another suggestive instance of the early transfer of traits constituting "personality style" appears in the work of L. R. Martson, who found even among two-year-olds that habits of persistence in the effort to make contact with a grownup ran through the test battery, individual children consistently overpowering obstacles and getting the adult to play with them, or consistently remaining shy and struggling along without adult help. Granted that constitutional factors enter here, as they do everywhere, the habits of adjustment to grownups are specific enough to be seen in the light of specific conditioning experiences; though the adult in the experiment is a stranger, he elicits conditioned responses transferred from earlier situations.

There are a good many useful suggestions regarding the transfer of *aggressive* patterns to a wider and wider context of play relationships. J. E. Anderson has offered a well-formulated suggestion on the transfer from the home situation to the school situation, as evident in the first grade. Many a child who through trial and error has found ascendant behavior, or sheer bullying, to be the one effective and workable way of handling parents and siblings appears ready, on coming to school, to use on the teacher and on the other children the responses to which he has long been conditioned at home. Most children who have found retreat the only workable pattern at home continue in school to retreat as before. Not all children show such direct transfer, and so broad a hypothesis may seem extreme; but something of the sort is actually implicit in practically all clinical theories. The Freudian conception of the mother substitute and of substitution in general is based upon a similar conception of wide transfer, and the Adlerian conception of utilizing both one's own body and the bodies of others as instruments of ever broadening compensation is shot through with assumptions of the same type (cf. Chapters 23 and 24).

Thus far, we have dealt with transfer in general, a type of response of which all children are capable. There is, however, a high degree of *individuality* in transfer. Shirley found a great deal of this in her personality study of the first two years. All the children had been conditioned to sit on laps, to say "thank you," and to ring doorbells; but the new situation, particularly the new test materials, brought out considerable transfer from some of them and very little from others. In McGraw's study of "Johnny and Jimmy" there seems to have been a greater subtlety on Johnny's part, a capacity to note resemblances which his brother ignored. We should expect in general that the intensity of the various drives, the complexity of the organism, and the momentary factors leading to excitement or relaxation would facilitate or inhibit the transfer tendency.

DIFFERENTIATION

If all conditioning leads to transfer, it is no less true that as stimuli vary, all conditioning leads to *differentiation*. The Pavlov technique for the study of differentiation (page 204) is worth recalling. When salivary conditioning has been established to 256 double vibrations per second, any tone higher or lower evokes the response; differentiation of response becomes clear cut by training with another stimulus *not* associated with food and by reinforcement through feeding when 256 is presented.

Differentiation of exactly this type clearly develops in responses to social situations generally. The first step is always generalization; but when the transferred response ceases to be relevant—that is, when the drive is no longer satisfied—its extinction follows. And the more active the interference (the more plainly the principle of dominance has an opportunity to work), the more rapid the differentiation. In this way the child rapidly learns appropriate distinctions between classes of people wearing certain types of clothes; he learns to tell a policeman from a fireman, a garbageman from a milkman, a white from a Negro, a boy who belongs on "our side of the tracks" from one who belongs "across the tracks." Consistently, and practically without exception, the first step beyond simple conditioning is transfer. The child calls the policeman a fireman if he has encountered firemen but has had no experience with policemen, and he plays with the boys from across the tracks or with the Negro boys; he transfers to them his reactions to his own playmates. In the same way he transfers to himself whatever is appropriate in handling others like himself, and he transfers to them whatever is appropriate to himself. It is only by embarrassment or reproof, or the awkward consequences of his transfer, that differentiations are effected. For example, so far as children are an undifferentiated group, they transfer to all children, boys or girls, the patterns of response which are appropriate to children. But eventually the boy usually discovers that responses to girls on the familiar basis bring reproof. One mustn't fight them, one mustn't take their toys; on the other hand, there is no interference with such behavior if another boy is concerned. By this process of endless differentiation, forced upon him by practical cultural demands in terms of age, size, sex, neighborhood, parental status, etc., he builds up a systematic pattern of appropriate reactions to himself; he learns to classify himself in exactly the same way. Every one of these patterns involves categorizing, placing himself in a group with someone else and in a group different from someone else. The process by which the self, in a broad sense, emerges is this process of the differentiation of conditioning.

The extraordinary richness of such differentiation when pressure is constant and clear is suggested in Welch's work with the differentiation of shapes and sizes; he found that children as young as fifteen or eighteen months acquire appropriate differential responses to slightly differing objects. This richness also appears in such tests as the Vigotsky test, in which children of school age quickly differentiate blocks on the basis of three categories at a time; they must find which number is appropriate for a block of a given size, color, and shape. Such a procedure, or any performance test with children or adults, shows well how the transfer tendency outstrips the differentiation tendency; the individual makes constant excursions in the direction of generalization but is constantly brought to a full stop by failure, whereupon a new procedure becomes necessary.

The experimental situation is usually so set up that transfer becomes an all-or-none matter; things either belong solely in one category or they belong in a completely different one. For the most part, society does the same thing; you are either an X or a Y, and in consequence you must do either A or B. There is of course no objective basis for most of these absolute rules. The teacher may say flatly that A is wrong and B is right, and this may be clear enough in the schoolroom. But the dividing line in a tenuous situation at home may fall elsewhere; this brings to mind various experimental animal neuroses (cf. page 299). The difficulty is not in the mechanism of transfer, nor, in the case of human beings, does it usually lie in the mechanism of differentiation; it is rather the presence of complicating background features in the situation that lead to uncertainty whether the rules applying to situation A or to situation B are in force. Moreover, the same problem arises when one is deciding who and what he is; the fear and unhappiness of children as to themselves and their acceptability, their struggle to find a niche where they are completely adequate, are often of the "experimental neurosis" type. It is not difficult to be acceptable to the gang or to the crowd at school or to the dancing-school group; difficulty may appear when one meets members of all three groups at the drugstore. It is not difficult to do what the parents or the grandparents or the teachers want, but a child often has to please all of them at once. He is constantly encountering obstacles when the stimulus patterns permit adequate transfer in several different directions, but each transfer leads into territory which is tabu from another point of view.

The term differentiation is currently used also for a somewhat different thing, the fact that intellectual processes become more and more compartmentalized. All mental tests at the five-year-old level are apparently so intercorrelated as to permit no very sharp differentiation of memory aptitudes, thought aptitudes, following-directions aptitudes, etc. By eight or nine, however, special abilities and disabilities—in other words, greatly reduced intercorrelations between items belonging to different functional groups—have become evident, and by early adolescence they are striking. By the freshman year in college, though intercorrelations between all verbal patterns and also between all numerical patterns are high, the two groups of skills are not very closely related. It is possible that this "differentiation" is the same old "differentiation" that we have encountered in the conditioning situation. There is, of course, the possibility that we are dealing primarily with neural maturation (the electroencephalogram goes on changing during the 'teens). But when we remember that the differentiation (as we measure it) follows the differentiation of the curriculum, the specialization of the training process itself, it becomes probable that we are dealing to a considerable extent, at least, with the process of transferring to new situations those patterns of response—including attitudes and interests—which were adequate within a given sphere of activity. The fact that the child has worked out an adequate system of interrelated responses with words points to a drive toward verbal skill, the prestige of verbal accomplishment, the need to identify himself with verbal parents, etc.; and it is evidenced more and more articulately in greater reading and spelling proficiency. But there is no magic by which such skills can generate interest in or identification with mathematical or other pursuits. In other words, the personal value system is reflected in the differentiation.

Now if what has been said regarding sheer motor and verbal skills holds true during the growth period, it must hold true regarding spheres of adult competence. The individual acquires useful generalized habits in appraising the manners, clothing, or social tasks of others and becomes socially expert; or he acquires such habits in appraising the ways of wheels, shafts, and cams, and becomes a budding student of engineering. In all such cases early interests (based as usual on drives) play a part. But transfer depends in large measure on specific vehicles provided through the use of common terms. For the most part, the niceties of gracious language, the finesse of social discrimination, permit little or no transfer to engineering; the know-how of the engineer does little directly to influence his social skills. On the whole, interests and attitudes are departmentalized as the life requirements would lead us to expect, but no more so.

But all these processes directed toward the outer world are directed at the same time toward oneself. One builds up a sense of competence in social affairs or in engineering, and the transfer of attitude from one to the other is seldom much encouraged. In short, the process of personal differentiation, involving the development of worlds of interest and worlds of self-attitude, appears to be analogous to the differentiation of skills at a much simpler level. Even the widest generalizations of all, such as those reported by Pallister in relation to a general undiscriminating attitude toward oneself, appear to follow the same principle. Pallister used the term "negative or withdrawal attitude" to define in general the fear of persons or the need for inner safety, as contrasted with active social participation. By means of a long questionnaire which had to do with family relationships, relationships with one's own and the other sex group, relations with teachers, and attitude toward the self, she showed that every one of her types of escapism, or fear of social contact, correlated substantially with the others.

The issue presented here leads immediately to a contrast between two concepts of therapy, which may be called therapy through differentiation and therapy through reconditioning. Transfer based upon the neglect of significant distinctions leads, according to Hollingworth, toward neurotic and generally inadequate responses; it follows that therapy lies in discovering the *region of appropriate transfer*. The psychoanalytic doctrine is in large measure directed to the same effect. Thus an individual reacts to his specific failure as to a demonstration of his total worthlessness. Authority patterns involved in imposing tabus could function quite properly if related to specific prohibiting attitudes of the father; but since they are applied to oneself *as a whole*, they come into conflict with the positive affective attitudes toward the self, and conflict results. On the other hand, therapy through reconditioning, therapy that makes use of the dominance principle, as described above in the work of M. C. Jones (page 197), has the advantage of taking the child at his own level, with all his failure in differentiation, and, despite it all, loading the dice in favor of the therapeutically more helpful pattern (cf. also Munroe, page 224).

The same problem appears in somewhat different guise in the Character Education Inquiry, which showed the progressive extension of attitudes of lying, cheating, and stealing in an underprivileged group studied from the fifth to the eighth grade, and the rapidly increasing resistance to lying, cheating, and stealing that appeared in a favored group during the same years. We should expect, moreover, that the *degree of generality* of honesty, the intercorrelation of honesty items, would be in large part a question of the age and environment of the child. This hypothesis is strikingly confirmed by the rapid rise in such intercorrelations in the favored group, so that a high consistency of individual honesty patterns is exhibited at the eighth grade. This is the more striking if we bear in mind that the specific honest acts— e.g., refusal to erase one's errors on an examination paper or to embellish the story of one's athletic prowess—are highly dissimilar. The transfer occurs either because *the child verbally brackets a wide variety of acts under a given caption* to which he gives his generalized adherence or because, in the parental indoctrination, *the parents' own verbal standard or cliché knits the various patterns together;* more likely, it is because of a combination of the two.[1] Both factors are emphasized by the neighborhood and social class membership of the favored child.

An even broader assumption as to the role of transfer now appears to be warranted. Remembering that constitutional factors predispose

---

[1] Transfer may occur in reference to any element in a complex pattern; the scope for it is therefore very great. But transfer can occur only when the element or elements of a present situation are dominant over competing situation patterns. A child may recognize in one situation a feature common to a situation in which honesty brought satisfaction, and may behave honestly; failing to recognize such a feature, or being overpowered by a stronger appeal, he may do the opposite (cf. Chapter 34).

to one or another conditioning, we might tentatively define personality traits in general as transferred (and differentiated) conditioned
and canalized responses. A trait is not a specific learned response; it is
a generalized response, due account being taken both of the variations
in stimulation and of the cross-conditioning factors which induce variations in response. "Shyness" or "aggressiveness," for example, when
arising in specific conditioning situations, frequently generalizes to a
wide range of situations.

In an earlier chapter we noted the feasibility of defining traits as
organic dispositions, or as upper and lower thresholds predisposing
the individual in one direction or another. For the most part, the
recognized personality consists of these organic dispositions *canalized
or conditioned to specific areas*, the areas being defined by generalization and differentiation. The traits, then, are the organic dispositions
in the areas in which they have been allowed to spread.

We need, however, to distinguish between regional or segmental
conditionings, however generalized, and those which reach beyond the
segmental modes of organization. We might refer to the former as
"localized" personality traits; loud or mellow speech, for example, is
localized in this sense. Gestural behavior or, more broadly still, one's
social manner, involves broader aspects of personality style. We have
seen that both the localized and the more complexly structured patterns develop through a long process of generalization and differentiation, and that it is the region of differentiation that marks off one trait
from another. One child is honest at school, dishonest on the play
ground; another is honest in both situations but dishonest with the
school principal. There is no such generalization of behavior as the
adult has in mind. Honesty can also be highly generalized; it is
often found to be a generalized trait if the child's background has
inculcated transfer and if the test situation is such as to permit the
transfer that will bring it out. The fact that this or any other generalized pattern can be broken up by new circumstances counts against
any theory of homogeneous, indissoluble traits. The possibility of
transfer depends, moreover, on the present organized situation within
the individual as well as upon the organized situation outside of him.
Thus in playing with toys that are real objects in miniature, an atmos-

phere that permits emotional release allows transfer from home experience to the play situation, but in its absence play may be more rigidly determined by the sheer form of the toys. Warming-up in the exercise of any adult skill similarly consists in part of a reorganization of kinesthetic experience which permits old habits to enter usefully into a present task.

Transfer goes on year by year, and consistent generalized traits are as a rule better defined in adults than in children. It would be tedious to review the hundreds of studies of adult traits which have revealed a high generality of behavior and attitude. It is sufficient to mention as typical the evidence of Donald Johnson that *confidence* is a generalized trait appearing through a variety of test situations; Efrón's studies showing that one's habitual gestures are transferred from one conversational setting to another and Howell's data indicating that *persistence* carries over from laboratory to classroom (cf. page 553).

But transferred conditioned responses, like all other conditioned responses, need frequent reinforcement if they are to persist. It is well to remember that the child may expect from a stranger what he is used to receiving from his parents; if the stranger does not fit into the expectation, however, this transferred conditioned response of the child rapidly disappears. Whenever transfer occurs, the consequences determine whether there is to be reinforcement or extinction. As we saw above in discussing generalization, it is the food or non-food that determines whether the salivary conditioning is to appear. It is well for personality theory to look constantly for transfer; but it is not helpful to suggest, as is often done, that transfer persists and spreads steadily without continuous reinforcement through appropriate experience. Personality is grounded largely in the experience of satisfaction and frustration; it is not capriciously extensible in all directions.

SUGGESTIBILITY, IMITATION, AND SYMPATHY

Conditioned motor responses to words and gestures are usually treated as instances of *suggestibility*: indeed most manifestations of childhood or adult suggestibility are simply conditioned motor responses with which there is no interference. Someone shouts "Look!" and we look; on the door is "Push" and we push. In these instances, another set, whether of disbelief or of challenge, might make us ignore the signal. In many phases of life, as in our response to tall tales about fishing or enemy radio reports, it is a standardized pattern to disbelieve and challenge. Such "negativistic" attitudes prevent the operation of the conditioning stimuli, as in any other case of dominance (cf. page 199). In other instances the preparatory set is favorable, reinforcing; we are told that we shall hear a true story about fishing from the piscatorial certification committee, or an impartial analysis of enemy broadcasts by the broadcasting company's military expert. The words then find their path well cleared. Later, one can relate the authentic information as his own; and its authenticity, thus vouched for by oneself, is subsequently unimpeachable. The clue to suggestion lies in the preparatory dispositions and their dominance roles. On this basis suggestibility or proneness to it would result from transfer and generalization, but the critical question would be why the transfer occurs in any specific case. This, as suggested above (page 202), appears to depend chiefly on the degree of freedom from interfering factors. For one thing, the younger and the less intelligent the person, the greater the suggestibility. This expected result is thoroughly confirmed by many studies. Previous conditionings in relation to the source of the suggestion will pave the way for acceptance or rejection in any given individual. Suggestibility varies largely with such conditionings, especially conditioning to authority sources. This is a way of saying that the trait of suggestibility depends both upon transfer and upon dominance. To bring out these relations more fully, it will be well to look at the evidence from a study of the trait called "negativism," the inverse of suggestibility.

Negativism or resistance to suggestion appears in measurable form by eight or ten months, in relation to even the simplest situations calling for the child's adjustment of posture to meet the adult's needs; it mounts fairly steadily until an age which, despite individual variations, can be put at about two or three years, and gradually declines thereafter but of course never disappears. Let the individual be carrying out any activity interesting to him (and for the two-year-old the new world reached through language and locomotion is too absorbing to be given up easily) and adult interference, admonitions, and restrictions will have to be pretty powerful to have any result. If they are not powerful enough, the child goes on his way and the adult admonitions and pressures become non-dominant elements in a conditioning situation. To the instruction "Do this" the child acquires the conditioned response of going on doing more actively what he was already doing. Unless the pressure is sufficient actually to redirect him, a normal child acquires in this way consistent and well-defined *habits of ignoring* and proceeds valiantly in defiance of whatever is suggested, just as Razran's third group of subjects succeeded in "conditioning in the wrong direction" (page 200). So far as their habits are reinforced and generalized, we may, in time, find ourselves dealing not simply with negativistic responses, but with a "negativistic personality."

The personality trait of negativism should on this basis be rather highly generalized, and this was the case when Reynolds measured it. It will, in fact, be as highly generalized in the child as is the habit of giving constant but weak instructions in the adult; and conversely it will be as narrow and specific as are the specific and exceptional absent-minded remarks of a consistent parent who through fatigue or inattention departs occasionally from his own general plan of training his child.

Under some cultural conditions, at least, and in most children, there is apparently an accentuation of negativism at puberty. This seems to be due partly to the inability to tolerate instructions from parents during this period of marked physiological changes and intense interests of one's own. Negativism appears, however, over and over again at *any* period in which the external interference is insufficient to redirect behavior but is sufficient to necessitate an extra effort in continuing one's own activities. Thus, for example, the schizophrenic patient's negativism becomes more and more marked as the world of family or hospital interferes fatuously but irritatingly with the development of a delusional pattern of life. And it appears regularly in normal people who have lost their job, and in refugees who are unable in the new country to carry out the patterned plan of living ingrained in them under the happier conditions of their earlier life in Europe. Without the principle of dominance it is hard to see how the trait of negativism could arise; without it there would be sheer failure to respond, sheer ineffectiveness in the redirecting of energies. But negativism is no such passive process. It is the reinforcement, the reactivation of patterns to which outside interference can offer no obstacle; *and as in the case of many other dominant responses, inadequate stimulation produces not more of the weaker response but more of the stronger one.* Without dominance, a gradual increase in the strength of the competing response would in time sap the strength of the stronger one. Nothing of the sort occurs; a change of pattern can be produced only by guaranteeing at a concrete and specific moment in time (under specific conditions of fatigue, irritation, etc.) the physiological dominance of the new response at the expense of the old.

Attempts to alter the existing negative patterns usually lead to new manifestations of the dominance principle. Let the well-meaning big brother or sorority sister try to overcome an adolescent's escapist tendencies. The result is no melting-down of contradictories, no compromise; either he clears the hurdle altogether and gets the adolescent started on an undreamed-of career of social activity, or he fails by a hair's breadth, succeeding only in frightening him further and proving to him more than ever that he is safe only with himself. Success must come the first time or ground is lost; pushing and poking a little harder each time strengthens the opposing forces. It is like the production of antibodies—if the danger comes slowly, a defense is built up to meet it; it is the sudden overwhelming impact of toxic bacteria that knocks one flat. In immunizing against certain diseases the serum has to be injected in large quantity, for unless there is a "reaction," no real resistance can be established.

The phrase "a hair's breadth" just used suggests the presence of definite distinctions, cleavages, between persons, in contrast to the smooth continuity with which the statistician usually prefers to deal.

If the hypothesis developed above is sound, we should expect the child either to obey at any given time or to be sharply negative; we should expect the radio listener either to believe the propagandist or to be sharply resistant; we should at least expect to find a tendency to discontinuity under conditions of uniform stimulation. The same person may shuttle back and forth between two opposing reactions, or when tested on a number of items may be markedly cooperative on some, markedly resistant on others, depending on their meaning for him in the light of specific past experience; he will seldom be near the mid-point. More frequently, a given individual will stay near one extreme, avoiding the other. Thus, when a large group is studied, discontinuity will be found, or clear-cut bimodality. Experimental data are unequivocal on this point. Tests of suggestibility yield normal distribution curves only when the suggestion situation is impersonal; the moment that the experimenter permits opposing attitudes to himself, as when he tries through his prestige to impress the subject, marked compliance and marked resistance manifest themselves. This gives a U-curve rather than a normal curve. Such a result is clearly manifest in the two studies of suggestibility that have distinguished between naïve suggestion and prestige suggestion. Propaganda studies also bring out the tendency of audiences not merely to move in the direction of the propaganda but to be split by it, one contingent moving with it, another away from it. The thesis offered here does not mean that an all-or-none principle appears in relentless and uncompromising form (cf. page 197), but only that the stronger tendencies tend to drive the weaker out. Imbalance seems to be a less stable condition, complete dominance a more stable condition.[2]

Negativism in a broader sense—namely, a negative attitude toward society at large—appears to be due to the same principle that was brought out in Pallister's study mentioned above (page 213). But here a broader type of generalization, or negative or escape reaction, is involved than was the case with the infant or the three-year-old. One has been hurt not by a single individual but by many; and in

---

[2] A further study of suggestibility is given on pp. 347 ff.

consequence of this original hurt or series of hurts he has developed a diffuse insecurity in all social situations. This is in fact as highly generalized a trait as we are likely to find. As is to be expected, however, this negativism or withdrawal usually proves to have a positive aspect. By developing attitudes that favor activity requiring no social participation, by devising ways of thinking, feeling, and acting which make him relatively independent and adequate in his own eyes in non-social situations, a person develops areas of individual security which depend only little on other individuals (cf. pages 600 ff).

Imitation at its most primitive level likewise appears to be a matter of conditioning; its mechanism is apparently based on the *circular response*. Some inner event or stimulus (S) makes one respond (R); one perceives (P) the R as it is carried out; all three events—S, R, and P—overlap in time, so that each repetition of R leads to P and hence to another R. When one has imitated oneself, functional relations are ready between the perception of one's own activity and the reiteration of the same activity. Having splashed the water for whatever reason, the two-year-old continues to splash it. On a later occasion, big brother in the same tub splashes it, and little brother does likewise. Guernsey's twelve-months-old subjects all raised their arms when she did. Repetitive vocalizations go on for months or years, apparently depending only on freedom from interfering patterns; in extreme fatigue one reacts with mechanical imitation, as in echolalia and echopraxia. When there is no interfering set, the hypnotizer, the leader of the excited crowd, can elicit such "echoes" as easily as commanded acts. Deliberate imitation is a more complex affair, involving closer perception of detail, greater integration of movement, and, above all, a set toward the end result, just as in the delayed reaction (page 247). One investigator was interested in measuring imitativeness as a general trait, as contrasted with suggestibility. In this one study (in nursery-school children), the trait appeared in well-defined form.

Humphrey has shown that *sympathy* appears also to be, at its most primitive level, a manifestation of conditioning. Having burned my hand on the radiator and having later cringed when near the radiator,

I see another hand pass near it and I cringe. Attitudes of identification (cf. page 491), however, seem to reinforce, and attitudes of ego isolation and hostility to inhibit, these primitive responses. The American child, for example, learns to treat his pet like a person, identifies himself with it, and is sympathetic when it is injured; the Hopi child, to whom a pet is a plaything like a stick or a doll, mauls it mercilessly. Not much about the *more complex* types of sympathy can be learned without recourse to the concepts of empathy (page 494) and participation (page 382).

Primitive sympathy—weeping at injuries to parents or pets, apprehension lest little sister be lost—is usually well defined by the end of the second year, and it is rather common behavior at nursery-school age. But the amount of sympathy cannot be well predicted in terms of chronological or mental age; it is much more closely related to personality factors which appear at every age. Among nursery-school children, general activity level and social outgoingness are clearly related to sympathy; indeed, this trait is substantially related not only to cooperation but to aggressiveness. While sympathy as a general trait is well defined, the specific behavior manifestations are manifold—staring with an anxious expression, rushing to the defense of an injured child, etc. Any one of these specific behaviors may appear without the others. This is what we should expect in view of the fact that each act is determined by a multitude of factors with a limited overlap. The specificity of such factors is shown by the fact that punching a child who is down is correlated positively with punching aggressors of the weak, and that the outstanding pugilist in the group is the outstanding protector of the helpless. The *general* factor is brought out equally clearly by the fact that sixteen sympathy items have a corrected reliability of .88.

These three mechanisms—suggestibility, imitation, and sympathy —have an important role in the early stylizing of behavior around cultural norms, especially as these are conveyed to the child by the family. To the little child the prestige relations are so important that all of them are more easily aroused in relation to parents and older brothers and sisters than to contemporaries. For the older child, however, his contemporaries and immediate seniors at school and play become important models, and he brings home many fond imaginings about cosmic structure or human reproduction that are so certainly "known" to be true that they stand up well against his "ignorant" parents' agitated protests. For adolescents in our culture, according to the documentation of the California Adolescence Study, it is more important to accept and imitate the norms of one's peers than those of the new, strange, or even hostile world of adults. Among many human groups the role of parents as models is systematically limited for a portion of the childhood period. The Manus child, for example, is buffered from the adult world, the boy having contacts primarily with older boys, and the girl (after about seven) with older girls; the children are prevented from taking over too many parental patterns before adulthood is officially announced.

10. The Hierarchy of Conditionings

WE HAVE several times hinted that the pattern of conditioned responses exhibits structural relations; there is a system, an architecture of conditionings. We must now try to suggest the dynamics chiefly responsible for this architectural organization.

When a conditioned response has once been established, a functional unit exists which in many respects resembles the functional units apparent in the newborn. In particular, a stable conditioned response may serve as a base for new conditioned responses superimposed upon it. Sights and sounds which accompany or precede the regular substitute stimulus may themselves give rise to the original unconditioned response. Although such "second-order" conditionings appear to be less stable than first-order conditionings, Munroe found them still capable of enduring for a matter of weeks. There may indeed be third-order conditionings, and conditionings of a still higher order. The learning process of the normal child probably involves an interwoven texture in which primary conditionings are difficult to separate from the various types of conditionings of second or higher order.

Of special interest is Munroe's suggestion that the second-order conditionings are broken down with considerably greater ease than the primary, and that the normal person is freed of his useless conditioned responses through the constant stripping-off of higher-order patterns that are no longer useful (drive-satisfying) in new situations. One class of conditioned responses, however, notoriously fails to be extinguished. This is the trauma, the shock of overpowering distress which some stimulus to fear, shame, or disgust may once have occasioned. Because of a terrifying experience in childhood, the sight of a cobbler's hammer or a "harmless necessary cat" may for the thousandth time, with no intervening reinforcement through new contact with the original stimulus, hurl one into anxiety or revulsion. Munroe suggests that the profound upset, the traumatizing fear, cannot ordinarily be removed directly, because no stimulus that can be used practically in reconditioning is as strong as the traumatic stimulus; such methods may even make the child afraid of the therapeutic technique itself (cf. page 197). The second-order responses are weaker, and reconditioning is feasible in dealing with them; it is continued until they have been so completely dominated by the therapeutic response that the strengthened therapeutic response can be utilized for the conquest of the trauma itself.

The establishment of a conditioned response means the establishment of a functional relation between a stimulus and a response not ordinarily associated with it, and it must therefore involve the removal

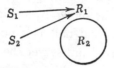

or inhibition of the response which would ordinarily follow that stimulus. Diagrammatically, S_2 will lead to R_1 only through a mechanism which at the same time provides that R_2 will disappear. The term dominance has been used throughout our discussion to indicate this kind of functional substitution, the term implying that one response must in fact dominate another if it is to appear as a new pattern.

We should suspect, if this is the case, that the ease of establishing conditioned responses will depend upon the biological situation of which the responses are aspects. We should suspect that if hunger is keen, a salivary response to an electric shock can be built up, whereas if hunger is slight the electric shock will lead to withdrawing movements of the member to which it is applied (page 199). If now we deliberately simplify the situation so that the organism cannot simultaneously carry out a food-getting and an avoiding reaction, we shall have a situation in which the relative strength of the food need and the escape need determines which of two all-or-none responses will be made. Most of the evidence on dominance (cf. page 195) is based on instances in which the organism is confronted by an all-or-none "choice" situation. Indeed, if there is no conflict or struggle for final common paths, there is no more occasion for dominance than there would be if two animals drank from the same spring at different times in the day. One test of animal "dominance" is thirst when many are thirsty and water is scant; the test of the theory of dominance in conditioning is the presence within the organism of stimulus patterns which, *when evoked separately*, give rise to a series of distinct responses, but which under conditions of joint stimulation make the simple integration of the responses impossible.

The clue to the architecture of the effector patterns appears to lie in this matter of dominance relations between primary and higher-order conditioned responses. The evidence is particularly striking in the case of language patterns, as shown by association tests. Each word or phrase or other higher verbal unit is a potential stimulus to many other words or other verbal units; yet the process of speech moves forward, for the most part, smoothly enough. Choices between equivalent terms are quasi-automatic; responses to one's own previous words and to those of one's interlocutor occur for the most part without abstract thinking but are manifestly determined to a great extent by the dominance relations, i.e., by the relative strengths of the tensions involved. For the dominance relation operates in exactly the same way in responses which are "means" to ends as in those which are "drives"; all acts are aspects of tension systems (page 193).

Just as conditionings are established on the basis of existing motives, so they operate and serve as bases for other conditionings in terms of the *quantitative attributes*—intensities, extensities, and durations—which they possess. To be set for food is to associate verbally in terms of food symbols. To be set for or against another ethnic or religious group is to be activated in such a manner as to exhibit an already existing pattern of conditioned responses that is quite different from the one called forth when the mood is different.

Striped- and unstriped-muscle dispositions play a part in determining the dominance relations from hour to hour and from day to day.

This is exactly the process demonstrated by Razran under the term "attitudinal control of the conditioning process." Razran's experiments, already referred to (page 200), suggest that attitudes favorable or unfavorable to the experimenter may determine whether the expected conditioned response will appear. *Attitudes—which are themselves conditioned responses- -determine what responses may later be conditioned.* We should expect bimodal curves or their equivalents, the U-curves, or even a full-fledged discontinuity of response, to appear whenever incompatible action patterns are involved, so that dominance relations must result in one or another contrasting category of behavior. Over and above the all-or-none pattern which provides the basic cleavage, there are always individual differences in the complicating circumstances, since behavior is not determined by a single variable. The variable with which we are chiefly concerned at any given moment lends itself, whenever dominance is present, to the type of discontinuity upon which bimodality and U-curves depend. The same discontinuity, the same gap between what we are at one time and what we are at another, appears in each individual. In its basic building constituents at any given period, personality consists of discontinuities—of all-or-none, mutually exclusive responses—that depend upon dominance relationships.

It is always possible to complicate the process by exposing the organism to more and more sources of stimulation, forcing the bimodal curve to resemble the normal distribution curve more and more. For a precise analysis, however, we must look for the functional units that are observable when simple stimulus patterns give rise to simple identifiable responses, and here we find that continuity holds for elementary responses, discontinuity for competing conditioned-response systems.

The question may be raised whether this situation, as exemplified in Razran's experiment, arises from the very fact that there is a set, a well-defined attitude at work. Suppose there were no attitude at work; suppose the perception and response were "unloaded." The reply is that *loading is always present* because, as we have seen, there are always nodal points, centers of high tension. "Free association" has proved to be controlled association in which the control, or set, is not clearly recognized. The fruitless quest for freedom from dynamic causation, the attempt to be spontaneous in the abstract, has shown merely that unrecognized or unverbalized sets or tensions have stepped in to replace those that are better recognized. We may be conscious or unconscious of set, conscious or unconscious of the tension system of which our behavior is an expression; but there is always a set and consequently there are always dominance relations.

Dissatisfied with this reply, our critic may well bring forward a more trenchant, probing question: Have we not overdone the nodal points; have we not ignored the fact that the organism is always subject to multiple stimulation, and hence exposed to the joint activation of multiple conditioned responses? Does this not mean in practice that a multitude of dominance relations must exist, and ultimately a network of action patterns, all of which give and take energy and result eventually in an integrated pattern in which many components are expressed? If so, do we not come back to continuity and imperceptible gradations?

However trenchant the question, the answer is in the negative. Dominance is defined empirically in terms of that response to a given situation which is biologically stronger than every other competing response tendency. The functional unit is therefore dominant not merely over one system, but over all others. Let a thousand identifiable stimuli be acting on the child as he is dropped from his mother's arms; the fact remains that he wails and clutches, these being perfectly compatible responses, and that a great variety of incompatible responses are completely eliminated. Similarly, the adult is called upon to make a complex decision that affects his entire life; much thought and much exploratory behavior may follow, but the final response is a matter of acceptance or rejection, affirmation or denial of some critical possibility that exploration has revealed. The end response is unitary, despite the multiplicity of stimulation. Even indecision or vacillation represents at the moment a simple and unitary response; as Hamlet and many another sick soul show convincingly, such behavior is itself as simple and unitary, is as much a form of decision, as any overt behavior is.

The process of achieving a unitary response necessarily involves a series of preliminary subresponses, each of which upon analysis proves to be based on a response as simple and unitary as is the final outcome. Experimental studies of the thinking process and the decision process always eventually reveal the discrete all-or-none character of the critical steps, the exclusion of some cues and the following of others at each point in the venture, each step revealing the dominance relations within the pattern at each moment.

None of this, however, denies in any way the basic significance of the clues that have been offered by the concepts of facilitation and inhibition. The threshold for a response depends upon the whole stimulus situation. It may be lower when two or three stimulating factors are present than when one alone is at work. Three annoying remarks, each from a different person, may lower the threshold for a blowup as effectively as one direct insult. The fact that many motives are jointly involved and many outer stimuli are being jointly received means that the presence or absence of a given final reponse will depend upon reinforcement among the stimuli. Thresholds constitute just as central a clue in multiple stimulation as in unitary stimulation. It is necessary only to define the situation completely and indicate the functional value of the various components, to understand why a multiplicity of stimuli evokes the response when a single stimulus fails. The all-or-none principle and the threshold principle hold for the final common path, whether the act is simple or extremely complicated. In the same way, inhibition arises from the fact that the presence of one stimulus makes impossible the effectiveness of another; indeed, from the present point of view, inhibition is simply a name for the fact that a non-dominant stimulus cannot for the time being successfully compete with the stimulus or stimulus pattern which is activating response through the final common path.

These guiding principles emerging from laboratory situations appear to help a good deal in understanding the more complex dynamics of social participation. Elements in a complex pattern leading to a given social response, like kindliness or aggression, may be present and constantly reinforced, but the final pathway to action or even to consciousness may be blocked by the dominant response to some other element in the pattern. Any shift in dominance may thus cause a dramatic shift in overt response to the configurational stimulus. For instance, fear of and contempt for the Negro, constantly reinforced in some communities, may be submerged by rational or idealistic or affectionate attitudes until something happens either to increase the fear or to diminish the strength of the favorable attitude. Temporary shifts in dominance in at least some members of a lynching posse appear; more enduring shifts may appear during a period of unemployment, where the rational attitude of tolerance must withstand the quasi-rational desire to eliminate a group of competitors for the jobs available. During such periods the reaction of the white worker is typically not one of frank pursuit of his self-interest, but rather a release of violent anti-Negro feeling. This reaction is inadequately explained as hypocrisy or simple rationalization (although these factors doubtless contribute and may be dominant for a few demagogues). The explosiveness of the race riot, the stubborn irrationality of race feelings, suggests rather that we are dealing with a conditioned emotional response which was started early in life, was reinforced by countless small impacts, and is easily assimilable to other conditioned responses. "Normally" the hostility to the Negro is blocked or at least controlled by other conditionings. No demagogue has yet suggested a pogrom against redheads, who are easily identifiable as potential scapegoats. A pogrom must build upon a well-established conditioned response system, even though to the naïve observer—or to the scientific observer—the signs by which a Jew is to be identified are no more indicative of inimical traits than red hair. The sudden emergence of anti-Negro feeling in a factory, of anti-semitic feeling in a whole country, is perhaps most easily explained as a shift toward dominance of aspects of a complex pattern which were previously blocked.

Probably most of our major culture concepts are of this sort; i.e., complex organized tendencies to action are touched off by a symbol: Our Country; Fascism; Communism; Free Enterprise; Motherhood; etc. All these concepts have a configurational unity which is, in part, a verbal convention, but which often demands forthright action of an all-or-none character. The generalization is made by the social group. The individual experience, however, which goes into the making of such concepts by the process of generalization and differentiation, is extremely diverse. No two persons have had the same experience of the Negro, of free enterprise, or even of motherhood. Nor, on the other hand, have the experiences of individuals been so completely haphazard as to produce *no* uniformity as regards direct conditionings. Typically the child encounters certain *groups* of experiences in relation to any one of these major abstractions which tend to build up relatively well-defined separate constellations of potential response, and which may be in sharp contradiction with each other.

"Mother," for instance, as the chief exponent of sphincter control and property rights against the natural impulses of the child, becomes the focus of a pattern in which resentment, hostility, and fear must play an important role. "Mother" as the source of food, of pleasurable contact, and protection, becomes a focus for generalization in a very different direction. The infant reacts now in terms of one pattern, now in terms of the other, with *relative discontinuity*, his own feelings of frustration or gratification preceding an appreciation of the mother as agent in an enduring, object sense. As the child grows older, "mother" as a recurrent fact of everyday life in a social setting requires a much more consistent pattern of response. It is unlikely that either of the intense infantile responses can simply vanish. It is more probable that the later configurational response to "mother"— and to stimuli which have somehow got tied into the earlier foci— will often be an unstable affair, based upon a blocking-off of unacceptable subpatterns rather than their complete elimination. These patterns cannot compete successfully for the final pathway to overt expression, and must often be "unconscious" as well. The resentment of the infant toward the punishing mother is, of course, very hazily related to the objective women he comes to appreciate later. Rather, the adequate stimuli for such a pattern are likely to be such fragments as were vivid in infancy and typically appear to the adult as fortuitous. They may remain adequate stimuli for hostile behavior—which can be freely expressed so long as the relationship to the later mother image is so obscure that it does not involve competition with patterns of behavior dominant at a later stage.

Thus the configurational conditioned response to a dynamic abstraction like "mother" is highly complex, with many structured potentialities not expressed in overt action at any given moment. A rather well-articulated system of hostility and resentment (or infantile demand for gratification) may be simply cut off from expression, and be ready for appearance with a shift in the equilibrium of dominance—as in the above example of the sudden appearance of violent anti-Negro feeling. Or these patterns may receive regular expression, while the provoking stimulus is not recognized as part of the "mother" pattern and therefore does not simultaneously arouse those reaction systems which would then preempt the effector pathways.

This analysis of the likely structure of the conditioned response to a complex stimulus strongly suggests the formulations arrived at independently by psychoanalytic observers: unconscious hostility actively repressed by other factors in the first case; unconscious hostility expressed in disguised form in the second case. (Or, just as easily, intense longings for pleasure and unqualified support.) Psychoanalytic theory as such will be considered later (Chapters 20–23). It seems important here to suggest the possibility of a basis for such formulations essentially similar to that developed in the laboratory.

Configural Conditioning

Is the joint influence of many stimuli in determining a response a matter of sheer summation or of patterning? It is both, depending on the state of the organism and the spatial and temporal arrangement of the stimuli. A single drop of acid on the flank may fail to elicit the scratch reflex, but temporal summation may be produced by applying a drop every thirty seconds, and spatial summation by applying a drop at many points. Similarly, we may not "mind" a dozen bantering remarks but crack up at the thirteenth. It is also frequently observed that the arrangement of appropriate patterns of stimulation gives rise to response, whereas the separate raw components in another arrangement have no such power. This problem, which was posed by Gestalt psychology, is defined by Razran in terms of "configural conditioning."

Most conditionings are conditionings to *patterns*, not to isolated stimuli. The transfer or generalization is based upon the recognizability of identical or similar patterns. Razran has shown that there may be good transfer from one pattern to another without any transfer from the isolated elements of the first pattern to similar elements that appear later. The converse process, the process of recognizing and responding to similar elements and ignoring their contexts, has also been demonstrated experimentally. In the former case, the dominance of the pattern depends upon the interrelations among all the stimulating factors; no one of them alone exerts any clear control over the organism. In the latter case, a single stimulus item does the work; a response to a pattern continues in full force when only one ingredient in the pattern is presented. This is Hollingworth's redintegration principle. Since many components of the stimulus pattern have been exercised in relation to the given response, it might be argued that each part could serve as well as the whole. This, however, seems an exaggeration; to determine which parts can thus serve is an empirical problem.

Complex conditioned responses to a pattern strongly suggest that *unnoticed* features of a complex situation may play an important part in determining the response. The rapid, unanalyzed evaluation of a person or situation (constituting part of what is meant by "intuition") may be due to single or multiple elements, or to their configurations, which are not consciously noted.[1] It is probable that the everyday

---

[1] There is some evidence, indeed, to suggest that conditioned responses may be established to *subliminal* stimuli, but this has not been confirmed. In any event, this issue is apparently not involved in configural conditioning.

acquisition of a personality pattern depends more on the configural situation than on the conditioning to isolated stimuli. The child acquires his patterns from patterned social stimulation for the most part; he does not need to verbalize the separate phases of the situation, for it is their configuration which carries social and personal meaning. The instantaneous sizing-up of the needs of others, the instantaneous recognition of one's own predicament, appear to follow this principle.

The configural responses appear to be long-lived and to die out at a rate which becomes increasingly slower as the number of elements capable of being reinforced increases. Spontaneous recovery, a phenomenon characteristic of most types of conditioning, can easily occur whenever any phase of the complex is reinforced. Variations within the organism and within the background factors of the situation occur even when the obvious "stimulus" does not vary. Spontaneous recovery of personal and social attitudes which apparently had disappeared is commonplace in fatigue, strain, or emotional upset. The fact that the various elements in a configuration reappear frequently under the ordinary conditions of daily existence probably results in their receiving much more reinforcement than is given to specially prepared, isolated stimuli.

Razran's experiment remains within the relatively simple domain of spatial arrangement. Most personality integration involves the patterning of stimulation from various modalities, a patterning in which sensory modalities are combined with complex ideational and affective elements. The final response, unitary as it always must be, is a function of the configuration itself; in the configuration the patterning of outer stimuli, complex as it may be, is still simpler than the patterning of internal visceral or muscular or cortical components.

One important form of personality integration consists of the patterning of internal tensions which permits a specific end result, to the exclusion of competing end results; integration appears both in the preconditions of response and in the response itself. There are, of course, many other problems relating to the dynamics of the integration of responses, e.g., the spatial, temporal, and other patterns which serve as a recognizable basis for the individual's personality style; to them, however, we shall return later (Chapter 26).

The Persistence and Continuity of Conditioned Responses

It is time to state and dispose of an apparent contradiction. Simple motor habits of the conditioned-response type—like responding to one door rather than another to get one's coat—arise in the service of temporary needs and are very unstable; they tend to disappear as rapidly and as easily as they appear, for they come whenever a new stimulus is attached to a need situation, and they start to disappear as soon as the stimulus is detached from the situation. On the other hand, we live our lives largely in terms of conditioning; from the time we wake up until we go to sleep (and even in our sleep as well) our acts are a continuous series, a never-ending web of conditioned responses—to our clothes, our breakfasts, our razors or our hair nets, our trains or autos, our jobs or recreation, our mates, our children, our names, our pictures of ourselves. These responses are tough; they do not disappear, they wrap us up in an ever-tighter ball as we grow older. Conditionings express for us not the evanescent but the continuous in life. It is hardly sufficient to say that they persist because they "serve needs." Whence comes all this continuity?

The major clues to this continuity are really not hard to discover. One is the fact of the time lag in tissues, any tension giving way only slowly to modifying conditions. And energy within a biological system passes from one point to another; most of it is not dissipated out of the system but goes into other parts of the system, the system as a whole losing its energy only slowly. By way of postures or words which keep a person set in a given direction, moreover, many of the internal factors involve circular responses in which the carrying out of an act or even the naming of it keeps the set constant and leads to continuity or repetition.

Let us look at these mechanisms more closely. The situation, whatever it be, that gives rise to a response tends to overlap in time with the execution of the response in such fashion that one experiences the response while the original excitation is still present. Whatever fragments of babbled or gurgled response are heard by the child are necessarily heard while the responses are still being activated. He becomes conditioned to his own vocalizations and repeats them almost indefinitely, being thus provided with a full-fashioned set of vocal tools which later become words and patterns of words. In the same way, whatever activity he embarks upon is experienced through the sense organs at the very time that he is embarking upon it. He begins crawling and keeps crawling; he begins humming and continues to hum; he laughs and goes on laughing. He is, we say, *perseverating*, a term for that type of circular response in which the activity is continuous rather than phasic. But in either event, whether phasic or continuous, activities which begin as a result of some trivial detail of stimulation may be incorporated within the structure and become stable features of more and more complex acts. They may, of course, be extinguished if these more complex acts are extinguished; but circular or perseverative activities become an essential feature in a larger act which is itself constantly elicited. There is, then, from the simplest stomach cramp to the prolonged effort toward a goal, a physiological and psychological continuum, a process of self-reinforcement. All personality structure is replete with cramp-like perseverative trends of this sort, and as far as we can see they belong clearly to the category of conditioned responses. They are all, even the most "mechanical" expression of tension, motivated, dynamic; but more tension is involved in some than in others.

Regarding the whole problem of perseveration and the circular response, Holt's view is exceedingly clarifying. When any tension within the body arouses restlessness from which action follows, the action propels the organism into new aspects of the environment. These new aspects act upon the organism while the tension is still at work; their stimulus energies converge upon the channel which is already in use, namely, the channel from tension center to bodily movements. These new aspects thus become stimuli which can later initiate the bodily movements. Whatever the organism has got itself into acts later to draw the organism to it again. One does more of what one has already done. Holt calls this principle *adience* (cf. page 167).

As far as a further principle underlying the persistence of conditioned responses is concerned, we have suggestive rather than convincing evidence. Ordinarily perseverative trends are fairly easily broken by factors which force changes in the overt responses, changes that render physically impossible the continuation of the muscular activity. There is, however, at least one striking exception, the phenomenon known as "autonomic locking." Unstriped muscle may undergo tension for an extraordinary length of time beyond the original excitation; even a powerful interfering agency (for example, large doses of opiate in the gastrointestinal muscles) may fail to break the grip of the tension. It appears likely that this locking of muscles under autonomic control depends upon an all-or-none mechanism; i.e., that it will occur as the excitation reaches a certain level but not if the level is slightly lower. Under such circumstances the tense system of muscles cannot be relaxed by any ordinary combination of slight psychological or physiological sedatives.

Another type of circular mechanism has recently been carefully studied. A surface scratch, as by a bullet, may initiate a constant and progressive pain that persists for months or years. A practical therapy depends on cocaine, which quickly cuts into the circular mechanism for pain and permits restoration of normal function, whereupon the drug can be discontinued. We have only begun to learn about the many circular, self-maintaining systems of the organism.

The facts of transfer, cross conditioning, and hierarchical structure mean that dominant features remain although others are lost. They may even mean, as details drop out and new ones are added, that there is continuity of the *structure* without continuity of the *parts*, like Aristotle's celebrated knife which was still the same even though on one occasion he had replaced the handle and on another occasion had replaced the blade. The formal continuity of the body as a whole, though every molecule of its structure is replaced from time to time, is paralleled by the formal continuity of personality structure in this sense.

One more reason for the longevity of conditioned responses calls for emphasis: The continual expression of the tension system is likely, as Holt has so well shown, to keep the individual in the very situation in which these particular responses were elicited. The hierarchical pattern of adult conduct, being more integrated than that of the child, tends to keep the adult in contact with those aspects of the environment which lead him to continue doing the things upon which he has already embarked. Not only is the adult less "plastic" than the child; he is less likely to do things which would throw him out of contact with the environment upon which the continuous and repeated acts as a "stable personality" depend. Many conditioned responses persist notoriously, though they do not give pleasure (e.g., a "foreign" accent, maladaptive mannerisms), and many interfere seriously with living (e.g., neurotic habits); but they all express conditioned tension systems. On the positive side, their persistence is a major factor in giving personality substance and strength. (This issue will lead to the discussion of further problems, especially in Chapters 11, 12, 13, and 30.)

This continuity inevitably maintains some of its focus, some of its dominant elements and their interrelations. Despite the interflowing, the relative permeability of traits by one another, the total must hold its focus to some extent—partly because, as we have seen, the hereditary dispositions have their own relative strengths, partly because the intensity and amount of reinforcement of their conditioned phases are preserved in time, partly because the same broad environment which played its part in establishing the hierarchical structure tends, on the whole, to persist. There would have to be some continuity of traits and of total structure even in a whirling environment, but there would have to be some continuity in response to a continuous environment even if inner structure had very little rigidity.

At least until the point of the active acquisition of language, the definition of enduring personality traits appears to be given by the principles thus far discussed—constitution, adience, hierarchical structure, and environmental continuity—taken jointly. The personalities of newborn children show considerable continuity from month to month by virtue of these factors; children transplanted to new environments show some but much less continuity. The social traits of three-year-olds are rather stable if the group and the teacher remain together, but with a shift to a new group the individual child may change markedly. It is of the nature of the growing-up process to achieve ever-greater stability, continuity; this is certainly in part a matter of the disciplines, ego structurings, responsibilities that go with marriage, job, and place in community.

It is through our own responses to these personality constants or continuities that we evaluate or change the characters of small or adolescent human beings. It is through observation of their persistent temperamental idiosyncrasies and their areas of generalization and differentiation of conditioning, and through knowledge of the background and foreground of their social environment that we appraise them, compare their drawings or their finger-painting with their gestures and play preference, write character sketches of them that are recognizable by those who have known them in other situations or in terms of a Rorschach record. Usually, of course, we use all these cues at once; in other words we, as judges, make transferred conditioned responses based on our own experience with children, differentiating as the situation requires and hierarchically integrating the multiple cues which each behavior disposition affords.

The Elaboration of Motives Through Conditioning

In view of the elaborations that have been introduced in the past few chapters, it will be well now to look more closely at the theory of motives that was sketched briefly in Chapters 5 and 6. We have seen that no drive is absolutely fixed or independent, like an organ stop in the vast panel of individual motivation. Some drives are more distinguishable than others; others, like the activity drives, are almost infinitely fluid. All these drives are conceived to be quantitatively modified by the very fact of their canalization and conditioning, and the cross conditioning of the various phases in the activity stream serves further to interlock them. It begins to appear that drives are independent to the same degree that muscular reactions or sensory responses are independent. Just as heightened tonus at one region means the heightening of some and the lowering of other tensions in the body, and just as a sensory stimulus produces intersensory effects (cf. page 334), so the sheer activation of any tension system involves a reshifting of tensions. There are, then, no pure drives. It consequently follows that organic techniques (page 130) will often be helpful in studying some of the drives because through such techniques the inner process of the relative differentiation of a drive can be more clearly seen; the mode of the environmental molding of tissue development can also be better understood in the light of such measures. Often, notably in the case of the activity and sensory drives, these organic techniques are very limited, the psychophysical totality being approached more easily in terms of the environmental pressures which we can observe. In these cases we can more easily witness the process by which a momentary sensory or activity pattern becomes consolidated or crystallized into a motor set, to form a persisting drive which in some individuals may be regarded as the chief motive or central value.

An example is the curiosity motive, always present in normal infancy, and easily observable as *anticipatory response* and *delayed reaction* become more marked. Not only is the individual stimulus object pursued when absent from the senses, but a *generalized disposition* is established to follow all that recedes from the senses. With the rapid gain in both sensory and motor contact with the world, the number of these pursuing reactions multiplies astronomically; the child is "into everything" and his "Why" questions dominate all others. Curiosity, then, is "instinctive" in the broad sense that one inherits sense organs, a peripheral nervous system, and a brain which permits symbols to persist beyond the action of the objective world that gives rise to them. Curiosity is "learned" in the sense that the type of objects which come and go, and the type of pursuit of them, as well as the general tendency to persevere in this quest, depend largely on the way in which the social order handles childish needs of this sort.

Gregariousness—the primitive satisfaction in the presence of bodies and voices—is evident even in children a few weeks old; satisfaction in contact and persistent stimulation leads to canalizations upon others, and is generalized so far as persons are satisfying rather than frustrating objects. The gregariousness of chicks and mice, in this broad sense of a positive response to the form and vocalization of others, appears very early, depending a good deal on temperature satisfactions as well as on those of sight and sound. The same general pattern holds for infants who converge upon one another as a result of the simplest stimuli of sight, sound, and touch, and who through adience do so more and more, at the same time that they develop more complex satisfactions in give-and-take and in the more complex types of play which necessitate this give-and-take.

Acquisitiveness or possessiveness appears when the momentary possession of objects for their own exploitation proves insufficient; when the child develops a tendency to anticipate the future, wanting to make sure that the object will be there for him when he comes back. The trait occurs in proportion to the ego enhancement which possessions bring in a society that evaluates an individual in large measure through the size, number, and value of the objects which cluster mystically about him as parts of himself (cf. pages 493 ff.). Whenever there is need for the sustained and unchallenged control of an object, there will be acquisitiveness; and whenever possessions enhance the self, there will be acquisitiveness in marked degree.

One might, in this way, briefly sketch the probable genesis of many of the social drives. Two types of response, however, are of such supreme importance in personality structure as to require a more elaborate theoretical treatment: first, the development of generalized sympathy or cooperative attitudes, or attitudes of identification with other members of the group; second, the genesis and elaboration of the ego needs, the needs centering in the craving for personal adequacy and recognition.

A major clue to the former patterns lies in primitive gregariousness of the type just described. A second is the reinforcement of the child's satisfaction in himself through parental approval and encouragement. A third is afforded by his strong affections and powerful canalizations upon his parents and playmates. A fourth is derived from his intense need of support, his concern about others because he needs them. A fifth lies in the mechanism of the primitive sympathy response (cf. pages 221 ff.), which makes the distress of others precipitate a response like that to his own distress. Finally, over and above all these factors, there is the diffuse glow, or affection, or love, or "positive response" that the healthy, non-frustrated child is ready to pour upon the world, which C. H. Cooley called "primitive kindliness."

These six principles would be sufficient to account for a powerful tendency on the part of the child to treat the joys and distresses of others as if they were his own. But this raises the following problem: Since sympathy is present and grows apace with these contributing factors, why does it fail? Why are children sometimes unsympathetic? And why do they sometimes become less rather than more so month by month? Such questions give an opportunity to show in practice the difference it makes whether the principle of dominance is or is not used. The child turns suddenly from affectionate sympathy to a violent hostility in which every sympathetic element is lost, if the primitive processes upon which his life depends are interfered with because of a stomach-ache or adult interference. Generalized disturbances, organic or social, can produce a generalized blockage of sympathy; the most sympathetic child may become either sullen or violent. By the same token, the enlargement of the world of happy contacts may generalize a sympathetic disposition, so that such attitudes toward human beings and animals prevail in general without discrimination. Furthermore, sympathy shows itself so far as transfer of response from self to other is possible. It stops when the similarity of self to other is not evident, or when the principle of differentiation has stepped in (cf. page 209) and made further generalizations impossible. "We are nice to the X's; we hate the Y's." The individual will consequently vary not only with respect to the specific people with whom he sympathizes, depending on nearness and dearness, but in the range of his sympathies. It is this range of sympathies that we shall treat below (page 810) under the head of *cooperative habits*. Individual differences in organic make-up, notably those expressed in health and well-being, are important, but the major clue toward understanding so important a trait is apparently the opportunity given the child to transfer broadly to all kinds of people the early sympathetic responses of which children are capable.

As to the ego needs, we noted earlier that canalization upon the self usually accompanies and augments most other canalized responses; indeed, it often overshadows in importance the wish or endeavor directed toward the external canalized object. At its simplest level this may mean that the value of these outer objects lies chiefly in their enhancement of self-esteem or self-love, or in the protection of the self against injury or humiliation. The term *prestige* may be used very broadly to define this self-enhancing struggle; if no rigid conception of class roles is involved, the term *status* will serve well. The quest for prestige in a competitive society like our own usually proves to be a quest for acceptance, for full membership as a peer, or, if it goes further, a quest for preeminence and the leader's role.

There appear to be ego needs of this sort in all societies, but their intensity varies clearly with the cultural situation. Among the Arapesh of New Guinea, acceptance as a member of the group is apparently the sole desideratum; indeed, positions of preeminence are avoided when possible. The Maori of New Zealand apparently considered it enough to be one of the horde identified with the leader, through whose prestige the individual's ego needs were vicariously satisfied. In the economically competitive societies, whether of the South Seas or the Mediterranean basin, class and family prestige are augmented by individual prestige.

Prestige is by no means always conveyed by economic success; the quest for gain may at times bring reproof, and many of the positions that carry the highest status are bestowed on those who have removed themselves from the current economic competition. Nevertheless, the mainspring of the cultural institution of prestige-seeking seems intimately related to the quest for gain, and no one could possibly view the two needs in conjunction without suspecting a cogent and necessary relation between them. For the present we shall defer any attempt to say (with the economic determinists) that competitive economic institutions predetermine the prestige values of the various forms of success, or (with some of the psychoanalysts) that the ego structure may itself be fundamental to economic as to other institutions. It is only necessary to insist here that the two needs, the need for gain and the need for prestige, are psychologically as distinguishable as are any two other needs; and that while the two bear an intimate relation in our own society, this is by no means true of all human cultural arrangements.

A third need, however, has an intimate relation to both of these. This is the need for power. The need in a little child to dominate what threatens him, to forestall attack—the security need—is interwoven with joy in manipulation, control, and creation. Their interweaving in the various forms of striving for power takes place so early that we can say little about the components, their relative strengths and their mode of integration. Manipulation of material things must of course be included among the activity drives; but it is evident very early that manipulation occurs not only for the sake of being active, but for the fun of seeing the emerging product, as the child draws, models, or puts together objects which delight him. His diffuse infantile writhings have been replaced by organized control of the environment; the ego *underlies*, or perhaps we should say the ego *is* this organized control of the environment (cf. page 523). He is soon busy also in manipulating and controlling people, both for the primitive manipulative satisfactions and for the fun of the end product, the dramatic scene or specific play group which for one reason or another he wants to set up. The power need in all its richness is evident enough in the three-year-old.

It is usually assumed in discussions of our competitive society that the power need and the prestige need are the same. But the three-year-old can teach us a great deal on this point. There are many types of passive enjoyment of prestige situations, as when a child suns himself in the admiring gaze of those whose comments on a new toy or suit give him momentary status. Often the prestige need becomes deeply ingrained, and in many such people the efforts at mastery or power arise merely as devices for the achievement of prestige satisfaction. One overpowers one's playmates not because of aggression or sadism, but as a means to achieving the resulting prestige of the victor. On the other hand, many children care far more for power than for status; they expand their manipulative tendencies to a point that involves the outright control of others, without seeming to care in the least about the prestige attached thereto; their enjoyment of being the power behind the throne may in time be so completely adequate that their identity as individuals is lost. So among adults, one quickly spots the political boss whose satisfaction is almost a pure exploitation of power, and the many professors and ministers who care much less for gain and power than for pure prestige.

Just as the prestige need and the gain need are in time woven together and almost assimilated to each other, so in our society the power need tends to integrate with the other two. Individuals manifesting one of these needs but not the other two are decidedly interesting; but to most persons most of the time the quest for a "better position" means their simultaneous elevation to a position of greater gain, greater power, and greater prestige. Frequently the stimuli for any one of the three touch off all three together. There may be something a little deeper than this, an actual *fusion* of the various wants along the lines already discussed (pages 89 ff.); e.g., men may compete for all three without the body's making a sharp distinction in terms of three physiological mechanisms. Hence it may prove sociologically more accurate, in connection with certain cultures, to speak of a competitive society than of the specific types of competition for the three goals involved. For *individual* analysis, however, it is frequently important to specify the areas in which the individual vehemently competes and those in which he is relatively or absolutely indifferent. In many a satisfying job these social needs combine well with sensory and activity satisfaction—the forester who loves the woods—and all may combine with the ego needs (Chapter 20) based on a picture of the self.

But as we shall see later in more detail (Chapters 32 ff.), there is a huge difference between limited and unlimited demands, between a "fair share" which is socially defined and a free-for-all competition for what one can get. In all societies known to us, the individual craves to be accepted, needs self-respect; he needs a modicum of material goods and of power over his own environment. These demands, however, can be easily satisfied; and when they are satisfied, the balance of his life may be governed by a philosophy of "live and let live." But in certain societies the demands for gain, power, and prestige are so organized that success feeds upon success, and no bounds are set on the expanding empire to which these demands may lead. This may be contrasted with Nehru's statement regarding India: "An attempt was made to prevent the joining together of honor, power, and wealth." To this theme of individual organization we shall return in Chapters 19 and following, when the development of the individual outlook and point of view has been considered.

11. The World of Symbols

PERSONALITY differences are in large measure individual differences in response to symbols. A word, a gesture, a nod symbolize different things to different people. Two children in the sandbox live in two different worlds; two men behind roll-top desks respond utterly differently to the same appeals for charitable contributions.

Yet we have told only half the story when we say that individuals respond differently to different symbols. People carry around within them their own symbols; their own inner cues keep them oriented to distant objects. These devices for orienting to objects not physically present have been clarified by experiments on the "delayed response." A light, for example, is exposed above a door that leads a small child to a toy; there are other doors, unlighted, that do not. He learns by trial and error that it is only the lighted door that takes him to the toy. He is then restrained while the light is exposed, and for an interval after it has been extinguished; but on being released he makes for the right door. He chooses it correctly, although there is no light now to guide him.

In a delayed response, a response to objects after they have ceased to act on the senses, "representative factors" within the organism guide its conduct appropriately and bring it into contact again with the goal object. The object has left something behind, a trace, a tissue modification in the organism, and to this residual trace a response is made as if the original object were still present. The stability of these inner cues which maintain or reinstate adjustment varies greatly with the species, and among human individuals. A conditioned motor readiness, or motor set, of the body is often sufficient for the purpose; a verbal symbol may be substituted for or combined with it; a visual schema may be introduced, especially when the kinesthetic or verbal pattern, strung along in *time*, would be cumbersome as compared with a visual "map" portraying the whole situation at once. The important thing is that such inner schemata, whether fully visual, or fully kinesthetic (as in certain painters studied by Galton), are as

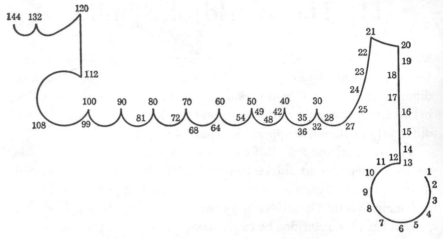

distinctive of the individual as are his expressive movements. Galton published a number of examples of the ways in which people visualize numbers. The accompanying illustration shows the "number form" of a person who started with the numbers as they appear on the clock face.

As life goes on, people develop more and more internal symbolic activity of this type, activity that refers to the world with which they deal; the personal world is largely comprised of the idiom of these personal systems of symbolism. The stuff of such symbolism proves, in most people, to be largely patterns of *words* acquired early and constantly enriched and complicated through use in a wider and wider variety of situations. It becomes necessary, then, to look more closely at words, and to consider them first of all simply as conditioned motor responses, for it is in this form that they first appear.

The Acquisition of Language

Among the infant's effector mechanisms which are active a large part of the time—partly because of external stimulation, partly because shifts occur in inner tensions—must be mentioned the vocal cords, the respiratory muscles, and the muscles that alter the shape and position of the lips, tongue, and soft palate. A blow, a flash of light, or a hunger pang may bring forth a whimper or a moan; a rustling sound or a gentle touch may give rise to a gurgle. Dozens of sounds and hundreds of sound combinations, at first utterly without symbolic value, are made during the first few weeks of life.

The sounds are in general more likely to occur in active than in quiescent states, and they tend, without the infant's knowing how, to be followed by more or less consistent results. Some tend to bring one kind of result, others another. Sounds that are made very easily and frequently (e.g., the "ma" which results from the opening of the lips when breathing out) may be rather uniformly found to bring similar results—for example, maternal attention—all over the earth, apparently because the person nearest at hand appropriates this common repeatable syllable as a name for herself. In most cases, however, the sounds bring different results in different places. Each child must make many responses until he hits upon one which leads to tension-reducing results; ultimately he acquires a speech pattern which, like other motor patterns, is the end phase of a long process of elimination and fixation, a whittling-off process which leaves at last one satisfying pattern. The same is true of word combinations. At first, words tumble out, but one pattern brings better results than another: "trial-and-error," as in many other learning situations.

The process is socially controlled at every stage. It is not enough that the child makes himself understood; he must talk like one of us. The slightest ridicule acts as social pressure; and if not the adults, at least the older children in the group will see to it that baby talk, or any kind of "funny" talk (relative to what is expected at a given age), achieves unsatisfactory results for the speaker. Baby talk may be perpetuated by older brothers or sisters who think it cute, in spite of adult effort to remove it; but it is usually eliminated as the child tries to meet the standards of "talking right" which the adults' corrections imply. So far is the social control of childhood speech carried that, in the matter of accent, adults learning a foreign language cannot compete at all with the little child's phonetics. The adult, having learned one way, would have to work long and hard with every position of the speech organs to pronounce the new language correctly; there is no such *pressure* on him to break the existing habits of articulation and organization.

Moreover, early in this babbling or bubbling stage, the infant imitates himself, echoes and reechoes a fortuitous combination (page 221), and similarly echoes what others say. If they are doing something while they name the act, the sounds used by the child come to be the means of making the act occur again (a very reasonable form of "magic").

More or less simultaneously with these processes of acquiring *active language*, the child encounters verbal symbols uttered by other persons and embedded in contexts of things and acts, so that the verbal symbol comes to stand for the thing or act; this is *passive language*. When looking at a ball he hears "ball"; while eating, he hears the word "eating." The word becomes a symbol for the object or act; the words of others can now set going the action patterns tied to them. One says to the infant, "Where is your ball?" and he starts hunting for it. In time the action patterns are abbreviated and appear only as inner adjustments, preparations, localized primarily in the appropriate muscles. Indeed, the meaning of a word appears to lie partly in such motor adjustments (cf. page 265); the little child knows what a ball is partly because when it is mentioned his hand tends to clutch, his arm to throw. The behaviorist hypothesis that a trace of such action patterns remains ever after may well be correct.

Through the delayed response, the child comes also to be able to sustain verbal reactions to, and thus to make contact with, an object after it disappears; he says the word over to himself. An infant whose ball had rolled out of sight maintained her orientation to it by saying "ball" repeatedly until she had crawled around an obstacle and rediscovered it. As the child grows, he can for longer and longer periods maintain such symbolic contact with things not present. The residual trace of the object, perhaps in the form of an image, may serve this purpose; the maintenance of set toward a distant object appears in most cases to depend upon postural (kinesthetic) and other non-verbal factors as well, but as a rule either the utterance of the word or its schematic inner rehearsal is a necessary conditioned stimulus for adjustment to or pursuit of the absent object. The true difference between man and other animals in responding to things that do not act on the senses is in large part a matter of words. Even with the two-year-old child, the word for anything he wants is likely to recur just as it will with the adult who has lost his way or his watch. The verbal elements do indeed appear to be superposed upon a deeper constancy of muscular orientation which accompanies and enhances the appearance of words. But the more complex the adjustment to a distant object the less adequate is kinesthetic orientation and the greater is the reliance upon the use of words. If there are two or more absent objects, the two may be symbolically joined or related, and reflective thought has begun.

There is, however, much individuality in all these aspects of speech. This appears first in the shape and strength and tissue relations of the organic responses. Just as the physical structure of the "roller" canary gives him a definite "tone" that differs somewhat from that of the "chucking" canary, the vocal apparatus of the child is distinctive in the earliest weeks. Individuality of voice is recognized even when experimenters seek common qualities appropriate to common external pressures. Moreover, the intensity, pitch, timbre, and time relations vary not only with structure but with the energies, the rhythms of expression; the voice total becomes "self-expressive" (Chapter 27). The selection of one of several possible words, the arrangement of words in any one of several possible ways, become evident marks of individuality as soon as the child passes beyond the one-word sentence. Each child acquires language in his own way, some by precise acquisition of specific words later strung together, others by imitating the rhythm of adult phrases first, then approximating the articulation more and more until something is recognized by the adults. Idiosyncrasies of pronunciation, emphasis, phrasing, continue to be dramatic through the pre-school years. Even at two and three, vocabularies differ greatly. Between three and six, vocabulary may be an especially revealing clue; some children frequently use feeling-tone words which are never used by others. Even at college age it is possible to formulate a picture of personality comparable to what is available through formal projective tests (cf. Chapter 28) by systematic analysis of language patterns. The amount of social stylization in all this is great enough to permit "placing" people by their dialect and conversational style, but not enough to prevent recognizing individuals speaking over the telephone or the radio. Even more important is the individualized mode of using the inner symbolic apparatus to define the different worlds which are real to different persons (e.g., in phantasy); to this we shall return at a later point.

The Retention of Symbolic Elements

If we are dealing with configurations of both stimuli and responses, we shall expect some conditioned responses to be preserved much longer than others. The extinction rates depend upon the intensity and frequency of exercise, but perhaps most of all upon the degree to which a muscle-action pattern is restricted to a specific situation, so that it is free from the extinction effects induced by other habits (cf. page 199). The more widely the action pattern is used, the likelier the general phenomena of interference. For example, as one forgets nonsense syllables largely through the interference to which they are subjected, so he loses muscular action patterns in proportion to their involvement in a variety of situations, i.e., the development of inhibition through dominance. Responses like skating or pedaling and balancing a bicycle, which are used specifically in very specific situations, are notoriously long lived and require minimal reinforcement. Verbal patterns which shift with the needs of life, such as memorized street addresses or the vocabulary of a foreign language, are notoriously short lived. We might consequently expect to find that the higher and more complex symbolic life would be obliterated when not constantly reinforced.

But there must be some other principle at work, because motor and visceral responses to words, and word responses to word stimuli, appear to be extinguished less rapidly than similar responses of non-verbal material. Razran found that conditioned salivary responses to words had a longer life than comparable responses to nonsense syllables; many a well-learned poem or Bible passage may come back after years of disuse, despite the fact that the constituent words have occurred in a thousand situations and have had abundant opportunity to produce interference. At least two factors are probably important in giving language such a favored position. First, it is human; being produced by the modulation of the human voice, it has more appeal than most other things. This may be a partial explanation of Harold Burtt's findings. He read Greek verse aloud to his infant son; when the boy was eight years old (with no rehearsal and of course no "use" of the material on his part) he learned this material significantly faster than he did another Greek passage used as control material. Second, in all probability the verbal systems which are constantly reinforced by being used in life situations as keys to major tasks, duties, and value are strengthened and come to constitute an impor-tant part of the core of personality, whereas the interconnections of words which are not thus reinforced are subject to ordinary extinc-tion. Moreover, deeply ingrained attitudes, sets toward words as *meaningful* sounds, seem to give them a special advantage (cf. page 259).

A further clue to the importance of language is to be found in experimental tests of the psychoanalytic hypotheses about the tendency to forget symbolic material. Thus when shocks were administered in connection with certain words, and the accompany-ing galvanic responses were studied, conditionings were established which outlived memory for the words; the material was *consciously* but not *organically* forgotten. It is quite possible that other factors, such as repression, are at work here, resulting in splitting or dissociat-ing[1] the person into two more or less independent systems (page 325). It is also possible that repression itself may prove to be a special case of interference between symbolic activities. Paralleling this experi-

---

[1] A discussion of various kinds of dissociation appears on pp. 67 ff.

ment is unlimited clinical evidence as to the extraordinarily abiding value which conditionings, especially to words, may have, even in the face of the individual's testimony that the situations occasioning them never occurred.

The mechanism just described does, however, show considerable individual differences. It is possible that these differences obtain with reference not only to the retention of symbolic responses but to the capacity of the individual to function as two more or less independent, dissociated systems, as a result of repression. The greater the dissociation, we may suppose, the greater the discrepancy between conscious remembrance and physiological retention.

This mechanism may be a partial clue to the clinical fact of "trauma." A disturbing incident is not put aside or forgotten; it continues to make trouble—indeed it may do so even when completely forgotten. A child who has been forbidden to play in the water and disobeys, with disastrous consequences, forgets the incident yet is disturbed thereafter whenever she hears running water. Traumatic situations of fear, guilt, and humiliation appear particularly likely to encounter interference at the symbolic or conscious level, i.e., to be non-attended to or even forcibly kept out of consciousness, yet they may enjoy extraordinary longevity as troublemakers. Perhaps we are dealing here, in some of the more extreme cases, with the actual maintenance of unstriped-muscle tension of the type mentioned earlier as *autonomic locking*, or we may be dealing with a *sensitization* of such tissues which permanently lowers thresholds for their fresh activation upon subjection to a new disturbance. Neither of these hypotheses is absolutely required by the evidence, however, and in many cases of trauma they are out of place. The traumatized individual does not ordinarily carry his trauma actively with him in all situations, nor do the tissues react as if they were thus sensitized in a general promiscuous fashion. On the contrary, when certain specific situations are presented analogous to those of the original fear or humiliation, the tissues are thrown into their original state of upheaval; the phenomenon is like a full-fledged normal conditioned response. This looks much less like autonomic locking or sensitization than like physiological retention of an action pattern through sheer intensity and because of the important fact that *interference with it—in other words, extinction—has not occurred;* the trauma persists because there has been no reconditioning (page 224). This in turn occurs because the trauma is an isolated response system, functionally dissociated from the person's main activities, as is attested by his inability to recall the conditions of its origin. Pocketed off, it cannot be directly reached by the reconditioning situation (cf. page 197).

Yet the symbol that is the key to the trauma may at any moment rearouse the visceral and striped-muscle components and keep the trouble going. Anderson's little girl, frightened at twenty-one months by a dog, illustrates the process well. For nearly a year after the frightening episode, she seemed to be practically without animal fears. At thirty months she had a nightmare about a dog; and during the next few days she was, for the first time in a year, terrified by dogs. The "spontaneous recovery" of the fear response in the dream did indeed bear a relation to a dog encountered during the preceding day, old patterns being reactivated. They could hardly have been reactivated, however, had not the symbolic life maintained them. And apparently it was the symbols that started the trouble again; the objective waking situation did not notably reexcite the fear. We shall attempt later (page 281) to indicate why the symbolic life must necessarily lead back constantly to the past, digging up and exploiting not only past joys but past distresses. Here it is important only to show that the conditioned patterns upon which early personality structure depends are often of a symbolic type which not only complicates the simplest physiological responses but often manifests dominance in relation to them, even to the degree of interfering actively with their execution.

Higher-order conditioning (page 224) probably exists in most children two or three years of age without benefit of verbal symbols, but most learning of this order of complexity appears to depend upon mediation of words. Indeed, much that passes for higher-order conditioning is simple first-order verbal conditioning. Suppose, for example, that the pairing of metronome with sugar lump produces salivary response to the metronome. Next the pairing of color wheel with metronome produces salivary response to the color wheel. This may look like second-order conditioning. But in most such instances of which we have direct knowledge, the stimulus twice removed from the original stimulus, e.g., color wheel, even when first presented instigates a verbal reference to the metronome and a verbally expressed expectation of sugar lumps, and consequently may be *directly* linked (first-order conditioning) with the sugar lump. Language is the supreme method of making such short cuts, and it is likely that it is far more often an instrument for such concatenation of conditioning than a true vehicle of higher-order conditioning. If human beings could easily establish and retain conditionings of the second and third order (or even, as one Russian study asserts, of the tenth and eleventh), it is hard to see why the linguistic structure should be so all-pervasive and so utterly necessary in most human acts of any degree of complexity; the linguistic structure serves perfectly to reduce such complex situations quickly to first-order conditionings.

Some non-verbal conditioning of a higher order, we have suggested, probably *does* exist in early childhood, and if so there is probably more of it in the adult. But its role appears to be of minor importance as compared with the role of the deeply ingrained verbal conditionings which, though of the first order, arise under circumstances requiring the establishment of a connection between responses that in themselves are not easily held together. Thus, when a transferred conditioned response fails, as when one tries to use an old habit in a new situation (e.g., "which kind of skeleton key would fit this lock?") he verbalizes the point of similarity between the old situation and the new; if verbalization fails, transfer may fail. In the serial ordering of acts, moreover, he resorts constantly to verbal cement in order to guarantee the proper timing of the sequence (e.g., opening a locker combination, he says to himself, "twice around to the right and then stop at sixteen"). The verbal response, then, is set up in relation to one element and as a regular antecedent or conditioned stimulus for the next. The intervening verbal element may often drop out, just as, in any series of links in a motor pattern, some of them may be dropped because of the adequacy of a new element A to activate not only B but C and even D. But on the slightest failure, the omitted verbal elements reappear and are relied upon.

For all these reasons, there is every cause to be skeptical regarding the frequently encountered assertions that personality traits at the verbal level are unrelated to the deeper personal orientation, regardless of whether these assertions are based on a disparagement of conscious life or on cultural emphasis on the value of language as a means of evasion or escape. It is indeed true that the *particular words* used are often irrelevant or evasive; but it does not follow from this that all words are irrelevant or evasive. Language may be given man "to conceal his thoughts," but by this very process it liberates and puts into circulation other thoughts; symbols control one's own conduct and that of others just as much when used in an unexpected or unfamiliar context as when used in the most naïve communication. It is the symbolic life that gives rise to the need of evasion or escape; hence to disparage the symbolic elements becomes meaningless.

It is not true that the world of symbols and the world of action are different worlds, or that dissociation lifts the individual from the behavioral world into a non-behavioral world. Even the rigidity of the catatonic, who lives in a world apart, is behavior—and behavior with distinct social implications, by way of protest and the construction of an alternative world. The world of symbols comes from the world of action and returns constantly to the world of action. If it fails to do so, even its tough fiber yields to the extinction principle. The fact that extinction is so slow and so difficult is one more bit of testimony to the intensity with which the symbolic world fuses on all sides with the behavioral world, one more reason why personality as conscious system and personality as action system never really drift apart, never exhibit ultimate dissociation. Under ordinary conditions of social living, symbol and act bear about the same relation as the right and left hand in the execution of such tasks as sweeping or shoveling, where one member, the more skillful, directs and limits activity and the other does more of the muscular work. The differentiation is of course sharper than it is between right and left under most normal conditions, but reciprocity of word and act is the rule.

Since outer stimuli are presented in temporal order, the words which become conditioned to them tend likewise to be linked in temporal order; the words "On your mark—get set—go" correspond to a necessary and irreversible outer sequence. Consequently the words themselves are soon linked in this order; the words "on your mark" become a conditioned stimulus for the utterance of "get set"; "get set" is a conditioned stimulus for the word "go." But even more important in the temporal linkage of words is their *cultural* ordering. In English, an adjective expressing color precedes its noun; in French, it follows. The important thing is the sequence of experience as ordered in the learner.

The principle of dominance, as we saw it in the extinction of children's fears (page 197), appears to apply to verbal conditionings in competition with other verbal conditionings, and to verbal responses in relation to overt behavior responses. One word crushes another as one act crushes another, and often enough a word crushes an act. It is in fact characteristic of words to dominate acts, both in the sense that a word overtly or implicitly uttered liberates one act and prevents the occurrence of another, and also in the sense that each word gives rise, in the associative stream, to one word rather than to another competing word, depending upon the dynamics of dominance. Words are examples of interfering responses of the type mentioned above. It is Jones' rather than Long's principle (page 201) that is involved. The presence of one associative link involves the impossibility of another at the same instant; and if the two occur together often enough, the second potential link drops out, is extinguished.

If a human subject is conditioned to a word—if he salivates when the word "bell" is pronounced because it has regularly been followed by a mint drop—will he salivate to a comparable degree when the word "ball" or "bill" is pronounced? On formal physiological grounds we might expect so; if dogs salivate 10 drops per minute to a tuning fork at 256 vibrations, they may salivate 6 drops to a fork at 260 vibrations. The physical resemblance between stimuli should lead to some physical resemblance in response. The evidence from human conditioning, however, suggests that similarity in the sound of words is of minor, often negligible, importance. But if a person who is trained to the word "bell" hears the word "gong" or "ring," which has no phonetic elements in common with "bell," he shows considerable salivary response, comparable indeed to that which appears to the training word itself. This response to meanings as contrasted with formal physical similarities is called semantic conditioning.

Because salivation is subject to complex central factors, it is conceivable that immediately upon the impact of the word "gong" or "ring," associations with the subvocal word "bell" are activated which in turn initiate salivation. This would reduce semantic conditioning to two consecutive conditionings. It will be valuable, therefore, to explore this further along two lines: first, by using a response that is more nearly at the reflex level (e.g., not subject to voluntary control), such as the galvanic skin reflex; second, by using young children whose associative mechanisms are at least considerably simpler than those of adults. B. F. Riess has recently obtained semantic conditioning of the galvanic skin reflex with children at all ages throughout the elementary school period. In the case of the younger children, the opportunity for intervening verbal associations—thinking of the word used in the original conditioning series—is reduced. This does not, however, rule out the possibility that any word heard, e.g., "gong," will excite a pattern of inner responses which overlaps with the one aroused by the conditioned stimulus already used, e.g., bell. Hence, when a conditioned response to "bell" has been established, "gong" will call it forth in whole or in part. (Cf. the discussion of conditioned responses on page 224 in connection with Munroe's work.) The possibilities here are enormous and call for much more research.

FROM OUTER TO INNER SPEECH

A word impressing the ear leads to the little child's repetition of the same word, or of another word, in accordance with dominant motor sets (page 201). Since words are being consolidated as the instruments of wants, the words which are conditioned to the want situation soon become dominant, and sheer repetition of the stimulus word is replaced by the use of speech in the service of major needs. Speech comes to serve these needs as well as, or better than, the earlier non-verbal techniques. Social intercourse as seen in the nursery school shifts from the non-verbal level of smiles, looks, pats, and shoves to "Can I?" "What's your name?" "Don't do that!" The friendly or quizzical or hostile attitude of the questioner predisposes to the arousal of an appropriate attitude (conditioned to this specific approach), and the "Sure," "What's yours?" or "Why not?" answer comes back.

But the words spoken *overtly* are often clumsy and give away too much; so they are in time subdued, truncated, converted to whispers. According to Lorimer's observations, they may sink, at five or six years, from inaudible whispers to "inner speech"—which can still be caught at times by devices that measure lip, tongue, and other speech tensions. Perhaps the muscular components sometimes drop out altogether, only a cortical action pattern remaining. The important thing for personality organization, however, is not their locus (in the speech mechanism or cortex, or both), but their continued capacity, as words, to initiate other words and to carry on the stream of inner speech, the scaffolding of thought, and hence at any appropriate moment to initiate overt action. One is forever signaling to himself.

If we could know the entire activity stream of an adult, including the role of inner speech in this stream, we would, according to the hypothesis, find nearly every emotion, nearly every overt act, traceable in some measure to an inner conditioning in which verbal elements play a vital role. We must here gratefully borrow a formulation which, though undoubtedly oversimplified, has an immense value in the conceptualization of the inner symbolic processes. William James gave us the classic conception of a "stream of thought" (moving forward with a central impetus, but with a thousand eddies and whirlpools), and J. B. Watson, with his "activity stream," puts this into behavior terms. Effector responses, Watson suggested, are of three varieties: (1) the responses of the viscera, comprising unstriped muscles and glands, which we shall call V; (2) the skilled and unskilled movements of the striped muscles, especially skilled manual movements, called M; (3) the skilled movements of the larynx and the entire speech apparatus, designated L. In terms of this schema, the activity stream of the individual appears as a complicated cross-flow of these responses, connected to each other by their conditionings. Late on a summer morning I sit thinking (L_1) of going swimming;

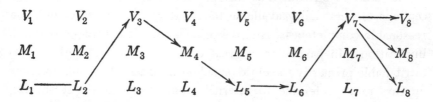

the noon whistle blows, so I realize that there isn't time (L_2) and am irritated (V_3). I start shaving (M_4), shout (L_5) to my brother to get dressed. Soon I am reading the newspaper (L_6), am elated (V_7) to see that the Red Sox won, and with pencil in hand start excitedly to figure out how soon they can reach first place (the response pattern $V_8 M_8 L_8$).

The advantages of the accompanying figure (adapted from Watson) in schematizing the *crossflow* of influences which go on simultaneously with the *forward* flow are evident at a glance. It will be noted that without the principle of dominance the scheme will not work; to each laryngeal response there are many other laryngeal responses, and a host of visceral and manual responses, ready to jump into activity—the words would jumble, the acts would clash, the emotions would be a mincemeat of confusion. The normal course of thought, feeling, or action is hierarchical, integrated, unidirectional, simply because a configural stimulus brings out a configural response, either an old one that occurred before in that configuration or a new one representing a hierarchy of compatible dominant features. Without synergy, compatibility, there would be no dominance; and without compatibility among the potential action patterns there could be no integrated total by which the personality could be recognized either by another or by itself. There must be organization at every instant. The cross section of the stream, as well as its forward flow, is organized. In this important respect it is entirely unlike a stream. There are no real cross-sections, no slices, any more than there is a static balance. If we must think of slices, they must be organized slices which melt into adjacent slices; the forward flow is not the flow of particles, but the gradually shifting equilibrium that achieves new organization momentarily.

The activity stream, thus interpreted, is one of the major conceptions of personality available today. It gives a sense of unity, a reasonable completeness. And the principle holds enormous research implications. In particular, a great deal which at first sight seems attributable primarily to subtle or unknown external stimulation now appears to be referable to internal stimulation, to slight shifting muscular tensions, to inner cues that act as conditioned stimuli to further inner responses or to overt responses. The vitally important role of kinesthesis, muscular circuits, postural and symbolic cues is suggested. Man differs, indeed, from all other animals in being relatively free of direct dependence on immediate external stimulation. Through his inner system of responses, he can adjust to what is absent in space, and plan for what is remote in time. He lives in a symbolic world. Though some of his symbols are visual or auditory images, many are proprioceptive; civilized man is in considerable degree a proprioceptive animal.

While this proprioceptive machinery is being established in the child, its components and its gradual progress toward organization can be observed. And though we should again note that the adult may manage to make many such responses by means of unaided cortical processes (cf. page 260), such processes must, for all that, bear the mark of their original proprioceptive form. Though Watson was certainly wrong in playing down the importance of cortical elements in the adult, we must emphasize that what the "motor men" of 1900 (the early students of the relation of action to consciousness) did to bring psychology closer to evolutionary biology by stressing complete acts, Watson continued to do by stressing the enormous significance of the symbolic apparatus residing in the proprioceptive system and by showing the role of the conditioned response in the establishment of this apparatus.

Symbols, then, become inner cues to action. The outer symbols used by society have been "internalized," "interiorized." Since symbols are definite organic events with a definite locus in a functional context, they act as precipitating and organizing agencies, precipitating in that they initiate action, and organizing in that they simultaneously or successively control a number of responses. They are themselves tension systems, and each one of them arouses the tension system of an act or of another symbol. Just as the symbol arises when its associated need state appears (Sanford's hungry subjects give more "free associations" relating to food than do his satiated subjects), so it may, when once active, initiate need states; thus one's mouth waters at the mention or thought of beefsteak. Two-way associations of this sort are found even in simple motor conditioning; and in the case of speech they are omnipresent.

We have seen that the individual acquires words as he has need of them, and that, once acquired, they can perpetuate and elaborate a need, or divide it into a cluster of distinct related needs, as one does in planning an appetizing meal or a program of music. The symbolic organization of the person becomes both a key to, and a factor in the further shaping of, his personality organization. Much of this is exemplified in the free-chain association method. In a subject who is overwhelmed by a given mood or dominating idea, any chance word touches off a series of terms which may at first appear to move at random but which soon revert to the area of his preoccupation. The word "chair" brought the following sequence from a man brooding over the war: chair, table, operation, wound, bleed, transfusion, cell, prison, captive, camp, Himmler, torture, death, catastrophe, accident, slip, dress, neat, nurse, hospital, etc. In a subject of Luria's who had been hypnotized and told that she would think of birds upon awakening, the following chain appeared: winter, jackdaw, sparrow, eagle, etc. A subject who had been told under hypnosis that he would make up a story when he awoke told the following: "Here in our village was a factory, and near it stood a house. There we met, played, and from the fields came the songs of nightingales." (He did not remember the instructions given him in hypnosis; the mental set operated "unconsciously.") Just as a specific set induced by the experimenter can control the association, so the mood guides the association stream; typically, a minute or two of free association brings the subject back several times to the center of stress. Unconscious stresses, as in the free association of the psychoanalysts, appear to operate here as do the dispositions closer to the level of introspection. From sequences and recurrences such as these, we can observe the superficial play of momentary word associations against a background of sustained tension; whether it be love or fear, the mechanism is the same. The individual is caught in a state of circularly maintained (perseverative) preoccupations or worries. Dominating interests, which, as Thomas Mann puts it, lead "one knows not how, to speak of one knows not what," differ not a whit from the anxiety state which will not let one rest. It makes no difference whether one knows all the original circumstances of his preoccupation or fear, or even that he has such a preoccupation or fear; the tension is there and it suffices. If life presents some huge problem, or ardently desired consummation, or ominous threat, the theme may run through one's fancies, one's dreams, one's words, and even one's mannerisms. The playwright or novelist may have to write his own life struggle over and over again in the lives of his characters.

WORDS AND VALUES

One phase of man's value tendency has been briefly sketched above (page 182) in connection with canalization. We value not only the present but the absent. The symbolic cue sets the stage for behavior which occurs long after the symbol has been removed. We have already referred to the delayed response (page 247). Hours or even days after associating light with toys, the small child, when placed in the situation again, goes to the compartment at which the light formerly appeared; he has conserved the disposition which was set up in the original situation. Allen found that nearly all of the one hundred infants twelve months old whom he studied could maintain this type of set for at least ten seconds.

That the capacity for prolonged maintenance of set is not solely a question of language, but a question of the complexity of nervous organization, is clear; the immense superiority of the infra-human primates over other mammals is shown by the success achieved in training chimpanzees to symbolic behavior involving token rewards. There is likewise the steady development of such capacity in the little child before the advent of language. After the appearance of language, say by two years of age, these sets are maintained for days, the child typically naming the object toward which the set is established. At this age he is beginning to embark upon the vast realm of symbolic linguistic behavior and is in good contact with features of the environment which do not impinge upon his senses. It would appear, then, either that language is a "symptom" showing that a capacity for long-range delayed response is appearing, or that language is itself the clue to the maintenance of such long-range orientation, or that both factors are at work. Judging by the helpfulness of acquiring special vocabularies for dealing with complex tasks, it is likely that the second factor is of overwhelming importance. Perhaps by exploring the world by symbols we may be able to ascertain the techniques by which the individual makes of himself an ever-renewed storehouse of long-range orientation tendencies, and at the same time indicate the reasons for the vast differences between individuals in their capacity thus to substitute the symbol world for the world of immediate stimulation.

Language, moreover, as Lorimer has shown, involves the sharpening of focus, the narrower delimitation of the goal object toward which orientation is maintained. We may, then, set up as a working hypothesis the suggestion *that continuity in goals is in the first instance an expression of "representative factors," the capacity to go on responding to what is no longer present to the senses*, inner linguistic cues playing a huge role among such factors.

Since goal objects are reacted to with some degree of consistency as regards vocalization, posture, and gesture, the process of the transfer and generalization of such responses goes on apace in infancy, so that certain classes of situations that involve satisfactions and frustrations evoke vocalizations, postures, and gestures which parents understand. There is some verbal stereotyping of the classes of satisfying and annoying objects. This classification is at first expressed in the child's own idiom; the mother or big brother or sister must often explain to others how the infant feels about cats or thunderstorms. The use of language by the world surrounding the child produces, however, a modification in his symbolic apparatus, first, as we have seen (page 257), by helping him to make use of the current coin of communication. But he is highly selective in this process; he learns some words more quickly than others, and develops a rich fund of specialized terms which are his own and which portray the deep idiom of his own outlook. He is outwardly and inwardly referring, much of the time, to the goal objects which mean most to him; they are his values and he is *defining* his values; to do this it is not in the least necessary that the goal objects be physically present.

Language is, then, one of the richest personality clues that we possess. Plenty of material has been collected on the speech of early infancy, but this material has almost invariably been organized with reference to levels and forms of communication rather than in terms of the idiosyncrasies of persons. Our interest turns now to the latter. We must ask: In what way does the individual choose from the standardized language of his environment the specific terms that are symbolically needful for him? The first answer, in Piaget's terms, is that he chooses the terms which refer directly to qualities of his own living; there is tremendous emphasis on positive and negative feeling, with interest in purely cognitive distinctions playing a secondary role. Many of the first words represented confused affective, impulsive, and cognitive expressions, the cognitive factors not being sharply defined. To this primitive type of experience Heinz Werner has applied the term "physiognomic"; for our present purposes, this is equivalent to Piaget's term "egocentric." Thus we can tell from the physiognomic or egocentric values of words what the world of the child is like. A sharp-cornered figure is "cruel"; a camera tripod standing erect is "proud."

The second answer to the question about individual idiosyncrasy is in terms of the way in which the medley of stimulating energies is grouped, first with reference to the recognition of common qualities and the formation of abstract terms, and second, with reference to the spatio-temporal grouping of such qualities in the form of objects. The cultural mold of language assists the impulse to discover common properties, and inhibits the ability to note other groups of qualitative similarities (page 278). Thus the similarities and differences experienced by the child, though inherent in the properties of things, are nevertheless accented (or minimized) so that they are perceived in a far from naïve fashion. The people whom he knows, especially the family, mediate to the child the proper way of grouping things and of naming such groups. To some degree the recognition of resemblances depends on personal wants, personal experience. But the cultural mold ordinarily honors the principle that the spatio-temporal grouping of elements shall be made in accordance with general utility; things that stay together and are used together are "real objects." Consequently, so far as the child's needs coincide with the needs of those who convey language to him, both systems of classification, that in terms of utility and that in terms of his personal wants, are acceptable. It is at the point where his needs cut across and alter the general cultural classification system that his own individuality is best revealed. The study of "children's secret languages" and of everyday baby talk has been rewarding, especially with respect to the richness of the sensory world; the child coins a dozen terms for visual, auditory, and tactual experience where adult language is poor indeed. "Father talks just like Santa Claus . . . boom, boom, boom! As dark as night . . . ! But we talk light, like the daytime . . . bim, bim, bim!"

It takes the culture several years to prune off these luxuriant excrescences of childish inventiveness and put in their place the fine distinctions which western culture—in particular, its science and technology—has created. Language is, in other words, an isolating process; and when the child has learned to group and to isolate qualities as the culture requires, he is ready, other things being equal, to put aside childish things and to forget how the world first looked to him. He may in later years learn a foreign language and live within it, yet fall back, he knows not why, into his mother tongue when the world calls for an affective structuring which his adopted tongue fails to provide; or he may, as dreamer or poet, produce, at the level of a William Blake, a grouping of words which is at the same time both infantile and magnificent. Even the humbler exploits of everyday conversation are perennial protests against the rigidity of hardened language. Every venture into slang is evidence that the qualities of things have failed to be registered in formal speech; and every experiment that shows the positive value of language in crystallizing perception and memory shows at the same time the rapid loss in perceptual and memorial richness which the mere presence of the word entails.

The world is indeed cut up and pasted together, its pieces made uniform, its patterns stereotyped, by virtue of the very mechanism which makes it manipulable by the individual and sharable by the group. In almost a dialectical movement, we may say that genuine individuality or personality in verbal expression depends first upon the asocial, physiognomic response of the child; second, upon its antithesis, the stereotyping and freezing of formal linguistic structure; third, synthetically, upon the capacity to transcend both asociality and sociality in individual creative expression.

Students of language have long recognized that the basic "feel" of individual speech tells much about the speaker which the *content* of his discourse leaves undisclosed. In Nietzsche's *Genealogy of Morals* and Veblen's *Theory of the Leisure Class* we learn that men are grouped not only in accordance with what they are and how they are placed, but in terms of their prevailing outlook upon themselves; something of their fundamental attitude gets into the form of their language. Kurt Goldstein has shown that in the aphasic the basic patterning of the world is beautifully revealed in deviations from the standard nomenclature and in the retention of terms here and there which betray how things *feel* to the user, his attitude toward the ways in which they may be used. Each cultural group develops idioms, essentially untranslatable, for the way things feel. In the same way, the language of the individual is a clue to personal affective responses and to the basically distinct ways in which, from his point of view, things can be used.

This individuality in speech is highly stable and firm in spite of outer pressures. Though language is an ever-changing dynamic thing to which additions are always being made, yet from childhood intelligence tests to studies of senility we have convincing evidence that the language structure is among the most highly organized, the most resistant to life's vicissitudes. Except in the more profound personality disturbances, words and word patterns stand firm; the normal subject maintains the same verbal structure, the same symbolic system, year after year. This highly stable and dominant structure is a central component of personality structure as a whole.

12. The World of Values

THROUGHOUT the study of motives and the learning process we have been finding not only that individuals want different things, but that they set up complex personal systems of wants which are relatively enduring and are maintained even in the absence of external reminders; they carry around within themselves personal systems of values. Personality is in large measure this personal value system; hence the latter calls for closer study.

A good deal, although not all, of this personal predilection is illuminated by the study of language. In the preceding chapter we traced the relation of the world of symbols to the world of activity. The continuity of language may be viewed not only in terms of the sheer continuity of available tools—as one keeps the same saws and scissors for recurring needs—but also in terms of the constancy of those semi-conscious or unconscious sets which mark off what is really *important and valuable*. The maintenance of individual language is a clue to the maintenance of stable life values. Let the life outlook change catastrophically, as in Tolstoy's conversion, and words instantly mirror the fact; they begin to "laugh and cry" in a new way. The symbol pattern reveals the value pattern.

But words not only *mirror*; they also help in some degree to maintain and organize sets or values. They define what to expect or what not to expect, what is to be emphasized or not emphasized (i.e., they inhibit outer response). They help to maintain constancy of attitudes to *want* or *not to want* (i.e., to value or not to value). On the basis of the more or less random utilization of words provided by the culture, one discovers for himself which words provide, in terms of denotation and connotation, the most effective service with respect to these three functions. We should therefore expect that the fineness of distinctions, the number of terms indicating varieties within a species, would portray the richness and intransigeance of individual wants. The richness of terminology reflects the subtlety of needs. An individual's language will be richest where central values, through manifold expression and long experience, have called for the greatest specification. We all want color; but the handicraftsman usually needs color more than the engineer, the poet more than the handicraftsman, the artist even more than the poet. It is because the poet and the artist actually *need* color, not simply because they have been conditioned longer to color terms, that they have actually enriched the language.

The maintenance of set, as we noted earlier, is partly a matter of conditioning to inner stimulation. The words spring to the tongue or pen as the old need springs to life again. The words, however, have a second function; they establish, again through conditioning, their own inner circuits, their own linguistic supplements; they come back in droves as a single dear old word activates the constellation of which it was once a part. Through a process of cross-association, any word partaking of a given flavor or aroma in terms of the qualities felt tends to bring back all the words of that familiar affective type.

This is peculiarly true of affective dispositions which take hold of the individual compulsively, which drive him forward to reiterate his old demands or to crystallize ever more rigidly his old anxieties. The pathology of rigid personality structure is partly the pathology of such inner circuits. Let a dietetic indiscretion or a poorly ventilated bedroom produce a vague distress, and one awakens with a word or word pattern that takes the conditioned form of a specific worry for the day; and the worry, ramifying into all the day's events, serves like a cramp to maintain the anxious state.

We should expect, if this is true, that verbal conditionings, being profoundly overlearned, being dovetailed into a system of mutually reinforcing associations, and being intimately related to the value world of human society, would be fraught with richer consequences than the conditionings which are based on symbolic elements that are not parts of the world of words. An experiment was designed by Razran to test this hypothesis. One group of subjects was given a nonsense syllable as a conditioned stimulus for salivation, no information being supplied to indicate anything special or peculiar about the syllable. Another equated group of subjects was given the nonsense syllable and was told that it was a word from "Benga, an African language." Apparently because a real word, part of the profoundly significant symbolic system of human beings, carried richer connotations, the conditioning process was established more quickly and more firmly in the second group, and extinction was slower.

The Development of Values

When simple canalizations are thoroughly established, they may be called values (page 182). Most values, however, have to do with objects that are physically not present. By virtue of representative factors (page 247), such wants may persist despite long separation from their goal objects, and symbolic activity may keep them at a high pitch of intensity. Ordinarily, indeed, activity in pursuit of value objects is maintained partly by symbols. Need may give rise to inner symbols, as in fasting subjects who, as their hunger increases, give more and more verbal associations referring to food; the symbols in turn circularly reinforce the intensity of the need, so that the ravenously hungry man is told to resort to distraction, to think of something else. But though symbols greatly complicate the process, the central fact about values is that they arise from definite wants, of all the types described in Chapters 5 and 6.

The relation of values to motives is clear. Values are not imposed on an unready individual but, like all other expressions of motives, are developed by organism-environment interaction and can never reach beyond the tissue needs from which they originally spring. The tissues themselves, however, have changed as the drive developed (page 111), so that it is a different individual who now wants the Bach music or the Masefield poem.

Since symbols play so large a part in the life of values and since they are for the most part conditioned stimuli, it should be stressed that values normally involve both canalization (the heightened drive tendency toward specific goals) and conditioning (the connection of the goal object with a symbol). Continuity in values is provided both by the general inextinguishability of the canalizations and by the frequent reinforcement of the conditionings. This continuity of value-seeking behavior in the physical absence of the valued object appears in every act of anticipation, from the simple conditioning setup or the maintenance of muscular tone to the preparation for a period of trial far in the future or for a happy escape from otherwise unendurable distress. One lives in some degree as if he were already about to enter upon, or were actually embedded in, a world of satisfactions which has no existence at the time. Such anticipation meets the specifications for conditioned responses; it can be put down as a form or a rough equivalent of motor set. It is subject to extinction, reinforcement, and spontaneous recovery; it can be built up with other anticipations according to a hierarchical scheme. One anticipation is dominant over another, absorbing the competitor when the two are antagonistic, and articulating with it if the two are compatible. All such anticipation, or preparation, or set is a response to continuing bodily activity, not merely an aftermath of previously existing overt stimulation. The child may not, like the mouse, need to keep his nose pointed in the direction of the expected reward, but he keeps *himself* pointed or focused—his fantasies and dreams prove that.

Is there not a difficulty here? The process of valuing, by its definition, gives satisfaction. But if the value system is maintained symbolically, *without* satisfaction from the goal object, why does not the symbolic pattern, a sheer system of *conditioned* stimuli, gradually die out? How can drive satisfaction be derived from the inner play of symbols when the symbols serve in no way to advance the attainment of a goal? I may play delightedly with symbols of a vacation when they advance the effectiveness of my planning and so make the vacation more complete. But this does not explain why such images are manipulated in the absence of any possibility of having any vacation at all, or even why they are persistently developed, as the psychiatrists show, as compensation for vacations which manifestly will not be given.

The answer lies perhaps in the fact that under certain circumstances internal symbols may play a much richer role than that of mere preparation for future activity. If the vacation scene I call up is one from a previous year, it is quite possible to regain some of the earlier pleasures by touching off some of the internal responses which made the other occasion a happy one. The fantasy projected into the future may be merely an elaborate form of reliving, together with a little wishful elaboration. The canalization and conditioning principles are appropriate for the illumination of a wide variety of repetitive inner behaviors, as in the case of other forms of reliving, such as haunting fears or pointless recapitulations of old behaviors (page 235). The greater the stress of present circumstances, such as solitary confinement or cold or hunger, the greater the futility of any overt response, the greater the blockage in activities which are manifestly futile in removing the outer threat, the greater becomes the relative strength of the repetitive patterns of response. Under such circumstances, there is indeed time and opportunity for much reliving, with additional decorative details which the possibility of eventual departure from the prison or what not may encourage. If, moreover, it is satisfying to contemplate a geometrically or esthetically adequate pattern before one's eyes, it is satisfying to contemplate a similar pattern in the mind's eye, the symbol world. The inner world is literally the external world with simplification, elaboration, or distortion in accordance with local blockages or facilitations.

Furthermore, if hard experience has taught that the reality is never quite as good as the foretaste which an indulgent imagination has presaged, the habit of depending upon the latter, distrusting or even paradoxically refusing contact with the external, can become deeply ingrained. The dreamer and the delusion builder are not necessarily so foolish; under certain conditions the value world is dealt with more safely and completely when most of it is anchored deep within the skin. That it is never completely isolated from the external patterns we shall hope to show when we discuss the personality mechanisms of the socially isolated person (page 890).

When the absent object continues to be valued, the tension related to it is evident in proportion to one's eagerness, but we have just seen that symbolic response (as in talking or thinking of the object) may be satisfying. And since the satisfied value response, being based on canalization, seems not to be extinguished but to be maintained through each repetition, the symbolic conditionings attached to it (so as to lead to satisfaction) cannot extinguish; for with each rearousal of the original drive by the conditioned stimulus there will, by definition, be some satisfaction of the drive (page 169). The low-arched doorway that leads to the mysterious attic, the fading green envelope that the absent friend addressed are conditioned stimuli that will not be extinguished because as they are experienced they lead to renewed inner symbolic satisfactions. But if they frequently appear in *other contexts*, involving a different response, and are non-dominant in the resulting competition, they can readily die out. It is easy to forget that the response to the absent valued object ordinarily continues and that the number of such objects and consequently of their possible patterns of comparison, their hierarchies, constantly increases. A life worth living becomes more and more topheavy with absent but cherished things. This habit of living with absent things may broaden into the inventor's or the poet's continuous preoccupation with beloved possibilities.

One of the chief facts that needs to be known about each enduring value tendency is whether it does its work by virtue of continuous, *persisting* internal tensions, constantly activating behavior, or whether it is only a tissue disposition, a potentiality for response, which remains *ready to discharge* when and only when externally aroused. A person grows thirsty on a warm day whether there are bubble-fountains nearby or not; the continuing tension makes him seek them. But one who has seen no potato chips for a month may suddenly "hunger" for them when, and only when, he sees them. It is not extravagant to say that the body is thirsty because of its own tissue situation, but it would be extravagant to say that before it encounters potato chips it is hungry for them in the same way. The fact that both classes of motives exist needs hardly be labored; but the issue as to classification is important, for otherwise we might forever be assuming that whatever men do springs from something already wound up within them. A single example of the magnitude of the issue at stake: Do we mean by an "aggressive" man one who is ready to fight when stimulated by external pressures, or one who is constantly "spoiling for a fight?" There are both kinds of aggressive men; and the same distinction holds in relation to almost every impulse. The chief practical difference between the two appears to lie in the maintenance, in the one case but not in the other, of continuous symbolic machinery that activates the tensions leading to overt behavior. One "carries around" aggression; the other does not. The projective methods (Chapters 28–29) are especially contrived for the study of what is "carried around."

Phrasing the matter in this way immediately suggests a third possibility. Sometimes the inner disposition sensitizes the action patterns, but nothing further happens until the external push is given. Both the delayed-reaction experiment and the persistence, during long years of toil and privation, of goal-seeking tendencies which will be fulfilled when one's ship comes in indicate that in man there is a system of events which somehow tends to obliterate the distinctions that must be drawn sharply at a simpler level. One may nurse a grudge or a dream; he may not only sensitize himself for the future moment when an expected stimulus will come, but act as if that stimulus were already present.

It is important not to think of anticipation as necessarily a fixed and abiding tissue disposition left over, once and for all, from a past era. Rather, it exhibits some elements of relative continuity, many elements of cross conditioning and inner reinforcement; it is constantly strengthened or complicated by new external stimulation, and abundantly enriched or modified by other anticipations, whether in verbal or other form. Consequently, anticipations change in accordance with the dominant stimulations; in other words, they show the phenomenon of trial and error, the constant change of response to outer objects though the inner need remains unchanged. Let the need reach a certain pitch, and the act to which it leads may become and remain dominant, the usual shifting patterns of trial and error being inhibited. Hamilton's human and animal subjects, when frustrated after making wrong responses, were sometimes in such distress that the need to escape mounted, the inner factors being reinforced and the outer cues serving no purpose—they went on furiously doing the wrong thing time and again. The sheer stress of a situation may prevent the ordinary lability to which the term "trial-and-error" learning is applied. The child or adult may fixate, because of suffering, the very response that causes the suffering. The "rigid," the "cocky," the diffuse, the "irritable," the "withdrawn" personality are not necessarily end results of successful adaptation to environment; they are often crystallized expressions of *failure to adapt*.

Huge individual differences in the lability or fixity of such orientations, the capacity to shift one's instrumental activity as the need persists, are among the most important factors in personality; hence it will be well to find out what is known about their origin. The hints about perseveration given earlier (page 131) are of some use; negativism (page 217), the resistance to outer pressure, is of more importance. The complexity of the nervous system and the number of acquired skills available play an important part; the richness of verbal means of constructing alternatives is more important still. Beyond it all there may well be a disposition of the type discussed by Rorschach, a basic tendency toward the maintenance of set; a basic rigidity, perhaps, as contrasted with the proneness to attention shift.

It is anyone's guess as to the exact structure of this complex of factors that make for persistence or the lack of it; hence one more guess may be ventured here by way of a first step toward a hypothesis. Our guess is that repeated and intense frustrations have not taught the individual *only* that this and that particular act get him nowhere; his response is much more generalized. The pattern is: "Whatever I do is wrong." This is exactly the pattern which some animals suffering from experimental neurosis (page 311) have shown—a cowed defeatism, a form of "rigidity" which may even mean muscular rigidity, or another manifestation of the same inability to do anything about the situation, namely, "waxy flexibility" of the extremities. This might be defined as a generalized withdrawal attitude (of the sort mentioned above on page 213) which in some cases takes the form of passive helplessness, and in others (where there is some record of a successful struggle against the outer world) prolonged defiance. There may, however, be pressure to escape not only from the outer world but *from one's own patterns,* and the result may be extreme vacillation, a grasping at every straw in the outer world. The extreme spotty "extratensive" pattern (the jumping of attention from one to another external object) may well be a pattern of escape from an inner symbolic world which, no matter how one looks at it, is frustrating. In contrast to the "flight *from* reality," is the "flight *into* reality."

It follows that rigid or stereotyped persistence and utter lability may prove at times to be not extremes on a continuum but contrasting forms of the same thing. In any event, the persistence of set, as both a qualitative and a quantitative problem, is among the major tasks upon which a theory of conditioning should shed light. Perhaps such a theory will prove inadequate to cope with problems at this level of complexity; at any rate, its use in personality study cannot be pushed very far until a way is found to predict, from a knowledge of persisting dispositions, which among a variety of outer conditioning situations will "take effect" upon the individual.

Value tendencies, then, arise not only from the direct confrontation of valued stimuli but from the cues associated with them. Two forks on the table suggest pie for dessert, a value through which the expressed attitude is activated. In other words, conditioning applies to value tendencies and to attitude tendencies (the fork is the symbol of the pie). Most symbols in the attitude sphere are verbal. In a complex symbolic world the conditioned stimuli are likely to confront us more often than the originals. The people of our own group are just ordinary people; they need no classification tag, and for the most part call for none. But members of out-groups—those who live across the tracks—are less frequently met, need to be symbolized, may be confronted in generic terms in every conversation or newspaper. Since generalization is a usual attribute of conditioning, such symbols normally control generalized attitudes. Skin color or accent or clothing may have served as a conditioned stimulus in a disturbing situation; similar though not identical skin color or accent or clothing may precipitate a response. So, too, since language seeks largely to crystallize the general that arises in a series of particulars, the verbal terms applied to a group, anchored upon a general criterion such as skin color, may touch off in the listener the general responses to the entire group designated.

Attitude

As one looks at the development of attitudes in the individual child, he finds them first appearing in the form of conditioned postural responses, including elements of attack and escape, and dispositions to modify the stimulus world. Affective and motor elements are integrated or almost fused (page 89). From these earliest attitudes of acceptance and rejection, which in their affective form we may call attitudes of outgoingness and of repugnance, wide generalization is to be expected and does in fact occur; it proceeds here, like all generalization, until differentiation is forced upon the individual (page 209). The child structures a world of positive and a world of negative orientation, regions of safety and of danger; and with repetition the affective and conative features have an opportunity for deep fixation. The symbolic elements in the configuration which touch off the attitude behave like other symbolic elements; a term of opprobrium regarding one's own social group may thus touch off a hostile reaction after many years of friendly contact between that group and another. It is even possible that the sudden interjection of verbal cues will touch off components never otherwise seen, as when a light-skinned Negro who has passed for white and lived as a white among whites is labeled "nigger" by those who know his genealogy, and a sharp shift in the behavior of whites toward him ensues. According to the theory developed here, a complex of canalizations and conditionings connected with satisfying and frustrating experiences was early established toward the group designated by a given skin color; but this complex of responses was tied to verbal symbols, so that the whole force of the conditioned response to "nigger" is available when the verbal conditioned stimulus is given. Or, on discovering that the verbal stimulus was inappropriate, that is, that a mistake has been made, the individual may revert to the earlier patterns. The basic canalizations toward social groups in terms of the drives which they activate remain in force, but they are manipulated by verbal symbols. A method similar to this was used in Hitler's Germany to reactivate attitudes toward Jews, Czechs, and Poles, with whom, in German communities, most Germans had lived reasonably amicably. The least desirable aspects of the stereotypes about these groups were emphasized and a generalized conditioned response was established in the form of each of these stereotypes; the individual Pole, Jew, or Czech in each town and village, despite earlier good status, then suffered from the transfer effects of the stereotype.

The principle of dominance applies as much to the verbal as to all other conditionings, and the attitudes of fear and disgust in relation to basic disturbances in the child's experience can be redirected toward the criteria by which a social group is recognized—mannerisms, gestures, speech patterns, etc.— which then serve as cues for these deeper dispositions. Were the canalizations less constant, were the individual less rooted in his basic social and personal needs and fears, he would be infinitely more plastic under the pressure of suggestion and propaganda; infinitely less effort would be required to remodel him through social and political pressures.

We have written as if the earliest social attitudes were rooted in the helpfulness or hostility of others toward ourselves, and in the safety or danger with which our dealings toward them are carried on. But, in reality, attitude toward the *self* is coeval with attitude toward every other individual. As we noted above (page 189), canalization upon the parent is of necessity canalization upon oneself, so far as there is any resemblance between child and parent, and such resemblance is of course magnified in many ways. There is also constant derivation of drive satisfactions from one's own person. The sensory and activity drives are largely gratified by sight, sound, contact, and muscular responses, all centered in the self; the little child plays happily with his toes and gurgles and smiles as he does so. Even the visceral responses are to some extent based upon the self, the simplest example being the thumb-sucking of the hungry child; a more complex illustration is seen in the self-satisfaction or vanity pattern of enacting little plays for one's own vigorous self-approbation. Consequently one develops attitudes toward others in relation to the developing system of attitudes toward oneself. Not only are other persons friendly to our physical existence, they are friendly toward the attitudes of self-enhancement which we need. Or, though not injuring us physically, they may thwart these tendencies—they may "hurt our feelings." Children's and adults' records of their earliest memories are as rich in humiliation episodes as in overt fear or disgust episodes. The child's attitude toward others is, then, dictated in large measure by the degree to which they develop or frustrate his own attitude needs in relation to his own person. It is indeed probable that adult enhancement of the self-regarding needs of the child underlies the generalized security or insecurity noted by Pallister (page 213); it is probably the adult tendency to tease or humiliate the child which offers the chief basis for the later withdrawal tendency.

Whether we dignify one group of symbols above another or not, symbols seem to owe their existence largely to dominance; and for that reason they are likely, as they lead to effective adjustment, to be constantly reinforced and maintained. If personality is a multiple-tension system, it should be possible to work out a gradation among the tensions in accordance with the depth and degree of permanence of their roles in the total. Certain striped- and unstriped-muscle groups that are activated by inner symbols referring to the self display exceptional constancy, invariability of response. While some parts of the body, such as the postural and locomotor muscles, may vary in a given person from very high to very low tension at a moment's notice, depending upon the context and the inner situation, others, such as the muscles of the arterial walls and the gastrointestinal canal, may show a much greater stability or rigidity because they are constantly excited by inner symbolic activity. Equally rigid, in other persons, would be certain striped-muscle patterns representing implicit responses toward the self, the matrix from which expressive gestures arise; the characteristic postural air of diffidence or self-esteem betrays itself in the muscles of the neck, chest, and shoulders. We should expect to find "hypertension" often due to chronic attitudes of aggression and fear, or cramps due to prolonged excitement or worry; all are rooted to some degree in chronic hyperactivity of the sympathetic system. That this is the case has been shown repeatedly, as in the recent work of Binger and his collaborators which emphasized a long history of violent pent-up aggressive tendencies prior to the first record of their patients' arterial hypertension.

Among the stable and frequently unconscious muscular dispositions related to attitude toward self are, of course, those of the speech apparatus. And the words most centrally located in the personal symbolic system are most easily activated. It is not only the poet who betrays himself in his favorite words; every person's favorite words suggest patterns for classifying the world and his relation to it. Within the matrix lie a few words which, because they represent ways of regarding the self, are among our most important clues to the study of personality. In describing the ego, Freud emphasizes auditory material. Although we need not go so far, nor do we need to deny the importance of non-verbal, indeed non-auditory, symbols of various types, we do, however, need to give the symbolic act of self-reference a prominent position in the symbolic system.

In spite of the great continuity of wants, especially those related to the self, that is implied by these examples, the frequent *changes* in the pattern of wants must also be considered. If one views enough ego levels and enough cultures, will he not find as great a need for novelty, for change, for the unknown, as for the tried and familiar? With satisfaction comes satiation, and the right of way is given to what is new. Man turns from one satisfaction to another. Caught between these two basic principles, the need to continue and repeat and the need to give up and change, he builds up habitual sequences in the pursuit of his goals; there is a temporal structure in his living that provides for the interweaving of connective tissue between his needs. Usually the needs tend to be set up in pairs, like waking and sleeping or working and playing; and these pairs become functionally ingrained so that habits of alternation are formed—the primal reconciliation of opposites, or logic of dialectic, that so delighted Hegel and Marx. At the human level, however, the opposites are only functional, not necessarily logical. They are reminiscent of a sonata, in which the second movement is not a "contradiction" but a contrast to the first, and in which the third, revealing and fulfilling both, shows their oneness as well as their contrast.

It is widely recognized that one's "interests" change more often than one's "values." The reason, we believe, is to be found in the difference between the types of learning process involved. Just as the concept of "attitude" seems to be clarified by both the "canalization" and the "conditioning" processes, so the concept of "interest" rests upon both processes. The relation of value to interest follows from the theoretical distinction made above between conditioning and canalization. Interests change rapidly as the mode of satisfying needs varies. I am interested in the program of a music recital because the Tchaikovsky that is to be played satisfies my own value; an extraordinary variety of programs may interest me so far as they are related to the value in question. Instantly upon hearing that the great conductor cannot lead or that the favorite pianist is ill, I lose interest in the sheet of paper announcing the program; the value is unaffected, but the piece of paper before me has lost its conditioned connection with the value. Interests, we suggest, are conditioned stimuli pursued because of their relations to goal objects which are valued. Interests in turn are extinguished, as all other conditioned responses are extinguished, when the relations to the drives involved are destroyed.

The Classification of Values

The number of values developed within the individual is never fixed, simply because no one ever finishes with canalization. And in the nature of the process, values overlap and fuse so that the classification of their ultimate types could serve no purpose. It is convenient, nevertheless, to put them into some sort of order, in the fashion, for example, of Spranger, who set up six basic value types. In presenting his scheme, we shall offer some simplification to adapt the system to the general framework developed.

The *theoretical type* seeks to grasp the nature of things. When the reality sought is not local and temporary but cosmic, we have the *religious type*. When not the abstract relations but the persons about one are valued, we have the *social type*. In the person for whom individuals are significant not for themselves but as pawns in a game for power, we have the *political type*. The *economic type* finds value in the relations of gain and loss. The *esthetic type* values the relations between sensory objects that are directly and immediately satisfying.

The chief usefulness of this classification for our present purpose is the fact that it can be employed to demonstrate the continuity of values within the individual from year to year, the relatively greater permanence of values than of interests, as called for by the theoretical distinction made above, and the close relation between values and the specific intellectual orientations of young adults. On this last point, for example, there is evidence from the Allport-Vernon test that students of arts are higher than students of business and engineering on theoretical and esthetic value.

Another much more complex classification of values could, however, be defined; the more complex, the more subtle, the more variegated it is, the better it will be for the description of individuals. As Spranger's scheme was devised expressly to describe types, any given individual incorporates in himself something of all the types and a great many more besides. Indeed, there are many values partly because it takes so long to grow up. The longer the period of immaturity, the period during which the organism is plastic, the greater the number of values it can form, the more complex the hierarchies it can establish in both its intellectual and its emotional life, the greater its opportunity for experimentation. What it learns during this period it learns with a less differentiated, less diversified nervous system. The values are values of the organism as a whole, and have a less compartmentalized character than those acquired later. In fact, this prolonged immaturity may be a reason why human nature is so complex, quite aside from the factor of greater intellectual power. Some have thought that the greater plasticity of the human drives might be due solely to this "prolonged infancy." We have attributed the range and subtlety of human motives to the great complexity of our nervous system; McDougall would ask whether the time required for the nervous system to develop might not be as important as the total complexity achieved.

The reason why values can be classified is that they transfer and generalize (page 168). Earlier we used the illustration of the hungry man and his *attitude* toward food; seated at the dinner table, he has a more specific attitude toward his favorite dish. The attitude is often visible behavior; the eyes and hands reveal it, and even in the well-behaved the salivary glands primitively betray it. At their core, attitudes are dispositions toward stimuli moving in the direction of more complete external responses. There are attitudes—incipient responses—toward *all* situations. Since every situation resembles certain other situations, attitudes are likely to prove general to some degree; but since each situation is definitely itself, differing from every other, attitudes are likely to prove specific to a certain extent. The behavior of attitudes suggests, therefore, that they are conditionings that exhibit the usual transfer and differentiation.

Attitudes are present dispositions which have developed through a long and complex process. Like all behavior, they are *motivated*, and they are adjustments to present situations. On all three counts they remind us directly of values; indeed, the more closely they are regarded, the more difficult it is to find any essential difference between values and attitudes. Current practice makes a convenient distinction in terms of the symbolic machinery expressive of the two; inwardly one pines for his old home, valuing it above his present home, but outwardly he expresses the attitude, as when he symbolizes verbally the fact that Centerville is a "dear old place." The value is conceived to be the feeling of which the attitude is the conditioned verbal expression. Attitude is defined by some as *value expression*. There is sense in this definition, for its central point embodies a canalization process; but the process is aroused by a word or some other symbol, and when aroused, the whole inner complex is likely to seem a conditioned stimulus for both verbal and behavioral expression. It would be more accurate to say that preverbal attitudes of the sort just described exist, and that words become a focal part of the attitude pattern. Value and attitude can be distinguished only by a convenient surgical separation whose utility is subject to doubt.

DERIVED SYMBOLIC TRAITS CONTRASTED WITH ORGANIC TRAITS

In Chapter 7 we noted that organic traits are sometimes susceptible to measurement. So, too, traits derived from the first organic dispositions through canalizations and conditionings are sometimes measurable; they are the same material, the same stuff, that we considered in Chapter 7, but they appear in new forms. Their measurement proves serviceable wherever life experiences permit the classification of persons in terms of similar experiences in drive satisfaction. Ratings based on recurrent observation of dispositions to satisfy drives in one way rather than another are likely to show interperson agreement in judgments, and consistency over the periods in which such dispositions could be expected to endure. The transfer and generalization of canalizations and conditioned responses permit the isolation of *areas* of behavior in which the traits appear, and measurement of the intensities, durations, etc., of such traits becomes feasible. These traits will of course overlap, both in the sense that the organic pattern responding on one occasion overlaps the pattern responding on another occasion, and also in the sense that different stimulus configurations may elicit rather similar organic responses. The abstractions which yield the traits have therefore naturally led to efforts at statistical simplification.

Even before the problem of learning was considered, the conclusion was reached that experimental determinations of such traits are as a rule more valuable than ratings (page 156); this view seems to be confirmed by the data presented here. The situation arousing the response can be more fully defined in the case of an experiment, and the response itself can be registered, rather than passing through the verbal symbolic system of the rater before it assumes numerical form. However, these advantages are often balanced or outweighed by factors that appear in ratings, notably the fact that a rating incorporates the results of many observations and hence gains in generality and reliability. The present chapter reinforces this view, because the verbal symbolic systems group together the socially related aspects of response even when these are objectively dissimilar. Thus a rater would include under "shyness" blushing, hesitation, and averting the eyes, although objectively they are not the same thing.

The study of learning seems then to have offered no reason for an essential change of emphasis in regard to method. The choice of method, however, depends chiefly on the kind of trait being studied. In the case of "organic traits" we made some suggestions as to the specific kinds of traits which can better be rated; but when such traits appear in their "derived" form, we must emphasize an exception. In the case of the strictly organic constructs that are based directly on primary tissue dispositions, it is doubtful whether the advantages of ratings can atone for their limitations. It is the organic root, not the structured pattern, that is wanted here. The organic disposition, if measured at all, should first be fully explored in relation to a known situation; it should be stated in general terms for other situations only when empirical observation warrants it. Although organic traits are subject to various modes of analysis, yet an experimental procedure that begins with a full-fledged demonstration and measurement of the trait in a known situation, and explores outwards from this to related situations to test the scope of its expression, is the *first* step. But when a trait involves any considerable degree of elaboration and relates to a characteristic way of appraising or orienting oneself with respect to a situation, the possibility of an organic definition of a relatively simple type is immediately lost, not because such responses are disembodied, free of the organic orderliness of inner bodily inter-stimulations, but because at present, even with the electroencephalo-gram, there is no chance of tracing such constituents. Most social attitudes, most evaluations of the self—most confessions of weakness, for example, which are used by the thousands in framing all sorts of questionnaires and trait lists—are released by symbolic stimuli and funneled in symbolic form. The situation presented in the question varies from the specific to the utterly general; and the processes intervening before a "yes" or "no" can be given, or a check mark made at one or another of five points, vary from the purely mechanical to the impulsive or chaotic "answer at random" or, at another extreme, the purely wishful (autistic). It is likely that these instruments are nonetheless essential for many purposes; our query relates not to their usefulness, but to the *kinds of traits*, the kinds of response uniformities, which can be revealed through them.

This does not mean that the organic and symbolic aspects of traits can be determined by inspection. Having begun with reliable ratings, we are steadily driven to the problem of the *origins* of traits. Certain masculine or masculoid characteristics, for example, such as aggressiveness or dominance, may in some men be genuinely "dependent on" endocrine function, developing rapidly at puberty and waning during involution. The same characteristics, literally the same, may well depend in another man upon *different endocrine* factors or indeed upon factors that are not endocrine at all; the possibility must at least be considered and excluded before any attribution of overt characters to organic traits can be tolerated.

Consider, for example, how complex a thing aggressiveness is at different developmental levels. At age 4, age, height, weight, strength, may be important in determining who can win in the simple physical contests at the nursery-school level. Age may give one either a basis of superiority through size, knowledge, etc., or just added time to acquire the skills. Aggressiveness at this age level is largely a matter of "bopping," pushing, biting. By 8 or 10, wrestling and boxing skills may be involved, and the ability to win in the fight may be a matter of who has learned, or been taught, or has naturally, the most efficient ways of handling the more elaborate "fight" situation. If you win the fights at 8, it may mean that you are more secure physically, have less need to criticize, bait, dispute, argue, etc., than the boy who cannot cope with physical aggression and substitutes verbal attacks. But you may have tied your security to success in physical combat, and thereby have a need to create situations through succeeding years in which you can demonstrate your superiority. Similarly, a vigorous personality may be frustrated by adult coercions at the age of 4, and show an accumulated aggressiveness which he does not need at 8, when the accepted freedoms of middle childhood remove some of the sources of frustration. Or a child who seemed to have little need to hit out at the world at the age of 10, when successfully absorbed in gang activities, might at 13, irritated by feelings of being behind others in the adolescent changes, or ahead and not allowed to use the new energies socially, become "impossible," aggressively destructive, messy, antagonistic, and temperish.

The ratings, then, will be supplemented by organic measures if and when the organic roots are found; and often enough roots of both types will be found. A reliably measured complex like "aggressiveness" often proves to be derived from such constitutional factors as age, strength, health; from factors of sibling rivalry and paternal discipline, or from factors of competition and social imitation. Canalizations and transferred conditioned responses may weave a compact strand that is very hard to disentangle. Traits generally overlap; most of them are complex composites. But for all that, the nucleus, the hard center that gives organization to the whole, often lies in a symbol to which some dominant conditioned response is anchored; there are key words—uttered by others or carried about devotedly by the individual himself—before which almost everything in him bows. There may be a temptation to call such symbolic tendencies less "fundamental" than the organic dispositions. But it must be remembered that the symbolic traits are based on tissue needs, tissue responses, just as all other traits are; the only difference is that the tissue responses are more complex and subtle, less obvious and less easily measured. This very complexity and subtlety works toward *stability*, and the fact that such symbolic systems are shared with the community means that each member of the group keeps on reinforcing the rest. This does not mean, however, that symbolic traits have structure only because outsiders group the various aspects of the trait together; the symbol is integrated inside the person before anyone else can make an integrated response to its presence. Symbolic traits, indeed, constitute a large part of the personality manifestations with which social psychology is especially concerned.

THE WILL

We have suggested (page 263) that inner signals of all kinds tend to initiate both inner and outer responses of a high degree of complexity. Sometimes a period of thought ends in a simple verbal summary from which a course of action follows. This overlaps a good deal with what we call the *will*. A man is said to be "making up his mind," and when a certain symbolic summary is achieved, he is said to have "resolved upon" a course of action, which then follows. Unless the term *will* is used to dignify sheer persistence, sheer continuity of action in the face of obstacles—which would be a strange usage in view of the fact that drowning caterpillars, and even plant tendrils, show this sort of stubborn continuity—a more generally satisfactory use of this word relates to a *symbolic process* in which a definable period of hesitation is known to precede an overt act.

The hypothesis that verbal cues intervene at the decision point and lead to the initiation of one response pattern rather than another is the background for an ingenious experiment which requires description; although the experiment does not touch all aspects of the hypothesis, it appears to settle the critical question whether inner verbal cues, as conditioned stimuli, can set the muscular mechanism going. Knowing that the pupillary reflex can be conditioned and its magnitude measured, Hudgins obtained pupillary contraction to a bright light, then conditioned this pupillary contraction to the sound of a bell, then arranged his apparatus so that the subject's contraction of forearm and hand closed the circuit for both light and bell whenever he heard the word "contract." In time the word "contract," uttered either by the experimenter *or by the subject himself*, elicited the pupillary contraction. A long series of conditioning sessions finally resulted in establishing a pattern in which, without benefit of light or forearm contractions, the word "contract," uttered aloud or even silently, led to the pupillary contraction.

This experiment suggests that control of the muscles through such inner symbols may be of great importance in volition. It is worth emphasizing that the process could not be established if the forearm contractions were eliminated. This may be due to the reinforcing effect of such muscular activity, just as the inhibited knee jerk may be brought out by sufficient activity—reinforcement—in other muscles. It may be, too, that contraction of the forearm plays a part by making the reaction *one's own*, that is, by bringing into the picture voluntary musculature long associated with the self (cf. page 187). This, while probably a necessary complication, would not invalidate the basic interpretation; it would itself be a form of reinforcement, just as the kinesthetic elements would themselves be integral features in self-awareness.

The experiment does, nevertheless, leave open the question whether the act called the will consists exclusively in vocal or subvocal activity. There is no special reason why vocal activity should be separated sharply from the other symbolic activities doubtless going on at the time. Fragments of imagery, postural adjustment, whether observable or too fine to be observed, are surely likely to have occurred. The conditioning process itself leads, as we have seen, to the interconnection of many processes. The experiment, moreover, does not deal with the process of *decision*, the resolution of conflicting action tendencies; this we should be inclined to subsume under the concept of dominance, but there is not enough evidence to settle the matter. The hypothesis that volition is a pattern depending upon dominant symbols is reasonable, and this experimental material helps to clarify and confirm it. But the point which the experiment settles —the capacity of inner symbols to arouse muscular contractions—is perhaps not the full flesh and blood of the volition process.

Another way of phrasing the problem of the will is in terms of Razran's "attitudinal control." Attitudinal control is just what one uses when he is set not to wince at an otherwise adequate stimulus. The development of attitudes is a long-drawn-out process, the later phases of which are unconscious; this point is noted in textbook discussions of the "development of voluntary attention." Just as Hudgins' subjects succeeded in voluntary control of the pupillary reflex through saying the word "contract," it is likely that voluntary control of the arm-raising mechanisms is a residual unconscious process that no longer requires explicit verbal cues; one *wants* to raise the arm and it goes up.

And since attitudes are never entirely "specific," never entirely "general," it should be true that each individual has some general degree of "will power"—we know rather well who will "break" under the stress of a threat, and who will not — and also that specific situations must make a difference, so that those who will not break under one threat may do so under another. Every police court studies the general reputation of the accused; but at the same time it seeks, and usually finds, places where the "hard" man will crack—in other words, where his *will to reveal nothing* can be broken.

The term *"will"* is sometimes used more broadly, and some of its other components need definition. The problem may be studied in terms of early development patterns. The infant struggles when restrained, shows compensatory effort. He may indeed do more than compensate; his response may more than balance the pressures applied to him. Internal stimulation mounts sufficiently to block or remove stimuli applied from without; there is protest, a generalized tendency to push back upon the environment. This process, moreover, is subject to learning; he integrates more and more of his struggle reactions, achieves a better and better organized struggle process. At certain periods in life, outside interference is likely to appear at an accelerating tempo; the world of cultural pressures comes down like an avalanche upon the child's gradually achieved integration. Thus as he achieves locomotion, he suddenly presents a hazard to himself and to his parents' possessions and equanimity, and brings upon himself interference with his newly achieved gift. The protest appears not only in more and better locomotion, but in generalized "negativism" (page 217). The negativistic action patterns are accompanied by the rapid growth of speech, and "I don't want to" takes on more and more articulate form. Not only do words accompany the bodily patterns of resistance; as the child discovers that the parents' words are leading to things which interfere with his own wishes, he discovers that his own words have the value of delaying and complicating the interferences and increasing his chance of holding off until the issue will no longer be pressed home. Many studies of childhood negativism show that it is precisely at periods of rapid gain in locomotion and speech that this trait is most marked.

We have been considering the aspect of the will that is involved when one sets himself against social pressure. In its positive aspects, however, the will must be regarded as an expression of the value system, as described above (page 182). This is another way of saying that while resistance to outer pressure constitutes one identifiable aspect of the will, there also develops in the individual a long-range symbolic orientation to goal objects, whether present to the senses or not, these "delayed responses" being maintained by virtue of self-excitation, especially of the verbal type. But we are ready for an appraisal of the exact role of symbols in the individual case *only* when we know the tension system which is being maintained with reference to a goal object, and its relation to the symbol system. Further progress in understanding the structuring of goal tendencies can come only when the nature of ego organization, with special reference to unconscious factors, has been discussed (Chapters 20–23). For the present we may say, almost exactly as McDougall did, that the will is a group of canalizations (sentiments) organized in behavior terms under the central integrating influence of self-canalizations (McDougall's "self-regarding sentiment").

THE CONTINUITY OF THE SYMBOLIC SYSTEM

Little attention has been given to the character of the inner symbols used. One person thinks almost exclusively in words; another makes generous use of images—inner pictures, sounds, etc.—direct residues from his earlier contacts with things experienced. To the word-minded it may seem axiomatic that it is through words that the deeper canalizations are revived and the determination made to return to a beloved scene or resume a beloved hobby; to others these inner symbolic activities appear to depend largely upon imagery. The problem is an interesting one, and we shall turn to some of its aspects in Chapter 16. Here, however, our interest is not in the content but in the form of the symbolic life, the processes of personal living to which symbols give rise. The vehicle through which continuity is maintained is for our present purpose a secondary question. It is possible for an individual rich in visual imagery to maintain his love of the fine arts as visual imagery fails and verbal and other types of striped-muscle control take its place. It is quite possible, through training imagery, to shift from a spatial orientation based upon kinesthetic elements to one based upon three-dimensional visual schemata. The formal patterns, the dispositions toward the self and the world, are so deeply ingrained and so tightly knit together that either type of symbolism, or both, may be called upon. Just as the man who has suffered an amputation may go on with his old pursuits—say tennis or bowling—using the other arm, so the system of symbols may be changed in mid-passage.

If the questions be asked: "What, then, is really at the pinnacle of the hierarchy of the symbolic system?" and "Is this not a confession that control is from below upward rather than from above downward?" the reply is that in a system so complex, whose parts are so intimately interrelated, any single feature may gradually fade, and the general style of organization be maintained. *Sudden* losses of words, *sudden* losses of imagery, do indeed entail gross disorganization, as instances of brain injury and cerebral hemorrhage abundantly show; but let the shift be slow, and the general outline of the personality pattern is no more profoundly affected than if a muscle group slowly atrophies as another takes over the function.

For most persons most of the time, symbols are in the position of generals; the muscles of trunk and limbs are the soldiers. If the general is killed in action, the army is disorganized; but if he *slowly* loses his health, the system of behaviors known as "the army" contrives to substitute a suitable commanding officer. Personality is organized largely through its symbols, but no symbol has absolute or coercive rights. The "wisdom of the body" as a whole sets limits upon the symbols which aspire to a central position. What is to be and remain central depends upon the three principles developed in the preceding chapters: the original constitution, the early canalization and conditioning patterns, and the field of organism-environment interaction.

An attempt has been made throughout this chapter to show that there is no real antithesis between symbol and act, between inner and outer personality manifestation. Personality begins in an activity stream, and the symbolic is a relatively stable and hierarchically well-placed form of activity. This may, if one likes, lead to the construction of a motor theory of the type developed by the early American functionalists. It is quite possible that consciousness itself, all the way from simple sensation to abstract thought, not only depends upon but is a direct expression of motor adjustment. There is, however, no way of proving this, and for our present purpose this last ambitious generalization is inessential. The important thing is to realize that the tension system is a primary reality which, in its relation to the world outside, varies more rapidly at some points than at others; in some regions it is more at the mercy of the momentary situation, in other regions it is more capable of perseveration and hierarchical control of the peripheral elements. No element in personality is absolutely continuous through time, and none is absolutely at the mercy of the environment; those to which the highest degree of continuity is attributable are the symbolic.

13. Conflict

TRAGEDY falls upon King Lear because he is an old man who cannot discern truth from flattery, and upon Othello because he loves not wisely but too well, but upon Hamlet because he is divided against himself. He will have revenge, but he wants to delay; when the thought of suicide comes to him as a way out, he craves it and at the same time fears it. Most tragedy, whether in the grand style or in the petty style of the daily suffering of common men or women, is a matter of a personality divided against itself. The awareness of conflict in oneself may be a major basis for self-reproof or self-pity, and the failure to become aware of it when it is strong regularly gives rise to "inexplicable" behavior.

Several kinds of "conflict" must be distinguished. First there are mechanical strains as extensor-flexor pairs of muscle groups are activated together; fatigue can occur even though little work is done. Yet such opposition of antagonists may be normal and satisfying, as in stretching after a nap. Conflict may also consist of balanced antagonistic nervous effects on the same muscle system, as in the sympathetic-parasympathetic control of heart and stomach tonus (page 116). But again, such antagonism is the physiological norm; indeed, the failure of one of the antagonists would constitute a pathological state.

This opposition of sympathetic-parasympathetic is, nevertheless, an important feature in many conflict situations. In a broad general way, as we saw above, the vegetative activities of the parasympathetic are disturbed during vigorous sympathetic activity, and during vigorous vegetative activity strong stimulation is required to arouse the sympathetic. There is a genuine antagonism, a genuine physiological competition between response patterns; the sympathetic system may defeat, or fail to defeat, the parasympathetic. The paralyzing effect of fear upon all interest in food or mates can easily be seen

[296]

—the x-ray shows that gastric activity has come to a complete stop— and those who have lived during a violent panic have frequently stressed the absence, among panic-driven people, of "human," that is, affectionate or generous, response. Fear regarding sex that stems from violent early tabus may mean lifelong incapacity for completeness in love. A strongly organized affection may *withstand* the impact of the panic stituation: "Perfect love casteth out fear." But, as other instances of violence show, perfect fear also casteth out love. We are dealing with a victory which is in many cases decisive; one autonomic component and all that it stands for achieves complete dominance over the other.

At a simple physiological level, then, the term "conflict" may refer properly to this opposition in which one component defeats the other. The use of this term, however, involves a certain forcing. Just as physiological balance is normal and commonplace, physiological imbalance is normal and commonplace. It is hard to see how the disturbed animal or man is any more in a state of conflict than a placid one. To be sure, he is not at the same moment frightened and amorous, or enraged and serene; but neither is he at the same moment running and standing, or sleeping and waking. These are mutually exclusive physiological states.

When two impulses are at work, the principle of dominance is still sufficient, at the animal level, to account for the prompt integration of behavior trends. Instead of starving, like the medieval ass, between two equally attractive bales of hay, the organism waxes and wanes with respect to one or the other or both, and a momentary decision is sufficient. That is exactly what you see when your dog needs both to obey your call and to chase off despite your commands; either he soon curls up by the fire or he is out of sight chasing the cat. There is no real suspense, no real balance; there is seldom any real conflict. This does not mean that the choice among alternatives need be instantaneous. Characteristically, when impulses are fairly evenly matched, the animal wavers, turns first to one, then to the other—the vicarious trial and error (VTE) of Muenzinger and Tolman. Tolman's "schematic sow bug," designed to clarify the situation, is a bit abstract, but serves well to show what not only bugs but rats and men continually do. The major orientation of the bug is toward a light, but at the same time another light strikes the periphery of its retina. As it moves toward the first light "satiation" develops, so that the ever-present pressures from the second eventually become dominant over the pressure from the first. The insect begins to swing and is shortly facing and approaching the second light. But satiation occurs once more, and the bug's "orientation need" swings it again toward the first. These orientation needs are the sensory drives described above. Thus the sow bug, by such "vicarious trial and error," explores the stimulus field without actually running through it.

The need for orientation is the need to respond to things other than the thing one is responding to; it is the antithesis of perseveration, the clue to diversity, inconsistency, heterogeneity in the life process, regardless of the intensity of external pressures or internal needs. "Adience" denotes the tendency to immerse oneself ever more deeply in the present situation; "orientation needs" provide a counterpoise, swinging the organism into new paths. But there is still no true conflict, no painful opposition of simultaneous wants. The mere fact of approaching one goal object often weakens that particular impulse and strengthens the other; in the very act of choosing, one finds that the grass is greener on the other side of the fence. (Indeed, that which is about to be relinquished takes on new gloss; blessings brighten as they take their flight, even when their flight is due to our own decision.)

IRRECONCILABLE IMPULSES

The question arises whether, if the term conflict is to be used for instances of physiological opposition, it might not be better to link it to those cases in which stimuli for two opposing patterns occur in such rapid oscillation, or act in such force simultaneously, that the normal physiological defeat of one pattern by the other is impossible. This can be done with animals by giving food and threats simultaneously, so that both patterns are vigorously aroused and a high tension level in the whole organism is established, and with small children by attaching grave and unknown dangers to cookie jars or assuring them that chocolate bars will "make holes in their teeth." The "experimental neuroses" induced in animals are sometimes of this type. A signal meaning food and a different signal meaning punishment may be thoroughly "built in" the organism, so that each arouses its appropriate response. By one or another device the two stimuli are then made more and more alike, so that they mean to the organism an intimation of "something coming," it knows not whether for better or worse. The experimenter may introduce "exceptions" so that, though a given signal usually means food, it may mean something else; the stimulus is *ambivalent*. The animal or child may break down under the strain, losing many other well-established habit systems and showing disorganized emotional upheavals.

We are thus forced, if conflict is to be made clear, to move beyond the realm of the simple organic conflict of physiological tendencies, which is not really conflict because it contains its own means of resolution. But there may be genuine conflict in response to *ambiguous signals*. Life is full of them; we are surrounded by signals that have sometimes meant satisfaction, sometimes frustration. If we maintain in readiness two physiological dispositions, neither of which can gain complete ascendancy, it gradually gets us down.

Even this, however, makes too much of the opposition of physiological systems such as sympathetic and parasympathetic; there are many other conflict situations in which no such simple physiological opposition can be demonstrated, and in which there is every reason to believe that it is not the ambiguity of the stimulus but its inescapable clarity, its inexorable directness and relevance for action, that makes the trouble. The student loves his chemistry and he loves his history; he is hesitating between medicine and law. Although his friends, being simple-minded souls, can make a prompt mechanical decision, he finds himself dragging out the decision over four years, getting into a worse and worse plight, unable to make up his mind. I have seen him, many times reduplicated, in my office. Like a system in balance, he moves in the direction opposite to that of any advice given and a sort of homeostasis is maintained. Like Muenzinger's and Tolman's rats, he exemplifies vicarious trial and error; he suffers an orientation need for that at which he is not, at the moment, looking. He is caught in a *conflict of values*.

Or consider the woman trying to decide between two lovers—to be specific, Brita in Bayard Taylor's epic poem *Lars*. She stands there between Lars and Per; both love her desperately; and she loves them both. When she cannot choose, the men decide that they will fight a duel until one of them is killed. She loves them still, still cannot choose. They fight, and Per is slain. In anguish she falls upon his body; it is he, she says, whom she loved. It would have been the same had it been Lars who was killed.

Life is crowded full of these inexorable choices where no decision can be made without renouncing an important value. The child who has been punished wants to strike back but will bring on himself a loss of safety and love. We want power and know how to get it, but we shall lose the respect of those who look on. Macbeth knows the way to be king, but he will lose the "golden opinion" of "all sorts of people." Children may know how to impress teachers; but they know that if they do as teacher wishes, their classmates will see through it all.

For our argument it makes no difference whether the valued objects are present to the senses or are merely maintained, kept "physiologically present," through outer symbols or even through verbalization and other inner symbols. And it makes no difference whether the two values are of the same type (two vocations, two lovers), or of different types (easy women and a wife's respect). The important thing is that the two mutually exclusive wants act together. Both may involve the same autonomic tensions (two favorite desserts on the menu), but both cannot be satisfied simultaneously.

It may of course be answered that the conflict really arises not from the two values, but from the fear that acceptance of one will mean automatic punishment through the loss of the other. The social code says that Brita cannot have two husbands; the choice of one therefore means the *loss* of the other, so that, after all, the conflict is between love and fear or something like it. Such a reply, however, becomes very forced when we consider the annoying choices that are impossible purely because of time-space limitations. I am free to hike or to skate this winter afternoon; there is no love in this problem and there is certainly no fear. I waste twenty minutes of good hike-skate time trying to decide. The conflict is inherent in the fact that value objects, like all other objects, are placed in organismic time-space. Life teems with such conflicts.

The case may be pushed somewhat further. Much of the supposed love-fear antagonisms, or other supposed antagonisms of the sympathetic and parasympathetic, appear in reality to be simply the need for two different satisfiers, the choice of one of them bringing about through social means the loss of the other. Still more often human choices involve two lines of conduct which have taken on the quality of being *our* potential conduct; in contemplation, they have become parts of ourselves; we have pictured ourselves doing the one and also the other thing. It is actually a curtailment, a mutilation of the self, to give up something on which we have set our hearts; the self is the poorer. What is lost is not just the goal object, but the canalized self in relation to it. The energy bound in it (Freud, page 186) must be dissipated, and no replacement is possible. In all serious cases conflict involves much more than a practical balance of impulses; it has become a question of weighing the value of two possible selves, one self following one course and the other self following another course. The magnitude of a decision, even regarding an apparently trivial situation, may be based on its relation to one's reputation; much of what one does is subject to certain people's disapproval at one time or another. The ego needs (as we shall see more fully in Chapter 22) are always tripping one another up. Although any difficult decision may delay one's action, the painful decisions are those involving the two kinds of person one wishes to be. The abulic patient is not really struggling over trivialities; he is struggling regarding the implications of two pictures of himself.

But conflict *need* not involve two objects. A single object involved in a decision can be the center of conflicting impulses. It is not just a question whether we need Object A more than Object B or one person more than another, but whether *desire for* or *aversion toward* a specific object or person is stronger—in our own aggression-laden culture, whether love for a person or aggression toward him is dominant. Powerful to-and-fro movements are involved in the manifest expression of a child's attitude toward playmate or parent. At the simplest level, this is motion toward or away from, and plenty of it is evident; at the symbolic level, however, the motion may be all in one direction, and behind it may lie contrary movements or eddies and backwashes of many sorts. To acquiesce in mother's demand for an exchange of endearments may mean acting like a little boy or like a sissy; it may mean being the kind of person that gives up easily; it may involve a promise not to do something which she has forbidden. After a pattern of conflicting attitudes has been somehow woven, the unconscious, unreflecting attitude may itself be full of ambivalence. Even if there is no conflict between the child's attitude toward mother and toward other persons, conflict may arise with regard to anything she asks or silently wants. She is herself a conflict object, and to sit in the room with her involves nervous wear and tear. The adult betrays the same mechanism. Sheer presence, without any requirements regarding overt activity, may be very fatiguing. Petty social events at which almost every word is dictated by social conventions are notoriously exhausting because of the inherent ambivalence we feel toward people on such occasions.

Guthrie has well epitomized this source of conflict that is inherent in the two valences of a given object. One of his laboratory cats found out how to escape from a box by backing against a pole that opened a door, but when near the pole it backed thirty-nine times without touching it, *as if avoiding it*. A basic quality of human conflict is to make contact with something without touching it, to move toward it and keep away from it at the same time. This second form of conflict is again adumbrated in ego stress; sometimes we cannot entertain the thought of ourselves as either taking or rejecting; both courses involve an ego blemish, a mortifying self-picture.

Either of these types of conflict may become more severe as a result of perseveration (cf. page 107). In perseverative tension, physiological strain may be visible in the face and in the postural muscles. The compulsions, grimaces, and tics of the extreme neurotic are usually expressions of these perseverative pressures. It must, however, be emphasized that perseverative strain does not maintain itself for any great length of time unless constantly restimulated by symbols (cf. page 235). One symbolically maintains a desire to appear to others and to oneself as a certain kind of person, but there are grave inconveniences in doing so. In most case histories it is apparent that perseverative strain arises from a dual and conflicting ego picture, not the dual picture from the perseveration. The same situation may prevail if one must choose between two kinds of worlds to live in.

Summarizing the argument thus far, we suggest that, in general, human conflict may be typically described as conflict between *drives in their canalized form*, e.g., love directed toward two individuals both of whom cannot be possessed, or conflict due to *ambivalent attitudes*—canalizations leading to contrary behavior toward a *single* object (including the self). The root of conflict is the fact that the very activity which brings us one satisfaction reminds us constantly that it is depriving us of another—and this is especially true of ego values.

The result of both these broad types of conflict is of course enormous strain, for the result of blocking an outlet is always to dam up energy. This is one of the points at which the pleasure principle, or any variations of the classical conception of hedonism, is difficult to apply. We might maintain that the two opposing impulsions are pleasure impulsions, and that the two negative factors are forms of aversion from pain, and thus claim, as Troland did, that hedonism is vindicated. But an essential part of the pleasure-pain theory in all its variations is the conception of the rational autonomy of choice. If the individual discovers that the course upon which he is embarking will bring more distress than satisfaction, the theory requires that he abandon it. But he does not. The nature of human conflict involves self-defeat of the gravest sort, an extreme incapacity to be rational or to make any such calculations as the classical theory requires. The data from clinical practice relate to opposed tensions and to means for their attempted but unsuccessful release. Though any isolated tension system may theoretically be governed by a simple pleasure principle, the actual hierarchical whole, the actual system of systems within the individual, rends the pleasure principle from top to bottom.

One major theoretical question remains to be cleared up. When there are two canalizations, two desires for persons or objects, both of which cannot be pursued at the same time, why does not the principle of dominance apply? Is it not inevitable that there will at times be a clear supremacy of one over the other and that a result will be reached in terms of dominance, with a consequent increased canalization upon one goal, an intensification which will gradually lead to more and more prompt and effective response? Will not the learning process gradually result in a complete fixation based upon sheer frequency of satisfactions? Some clinical records certainly support such a view; they do not all suggest that human beings must stall in a condition of neurotic abulia. With equal clarity, however, they reveal that even when such a solution is reached, attachment often remains in the background; the individual may sentimentally, sheepishly, or guiltily try to relive the past, to recapture the possibility of the other decision. We have, then, not explained at all why the defeated component refuses to give up the field and why it cannot be dislodged by the conqueror.

To give the theory symmetry, it would certainly be desirable to demonstrate, if we can, that this is due to the basic fact that canalizations are not subject to extinction. It should be possible to show that although one canalization can be progressively strengthened, there is no device by which an opposing canalization can be progressively weakened. To be sure, the individual may make decisions more and more promptly as the imbalance between the two increases. But the tension level will become progressively higher; and if, as we should expect, there are moments when the weaker competing element is strongly reinforced (as when, despite good resolutions, one "yields to temptation"), the second impulse will be strengthened accordingly. The result of the process over a long period will be not to eliminate through the principle of dominance, but to heighten the general tension level more and more. The principle of the inextinguishability of canalized responses is probably serviceable as far as it goes, but there is certainly something at work in ordinary normal persons which prevents the tension level from working itself up step by step to these unbearably high levels. At the level of sheer canalization upon objects, and without benefit of any further principle, it is not likely that an adequate theory can be presented; we shall, however, recur to this problem later.

FRUSTRATION

We have referred to impulses aroused and sustained, and in some cases satisfied, but we have not tried to explain what happens when the aroused impulse finds no outlet, when the tension can in no way be reduced. The generalized term which has recently become rather well standardized in describing this situation is *frustration*. The word is useful in indicating not merely the attainment of a state of suspense but the irradiation through the organism of a high tension, that is, a suffusion of stress to other parts than the one originally involved. It is important to emphasize clearly that this spread of tension is no metaphor. The tension can be followed step by step with Jacobson's technique for measuring the magnitude of muscle tensions electrically; waves of increasing or decreasing tension can be followed all the way from fingers and arms to the gastrointestinal canal. Stomach ulcers can be directly treated by reeducating the innervation of arm and trunk muscles. Frustration, then, is not only a negative thing, a failure to achieve; it is a positive augmentation of tension throughout the organic system.

We now need to describe what happens when the tension level is augmented in this way. *Temporary* consequences can be traced in random movements, that is, the outburst of poorly coordinated responses which occur because additional energy has passed across a number of new thresholds (page 101). Some of the responses, of course, reflect past habits of behavior resorted to under such stress conditions—"autistic gestures" Krout calls them, i.e., blind and unconscious vehicles of habitual impulse, originally directed more or less against the object causing the stress. Frustration involves more than the organism's relation to itself; it involves temporary or permanent *methods of dealing with the stress inducer*. As Holt has shown, the random movements attendant upon the earliest frustrations are likely, when first aroused, to knock the offending object out of reach; by the ordinary mechanisms of motor learning, skilled movements are progressively developed by which we ward off such annoyers during the time they are active, or even upon their first manifestation. Such movements are gradually ingrained; and the subsequent posture of aggression, escape, etc., as manifest in the form and extent of gestures, completes the picture.

There may be also relatively *permanent* consequences of a long period of frustration in terms of deeply embedded defensive expressions of face, arms, or total posture (cf. page 151). Such patterns show themselves in all the waking hours, regardless of the preoccupation of the moment; they are well caught, for example, in the business man or society woman sitting for a portrait, and in the Italian fruit vendor and Jewish tailor seen in Efrón's sketches. Here the piling-up of energy arising from lifelong stresses has led to habitual muscular innervations which are manifest even during moments of the greatest relaxation.

But to pursue more fully the long-range implications of these tension situations, is there no such thing as an enduring personality pattern related to early frustration, even when the frustrating circumstances have long since disappeared? Do not many types of nervous sufferers eat much more than they need, because as tiny children they were not sufficiently fed or because some other drive was frustrated? Are there not long-range compulsive expressions which arise not from the continuation of objective outer stimulation, but from the continuation of an attitude—preserved, perhaps, by circular reflexes or by verbal cues within the self? Clinical experience strongly suggests that infantile frustration shows itself in this type of continuity, this maintenance of an early attitude, throughout the rest of life, regardless of reconditioning factors and the patient's clear perception of the futility of such patterns.

Here, again, the animal laboratory has simplified the picture and given surprisingly clear support to a theory based upon clinical findings. Four equated groups of rats were reared by J. McV. Hunt for comparison. Two of these were fed normally throughout the developmental period; the third was fed normally in infancy, was fed scantily during the pre-pubertal period, and then fed normally again; the fourth group was subjected to feeding frustration in infancy but was given all the food it required through the later growth and early adult periods. They were all again subject to feeding frustration after reaching adulthood. The fourth group showed gross hoarding of food, laying up large quantities that were not needed, whereas the other two groups hoarded much less. This is the sort of sustained response to early frustration which psychoanalytic theory calls for. The tension appeared to be rather specific; it showed itself at the completion of the meal, not in other general patterns.

An even more striking description of adult response related to infantile frustration appears in animal studies by Alexander Wolf. The hearing of one group of baby rats was impaired by plugging the ears tightly; a second group was made blind by taping the eyes shortly after they opened; a third group served as controls. After a few weeks the restraints were removed. The rats proceeded to grow quite normally. As adults they behaved normally in their individual quest for food, etc., and in their relations to one another. Those that were blinded saw normally after removal of the tape; those that were deafened heard normally. But when the rats had to secure food in a *competitive situation* (several of them having to respond simultaneously to the food pellets), a clear-cut form of response to this infantile frustration appeared. The rats which had been blinded acted as if they could not see the food; they sat on their haunches and did nothing while the others promptly walked off with the food; they behaved, as Wolf says, like functionally blind hysterics. Those which had been deafened made no response to the tone which was used in the competitive situation as a conditioned stimulus for food; though they responded adequately to visual stimulation, when the auditory signal was given they acted as if they did not know it was dinnertime, remaining immobile. If we were dealing with human beings, we should say that these individuals were "inadequate" when in social situations, although they were perfectly adequate when alone. The tongue-tied or paralyzed person who is incapable of action when in a social situation behaves rather like these rats. One who has learned in infancy to give up because there was nothing else to do exhibits the same pattern as an adult, *if in stress;* not otherwise. But the giving-up attitude may in some persons transfer to a very wide area; and in these cases it is proper to speak of a generalized "passivity" pattern.

For theoretical purposes it is important to note that such frustration patterns at the adult level are as a rule specific. They repeat the frustration experience of infancy, as if a genuine impairment of function had occurred and had never completely disappeared. The impairment is too slight to do any harm when the stimulus-response sequence flows through systems not under high tension; but under the necessity of coping with competing individuals, the primitive pattern of approach to the goal object cannot be followed.

Lewin has studied similar instances in which an intellectual task had to be performed, first under easy conditions, then under fierce competition, and has shown that the impairment in the second case is due to a *disappearance of the functional barrier* (for us this is the actual free spread of tensions) between the immediately required act and the total activity pattern. One rushes ahead to do the immediately necessary thing, instead of holding the action in suspense while getting the over-all picture of what is required. Goldworth found similarly that the imposition of a time limit in an intellectual task produced disorganization and impairment of skill only when the limit disturbed the subject's picture of himself, that is, only when, for ego purposes, it was important to get the task done within a certain number of seconds. In all these cases the goal is pursued with an adequate show of skill unless a context of other pressures interferes—in other words, unless the specific tension system required for the act is inundated, confused, overwhelmed by other bodily tensions cutting across and leading in other directions.

If in the light of these experiments we seek the basis of the "frustrated personality," we must first seek specific frustrations in early life and look for the *transfer* of these specific frustration-induced habits. Although there *may* be persons who have never been severely frustrated in any one particular life area but are frustrated with reference to life in general, we have no direct evidence of this, and rather strong grounds for denying it. Even the most tied-up child can, we hope, be given confidence in some area over which he has control; furthermore, no type of neurosis, no matter how severe, has proved to be as absolutely refractory to specific therapy as the concept of the all-round "frustrated personality" would require. We are dealing ultimately with questions of transfer and generalization, and perhaps at times with problems of cross conditioning between different systems (page 239). There is of course such a thing as frustration which is *generalized* beyond the area of its original incidence; indeed, this is characteristic of most responses to frustration, and of most learned responses in general. But we must call a halt when the area of conceivable generalization has been covered. There is a place for both temporary and permanent frustration, and for both local and general frustration, but none for "frustration in general."

Disorganization

We have already touched upon the problem of experimental neurosis (pages 211 and 277). A wide variety of phenomena are catalogued under this head, some of which certainly call for more intensive study in connection with frustration, though we cannot, of course, do justice to the field as a whole.

We must first take account of ambiguities in the stimulus situation whereby two antithetical responses are permitted to be jointly aroused. In Pavlov's laboratory, the dogs were shown circles and were then fed; when ellipses were presented, no food followed. The ellipses were then made more and more like circles, until a critical point was found at which trained animals could no longer make appropriate discrimination responses and began to whine, yelp, bark, tear at the harness, and "go to pieces." At this first level we are dealing merely with opposed reaction patterns, which, as we saw earlier, do not always lead to conflict. Yet even at this simple level there is more than hesitation, more than oscillation between two patterns. The indistinguishability of the stimuli means that neither of the incompatible responses, approach and withdrawal, is fully aroused; yet both are simultaneously activated to some degree. There is, then, no mechanism by which the principle of dominance can work. The tension aroused by the two unresolved antithetical systems is great, and an effort to resolve it only increases it; the conflict state is acutely distressing.

This response is similar to human neurotic responses which arise from what we might call "universal" neurosis-producing situations, in the sense that any individual, no matter how healthy, may be expected to develop such behavior because of the characteristics of the situation. Thus, to be activated at the same time by the need for food and by the need to avoid punishment—as when there is social disapproval of eating—may become a stress situation if the cultural standards regarding eating are indistinct or poorly understood. This is a stress situation to which any perfectly healthy small boy or girl may be exposed. Let us say that dinner on Christmas Day is at two-thirty instead of the customary twelve o'clock, and that the rules as to whether the child may or may not slip into the kitchen and get a snack beforehand are imperfectly defined. To prowl around, grimace, or even cry or have a temper tantrum when the stimulus structure is not completely clear is not in itself neurotic, but it is of a piece with the neurotic behavior described. Some cases of abulia are doubtless stimulus-determined situations of exactly this sort in which the character structure of the individual patient need not inevitably arise.

A slight complication of the problem, but still on essentially the same level, appears in investigations such as those made by Maier. Having trained his animals to respond appropriately to one or the other of two signals by jumping through a window to their food, he made the problem insoluble by failing to feed them following the behavior that had been standardized as correct. The situation reached a point where literally anything that the animal did was "wrong," and many of them became nervous and confused. The climax was capped by a jet of air, which from other evidence we know is in itself a nervousness-producing stimulus. Whatever you do is wrong, and if you stand still in indecision you are punished. The situation differs from the Pavlov type of experimental neurosis only in the fact that the uncertainty due to the lack of clarity in the stimulus situation is complicated by an all-round apprehensiveness and a disposition to expect punishment as a sequel to confronting the choice situation. As a result of training, the tension level gradually goes up through the series of decision situations, until the process of deciding is itself brought into the conditioning picture. The very fact of confronting a decision becomes a conditioned stimulus, a symbol, that trouble is coming; whenever one finds himself in such a situation, the one thing that is certain is that the outcome bids fair to come out in the worst possible way. It would be a mistake to conclude that since this is absolutely sure, the need to decide adds nothing to the distress, i.e., that the animal acts as if its own conduct could neither aggravate nor ameliorate the situation, which must end in the same punishment in any case. The reason why this last point is not true is probably the fact that in animal, as in man, some furtive hope of escape still remains, a hope that, though slim, prevents the attitude of apathy and resignation (page 318).

The situation presented by Maier contains exactly the mixture of distress signals that marks the typical neurotic situation. One has sought many times to achieve love and acceptance from a variety of persons, and is almost but not absolutely certain that there is no formula that will please them all. He goes through antics not unlike those of the celebrated father and son in Aesop's *Fables*, who move from one level of ridiculousness to another in order to find a socially acceptable way to get their donkey home. There are actually, then, two tension problems; one a *decision* problem, the other the pure *suspense*, the sheer mounting painfulness of postponed but inevitable distress. Either one alone would shatter the nerves of healthy animals or men; the two together are sure-fire.

Hamilton's experiments on human and animal frustration (page 276) show a third system of mechanisms at work: the effect of tension upon animal, child, or adult who is learning a way of escape. Placed in a small room from which four doors apparently permit escape, the subject, mildly punished, tries one door after another; he soon learns which door can be opened, and after a few such experiences makes quickly for the correct door. Let the punishment be increased, however, by increasing the strength of the shock or by using cold water, and he reaches a tension level such that he strikes out blindly, repeatedly going back to a door already found locked before he has tried all the others. What is especially striking in Hamilton's experiments is that the distinction between the four doors does not involve the perceptual difficulty present in the circle and ellipse (page 309). It is a question of *disorganization* due to high tension. The tension level has become so high that the decision process itself is seriously impeded.

The chief problems of experimental neurosis, so far as they relate to the *individual predisposition* to break down, whether in animal or man, appear to concern the generality or specificity, and the temporary or permanent character, of individual tension levels. One of the clearest approaches here is the work of Luria, who has not only emphasized general tension problems but discussed critically the specificity of tension regions; his work shows that the higher the level (i.e., from reflex to cortically integrated response) at which conflict occurs, the greater the possibility of a solution. Conflict at the level of effector processes, such as the mere impulse to move or speak, may lead to paralysis, contracture, or stammering, whereas blockage at the cortical level, if the tension at this level is not excessive, may lead to the reshuffling of possibilities. A problem that is insoluble at a lower level may be soluble at a symbolic level. Even here, however, distress situations may cause so great an irradiation of tension that a complete blockage, almost a form of syncope, may result.

But the symbolic level is not only the most competent to effect an adjustment; under strain, it is the most vulnerable. One trembles or wails irregularly, one gasps or perspires, but it is at the level of speech that the disorganization due to tension is most severe. We might consider in this context the everyday problem of nervous stammering (aside from constitutional factors of lateral dominance and the like). Many children stammer to some extent, especially when word combinations, phrases, and sentences are rapidly increasing, or when tired or emotionally upset. The problem is complicated by inadequate sleep or excessive carbohydrate diet, but most of all, apparently, by reproof and general insecurity. In the same way, the adult who is "on the spot" is, like Hamilton's subjects, caught in a situation in which the tension level is so high that coordination fails; errors are repeated, new higher units are imperfectly formed. To put the stammerer in a special category as if he were different from the rest of us is first to overlook the high incidence of the same mechanisms among us, when physiological reserves are low, and second to neglect the specific and chronic characteristics of the distress signals that develop after repeated failures in any complex function. Hamilton's and Luria's subjects, caught in the impasse of their own confused behavior, did not learn the way out of it rationally. The stammerer, having found himself caught, having attempted under high tension to get out of his predicament, and having firmly fixed upon the symptom as an attribute of his own imperfect adjustment, his own failure to cope with a problem which most people solve, has no means of escape at his disposal. The general cultivation of self-assurance, the general reorientation which enables the individual to play down his stammering, usually lowers the tension level and gives some relief. Perhaps it is the sheer lowering of the all-round tension level that makes stammering less common at twenty-five than at fifteen, and rather rare after thirty-five. We should expect it to persist into the later years of life only in the most sensitive and most thoughtful people, and in those whose stores of energy fail to be depleted. The endocrine differences between men and women and the characteristic differences in muscle tone already described are closely related to the fact that stammering is only one-fifth as common in women as in men. The types of nervous strain, though equally acute, are much less likely to take the form of a demand for definitive and overt action, less likely to be of the overt, aggressive, and competitive pattern.

A number of other unintentional acts, comparable in some ways to stammering—compulsive gestures, tics, grimaces, etc.—seem also to be expressions of high tension which at the moment are out of control of the central, or dominant, or most highly organized systems. To say with the Freudians and Adlerians that these may be used purposively to express unconscious wishes is true; but even in the absence of such a purpose, the experiments of Hamilton and Luria show that an action pattern at a certain level of tension establishes circular reflexes which persist even in the face of repeated distress. It is not suggested that these have the deep roots, or the persistence, of a compulsion or a tic, but they may reveal circular mechanisms. The small boy at a family gathering of thirty sees the august grandfather at the far end of the table lift the carving knife as he says: "Will you have some turkey, Robert?" To be spoken to by the patriarch in the presence of the clan is unbearable. "No," he replies, "I never eat turkey." He is clutching at a straw in the hope that all eyes will be averted from him, but the clan turns upon him with mixed anxiety and amusement. First he protests that he really does not want any; then he stammers more and more petulantly that he really means what he says.[1]

Persistence in denying oneself what has been rejected through sheer agony of conflict may of course arise from pride—unwillingness to admit error—or from self-punishment. In terms of the present problem, however, the important thing is to realize that many neurotic patterns are established through early faulty adjustment, that they expand and are generalized through the symbolic system, so that the resulting chronic high tension cannot be eased. The neurotic is sometimes helped by transference (page 542) or suggestion (page 217); this may be another way of saying that reassurance lowers the tension level and makes possible a fresh attack on the problem.

Although the mechanisms described so far occur chiefly in the striped muscles, the same general dynamic is evident in unstriped muscular systems, as when the vasomotor or the entire circulatory system is thrown into a cramplike state of excitation. Thus the blood-

[1] The story is Prescott Lecky's; it relates to his own experience.

pressure indicators in the lie detector indicate the tension inherent in being "on the spot." Though the guilty individual knows that he is on the spot throughout the examination, he also knows that certain words refer specifically to the crime he has committed. The tension level of the innocent person is more or less constant throughout the session, because he has no way of knowing which of the words contains a concealed reference to the details of the crime.

Even more revealing of specific areas of conflict is the current work on skin temperature (page 154), a peculiarly good indicator of vasomotor instability as used by Mittelmann and Wolff. During the psychoanalytic interview the tension level can be made to sink to a point of easy conversational rapport, until questions arise in which the patient feels himself to be on the spot. Although this involves relatively little incoordination in speech, there is a marked drop in the skin temperature from the fairly even level indicated by control curves during normal conversation. One of the intended "control" sessions, however, proved to be quite illuminating; in this the subject was doing simple arithmetic problems, but the skin temperature dropped as if a psychoanalytic issue had been introduced. The comment afterward revealed that the subject thought that the arithmetic task was an intelligence test; she felt that she was on the spot. It was evidently not the hidden content, libidinal or otherwise, that caused what was essentially a fear reaction; it was simply fear. Fear aroused in this way produced the same result as fear associated with psychoanalytic resistance.

In relation to the *chronic* visceral expression of tension, Carl Binger and his collaborators have shown that the overdependent individual who desperately wants to break away from his parents but fears the loss of safety and love which this would mean, develops a subacute arterial hypertension which may, on the sudden accentuation of stress at the time of the breakaway, take the form of a full-blown clinical hypertension. The same general approach is apparently appropriate in some cases of gastrointestinal ulceration in which pathological overactivity of the circulatory system results from chronic overconcentrations of tension, especially through chronic fear from which there is no escape. Alexander and others have demonstrated that persons who have suffered deeply since infancy from a feeling of inadequate love and protection may show chronic peristaltic activities even though there is no food in the stomach. On the suspicion that this might in time cause ulceration, an experiment was carried on in which a dog with a stomach fistula was "sham-fed" over a long period, the food being ravenously devoured but never reaching the stomach. The activity of the empty stomach led to the expected ulceration.

INDIVIDUAL FRUSTRATION TOLERANCE

Just as the thresholds for rage, or affection or amusement show wide individual variations in little children and young animals, so there are wide individual differences in responding to the blockage of impulses when once aroused. As Rosenzweig well puts it, the individual shows a "frustration tolerance" all his own. But the energy of aroused response must go somewhere. We have just considered various outlets for it in the striped and unstriped muscles. It may, however, be diffused or scattered, lost in implicit movement spiraling down to acquiescence, resignation, or sheer inactivity. There is good evidence of constitutional individual differences in autonomic tolerance and characteristic tension level, for they are conspicuous in responses to the "standard" frustrations of hospital routine and in the experimental observations of Pratt, Nelson, and Sun. Individual differences in frustration tolerance are also undoubtedly related to several types of early experience.

Tolerance means here the relative absence of an observable disorganization in response to frustration; more broadly, frustration tolerance involves adequacy and efficiency of response despite frustration. In the adult, as we saw, all sorts of "blocked" or inhibited responses to frustration may at one time or another be observed. At one extreme we may put definite patterns of stoicism, self-control, will power, or whatever we wish to call the symbolic patterns which disperse the energy before an aggressive outlet is found. We may then pass all the way through a series of mixed states to the other extreme at which the blockage process appears to be due not to "self-control" but to the activation of powerful drives that lead to constructive behavior, so that aggressive expression is prevented by the law of dominance. Even if all these types of internal inhibition are ultimately of the same general physiological character, they differ in their feeling tone; e.g., the inhibition imposed from within may give much greater gratification or may convey a greater sense of distress and futility. The abrogation of a purpose by the intervention of a stronger one may seem to the individual an "act of God," something in which the ego feels no painful participation; or he may feel that he is betrayed by himself.

The problem is, however, still more complicated. It appears to make a world of difference whether the blockage is interposed between the aroused drive and its goal object, or before the drive is allowed to develop to its own normal physiological tension level. To describe the former situation, we may borrow from the Freudians and speak of aim-inhibited drives; the individual cannot have what he wants, although the drive remains in force. In the latter case, we may speak of drive inhibition; the blockage takes the form of preventing the full development of the drive itself.

Both processes are evident even at the animal level: (1) In frustrated rats a series of defeats in the competitive struggle for food leads to the abandonment of the effort whenever the competitors are nearby. A morsel of food within easy gobbling distance is not approached, and is scarcely even looked at, until the potential adversaries have left the room. The goal object has ceased to be a manifest goal object; the drive, however, continues. At a later stage, the rat will not eat even when alone; it carries the inhibition within itself in the sense that the food situation is a conditioned stimulus to inactivity. Up to this point we might say that withdrawal has become a generalized response to the goal object. (2) But the further process of drive inhibition, the gradual or sudden disappearance of the drive itself, must be noted. There seems to be a point at which distress in the competitive feeding situation ultimately imposes upon the weaker animal a blockage in the hunger drive itself; the stomach is involved in the "inhibition."

The same thing, of course, is found in hysteria, the term *anorexia* often being applied here; distaste for food takes the form not only of specific aversion to foods which have caused distress, but of generalized inability to become interested in food in any form. So, too, the traumatized lover, having found that love is not to be had, begins by avoiding the situations in which the bitterness of defeat is reinforced, but ends by disclaiming love in the misanthropic manner of Schopenhauer. This complete inhibition of drive may have had a part in the apathetic and quiescent pattern of the jobless in an Austrian village in the 'twenties (page 311); perhaps not only the expression of the drive but the *drive itself* was completely eliminated. Psychiatric practice makes clear that the inanition and, at least apparently, the destruction of almost any drive may occur under circumstances of this sort. In other words, the frustration has conditioned not only the appetitive behavior but the visceral and vegetative factors upon which appetitive behavior depends. The underlying drive may of course be merely masked at times, ready to return in full force when the obstacle is withdrawn; blockage may be continually reinforced by outer circumstances or by inner habit, and the effects of this blockage may be traumatic. (Over and above all this, the individual who fails to get what he wants may verbally deny his wants—the sour grapes mechanism—or even gloat in his martyrdom.)

Most human beings are subject to frustration of all the types described, and make some use of all of these methods of escape. In personality study we are especially interested in the frustration of ego wants. But people differ in the frequency and intensity of their use of each method. Rosenzweig's experiments (page 316) give a measure of the tendency of the individual, identifying himself with frustrated characters shown in pictures, to blame the source of frustration (extrapunitive response) or himself (intropunitive response), or to treat the situation impersonally (impunitive response). Such measures are apparently reasonably reliable; they seem to express some degree of generalization of behavior under frustration. Rosenzweig has also been able to show that the Zeigarnik technique (which tests the ability to recall *completed* as contrasted with *interrupted* tasks) is suitable for such purposes, the intropunitive individual tending more frequently to recall the situations in which he was interrupted during a period of experienced failure. The capacity to accept impunitively both the frustrating situations of everyday life and the experimental situations in which one experiences his own failure appears to be a clue to the absence of a neurotic disposition.

A number of types of conflict appear in more complicated people that are absent in those more simply organized; in their case the symbolic world offers a wider variety of conflicting restrictions, and it is likely also to seem more frustrating than the world of immediate physical reality. The more complicated person has more canalizations; and being more complicated, he is subject to greater involvement in situations by virtue of adience (page 167). The adience principle is especially valuable in the case of the sheer continuity with which the quest for a goal is pursued. One starts to eat breakfast because he is hungry, or to listen to a concert because he is "hungry for music." Caught in the toils of the circular response, he goes on reacting because he is in the situation:

> 'Tis you that makes my friends my foes,
> 'Tis you that makes me wear old clothes,
> But here you are right under my nose,
> So up with the jug, and down she goes.

He eats not only more than he needs to satisfy his hunger, but literally more than he "wants"; and he stays at the concert not only beyond the point of actively needing the concourse of sweet sounds, but even to the point of being almost literally sick with it. Like those in whose heads tunes run for hours or days beyond the point of deriving any delight from the process, we are haunted by sights and sounds, thoughts and fears, into whose circular systems we have been drawn.

This much is true even of organisms that are largely dominated by the pressure of events outside their skins, acting through their "exteroceptors." The autonomic nervous system and the unstriped muscles show, as we should expect, a considerable period during which excitement is maintained at a high level. In man, the cortical tissue and the voluntary musculature go on reacting for a while after being directly struck by the impact from the exteroceptors. Under many conditions the individual goes on seeing, he hallucinates; sometimes what he sees is a little less intense, and he wonders whether he is seeing something or just imagining something. Sometimes the impression is feeble and indistinct, and he calls it a picture in his mind's eye. The role of symbols, then, should be like the general role of sensation, and in fact it is. The fact that one imagines keeps him in the field, in the "behavioral environment," as Koffka would say, though the "geographic" environment has disappeared.

The chronic results often assume a maladaptive form. It will be recalled that many neurotics are prone to neurocirculatory difficulties (cf. page 137). Whatever the predisposing factors which handicap such people, whatever the present tensions, fears, and repressions, it is patent that many are in a condition of neurocirculatory instability which may be masked by the easy conditions under which they live, and that they have no reserve with which to handle even a slight strain. Here the concept of tension level, already developed (page 68), may be as important as the specific situation which is causing distress. This is by no means a statement that their inherited physiological constitution is "the cause" of their neurosis; we mean only to say that the background, the organized total of all that they are as individual organisms, is important with reference to any specific problem involving decision. The amount of effort required to solve a simple everyday problem may cause strain and even collapse, not because a neurotic attitude is necessarily exhibited in the decision itself, but because confronting any problem at all, with whatever slight increase of tension is inevitable, makes the individual go beyond his area of physiological safety. At times, of course, what seems to be a slight effort may be great, because of the symbolic meaning of the issue for the person (cf. page 301); but even the simpler decisions and volitions can be too much for one in a state of exhaustion or of neurotic high tension.

Throughout the study of conflict we have sought to avoid reference to "organic" versus "functional," and to "physical" versus "mental" sources of distress. The organic make-up seems not to work in terms of such distinctions. The organic source of trouble differs from the functional in the degree of its visibility to the observer, and the "psychogenic" factors differ from all other factors only in this respect: It is more convenient to use language of this type when we know more about symbols than about the tissue tensions (e.g., in throat, or brain) which underlie them.

This psychological conception, in which there is literally no place for a mind by itself or a body by itself, has been well phrased by Wolff and Curran in an effort to indicate the dynamics of a special class of psychic events, the process of delirium: "It is an idle and profitless exercise to discuss whether shadows, loud noises, failure in visual accommodation or tinnitus produced 'physiogenetically' or 'psychogenetically' their effects in the cases reported here. It is, however, desirable to formulate data in a manner which allows expression of the facts and which does not create divisions non-existent in nature and for which there is no pragmatic sanction." There are various "levels of integration," the cortical process necessarily involving more complex wholes than reflexes, but at no point marking the introduction of a new kind of substance into the life of the organism.

The difference between the traditional reference to organic and psychogenic factors in personality disturbance and the present psychobiological view appears in many of the current studies in psychosomatic medicine (cf. page 78). In such investigations the relation of injury, disease, or disability to personal living is never stated in simple cause-effect terms. The effect of any physical agent depends on the patient's personality; moreover, the personality moves in a given direction as a result of its problem; the injury must be mediated, reacted to, by the person. Similarly, no psychogenic factor can produce an effect in itself; nothing can be due directly and simply to a conditioning or an association; conditionings are embedded in the context of the organism's total tissue pattern and are different for different organisms with different tissue systems.

THE REDUCTION OF TENSIONS

The next problem relates to the possible ways of handling the tension which arises from frustration. The most obvious is the development of specific aggressive modes of coping with the frustrating object. Almost equally obvious is the method already suggested in Alexander Wolf's experiment (page 307): that of quiescence, apathy, the death feint or playing-possum response, crawling into one's shell, resorting to catatonic rigidity or waxy flexibility of posture and face. Finding that one cannot knock the offending object out of the way, one gives up and does nothing. In their study, already cited (page 311), of the behavior of people who had lost their jobs in an economically strangled Austrian village, Lazarsfeld and Zeisl found apathy and resignation; people no longer rushed about trying to find work or busying themselves with leisure-time pursuits, but acted like hibernating animals, like sheer vegetative systems showing few signs of human life.

It is true that this vegetative response is at times more active than it seems. As one plays dead, one thinks: "They'll be sorry that they picked on me." While withdrawing from social activity, one dreams of revenge or of new supreme achievements. This can, however, be insisted upon much too strongly. In the child who finds that despite his wails he must go to sleep, and in the adult who, despite pounding on the wall, has to face his solitary confinement, there is such a thing as a progressive reduction in the tension systems. A certain amount of steam has been let off through long protest; in fact, a learning curve can be traced in which the protests grow shorter and shorter as the defense reaction of "keeping still" becomes established more and more securely. Sheer apathy as a protective measure can develop, perhaps, without any psychoanalytic mechanisms, that is, without any indirect or veiled purpose; it can develop because tension has been reduced through trial and error. This general way of handling frustration can be either temporary or permanent; it can mark itself upon the face and posture of the "man with the hoe," or the defeated soul who has no outlet, no escape, and whose only protection against renewed stress is the maintenance of shallowness. A visit to an institution for the insane will probably convince the observer that absolute resignation of this sort is as common as are the more picturesque escapes found in delusion or in manic excitement.

A third form of response to frustration appears to be far more complex than the two already described. Most purely physical frustration can be handled either by aggression or by resignation; but frustration of a person's ego needs, conflict between his needs to see himself a certain way and the actual perceptual pattern daily brought home to him, permit other devices for defense. We mention elsewhere the "mechanisms of self-deception" (page 547) which are studied by psychoanalysis. These mechanisms are especially relevant in the present context, that of frustration. One means of escape is to reconstruct the picture of oneself so as to make it satisfying; a second is to reconstruct the picture of the aggressive world, so that it is no longer a threat; a third is to picture the self as superior to and capable of obliterating the threat. The typical delusions of the psychotic follow these three lines of symbolic escape; and the defenses of the normal person consist typically of milder and more subtly constructed pictures which enable him to achieve one or another of these three purposes.

Very common indeed, yet theoretically complex, is a fourth pattern, "displaced" aggression. The impulse against the offending object or person is itself blocked. There is, then, blockage at two levels: the individual cannot have what he wants, and when he tries to knock aside the intruder, even this act of protest is rendered impossible—the bully stops his mouth, holds his hands immovable. Mary Jane protests against rice pudding, and then is cracked down on because she "makes a fuss." The usual result is to seek another object for aggression. Animal behavior is full of displaced aggression; the primates, in particular, constantly vent their wrath upon an animal not quite so large and terrifying as the one who blocks the way. Deflected aggression of this sort is also common in childhood games and adult politics. The first step in the process is easily enough subsumed under the general psychology of transferred conditioning; the impulse toward the blocking agency is touched off at the moment that any similar agency presents itself—similar, that is, in size, shape, or any other aspect of appearance. Actually, however, the displaced aggression is by no means always directed toward a similar (substitute) object—the child frustrated by his mother may break the toy telephone. Perhaps there is a continuum in such behavior all the way from the primitive tension increase through which blind *random* movements smash everything in sight, to the other extreme at which nearby objects are purposely broken as a way of punishing the interfering person. Between these two extremes, however, there is a large area of displaced aggressive behavior which looks more like a generalized need to reduce to pulp anything and everything that can with impunity so be reduced, a generalized need to smash everything that does or might resist.

This must, in a sense, be called symbolic behavior. The child smashes his own tricycle, the adult shatters his own golf club or political reputation at one stroke, partly because it is something in sight that he can destroy. It is a way of destroying with one sweeping gesture all the annoyances of life, all the things that stand in the way, even all the "ambivalent" things. And even when a person is "cutting off his nose to spite his face," he has the momentary satisfaction of demonstrating a sublime indifference to all threats. In this respect the behavior resembles the passive or apathetic behavior in which the individual refuses to make specific protests (actually much ego defense is involved); but it also has a great deal in common with the highly generalized blowoff reactions in which he protests indiscriminately against everything. If there are pure types of anything, we should be ready to look for mixed types. This fourth type of response to frustration, this phenomenon of displaced aggression, is typically very complex indeed, with some obvious elements of transferred conditioning, and with other elements which from time to time assume varying weights.

Escape from Conflict

Thus far we have found the poor neurotic (and all of us have seemed to participate in the neurotic mode of response) caught in the toils of his own mechanisms. Difficult decisions are sure to be confronted in the world outside, and difficult decisions are sure to arise from his own inner system; and whether they impress us objectively as being difficult or not, they certainly must become so when the tension level reaches a certain point. The implication seems to be that though there are palliatives (page 322) there is no really satisfactory escape; the neurotic pattern is inevitable, and when it once appears it draws the individual more and more within the sphere of its power, so that he helplessly describes meaningless circles. There are actually, however, two broad categories of response—over and above changing the world that causes the conflict—which represent *genuine* escapes from the conflict. We may phrase these categories very simply: first, escape through dissociation and automatism; second, escape through reinterpretation of the stimulus field.

As regards dissociation, all individuals possess to some degree, and some to a higher degree than others, the capacity to split, the capacity to react on two levels, to carry out two lines of conduct which are unrelated, unintegrated with each other; one usually assumes the form of conscious and directed activity, the other is apparently involuntary and is generally not noted or is belittled and avoided as far as possible (cf. page 449). Indeed, the individual symbolically reinforces the stronger tendency and keeps the weaker one at bay; and unless he negativistically reinforces the weaker one at the same time, he has gone a good distance toward resolving the difficulty. The more nearly equal in strength the two conflicting impulses, the more reinforcements of this type will in general be needed to give the stronger one clear dominance. The state of the organism has much to do with success in achieving such dissociation; in sleep and sleep-like states victories are often all too easily won. This may be due to a proneness to dissociation resulting from a change in the physiological basis of bodily integration.

That a functional separation of habit systems is sometimes a physiological reality is demonstrated by the experiments of Girden and Culler. Using the drug curare, they have been able to show that experimental animals retain in the normal state the conditioned reflexes which were learned in the normal state, while losing those learned in the drugged state; and correspondingly that drugged animals preserve the responses acquired in a previous drugged state but lose those acquired in the normal state. There are, then, mutually exclusive action patterns, dissociated one from the other. Without speculating as to the exact relation of physiological dissociation to the ordinary dissociation of human experience, we may say that a mild form of dissociation is evident in the man who at church remembers all the events of the ecclesiastical calendar but has no interest in such things when engaged in business. A greater degree of dissociation apparently occurs in many normal persons subject to stress; they carry out acts which are independent of their primary consciousness (cf. page 449). The more elaborate forms of such functional cleavage will be studied at greater length in Chapter 23, in connection with psychoanalytic mechanisms.

The other device open to the individual for relieving tension is to discover a means of regrouping or naming the stimulus materials so as to permit an integrated response to the whole system, rather than mutually antagonistic responses whose reciprocal blockage constitutes a primary feature of neurosis. It is this device that constitutes the primary normal means of resolving conflict; and therapy as well as education consists largely in discovering such methods of grouping and naming. As E. B. Holt put it, a complex situation may arouse fear or aversion until some appealing aspect of it is noticed, named, and emphasized. The country girl with strict upbringing has been taught that the theater is wicked; among her city friends it is "recreation" and also "art." As she begins to discriminate and to name the things that fit with her own values she is able to shake off her original blind dread; the new experience is integrated with her earlier wants and attitudes, which are themselves somewhat transformed by the process.

Such integration, however, never genuinely involves the utilization of *all possible* responses, but rather, as usual, the all-or-none principle and the principle of dominance. The problem concerns the discharge of the accumulated tension, and suggests therefore that energy is taken away from conflicting tendencies which, being nondominant, can be allowed to subside. Much has been written regarding the supposed role of ethics and religion in permitting release, in integrated fashion, of *all* that the individual really wants. But it is of the essence of civilization that it leads to genuine conflict in wants; integration, in the naïve sense of permitting all wants to be realized, is chimerical. What is sound in an ethical theory like this is the fact that the individual discovers a device for recognizing a pattern that permits a dominant action pattern to express itself, competing patterns being shunted out.

One more step is, of course, required: a definition of the qualities of the configurations which make this unitary discharge possible. Probably they lie close to the central core of selfhood within which resides the greatest continuity and within which are involved most of a person's action tendencies. Integration, then, is not simply a question of finding a possible major means of resolution; it consists for the most part in discovering the qualities of the self which, being dominant over all else, must be enhanced and maintained through the decision.

Hence in order to answer the question about individual differences in the capacity to handle conflict, we shall need chiefly to know two things: first, what kinds of people, under what circumstances, will solve their conflict problems by resorting to dissociation, and what kinds of people, under what circumstances, will do this by restructuring the stimulus field and developing new integral patterns from which conflict is missing. Kurt Lewin speaks here of the antithesis between *rigidity* and *fluidity*. Part of the problem involves an original "cleavage capacity," or "capacity for splitting" (*Spaltungsfähigkeit*) as the Kretschmer school called it; part of it involves habits of splitting that have been developed in neurosis-producing insoluble situations; and a good deal of it appears from the foregoing to be due to the chronic tension level of the individual (at a high tension level all of us would tend to dissociation in the sense that higher integrations would fail).[2] Similarly, the capacity for integration seems to depend both upon constitutional factors and upon a life

---

[2] Remembering the three levels of development (page 66), we see that it is possible to regress from the integrated level to the level of differentiated but piecemeal activity; this is dissociation of the type discussed. It is also possible to regress from this level to the lowest level (cf. pages 145 and 548).

history of relative freedom from such tense decision situations, and partly also upon intellectual and emotional factors which have permitted successful training in the regrouping of tension-producing stimuli. Symbols within a hierarchically organized system probably also help in holding it together.

Apparently, then, there are countless problems behind the simple question as to whether an individual will dissociate or integrate. And beyond this question of individual differences in capacity to integrate lie such general questions as these: Under what conditions do thwarted impulses die out? Under what conditions do they remain active, pressing for expression? Under what conditions do they remain latent, waiting for a stimulus to activate them? How and when may their energies be redirected, so that new responses appear which on the surface have no relation to the thwarted impulse; how and when do they raise the whole individual tension level? Though we are far indeed from an answer to such questions, we may find that ego psychology (Chapters 20–23), especially as developed by psychoanalysis, can reach further than the rather elementary "drive psychology" so far considered, and that a structural approach (Chapters 26–31) can take us further still.

Part Three
THE PERSONAL OUTLOOK

14. The Perceiver

WESTERN man's basic ambivalence about his own make-up is beautifully illustrated in the way he talks about his senses. Although everyone knows that it is brutish to rely on one's senses and that the clear light of reason puts the senses in their place, the ultimate test of sanity and adjustment is nevertheless to have sense, common or otherwise. The paradox has led us to contrast the senses with sense; a man comes to his senses as he reflects and discovers that his senses have been misleading him.

This basic ambivalence, this urge to play both down and up at the same time the machinery by which we secure our impressions of the world, has come crashing into experimental and other fields of psychology. In studying the "higher phenomena," there has been pressure to disparage the importance of the sense organs; there has, at the same time, been an effort to prove that these higher processes are all essentially of the same family as the simpler ones, that perception and thought are governed by laws of impression and association as simple as those operative in smelling, tasting, and touching.

Yet despite the debate there appears to be a continuum in the cognitive processes all the way from the simplest to the most complicated, and language is so saturated with the recognition of this fact that nothing the psychologist can do can either obscure or clarify it to any great extent. For example, the reader glances over this passage with its not very well concealed dissatisfaction with experimental psychology and wonders whether it is in "good taste," that is, whether it should be compared with oranges or cod-liver oil; or he will close the book for a moment's dissatisfied reflection and say that the author "doesn't see it the way I do." In other words, he will use the language of sensation to describe the facts of thinking. People differ in "point of view" on the most abstract problems. The common man says he doesn't like the "smell" of a thing; the poet says the philosopher has lost the "common touch." It is altogether shocking, I think, that personality study has tried to get along without a study of the senses. The suspicion arises that personality study in terms of using the senses in relation to the world—for example, as in the Rorschach method—long remained unknown (or in disrepute) among psychologists largely because of a basic reluctance to admit that sensation and perception involve personality in any way.

But while personality research was once concerned largely with behavior manifestations, it is only fair to say that the last two decades have witnessed a steady shift to another approach, in terms of the individual's manner of perceiving the world about him, and himself in relation to it. If we understand the differences in *perceiving*, we shall go far in understanding the differences in the resulting behavior. The relation between the outer world and the individual is gravely misconstrued by the assumption that this world registers upon us all in about the same way, that the real differences between people are differences in what is *done* about this world. The contemporary point of view, developed in the past two decades by Piaget, the Rorschach workers, psychoanalysis, clinical psychology, projective tests, etc., has involved emphasis upon the basic notion that every individual lives in a more or less "private world" (L. K. Frank); there is no standard objective world except through our slow yielding to a rather painful compromise process (Piaget's "objectivity") that is often less coercive, less "final," than the private world. The structure of the private or personal world, then, is the problem to which we turn.

This problem can be broken down into a series of subproblems as to where such personal worlds begin and how they are constituted. They begin, of course, with the individual differences in receptors mentioned earlier (page 73), differences in their adequacy and subtlety, their upper and lower thresholds, their health, their resistance to fatigue and disease processes. Second, these personal worlds differ, in all these same ways, with respect to the nervous pathways that run from the receptors inwards and with respect to the interconnections between these pathways and the lower centers, particularly the interrelations of sensory and affective responses in the "lower centers" of the brain. Third, there is the variety of impulses arriving at the cortex; this depends upon the structure of the projection and association areas and upon the life history which has interconnected and dynamically organized them in one way or another. Last of all, these worlds differ with respect to implicit or explicit tendencies to action (including the intrinsic action tendencies of glands and muscles) in which all these processes of elaboration are expressed.

We might summarize the relation between this great complexity of the problem of perception and the false simplicity often assigned to it by saying that we do not really see with our eyes or hear with our ears. If we all saw with our eyes, we should see pretty much alike; we should differ only so far as retinal structure, eyeball structure, etc., differ. We differ much more widely than this because we see not only with our eyes but with our midbrain, our visual and associative centers, and with our systems of incipient behavior, to which almost all visual perceiving directly leads.

The only method of analysis which can safely be followed in all this complexity, in view of the sketchiness of the available anatomical and physiological data, is a genetic method, one in which the course of perceptual development in the individual child is patiently followed Although this method is itself sketchy in some respects, it has the advantage of achieving reasonable coherence through a system of cross checks and a formidable amount of experimental data that has been well summarized by Heinz Werner, and because data on the character of perception and on behavioral and neural growth stages now constitute a fairly harmonious and biologically intelligible unity.

PERCEPTUAL DEVELOPMENT

There are a number of reasons for believing that perceptual responses in the newborn are relatively diffuse; sensory projection areas being poorly developed, sense impressions are massive, blurred, incompletely differentiated. There is a rough quantitative difference between a big impression and a little impression, but there are prob-. ably no clear distinctions between colors or tones, or even, apparently, between color as such and tone as such. The mind as a whole is a blur; there are no sharp outlines within it. A loud sound and a bright light combined may produce an effect something like that produced by a much brighter light or a much louder sound acting alone. The qualities of sensation which do not belong to any *one* sensory field, the "intersensory" effects (cf. page 240) are well marked in infancy. Though the sense organs are for the most part active in the newborn and are constantly funneling energy to the central nervous system, the latter is not differentiated enough to register them independently. But differentiation and learning go on rapidly. Conditioned responses, as we have seen (page 193), can be formed in the first fortnight, and these probably involve some sort of perceptual distinctions. Canestrini reported that a child a week old responded differentially to his mother's voice in contradistinction to other voices, and Bühler and her co-workers found that by six weeks the sounds of banging, blowing, and tearing, which were at first not differentially responded to, were well differentiated, and that voices produced reactions characteristically different from those produced by non-human sounds.

The process of perceptual development seems, then, to involve marking off, reacting to element after element as a distinctive entity. From the blur, from the mass totality, emerge well-defined individual elements. For the most part, integration lags behind; there is so much to be discovered, and the means at the child's command are so inadequate, that two new experiences, like the *sight* and *tactile* impression of an object, may long remain unconnected. But by the fourth or fifth month he not only is consistently following moving objects with his eyes but is beginning to connect them with the tactual impressions which result when he accidentally touches the moving object; from this follow reaching and generalized eye-hand coordination. When the hands can cooperate with the exploring eyes, the world is broken down, its material assessed much more rapidly and effectively.

But the eyes do not suddenly reach the level of mature discrimination. Until the baby is eight or nine months old, the lady from across the street can play with him and be accepted, if she knows how to hold him; faces are more or less alike to him, and they are all more or less good. The typical shyness, the head-averting or hand-over-the-eyes pattern of the child nine or ten months old in response to a stranger is rather sudden and is reasonably clear evidence that he is beginning to distinguish faces, just as much earlier he distinguished voices. This pattern does not appear in babies who are "passed around." This means not that all women are equivalent, but that none of them is *strange*.

The process is still one of differentiating, separating, breaking down. It depends primarily upon sheer neural, especially cortical, differentiation; but to be effective, it depends also upon practice in coping with things that have to be distinguished, exigencies of the situation. It makes a difference in your action whether you differentiate or not; you get better results when you do. Learning to see parts, learning to break up wholes so that you can manage the separate components, satisfies drives and eliminates frustrations. The child is struggling to cope with his world, and one of the things that every hour or experience teaches him is that he copes with it better when he breaks it up.

The actual requirements of his particular family and culture determine what must be broken up. If, for example, he lives in a group in which all adult women are friendly to him, differentiating between their faces will be of small import; the same will be true if they are all about equally hostile to him. If he lives in a world in which mother is good to him and other people are careless or even hostile, the process of differentiation is accelerated. Individual differences can then be expected on the ground that cultural requirements differ and that within a subcultural whole individual mothers will differ. And, as always, the individual child will struggle in his own way, depending upon the intensity and duration of his needs as well as upon the rate of neuromuscular maturation.

The pathways from the receptors not only lead ultimately to the cortex but on their way pass through the lower centers of the mid-brain. This probably means that each sensory impulse is capable of arousing an affective response, because those centers are intimately concerned with affect. At any rate, a large part of the little child's stimulus world is good or bad, acceptable or unacceptable, comforting or frightening. If we were speaking of the adult, we might say that an "association" exists between the cognitive value of each impression and the affective tone associated with it, as when we find the sound of a cello agreeable, the sound of rattling cans disagreeable. We must remember, however, that the sharp differentiation between sense impressions has not yet appeared in the little child; he does not differentiate sharply even between sensory and affective elements. We are dealing with sense affects, that is, with global impressions in which the affect is a phase of the impression itself. This stage, in which the affective attributes of stimuli cannot be separated from the cognitive, Werner calls *physiognomic* (page 266). Material from diaries and copious experimental data show the perennial disposition of the child to perceive directly the beauty or ugliness, the goodness or badness, the lovableness or frightfulness of the things that act upon him.

The world is loaded with such prejudgments long before the stage of judgment itself is reached. And while differentiation apparently works against the deeply established tendencies of primitive experience engendered in the mental background, the physiognomic attributes promptly reestablish themselves in the relaxed, unpractical mood of fantasy or of poetry; the physiognomic way of thinking and speaking also returns in the heat of strong feeling.

Except for a somewhat different vocabulary, Piaget's stages in the child's mental development parallel closely those of the German experimentalists cited by Werner. *Indissociation* is the term used by Piaget for the stage of undifferentiated blur, when dissociation or differentiation has not occurred. Most stimulus objects deliver their energies to the organism in patterns which change from moment to moment. The size, shape, and color of a mahogany table and the inflection and timbre of the mother's distant voice are not fixed entities; in such a multiple stimulus the phases constantly change, so that their organization is perpetually on the march. For all that, the child learns to know both the table and his mother's voice. This is the problem of "constancy." One finds constancy in the thing, or the person, or the law, though nothing ever recurs in quite the same form. This has become today a very general and very important problem for experimental studies, such as those on size constancy, color constancy, and object constancy.

Piaget likes to phrase the same problem in terms of that great nineteenth century slogan, *conservation*. Despite the fleeting appearances of mechanical, electrical, and chemical systems, science learns to find in its equations a "conservation of energy"; despite the apparent disappearance and reappearance of substances, it finds a "conservation of mass." In a similar mood, historians may tell us that all our present-day ideas are mere refurbishings of ideas as old as Thebes, or indeed as ancient as paleolithic man.

A tangible point at which to take hold of the child's ideas of *persons* and *things* through the establishment of such constancies is the study of the capacity to recognize objects in changing contexts. As the contexts change, how and at what age does the child learn to demarcate them? This is Piaget's experiment: A watch is dangled before a child nine or ten months old, and he grabs for it. After he has played with it for a moment, it is placed behind a pillow; he dives under the pillow and comes up with it. The experimenter takes it from him a second time; he moves it across the child's field of vision; and this time he proceeds to place it under another pillow at the other side. The child is now free to dive again. What does he do? He dives at the spot where he *first* obtained it; though it was put in its new location before his very eyes, he seeks it in its old habitat. The child, says Piaget, is responding to the global situation—to "shiny-tick-tick-right-side," we might almost say, not to *isolated* shiny tick-tick. There is as yet no *object constancy*, no *conservation of things*. (It is in this stage of holistic response, of indissociation of the stimulus components, that Freud's "omnipotence of thought" and unstinted magical participation flourish; cf. page 382.)

It is largely through motor response, especially manipulation, that the various phases of the whole situation are separated, phases that the child can control, can *cause to appear* one by one and can use at will as they become distinct. Even the three-year-old hears many sentences as a blur; the what, why, how questions are often purely requests for repetition. Too literal an answer, at an equally rapid tempo, may lead to continued confusion; what the child needs is a short phrase that has *parts* so that he can take hold of one of them. Echolalia in three-year-olds, the mechanical repetition of the last two or three syllables of a sentence, suggests the presence of a circular-response mechanism unaccompanied by the capacity to break down the flowing sentence perceptually, even when the individual words are familiar. At a higher stage in understanding, a word is recognized and responded to. At an even higher stage, two components in a sentence may be grasped and each responded to, still with no sense of the relation between them. If they are repeated, the order and relation are controlled by the child's needs, so that juxtaposition and syncretism appear; he repeats the story with the elements intact but jumbled (real skill comes later, at the third level, the level of perceptual integration; cf. page 342).

We saw earlier that development from the first perceptual stage to the second is primarily an expression of experience rather than neural growth; the same thing is suggested by these instances of juxtaposition. For they occur not only in the little child, but in the adult who is confronted with a complex new situation; he detaches the recognized parts from the whole and strings them together in the chain of his own association. Perceptual differentiation in the adult appears to depend upon this sequence of experiences, especially those in which he has had to make a selective response to a phase but not to the whole. The stages are comparable for all of us so far as we all have the same needs. The world of things is fairly obdurate in imposing distinctions. All who have had experience with tables, with traffic, or with spoken English have been forced, up to a certain point, into making similar distinctions and reconstructions; we have been bludgeoned into recognizing that balls roll off of tables, that umbrellas will remain leaning against walls but not against cats (the two-year-old tries the experiment). So wherever our needs differ we literally *see* differently. Much of the process of individual perception depends on the force of *past wants*, the person's need to disentangle and restructure in terms of the situations with which he has had to cope. The fact remains, however, that we have *learned* to perceive as we do, and that needs play just as important a role in guiding the formation of our perceptual structure as in guiding the structure of our motor habits. The world of human relations is much less uniform than the world of nature; one can use logic at home that does not work in the town meeting or the court, but there is still a common denominator which we all share. In the world of fantasy there is a far greater place for individual patterns.

To be sure, the process of differentiation which we have described must inevitably depend to some degree upon general and local bodily changes; differentiation cannot occur until the body is ready. The same process is evident in the adult's daily confrontation of new situations. When he sees for the first time a Navajo ritual, a surrealist painting, or a cyclotron, he presses toward the isolation of parts from the melee, giving particular attention to relatively familiar elements; it is only after he has isolated the elements that he makes sense of the whole. It follows that the phases of bodily development are important only as a background for understanding perceptual development; the latter must occur every time that a new whole waits to be mastered. Differentiation takes place under conditions of need or stress—of an external need to find a means to an end, or of the need involved in the unresolved tension situation that we call curiosity (page 240).

Egocentrism

It is not surprising that at first the little child does not pick out from the flux of his own visual, auditory, and other impressions some sharp thing that is his *self*. Since for him there is no "thing constancy," there can be no continuity in that particular thing to which selfhood is attributed. He is thus "egocentric" in the sense that there is no frame of reference which permits him to look beyond himself as an entity distinguished from the rest of the world. Many corollaries follow from this lack of awareness of self; for example, in the light of the flow of his own stream of thought, he learns by experience that many things happen in thoughts in accordance with his wishes, and, as he watches the stream of outer events, he expects his wishes to affect its course. The child is magical in his thinking; seeing no fundamental difference between the manageable and manipulable flow of thought and the course of events in the outer world, he believes that thinking a thing will make it happen. This process of subsuming outer events under the category of mental activity Piaget calls *participation*. It is only as perception of the self is sharpened, and consequently a line is drawn between thought patterns and perception patterns, that the limitations of participation and mental control are grasped. The child's naïve acceptance of things as they look to him—*realism* is the name Piaget gives this process—is gradually replaced by *objectivity*, in which a world independent of egocentric appearances is sought. Freud's "reality principle" is thus closer to objectivity than to Piaget's realism.

Lacking any clear awareness of self and therefore of the dependence of his world of experience upon this self, the child assumes that what is evident to him is evident to another; his egocentrism takes the form of assuming that everyone sees what he sees. Children of various ages were Piaget's subjects for an experiment on this phase of ego-centrism. The child sees a doll that has been placed in the midst of a large relief map of the Alps. Around the walls are large photographs of the peaks from different vantage points. The request, "Pick out the photograph that shows what the mountains look like to the doll" leads the younger children to select the picture which shows what they look like to *him* from where he is standing at the time. Egocen-trism is evident also in the following: Arabella, aged two and a half years, lay in her bed in a room in a "railroad apartment" in New York City. She knew from his vocalizing that Paul was in his bed three rooms away. Arabella had proudly mastered the "tumbleset"; and since achievement calls for a spectator, she shouted the length of the hall, "Paul, see what I can do," and did another tumbleset for him to see. This was no summons for him to come down the hallway; his answering voice showed that he had heard, and nothing more was necessary for Arabella's happy continuance of the performance *in the presence of a witness.*

Paul himself at five noticed a scarlet tanager. His father remarked that some people couldn't tell a scarlet tanager from a grosbeak. "Oh, yes, they could; they'd notice his black wings, and he's redder," "But, Paul, some people don't know; they never noticed how red he is, or how black his wings are." Paul was not convinced. He had studied minutely the color plates showing the tanager and grosbeak, and he knew every detail; the details *were there to be seen*, and no one could miss them; everyone's experience was like his own. The fact that others perceive differently from oneself can come only later, after long experience with the differences in people's testimony as to what they perceive, and when the sharpness of self-awareness is brought into relation with these different worlds of experience.

From the same general way of thinking follows judging others by oneself, that is, attributing to them what is a part of one's own pattern of thinking and feeling. The nursery-school children who had been frightened in the course of Mrs. Holmes' experiment in "walking a plank" suspended on stepladders found it hard to believe that other children enjoyed walking the same plank. John had been frightened; hence when he looked at Ernest's beaming face in the photograph taken when Ernest was walking the plank, he said, "Ernest is afraid."

Piaget's methods also reveal, as do the German methods, that this simple projection upon others of what is a part of oneself is a long time dying, and in fact never completely dies. Indeed, though the *existence* of Piaget's egocentrism seems as solid a fact as any revealed by experimental psychology, his apparent belief that there is little or no egocentrism *in adults* is extremely curious. Almost all adult misunderstandings, arguments, and recriminations are colored heavily by egocentrism, by the assumption that the other fellow must see it as we do and is just perverse in not acknowledging it. A distinction could of course be attempted by saying that the adult is not egocentric but is indulging in wishful thinking or is autistic (cf. Chapter 15). Each party to the encounter is, to be sure, autistic; each wishes to cling to his own familiar, satisfying way of seeing; but this is also true of childhood egocentrism. The failure to carry on the laborious task of reordering one's experience, to see how it would look to the other person, is due to inability and to repugnance for the labor involved in striking out for new reference points and painfully structuring all over again the world to be seen. "I know I'm right anyway; I've been all through it dozens of times; he's prejudiced."

The present hypothesis may be pushed still further. Egocentrism is probably never given up at all except under pressure; the structure that autistically gives peace will never submit to remodeling except as the unfortunate consequences of the inexorability of the world or of other people's insistent wants gradually mount up. Piaget seems at times to put the case this way, in terms of increasing experience; at other times he seems to think that sheer chronological age, maturity as such, is a guarantee of increasing objectivity. The present hypothesis holds that all perceptual responses are maintained as long as they *work* well, that they are shaken down only when necessary to permit a working structure, and that egocentric percepts are exactly like all others in this respect, being given up, "de-ego-ized," only when life's demands admit no escape.

The "blur" stage of perception, stage one of perceptual development, is replaced by *differentiation* (page 334). A third stage is possible: *integration*, the articulation of the differentiated parts. All three stages are manifest in the child or adult whenever he confronts a *novel situation*. A visit to a factory is likely to mean, first, a vast blur; then a series of specific machines or of individual wheels, cams, shafts, pistons; and finally, but much later, an integrated pattern of how all the various pieces of machinery are integrated for production. Similarly to one hearing a strange language or an unfamiliar type of music, there is at first scarcely more than noise or undifferentiated tone. So far as it is worth while to make the effort, he proceeds eventually to disentangle the sounds; as usual he learns chiefly because it is worth while to do so. As fast as the parts can be disentangled from their matrix, they are ready for recombination and are organized; the tones from the various instruments are grasped as a unit. The ear which is at first able to hear only classical music can in time hear a new musical form. The practical music teacher must first break down (from the original blur) in order to build up, must inculcate analytical habits of perceiving in order to give a sense of freedom, appreciation, or creative power.

These three stages, then, are present even when the maturation problem is not involved in any way. But these are the same stages which characterize the process of maturation (cf. page 62) and motor learning (page 202). Since this is the case, it may well be asked why the stages should be the same in relation to these very different problems. The answer seems to be that the theory underlying the three stages is, as Herbert Spencer made clear, just a logical ordering of a developmental necessity. The theory proves to be nothing but an axiom; it has to be found in living things and everywhere else. No problem of development arises unless a thing changes; a homogeneous thing can only change qualitatively by breaking up into recognizably distinct parts; and it is only when such a breaking-up has occurred that the heterogeneous elements can be integrated into an articulate whole. Unless individuation follows mass behavior, there can scarcely be behavior units; and unless integration follows, there can scarcely be adjustment to the environment. In the same way, if in either childhood or adulthood the individual confronts something for which he has no preparation, the only thing that he can do is to look at it until he finds parts with which he can cope; and the only thing that he can do thereafter is to put them together in a pattern which mediates between himself and his behavioral environment. We appear to be dealing with a general principle of development. To be sure, the child cannot go through any such stages in confronting new things unless he has begun, through motivation, to be biologically disposed to some differentiating. But when he is capable of differentiating between things, he needs experience in carrying out the process.

It would be misleading to imply that the only thing that can be done with differentiated parts is to build a mosaic structure or "pattern," in which the component parts can still be recognized. Such structures are indeed common. Often, however, the distinguishable ingredients merge in a blend that almost completely defies analytical effort. Thus the culinary art, among others, is successful so far as the many ingredients offered to taste, smell, touch, and the temperature senses are not separately distinguished but are taken as a whole. Such blends of differentiated parts can be made anew, even though the neural development be as complete as it ever will be and the specific energies of the various cortical sensory regions be well defined.[1]

If the sensory components of consciousness are clear, how can they be melted down into a blurred totality? The answer is apparently that they constitute simply a return to the first undifferentiated state. Indeed, if we look closely, we find a continuum of activities constantly evidenced in the adult, from the mosaic type of integration to the blend type of experience. The teataster, like the orchestra conductor, trains himself to recognize qualities that are ordinarily lost in the total; he does exactly what one does when passing from the first to the second stage. At the same time, however, other aspects of the tea, or the music, are present; these represent new blends made at the moment. The fact seems to be that the adult mind is functioning all the time at all three levels, but that each individual has his own proportion, his own balance of the three. The same thing is brought out by a comment on Gestalt psychology to the effect that organized *structure* is one characteristic, but not the only one, of normal adult thinking, and, in particular, that the phenomenon of insight and the question as to whether insight is gradually or suddenly achieved must necessarily depend upon the general maturity level, the specific perceptual level regarding the matter in hand, and the specific individual disposition toward achieving structure as compared with remaining at or returning to either of the more primitive levels.

It must be stressed that forward movement from the first to the second and from the second to the third makes up a large part of what is ordinarily called "thought." In special reference to Freud, it is worth while to note that the progression is inevitably unconscious

---

[1] The sensory regions have been established in several ways, one of the most interesting being the experimental study of a patient undergoing a brain operation without general anesthesia, who, completely conscious, undertakes to describe the specific quality arising from different stimulus regions of the brain.

and reveals all the attributes of unconscious dynamics. The undifferentiated state can hardly know where it is going, nor can anyone know, on its behalf, what it should do; when the differentiated parts emerge, they are equally helpless to tell where they are going. Nor does it help to say that a mental set or predetermined tendency provides guidance, for such a tendency is itself merely one of the ingredients that is waiting to play whatever organizing role it may, along with the organizing role played by all the other factors. We can hardly bring in the unity of the completed process to explain what happens at the second stage before the parts interact; we cannot resort to a law of closure which finds within the components the one possible way in which they must reach the third level. There may indeed be one method that is the most tension releasing in a given process of thinking, but a great deal depends upon the circumstances of the moment. Many types of integration are usually available. A great many integrated third-level processes are constantly being discarded and replaced by others which function better at the moment, only to go their own way later into oblivion.

A factor often neglected in the study of perception and thought has been motivation. As blurred percepts give way to differentiated ones, and these in turn give way to integrated ones, the underlying principle is that of *need*, or *drive*, or *tension*. The latent aspects in a percept—as yet unresolved and lacking recognizable individuality —which have a stable relation to tension reduction, to satisfaction of a craving, tend more and more to stand out as figure against the background of other attributes; with each successive tension resolution and each change in the qualities of the total, perceptual sharpening is accelerated. If the blurred total is related, as it often is, to two or more needs, and if on some occasions certain parts of it are relevant to one need, other parts relevant to another, it is only by focusing the sensory and cortical apparatus at the time that the immediate need is cared for; only through neglecting some parts and emphasizing others is adaptive behavior possible.

The principle of controlling the perceptual processes through tension or needs is evident in the earliest childhood problem of differentiating between friendly and hostile voices, which, Bühler's photographs show, is still absent at three months. "Voice in general" is what is heard; and smiles and diffuse excitement are the responses. By seven or eight months "friendly voice" and "hostile voice" are heard; from the blurred total have been differentiated attributes of friendly or hostile import. Qualities in the latter make appropriate behavior consist in avoiding or placating the adult; in the case of the former the playfulness and laughter of adult patterns make playfulness and laughter appropriate responses. The voice has of course many other aspects besides friendliness or hostility. The child must learn to select and emphasize; he must organize in terms of figure and ground.

When a person has once gone through the three stages he can respond instantly in third-level terms; he can take in the meaning of a sentence before he attends to individual words. This aspect of perceptual dynamics is clear in the Rorschach procedure. The preponderant tendency is from whole to detail, and usually from large detail to small detail. Rorschach himself was keenly aware, as for example in his discussion of the personality structure of the pedant, that the need to differentiate in order to control, and the need to be systematic and orderly in such differentiation, reflect basic perceptual dynamics. In general, the details perceived as figure against the background of the rest of the ink-blot pattern (and the card as a whole) are directly suggestive of the individual's drive structure. Schachtel has shown the persistence, in both childhood and adulthood, of primitive global tendencies and of the trend to differentiate or fail to differentiate, depending upon the need of the individual, and has made clear that the contents of the differentiated response are related to personal wants. Thus a frightened child found comforting and protecting figures scattered through the test.

ANCHORAGE

As soon as differentiation has occurred, *anchorage* appears; this is the tendency of percepts to take on a form which gives one feature of the situation special prominence. This one feature, the "figure," stands out against the "ground," and it is upon the figure that the percept is said to be "anchored." Subjectively this is a phenomenon of attention; objectively it is the law of dominance (cf. page 195). The response that is dominant is the one that represents the prevailing anchorage.

To discover the dominance relations of drives is to discover the anchorage of ambiguous figures (cf. Schafer, page 371). Anchorage is also illustrated by the Skinner tautophone which Shakow and Rosenzweig used to bring out, in each individual subject, the tendency to anchor upon that aspect of a blurred stimulus which is most directly relevant to his personality (page 702). A phonograph record containing only vowel sounds is played over at such a distance or under such conditions that it is impossible to hear the record distinctly: the subject hears in the fluid sound pattern what his own needs and interests predispose him to hear.

Anchorage is not an ideal term for this process. Whereas a physical anchor leaves the structure of the anchored ship unaffected, psychological anchorage depends upon the entire structure of the perceptual situation; each aspect is part of the context of every other aspect, and helps to "anchor" the rest. The context of which we are dimly aware may help to determine the meaning of a sound which thereafter appears as figure; nevertheless the meaning, when once clearly perceived, serves as the anchor for interpreting other parts of the stimulus field.

The nature of the *context* or *ground* in giving a specific meaning to the *figure* is well illustrated in the "autokinetic effect." When a single star breaks through the mist on a dark night and is closely watched for a moment, it appears to move. The star may be brought into the laboratory in the form of a tiny point of light shining from a black box; the night, in the form of a darkroom. The light wavers or swings. At first, the movements seem chaotic. But they are remarkably responsive to the experimenter's suggestions; his instructions may cause the light to move rapidly to the right, slowly upward, etc. The movements are, moreover, very responsive to autogenous direction; the light moves as one expects it to move. This "autokinetic" effect, long explored by astronomers as well as experimental psychologists, has been used by Sherif to demonstrate that perceptual fields may be structured by social forces in a manner whose lawfulness and quantitative relations can be explored. The fact that *external* structure is wanting allows maximum play for *inner* structure-giving factors and for all those which arise in the subject from the verbal and other suggestions of those present. The phenomenon obeys all the laws of prestige suggestion and negativism. A mature and experienced subject, instructed to distribute his judgments around his own predetermined mean, influenced a young and naïve subject to bring her range of judgments nearer his own and to raise the mean. At times a subject, setting himself against the effect, saw no motion (cf. page 200). We conclude, then, that motives in the broad sense control perceptual responses exactly as they control motor responses. Voth has shown that different kinds of autokinetic responses characterize different psychiatric groups.

When there is a cumulative effect from several observers, resulting in a conflict due to the disparities in their reports, a nice problem arises in computing the resultant of forces. When, for example, three or

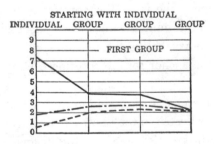

On the a-axis are indicated the four successive experimental sessions (one individual and three group); on the y-axis the number of inches the light was judged to move.

four subjects work together in the darkroom under uniform instruction, each voicing his judgment as to the distance traversed by a light, the discrepancies gradually decrease, and a "funnel-shaped" convergence of judgment may result. If no gross prestige effect brings the other subjects into line with a single subject, the result is simply a reduction of the "degree of individuality." This return to the usual type is what Metfessel found when a group of canaries whose voices had been studied in isolation were brought within hearing distance of one another.

The little child learns to see ambiguous situations much as Sherif's subjects learned to see the moving light. The greater the ambiguity, the more coercive the parental influence; and when others disagree, the child is *impelled* by opposing buffets to occupy a middle region, the safe region of the mores, that is as far as possible from the deviants, the "lunatic fringe." For in this and all other cases of anchoring, the figure-ground relations depend on the tension system; hence specific needs play a huge role in determining these relations, as we shall try to show in detail in Chapter 15.

The anchorage point depends upon variable thresholds, as the excited or fatigued man quickly demonstrates. A person loses his bearings; he forgets the point, the real nub of the situation, or he "loses perspective" in a moment of excessive zeal. The threshold varies with the intensity of the need and the intensity of the outer stimulus, since, like all thresholds, it is dependent upon organic conditions. But it is the property of the anchor to help to preserve continuity of outlook when once established. The intensity of a stimulus which has operated a while above the threshold may weaken later, and yet the habit, once established, may persist. Having learned to detect a sound as a significant sound in the midst of the blare of automobile horns, one hears it thereafter when it is weak. Inner voluntary factors also play their part; one can, with effort, *pick out* the sound previously unheard. In Schafer's experiment (page 371), some perceptual habits, once organized, persisted without reinforcement. Typical anchorage points are much more stable than are the thresholds manifest when they are first being established; this is another way of saying that dominance relations that are established within the organism as a result of a few outer and inner factors (page 271) are not at the mercy of momentary variations in outer stimulus intensities, but are only slowly adjusted to such outer pressures. The "constancy of the inner environment" applies as much to inner patterning as to biochemistry.

The other elements, in addition to the anchorage point, also have their own variable thresholds. We are dealing with *relative* intensity, as is always the case when dominance phenomena are involved. If we ask what, in an anchorage situation, becomes the anchorage point, we must answer that all the multiplicity of factors that determine what act will occur in response to a complex situation appear here; for anchorage is an act, and all the complex dynamics of action are present in the transformation from one act to another. If there are individual differences, constitutional and acquired, if there are degrees of generality and specificity in conduct, and of continuity and of spontaneity in action, so there are individual differences in the world of perception. The struggle and integration of impulses, the differentiation and integration of elemental parts in the perceptual field, and, above all, the phenomenon of accentuation through the anchorage process are the same dynamic phenomena appearing in the inner world as are exemplified in the outer world of manifest behavior.

The *internal* anchors must not be forgotten. Unstable though it may be, the inner organization has regions of relative fixity; one moves forward to the tune given by the organic condition, while moving also in response to the changing accompaniment provided by the stimulus field. The need to keep in intimate contact with the environment is thus the need to discover relevant anchors in the outer world —anchors that move to reduce tension. What is called the *psychology of attention* and is often treated without much reference to inner needs often proves to be the psychology of this quest for anchorage. Just as the structured world is the end result of the evolution of practical necessity (page 335), the selective awareness of the individual child or adult is less a matter of sense organs and permanent brain dispositions than of needs for peace, stability, satisfaction.

Thus in contrast to the common assertion that the Gestalt principle of organization has been overemphasized, we are inclined to say that it has not been emphasized enough. One of the attributes of outer stimulus fields which makes them capable of the organization described by Gestaltists is their dependence upon the character of inner fields. The principle of isomorphism which the Gestaltists have emphasized (the correspondence in *formal organization* between outer stimulus pattern and inner bodily response) is not merely an isomorphism of psychological and physiological structure. It is true that the same organizing principles are discovered with the tools of the physiologist as with those of the psychologist; but there is a still deeper unity of perceptual and motivational structure. This lies in the fact that the structure of motive patterns tends to become the structure of cognitive patterns; the perceived world pattern mirrors to a considerable degree the organized need pattern within. The more tightly organized, the better structured the world pattern, the less it can be controlled by the inner pattern; the more lowly organized, the more lowly structured, the more the inner pattern controls it.

This is not to say that a momentary need must take precedence over others which have functioned before. Personality patterns involve habituation, and cognitive patterns need much reworking in order to be stable, dependable satisfiers of enduring needs. Percepts solidify and resist change; new evidence, new phenomena are frequently unassimilable. Here is embodied what we might call the fallacy of expert opinion, or what Stefansson has called the "standardization of error." New ways of perceiving in science, as in other fields, must often be valiantly sought by the novice or the crackpot individualist among the scientists. Unless a new movement in psychology, for example, carries with it the immense prestige of the better-established aspects of the physical sciences, it is unassimilable. The poetic language and the uncontrolled clinical observations of psychoanalysis made it difficult for psychologists to settle seriously to the task of discovering what was there, whereas operationism, with all its halo of scientific respectability, has been assimilated in psychology much faster than it has been understood. A homelier example is the prestidigitator's comment, "Magic won't work with children." The child has not structured the world in the orderly schemata required for ordinary dealings with mechanical and social events; consequently he neither sees nor infers as the adult does; he does not have habits that can be systematically misdirected. The adult's cultivation of "naïveté" or spontaneity is arduous; it involves not only the painfulness of breaking an established habit, but a direct loss of prestige in the dignified world of adults, the educated, the sophisticated.

Individual differences in this capacity to be childish, this capacity for spontaneity and for relative simplicity or plasticity of structure, are enormous. They are what the Rorschach and projective techniques are far more likely to reveal than are interview or paper-and-pencil schedules, because the superficial manner of freshness and spontaneity is much easier to assume than a deeper, more unconscious freedom. But just as regression may go on without the individual's being aware of it, so the life situation of the overspecialized scientist or technician may lead unwittingly to revulsion and a renewal of primitivism, of the sort magnificently illustrated by Tolstoy's conversion late in life, and by John Stuart Mill's "failure of nerve." Our knowledge of individual differences in the plasticity and adaptability of the anchorage process is at present confined chiefly to such material as this on the effects of specialization and of emotional constraint in preventing plasticity of outlook.

Our recipes for the increase of spontaneity are therefore purely negative. We are able only to warn in a general way against habits of pigeonholing experience, of pedantically organizing each new aspect of experience in a preformed system of categories. The Moreno procedure for training in personal spontaneity consists of breaking the cold stereotypes of social attitude; similarly, the Rorschach data on "constriction" lead to psychological therapeutic suggestions regarding the breaking down of rigidity. But positive recommendations as to the ways of developing plasticity remain indirect. Suggestions about freedom, happiness, and richness of experience for children do not tell directly what kind of freedom, what sorts of happiness, what specific rhythms and varieties of experience. As Fromm puts it, we have learned to emphasize "freedom from"; we know little indeed about "freedom for"—freedom that guarantees a basic and generalized habit of mobilizing all one's energies to meet a new situation. If we knew more about the biological factors involved in the anchorage process, we could make recommendations for the preservation in the individual of the particular kind of spontaneity that is his.

We have been working our way slowly toward a definition of perception in bipolar terms, as an organized process which is both outer and inner, which is organized in terms of saliences both of the world without and of the world within. Organization is not molded exclusively by the need pattern or by the stimulus pattern. This definition, stemming chiefly from Koffka and Sherif, makes perception an *individual process*. The outer world can never be so completely unstructured as to make perception depend solely upon the perceiver; but it can never be so sharply and clearly organized as to obliterate individual differences among perceivers. Experimental techniques can therefore be formulated which cover the entire continuum from extreme fluidity, as in the autokinetic effect used by Sherif, to a definite structure, like an illuminated page of print, in which deviations of individual percepts from the "standard" are slight and can be explored only with patient analysis.

The cultural molding of perception must be viewed in these terms. It is true that group pressure can profoundly modify the individual's habits of perceiving or recalling or reasoning; but it must be emphasized that almost everything depends upon the clarity and tightness of the structure involved, and that there are huge individual differences in the clarity of the inner structure that is brought to bear on the outer pattern. Thus Lewis and Asch have shown that the effects of suggestion, marked though they may be in subjects who have only an extremely fluid inner social attitude, are negligible in subjects with clear-cut convictions. The latter respond in two contrasting ways: either by redefining the suggestion stimulus, giving it a meaning which makes sense in terms of their own inner structure and thus enables them to make sense out of it (instead of being bowled over by it), or by elaborating a fresh context to surround the suggestion stimulus and interpreting it as a natural mistake or a deliberate frame-up. When a Fascist-sounding slogan is attributed by the stimulus material to a political leader who in reality is far to the left, the subject reconstructs the situation; either the stimulus does not mean what it seems to, or it is part of some plan of the experimenter's which the subject tries to understand.

THE UNITY OF PERCEPTION AND ACTION

Whatever else perception may be, it is certainly an integrated act that involves the interrelation of components and requires the study of modes of interrelation. Typically, it is organized about a nucleus, more or less as a cell is organized about its nucleus. This nucleus is what we have been calling an *anchor*. Consequently, although there is an interdependence of parts, the dependence of some parts upon the nucleus is more easily observed than is the dependence of the nucleus upon the components. When the interdependence of parts is slight (cf. page 629), some elements in the structure may be said to be more essential than others, and some may drop out without disturbing the others.

In all these respects, perception is like a motor act which involves interrelations and nuclear phases. Whatever the ultimate judgment of psychologists may be regarding the motor theory of consciousness, it is plain that in practice the organizing principles for the two types of processes are the same. The electroencephalograph and myograph strongly suggest that the cortical process is organized and anchored in accordance with the general pattern of organized motor response; the same indices of "attention" or "relaxation" appear in the two types of records. In the same way, studies of the restructuring of the perceptual field, such as Stratton's classical work on learning to see normally when wearing reversing lenses, suggest that the visual space is reorganized at the same time that the world of muscular adjustment is reorganized. Schilder's data on the unconscious schemata by which one appraises the distance and direction of stationary or moving objects also bring out the influence of kinesthetic factors upon the organization of visual space. Individual differences in visual space, such as are described by Stern, make sense when the complete organic make-up is studied.

The visceral components, too, enter into the individual spatial schema. Psychoanalytic studies of the child's progressive discovery of his body, especially the parts associated with strong affect, and his frequently intense response to his discoveries, have sometimes proved useful in understanding adult visual space. Time as a system of divisions for the purpose of ordering the course of one's life is structured by the internal anchorages originally formed by vital experiences of simultaneity and succession. The world of personal time and space to which Stern has given such intimate study proves to be a world individually organized; it has the uniformities that are entailed by life requirements, but it retains much of the organizing power of early unconscious anchoring dispositions.

This unity of perception and action may be illustrated by studies of the conditioning of the perceptual response. For some decades it has been customary to speak of the conditioning of motor responses, and to some extent we are prepared to replace the language of association with the language of conditioning; nevertheless, the phrase "the conditioning of perception" still has an odd sound. Perception, being an organized personal totality, is touched off by any ingredient of the original stimulus configuration, or by details which never were part of the original configuration but are *similar* to the details of it. In the latter instance, we have no choice but to refer to the "transfer" of perception just as we could refer to the transfer or generalization of conditioning. (It is, in fact, this tendency of perception to develop like a motor system—to be conditioned, transferred, and organized in terms of higher units into new and more embracing perceptions— which justifies the studies of *personality style* in which generalized dispositions to certain types of motor responses are found to run parallel to generalized dispositions in the cognitive life; cf. page 632.)

Such transfer of perceptual habit is nicely shown, for example, in individual differences in "constancy." It was noted earlier (page 337) that it takes the child a long time to develop the thing constancy, size constancy, etc., of the adult. The experimenter defines the specific cues, and they must all be the same in order to be functionally equivalent in evoking responses. A good many years seem to be required by the average individual to acquire the normal adult constancies, that is, to build up the appropriate perceptual transfers and to learn what to emphasize, what to ignore. In spite of the extraordinary uniformity of the social pressure to see things in a given way, substantial individual differences in such constancies still appear.

Such constancies lead ultimately to the problem of the way in which things are to be grouped; e.g., shall a series of colored shapes be grouped by color or by shape? All things having a certain property in common are to be handled in the same way, regardless of the varying contexts in which this property appears; but what determines the criterion for the grouping? The answer is that grouping depends largely upon the practical necessities of life. But individuals vary in their needs. Nursery-school investigations show that when blocks and toys are to be handled according to certain definite rules, the child's intellectual maturity is the chief factor involved in the basis chosen for grouping; younger children group by color, older ones by shape. When, however, the rules of the game are more fluid, as in a projective technique, the "mature" basis may be "regressively" abandoned, boundaries between categories resolved, and new ones established as momentary needs direct. Adult reverie may permit one's needs to find an unconventional expression through the form of grouping chosen; thus a psychotic subject tested by Bolles grouped a variety of objects together on the basis not of shape, size, or color, but of their power to kill.

The same conceptual tools which are needed to understand the grouping of objects are useful also in studying social stereotypes. In the welter of individual differences between human beings, one learns to anchor upon the qualities of skin, cheek bones, hair, or manner, which are differentiating in the particular social context; and it is on these that the name and the organized emotional conditionings are bestowed. If different marks are hard to find, but the social need to differentiate remains, one may anchor upon proper names, or even legends of ancestry. And he does the same thing when the person concerned is himself; he groups himself on the basis of the superficial, the external. But just as Goldstein's brain-injury patients lost the ordinary principles of grouping, the member of a social class may in times of crisis lose the anchors which have differentiated his class from those above or below; the sharing of a present predicament constitutes a new anchor. In the same way a personal difficulty, an inner stress, may make some basis of classification other than the conventional one congenial; in crisis one recasts the figure-ground view of himself and finds a new classification.

The same approach is helpful in relation to the *intuitive* view of the self and of others, and of intuition generally. Intuition appears to be a matter of swiftly and effectively *classifying* a new experience under an appropriate head; and apparently is acquired just as the other capacities for classification are acquired; that is, by virtue of an appropriate anchorage. There may, in addition, be intuitive capacities based purely on original tendencies, and hence utterly untrained; but it is hardly profitable to make much of them at the present time, when so many lines of research point to the acquisition of perceptual and other organizing habits through the usual nature-nurture interactions (cf. page 5). The most important fact usually signalized by the term intuition is the role of unconscious or, if one likes, physiological dispositions in classifying a new experience. Whether a given aspect of the organizing tendency happens to be reportable by the individual is inessential. In this sense intuitive recognition of a person or intuitive classification of a bit of music may, as we have suggested (page 233), be the products of an organized activity of which only a small fragment flashes meteor-like through a corner of the conscious field. It is, in fact, unnecessary that any of the *modus operandi* be clear to the intuiting observer.

Although the intuitions of children and animals are probably even less conscious, they may throw some light on the process. Birds often instantly recognize and appropriately respond to the attitudes of other birds toward themselves, instantly divining the presence of hostile intentions of a guileful and indirect sort. In the background there are of course some ordinary conditionings of the Pavlov type; the problem here, however, is the nature of the perception. The bird knows "what is up" and prepares itself for danger. If this occurred in a man, we should call it intuitive and we should be puzzled by the fact that some people have better intuition than others. One man knows perfectly well that he is in danger, whereas another does not, and neither can define any of the specific cues which make him feel as he does. The bird on the ground "knows" that it is in danger; at the top of a tree it knows that it is not. But, in the ordinary sense of the term, such knowledge is "unconscious." If it means anything to say that an organism "knows" something of which, at the time, it is not conscious, the bird "knows" that it is in danger; it intuitively perceives the situation. It is doing what a human being does when he makes an integrated perceptual response to a very complex situation, no component of which reaches the level of a clear and reportable image. Our knowledge of others and of ourselves is largely intuitive in this sense; much of it is "unconscious," much seems mysterious, because there are no conscious anchors for us to take hold of.

Indeed, a large part of what we call personality structure is intuitive response of exactly this sort. It is neither the concatenation of images nor the organized conscious system of relations; it is the individual's unconscious readiness to differentiate, to classify, to organize experiences in his own way. This is why it is pointless to ask whether the psychoanalyst's unconscious processes really exist as "the unconscious," or whether memory images are "stored up" somewhere. The events which we call mental are to a large degree events which move too fast and in too complex a context to permit their recognition and reporting; most of them are the anchored and organized acts involved in appraising situations, and to this we have given the name *intuition*. A psychology of perception which neglects this intuitive matrix is a psychology of surfaces, not of solids; and a psychology of personality which considers only the conscious aspect of perceptual wholes is no better.

We referred earlier (page 266) to Werner's discussion of physiognomic response in which the distinction between cognitive and affective processes has not yet been made. Here, by way of a different route, we appear to be approaching the same kinds of processes. Though we think of the cerebrospinal axis, functioning with the sense organs and muscles, as showing us *our relation to* the world, and of our visceral and midbrain structures as giving us *our feelings about* the world, we seem to have come to a point where, from the point of view of the individual who is acting, intuitive responses must be recognized as involving a complete fusion of the two. Consider, for example, the psychology of values. Values involve tensions and tension reductions (cf. page 182). Value situations are perceived and felt intuitively, in what seems to be a single act; they are appraised and reacted to, exactly as are physical situations.

The Quest for Form

This system of conceptions may be put to the test in relation to the problem of individuality in esthetic perception, especially the esthetic value of form. The quest for form can drive a da Vinci or Bach or Picasso just as—for very different reasons—it can drive a compulsive child or an adult neurotic. Form is here a value; it is perceived, felt, and sought. If, instead of being approached by the geometrician or the carpenter in terms of the measuring rod, it is pursued by the artist in terms of *"feeling for" the form he wants*, the response is properly called intuitive.

The ordering of events in time and space gives satisfaction. During the first months of life, movements are smoothed out; symmetries take the place of jerkiness; a small intense activity, as in reaching, is balanced against a large diffuse activity, as in maintaining posture. All these form-giving processes are well known to the student of visual or auditory esthetics. All are tension-reducing processes. Since we have considerable evidence for large individual differences in the intensity of this form-seeking need very early in childhood, we are on reasonably safe ground in emphasizing native factors, although we have noted that we are not safe in defining these factors as the basis for the *enduring* anchorage tendencies. The problem of the early handling of form is, however, somewhat simpler. We do not know what specific method of organizing will be congenial to an infant, or how he will hit upon the methods he uses later; but we do know that the need for form and the manner of seeking it differ widely from one child to another. Some children move rapidly forward to sharp and clear organization, learning words as sharp and clear elements to be added to the vocabulary day by day; other children take in global masses of meaning and talk, geyser-fashion, in intelligible but unanalyzable sentences that are understood by older children "intuitively" in the sense noted. Clay, fingerprints, and blocks, and the specific acts involved in roller skating or walking on stilts are handled by some children through incisive piecemeal analysis and synthesis; others attack them globally, making many small acts of progress simultaneously on many aspects of the total. The ultimate achievement of the latter may equal that of the former, but it comes about through the gradual sifting-out of disorder rather than through the rapid accretion of orderly serviceable units. Conflicts and repressions may overlie all these mechanisms and create an artificial rigidity of structure or an artificial amorphousness as an effective screen against too clear a recognition of unconscious meanings. But the neurotic disposition will have to follow the original bent. It has been all too characteristic of psychological therapy to assume that the adult's entire quest for form, or dread of it, is a protest or reaction formation (page 551) against specific formal experiences;[2] on the contrary, part of it is in reality a continuation of, or a transfer from, the form-seeking tendencies of early infancy.

But it is not merely the *quest* for form which the student of personality must be prepared to recognize; it is also the *capacity to achieve it*. Just as children with the same drive to roller-skate may differ markedly in their success, depending upon length of legs, position of the center of gravity, and efficiency of the cerebellum, so the capacity to organize depends not only on the quest for form but upon an integrating power, *Gestaltungskraft* (Klages and Rorschach). This over-all organizing capacity cannot at present be measured, except in the

---

[2] For example, the child's confusion as to the spatial relations of tabooed parts of the body may appear, in certain individuals, to be the basis for their later preoccupation with spatial ordering; but it does not follow that all such order has such a root. Most of the sensory and locomotor problems of children, for example, are soluble only through mastering spatial order.

crude ways provided by the comparison of whole responses and details in the Rorschach technique. It cannot be effectively measured in childhood, because the imperiousness of the *quest* for form shows such huge individual differences that sheer *competence* as such cannot be appraised separately. By the time the organism is differentiated enough to permit a quantitative approach to organizing capacity, the data indicate capacities which depend largely upon the area of life that is to be organized, such areas, for example, as are indicated by verbal, numerical, spatial, and tonal material. There probably remains a generic organizing capacity behind these specific gifts, which probably plays an important role in what is called general intelligence; it is in fact close to Spearman's capacity to "educe relations," but it waits for clear identification and a measurement.[3]

The problem of form perception has been used as a rough test of the theory we have developed. Form perception and the capacity to respond to and use form appear to develop consistently in a direction partly determined by individual idiosyncrasy, especially idiosyncrasy in individual needs. The same is apparently true regarding all the kinds of tasks with which perception deals, such as the capacity to note details in a context or to observe distinctions within a relatively homogeneous field or to group things by virtue of their similarity. In every such perceptual function we find what we have found in the perception of form: constitutional adequacy, drive pattern, experience. Perception takes on a form reflecting the whole of what the individual is, just as does maturation or motor learning.

---

[3] Systematic experimentation and factor analysis already reveal some apparently deep-seated individual factors in perception which will eventually probably prove important for personality study. Thus Thurstone tentatively suggests a factor having to do with perceptual speed, a factor of speed and efficiency in perceptual closure, and a factor relating to the rate of reversals in perception. Hanfmann's data show interesting differences between those who approach a task *perceptually* (e.g., *looking*) and those who approach it *conceptually* (*thinking it out*). It is likely that this area, when explored, will articulate closely with the problems discussed in the text.

15. Autism

AS NIETZSCHE remarked, "My memory says that I did it, my pride says that I could not have done it, and in the end, my memory yields." This chapter is our attempt to show why, and how, memory—and all the intellectual kin of memory—*yield*.

Practically the whole folklore of western culture asserts that thought and feeling are utterly different things. Thus Aristotle, being a gentleman, put the rational soul, the motile soul, and the vegetative soul in harmonious hierarchical relation. Instead of bemoaning the lower wants, the animality of man, he ordered them in an aristocratic society; the motile and vegetative souls were "all right in their place." Thought, however, was supreme. Thought was not feeling; it emanated from an utterly distinct principle. The Christian philosophers had a hard time in stomaching this, because faith, hope, and charity, the love of God and of man, were not rational but impulsive and affective; and when through God's grace they were given to man, they seemed to come right out of the feeling life. The thinker, as such, was often dead to the true life of the spirit. St. Thomas achieved a thirteenth-century reconciliation.

With humanism and its children, much of the Aristotelian "class structure" of the little community within the self came back in one form or another. Rationality was supreme; feeling was at best the well-beloved servant of a glorious master. The deists went so far as to make rational man capable of discovering God and salvation by his own clear vision, without any gift of revelation through grace; and the agnostic intellectuals of the eighteenth century sharpened the distinction, until reason became the mark of humanity, in utter independence of and supremacy over animality. This was the basis for that great new idea of *progress* which optimistically ushered in the scientific era of the nineteenth century. To put it all physiologically, it was assumed that we think with the brain, feel with the viscera.

This dogma regarding the absolute separation of thought and feeling secured such a hold that Darwin's effort to show the animality of man's thought convinced the intellectuals only that they ought to do colder and clearer thinking about the origin of thought, and approach the Goddess of Reason with less feeling. This does not mean that philosophers and psychologists continued to hug the rational soul; quite the contrary, they disapproved of all hugging. They wrote copiously of the dependence of thought upon its evolutionary background, but they were like a humorless man trying to explain a joke. They saw no pertinence of evolutionism to the quality of their own approach, which continued to be analytical, verbal. No real psychologist would let feeling "interfere" with his thinking. James and Bergson, the two greatest advocates of full-bodied evolutionism, the two who saw the evolutionary implications most clearly, are full of examples of this tendency. James spoke perpetually and vehemently about the "sentiment of rationality," the "will to believe"; but he wrote a chapter on perception which assigns to the stimulus structure, the receptor structure, and the brain paths almost the entire task. His chapter on habit gives central and motor mechanisms almost complete say in the actual course of habitual conduct, without even a reference to autism; he wrote a chapter on reasoning that starts with recepts and ends with concepts. Bergson, from whom we might certainly expect a more biological approach, makes reason the process of cutting cross sections through a fluid reality, crystallizing as it goes, in sharp distinction to the tide of impulse that directs life. The textbooks today still serve up affect (emotion), impulse (conation)—the will seems to be disreputable—and, near the end, concept formation, thought, reasoning, as a completely different kind of activity, *sui generis*. Everything else in human conduct is supposed to be impelled by tension, impulses, needs; but we perceive, abstract, generalize because we have brains—and words. These processes require no motivation; they act by perpetual motion without new energy.

Psychologists have of course always been "of two minds" regarding the nature of perceiving, thinking, and remembering; for while as theorists they have striven to separate these cognitive processes from feeling and will, they have gone on living on the assumption that every man perceives, thinks, and remembers in terms of his economic interests, his religious and racial bias, his personal ego defenses. In a world wrung to a rag by an economic depression, each new palliative was regarded as a short cut out of the morass *or* as the ominous beginning of the total destruction of the social order; in a world timidly hoping for new creativeness from atomic energy and shaking in its shoes lest only destruction result, the outlook of men everywhere is so profoundly colored by hopes and fears that it is hard to be sure that reason will find its way through.

Nothing is more fatuous than the assumption that by making a voluntary effort, by "leaning over backwards," one can nicely separate thought from impulse and "correct" for one's biases. These mechanisms by which personal needs guide each individual's outlook go right to the bottom of personal existence; the more profoundly his needs are involved, the greater the danger of the complete captivation of the cognitive apparatus within their vise-like grip. Doctors, lawyers, ministers know this as they deal with men and women faced with grave and ultimate matters, with problems of life and death. Congressmen and statesmen know it as they read history or view men of other lands. But how often they see only a miscroscopically small distance into the process by which the inward aspects of their own determining motives guide their stormy convictions—perhaps about as much as psychiatrists and psychologists, who also frequently peer into other people's sorry tricks of self-deception with a microscope but remain well "defended" against too close a view of their own.

How does all this come about? Do we not, after all, have an elaborate machinery for making contact with *reality*, do we not have sense organs, brains, and action systems which lead us to adapt not to our whims but to our *environment?* Yes, perception depends upon the structure and function of receptors, and mediates the environment to us. In the long run, organic needs are satisfied through the adaptive behavior which results from the effective functioning of the reporting and communicating system. *But there is another way in which needs relate to perception.* Since all behavior is drive-motivated, the process of interpretation may fail to lead to behavior upon which adjustment depends, yet may, through past experience, pattern the perceptual world so that it conforms *directly* to the need. The molding of perception or thought or memory in the drive-satisfying direction follows directly from the satisfying or frustrating quality of past perception; one learns to perceive, think, or remember in this way or that because such a habit is satisfying, just as one learns to *behave* this way or that because such behavior is satisfying. All cognitive processes are apparently continually shaped in greater or lesser degree by the pressure of wants.

This movement of the cognitive processes in the direction of need satisfaction is called autism. The term comes from Bleuler, who was especially concerned with autism in adult psychotics, yet saw clearly the almost universal role of the process in human life. Although the individual drive patterns vary, and the learning history of each individual is unique, a cardinal problem in personality study is the acquisition of individual autisms.

The Beginnings of Autistic Response

At the first stage of perception, as we have already seen (page 336), drive satisfaction or drive frustration yields affects that are fused or blurred with cognitive dispositions in the physiognomic process, the whole being a global reaction. The child's language, frequently coined for the purpose, shows that it is the drive-satisfying or drive-frustrating quality that marks off one object from others; a "gunga" window, for example, is a window with a rich brown frame, like chocolate. At this stage there need be no autism as such, because the child is not pretending that he sees things coldly, objectively, as they really are. The fact that affective and cognitive processes are not distinguished makes for complete realism in Piaget's sense; the drive-satisfying character of the objects experienced is simply an aspect of the perceptual whole.

At the second stage, the cognitive structure begins to move into the foreground, and objects are recognized but are *acceptable* or *unacceptable* (or good at one time and bad at another, depending not

upon the cognitive structure but upon dynamic contexts, i.e., varying needs). Here, again, there is no occasion for referring to autism,
since the cognitive elements are relatively independent of the affective.

At the third stage, *affective elements are wrought into the total picture in which cognitive integration has been or is being achieved.* In the
bipolar organization of perception there is a constant shift between
emphasis on outer factors and emphasis on inner factors, so that there
is constant variation in the degree to which drive-satisfying qualities
act to influence the organization of the cognitive ingredients. It is
precisely when the affective ingredients markedly distort the cognitive
picture of reality, so that the observer is markedly misled by the distortion, that true autism appears. Typical autism is thus not merely an
expression of the third level of perceptual development; it is an expression of those phases of third-level perception in which the interaction
of affective and cognitive elements goes on without the observer's
being sharply aware of what is happening. As the blood stream, for
example, bathes the brain with varying endocrine products, one sees
(or remembers, or imagines) in accordance with the changing thresholds.

Since events at all levels of perception show a high degree of
individual idiosyncrasy, we should expect that the individual differences in proneness to autism would be to some extent generalized,
depending upon the type of intellectual training received, and also
that this proneness would depend upon the intensity of the immediate
need and the amount of experience, of opportunity for practice in differentiating and integrating. Such individual factors have an excellent
opportunity to influence the way in which the percept is anchored.
Studies of "affective anchorage," in which the affect is the aspect of a
perceptual pattern that serves as anchor, do in fact indicate that experimental subjects may become confused as to what is cognitive, what
affective, and may recall cognitive patterns largely in terms of
similarities in the affect associated with them. One pleasant restful
scene may recall another by virtue of the similarity of the inner
response to them, although the two may differ completely in objective content.

It is a nice question whether *all* cognitive processes are partly controlled by autistic factors in the absence of known visceral or emotional factors (page 355). We should still expect the relation between *sensory* or *activity drives* and each perceptual pattern to make some real difference; in particular, we should expect interest in or curiosity regarding each phase of a percept or image pattern to vary from person to person, so that it has a personal rather than a purely objective structure. In this sense we may well doubt whether perception, recall, or thought can ever be structured *exclusively* in terms of external factors; the structure would then lose its bipolarity. On the other hand, such individual factors accenting one or another phase of a total are often negligible in comparison with the uniformities of structure which result from our essentially uniform experience with the outer world—we all see flat tables, square rooms. Standard experimental studies of perception and recall are not greatly complicated by autism, for the experimenter can control percepts fairly well by controlling the external structure and giving the subject no instructions but to report what he sees or hears; the student of memory can obtain with nonsense syllables such uniformities as to suggest that autistic factors are of small weight in these situations. Similarly, when individual differences in perceiving are a direct expression of individual differences in *receptors*—as in color blindness or in tone deafness—consistent and meaningful results are obtainable without any reference to autism.

These situations that are devised to provide uniformity among subjects are, however, of precisely the type that yields least to the student of personality as such. The organism is segmentalized, deprived of its guiding affects. Whenever a situation that grips the individual's life is involved, autistic disturbances begin to threaten. The struggle to see things as they are objectively—as the lookout man does while watching for submarines—may long be successful but may become panicky as fatigue comes on. The man whose business is beginning to fail succeeds for a time in finding helpful solutions, but in a moment of unsteadiness he sees a "great opportunity" which under normal conditions he would recognize as a trap.

Progress in the quantitative analysis of the cognitive aspects of perceiving has been equaled only by the neglect of the autistic aspects. If the experimenter is to study autism, he must do two things: first, allow it to appear; second, determine, preferably by his own experimental procedure, what the autism shall be and how it shall be set free to operate. Suppose, for example, that a slight partial color blindness ("color weakness") appearing congenitally in one man can be measured and thus serve as a standard; can the experimenter induce an *attitude toward color* which will produce in another man the same form and degree of color weakness? When this has been done, we shall have begun to reduce the autistic factor to some sort of order.

Although many experiments deal with the pleasantness or unpleasantness of laboratory stimuli, their results are not clear in relation to our problem. For one thing, pleasantness and unpleasantness are abstractions to which even the trained subject finds it difficult to turn completely. The feeling quality of colors or odors, for example, appears to be unstable when the drives themselves are weak. We should expect a more clear-cut result from more powerful drives. Furthermore, the laboratory studies seldom tell us how the cognitive structure is influenced by affect.

To study autism, we want first to know whether an obvious visceral drive, such as hunger, can clearly and consistently influence the perceptual structure. In the pioneer experiment on this problem, Sanford's subjects, after being deprived of food for varying lengths of time, had to interpret pictures which had been so mutilated that it was not certain what they showed. The frequency of interpreting the pictures in terms of food increased with the time since eating. Sanford's second study, which followed the effects of food deprivation over a 24-hour period, confirmed the tendency to interpret more and more in terms of food as food deprivation continued. But superimposed upon this long-time trend were observed secondary cycles of waxing and waning frequency of food interpretation, in accordance with the eating cycle of the adult subjects.

Sanford's subjects reacted to clear but mutilated, and hence ambiguous, pictures; they interpreted the pictures as *meaning* food, but they did not *perceive* food. If further light is to be thrown on the dynamics of autistic perception, the stimulus situations should be loosely organized so that autism can supply organization to the percept. For this purpose R. Levine placed behind a ground-glass screen pictures of three classes of objects: food objects, ordinary household objects, and geometrical designs. Some of the pictures in each of the three categories were in color, the others were black and white. Each member of the experimental group was individually tested three, six, and nine hours after eating; the control subjects were tested soon after they had eaten. The curves reproduced in the accompanying figure indicate that every subject tended to make a large number of food interpretations at the three-hour interval in the case of the black and

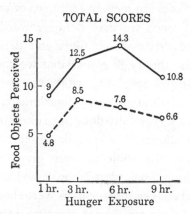

TOTAL SCORES

Solid line: black and white cards;
broken line: colored cards.

white pictures, and even more at six hours. For the colored pictures, the inflection in the curve occurs at three hours. Both with chromatic and with achromatic pictures, autism at first increases as the deprivation time increases; but as time passes and no food appears, the need to get out of the situation increases, and the curve goes down; the pictures (which are, after all not very satisfying) yield to a *realistic* attitude (in Freud's, not Piaget's sense; cf. pages 340 and 364). We should expect that the struggle between autistic and realistic tendencies would depend in some measure upon the realism of the pictures used, and therefore that the decline in the autistic trend would appear earlier with the colored pictures; this is in fact what happens.

The tendency to give autistic structure to poorly structured stimulus materials is by no means confined to situations involving the visceral drives. The need to conform was the apparent drive in Sherif's experiments in which naïve subjects were asked to make darkroom judgments regarding the movements of a point of light (page 384). In similar fashion Bartlett found that photographs of Army and Navy officers were interpreted by young males subject to military duty in terms of personal meanings; e.g., some of the faces seemed to embody threats or commands. Murray found that induction of fear in his subjects led them to attribute "maliciousness" to faces in photographs.

Since all these effects are merely examples of the influence of drive on perception, and since we may define rewards and punishments simply in terms of drive satisfactions and drive frustrations, we should expect, if the theory is sound, that we could develop autistic tendencies fairly simply by giving arbitrary rewards when the subject sees things one way and arbitrary punishments when he sees them otherwise. This was successfully done in an experiment involving lines of various lengths shown in a semi-darkened room; arbitrarily and without explanation, the subjects were given small quantities of money whenever long lines were shown, and comparable amounts were taken away whenever shorter lines were shown. After this training series, a test of their tendencies in estimating lines revealed that they had consistently moved in the direction of exaggerating; because they had been rewarded for "seeing long," they had learned to "see long." In a weight-lifting experiment they were given rewards whenever they lifted lighter weights, and were punished when they lifted heavier ones. Accordingly, they learned to underestimate rather than to overestimate weights. The data hint that it was no mere modification of verbal reports but a modification in *perceptual structure* that was involved; subjects who had merely learned what to say could scarcely have complained, as some did, about the poor light.

Generalizing, we may suggest that the figure in a figure-ground presentation may be quantitatively changed by the autisms which

serve as part of the context. Since autism relates ordinarily to alterations of structure (page 366) rather than to the creation of percepts
out of whole cloth, such experiments may indicate that the specific
means by which autism operates is the control of figure-ground
relations. This hypothesis has been tested by Schafer, who provided
stimulus patterns that could be broken into two parts, one of which
was made consistently "satisfying," the other consistently "frustrating," in order to determine whether the satisfying part tended to
become figure. Within each of two circles were drawn contour lines

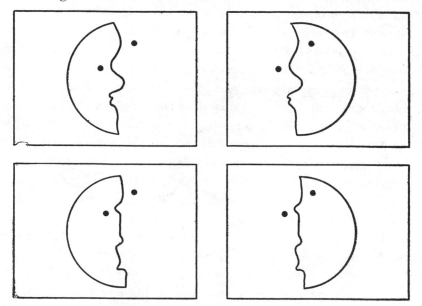

such that a "face" could be seen in either half of the pattern. Half-
figures, in the form shown in the accompanying figure, were presented
to each of a group of three subjects along with a small money reward;
when the complementary face was shown, money was taken away
from them (punishment). Two other subjects were rewarded in
the situation in which the first group had been punished, and punished
when it had been rewarded. After this training, all the subjects had
learned to perceive within the *double figure* (the complete circle) the
face which had been rewarded, and to ignore the other. No subject
was aware either of the other face in the stimulus situation or of the

fact that his perception was dictated by autistic factors. This study indicates that the structuring of figure and ground can be influenced by autistic mechanisms.

It will be noted that in none of these cases is any element in the percept lost, nor is cognitive structure completely obliterated. Rather, as Sherif pointed out, the drive factors influence the cognitive elements in the total situation. The balance is upset, but it is unnecessary that the pattern be completely redefined. The autisms of daily life are matters of relative displacement, of figure-ground modification, of new anchorage points. At times, however, complete obliteration or repression of a part is the only means at one's disposal; the autistic impulse must be strong to effect such a result. Or, instead of responding autistically the individual may dissociate (page 325) and fail utterly to perceive. Mere modification of the perceptual response does not serve; the only thing that does any good is to block out the danger. But, fortunately for our sanity, we are also commonly capable of mobilizing our energies under frustration so as to move in the realistic direction, as described above (page 326). We have, then, a variety of means for the perceptual handling of an affect-dominated situation, but we know very little about the factors that determine for the individual at a given time which of these means will be used. A beginning has been made in Rosenzweig and Sarason's hypothesis (page 562) regarding the relation of repression to other personality tendencies.

Thus far we have considered autism in the process of perception. But since memory is the continuation or reactivation of central processes after the outer stimulus field has been removed, we should expect the dynamics of autism in the memory process to be the same, and this is apparently the case. Bartlett's studies suggest what happens as the drive patterns gain an opportunity to distort the original presentation in the total pattern of recalled material; the drive-satisfying feature stands out. If this happens several times, much of the material in the original ground may drop out altogether. In an experiment by K. B. Clark, a story describing a struggle for status between a man and a woman was recalled differently by the two sex groups. "She's quite a handful, that woman," began the story, in which a burly Amazon challenges our hesitating masculine hero to make the rounds with her as she delivers huge sacks which most men could not carry. In recalling the story, many of the men subjects identify with the man, often putting the narrative into the first person ("I thought," etc.), although the third person was used in the original; the women, on the other hand, find it difficult to identify with the woman and hence keep the story, so to speak, at an impersonal level. Jerome Levine was able to demonstrate that the curve of learning and the curve of forgetting controversial material both showed the consistent operation of autistic factors. Strongly pro-Soviet and anti-Soviet groups of American college students undertook to learn passages which were very favorable and very unfavorable, respectively, to the Soviet Union. Each group learned more effectively the passage in harmony with its own attitude, and the difference persisted through-out the entire learning—and the subsequent forgetting—period.

Seeleman gave her subjects a schedule of questions on attitude toward the Negro. Later she showed them a set of photographs of white students from a Columbia College Yearbook, and of colored students from a Howard University Yearbook. Still later she showed them the same photographs of the white students mixed in with others not presented before, and the same photographs of the colored students mixed in with some new ones. The results showed that the subjects favorable to the Negro were more competent in differentiating new from old faces in the Negro group, and that those unfavorable to the Negro were more competent on the test with the white photographs; it was as if they failed to respond to the Negro faces as individual faces. Although this was a test of recognition, it is likely that the autistic factors—the urge to find differences in faces and not to find them—operated at the level of perception. This is especially impressive in the light of Allport and Kramer's evidence that anti-Semites distinguish Jews from non-Jews better than others do; their sensitivity is perhaps to the group as a group rather than to individuals.

The same general point seems to hold also for Postman's study. Children who had indicated their attitudes on social issues were required to memorize and reproduce pairs of words which were in varying degree compatible or incompatible with their attitudes. Thus one of the attitude items was to the effect that in spite of the Nazis the Germans are a kindly people; the pair "Germans—kindly" is compatible for those agreeing with the original statement, and incompatible for those disagreeing. Postman found a clear tendency to recall compatible better than incompatible pairs; this probably indicates autism in the original perceptual response as well as in recall. But intensity of attitude was also a factor. When intensity and compatibility are both considered, the result is a U-curve (affectively neutral items having lowest recall value), as in forgetting pleasant and unpleasant material. Affective factors have an influence proportional to their intensity, but the satisfying has an advantage over the unsatisfying. The same general principles cited in the case of perception, recall, and recognition hold throughout the whole realm of the more complex cognitive processes of thinking and imagination, as we shall try to show in detail in Chapters 16–19.

THE THEORY OF AUTISM

Lest it be inferred that autism is a *deus ex machina* unrelated to the principles discussed in Chapters 8–12, it may be worth while to examine more closely the way in which autistic habits develop from individual canalization and conditioning.

Since drive satisfaction is always involved in canalization, we should expect the focus of tension reduction to lie in that phase of the perceptual field (or the field of memory, thought, imagination) which represents the satisfying object. Similarly, a conditioned stimulus associated with past satisfactions would be expected to appear in focus, i.e., as *figure*. This follows directly from adience (page 167) or orientation to drive-related stimuli; no new principle is involved.

When appetitive behavior is aroused and sustained by conditioned stimuli, it is, for rough purposes, correct to say that the organism is "seeking satisfaction." To be sure, it may not know exactly what it is seeking; certainly it seldom knows enough to formulate the abstraction that it is "seeking satisfaction," but scientists may make the abstraction for it. Practical men manage one another, as they do their dogs, in terms of holding up rewards and punishment. Since, according to the present conception, it is the drive itself that is conditioned, and since the drive is an appetitive or defensive trend, it is sufficient to say that satisfactions and frustrations, joys and woes, operate as motivators. There is no need for a pleasure principle, a law of effect, in which the hedonic tone consequent upon an act has in its own right an effect upon behavior. Conscious pleasure or unpleasure may indeed be present, and important; but according to the present working hypothesis they accompany appetitive and defensive strivings without being independent agencies.

There is indeed a certain sense in which we are better off without these pleasure-pain conceptions than with them. Much else besides conditioning goes on in the motive situation. Sometimes high tension is increased by failure and frustration, so that the animal or man repeats in confusion or the heat of passion the acts which have just brought distress. Motor mechanisms as well as the viscera are in a state of upheaval; nothing can make them behave according to the algebraic sum of past experience or a felicific calculus of the future. At times one does what one *fears* to do because, during the confused organic upheaval, the preparatory tensions associated with escape tend to be incompletely separated from the tensions of agonized anticipation; this may be stated in psychoanalytic terms if necessary. But the central fact is that the tensions that lead to behavior are many and intertwined, so that selection and emphasis upon those that happen to be reflected in consciousness, and the identification of motivation with these conscious factors alone, make conduct appear both more rational and more coherent than it is.

There is, nevertheless, a place for consciousness in the schema of motivation, and a very important one. We have seen that in the trial-and-error process there is more and more elimination of the frustrating and increasing adience in relation to the satisfying. A person spends more and more of his time, if he can, in situations which are satisfying. If there is within his body an event which symbolizes the satisfying world, he may be happy to live with the symbol. If the symbol is in itself a satisfying aspect of a satisfying world, as when the poet's image is as rich and as dear to him as the glen or the rose which his eyes report, he may, like Chatterton or Lanier, swoon in exultation, needing nothing that the outer world can give. If the child's imaginary companion is a full-fledged playmate, he may be as good a companion or a better one, than the boy across the street. One can live in one's symbols.

More often, however, the symbol is incompletely satisfying. Even in the case of esthetic satisfactions it is seldom an adequate substitute. In the case of the visceral drives it may give some satisfaction, but the motor tendencies press forward, and the failure to provide all they want leads to greater distress than before. Thus it is a joy to hear that there will be steak for supper, provided that the mounting tension within can be handled in the anticipatory fashion; but when there is a long delay in the kitchen, repeated mention of the feast may become more and more annoying. When the satisfaction is remote, dwelling upon it may become torture—another instance of motivation directed by a learning process, but in itself hardly subject to a simple pleasure-pain interpretation.

In general, tension reduction is satisfying. But we must stress in the same breath that one can structure it also in terms of one's fears. (Postman's experiment showed the autistic role of the markedly unacceptable experiences; page 374). The mechanisms of escape, when activated, are conditioned to aspects of the ambiguous situation; if terror is sufficient the doorpost may become a specter, the ambulance's purring motor a bombing plane. Such mechanisms may help to activate escape from danger, and hence may be useful. We must, however, distinguish two phases of the autistic process: first, the ordering of the percept in terms of inner stress, whether the drive is toward or away from the object; and second, when life permits and the object recurs repeatedly without destroying us, the trial-and-error approach and the gradual ascendancy of the wish-fulfilling percept over the fear-arousing percept. Eventually we come to assume that the object portends good; hope springs eternal. There are pessimists, but they may well be enjoying their status as kill-joys. Practically all farm years are "exceptionally bad," much California weather is "exceptionally cloudy." *The best is the norm.*

Throughout this discussion we have striven to indicate why autism need not modify sensory elements; it need only alter structural relationships. We may speak of the cognitive structure in terms of the dominance relations of the various elements in the representation (due to such factors as sheer intensity or sharpness of contour), and of autistic structure as derived from the drive pattern. We may say, then, that the individual's attitude toward the world about him is a function of the interaction of these two structural systems. This hypothesis can be directly tested by asking people whose drives are known, to specify, on the basis of given information, what outcome will occur. Douglas McGregor, supported by studies by Israeli and Cantril, asked his subjects to make predictions about future events on which they had limited but clearly organized information. The *amount of information* and the *intensity of desire* were compared with the predictions made, and the following rule was formulated regarding the relative influence of the two structural components: As structure becomes fluid through the reduction of information, autism becomes more marked (cf. page 353). The McGregor study suggests that it is only in regions of considerable fluidity that autism as an individual mechanism can be given great scope. Not only does the cognitive situation shift constantly; the drive situation is similarly fluid. In Sherif's terms, we should expect unstable rather than stable equilibrium, the perceptual field moving subtly or sharply as situations and needs adjust to one another.

It must, however, be borne in mind that the *existence* of needs precedes their expression in perception. Needs are present before one opens his eyes, before a voice strikes the ear. Needs determine how the incoming energies are to be put into structured form. Perception, then, is not something that is first registered objectively, then "distorted." Rather, as the need pattern shifts, the stage is set, minute by minute, for quasi-automatic structure-giving tendencies that make the percept suit the need. The need pattern predisposes to one rather than another manner of anchoring the percept around one's needs. *Needs keep ahead of percepts.*

Wayne Dennis' account of the foot race run by the Hopi children provides a simile for an analysis of this relationship. As he runs, each child kicks a stick before him; the sticks are the real competitors. In a close race one child may win because his stick reaches the goal a second before another stick, though his own body may be slower than the other child's. In the same way, needs push perceptions ahead of them; although perception does in a sense convey reality, nevertheless what will appear in the *next* instant in perception derives in part from *present* needs. The needs are always controlling; perception, instead of being the lawgiver, takes orders from the need. As one wrestles or plays with a problem during creative thinking or casual fantasy, memory and constructive pictures are thrown on the screen constantly as the inner activity stream requires. The thinker confronted with the questions "Why did you think that?" "How did that come to you?" replies that it was an "association" from previous "ideas." To be sure, chronologically, it seemed just this. Actually, however, each perceptual pattern alters the need structure, and from the new need structure follows a new perceptual pattern, as the accompanying diagram seeks to show. It may be felt that this statement gives needs too big a role, that our own preference for bipolarity should keep the balance between outer and inner control. There are indeed two consuls, each acting as a check on the other, as in the Roman system. The issue here, however, is different. *When once we face* a perceptual

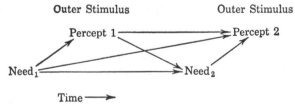

situation the control is indeed consular; but it is the need pattern that plays the chief role in determining *where we shall look*, to what outer stimuli we shall attend, what other factors shall be allowed to enter the control box.

SOCIALLY SHARED AUTISMS

So far as individuals share the factors that make for uniformity of outlook, they share their autisms. And not only do they tend to anchor perception in the same way and to derive the same satisfactions for their way of seeing the world; their community status depends in large degree upon their being able to see as sound, sensible people see. It should be easy, if this is so, to define and measure experimentally the autism of a socially defined group. Such an attempt has been made in a study by Proshansky, which aimed to evaluate the end result of the three types of autism which we should expect to discover, namely, autism of perception, of memory, and of thought. College students whose social attitudes had been measured were briefly shown pictures of social situations which they then had to describe in five-minute essays. Autistic factors were evidently present all the way through from the first appearance of the picture on the screen to the last word of the written report. Thus, commenting on a picture of "poor people," one subject says: "They seem to be messy, sloppy people, who seem to enjoy dwelling in their own trash."

As we turn to the way in which individuals come to share the same autistic outlook, we find abundant evidence in observations of children, which show that if an adult calls a child's attention to a feature of a complex situation to which the child already has a strongly positive or negative response, through anchorage the whole perceived situation becomes good or bad. But even if the child has no predisposition in the matter, an adult can supply it by strongly indicating his own attitude; the child by identification with the adult (page 491) both anchors when he does and assigns a disvalue when the adult assigns it. If we are interested in observing quantitatively the way in which an adult comes to share the outlook of other adults, data from Sherif's original experiment (page 347) answer precisely this question. It will be recalled that when three experimental subjects were jointly tested in the darkroom, giving their judgments orally, each tended quickly to assimilate his judgments somewhat to those of the others, the one giving the largest estimates and the one giving the smallest both moving toward agreement with the subject in the middle position. This "funnel-shaped relationship" seems to be characteristic of most group conduct, for the individual's approximation to group standards must occur gradually. Such data suggest indeed that security, the need to be safe in the midst of the group rather than be a lone dissenter, is the central motivating factor, and that socially shared autisms in general, as brought out in the studies of Horowitz mentioned below (page 721), derive basically from the need to be accepted by others.

From this point of view we can hardly be surprised that the individual who has built up his autistic perceptions in the group retains them, at least for a considerable period, when tested in isolation. Socially shared autisms express chiefly the needs that relate to commonly accepted standards of social adjustment. When a need is as compelling and continuous as the need to be one with one's group, we may expect autism to have much greater liveliness and longevity than the autistic patterns that appear in food-deprivation situations (page 349). One of the clearest and most important features of Sherif's findings relates to the considerable individual differences in response to his suggestion and to the judgment of others, and to their stability throughout the course of the experiment. Indeed he was led to approach leadership in terms of the greater inactivity of some people to group pressures, and the greater susceptibility of others.

The processes involved in the consolidation of percepts are of course much more complex than this brief account suggests. But before we go on, we shall consider a type of drive-satisfying process which at first seems to differ from autism, at least from the familiar form. The Schafer experiment (page 371) dealt not only with the influence of "rewards and punishments" but with the gradual consolidation of responses neither rewarded nor punished. The rewards and punishments were discontinued after the sixteenth trial. Since the situation was analogous to a conditioning situation (substitute stimuli being connected with drive satisfaction), we should expect the discontinuance of the rewards to lead soon to the extinction of the acquired responses. This was in fact what happened; all the subjects proceeded to lose the figure-ground structuring tendencies which the rewards and punishments had built up. But they began to do something new on their own, for every one of them, as the trials continued to the sixty-fourth, began to move away from the chaotic or irregular habits of response which followed the extinction period, and consolidated a consistent way of seeing the pattern. They always saw one face, never the other; in the case of some of them it was the face that had brought the reward; in the rest, it was the "punished" face. Apparently something about an individual's perceptual organization leads to a consolidation, a perseveration which derives some satisfaction from drives less obvious than those used in the first part of the experiment. As Schafer pointed out, each response was, after all, a sure, swift, and correct response; hence each was "rewarded" whether money was used or not. Each subject experienced the satisfaction of solving the task imposed, and *kept on seeing* with a deftness, skill, and freedom from confusion which typically characterize the trained rather than the naïve laboratory subject. Part of the satisfaction was probably ego satisfaction, satisfaction in "knowing how to do this," or perhaps in recognizing the familiar. At any rate, the subject had freed himself from the tension and confusion of an ambiguous situation. It is likely that ego dynamics of an elementary type are partly responsible for autistic structure, even when no "prestige" or more obvious reward for a social drive is provided. But prestige, as several recent studies clearly show, is a major source of autism; the perceiver recalls that which enhances or defends the picture of the self. At the same time, there is often a need to avoid being conspicuous. Thus in Marks' study, very dark and very light Negroes rate their own skin color nearer to the *average* point than other Negroes rate these individuals.

A word must also be said about the way in which attitudes toward the self structure the perceptual field. At least since the time of Demosthenes, orators have consciously striven to make points of view appear to their listeners as being the outcome of the latters' own autonomous activity. This is not a question of flattery; it involves the problem of enabling the hearer to infuse the suggested attitudes or opinions with a quality of "ownness"; it is essentially a matter of conditioning the proposition to one's own self-image and transferring the warm self-attitude to the proposition. If the listener can be led to take *active steps* and reach the conclusion with a conscious sense of participation, so much the better.

> Men must be taught as if you taught them not,
> And things unknown proposed as things forgot.

The suffusing of any attitude or belief with a self-quality carries over three-quarters of the way toward its acceptance as valid. The Iowa housewives who heard a solemn talk on wartime nutrition agreed that it was necessary to buy in accordance with a new pattern and went on buying as they had before; but when they discussed among themselves what the situation called for, and reached their *own* decision, they acted upon it. In all education the problem of preparing for life consists not simply in reading or in acquiring skills but in making them actively a part of oneself. This is "autistic" in the broad sense; but such autisms geared to life may integrate rather than "distort" individual reality.

At this point the relation of autism to those magical habits by which we try to control the world through our thoughts becomes clearer. It will be helpful to borrow and adapt Piaget's formulation of the problem. The term Piaget applied to the first phase of perceptual development is *indissociation* (page 336), that is, the lack of the dissociation or differentiatedness that characterizes adult awareness. Indissociation implies a lack of distinction not only between external objects but between the phases of the self; in particular, the absence of boundaries between such "inner" experiences as the kinesthetic and organic on the one hand, and such "outer" experiences as the visual and auditory on the other. There is as yet no inner or outer, no self or not-self. The motor, and consequently the kinesthetic, tendencies follow the stimulus patterns without regard to their assigned status as *your* or *my* behavior; empathy and mimicry follow channels of earlier experience without any need to ask whose effort or activity is in progress. This is the process of *participation*, the flow of experience which goes on before the dam of selfhood has been built. Imagery and anticipatory behavior are followed by a changed external world;

the individual's own activity has effected the changes, but he does not as yet think in these terms. Consequently when imagery and anticipatory movements accompany the observation of another's activity, he expects similar consequences. Indeed, in accordance with the usual principles of trial and error and the redirection of drives (page 249), he carries out the anticipatory movements with the expectation that the accustomed results will follow. This is full-fledged magic—the "omnipotence of thought," the control of the world by "autistic gestures." The process continues despite the gradual formation of the self. The self is a region more suitable to magical control than the outer world; but even in the latter there is still considerable magical effort, especially when wishes are intense. The magical effort of the spectator to push the runner forward, or of the crowd at a football game to help block the kick, is typical autistic participation.

It is clear, then, that the imagined magical control of the outer world is based partly upon failure to distinguish outer from inner, partly upon the empirical fact that one can to some degree control the inner world and transfer the "control attitude" to the similar phases of the outer world, and partly upon ordinary autisms, the continual structuring of life situations in terms of the ways one wants them to be. It is equally clear that emancipation from such autisms comes not by sheer growing up, but primarily from the discipline of experience and the intensely frustrating consequences of following these magical tendencies. Such tendencies are still with us to some degree in adulthood; the huge individual differences in them, as shown in tests, are, in some measure related to the individual frustration tolerance (page 316), as well as to the areas of thinking in which specific realistic disciplines have been at work. A well-known Biblical critic is known as a gentle soul who "believes *anything*, provided it is not in the Bible."

THE AUTISTIC GROUPING OF PEOPLE AND THINGS

In every confusing situation one looks for an anchor, for something familiar and tangible, a core about which to structure a bewildering welter of new detail. And the second of Schafer's results (page 380),

the tendency to develop individual habits of perceiving even without external *reward*, reminds one of many life situations in which
structure takes place in the absence of obvious autisms. Along with
the desire to see things as we wish to, it is likewise very human to
expose ourselves, in somewhat helpless fashion, to an unformed situation in order to see what "takes shape," the result being determined
largely by what has habitually been seen, rather than by present
"wishes." But the fear of the strange and the need for the familiar may
also properly be included as autisms, and even a "cold" and "passive"
situation may have its share of the autistic. In our scientific technical
age, to see a thing "cold" is a "good" way to see it.

This process of looking for the familiar has further meanings for
personality structure. It may play a large part in the tendency to
connect things because they are *alike*. Association by similarity, as
defined by Plato and Aristotle, involves the tendency of the mind to
move from one object to a "similar" object. But the capacity to grasp
resemblances, which James regarded as the highest evidence of genius,
seldom depends upon the sheer ability to slide forward casually
from one element to a similar one; it depends almost invariably upon a
drive—or even on a focused effort—to discover the element in a
given situation *B* that has been observed in another situation *A*.
Experience with *A* and the beginning of experience with *B* leads one
actively to ask whether *B* contains the quality he has already learned
to know in *A*. This becomes one of the major opportunities for autism,
namely, classifying or grouping persons or things. Almost any two
things in nature, or almost any two people, are similar in some respect.
While the problem of science consists in finding out which types of
similarity are useful for classification and prediction, the ordinary
daily quest for similarity, as a relatively undisciplined impulse, leads
to a more casual classification of one object with another, or one
person with another, and one finds the kinds of similarity between
them which he wishes to find.

Consider, for example, the human being whose attributes of mind
and heart and body are rather well described, and who is discovered to
be a creative artist of great talent. At this point, however, it is noted

that he has a yellow skin; it is then possible immediately to classify him as belonging to such and such racial group. There is no intrinsic rule by which the similarities serving to group people can be called important or unimportant; it all depends on the purpose which is served by emphasizing them. If the educator, the propagandist, or the statesman wishes to stress certain similarities which lead to people's being bracketed together, he will find it easy. The process by which the specified individual is now seen as "Oriental," or whatever generic term is used, brings to mind a host of other attributes, real or unreal, that are associated with the similarity which has been defined and looked for.

This is a way of saying that autism, involving the quest for similarities, can and usually does *select which similarities are to be used in terms of the drive structure of the person making the comparisons and groupings.* The world of the individual is made up largely by classifying groups of things and persons. To be an autistic world, it need not be a "fantasy" world; it need only be structured in terms of his affective system, or, more accurately, in terms of the way in which that system contributes to the organization of the cognitive pattern. Experiences, moreover, are grouped in terms of the "membership character" (page 513) that is gradually acquired by each component in a pattern, so that in time each element—for example, yellow skin—has the affective tone of the total. The total comprises central nervous system, viscera, etc. But because of the affective tone that is anchored to the physical criteria of race, it becomes unthinkable that an individual with yellow skin could be a great philosopher or statesman. This type of thinking, chosen simply because of its commonness, pervades the reasoning processes of scientists and laymen alike, specific training in making distinctions having unfortunately no demonstrable carry-over when new areas of social intensity are confronted.

The whole process is of course abetted profoundly by the fact that all the young members of a given group reinforce one another as they move toward accepting the standard autisms of the group. At the same time, the process is facilitated by linguistic factors. Just as the cultural situation emphasizes the elements of similarity which are to be stressed, so the fact that they can be labeled with the same term facilitates the process of identifying the two experiences as belonging to the same basic type. Both factors lead inevitably to the social standardization of autisms, the "standardization of error." (Stefansson.)

In the same vein, the patterning of individual attitude after the standard set by the group leads to a similar tendency to structure reality in terms of the *rightness* of one's own group. Studying the attitudes of boys in French-speaking Switzerland, Lerner showed that the norms of Geneva had, for Geneva boys, the same unchallengeable rightness as their personal attitudes did when in conflict with those of other boys. Side by side with egocentrism there was sociocentrism; the boys who played their games differently over there in Lausanne just didn't know how to play. A widening circle leads thence to ethnocentrism (tribalism), or to nationalistic standardization of ethics and law.

If to these mechanisms be added the sense of righteousness in the moral sense, and its converse, the sense of guilt, one has all the raw materials from which to make "moral realism" as described by Piaget; here the definition of reality includes the tissue of super-individual morality as well as the cognitive outlines of cold facts. Piaget's children discover from the grown-up world what is right and wrong, exactly as they discover, when coping with tricycles and street traffic, how things work. Morality has none of the character of inwardness which the philosopher describes. Piaget reports that moral realism yields gradually during childhood to an ethics of reciprocity; what is right is now defined not in terms of self-evident and inherent necessity but in terms of a sense of balance or justice. Rightness is a matter of the mutual consideration of needs. Even this more subtle process is, however, still autistic in the sense that needs give structure to the cognitive situation. For just as the little child measures the wrongness of a careless act by the amount of broken china, so the older child or the adult, measuring wrongness in terms of unfairness, judges in terms of his own needs, as if things like unfairness were independent objective data. Here, moreover, the entire community supports the legal processes which regard offenses against others or against the state as having an inherent quality of wickedness that requires objective retributive measures. The world of ethics is one in which, to this hour, almost no progress has been achieved toward sharp cognitive definition in the average adult's mind. Indeed, the problems of ethical behavior are handled in the most subtle modern fiction, as in the yellow press, in full-fledged physiognomic fashion (page 266), with the heroism or baseness of individual conduct portrayed in three-dimensional completeness. The realists in fiction have been acutely aware of the difficulty but, as the use of the term "realism" indicates, have succeeded only in banishing one set of ethical postulates—namely, the standard ethics of the middle class—and falling into another, such as the "ethics of Hercules" or the "ethics of Nietzsche" or, rarely, the "ethics of the worker." Thus in Marx's notes on the Paris Commune, judgments are not made with the cold objectivity of science but are white-hot, with the intensity of a new categorical imperative. As fast as it has been destroyed by humanism and science, the need for absolutist ethics has returned phoenix-like, to plague the normative needs of civilized men.

Thus far we have followed Piaget's approach, and in a later chapter we shall need to consider the alternative explanations of the moral attitude presented by Freud; but at this point we must consider another approach from which much factual material has been gained and which has shed light on individual dynamics. Westermarck succeeded, by means of historical material, in plausibly defining three stages in the development of the moral attitude. First there is pure gratification or rage at the acts of other men who aid or injure us. (This is like the stage described above on page 366, in which affect *attends* other experiences but is not blended with them.) Second, as men learn that an *individual* or *act* that is dangerous to one may be dangerous to all, processes of transfer and generalization occur, and the use of appropriate symbols leads to the definition of certain classes of acts or persons as dangerous, and to the establishment of firm sanctions against them. Finally, the quality of being an aid or a menace to others is abstracted from the total, and the abstract conception of right and wrong appears. If Westermarck's hypothesis is correct, it suggests that strong feeling rather than social norms may be the root of the child's first quasi-moral judgment. If so, the first stages in moral attitude would not be, as Piaget asserts, naïve copies of parental attitudes but moral indignation springing originally from the child's own sense of injury.

Observations of small children certainly seem to support Westermarck as against Piaget. Almost every parent finds that the moral law which he invokes regarding "getting into" grown-ups' property or crossing streets or saying tabu words falls far short of achieving in the two-year-old a blind acceptance in terms of moral realism. Children have their own ideas, their own stalwart defenses of their own points of view, their own norms based on their own immediate satisfactions. The child does "catch" from the adult the attitude of moral indignation; he catches the music of the situation but he supplies the words himself. It is not until the full-fledged organization of conscience that moral realism can firmly establish itself, a point that supports Westermarck as far as it goes, and also the Freudian approach, as we shall see below (page 543).

The moral attitude is, however, a composite. Thus capital punishment is considered essential to social safety because (1) it expiates, removes the murder stain, (2) it protects us against the next would-be murderer, (3) it reasserts our own conscience against our hostile impulses. Indeed, within the same individual in a stress situation the Piaget type, the Westermarck type, and the Freudian type of attitudes appear furtively and fluidly as he looks for anchors to which to secure his need to defend himself. When a situation arises which requires both overt action and at the same time a defense of one's picture of oneself, one searches for an anchor that will permit an appropriate autism.

THE GENERALITY OF AUTISM

The persistent or enduring drive structure of an individual is reasonably well illustrated by what he makes out of a narrative or other verbal pattern in understanding or retelling it. The fantastic Eskimo tale of the "war of the ghosts" comes back from the English student as a simple quarrel among primitive tribes; the grocer's story of the fragments of plaster in the butter comes back from the sewing circle as evidence that spies are poisoning the town—first with plaster of Paris, then with Paris green. The personal limits of modifying autistic response are perhaps definable only when we confront deep-seated and relatively uncontrollable drive tendencies. In contrast with these indicators of enduring drive structure, *temporary* alterations in drive structure reveal themselves well in the free-chain association experiment. Thus the innocent stimulus word *camera* brought forth the following responses: camera obscura, dark, threatening, war, death, brother, blood, return, go back, backbone, courage, hope, charity, mercy, Red Cross, blood bank, powder, explode, bomb, atom, death, chaos, restore, return, faith, hope, charity, give, blood-sweat-tears, UNO, hope, strive. No long time or deep psychiatry is necessary for us to see the subject's worries sticking through all the crevices in the wrapper. In general, temporary variations in drive structure can be handled reasonably well by experimental techniques in which the intensity of the drive can be varied and the effect upon autistic perception measured.

In view of these many approaches, the student of personality will want to know to what degree proneness to autism is a generalized quality of individuals, to what degree it depends on specific situations. We should on the whole expect, as Bleuler originally pointed out and as direct observation suggests, that autism is at a maximum in infancy and that it gradually yields to a "reality principle" as the external cognitive structure becomes clearer. This is partly because the school of hard knocks has built up a second world in opposition to the first world of immediate impulses; but another factor is the drive to be socially correct, to see a thing "as it is." There is reason to suspect, however, that we are overlooking a source of error when we refer to childhood autism and let it go at that. It was noted earlier that not only the child's perceptual responses, but *every* mind in *every* new situation, passes through the three stages. The adult will be much more confused on first confronting a new situation than he will when landmarks of certainty have been discovered at the second level of perception, and he will be even less so at the third level, when a workable method of organization is at hand. Autism, as such, is, however, a third-level phenomenon (page 366); hence any effort to discover the degree of generalization in the autistic tendency of the individual, permitting us to place him on a continuum from autistic to realistic, must wait upon successful attempts to define the areas in which he has attained a given degree of perceptual proficiency in dealing with material. We are reminded here of the very natural autisms of primitive peoples when encountering complex events for which they have no cultural preparation in the form of science, and similarly of our own autistic thinking about unforeseen economic and political events because of our lack of proficiency in perceiving the complex of facts to be judged.

Another difficulty makes the measurement of any all-round dis-position toward autism peculiarly crude; the pressure to be "reasonable" (non-autistic) is connected with one's status in his immediate personal world. Among people whose respect a person does not need, or to whose opinion he is unresponsive, the effort to make objective sense out of a situation, i.e., to forego one's autisms, is relatively pointless; but in some situations status is highly dependent upon reasonableness. To measure all-round autism we would have to know how much social pressure is being applied to the individual to make him forego his autistic drive satisfactions. For all these reasons we should expect to find it practical to study forms of autistic expression within each individual, but we should expect to encounter difficulties in defining his *all-round proneness* to such habits. As the case stands now, we can be far more certain that individuals have their *distinctive patterns of autisms* than that generalized proneness to autism is a stable individual trait.

16. Imagination and Thought

IN THE last two chapters we have watched the process of perception taking shape under the bipolar control of outer and inner influences; the individual perceiver has proved to be as distinctive, as different from his peers, as is the individual actor. In the light of our study of autism, it has begun to look as if the thinker and the imaginer could be understood in the same terms, as if the same bipolar organization could be found in fantasy and creative thought, with individuality underscoring all the words in the text. It will be worth while, then, to look first at the elementary phenomena of the world of thought, and then to trace the more complex manifestations of individuality in the higher mental processes.

IMAGERY

All tissues take time to reach their maximal response to stimulation and to subside when stimulation is removed; this is easily demonstrated in the case of receptor and cortical responses. The perseveration of receptor and cortical cells always offers the possibility that the stimulating object will in some fashion seem to remain after the stimulation from it has ceased. And after the object is gone, it may somehow be reinstated. To discuss the physiology of such processes would not be appropriate here; the essential thing is to emphasize that there are marked individual differences in sensory responses and in their tendencies both to perseverate and to reappear in the form of memory at a later time. These later appearances, similar enough to their originals to be called "images," were among the first psychological events to be studied from the standpoint of an interest in individuality. Francis Galton asked his respondents to call up a visual, olfactory, and auditory impression of the scene at the breakfast table one morning, in an effort to calibrate vividness of imagery on a scale running from zero (no image whatever when thinking of the object) to 100 (having the vividness of the original sense impression). Later studies have more modestly sought only to obtain estimates in terms of 0, 1, 2, 3, 4, 5, but have used many samples from each sensory modality. The abundance of zero's in all such studies, despite the fact that the items are somehow recalled, makes it clear that imagery is not the *only* persisting symbol of the percept, and the abundance of 5's suggests strongly that many subjects live in a world containing items of almost perceptual clarity.

Certain reservations are necessary. The physiological process upon which an image depends may be too weak to yield a reportable image but it may go on functioning, serving perfectly well as symbol, or substitute stimulus, or initiator of an association chain, and at any moment it may rise to a level of vividness that permits conscious recognition. At the other extreme, the image rated 5 may pass muster as akin to a sense perception, yet on inspection prove to have uncertain boundaries and to lack much of the detail that characterizes the percept.

There seem, nevertheless, to be at least seven classes of images in normal persons which are virtually indistinguishable from percepts: (1) the most obvious, images of the dream; (2) the "tied" images of familiar percepts, as instanced in the sixth finger of the conjuror; (3) the images developing from a neutral matrix, like voices sometimes heard in the conch shell; (4) the images, ordinarily called hypnagogic, which realize themselves as one is about to fall asleep, see below (page 395); (5) the hypnopompic (page 395), which are similar to the hypnagogic but appear as one awakens; (6) full-fledged hallucinations, usually in the form of a visual presentation of a person or his voice—at least one normal person in ten experiences such hallucinations occasionally; (7) the eidetic images, which are so vivid and so "external" that they are often confused with percepts; they are most common in young children.

To make clear the nature of eidetic imagery, it is useful to distinguish between two ways in which complex perceptual wholes are remembered. Almost all adults and older children recall things largely in terms of their total organization and meaning, with abundant use of verbal labels. In testimony experiments, for example, the individual recalls what he attended to; he does so not by reading off from a photographic visual pattern established in his mind, but by specifically bringing back step by step (with the aid of words) items upon which his attention was focused. Imagery is frequently fragmentary, and almost invariably too schematic to be relied on for accuracy. However, certain adults and a much larger number of small children do have a capacity to bring back a perceived situation in the full richness of its original occurrence. Thus a child is shown a picture of a garden scene for ten seconds, and some hours later is able to *see* the scene, reading off from his memory panorama more and more details which he never noticed in the original during the period of exposure. Such images may be poured forth in a volume that is immense in comparison with what can be produced by the ordinary methods of remembering and verbalizing. They also obey optical laws too complex for the child to understand, indicating an orderly perceptual process which is continued in full force long after the removal of the outer stimulus. There is some evidence that eidetic imagery can be grouped according to *types*, e.g., that a rich and plastic imagery appears in people inclined to hyperthyroidism, the images being expressive of mood and attitude, whereas in those inclined to parathyroid defect the imagery is brittle and unresponsive to prevailing moods.

In each human stock there are probably family and individual differences in eidetic tendency. So far as we may speak of eidetic types in the constitutional physiological sense, we are perhaps dealing with endocrine patterns that are somewhat dependent upon gene structure and, as noted earlier (page 98), are profoundly influenced by cultural factors. A person may love or hate his own eidetic tendencies, and for both practical and autistic reasons he may cultivate them or seek to inhibit them; thus, if sensory experience delights him, he may prolong and vary it. Some famous European eidetics, such as Blake and Goethe, have cultivated their imagery and lived largely in an eidetic world; others have been, as it were, harried and haunted by such experiences. We should expect that the fluid type of imagery described above would to some extent be subject to voluntary control, so that over the years the imagery pattern would more and more resonate to the need pattern, especially the individual's sensory need pattern. This would mean the maintenance and elaboration of imagery that is satisfying, the creation of a congenial inner world; at the same time, however, it would mean the autistic reconstruction of events actually experienced. The fluid character of such imagery would permit the individual to relive each good experience, making it better yet, and to transform hateful experiences to give them a quality acceptable to the ego.

Hence we should expect to find that the influence of experience and practice may reveal itself in the enrichment of eidetic imagery in the schools which deal with concrete and personal materials, and that attrition and repression of such imagery may be expected in schools which stress the formal and abstract. The German folk school and the classical school are a case in point; apparently the folk school during the Weimar period did in fact intensify and prolong eidetic phenomena, whereas the classical school inhibited them. This is reminiscent of Galton's discovery that mathematicians and logicians are weak in imagery, especially of the visual type, their training in abstract thinking having made imagery less and less useful. Verbal habits appear to weaken or destroy images, perhaps because the attention to words reduces the practice given to images, perhaps because the reality attitudes required for verbal report inhibit the fantasy attitude necessary for imagery.[1]

---

[1] Tissues that are used tend to differ more and more from those that are not used. Muscles thicken and harden; those surgically deprived of their innervation tend to atrophy. Something like this apparently happens also in cortical cells; at least, the sensory projection areas of the blind and deaf show cell degeneration. It would seem a reasonable speculation that the cultivation of imagery is in part the physiological cultivation of certain cortical functions; in view of the doctrine of specific energies, such functions are probably localized. On the other hand, Jacobson's work suggests that muscle tone plays an important role, perhaps as reinforcing agent, the kinesthetic impulses summing with those from other receptors; in general, the all-or-none law seems to weigh somewhat against the idea of training the cortical cells to yield responses that are qualitatively or quantitatively different. The physiological mechanism of image cultivation must for the present be put to one side.

In the light of all this, it would seem that mood or need pattern (page 105) can intensify and enrich the world of images, determine figure-ground relations, and serve as the basis for the temporal flow of imaginal material. Perhaps eidetic imagery is here simply a prototype of all imagery; indeed, we may find that all the materials of thought and imagination are similarly responsive, and in exactly the same way, to the individual need pattern.

To most normal adults eidetic imagery sounds a bit spooky at first; they are disinclined to believe that the creative artist or the child can actually preserve past experience so perfectly. But when one reminds them of the world of dreams and points out similarities, their attitude becomes more open-minded; fortunately, with any large group of normal adults, one can prove to a quarter or a third of them that they have had certain types of experience which are very similar to certain classes of eidetic experience. These are the hypnagogic hallucinations which sometimes appear as one is about to fall asleep; they stand out sharply as one lies relaxed with his eyes closed. Though many of them are residues from the day's experiences, they are frequently so original that their source remains unguessed; in most people they resemble the rigid and unmodifiable rather than the fluid type of eidetic imagery. Somewhat less common are the hypnopompic hallucinations that appear as one awakens; these are sometimes continuations of dreams, sometimes continuations from the hypnagogic experiences of the previous evening. This material does not fit easily into the picture of eidetics; however, it serves as a preliminary which, for the time being, may to some extent normalize or naturalize the phenomena of full-fledged eidetic response.

While eidetic images, and even dreams, may seem to partake of the character of the exotic, the great bulk of humanity has images of the ordinary garden variety, memory images. The man in the street has pictures in his mind's eye, and he can hear the voices of childhood friends as if it were yesterday. The capacity for memory imagery in the various modalities, and the richness, intensity, and duration of these images, apparently depend both upon constitutional disposition and upon training. Although data on parent-child resemblances in intensity of imagery are lacking, the state of imagery in early child-hood is the best source of information on the constitutional factors, and studies of the progressive enrichment of imagery in creative artists offer the best available data on training. Some incidental evidence is offered by cerebral damage, whether through drugs, tumors, or toxins; for since imagery may be impoverished or intensified by such factors, it becomes reasonable to believe that enduring cerebral dispositions, whatever their origin, may have a similar effect.

The exclusive emphasis on the constitutional factors in imagery has come down from a period in which it was believed that one's endow-ment in one modality of imagery must be negatively related to his endowment in other modalities. According to this theory, people fall into imagery types; he who has rich visual imagery is weak in auditory and tactual images. But introspective studies in which images are calibrated on an intensity scale suggest a positive rather than a nega-tive relation between the various modalities, for people with strong visual imagery are apparently more likely to be well endowed in auditory and other fields of imagery.

An individual's proneness to a specific modality can, however, be seen in many cases of synesthesia. To the visual-minded, tones are conceived to be of various colors; to the auditory-minded, colors are conceived to have various tone properties. For some persons, colors and tones bring to mind varying geometrical shapes so tightly linked with the original sensory elements that the sensation cannot be experi-enced without experiencing the accompanying image. Many syn-esthesias indicate that one type of imagery introduces itself into all other sensory patterns; thus the visual-minded cannot hear or touch or smell without experiencing an imaginal visual counterpart jointly with the stimulus. Though the evidence is not clear cut, this appears to be due to the same general type of dynamics that we considered in connection with "physiognomics" (page 266), namely, the person's failure to complete the process of disentangling the various elements in childhood perception. Synesthesias appear to be common in child-hood and are apparently slowly broken down by fresh associations and the progressive recognition of the irrelevance of the associated images.

Although the discussion thus far has emphasized past associations, present attitudes or sets are also important in this connection. We have already described, in terms of internal reinforcement, the process of *set* which plays so large a part in perception (page 354). This factor is also operative in the arousal of imagery. Just as the conscious acceptance of a task brings about, through inner conditioning, the incipient movements required to execute it, so a person may, as a result of a mood, unwittingly begin the completion of a task that realizes the mood in external form. As a composer's *moods* vary, the *musical form* he chooses follows suit. Indeed, several experimenters have succeeded in inducing in their subjects various moods which appear in their musical compositions and paintings. The richness and form of the imagery depend upon the specific way in which training and the broader cultural emphasis have enriched, intensified, or inhibited the imaginal processes of the individual.

It is likely that imagery is maintained or lost, and that recall occurs or fails to occur, for the same reasons we brought forward in our discussion of perception. The image comes or goes as the need pattern requires. Recall follows from the joint operation of the outer situation and the inner stress system. The general dynamics of conditioning and association, with the all-or-none principle, the principle of dominance, and the principle of hierarchical organization following the three-level patterns of perceptual development, clearly applies to the inner world of imagery and recall in the same way and with the same cogency as when objects are first perceived. In particular, just as a percept is a structure resulting from outer and inner patterns in a state of fusion, and just as it follows rather than precedes the need pattern with which it is linked, so the inner world of imagery and recall represents a fusion of outer and inner—but with more accent on the inner—and responds moment by moment to the individual need pattern. In this sense, persistent individual differences in imagining and recalling are to some degree expressions of whatever continuity the individual need pattern possesses. Individual differences in these and other cognitive functions are indeed only secondarily an expression of the fixed properties of neural tissues. Primarily they are expressions of the individual's *long-time needs* upon which are superimposed the immediate consequences of *momentary needs* acting reciprocally with intercurrent stimulation from the outer world.

The Course of Imagination

Perception is a screen held up before the groping organism; it is usually a spatial and temporal ordering of the manifold of environmental objects to which response in ordered form must be made. It is constantly guided both by the changing environmental relationships and by the inner complex of needs. Imagination, however, is free for the moment from the coercions of the outer world; it can yield far more to autisms. When we actually walk through the external world, we note its patterned images closely; but if we lie idly by the wayside, we can turn it to and fro, finding in it dreams of the way we should like to go. Imagination is never absolutely free; but the reality world to which one returns after the fantasy is sometimes distant and can be held stationary as a "thing" rather than an unceasing process. The stream of imagination can be guided for a while by a process of rehearsal or creation; the individual is a stage manager who is responsible to no audience but himself.

To illustrate an earlier point we used the Hopi Indian boy who kicks a stick before him as he runs a race; it is not boy, but stick, that must reach the finish line (page 378). This applies also to the nature of fantasy. Fantasy is pushed forward as a person runs his race; imagination helps to "guide" drives, but in the first instance it is also guided by the drive process. Our hypothesis, then, is that imagination is the same bipolar process that we encountered above (page 349), but that the relative freedom from outer constraints means a relative intransigence on the part of inner needs. In other words, there seems to be no place for free, non–drive–directed association, no easy-running succession of casual ideas on the basis of the laws of association acting in a sovereign capacity. Let us see where this hypothesis leads. What do thought and imagination look like, when regarded as expressions not of *association* or of Gestalt *structures*, but of individual drive dynamics? There is no need to throw association out of court as is done by Gestalt psychology, or to discard Gestalt principles in the manner of modern associationism; both conceptions are necessary. But the present hypothesis holds that *both* association and structural whole- ness are intelligible only in the light of individual needs acting to determine figure-ground and dominance relations.

It will be apparent that the simplest patterns of imagination and thought, the building stones which enter into higher units, are them- selves composites of words, images, motor impulses, and other ingredients; the laws of association, of dominance, and of organiza- tion play a part in the formation of each such complex structure. Special importance, however, attaches to words, not only as ingredients in these structures but as devices for labeling each recognizable func- tional unit. It is natural, therefore, that a superficial examination of thought has given the impression that it "consists of words"; in fact, thought is usually reflected in words. But the labeling process has induced some to regard the thought as comprised of the labels, whereas in reality the labels denote certain elements which are them- selves non-verbal, and principles of organization which lie much deeper in the matrix of the mind than any symbolic process can be.

As to the flow of thought, imagery and other ingredients may be directly aroused by *sense impressions* of another modality, as when a tone calls up a visual image of the musical instrument, and by other images, so that trains of images appear. Such trains are of course governed by similarity and contiguity of the associated elements, and by the recency, frequency, and vividness of their connection. The laws of association operative during thought are necessarily the same as those already reviewed (page 345). They involve on the one hand certain principles regarding piecemeal connection and on the other certain principles as to organization; the discussion whether they are to be viewed atomistically or totalistically depends upon the types of experimental data to be emphasized. Cameron's data are replete with evidence of both piecemeal and integrated action, and Durkin's study showed a continuum from "random" or piecemeal association to full- blown "insight." But the patterns of thought are governed also by the individual determining tendency or set, which appears to be the same as Razran's "attitudinal control"; this may govern both the *establishment* and the *later recurrence* of an association. Such controls have already been noted in the case of perception (page 354); they appear both in the recombination of image patterns and in the sequence of these patterns. When the determining tendency alters the cognitive structure, we may refer to autism; its essential structure, as we saw, apparently lies in the dominance of satisfying over unsatisfying trends, as in motor learning. The first thing, then, that we hope to learn when a recorded pattern of thought is spread before us is what determines the course of operations, the "trains of association" which mark continuities of mood or progress toward goals. Such trains appear to begin with the anchorage (page 346) of percepts at particular points; and these anchors, being dominant elements, serve as conditioned stimuli for new patterns that appear in response to present need patterns.

Whether dealing with random associations, daydreams, or creative thought, we are always confronted with the problem of determining empirically what the operating needs are. In particular, it is important to do justice to what we earlier called the activity needs (page 107), especially the tension patterns of striped muscles. These play a large part in the control of thought, a phenomenon that Lasswell speaks of as "postural control." As one tightens the fingers or arm of the hypnotized subject, or merely gazes fixedly at a dot on a card, the course of association quickly responds to the tension. To relax locally or generally involves the cessation of certain types of control and the liberation of others, particularly those organized around images. It is for this reason that daydreams are rich and night dreams richer still, and that the psychoanalytic method has depended upon the subject's reclining on a couch so as to set free the inner, especially the cortical, tension systems and remove them from the coercive control of the skeletal musculature.

The thinking process is therefore guided (as are all other processes) by both the objective and the autistic aspects of the stimulus pattern, whether one is thinking "with a purpose" or merely "randomly." To be sure, voluntary thinking may necessitate a greater constancy of the goal and the use of larger blocks of material, so that higher units are more conspicuous. Unconscious controls by postural, visceral, or other factors may at times, however, necessitate the same striking continuity of goals and the same use of higher units. Continuity in the thought process may result from continuity in the pressure of needs and in the tension sequences which arise from the entire need pattern; this makes sense in view of the fact that one is often unable to trace back the content of a given thought to its source. "Unconscious thinking" has been subject to considerable mystery as an apparent contradiction in terms. But all thinking is both "unconscious" in the sense defined above, and at the same time conscious in the sense that as the tensions readjust there is thrown upon the screen of awareness the representative expression of the situation confronted (just as, in Plato's *Republic*, shadows are cast upon the wall of the cave by figures that pass to and fro).

This unconscious control appears, for example, in the dreams of arctic explorers. These dreams, as recorded by Rasmussen, show that verdant pastures, a warm sun, refreshing streams, and a variety of fruits and other tropical foods continue to appear month after month, as life goes on in the steady cold, darkness, and deprivation. So, too, in the daydream, images of all the good things which were satisfying in the past come back as the present situation fails to satisfy; fantasy is a mirror in which the need situation is reflected. As far as we know, all needs operate in this way. Studies with the Thematic Apperception Test (page 670) suggest that a variety of definable needs can be ascertained, indeed roughly measured, by the fantasy-releasing process. As a rule, more than one need is evident; we should expect the more complex need patterns to lead to more complex imaginative expression, until a point is reached in which one pours the entire system of his wants into a single unrestrained outburst. The needs include not only the physical, esthetic, and social wants, to which attention must always be given, but the wants that relate in a deeper sense to self-realization. The need to complete and enhance the incomplete and unsatisfying image of the self may, under conditions of extreme vigor, produce unique experiences of otherworldly meaning; the mystic becomes one with the universe, enjoys "cosmic consciousness."

Here there arises a question of dynamics concerning the interrelations of three types of phenomena which appear in the thought process—mood, belief, and imaginal process. Which comes first, which second, which third? We shall use as illustration the presence in psychotic patients of mood disorder, delusions, and hallucinations. The layman, noting that all three are present, is inclined to suggest that the hallucination or faulty perception gives rise to the delusion, and that consequently a mood takes shape which is appropriate to the belief entertained by the patient. Clinical study, however, shows that the reverse order usually holds. A gay or somber mood leads to the autistic anchorage of one's responses upon a satisfying or depressing element; the situation is structured to yield an appropriate delusion. The delusion, in turn, constantly fed by the mood, makes possible anchorage upon certain phases of the imaginal field, so that hallucinations develop which accord with the delusion. This sequence in the psychotic in no way indicates an abnormality, but merely an intensification of the phenomena usually encountered. The ordinary relations of mood, delusion, and hallucination are apparently the same in all normal conduct. Personality is first of all a drive system, of which mood is a prominent aspect. The drive system determines a person's way of thinking and believing. Dominated by these need patterns and beliefs, he perceives, so far as the objective stimulus structure permits (page 372), in such a way as to round out and implement the belief.

FANTASY AS AN EXPRESSION OF INDIVIDUALITY

Egocentrism, in Piaget's sense, must of course appear in thought if it appears anywhere. We should expect to find less of it in the older child than in the younger; we should also expect that the development of socially accepted methods of thinking would steadily reduce the more primitive types of fantasy. The individual would consequently be expected to lose, year by year, the elementary habits of autistic thought which were so deep a solace in his earliest years. But he may in turn learn gradually to stereotype his fantasies in the form of the smart, the rich, and the powerful, or the homely, the honest, and the folksy, all of whom appear in comics, pulp magazines, and soap opera. Or he may learn to escape into the idiosyncrasies of another world which is uniquely his own. A few historical examples will be helpful in indicating the dynamics involved.

Through Jeanne d'Arc's native village roamed French and Burgundian soldiers, and cattle driven from burning and pillaged hamlets —symbols of France's danger. At home a devout father and mother told the young girl about the Virgin; she listened and loved. When the other children played, she went to pray; when they taunted her, she prayed the more. On Saturdays she went alone to St. Tiebaud's fountain, buried herself in an intensity of prayer, was found swooning in ecstasy. The world of the Virgin and the saints came nearer and nearer to her. One day she came home, believing that her mother had called her. No, she had not—then perhaps it was a voice from another world. "At noon on a summer's day" when she was twelve, a voice which later she accepted as St. Michael's told her that she was to rescue the king; and soon St. Margaret and St. Catherine were coming frequently to her. Her duty and her way to achieve it became clear. During her trial at Rouen the learned judge asked whether, and how, she had seen them. "I saw them, sir, in exactly the same way that I see you."

Around William Blake's boyhood loomed the "dark satanic mills" of the new industrialism, driving mercilessly into the moors and hedgerows of his beloved countryside. Nursed in the vital imagery of the Hogarth school, Blake served an apprenticeship as an engraver. The grand apocalyptic figures of seventeenth-century evangelism broke upon him in Bunyan, as did also, a little later, the epic mysticism of Jacob Boehme. He cultivated these images, dwelt more and more with and within them, until at last, as in Jeanne d'Arc's case, they were as real to him as father and mother; they inhabited his world, spoke to him with authority. The divine "new day" and the Satanism of the "tiger" are an expression of his yearnings and his dreads. The engravings and verses poured out of a creative mold which was too big, too surgingly alive, for conscious control; he put the images down as he saw them, wrote what they commanded.

The young philologist Friedrich Nietzsche lived in the languages and sacred books of the East. Bitterly competitive, he became increasingly involved in his own interpretations. The anguish of gastric disease tensed him more and more; long walks only aggravated his agony. The world of his dream became the world of a real Zarathustra and other spirit forms from the unseen, which commanded and goaded him. According to his sister, sometimes he said that it was not he who wrote; he simply put down what the spirits said. Nietzsche, like Blake, listened while the invisible forms dictated; he became a scribe for their imperious messages.

These three brief accounts suggest that the individual has in a sense voluntarily controlled his own evolution; i.e., that the product of fantasy is no mere expression of a momentary need, but rather a continuously renewed fulfillment of a lifelong wish. This is clearly the case in most instances of great creative fantasy; childhood wishes, enriched through growth and learning, call the tune through later decades. There are, however, some apparent exceptions. Thus Swedenborg, the physicist and biologist, at fifty-five had attained a commanding position as a savant. Teeming with information and revered for judgment, he constantly sought the meaning of life in observation and experiment, in reflection and debate. One day, when he was alone, a man appeared to him; when the figure was gone, he knew that it was Christ. Soon thereafter other figures came to him and spoke; he once tried to settle an argument at a scientists' dinner by assuring his opponent that St. Paul had explained the whole matter to him. This "prosaic Swede" became a seer whose *Arcana* revealed both the world above and below our earth, and the course of human destiny. It may perhaps be maintained by the psychoanalyst that even in his case childhood wishes had taken hold to produce a structure not at first apparent in the adult man of science; perhaps physical or social circumstances intensified the need in the older man, or weakened the inhibitions, although he was at the height of his intellectual powers. It would be franker to say that creative imagination sometimes breaks out, as in this case, with a force for which there is at present no explanation.

We are usually prone to disvalue the imaginative act, the fantasy, the daydream, not only when it leads to hallucination but also when it merely diverts time and attention from the tasks of the workaday world; but the instant it proves that it has had practical worth in preparing for action we forgive the daydreamer his idle eccentricity. Although our culture has tended to disparage the chronic dreamer, it is also true that we have had respect for the boy with "the long long thoughts," nor have we been unmindful of the values in daydreaming, provided the daydreams stay within suitable limits. Daydreams which ultimately lead to action, which are tested by reference to the question "How can we really do this?" which lead to passionate persistence in working on a problem, as in the case of the Wright brothers and their early daydreams of airplanes, are deeply respected; a person who never dreams up any new issues is criticized as dull and unimaginative and perhaps not quite in the American tradition.

CURIOSITY AND THE PROCESS OF THINKING

Like all organic events, imagination and thought are tension-expressing processes; like all human events, they are directed processes, the direction becoming more constant, more specific, with experience. The tension initiates the original activity; the direction is clear or obscure, simple or complex, depending upon the character of the wants and the experience in dealing with them. The wants evolve, however, as the activity goes on, and the images and processes involved may be valuable in their own right, so that it is *fun* to think. The solution of problems may be appetizing in its own right, and any degree of playfulness or autistic delight may attend the movement to the goal, so that the sharp distinction between autistic and realistic thought becomes fatuous. Curiosity is at first an activity drive that is notoriously non-specific in direction. Puppies, monkeys, men are forever poking their noses into what does not obviously concern them—that is, what does not concern any previously aroused drive.

but very much concerns the completion of a perceptual or activity pattern. And when one activity is completed, a person finds himself already involved in the next. Curiosity behavior, orientation needs (page 298), perseveration (page 107), the need for more experience of the same general sort push us into the "irrelevant." This need can be compelling; it can be strong enough to keep the hungry child exploring for hours past lunch time. Though often mixed with other needs, sheer love of exploration may, in a complex creature like man, be an autism of tremendous strength. (The term "autism" implies no "irrationality"; it continues to be used in the sense of movement of cognitive processes in the direction of drive satisfaction.) It is the only autism known that has any chance of lifting the individual out of the surging pressure of his practical needs; the only kind of thinking that, purely by its willingness to take orders from outer as well as inner stimulation, has any chance of blowing to pieces the mass of super-stitions, shams, hypocrisies, standardized errors, and stupid conven-tionalities that human flesh is heir to; the only kind of thinking in an ordered, normal society that has any chance of cutting through the suave logic which makes the familiar always right.

One must, then, distinguish between thinkers in terms of what they *basically want* to do. Since one of the many things they may want is to make contact with reality, we may, if we wish, utilize Bleuler's dis-tinction between fantasy and realism, if in doing so we make clear that the reality "set" or the reality "feel" is one of many drive-deter-mined qualities of the thought process. Just as William James found the quest for truth springing from the "sentiment of rationality," so Asch, experimentally studying the process of thinking, may find the affective and conative struggle to "see things as they are," rather than as others insist they are, one of the compelling human motivations. Asch has raised the question whether the blind suggestibility to which students of group behavior have so often referred must actually appear when the individual is thrown into a situation in which his own eyes convey the truth to him in one way and the testimony of a half dozen comrades insists upon a different interpretation. Asch showed that the united group testimony of companions typically produces merely nervousness or tension in an observer who nevertheless sticks to his guns, sees the matter in his own way, and says so emphatically. These findings do not maintain that a cold cognitive attitude shifts for itself without aid from affective factors, but rather that the *drive* to make contact with reality may at times be the drive that counts most.

The quest for reality, however, is seldom simply a quest for something to fill in a spot marked by ignorance. It is, as Spearman showed, a search for missing parts and missing relations. What is given is experienced as a series of clues, not a complete datum with which to deal. As we face such incompleteness, tension increases and the need for the whole activates the associative bonds already present. Similarities are exploited, new contrasts are actively sought, or old contiguities are pressed into service. "What came before? What came after?" we ask. And we round out a satisfying whole.

Whether the thought process moves toward reality or fantasy, it always moves toward the satisfaction which can be achieved only when the sensory and activity drives directly encounter patterns that will reduce their tensions. Regardless of whether the pattern that will achieve this is outer or inner, or a composite of the two, motivation moves forward in terms of such achievement. In spinning a yarn or writing an epic, the satisfactions are achieved moment by moment, and they always lead to the setting up of new problems and new solutions.

Each such thought or fantasy process establishes new structures in the mind of the thinker; in other words, one learns to think. Unfortunately there is no one way to think, no one "art of thinking," no one thought craft that every craftsman can acquire. Rather, there are various types of logical thinking, various types of constructive and analytical thinking, each of which follows a series of disciplined efforts leading to the acquisition of specific skills and hence to the increasing rigidity of the thinker's mind. Darwin at sixty could no longer read Shakespeare; his mind had been trained to cut from the tissues of reality a cloth of quite another pattern.

To this negative aspect of the process of becoming rigid there must, however, be added another factor, namely, the common tendency of curiosity to pursue more and more specialized goals. While the high-school student is mildly interested in solving a mathematical or chemical problem, many an adult mathematician or chemist cannot eat or sleep until he finds the answer. All the learning processes discussed above lead to deepening and also to narrowing; that is the price of learning, i.e., movement toward greater and greater specificity, so that it is not surprising to find that functional cleavage often becomes sharp. The fact that a person is exercising a narrow skill on a topic of real pertinence to himself means that all else is lost for the time being, and thè more time he spends at one kind of task, the less expression there is of other interests. The process of creative thinking, no less than the process of daydreaming, involves shutting out or thrusting aside part of one's make-up while emphasizing another part—in other words the exaggeration of the distinction between figure and ground until the ground is lost. There are obviously large individual differences in the tendency to such "shutting out" or dissociation. This leads to the question: If we are all characterized by dissociation to some degree, are we also characterized by degrees of capacity for organizing or integrating our activities? The Rorschach data at first suggest an affirmative answer; there is considerable evidence that some kinds of whole responses are a gauge of organizing power (*Gestaltungskraft*), but it is not certain that the capacity to organize is the opposite of the tendency toward cleavage. These data suggest that the focusing or centralization of function makes possible the best-integrated behavior; but it is this same focusing that may induce cleavage. Just as progressive centralization in policy-making goes with decentralization in administrative functions (in the modern state and in modern industry), so it would appear that the individual capacity for concentrated endeavor is actually greatest in those for whom the short-circuiting of all other activities is possible.

This would mean, however, that the cleavage capacity is to only a small degree a fixed constitutional mark, a "stigma of degeneration" in the sense of the Italian school, related to those great wits who are so close to madness. It would appear that dissociation based upon constitutional factors is augmented by the acquisition of skills which permit highly organized activity, and that the type of cleavage resulting is in almost every respect different from the cleavage that results from the conflict of motives. In other words, we should expect to be able, through education, to develop a certain type of functional cleavage in which no conflict is involved.

This is what the autobiography of John Stuart Mill plainly shows. At times his father overemphasized the drill process in John Stuart's education; at times the boy's capacity for feeling was actually weakened. But his later life showed clearly that the three spheres—logic, economics, psychology—in which he had been taught to think were the ones to which he later made epoch-making contributions with the normal zest and affect of an integrated person. However, his mind, like Darwin's, had been narrowed, so that neither cognitive nor affective response was possible in relation to many of the issues with which educated Englishmen were concerned during Mill's era. Although overwhelmed by the theory of evolution, he could not think about it in a sustained way.

In studying this process of the progressive organization of the power to think, it has seemed unnecessary for us to debate the issue of wholes vs. parts. The nature of primary components and the character of dynamic interrelations are of equal significance. Our needs for building-stones and architectural principles are equally pressing; hence no controversy regarding the reality of insight can be half as useful as the direct recognition that both association and Gestalt structuring are patent aspects of the creative process. We are especially encouraged in so bold a statement by L. W. Max's evidence on "imageless thought." The thoughts without sensory content which appeared in his experimental subjects—deaf people who used their fingers in thinking—developed at moments when kinesthetic impulses were too weak to be consciously recognized but were still strong enough to be picked up by the electrical record. Although the elements in the thought process may be too weak to be individually detected, this physiological clue suggests that there are always sensory components and always structured interrelations.

PERSONALITY

THE INDIVIDUAL QUALITY OF THOUGHT

There still remains the question of the *quality* of thought, the basic feel, or, as Santayana puts it, the odor of the individual thinker's mind. The clue to this individual quality has been sought sometimes in content, e.g., in organic sensation, and equally often in form, e.g., in the temporal flow (smooth vs. jerky, etc.). The whole sequence of studies from the time of the Greek "psychognostics" to modern work on "personality style" seems to indicate that individual thought behavior should be unique in content or form, or both, and with this we must agree. But experimental proof that we can recognize the authorship of musical compositions or scraps of handwriting strongly suggests that sensory elements and their interrelations play a predominating role in such individuality. The thinker starts with motives, largely esthetic, and with activity drives, including curiosity and prestige and power needs, which help to organize particular sensory elements (page 371). Familiar elements cannot be abolished or overridden any more than the drives can; hence he wittingly or unwittingly uses the old similes, rings changes upon the old word pictures. The individual quality of thinking is the composition of the photograph in which one's own special point of view is manifest; and though the student of motor expressive patterns has important clues, a simple and direct probing of the sensory structure of the thinker's mind may in the long run be even more useful.

Indeed, the molding of the mind by cultural processes is a matter of supplying and organizing sensory and affective material. Each adult mind is in some measure a culturally imposed pattern as regards both its form of response and its basic content. But, because unobserved by others, the way in which each thought is *felt*, in terms of the organic and kinesthetic sensations, the inarticulate feels and stresses of each moment, is perhaps less closely controlled by culture. Neither the poet nor the common man can tell clearly what each feels within himself; he can tell only the outer things about which he is thinking, not the quality of his thought. In the struggle to communicate with his psychiatrist, every neurotic and psychotic patient finds that he can convey the *situations* and the *behaviors* with infinitely greater ease than the resonating but unnamed qualities that make up so much of the quality of his own experience.

Thus far we have regarded all thought as alike, in the sense that it starts from needs and moves toward need-satisfying goals. We have yet to deal, however, with one great challenge, the specific challenge of the psychoanalysts which has been stressed by Lasswell: Is not the relaxed, image-rich thinking of the person on the psychoanalyst's couch *fundamentally* different from ordinary thought? Is there not a difference between the two kinds of thinking, not merely in drive and goal and content, but in the very nature of the thought process? Is the individual who thinks in undirected fashion free of all the principles we have sought to define? We believe that Lasswell is entirely correct as regards the richness of a type of thinking that sober daily life ignores, and in succeeding chapters we shall try to do justice to this inner world. But we cannot see that the second type of thinking expresses the unconscious more than the first. All thinking, as we have constantly tried to make clear, is in its core unconscious; it is only its shadow which is conscious, and this is true of free as of directed thought. To be sure, in the one instance the person "knows" where his thinking is tending; he is thinking for a verbally expressed purpose. In the other instance he does not know where his thought will lead; he has not stated his goal. But this does not mean that there is more goal direction in the one situation than in the other. Both processes are perfectly goal-directed; both are perfectly "physiological" in their movement toward this goal. They differ in the fact that the shadow thrown into the consciousness includes in the one instance a symbol defining the goal, whereas in the other the goal remains hidden. In this sense the two, as Lasswell defines them, are distinct indeed, even mutually exclusive. But since goals may be half-articulately known and since there are all degrees of awareness as to why one thinks as he does, we regard Lasswell's dichotomy purely as stating the apparent extremes within which thinking must move, not as establishing an eternal chasm between two utterly distinct activities.

We have, then, completed the tentative answers toward which we aimed. The author's own need pattern has confronted the problem of assimilating the symbols "thought" and "imagination," which in the past have so often been included in studies of personality. He found himself bringing in, step by step, all the half-conscious storehouse of material on motivation, canalization, conditioning, perceptual structure, dissociation, and organization to which reference was made earlier, the integration of which was obviously required. As a result, he concluded that thought and imagination are merely the more complex organized expressions of all the tendencies which we see in humankind, even when off guard, in undirected and "thoughtless" form. From the delayed reaction to a lifelong quest for a scientific answer there is a continuum of responses, a hierarchical progression, in which fortunately most of the steps have been studied experimentally so that a reasonably articulate answer is at hand.

The actual substance of imagination and thought thus comprises both the quest for reality and the effort to escape it, both curiosity about the world and the need to improve upon the world. The factors that give rise to each new step in the process of imagining and thinking always constitute a network of interacting influences with nodal points and backgrounds, and what occurs by way of response is a new and complex pattern. But the response pattern also exhibits the threshold or all-or-none principle; "a new idea" is likely to come as a whole, or to fail to come, depending on the circumstances of the moment. Thought moves forward in chunks, undergoing some splitting and some new accretions and organizations, but always subject to the need pattern at the moment, and always leaving residues in terms of habits of thought and imagination upon which these processes will inevitably draw.

Hence thinking becomes highly individualized. But since the peripheral circumstances which determine thought are likely to be much the same among people in the same subcultural situation, the actual richness of individual differences in thinking is supplied largely by the aura or, if one prefers, the "stuffing" of specific drive material which the individual supplies. This "stuffing" may be very explicit, of the "I want my dinner" variety, or it may be very diffuse, as in the "atmosphere" of thought. In the experiments of Sells and of Morgan, the words used in a sentence touch off *attitudes* which are not really relevant to the matter to be judged, yet affect the reasoning process. Thought here reflects diffuse unverbalized attitudes. Generalizing, we may say that into thought enters the attitude syndrome of the individual, and this is almost a way of saying that all of the person is expressed in thought. For the life of attitudes is limited only by the life of motivation, and this is as broad, complex, intertwined, and overlapping as is the life of the tissues themselves.

17. The Dreamer

JUST as reverie can portray both the content and the style of individual autism, so the full-fledged dream can speak volumes about the present meaning of one's past, the future meaning of one's present, the structure and feeling of one's wants.

The dream, however, has more to say than this. Just as the artist creates because he wants to create, and not merely because the canvas can perhaps be sold, the dreamer dreams not only because he can in this way put some of tomorrow's goods on to the dream stage for present contemplation, but because the dream process is itself a good, a value, a thing worth while. Many wishes may struggle with one another, some relating to the future, others remorsefully to the past, others—as Holt has so well shown—being simply modes of escape from predicaments. But all these scattered wishes are ordered, given a unified dramatic vitality, because there is a need for it. If it is true that wishes are clues to the appearance of the dream fragments, they are also clues to the dramatic wholes. Many a commonplace person finds some degree of fulfillment in dreams with melodramatic, lyric, or epic splendor of a sort which he could never for the life of him compose in the full light of his "senses." There is a need at work, and a full-fledged activity which has an organic meaning; there is a kind of creativeness which is indulged for its own sweet sake.

Perhaps the fact that it is a thing one resorts to when he is not under any immediate stimulus compulsion from outside is evidence that dreaming is a thing he very deeply wants to do. Perhaps this epic or architectural building activity is something resident in human tissues and very imperfectly expressed in a practical civilization. General testimony indicates that imagery is usually richer, affect stronger, dramatic plot more complex in dreaming than in waking reveries. And if, as appears to be the case, one can in a private world create according to his heart's desire, in his own idiom, and for his own delectation, with no need to play to the grandstand, to please the boss, Mrs. Grundy, or the American Legion, or even the sound sense and good judgments of the "best people," there ought to be in the dream process a revelation of individuality that is not to be had anywhere else. The best we have been able to do up to the present is to half-persuade the person to be his private self; this is the value of the projective methods, the Rorschach test, the analysts' free associations. But half way is not enough; perhaps the dream can go further. It must be caught, cultivated, tissue-cultured, or, best of all, placed—while in full vitality—in a vivarium where its macroscopic and microscopic tissue changes can be studied.

This is not to say that the private world is the "best" world. Most of this book concerns the aspects of personality that appear in a social world; it is the work of an American who has listened like the rest to the pioneers and entrepreneurs, to the big doings of Paul Bunyan and Henry Ford, to Horatio Alger's success stories, to the be-not-weary-in-well-doing of the Lions Clubs, to all the excellent cultural-molding-of-selfhood doctrines, to the group altruism of Jane Addams and John Dewey, to all that is up to date, socially-minded, and progressive. All these influences and most of the books on personality by psychologists are so top-heavy with sociality that the little self is timidly hidden under the mass. But there is a *private* world, and within this a *private private* world, a world of dreams, in and for oneself. When it is discovered, when its richness, strength, and individuality are studied as objects of value for science and for art, there will be a psychology of personality more worthy of the name.

Almost everything in our culture has been given an "economic" interpretation; everything we do, say, or feel is traced to our mode of production and distribution. One portion of our humanity, however, has like Pandora's little "hope" been left in the box, so unimportant, so unworthy that it was not even thought fit to be shaken down into its economic role; the economics-minded have perhaps been so sure of their economics that anything so clearly without value as a dream could be ignored.

[415]

Pandora confronts the world of the sleeping person. Everyone knows that sleep is physically necessary; we wail at the wasted time but we perfect our mattresses. Dreamless sleep is "better for" us; the "real" things of the waking world can be done better if we consecrate the resting hours to a new attack upon them. Most of what we dream is forgotten in the first few minutes; only if it makes good conversation or "bears upon" the day's tasks is it worth a thought. Psychoanalysts say that dreams "mean" all sorts of things, i.e., in terms of waking; the individual fears to tell his dreams for fear of waking reproval. The psychoanalysts are, however, completely harmless, for they, too, are awake. They agree that sleep is nothing but escape, and that dreams are guardians of the escape process, letting us dwell in disguised fashion upon the possibilities in the waking world, so that by make-believe that is not too realistic we may be strong enough in the morning to go on with our usual self-deceptions, and when necessary walk through the shams of life with a finger on Ariadne's "reality principle."

A third of life for us all, then, is a sad psychological waste that has no economic value except as a hostage to tomorrow's toil; its psychological product is industrial waste, occasionally salvaged by the psychoanalytical chemist, but for most people most of the time so gross that it is not commercially worth the cost of reclaiming it. This, I think, is the honest attitude of our practical society toward the world of sleeping and dreaming. It is the attitude of the business man who gets things done, and of the worker who gets the things done for him. Nobody wants a "dreamer." Let's stick to business.

This attitude has resulted, I believe, in one of the greatest instances of myopia to be found in contemporary psychology. Indeed, from a respectable psychological point of view, the waking events to which we have been attending throughout the preceding chapters are ordered with reference to the struggle to exist or to maintain a standard of satisfaction in existence. Psychological events, in other words, occur for the sake of something to be achieved thereby. The means-end relationships color everything; when once the author has given you his pet theory of drives, the remainder of the book consists in seeing how the drives are satisfied. The Ways and Means Committee, as always, is the center of the structure. The one psychological world at the center of which each individual, spider-like, watches for prey is a world in which psyche waits upon soma, ministering to its every need.

Now this is very extraordinary biology. The arm does not exist to keep the stomach alive, nor the stomach to keep the heart alive, nor the heart to keep the genitals alive, nor the genitals to keep the brain alive. Every organ needs to function; and the functioning itself is a life process which may or may not have a practical value in itself. Kittens will play, boys will be boys, men will go fishing, women will talk over the back fence, and all of us will dream and dream. Dreaming, in other words, is the realization of a biological function for which there is a need; it occurs because universal and important activities are expressed in and through it. Although it may be in part preparatory to waking tasks, this helps but little in defining its *modus operandi*. We smilingly approve of Junior's playing football, for it will make a man of him; but he does not play because it will make a man of him, but because it is fun. The rules by which he plays are determined not by the kind of man he is going to be, but by the inner necessity of the activity. Books about football are not tracts on the business world for which football prepares. Yet dreaming—exquisite, rich, beautiful, terrible, insane, furious, trivial, ineffable, silly, ravishing world that it is—is treated by psychologists, psychoanalysts, fortunetellers alike as a "nothing but" world; it is "nothing but" a repetition of or preparation for waking experience, nothing but an odd befuddled form of imagination. Sometimes one wonders whether the practical psychologist has ever allowed himself, on waking, to try to reconstruct an entire active dream in all its fullness, or set himself, as he retired, to the task of dreaming a particular kind of dream; whether he would ever dare come near enough to a whole dream to get the feel of it; or whether the psychoanalyst has ever allowed himself to see anything in the dream except the symbolic play with the phases of the waking world of which his patient is wishfully afraid.

For the dream may not only run parallel to but bring to its finest fruition that which is outstandingly original or beautiful in the waking state. As De Quincey, most magnificent of dreamers, describes it:

When I lay awake in bed, vast processions moved along continually in mournful pomp; friezes of never-ending stories, that to my feelings were as sad and solemn as stories drawn from times before Oedipus or Priam, before Tyre, before Memphis. And, concurrently with this, a corresponding change took place in my dreams; a theatre seemed suddenly opened and lighted up within my brain, which presented nightly spectacles of more than earthly splendour . . . as the creative state of the eye increased, a sympathy seemed to arise between the waking and the dreaming states of the brain in one point—that whatsoever I happened to call up and to trace by a voluntary act upon the darkness was very apt to transfer itself to my dreams; and at length I feared to exercise this faculty; for, as Midas turned all things to gold that yet baffled his hopes and defrauded his human desires, so whatsoever things capable of being visually represented I did but think of in the darkness, immediately shaped themselves into phantoms for the eye; and, by a process apparently no less inevitable, when thus once traced in faint and visionary colours, like writings in sympathetic ink, they were drawn out, by the fierce chemistry of my dreams, into insufferable splendour that fretted my heart.

This kind of full-bodied reality offers the starting point. Analysis is excellent if it does not forget what is to be analyzed, or insist that the many fragments discovered are all that there is in the organic totality. Let us try, then, the method of dissection, then return to the problem of dream structure. Dreams are a form of association (covered by laws considered in Chapter 16) and are related to the days which have gone before; and they are a form of wishing and they relate to the days ahead. The interconnectedness of life processes requires that. So—and also because dreams have been collected and published with these simple principles in mind—the analysis of dreams as personality indicators will have to begin with studies of the association and wish-revealing properties of dreaming, for each dream shows personal idiosyncrasies, motivation, and structural properties. Abundant records of children's dreams, as in Piaget's and Kimmins' work, make very clear that both the content and the form of the dream reflect the mental level of the dreamer, complexity coming with complexity of mind; Sarason's comparisons of the dreams and the waking fantasies of subnormal girls bring out very striking parallels of the same sort. Since the dream is a turned-in or introverted process and hence suffers from the general disvaluation to which all introverted activities in our society are subject, we should expect to find a greater richness in dreaming on the part of those who, for whatever reason, have learned to find their deepest satisfactions in the inner world. In a similar vein, we should expect to find that those whose autisms can give rise to plastic and productive fantasy while awake will, other things being equal, dream most magnificently. We should expect to find individual differences in the sheer skill or artistry of individual dreaming to which the great dreams of De Quincey and Coleridge bear witness.

One of the most skillful realizations of dream autism is the process by which little is made to stand for much. The dream is a condensed or truncated picture; it must say much in few images. In response to an outer stimulus it may fabricate by a method of successive high spots what would in waking life take months or hours to produce. Thus in Welch's study of the time relations of hypnotic dreams, an event which would take about seven minutes (walking to Mill Lane) is run through with reasonable clarity and convincingness in a half minute, or in two minutes at most. Naturally we raise the question whence this convincingness comes; and if we look closely, we find a "dream pantomime," or make-believe, by which the truncated performance is taken as if it were the whole. Few dreams, except the rather rare, starkly realistic dreams and nightmares, have the full *structure* of waking fantasy. One of the things which makes the dream less realistic, one of the devices by which a person knows when awake that he is not dreaming, is the fact that the dreamer keeps at arm's length the disturbing details which would interrupt the symphony of his autisms; he is vaguely aware that he is *schematizing* rather than photographically recording. There are thus all degrees of self-deception, all degrees of effectiveness in parrying life's threats, in keeping just out of sight those attributes of the dream which would defeat the essentially autistic character of the process.

The heart of the normal dream is apparently the physiological excitation of tensions, in other words, unsatisfied needs, as suggested earlier (page 401) in reference to the dreams of explorers. Various nineteenth-century experimenters induced dreams by placing the limbs of the sleeper in such positions as to cause discomfort, so that dreams of activity ensued, or by producing tactual discomfort leading to dreams of escape. Klein's subjects dreamed of falling head first or feet first, as the experimenter pressed down the head or foot of the cot. So, also, the studies of Watt and Horton have shown the simplicity of the connection between physical stimulation and dream elaboration, inducing dreams of flying or of being scantily clad by manipulation of the dreamer's environment.

The dreams of children, as both Freud and Kimmins have shown, are often centered in the wishful continuation of daytime activities. The drive, as we have sought to show (page 400), is associated with the features of the environment which tend to satisfy it. A child, skating to his heart's content, is called in to supper; in that night's dreams he goes on skating. Surface needs are also frequently evident in adult dreams. A man hearing the alarm clock ring at 8:00, and having a distant appointment which he must keep at 9:00, falls asleep again and dreams that he keeps the appointment, thus satisfying the sleep need and at the same time autistically satisfying the social-respectability need; he sees himself as an appointment keeper. Clearly a "comfort dream" of this sort is a purposive dream. However much we may be impressed by the "association by similarity" which occurs in dreams, by their symbolic portraiture, their capacity to mirror or to distort waking reality, they clearly have the additional quality of aiming at something, of achieving a purpose.

Freud's Dream Interpretation

In terms of the whole conception of motivation developed here, *every* motive, every tension, is likely to influence dreams, and every tension which reaches a high pitch is likely to be *central* in dream determination. On this basis, for example, sex dreams should be common in adolescence and early maturity, rarer in childhood and old age; and this is evidently true. On what grounds we should assume that dreams not directly suggesting sexuality must derive from the sexual is unclear; but there is clear reason for such interpretations if we look at the historical conditions under which this approach was developed. In recounting his early days, Freud tells how, on discovering the regularity of overt or covert sexual aberrations in the lives of neurotics, he undertook to give a systematic report to the Viennese Neurological Society. The audience froze him out; they did not want to learn from him; he was a moral leper in their eyes. The result, as he makes clear in no uncertain terms, was to make him determine from that time forth unswervingly to seek from every patient the sexual origin of his neurosis. He determined to find sexuality. This is a clear and honest statement of autistic perception, and the dream was a major datum to be perceived in this way.

In his masterful *Interpretation of Dreams,* the result of this quest, Freud contrasts *manifest* dreams, as recalled by the patient when awake, with *latent* dreams, made up largely of sexual wishes, which, owing to a process of censorship, must be disguised in order to allow the sleeper to escape the anxiety which would be aroused were he to confront them directly. The disguise is effective through symbolism (a dream of water refers to birth, etc.), condensation, transposition, and other forms of elaboration of the events portrayed in the original (unconscious) wish. The free associations given by the patient after recounting the dream help the analyst to find the "sexual origin of the neurosis." But when he finds it, he does not go on to find other cognate or even more important tension systems that may be at work in dream etiology. A mountain-climbing dream is held to be *interpreted* when mountains are seen as breasts, etc.; there is no interest in the empirical possibility that mountain-climbing as a canalized activity drive is fun per se.

This point of view was conveyed to the pupils who thronged to learn the new approach. In his history of the psychoanalytic movement, Freud wistfully refers to the years just before the close of the nineteenth century when he worked in isolation and was thus free to follow his own ideas. The publication of the *Interpretation of Dreams* in 1900 altered the scene. He was now a celebrity, a teacher at whose feet young physicians sat for guidance in the new method. They soon overflowed his office. Over their coffee they learned to seek out the clues to hidden motivation and censorship, the subtleties of transference and the skills available to the analyst. This way of looking at dreams came into medical and then general folklore, and is as hard to view objectively as is most folklore, especially since Freud's point of view is in many fundamentals corroborated by clinical evidence. The task of disentangling fact from fiction is difficult indeed.

Among all the flashes of genius in Freud's work, none is more compelling than the distinction between the latent and the manifest dream, for this provides the one necessary clue to the relation between the physiological world and the psychical world. The latent dream is the tension system. There is no one way in which the tension system must be discharged; on the contrary, there are many alternatives and many possible combinations. The *dream work* is the process by which the tensions, in their facilitation and conflict, actualize, through the familiar autistic mechanisms and figure-ground relationships, a perceptual whole. The result usually takes a three-dimensional form, conveying reality to the dreamer, but it is fluid with respect to time. Hence, as we have seen, events are transposed or condensed. The architectural quality of thinking also appears here, with genuine higher units and a definite dramatic plot. The dream as we experience it, and especially as we remember it, is therefore much more than a clue to the needs that dominate at the time; it is a clue to the architecture of our minds as well.

Freud realized early that the events of the day preceding the dream are of some secondary importance, in that they provide some of the raw materials for the manifest dream; at the same time he inferred that materials registering on the periphery of consciousness will be more likely to be used in this fashion than materials accepted by the ego and woven into the ego system of waking life. Both interpretations were strikingly confirmed by experiments indicating that of the material exposed to experimental subjects that which was never noted was in reality used more frequently in the dream than that which was noted and commented upon.

The presumed relation between latent and manifest dreams necessarily involves the use of substitute responses of the sort noted below in studies of displacement (page 549) as well as those appearing in transferred conditioned responses (page 204). Such substitutes are called "symbols;" the manifest dream is a texture of symbolic material. The man who wrote about Joseph's interpretations of Pharaoh's dreams fully understood the mechanism, and Aristotle gave it a trenchant description; but it remained for Freud to show the inevitable and universal role of these symbols if the physiological world is to enter meaningfully into the shadowland of imaginary portrayal. We should expect to find the summation or integration of the physiological impulses resulting in the utilization of symbols that kill two or more birds with one stone, or, to put it the other way around, symbols arising because multiple factors lead toward them. This mechanism Freud calls *overdetermination*. Although it is omnipresent, it is particularly forceful in making clear that experimental analysis is the only device by which the different determining components and their varying contributions can be ascertained.

If it is true, as we have argued, that all motives interpenetrate and that all motivation is complex, it follows that there is a sexual phase in most activity patterns, just as there is an esthetic and an activity phase. To anchor one's view of the dream in terms of any one motivation is perfectly sound if thereby he means temporarily to limit the field of observation, as in a microscope. But if he forgets that he has done this, the result can in time damage his whole picture of the dream. There is, indeed, high probability that direct or indirect sex impulsions appear in a great variety of normal human relationships as plainly in waking as in sleeping life, as poets and novelists and kind hostesses and the gentry of the courts have always known. We can therefore offer no objection to the complex arguments which the Freudian dream interpreters use to discover indirect sexual references in most dream material. But the fact of such indirections must logically be considered in relation to all the other motives as well. Freud could have used the occasion to show that sensory and activity drives, and particularly ego satisfactions, may frequently be indirectly satisfied through direct sexual expression, so that the argument cuts two ways. Just as sexuality may be hidden beneath a purported esthetic impulse, so an esthetic need may be masked by the crudely elaborated symbols of sexuality.

From this it follows that there is no final interpretation for any dream. Almost as soon as the cigars and coffee had been handed around, the neophytes who had learned how to interpret dreams began to quarrel with the master and with one another, asserting not only that they had found better interpretations but that they had found better *ways* of proceeding. Many of the splinter movements which from time to time have drawn off numerous members of the group have been activated by such quarrels about the interpretation of dreams. Just as Stekel discovered the true meaning of dreams in 1911, so Horney has recently found better methods for getting at what the dreamer is really up to.

These differing approaches to the dream depend partly upon our conception of the task of interpretation. If the analyst wishes to *reduce* the dream to its sensory and physiological basis, the experimental method is the only safe one, as Klein's work (page 420) has made clear. If, however, he wishes to determine the full *significance* of the dream, to read between the lines, to immerse himself in a world between earth and heaven in which everything tentative is real and impossibilities become possible, it may be better for him (at least for the time being) to dream along with his subject, to allow a certain tentativeness to lead him slowly into a semi-mystical world in which anything that appears to be a hypothetical possibility becomes for the moment an immediate reality. Exactly this path was trodden by Jung in his amazing *Psychology of the Unconscious;* its method—it is no more than a friendly exaggeration to say this—is to argue that because A is somewhat like B, and B can, under certain circumstances, share something with C, and C has been known on occasion to have been suspected of being related to D, the conclusion in full-fledged logical form is that $A = D$.

As the language of *science* this is meaningless; but as the language of the dream, which for the time being the analyst shares sympathetically it is as eloquent as any poetry. "Dream interpretation" need not involve a catalogue of the source materials of dreams; it may mean the process by which the student, himself wide awake, can recapture the essence of the dream's intent. One cannot live in this egocentric, non-logical world of the dream unless he has taken a round-trip ticket to a place far from the demands of waking existence, knowing full well that he is going away and will return later. To do this requires an active putting aside of the waking point of view. We saw in the discussion of conflict (page 325) that this process of dividing ourselves between two worlds of activity may be achieved by dissociation, the functional splitting of personality. The dream is an especially clear-cut example of such splitting.

The splitting may go far, as when one part attacks or makes fun of the other. Humor and terror dreams in particular have attracted the attention of those who have suspected not only that there is dissociation but that one compartment of the personality is taking the other part for a ride. The humor of the dream is often a take-off upon oneself. As the solemn man dresses himself up in Puritan or even Messianic costume, the feeling tone is of that confused *ambivalent* type which we have when we feel *impelled* to read in the newspaper (and enjoy reading) something that we verbally insist is *repugnant*. So the Puritan and the Messiah are looked upon by the dreamer as his good old self, somewhat glorified, and yet not quite as glorified as he expected. As he wakes, he breaks into a laugh when he realizes how perfectly his own pretensions have been portrayed, yet with such restraint that the Puritan or Messiah in the dream did not give up the whole show as a bad job. In the same way, as the nightmare descends, the dreamer succumbs properly to the intended terror but is seldom as completely terrified as he "ought to be." His feet may drag heavily as he tries to escape the bear, but the bear's claws do not actually take hold. Often, indeed, the "stage manager" who is directing the show works up the terror step by step, as if he were applying thumbscrews until just enough fear was produced to wake the dreamer. There is a certain quality here as if he said, "This fellow is stifled by too many bedclothes over his face. Let's see how much scaring he needs to wake up."

Before we embark on any theory as to the nature of the dissociation oi the selfhood shown in such performances, we should realize that it is a primary task of the dream to *deceive* the dreamer. And though deception is usually a clumsy process, it seems somewhat smoother, it is less frequently "seen through" than is the case in waking life. Everything is *as if* there were not merely physiological impulsion but definite design. The design is evident only in waking retrospection, because the consciousness of the dream state is the unitary, self-deceived consciousness of participation in a make-believe world.

It might well be argued in connection with this view of dissociation that the physiological dissociation of sleep merely renders part of the personality inactive, so that there is, as it were, a reduction—a sub-amputation rather than a splitting. But though the dissociative effects of sleep need not be denied, there is much to indicate that as one runs away from the waking world, he actively pushes away many of its attitudes. It is largely because he does so that he can give himself a clean canvas for dream creations.

DREAM CREATIVENESS

Partly because the outer world is not there to say no, partly because the senses can contribute only few and feeble interferences, partly because one has at his disposal the entire material of his life, and partly because no critical standards, no acid test can be invoked, the dream typically reaches heights and spreads out over areas which the disciplined mind of the civilized adult would not dare to scan. If for no other reason than the richness of the available materials, the degree of creativeness achieved may altogether transcend even the wild fancies of the fanatic, the intoxicated, or the delirious.

Such creativeness, however, is in no sense purely a matter of being as different as one can from what he is in his waking life; it may be creativeness in the sense of making the most orderly and intelligible pattern out of existing materials. In other words, it may, according to the standards of waking life, outdo the dreamer's best intellectual standards when awake. Few have a better right to appraise this than Stevenson, who marketed his dreams on a large scale. In his judgment, "The Brownies" who created his dreams were often far ahead of "his own" achievements. He tells how his dreams came to produce stories for him much more rapidly and effectively than he himself could; "the Brownies," the "little people," not only could create a good plot in a few moments but could hide the solution from the dreamer, so that not until the final moment of the story could he catch the purport of the whole; then he would be startled by the simplicity of the solution. The Brownies gave no unnecessary hints. "I will go bail for the dreamer (having excellent grounds for valuing his candour) that he had no guess whatever at the motive of the woman —the hinge of the whole well-invented plot—until the instant of that highly dramatic declaration. It was not his tale; it was the little people's! And observe: not only was the secret kept, the story was told with really guileful craftsmanship. The conduct of both actors is (in the cant phrase) psychologically correct, and the emotion aptly graduated up to the surprising climax . . ."

What is the *dynamic,* the *process* of dream integration?

Several steps are required in answering this question. In Stevenson's words, "Who are the Little People? They are near connections of the dreamer's, beyond doubt; they share in his financial worries and have an eye to the bank-book; they share plainly in his training; they have plainly learned like him to build the scheme of a considerate story and to arrange emotion in progressive order; only I think they have more talent. . . . Who are they, then? and who is the dreamer?" For one thing, he believes, they are wiser than "the dreamer." "I cannot but suppose my Brownies have been aping Bunyan, and yet in no case with what would possibly be called a moral in a tract; never with the ethical narrowness; conveying hints instead of life's larger limitations and that sort of sense which we seem to perceive in the arabesque of time and space." They seem, then, to be the artist freed of many of his temporal, local, and cultural constraints. Their imagination is the artist's normal imaginative processes broadened, enriched, and deepened.

Occasionally we are fortunate enough to have a closer view of the thaumaturgy of dream creation in the form of a detailed autobiographical record of the process by which a dream solution of a problem oversteps the achievement of the waking mind. A classical instance of this type was offered by H. V. Hilprecht of the University of Pennsylvania, who had ineffectually struggled to decipher a cuneiform inscription upon a broken clay cylinder:

The whole problem passed yet again through my mind that March evening before I placed my mark of approval under the last correction in the book. Even then I had come to no conclusion. About midnight, weary and exhausted, I went to bed and was soon in deep sleep. Then I dreamed the following remarkable dream. A tall thin priest of the old pre-Christian Nippur, about forty years of age and clad in a simple abba, led me to the treasure-chamber of the temple, on its south-east side. He went with me into a small, low-ceiled room, without windows, in which there was a large wooden chest, while scraps of agate and lapis-lazuli lay scattered on the floor. Here he addressed me as follows: "The two fragments which you have published separately upon pages 22 and 26, belong together, are not finger-rings, and their history is as follows. King Kurigalzu (*circa* 1300 B.C.) once sent to the temple of Bel, among other articles of agate and lapis-lazuli, an inscribed votive cylinder of agate. Then we priests suddenly received the command to make for the statue of the god Ninib a pair of earrings of agate. We were in great dismay, since there was no agate as raw material at hand. In order to execute the command there was nothing for us to do but cut the votive cylinder into three parts, thus making three rings, each of which contained a portion of the original inscription. The first two rings served as earrings for the statue of the god; the two fragments which have given you so much trouble are portions of them. If you will put the two together you will have confirmation of my words. But the third ring you have not yet found in the course of your excavations, and you never will find it." With this, the priest disappeared. I awoke at once and immediately told my wife the dream that I might not forget it. Next morning—Sunday—I examined the fragments once more in the light of these disclosures, and to my astonishment found all the details of the dream precisely verified in so far as the means of verification were in my hands. The original inscription on the votive cylinder read: "To the god Ninib, son of Bel, his lord, has Kurigalzu, pontifex of Bel, presented this."

Thus Hilprecht's problem was at last solved. But verification was needed, and it soon came.

. . . In August, 1893, I was sent by the Committee on the Babylonian Expedition to Constantinople, to catalogue and study the objects got from

Nippur and preserved there in the Imperial Museum. It was to me a matter of the greatest interest to see for myself the objects which, according to my dream, belonged together, in order to satisfy myself that they had both originally been parts of the same votive cylinder. Halil Bey, the director of the museum, to whom I told my dream, and of whom I asked permission to see the objects, was so interested in the matter, that he at once opened all the cases of the Babylonian section, and requested me to search. Father Scheil, an Assyriologist from Paris, who had examined and arranged the articles excavated by us before me, had not recognized the fact that these fragments belonged together, and consequently I found one fragment in one case, and the other in a case far away from it. As soon as I found the fragments and put them together, the truth of the dream was demonstrated *ad oculos*—they had, in fact, once belonged to one and the same votive cylinder.

In the case both of the Assyrian scholar and of Coleridge's Kubla Khan it is clear that the materials lay scattered over the whole floor of the dreamer's mind. In each case the materials were swept with a single stroke into an articulate and architecturally perfect form. Just as the Assyrian scholar had the necessary *information* but could not organize it when awake, Lowes has shown what materials lay strewn in Coleridge's mind awaiting their opportunity in the dream. But despite such studies of the *sources* of dream material, we are left almost as puzzled as we were originally regarding what gives the materials form.

When comparisons are made between these almost instantaneous creations and the works of genius that are hammered out in the sweat of one's brow, we find that the element of strain or volition is conspicuously lacking in the former. The contrast between the Assyrian scholar's failure while awake and his success while dreaming is equaled only by the intensity of effort in the one state, the perfect effortlessness in the other. This may perhaps have been due partly to the removal of outside interferences, partly to the sheer fact that the muscular postural system is involved in the one case and shunted out in the other. But apparently the highest creation may be the consequence of involuntary activity, albeit often following long periods of voluntary concentration; and to consider the dream a supremely involuntary expression might cast some doubts upon the commonplace of popular morality, that it is effort which makes the good, stress which gives dignity. It cannot indeed always be shown even that a *preceding phase of effort* is necessary to the dream. A supremely casual attitude seems actually to be the source of many of the greatest and the richest departures from the grooves of daily routine.

This relative effortlessness may mean that *more of the self* is involved in the dream, or at least in many dreams, than can be involved in the acts of waking life. Waking life is an alternation or oscillation between mutually exclusive centers of activity; a perpetual nervous recentering, with a new quest, moment by moment, for drive-satisfying points of anchorage. This must, of course, be true in some degree of the dream also. But the more creative dreams succeed in being creative just because they use a wider range of materials; they allow the dreamer to confront simultaneously a wider variety of appealing materials from the storehouse of his memories.

This is the reason why it has been suggested that the dreamer is a "larger self" than the waking man. Mitchell similarly believes that the hypnotic consciousness is wider than the waking consciousness of the same person. The dream may often be, among other things, a quest in the direction of self-realization, fearing nothing, ashamed of nothing, bogged down by nothing, playing with new poses, trying new combinations, picturing the dreamer as hero and as villain, tasting all the possible and impossible qualities which might conceivably be encountered or never could be encountered in this or another world; in this sense the dream is supreme selfishness. On the other hand, H. E. Starr suggested that over and above the more simple and obvious motives there exists a self-realizing motive based on identification with humanity, that the sociality of man leads to the all-embracing motive of unification with the human family. He called this motive the "Promethean complex." The dream can apparently be anything from the narrowest to the most expansive portrayal of selfhood. It is because the narrower phases have been most intensively studied that we have here deliberately voiced the suspicion that the other pole in the dream continuum, to which experimental access is difficult, lies far indeed from the individualistic and competitive selfhood which western psychology has consistently stressed.

THE DREAMER

This continuum from narrow to broad is one of many upon which the dreamer may be located. Probably no sphere of personality expression is richer with individuality than dreaming. And if it be argued that people differ only in their manner of arranging the same universal raw material, only in the interrelations between the old familiar themes of human passion, interest, and ego need, the answer again is that dreams differ in every respect in which waking behavior differs—in motivation, in feeling tone, in canalized and conditioned patterns, in figure-ground relations, in hierarchical structure. One man's dreams are little sketches or skits, little flashes of humor. He awakes with a smile on his face and laughs for a moment at the ridiculous nonsense which his involuntary self has dished up; indeed, many a child laughs in his sleep, and often has a fragment of delicious fantasy on his lips in the morning. To others the dream is a chronic and insistent threat; as child or as adult they fear to sleep because of the regularity with which night terrors descend. For one person the dream is a monologue, for another a five-act play. When the projective methods can be adequately compared with dream analysis, the two methods will probably yield not only comparable data on individual drive patterns, but also mutually confirmatory data on the interrelations of drives, the varying feeling tones, and the other personality dimensions, already explored (page 419), which distinguish dreamers.

We should expect to find, and we do find, much parallelism between a person's waking fantasy and his dreams. We should expect that individual differences in intelligence and creativeness, as displayed in the dream, would agree well with indices of intelligence and creativeness based upon waking skill in problem-solving and in fantasy. But the dream *outdoes* the waking fantasy in many respects. The material is more vivid—hallucination replaces image—and more elaborately dramatized. Thus the dreams of the blind who have developed keen tactual and auditory discrimination follow the familiar lines of waking imagination but may draw more richly than waking life upon the memories of days before the sight was lost. Where life experience has enriched a modality, as tactual experience was enriched in Helen Keller, the enrichment is preserved in the dream; this "compensation" of one sense by another may be carried even further in the dreaming state than in the waking. When such compensatory skills in manipulating images are supplemented by well-preserved memories from the days when all the senses were intact, the result naturally is likely to be a richer product than the waking life can yield. But just as the waking fantasy tells a story which behavior would not know how to tell, so the still greater removal from reality permits still greater richness, a wider variety of personal idioms, in the dream than in the waking fantasy. The dream, being the least social, is in a sense the freest of expressive acts. It is true that many people carry their consciences with them into their dreams and censor their dream novels; it is likewise true that many dreams are so frank that they are told or even recalled only reluctantly. This matter of moral restraint is only one of a dozen kinds of restraint that waking life imposes. Most dreams have a lush or lavish quality which unambiguously bespeaks greater psychic freedom and creativeness.

It is clear, then, that despite the many overlapping aspects between sleeping fantasy and waking fantasy, the dream is not just a duplicate of any other personality experience. It has the supreme advantage of occurring when we are socially isolated, when the environment provided by sight and hearing is cut off, and when many of our impelling needs to act in one way or another can for the time being be successfully ignored. Autism has much fuller play, and dissociation of many memories and many habitual attitudes occurs. There is some dissociation in all sleep because of physiological factors (page 326), but the process is greatly augmented by the autistic exclusion of all that would interfere with the enactment of the scenario. For this reason the dream is often one of the most eloquent spokesmen regarding the content and form of individual personality; but being a special pleader like all the other spokesmen, it must be seen in full articulation with all the others.

18. Multiple Personality

OVER a hundred years ago Mary Reynolds fell into a long slumber; upon awakening there appeared a person who shared no memories with the previous self, and the temperament was also changed. At times, however, she fell back into her earlier self, and for some years alternated between the pre-sleep and post-sleep character patterns. There were many similar cases in the nineteenth century; in particular, the French psychiatrists of the great classical period which began about 1870 succeeded in discovering and describing a number of instances of dual and multiple personality. Utilizing hypnosis, they found what they regarded as levels of personality far beneath the personality of waking life, and they devised methods which permitted these latent personalities to come upon the stage of consciousness and action, pushing aside the usual self. For a while, alternating personality became a dramatic expression of the new psychiatry, especially of the new hypnotic methods used in therapy; there was a premium upon the dramatic value of mutually exclusive selves inhabiting the same organism. Stevenson's *Dr. Jekyll and Mr. Hyde* put the capstone upon this achievement of the French psychiatric school, and the educated public came to accept the idea of the same flesh being inhabited by two or more selves as a central fact of the new psychology.

Our first problem is to obtain clear descriptions of just what occurs in such cases; our second, to see how far the concept of dissociation is serviceable in bringing understanding; our third, to probe the factors of motivation that may possibly underlie the manifestations. As to the descriptions, we shall begin with a brief summary of two contrasting cases.

Ansel Bourne disappeared after a visit to the bank in a little Rhode Island town. Two weeks later a stranger, "Mr. Brown," appeared in a

Pennsylvania village, set up a shop, and proceeded to live quietly and normally in his new community. After six weeks, Bourne woke up in this Pennsylvania village wondering where he was; he had no memories of events since he had hitched up his team. He made his way back to his Rhode Island home and took up his old life again. Hypnosis recovered part of the Pennsylvania episode, enough to suggest that the different personalities were not so sharply and irreconcilably separated as they seemed. Hypnosis appeared, then, to be a way of leading from one personality to another.

Morton Prince's "*BCA*" case, who after recovery wrote her autobiography as a double personality, illustrates another type of cleavage. *A* was sober, serious, reserved, afraid of life and of herself, "full of metaphysical doubts and fears, full of scruples." *B* was jolly and carefree, healthy and vigorous. When *B* suddenly disappeared, *A* was often shocked to find herself confronting a wineglass or a cigarette. *B*, however, knew all about *A*, pitying and despising her thoughts and attitudes, of which *B* always had complete and direct knowledge.

Most cases of double personality can be assigned to one or the other of the two broad types illustrated by these two cases. In Type I the two personalities maintain, in their alternation, complete independence of each other; Ansel Bourne is an example of this type. *A* knows

nothing directly about the thoughts and doings of *B*, and *B* knows nothing of *A*; they do not overlap. In Type II, of which the *BCA* case is an example, *A* is ignorant of *B*, but *B* is well aware of *A*. *B* remembers what *A* has done and thought; and, while *A* is in the ascendancy, *B* may even claim to be consciously active, controlling some of the motor mechanisms. (T. W. Mitchell.)

MULTIPLE PERSONALITY

DISSOCIATION

Now as to the mechanisms responsible for double and multiple personality, the one longest known and most clearly understood is dissociation, of which we have already had some discussion (pages 325 ff.). We have seen that integration is frequently incomplete, that there is often a tendency to be active in one region, inactive in another. The man who is utterly absorbed in a task or sunk in a "brown study" is dissociated; he may do things of which he is unaware, and later deny that he has done them. In such moments of "concentration" there is paradoxically a liberation of many parts of the personality system; relative autonomy is given to processes of speech or action which usually stand closer to the core of the self. Regions of tension lead, during dissociation, to segmental response. There is also an opening of the sensory inlets so that much is registered for which the thresholds would ordinarily be too high. Oddly enough, the reality of such mechanisms is still sometimes contested. The issue is not whether skilled acts can ever be carried out without conscious direction, for there is too much direct evidence on this, but rather, whether highly organized, focalized acts which usually require conscious control can be carried out at the same time that organized conscious control is being given to other activities.

These mechanisms are beautifully exhibited in one case history carefully reported by G. M. Stratton. A flier forced down from a great height in 1918 began to relive the scenes of his boyhood. These memories persisted vividly while he was carrying out an exceedingly complex and difficult landing operation, an operation so complicated that it is hard to see how he could have achieved it by the mere concatenation of simple conditionings. His behavior was highly integrated; he was apparently fully conscious. According to his testimony, however, he was also occupied with boyhood memories during those critical moments. This kind of dissociation seems to be due not to conflict, as discussed in Chapter 13, but solely to intense concentration. Such marked cleavage between integrated activities is uncommon and may well depend on a personal idiosyncrasy, but lesser degrees of it are by no means rare.

Indeed, we may legitimately use the term dissociation in the sense of incomplete integration, which is excessively common. The forms it takes (consisting of a return from stage three to stage two, as noted on page 344), are very expressive of individuality; some of them are similar to the examples of autism given in Chapter 15. At times the perceptual apparatus may function by accenting one phase and dissociating another phase of the stimulus to produce an acceptable and complete percept. The hopeful or alarmed person observes in definite response to an indefinite ambiguous stimulus. But the determining tendencies most relevant to the percept are often completely unknown to the perceiver; they may be his ingrained habits or his momentary predispositions. A conch shell held to the ear, instead of yielding only its normal continuous roar, begins to yield words, more and more distinct, more and more completely articulated. The result may be a fantasy, a simple wish fulfillment, or a complex creative whole. Similarly, a crystal, a drop of ink, the shiny surface of a pool may lead to a well-defined percept; the surface usually clouds over and upon it clear and distinct hallucinations appear. Such experiences have classically been known as "sensory automatisms," automatisms in the sense that they come from strata somewhat dissociated from those of the dominant reality-confronting awareness. The expression will serve well enough, provided we remember that unconscious dispositions are always at work in all perception and thought, and that automatism in this sense is a question of *degree*.

Another form of dissociation that is commonly found among normal people is the execution of movements without the intervention of the will; to the individual, the hand or voice seems to act of its own accord. Automatic writing may begin unexpectedly; more often, however, the subject sits, pencil in hand, waiting for it to appear. At first it is clumsy and halting, but it develops slowly like other habits and eventually becomes a structured and creative whole. There is usually no great difficulty in tracing most of its content and its general style to the writer's disposition, although at times its facility (and felicity) of expression far outdo that characteristic of his conscious level of activity. This appears to be due, sometimes at least, to the release from self-consciousness, indeed the release from the hundreds of mechanical associations needed by the prosy man in making contact with reality; the automatism is released by a set that is bent on something genuinely new, genuinely beautiful, which the "sane," "conscious" man would fear to approach.

The wishes and scts that operate when free from conscious control may be incoherent, or voluptuous, or malevolent, or whatever is waiting to force itself into expression; thus some of Anita Mühl's patients write automatically in the persons of entities purporting to be malevolent spirits that are dangerous to the writer. We might be inclined to say in such cases that "the real person will out" in the guise of automatism, were it not that so many different real persons will out, not only in automatism but in ordinary writing, not only in sensory automatism but in all perception. Whatever is in us, by way of a past or a present potentiality for synthesis or creation, may appear in the speech and act of every one of us.

Alfred Binet went further, when, from his study of automatism he came to the conclusion that there may exist in the same person at the same time not only two independent activity streams but two centers of consciousness; indeed, it was his belief that he had experimentally induced these states of double consciousness. To a subject writing automatically Binet whispered instructions which were to be followed by oral response; the writing and the oral response went on independently, neither betraying any reflection of the other. Morton Prince later undertook to demonstrate the same process; the hand that was writing automatically occupied itself with the answers to arithmetical problems while the oral mechanisms were busy reading aloud. Neither activity seemed disturbed. And Burnett apparently confirmed the existence of a true "splitting" of consciousness. These studies failed, however, to measure precisely the degree of independence of the two functions, as might be done by comparing their ease and speed when executed under unitary consciousness and when executed during the concurrent activity of another consciousness. When Messerschmidt required her subjects to read aloud while carrying out posthypnotic instructions to solve arithmetic problems, both the reading and the computing suffered immensely; in fact, they went on not concurrently but in alternation, and when the alternation was rapid the two were grossly scrambled. Similar results have been obtained by other experimenters. Pattie found that hypnotic blindness of one eye is not genuine blindness; careful tests show that the apparent dissociation in such cases is unreal.

It is, of course, conceivable that the subjects who gave these negative results were not truly somnambulistic but, like the subjects in some of the published reports on hypnotic results, were merely in a "foggy state." It is likewise conceivable, however, that the subjects of the earlier studies were in a different type of foggy state which prevented their giving clear and accurate testimony as to the oscillations of attention which actually occurred. But although the experimental studies show the difficulty of obtaining true dissociation, many cases of the Stratton type (page 435) serve to warn the critical reader to suspend judgment. Perhaps spontaneous life experiences can produce a more clear-cut cleft in personality structure than the hypnotic techniques usually produce. A fairly common kind of "double consciousness" involving less sharpness of separation than Stratton's case occurs when one knows that he is dreaming but continues to take the experience seriously, from the point of view of the dream consciousness. A close parallel to this appears occasionally in experiences with drugs; although the world seems utterly strange, the individual knows, in spite of this, what the reality is.

In the meantime, if we grant that full-fledged dissociation occurs, not only of activity but of consciousness, we need definite evidence as to whether we are *all* dissociable in this sense, and we need a means of finding out whether individual differences in dissociation move through a continuum from one extreme to another or whether a gulf separates the markedly dissociable person from the rest of us.[1]

Let us see how far the concept of dissociation will help us in relation to the problem of multiple personality. We shall borrow freely from the French school, for these men were predominantly "associa-

---

[1] Degrees of dissociation are suggested by the Kretschmer school (cf. page 59) but the data are not clear cut.

tionists" who looked upon association and its counterpart, dissociation, as primary clues to all problems of personality. They pictured associations as mosaic pieces fitted together according to temporal as well as spatial design. Associations are made or broken as elements of experience are combined in new ways. Each sensory experience, each motor impulsion, each memory may be functionally split off or lost to the individual; in amnesia, for example, a memory or a block of memories is lost. When a person loses from his awareness some of his characteristic feelings or attitudes, his personality is radically affected. Hence this school believed that the clue to multiple personality lay in the sundering of the associative linkages that permit the integrated expression of all that the individual is.

Needing a name to describe each form of dissociation in this black-white pattern, Janet suggested "monoideism" for the relatively simple condition in which a single idea dominates the consciousness, all else being dissociated. This is exemplified in the case of Irene. After months of tortured devotion to a dying mother, Irene proceeded, immediately after the mother's funeral, to forget the entire illness and death; she shut out the idea. At other moments, however, it sprang back to reality; she lived again as the mother's filial comforter, moved back and forth in the imagined sickroom, and was blind and deaf to everything that interfered with her task.

To put this in the simplest possible language, Irene's case is reminiscent of the extreme cases of absent-mindedness in which the individual denies doing a complex act that must have required integrated intelligent activity; he looks at the signature he wrote yesterday and protests to the last ditch against the possibility of his having written it. Attitudes and interests are focused in one activity stream; even if they seem to the observer to be all-absorbing, the center of self-awareness finds no contact point with the alien stream. Thus a French officer, separated from the woman he loved, found himself overpowered, a thousand miles away, by images from the past, images that Janet calls "memories which are too real." As the cleavage extends and more and more elements are blocked out, the individual loses enough of the context of his life to forget his family and his work; he wanders to new surroundings and begins life anew. Janet refers to these states as "fugues." As the cleavage proceeds, the individual loses not only the perceptual and memorial elements, but some of the temperamental elements which constitute the everyday self, and a new functional whole is established. The personalities may be only slightly different or profoundly antithetical. In another classic case, Félida lived a life of temperamental contrast between vivid, eager, and gay young womanhood and the solemnity and despondency of a bereaved matron.

A recent case that illustrates dissociation beautifully and involves rather slight personality differences between the main components of the individual, is the one entitled *Persons One and Three*. In one state the patient remembered only what had occurred since early in 1915; in another state, only events up to the fall of 1914. The shock of a mine explosion in Flanders was apparently responsible. The device by which Franz, the therapist, finally succeeded in weaving the two together was the simple reeducation of associations. Inferring from circumstances that the patient had served in East Africa, Franz spread out before him a map of the area. When the patient's eyes fell upon the little town of Voi, his face brightened. "I had a monkey." There rushed back into his mind an episode in which his pet monkey had been chained too far from camp and had been killed by a leopard. As soon as the emotionally distressing episode was recalled, old memories came flooding back like the waters when the dam is broken. By associative procedures of this sort, the two memory streams were ultimately combined.

MOTIVATION

There seems to be no doubt that "dissociation" is a useful label for these processes. Associations can be broken and a genuine splitting of individual activity occurs. Dissociation, as we have sought to show, occurs in normal persons (page 326); and it can be experimentally induced (page 449). But this does not mean that dissociation completely clarifies the problem, for we still do not know why dissociations take the form of multiple personality. If it is true that needs—motives—are fundamental in any personal act, this will be true with a vengeance when something occurs in the individual which results in two or more personalities in place of one.

Morton Prince's "Sally Beauchamp," a double personality who became a quadruple personality, clearly demonstrates that the cleavage does not involve merely an accidental dropping of bits of mosaic, but is rather a question of conflicting drives. The imp Sally could not live in the same house with the staid Miss Beauchamp. This is likewise well brought out in "BCA," already mentioned. Here a morbidly conscientious personality alternated with a free, vivid, and alert one. As they functioned, the personalities were mutually exclusive. The constricted personality talked very seriously, the gay one casually; the former was full of intense emotion, the latter interested only in sports and a good time. Whereas the conscientious personality knew the free one only by inference, the free personality was present all the time that the solemn one was present, knew her every thought and memory, was amused at her, and treated her like an odd stick that it would be convenient to eliminate if possible. T. W. Mitchell's studies of such people (page 434) suggest that in all such cases of one-way amnesia there is a constricted personality and a relaxed personality. The constricted self is in reality narrow and constricted in its perceptions and memories and cannot allow itself to remember the more casual attitudes. The relaxed self is ready to make contact with anything and has no trouble in recognizing the activities of the narrow self. In other words, the case of "BCA" is a prototype for all.

Subtracting a little of the mystery, we may say that the case is suggestive of the normal alternation between states of narrow, self-reproving consciousness in which a person knows rather little of himself (because it would be disturbing to know more) and those breezier, more casual states in which he remembers the straitened self with amusement or scorn. In one state he can afford to remember; in the other he cannot. By this we do *not* mean that this analogy with the normal oscillation of moods provides all the necessary clues to the more unusual fluctuations. For one thing, there appears to be in all these cases a deep dissociation, a capacity for cleavage which most of us lack. But perhaps the normal personality is more dissociable than we suspect, and the pathologically dissociated is a bit played up, dramatized by patient and doctor alike.

The motivation which provides the basis for the dissociation is still not altogether clear; we must seek the drives that lie behind the separation of the two activity streams. The BCA case will continue to serve us here. There had been a conflict about an emotional—very likely, from the context, a sexual—problem. She felt that her life situation was unbearable; indeed, this attitude was part of a morbidly severe system of attitudes. Around this attitude the A personality took shape. The other attitude was relaxed, easygoing, afraid of nothing, and around this B was built. It is easy to see why B was the more inclusive, the less constricted in awareness. If Mitchell is right in saying that in most or all of Type II double personalities there is a sober and a carefree self, we should expect to find the carefree, less inhibited self more complete, the one with the broadest field of consciousness. Thus in one of Mühl's patients, the imp "Tookie" calls the other personality, Lizbeth, "horrid and prim"; "her wouldn't speak to the flowers or anything."

There is of course something suggestive of the histrionic about these cases, something which reminds us of a pose. But we are likely to forget that all the attitudes maintained in a social context have a histrionic quality. They serve a social purpose and become crystallized as mutually exclusive social roles. It is hard for a person in the midst of a shrewd deal to remember his sentimental moods, and it is easy to deny them; as actor in one role, he cannot admit the possibility of another role. As when Peter denied that he was of Jesus's company, the accusation that one has another selfhood creates stormy protest. Nor is there anything about the histrionic character of the double personality that cannot be examined experimentally by the careful student of hypnosis. Not only names but a cluster of attitudes can be shunted in and out.

Looking still more closely, we may well wonder just what the conception of a pose means in these instances. The hypnotized person is told to become a dog, and he growls appropriately. Does he "really believe" himself to be a dog? He behaves, rather, like "man acting dog." The two-year-old plays dog, arguing volubly with his play-mates that he really isn't Roger, he's a dog. Apparently self-aware-ness is labile; one can combine some phases of the ordinary self with some imagined phases of other selves, and the imaginative processes may be rich or meager, true to reality or utterly fantastic. It is likely that every kind of histrionics is present in the double personality. Yet, for all that, the reality of the dualism in the self must be admitted. The term "pose" is likely to assign to the associa-tive systems a quality of voluntary control which they partially or altogether lack. In full-fledged hypnotic dissociation the futility of "will power" is evident; the same thing appears in the well-organized patterns of double personality, for it is not the will that settles whether or when a personality change will occur. We are dealing with an attitude shift which, like most other attitude shifts, follows upon a com-plex constellation of factors; it is likely to be as sudden as the case of sudden insight discussed on pages 428 ff.

Actually the main dynamics in most cases of double and multiple personality seems to be an exaggeration of a conflict situation which is present in nearly all of us, namely, a conflict between a conforming and a guilty non-conforming trend. While the increasing complexity of our culture offers increasing opportunities, it also imposes increas-ing constraints. A person has to learn very early in life to stay "in the groove"—indeed, in many grooves. Cribs, playpens, play fences, and the like surround the child with barriers from his earliest months. Later he has to ride the trike and then the bike, then drive the car, within very narrow limits. Although there are increasing varieties of vocational possibilities, it is doubtful whether an equal range is permitted in personality development. The demand to be "well adjusted" presses on the child from his nursery years through ele-mentary school, college, and vocational life. Being temperamental or eccentric may cost a person his job, his status, his place in the group. Some individuals can absorb these pressures to keep feelings and behavior within limits more easily than others. Some try to conform to the expected pattern, but only succeed in building up a shell of surface conformity under which seethes a fiery or passionate or adventurous personality, as the case may be. It is noteworthy in this connection that in most of the cases of multiple personality that have been most carefully studied, the split which divides the overrestricted from the free and spontaneous personality of the patient has been found to come at just this point. Less extreme degrees are familiar to many school and college teachers, whose chief concern may be to free the individual for more complete fulfillment or to help him "find himself" or realize his "full potentialities."

Integration of the Associationist and the Motivational Approaches

We seem, then, to have evidence for both the associationist view and the conflicting-motive view of the cleavage process, and hence we may wish to find out whether both principles are ever operative in a single case, and to make clear their interrelations. Several such cases have been reported, one of the most satisfactory, because so intimately portrayed, being an anonymous autobiographical study entitled *I Lost My Memory*. A professional man, broken by unemployment during the depression, disappears in a railway station as he goes to buy some tobacco. After three days he awakens, like the subject of Keats' poem, on a "lone hillside," haggard, hungry, and confused. From a newspaper fragment borne by the wind he makes some deductions as to what has happened. Walking to the rifle range nearby, he manages to make contact with a friendly sergeant, who recognizes some of the names which have come back from the patient's boyhood. The man's family is reached and he is taken home. The physician who studied the case used the associative weaving technique, as did Franz, but both he and the author make clear that *emotional conflict is the central factor*.

It thus appears that the association and conflict principles can be integrated. We ought, however, to ask whether there is really any duality in the dynamics, whether association and motive are really mutually exclusive principles. We have already tried to show (page 398) that associations are not beads arranged on a string, or pieces in a mosaic. All associations are dynamic; all elements are functionally bound through tension systems to other elements. Sensory bits do not adhere, nor do motor bits coalesce. The action patterns with which they are bound come into dynamic facilitating or inhibiting relations. There is indeed perfect unity between the modern associationist view and the dynamic view. If we look more closely at the dramatic incident of the pet monkey cited by Franz, we see that the network which made possible the reestablishment of unity was a dynamic network, the elements that represented the deep needs of the patient being most active. All the elements are synergic (page 202) or in conflict (page 198) with other elements, and the momentum of their movement is the system of values which express the underlying drives. Unity or conflict of values is the clue to the unity or disunity of the person.

The documentation of this thesis may be sought in the case history of Doris Fischer as reported by W. F. Prince. The most fully reported case in all the literature of multiple personality, it embodies all the principles already described, and more in addition. As a child of three, Doris had been hurled to the floor by a drunken father; thereafter she had had a sober self and a carefree self in a Type II relation. The sober self, "Doris," knew only her own thoughts and memories, but from what she saw when she came back into consciousness, and other evidence, she found out about her co-self. "Margaret," the carefree one, was a veritable imp who despised her dutiful alter; she laid traps for Doris to fall into, and clawed her skin if she played thoughtlessly with Margaret's dolls or other property so that Doris would learn a lesson. Doris studied her lessons faithfully; but when Margaret was in command, she refused to be bothered with most school work. Sometimes she would make her psychological exit in the classroom just in time for poor Doris to be reprimanded for Margaret's misdemeanors.

When Doris was sixteen, her mother, to whom she was utterly devoted, suddenly died, and in Doris' state of shock there appeared a new self, later called "Sick Doris." Sick Doris was a narrow, soulless, wooden creature with no imagination; she was entirely willing to be a drudge and showed extreme competence in the role. The struc-

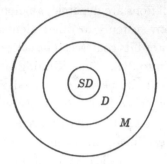

tural relations of the three are suggested in the accompanying figure. Sick Doris was the least inclusive, knowing only her own states, whereas Doris was fully acquainted with both her own state and that of Sick Doris.

Prince one day undertook a hypnotic procedure, which he understood imperfectly, in an effort to weaken and drive out the tendencies interfering with Doris' normal unity. After he had hypnotized her, he said "I am going to take away your power." The effect was directly evident in the weakening of her pulse; she turned blue. Suddenly her lips opened and a voice declared emphatically "You must get her out of this. Walk her! Walk her!" By walking her back and forth Prince managed to restore her circulation, but he did not try hypnosis again.

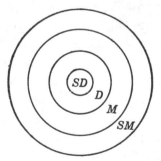

Thereafter, whenever necessary during therapy, this resolute self which had directed Prince what to do—the "sound sense" of the organism, we might say—came back; following her advice was an aid in the treatment. This fourth entity was called "Sleeping Margaret" because the eyes were closed when she spoke; she was more extensive than any of the others, as the accompanying figure shows.

The therapy emphasized the consistent shortening, week by week, of the amount of time allowed to Margaret and Sick Doris— they were badgered and pushed if they overstayed their time—and extending the amount of time allowed Doris until she was present constantly. After three years of patient work, restoration was effected. The Sick Doris memories were assimilated in those of the real Doris; those of Margaret were not, for when Margaret was driven out her memories "went" with her. The Sleeping Margaret personality was not driven out, and was thereafter available for conversation during Doris' sleep; Sleeping Margaret gave a clear retrospective account of her case to a number of psychologists who were invited to talk with her.

We should be tempted to call the case "weird" were it not for two considerations: first, that the "histrionics," as we have called them, though extreme in this case, are different only in their elaboration, not in their quality, from those present in other cases, such as BCA and Miss Beauchamp; second, that in times of grave threat to the organism, the soundest sense of which Doris was capable—we have suggested that this is what the Sleeping Margaret personality represents—was marshaled and focused. We have already noted that the most *inclusive* personality is the one most likely to have the best potentialities for mental health. None of this implies that we understand this case or any other case of double or multiple personality; however, as usual, we must carry forward as far as possible the principles which have stood extensive testing.

Most of the facts in Doris' striking case, as in all the others we have described, seem to fit in with a point of view that is congenial to most students of personality, one which demands a search for all the unity that can be found underneath the apparent multiplicity. In such cases it is as if the unified plan for living, which most of us strive to maintain, has become demoralized and been replaced by a series of blind stabs into the unknown; genuine conflict of purpose leads to genuine conflict in the individual's pictures of himself, and the exigencies of the situation lead to the unconscious setting-up of conflicting poses. Such poses may be accepted, believed in by the individual, in the same degree—if not indeed in greater degree—that actors *immersed in their parts* "believe" they are actually the characters they portray. To say that beneath all this there is complete and genuine unity does not mean much, for such unity is potential rather than actual. It does, however, mean a great deal to say that the poses, the various "looking-glass selves," are at first experimental, tentative efforts at adjustment and that in one's sober sense one does, at a very deep level, know that they are poses.

So far, so good. Unfortunately, however, this way of thinking, which we should all like to accept as final, does not cover all of the patiently described facts in Doris' case. Specifically, it fails to answer the question about the nature of the Margaret personality which, when "driven out" during the processes of synthesis and therapy, left no baggage of memories or attitudes and showed no signs whatever of fusing with the rest. But certain later phenomena, not part of the original study, do appear to square with this broad interpretation. The Princes had adopted Doris and, after Mrs. Prince's death in 1923, the girl became the center of her foster-father's life. It was he who made her well, he who supported her and gave meaning to her life. Following his death in 1934 there was a sudden and painful disintegration, involving vivid automatisms purporting to come from malignant spirits. Elwood Worcester, who had known Prince and his work intimately, knew that therapy for Doris lay in making contact with Sleeping Margaret; once this was done, she gave him therapeutic clues which led rapidly to restoration. It would appear, then, that we are dealing with lifelong dissociative tendencies which were patched up but not completely removed by the earlier therapy, and that various unconscious purposes were served by these dissociative phenomena. The more malignant expressions may be poses and may be made intelligible if the full force of the catastrophe in 1934 is envisaged; the healing presence of Sleeping Margaret may constitute stabilization on the same basis on which Prince had built solidly twenty years earlier.

Rarities of this type, as was noted earlier, are made less incredible by the discovery of transition states, dissociations less marked and more temporary, which display, in a manner not so different from our own brown studies and minor automatisms, the disposition toward psychic cleavage which we all possess. Especially instructive here are Mühl's studies of incipient multiple personality revealed in automatic writing and developing through the expression of malignant entities into a hornet's nest of moral contradictions (page 437). Mühl emphasized the conception of unwitting, hidden motivation; what is repugnant to one personality may lie at the very core of another. Her studies provide a gateway to the psychoanalytic conception of multiple personality.

Here we must pause, contenting ourselves with emphasizing the relative unity of the deep-level self, and making rather free use of the concept of unconscious histrionic power, of which the normal person has plenty when the self-consciousness of daily living is abrogated. It would appear that the dissociations of most multiple personalities can be dispelled when appropriate motivation for renewed unity is supplied, and that the major clue to most of the phenomena is given by a study of the impulsions which make the dissociable person need a system of selves rather than a single responsible self.

There still remains, however, the evidence (there is a great deal of it) from Rowland, Wells, Brenman, the Ericksons, Harriman, and others that dissociation of a deeper type exists; organized purposive behavior may be carried out unknown to the usual conscious self. There is a tradition in psychology that the hypnotized individual will do nothing alien to his personality; but Rowland, Wells, and Brenman have taken the bull by the horns and have led normal, stable people to do immoral and criminal acts. Such studies offer ocular demonstration that we can no longer say so confidently that the hypnotized person "does nothing contrary to his deeper self." We therefore have to recognize that dissociation may at times produce action patterns which are genuinely and fundamentally outside of the major system familiar to the personality.

In the light of such evidence, the Margaret personality and some of the phenomena of full-fledged somnambulism suggest that an incubation process has developed the germ of dissociation into a full-fledged, independent entity, a foreign body within the psychic structure, so that acts are committed which not only are inconvenient in terms of the pose of the moment and of all the other characteristic poses of the person, but are basically and fundamentally expressive of a personality system distinct from that of the normal personality.

Indeed, if we treat the evidence honestly, we shall have to take one final and very difficult step, one that is repugnant to our deeply ingrained philosophy of the person. We shall have to admit that two or more egos, two or more self-aware autonomous individualities, each not only historically but fundamentally hostile to the other, may in certain rare cases exist within the same living organism, either in alternation or concurrently. The Margaret personality cannot, even with autistic effort, be made to fuse stereoscopically with the Doris personality; and when Margaret is beaten, she retreats in full order, leaving no booty for Doris.

Physiologically and psychologically, there thus appear—very rarely—to be genuine rifts in the organic structure—vertical rifts, so to speak, which permit independent organized activities to proceed without intercommunication. Philosophically this is a good deal to stomach, but apparently it is a fact. We may make the best of the Mitchell hypothesis (page 434) and with it push on almost to the goal of complete explanation; however, we must concede the existence of dissociation, both of functional units of high complexity, and even of the mechanisms of self-awareness.

We gladly agree, of course, that these latter phenomena are "abnormal," a point that is not so very far removed from Kurt Goldstein's admission that, despite the unity of the organism, certain processes may at times be "isolated," functionally independent of the normal integrating processes. In diseases of the brain or even during neurotic strain, parts may be wrenched free of the main system, and the resulting abnormalities of conduct may give us clues as to the basic integrity which normally obtains. To grant this much would not be out of harmony with the recognition, following Piaget, that real functional unity at the symbolic or ego level is achieved only slowly in individual growth. In a certain sense these phenomena, abnormal though they are in the adult, are like the manifestations of multiple egos in the little child who literally has not yet determined who he is to be. In a broad sense they are like the regressions of psychoanalysis. In certain rare cases they constitute the most feasible device by which the frustrated adult organism can resort to the cleavages that characterize the second stage of perceptual development. The depersonalization described by the psychoanalyst and the loss of selfhood which occurs in many cases of melancholia are similar instances of the breakdown of the integrative mechanisms. There is a collapse of behavior at the third perceptual stage, in which the individual normally sees himself as a unit, and a temporary or permanent reinstatement of genuine, mutually exclusive pictures of the self. Such a fissure in the organic make-up can occur only when to constitutional dissociability there are added two or more warring impulses, so that a weak sense of unity gives way to two or more ego systems organized around different needs. Rarely indeed is this construction of forces found. Most cases of multiple personality appear essentially to represent the organism's efforts to live, at different times, in terms of different systems of values.

19. Creativeness

NEWTON as a small boy had begun to be enamored of the relationships of the physical world. He improvised little experiments such as jumping first with the wind, then against it, and computing the velocity of his jumps. This interest in "natural philosophy" pursued him through school and university. While at home during the great plague that struck during his first term at Oxford, he laid down, on deductive grounds, the three principles which we know as the laws of motion. At the age of twenty-four, it occurred to him while he was grinding lenses one day, to prepare a prism that would separate white light into its spectral components. He attacked the integral calculus before he was thirty, and completed it within two years.

By the time he was five years old, Mozart had assimilated the structure of music and was writing compositions that are still used in piano instruction; at seventeen he was the composer of immortal harmonies. Whence comes such achievement even before a man is grown?

SENSITIVENESS

On the basis of such cases, the first great phase in the evolution of the creator appears to be extreme *sensitiveness* to a specific form of experience, usually sensory; it is especially likely to involve sight, sound, or the muscle sense. It embodies delight in these experiences, a need for more of them, a curiosity into their relationships (page 240); in other words, we are dealing with sensory and activity drives (page 113). Such a person dwells more and more upon these experiences, exposes himself to them, and as far as possible controls them so that at will he can have what he wants. He tries them in combination and selects the most delightful combination; creation thus flows out of the original need for a form of experience.

CREATIVENESS

Sometimes it is not the sensory properties as such, but some persisting or recurring relation between them that intrigues him—a symmetry, a contrast, an ordered appearance and disappearance of one or more aspects of a whole. These relational experiences may at times prove also to have a sensory basis; symmetry, for example, may be a form of kinesthesis. In any event, they are important in their own right; e.g., the order or relations of tones may be far more compelling than any single tone quality. Sometimes the response to the sensory and relational experience is engulfed in a need for a still more complex ordering of such experiences into perceptual and imaginative wholes, so that the individual becomes involved in the pursuit of hidden relations, as in exploration or scientific activity. The delight in the process may increase in intensity and ramify in every direction until a full-blown passion is aroused, and, as we saw in Chapter 10 (page 240), this may siphon into the affect from other systems.

There is then at the beginning a controlling drive and a resulting inveterate habit. It is true that necessity is the mother of invention, but the necessity is as much the creative thinker's own need of experience as it is the community's need for more goods. Among most human groups, there is far more invention in the form of folk music, epic poetry, religious philosophy, embroidery, and decorative wood-carving than in the form of tools to serve economic needs. The need for devices to keep the wolf and the plague from the door is tremendous, and the need for better weapons for war and the chase is usually great. But in most societies these skills generally remain at a level that is "just good enough," whereas creative energies go into the arts. The Russian muzhiks of the fifteenth to the nineteenth centuries needed so many things that humanitarians wept on their behalf; they went blindly through their supposedly sheep-like existence, but they created through the centuries such folk dances and folksongs as have seldom been seen or heard upon the earth. We know from watching children in progressive schools that the desire to create must be almost universal, and that almost everyone has some measure of originality which stems from his fresh perception of life and experience, and from the uniqueness of his own fantasy when he is free to share it. Fantasy ideas are as much a function of a healthy, active mental life as motor achievements and skills are of healthy muscles. Just as postures, gaits, and gestures may become stereotyped and rigid as a result of repression, anxiety, or overconformity, so thinking may become stereotyped, banal, or rigid because of overconformity to conventional pressures. The potential creativeness in any group is far greater than what is actually realized, especially in these days of narrow standards regarding what is correct or in good taste or "well adjusted," regardless of whether thinking or behavior is concerned.

There is danger here in isolating the individual from his fellows, for sensitiveness arises and is nursed in a social context. We have long paid tribute to the enduring contributions of the genius, but only recently have we realized clearly the equal importance of the creativeness of whole peoples, whether expressed in the arts of primitive cultures, in folk music, in the rich musical traditions of Germany and Italy, or in the literary productiveness of a group such as the romantic poets. We shall need to try to understand both the forces underlying the highly focused creative activity of a genius who blazes new trails for other creators to follow, and the forces underlying the culture-wide creativity which has characterized some peoples for long periods. Sensitivity varies from one individual to another, but it may also be stimulated or repressed culturally. It must be this cultural fostering of this quality in certain areas which accounts for the fact that in the Hebrew culture sensitive people produced great literature, while across the water in Greece great sculpture as well as literature was being created, and in Egypt the creative works in stone outshone those in words. Society gives appreciation, status, and a role to the potentially creative individual; or it may fail to give them, in which case potential creativeness withers at the root. One culture group may expect almost everyone to be able to sing or play an instrument, whereas another group warns the young away from such eccentricities: "Don't go in for art unless you really think you can be a great artist." Within one culture the creator finds a ready-made audience, with patronage, and even with "schools" or groups of fellow creators; another lets him fend for himself in an attic. Where there is a generation of creators, as with English poets, German musicians, and American novelists after the First World War, there is mutual stimulation and release through understanding. Not only the culture's art values but its deeper experiences provide or withhold nourishment for art. A cultural soil rich in experience of love, hate, suffering, triumph, offers nourishment whether for Hebrew psalmists or Negro folk singers. Freedom to live and feel may also be involved; repetitious factory work may not be so conducive to creative work as the rich sensory and muscle experiences of farm life.

Not only the simpler qualities of the senses and of their relations, but those complex personal wholes that the child confronts in the form of parents, brothers, sisters, and friends are objects of delight and curiosity. The passion to immerse oneself in personal relationships may be the mainspring of genius, just as is the passion for impersonal things. The embryo dramatist or novelist may live in a world of simple manipulation of personal relations until, like colors and tones, they realize for him more and more complex and satisfying wholes. Similarly, the delight of watching the panorama of personal life may fuse with the delight of achieving power over people and of receiving recognition or applause from them, until one becomes a miniature statesman in his neighborhood or boy's club or fraternity, and goes on to a diplomatic or parliamentary career. If this delight in ordering human relations is combined with the chess player's delight in a complex balance of forces to achieve victory, a military career may be the most complete fulfillment; if power and prestige needs are overwhelming, the individual may become an emperor, a dictator, or a despot. There is no doubt that early frustrations may accentuate these drives, as Adler has said; but there is likewise no doubt that the drives are present before they are frustrated. It is for those in whom the drives are strong that the frustrations are important, and such people may move forward to their goal without being greatly frustrated, so that success feeds upon initial success as well as upon initial failure. Creativeness begins with impressions, sensitivities, wants, energies. Blockage of one's life demands may engender the struggle to contrive an unusual way out, but it can scarcely be put down as a universal clue to creative achievement.

PERSONALITY

ORGANIZING THE MATERIALS

So far we have considered only the drives, not the means to the realization of genius. Human needs may be so intense as to bring an agony of hunger for experience without leading to anything especially new or creative (as in Richard Jeffries' struggle to tell about his passion for the world of nature) or even to skill sufficient for the copying of existing works of art. One may, like Sidney Lanier, swoon at the beauty of the music of the violin but see or hear nothing articulate enough to record. For every Wordsworth who can put into words the outline and feeling of experience there are thousands who look into nature, into the gorge of the Yosemite and the blue of Crater Lake, and are able only to say that it is beautiful and that they will love it forever. Even if we are not dealing with a lack of richness in the complex of induced feelings, we encounter limitations of associative richness and organizing skill.

In other words, there must be *a pattern of creative skills*, a pattern which, if the needs are strong enough, may be gained by persistent practice. Those able to discover relations between sensory experiences must also be able to manipulate them so as to restructure their relations, to complicate them, and to improvise new ones. Sensitiveness and skill often coexist; those who see most deeply into the various orders of experience or systems of natural relations are likely, in the long run, to be capable of the richest creation; but there is no certainty that this will be the case. There is no guarantee that sensitiveness will be attended by this skill, but it is certain that both must be present if the work is to reach the level commonly accepted as that of genius. Since skill of this sort is doubtless dependent on general intelligence and on various special abilities, we shall content ourselves with the banal statement that an intellectual feature must be added to the affective factor. For some types of creative labor a third group of capacities is needed, namely, motor skills. But the poet and the novelist, the economist and the statesman, the mathematician and the philosopher can achieve the pinnacle of genius with no motor skill.

[456]

We have, then, set up the following hypothesis: At least three major, and largely independent, factors contribute to genius, one affective, one intellectual, one motor; and all genius involves the integration of the first two, but that some forms of it can dispense with the third. This is only a hypothesis that is suggested by biographical materials; much more complete data are needed. Some evidence that assists in its verification or refutation is at hand in Bühler's and Cox's studies of the childhood abilities of men and women who were destined later to outstanding distinction. Cox found that evidence of intellectual precocity, based on the school record and other early attainments, is closely linked with adult achievement in mathematics, philosophy, and science, less closely with achievement in the fine arts and music, and not at all closely with military prowess. What we have called the intellectual factor appears with a high "saturation" in some fields, with slight "saturation" in others. Her study of the interrelations of outstanding abilities led Cox to conclude that success in one intellectual sphere is substantially correlated with success in others, and that success in one esthetic field is correlated with success in other esthetic fields, the degree of correlation depending on the relatedness of the fields.

Cox's studies appear to support the hypothesis that the creative worker in esthetic fields must make good use both of esthetic sensitiveness and of intellectual endowment. The genius may at times feel no more intensely than do other people, but he must analyze, fractionate the cognitive situation more finely; in other words, he tends to be more subtle in his analytic response to the affective situation. It might also be suggested, though it cannot be proved, that intellectual powers directly enrich the sensory satisfactions. But even if the principle is sound, it would hardly suffice to lift an insensitive person into the category of the creative.

These data are based on such an extreme group of subjects that no general statement regarding the interrelations of intellectual, affective, and motor gifts can be attempted. In general, a person would have to be highly endowed with both intellectual and affective gifts to be included in a roster of geniuses, and the fact that these gifts appear together in Cox's data does not prove that they are correlated in the population as a whole.

CONSTITUTION AND ENVIRONMENT

There are rather strong a priori reasons for believing that the sensory and activity drives, as well as the glandular and autonomic make-up, are dependent in some degree upon constitutional factors (page 57), but that these dispositions depend not on single genes but on complex multi-gene determination. This is apparently also true of the intellectual factors that enter into creative work. If unlinked genetically,[1] the two gifts in high concentration would rarely coincide in a given individual. Moreover, it is unlikely that all the genes related to such gifts would be dominant (cf. page 61). It ought, therefore, to follow that only rarely does a genius who is married to a person of ordinary endowments transmit all the necessary components of the two necessary systems to a child. This kind of "hereditary genius" should be exemplified by the merest handful of cases through all human history. If, in addition to these considerations, we remember the huge role of the environment in cultivating the spark of genius, the peculiarly favorable soil in which alone it has a chance to flourish, we might expect this rare combination of genes to be realized in adult genius in hardly a single instance. The Bach family has been cited as the best example of true hereditary genius. This is, of course, permissible if we include as geniuses such sound and competent musicians as the son and the grandson; however, only Johann Sebastian is commonly recognized as a "genius" in the accepted sense. The question is thus entirely one of definition. If we limit the term to creative minds of the first order, it would be more honest to say that there are no cases in all our history. But a brilliant and creative mind is much more likely to appear in the family of a genius than elsewhere, and enormously more likely if both parents are highly

---

[1] Linkage is the association of two genes in the same chromosome. We know exceedingly little about the linkage of human genes, except in the case of sex-linked traits, i.e., those in which the sex-determining chromosome carries other identifiable genes. Cf. Burks, p. 50.

gifted. The case is analogous to familial traits exhibited in stature and body form, but it is much more complex. Barring gross pathology or deformity, the seven-footer is more likely to occur in the family of giants than in the family of mere six-footers. Even so, with everything in his favor and with a diet and regimen pushing growth to the utmost, there are not likely, even in the giant family (say six-foot-four), to be any seven-footers; there will, however, be more six-footers in such families than in ordinary families. If one sets such a standard for genius as is set for giants, there will in all history be few if any cases of hereditary genius, but there will be far more *near-geniuses* than chance expectation would allow. The exceptional mind and the exceptional creative gift appear in families containing other minds that are akin to them; but since they have been chosen as the greatest deviations, we must be content to find approximations rather than duplicates as we scan their kindred for resemblances. If the bars are let down enough to allow, let us say, John Adams and John Quincy Adams or James Mill and John Stuart Mill to pass, the examples of hereditary genius will be plentiful.

A reinforcing factor of enormous weight is parental example, direction, encouragement, or coercion. The parent provides the atmosphere, the objects to be attended to, the fields with their anchorage points, the experience of watching the work in art or science when it is in the making, and the chance to participate early in the creative process. This may captivate the first-born son's imagination more than that of the others because of the greater time and interest, the greater enthusiasm and freedom on the part of the father; similarly, after the mother has for some years borne no more children, the last-born may be closer to her and to the father, and both economically and emotionally more richly endowed with those advantages or personal treasures than are the intervening children. This may well be the interpretation of Havelock Ellis' data, which indicate that eminent men in Great Britain tend to be the eldest or the youngest child in proportions surpassing their fair share among all the children considered.

The effect of special training upon the work of the genius requires closer attention. We have seen that the genius not only dwells in but manipulates the material which he loves, both stumbling upon and—as his skill increases—foreseeing the products of his acts. As in all other skills, there is huge transfer. The composer of gavottes or *Lieder* quickly learns to compose more exquisite gavottes, more touching *Lieder;* but he has also learned something about composition in general, something about the broad architecture of music. It is among the composers of sonatas and études, not among the builders of bridges, that the creators of opera and symphony arise. Although the long training process may depend at first on parental stimulation, it brings the joy of mounting capacities and of the constant creation and fulfillment of new wants because an autonomous compulsion eventually appears. One must go on to new forms, to the solution of new questions put to nature. This is the "creative mastery" to which students of esthetic satisfaction have paid tribute.

ILLUMINATION

Up to this point we have contented ourselves with reference to skills that proceed gradually from simpler to more complex units. Step by step, the individual makes ready for bigger achievements; he remains in control of the lower units as the higher integrations are painfully achieved. One regularly recurring feature of creative thought, however, is its tendency to get out of hand, its habit of rushing uninvited upon the scientist or inventor or composer or dramatist with a new and unexpected pattern of articulate expression. A great many thematic patterns, a great many higher units of color and form, knock suddenly at the doors of the trained mind, no matter how absentminded or how deeply engaged in other matters it may be. Indeed, not content with knocking at the door, such material may suddenly fall like a landslide into the very center of the mind. Many of Blake's finest integrations, for example, took shape as wholes hurled at him by forces which seemed to him to stand beyond the limits of his own selfhood. This process of being overwhelmed by accumulated unconscious or subliminal material is the heart and core of genius as defined by F. W. H. Myers in terms of a rush of material from the subconscious, a *"subliminal uprush."* Such an uprush, the climax of creativity, can appear under somewhat more deliberate control. One can never tell it just when or how to come, but he can dig deep into or ponder through the meshes of a problem and, either in a moment of heightened concentration or, more usually, in a relaxed moment *after* such concentration, catch the illumination, the solution of the problem, the answer to the scientific question, the appropriate denouement for the story.

The term *subliminal,* or the emphasis upon unconscious factors in the attainment of illumination, may suggest one or the other of two quite distinct processes. Exactly the right set, together with a vast fund of relevant organized material (only a little of which is conscious), may be touched off by a slight or even a subliminal cue, so that one reacts to many relevant phases of a problem all at once, exactly as in the perceptual experience of insight described in Chapter 14 (pages 399 ff.). There may be false percepts, misleading insights, illuminations that are actually steps toward the darkness. This is rather common in science and invention, but with experience one fumblingly learns to discover the earmarks of productive clues. In the arts, however, the standards by which a true and a false illumination are distinguished are more complex and more unstable; and though many cues may be discarded, many that another age will reject as the nodding of Homer are accepted by the creator himself as genuine. Thomas Gray scratched out from his *Elegy* many lines which lovers of English verse today would prefer in place of some that he retained.

We do not mean to imply that illumination comes by accident, for nothing in the organism happens accidentally. We do, however, mean that the tension release is so great that it is impossible for the artist to make a completely autonomous judgment of the project at the time. Nevertheless, the experienced creator experiences much that seems to arise outside the focus of voluntary control; as Pater made clear when he distinguished between the fine frenzy and the quiet eye, he makes his critical judgments with an apparatus which is not identical with that from which the creative impulse came. The same holds true, of course, in all creative work, indeed in all skilled work. Much of this impulse comes from the unconscious, that is, from a realm not in consciousness at the moment. The more complex, the more unstable the creative process, the more difficult is the analysis of this unconscious, integrative process and the architectural forms upon which it depends.

There is another sense in which illumination may come from the unconscious. It may arise, full-fledged, from a realm of genuine creative activity which for the time being runs parallel to and is unknown to the primary awareness. The creative act is carried out not by a conscious self working with ready-made unconscious material which leaps into new conscious form, but by an unconscious level of the personality which carries out a sustained creative activity unknown at the time to the conscious self. Although such cases are relatively rare, there is considerable evidence of them in biographical material (cf. the dream materials mentioned on pages 428 ff).

Much of the evidence for such "coconscious" activity, as Morton Prince called it, is likely to be ambiguous, as we noted on page 437. The full-fledged literary creations which appear in written form at a conscious level or through automatic writing may actually be coming into existence at the very time of their manifestations, and not be preformed at all. This basis for rejection hardly applies to visual schemata. Unlike a time art, a space art may throw upon the conscious screen a single whole so complex that a series of directed creative processes, rather than blind fumbling, must be presupposed. No one of these processes, however, has had any opportunity to appear until the end phase suddenly inundates consciousness; they are like the geometric solution of a problem conceived algebraically.

Although such instances add something to the suggestive evidence, already considered, regarding a genuine coconscious process, this is not the basis for our present interest in them. Their special importance for us lies in the light they throw on the processes of subconscious preparation or incubation. In the case of the genius, the full creative process, when traced over a period of years or decades—the accumulation of knowledge, skill, and higher units of both knowledge and skill being brought out—occasionally shows the operation of such *dissociated creative activities*. The warming-up processes that bring the incubated material near the hatching point can be watched. Thus to Thomas S. Jones, author of the *Rose Jar* and other sonnets, there came, in middle life, the gift of automatic writing. Under high tension and with rapt expectation he waited to see what the swiftly moving pencil would indite; in an average time of ninety seconds, the Petrarchan *Sonnets of the Cross* appeared. It will be remembered that in a Petrarchan sonnet some consciousness must know what the concluding lines are to be; but this poet simply waited to see what the script would say.

The psychology of such creation requires all the direct light we can get. Until recently we have had to rely on biographical material. Most of the material on this problem, however, has three disadvantages: (1) It was recorded long after the events occurred; (2) it was recorded before the more careful methods of sifting evidence came into vogue; (3) it was recorded haphazardly with no prearranged plan or hypothesis to be verified or refuted. Furthermore, it is almost always infected by the autistic impulse to add, subtract, or reorganize in terms of adoration or, less frequently, cynicism on the part of the narrator.

Two methods have been developed to minimize these drawbacks: Hutchinson's interview method and Patrick's experimental method. Hutchinson interviewed well-known authors, scientists, and other modern celebrities regarding the form of their creativeness. Patrick succeeded in getting artists and poets to devote themselves to their accustomed creative tasks in response to prepared stimulus materials while she herself took notes on the process. Although both of these methods have obvious limitations, Hutchinson's method appears to reduce the first difficulty and to remove the other two completely; it serves also to bring the autistic complications somewhat under control. Patrick's method completely removes the first two difficulties and almost completely scotches the third; moreover, it reduces the autistic problem to the dimensions ordinarily present when a subject talks about his "desirable traits," and it holds the artist's comments in line with the visible attributes of a product that he has just completed. It is true that the people Hutchinson interviewed may not be typical of all the varieties of genius, and that Patrick did not succeed in getting the greatest living poets and artists to write and paint. But such objections are somewhat like those of a student of explosives who would reject the chemist's explanation of the popping of a hydrogen bubble because the chemist will not seat himself beside an atomic bomb that is about to explode. These two methods clearly reinforce the classical conception of sudden creation or illumination. Both investigators present plentiful direct evidence on this point, for the sudden emergence of creative wholes runs through the work of both of them.

Polishing

It is tempting, in accounts of inspiration, to treat the great event as a full stop, the close of a period, and to dwell only briefly upon the need for a little polishing up, hammering out, "filing and fitting" to make the product complete and presentable. This polishing process must not, however, be undervalued. The dramatic quality of insight, born in an ecstasy or in an agony of creative intensity, often leads the artist to forget that the baby must still be brought up. The toil may be arduous, for a great deal has to be changed completely; indeed, the painting or drama may take a constantly changing form, and there may be many further insights along the way. The quality of the genius' mind is shown nearly as much in the capacity for masterful polishing as in the gift of sudden illumination. Literary and artistic history, and the history of science and invention, are strewn with the wreckage of brilliant ideas not carried through.

This polishing process is also peculiarly interesting in showing the intimate interdependence of attuned possibilities, the literally inter-individual or super-individual character of the creative process itself. What is incomplete in one mind may be fulfilled in another. In the space arts, where the vision of a painting or statue or cathedral may come all at once, the finishing off is sometimes left to others who are acquainted with the master's style. This was apparently the rule, for example, in the school of Botticelli and in that of Rembrandt. Although this is not an accepted practice among musicians, they follow a rather similar process in arranging, rescoring, or orchestrating earlier works. It is "correct" for any competent musician to arrange and rearrange the work of his predecessors, and such compositions as "Meditations on a Theme by _____" permit thematic material to be endlessly reconstituted in work which gradually ceases to represent a polishing process, becoming instead a new cycle of creation. In the verbal arts it is likewise common for one man to take another's plot. The Greek dramatists asserted that their works were "tidbits from Homer's mighty feast"; Shakespeare never hesitated to rework the dramatic fragments of the medieval and early Renaissance periods, and Eugene O'Neill is in the true dramatic tradition in recreating Electra in a nineteenth-century setting. Just as in the individual's life history one good stroke suggests another, so many a forward step in the creative process may be regarded as either a minor embellishment or a step toward fresh illumination. One creative mind may adopt and develop the work of another and, depending upon its own caliber, imitate, elaborate, parallel, or altogether transcend the original. One of the greatest of all pictures of Jesus that is known and loved throughout the western world hangs in the gallery at Milan with only the caption "Imitator of Leonardo da Vinci"; similarly, one who had a different ax to grind might set up a statue of Jefferson with the inscription "Imitator of Montesquieu."

Although the individuality and weakness of the artist is forever prized and glorified, so that his place as a *member of the community* is slighted and forgotten, this forward step in the creative process, this development and completion of the intuitive vision, shows in two respects to what degree he is one with his cultural group. First, he must be open as a child to the great impulses of his age, so that he may make full use of its art forms and the accepted canons of the world. Second, no matter how glorious his isolation, other men must use him, develop him, and try as best they can to surpass him. His work is both a fixed crystallized image to be revered, and a living expression whose remaking is demanded by him and by others. Not infrequently the artist defines the rules of Platonic completeness by copying his own paintings with notable changes, as Leonardo copied and altered his Madonna of the Rocks. The completion process is therefore no tag end, no mere lapse from the transcendent level of the master to the puttering level of the semi-skilled worker; it is usually an integral part of the creative process. It expresses the full force of the same incubation which preceded the illumination, and the direction and vitality of its achievement is consonant with that of all the preceding stages.

We are now ready for a summary of the more evident creative processes. There is, first, sensitiveness, the presence of a need that satisfies itself and feeds upon more and more material of a certain type —color, space relations, tone, rhythm. As satiation (page 298) occurs, the need sets itself a bigger, more complex goal of the same type; and the individual *learns to create*. Second, there is a long accumulation of experiences which mediate richer and richer contact with the material needed; this is a period of acquisition, strain, and unfulfilled desire. Third, usually in a moment of excited self-direction toward the goal, an integration of the accumulated material takes place in which both conscious and subconscious storehouses of experience are drawn from. A whole that is the answer to the long quest is made manifest in a moment often characterized by the term *illumination*. Finally, as the need and the achievement are relived again and again, it becomes clear that the need is not perfectly fulfilled or that secondary needs are still frustrated, and the work of art or of science is accordingly hammered out until it is more adequate. When J. J. Rossman, on the basis of his experience in the Patent Office, undertook to define the stages through which the thoughts of inventors passed, he found the same recognizable steps as those reported by Hutchinson for writers, composers, and artists. The motives were predominantly those of practical achievement or curiosity, or both, rather than being predominantly esthetic, but the process was substantially the same. Indeed, all these phases of genius or high creativeness have been noted many times by modern writers. And they may of course be present in rudimentary form, as when a two-year-old who loves paint dabbles his way slowly into a "picture"; there is a continuum from such creativeness to that of a Michelangelo.

"GREAT WITS ARE SURE TO MADNESS NEAR ALLIED"

There are at least four factors in the creative process which involve nervous wear and tear on the individual. First, his craving is intense. He may rest perfunctorily because it is good for him; but he takes his incompleted work to bed with him, and while others sleep he leaps downstairs two at a time to add a stroke or a phrase or, like Leonardo, he crosses Milan to put a touch of blue on Matthew's restless figure in the Last Supper. The intellectual processes are screwed to a pitch which would batter any nervous system. Of course, all sorts of states may masquerade as nervous fatigue, but it seems hardly fair to deify the genius to the point of denying that his nervous system needs rest, or at least a bit of sound sleep, on occasion.

Second, not only is the drive sustained without release, but it may take the individual out of context with most of his environment. Just one thing, one's creation, is of value. When Gauss locks himself up for two days in his attic, or Newton, having dined, demands of his servant that dinner be served, or Archimedes runs naked from the bath shouting, "I have found it," we cannot avoid the impression that the mind not only turns ceaselessly on its narrow pivot at a pace which allows no rest, but also permits itself no contact with the normal world of perspective and sanity. Frequently the creator is outside the orbit of social reality. Artists who, like Sinclair Lewis or Grant Wood, immerse themselves in the social reality of which they are a part are less prone to such madness.

Third, the genius may be so engrossed in himself—so patently supported, after his first achievements, by some social recognition of their value—that his head is turned; he may consider himself subject to no common rules, defy the conventions of health, courtesy, and ordinary living, subject himself to an artificial existence centering more and more in one narrow preoccupation.

A fourth factor is the inevitable frustration involved in the very process of moving forward. The individual sees dimly ahead the pattern toward which he struggles, but is still unable to move consistently toward it; it is always both near and far. When a solution actually comes his way with a surging sense of its superhuman value, he must struggle to *seize* it and may, in a moment, do so; but as he grasps it, other visions crowd forward in their turn and beyond them others loom darkly ahead. He may glimpse with ecstasy, but most people create in agony. "The work draws blood," said Johannes Müller, as he came from his laboratory.

The old surmise regarding the frequent nervous instability of geniuses makes sense in view of all these considerations. Though clear enough to the historian and biographer, it remained for Southard to conceive a systematic study to discover the actual degree in which genius is prone to mental disorder. Southard and his pupils selected the thousand individuals to whom most space was given in the *Encyclopædia Britannica*, excluding those who owed their position solely to the accident of birth (not indeed that space in an encyclopedia is proof of genius; however, some objective standard must be used). The work, incomplete at the time of Southard's death, was said to indicate 150 clearly disturbed cases and 100 more whose behavior was in doubt. Unfortunately, nothing was published, and comparable control figures for ordinary people would be hard to obtain. It must of course be conceded that in some individuals the instability was probably neither the consequence nor an attending circumstance of the creative powers, but in a number of cases the mental disorder seems psychologically connected with them; it seems to derive in part from them, but in turn it colors, accentuates, and deepens the existing marks of genius. Though it would be ridiculous to deny the heroic proportions of Coleridge, the fantastic brilliance of Poe, the disorderly splendor of Nietzsche, there can be no doubt that opium, alcohol, and syphilis played their part in exaggerating or luridly lighting up the high peaks of the already conspicuous creativity of these men. This is certainly due at times to the sheer *release* which drugs and disease sometimes offer from the binding restraints of common sense and common social response, the escape from the monotonous roads of accepted thought, the removal of painful self-awareness. At other times extraordinary creativeness seems more clearly due, as in De Quincey's visions, to a summation effect, the reinforcement, by a toxic agency, of imagery already more splendid than that of the common man. All of this does not in the least mean that *most* geniuses are abnormal; only that nervous wear and tear are not uncommonly associated with high creativeness.

Insight, Psychodynamics, and Association

Both in the last few chapters and in the present one we have used jointly, or even simultaneously, the Gestalt doctrine of insight (page 399), the psychoanalytic principles regarding psychodynamics, especially unconscious drive (page 401), and the associationist doctrines regarding the gradual forging of mental connections (page 399), transfer of training (page 204), summation (page 123), and dissociation (page 325). Under one name or another, these principles have forced themselves on the attention of most of those who have studied creative thought. Psychological schools may fight about them, but the conflict is not in nature, but in scholastic schemes. Although the present venture may well be mistaken at many points, its aim is not to force together incompatible elements wrenched from different systems; it regards all the aforementioned principles as existing very compatibly in the organism. If one feels that they are in their essence incompatible, this will almost certainly be because he considers that associationism fits poorly with Gestalt and psychoanalytic principles. It will therefore be worth while to give a little attention to the place of the associationist doctrine in relation to the problem.

If associationism be regarded as a prison, a self-contained system from which no escape can be found, the reason is to be found in the fact that the prison is none other than the universe itself. The psychological system evolving within the individual is directly open to the culture and to the minds of others. Through language and symbol, through pictures and the cultural residues of art and technology, it becomes a process of endless fluid interchange with all that men have thought and felt. Barriers there are indeed; but they are static and arbitrary barriers in the form of geographic or cultural walls which separate the thoughts of some men from those of others. There is nothing about the process of association that imprisons the individual. To avoid such restraints and to use the system of associations both for the enrichment of the individual mind and for the cultivation of the broadest possible means of communication between mind and mind, was the intent of the earliest practical efforts of associationism, all the way from the intellectualism of David Hartley to the romanticism of the early mesmerists. The advocates of associationism in its heyday undertook to liberate the mind, not to fetter it. In the hands of French psychiatrists, it gradually became a device for restoring to the individual those patterns, those capacities that his own psychic conflict had lost for him; hypnotic reeducation was indeed the first step in psychoanalysis. That psychoanalysis as a system is founded squarely upon association psychology is usually forgotten. The drive psychology of the early and later Freudian period integrates well, as we have constantly tried to point out, with dynamic associationism of the Aristotelian type. In fact, a drive psychology could hardly be constructed were not the classic outlines of association psychology at hand for use.

Associationism has been misunderstood in two respects: first in being set off against dynamic psychology, and second in being set off against the principle of form or organization. But both psychoanalysis and organicism are salutary largely because they bring out aspects of the association doctrine which had been forgotten. It is through the revitalization of the classical associationist theory that the dynamic and Gestalt doctrines achieve their message, just as it is through the quantum and relativity principles that the Newtonian conception of a world of ideal mathematical relationships is realized. Where Newton was categorically wrong, he has been set right; and similarly, where the association doctrine was categorically wrong, as in its emphasis upon the value of isolation and repetition, it has been set right. Its task, however, is to reveal the structural properties of the psychic process wherever it occurs, to make clear the interrelatedness, the systematic interdependence of all psychic entities. And when, as has so often been the case during the past few decades of psychological writing, the entities are dynamically conceived, their systematic interconnections can be studied only when the basic principles of connectionism are sought.

THE EXPERIMENTAL ENRICHMENT OF CREATIVENESS

We can, I think, go much further than these timid beginnings have suggested. In contrast with the bold associationist prophecies of Herbart on the one hand and the mesmerists on the other, we have in recent decades sought to add to the understanding of the mind by using the medicine-dropper technique. We have feared to engulf the mind with real richness; we have feared to use that most powerful of all instruments for the discussion and the reconstitution of psychic structures, namely, the experimental hypnotic techniques and those closely allied techniques that cultivate the study of fantasy and the dream, reverie and projection. The story of psychoanalysis and of experimental hypnosis is one of such overpowering significance that psychologists have hesitated to make real use of these techniques. The psychoanalytic technique, as contrasted with psychoanalytic schematization, is still employed almost exclusively for the healing of sick souls, not for the exploration of the normal mind; and experimental hypnosis is still used to answer certain technical questions on the nature of dissociation and suggestion rather than to show the half-hidden contents and forms of psychological activity which reveal that vast dominion of the mind to which introspection has lost the key. The psychoanalysts are slowly and cautiously beginning to move in the direction of a systematic experimental study of unconscious association, upon which ultimately all creativity depends. Experimental hypnosis has possibly an even greater mission; it may well bear witness to a psychic dynamics of a subtlety and complexity compared with which the orderly dynamics of waking life are but narrow and puny. As one studies the functions of memory and fantasy in the hypnotic consciousness, he begins to glimpse a storehouse of energies—like the energies within the atom—from which a tempest of creative force may be siphoned off or, under wise control, directed to the great improvement of the caliber and accuracy of human thinking.

The coins of medieval Spain bore a Latin phrase referring to the pillars of Hercules, which mark Spain as the end of the world: *Ne plus ultra*, there is nothing beyond. He who sailed from Cyprus to the west was confronted by this last frontier of water, the gateway from the safe world to the outer brink of the unknown, the non-existent. After the Portuguese and Spanish mariners of the fifteenth century opened the seas to the traffic of Europe, the single word *ne* was stricken from this inscription, so that it read *Plus ultra*, there is more beyond—thus words that told no longer of the closed frontier but of the limitless world beyond. Thus we may say that the associative structures of Hartley and of Mill have been liberated through psycho-analysis and experimental hypnosis. There is no apparent limit to the richness of associative networks. Inhibitions once removed can be rearticulated. A person can train himself to pass on to higher units, to see more subtle relationships, to define for himself goals of esthetic or practical mastery to which no longer a mere fragment of the self but a whole living system may be devoted.

When once the laws of the associative system are as well understood as the laws governing the physical world, the educator may well hope to order human personality in terms of its real potential rather than in terms of the surface context and casual time-space connections which actually constitute the educational process in the early years. The problem is one of barriers and of goals. Laws relating to the barriers are already beginning to be formulated, and we have begun to find, in the deep release and self-realization of the child's mind, the methods for their removal. Somewhat more timidly, but still in articulate form, we begin to see the principles that underlie the free utilization of all the limitless storehouse of psychic interconnections to which the normal human mind may gain access. We marvel at the sudden tide of creativeness that may surge up in a frustrated delinquent child when treated humanly, when set free to paint or to draw in terms of his heart's desire. In the same way, when once the barriers are removed and the unconscious goals are defined, we may hope to draw into the vortex of individual creativeness no mere fragment, but an energy system, the utilization of which will be not simply a drive expression but a genuine personality expression.

In our discussion of autism we sought to show that one thinks in terms of needs, and that the attainment of intellectual freedom is not merely a negative problem of removing distortions, but a positive problem of setting free the wish to understand. We are beginning to see that intelligence is a released *capacity to understand* that expresses the free rather than the frustrated associative systems of the individual. In the more important human creative situations it is as a rule not the stupid but the autistic, the paranoid thinker, who, equipped with adequate material, comes perversely to the wrong conclusion. When once the thinker is set free, his intelligence takes on a driving power which overwhelms the obstacles of nature. Experimental studies of the freest types of association—namely, those involved in fantasy— that are already available show that the more serious impediments to effective thought result from self-imposed barriers; for one error due to stupidity there are a dozen due to dispositions within the individual which are essentially protests against the social meaning of the task or against his own relation to it. We are reminded of Ruger's classic demonstration that when an objective task lies before one, the "problem attitude" releases capacities that had previously been tied up in various self-conscious attitudes; but even Ruger's subjects had begun to utilize only a fragment of their potentialities. White's recent studies make it clear that when once the nature of *unconscious obstacles* is evident, everything in the psychic apparatus, from sensory thresholds to the capacity for higher creative units, is recast. As Lasswell has put it, there are types of release from constraint which suddenly open a new world to the thinker. But all real education is fraught with release opportunities of many different kinds.

If creativeness can thus be so greatly enhanced in the adult, what can be done in childhood? If it is true that we learn to create, using in each creative act both the content and the habits acquired earlier, can we not develop an experimental science of personality liberation which can be applied at the very beginning of life? The answer is yes; and considerable evidence points in this direction. Much good has come from the economic approach, which shows that economic deprivation and competitive strains warp the child's creativity; much good also has come from those who explain psychoanalytically the earliest constrictions that are due to blind tabus, and from those who as educators aim to provide a releasing and enriching environment; all are working on interrelated aspects of one enormous problem.

There are, however, no short cuts in the educational process that leads to such release. What has been said here relates to the goal of free creativeness; the process of aiming toward such a goal must be continuously implemented, year by year. Progressive education of the type which allows the child to specify his own goal, and especially of the type in which the members of the group assist one another in specifying their goals, has manifestly increased both intellectual and artistic powers. What it has accomplished appears to be the removal of the more obvious social fetters upon the educational process and the encouragement of spontaneity in the student. With the beginning of rigorous and systematic research with projective techniques during the course of each individual's education, we may hope that a generation of children will not only pass through such liberating experiences but enable us to observe objectively just what is going on. In particular, there is need to observe the various *types* of release, the differences in the values of the various progressive *techniques*, and the *individual differences* in the capacity of children to make use of one or another form of liberation.

One method of liberation, the *spontaneity training of* J. L. Moreno, has received special study. *Spontaneity* is here conceived as the shaking off of the encrusted habits of the social routine, the setting free of impulses that are both naïve and organized. The child's first need is conceived to be the need for sociality, the need to respond to others and to be responded to by them. This means that for each individual the deepest, most naïve impulses are love and hate, and that therefore the first task of the educator or psychiatrist is to allow the individual, through the spontaneous selection of his own social world, to define the influences which enable love rather than hate to serve as organizing principles, or to direct and channel hate into the form of hating things that threaten humanity. The individual, however, cannot be spontaneous merely by resolving to become so; he incvitably has to learn the petty rules of social conduct, the small change of conformity or adaptation; he builds a shell about himself. The psychiatrist and the educator must see through this, must discover the intensities that lie underneath, must literally cultivate and make habitual the spontaneous manner of responding. In one who has learned to be non-spontaneous, only learning can restore spontaneity and give it its rightfully dominant position. Spontaneity training is therefore a systematic part of the psychiatric system established by Moreno. Sick and well, old and young, learn upon the stage to throw themselves spontaneously into the roles that fulfill them as persons—to be themselves, to reveal an individuality which life had taught them to conceal. The histrionic powers of the average man or woman trained in the routine manner are suddenly dwarfed by the forces liberated in response to the demand that he use the stage to act out not a "part" but himself, or some person with whom he identifies.

The Moreno technique appears, then, to support and supplement the techniques used in progressive education, experimental hypnosis, and psychoanalysis, all of which tend to show that there are vast energies within the core of the ego which have as a rule been left to accidental expression. Throughout all history there has been a sort of spilling-over of creativeness which we have eagerly lapped up and glorified in biography or history, but which until very recently we have tended to regard as beyond all understanding or social control. Creativeness, however, is not private property; it belongs to humanity, and wherever there is human material it can be nursed, cultivated, and brought to flower.

These conceptions do not lead merely to a definition of the type of education that might set free the general run of more or less average persons. Just as the inner forces are highly individualized, so the special environments most productive of release in exceptional persons must vary widely. Rare personalities may have special, individualized needs, as suggested occasionally by the educational theorists of western Europe and by Soviet writers. We refer not to the general run of "leaders" or "gifted children" but to those rare sports, those one-in-a-million eccentrics who do so much to determine the course of scientific, artistic, or intellectual history—who are often too brilliant, or too sensitive, or too rich in their originality to make good use of even the most individualized, the most progressive of our educational systems. So amazing is human individuality that it is quite likely that all the general principles about socialization to which most educational thinking must be directed will have but little meaning in such cases. It is hard to see in what way Newton or Gauss could have benefited by an "enrichment" of his environment. Each ran into himself rather than into the group, achieved the encapsulation which he unconsciously knew offered the only protection for the germ that was ripening. In some cases, as Hocking makes clear, an alternation between sociality and isolation may be the best educational device; forty days in the desert may be followed by a career of teaching, or Zarathustra may relinquish his aloneness to permit intimate contact with those whom he loves. The first phases of all education will inevitably be profoundly social, and in some individuals the social emphasis may suffice. It seems likely, however, that a sort of dialectical process may occur, social response yielding to a counter-movement of isolated self-fulfillment. Finally a synthesis is achieved; the inner resources are free to break forth because of their dynamic balance with the social responses that have been laid down in the original organizing processes of the early years, and self-fulfillment and social participation become one and the same.

Part Four

THE SELF

20. The Origins of the Self

OWING partly to the structure of the language and partly to religious and philosophical traditions, the term self is used in two contrasting senses, as thing acting and as thing acted upon. I *myself* saw him; here self is the agent. I have cut *myself*; here self is the thing acted upon. The same difficulty arose for Descartes, who from awareness of a thought process concluded that there must be an individual thinker, and for James, who struggled against a pure ego in favor of an empirical *me*. Although no purpose is served by tilting against language or philosophy, there is value in attempting the simplest possible formulation of a sufficiently complicated problem. From the point of view outlined in this volume, there is an organism, which among its many functions includes the function of observing and knowing. Among the things which it observes and knows are its visible surfaces, its vocal cadences, its muscular strains. Being a more or less integrated system of responses, the organism appropriately orders these diverse impressions into an integrated whole and agrees to call it by the name which others have given it, just as it accepts the names that are current for other distinguishable wholes. In the same way it begins to cogitate on the nature of this totality, paying more and more heed to those aspects of it which others fail to note; the inner world becomes important. From the diverse knowing and thinking processes a conceptual unity is deduced. The self is a thing perceived, and it is also a thing conceived; in both senses it is constantly responded to. A large part of the behavior that constitutes personality is self-oriented behavior. The system of *responses to* the self will be considered in later chapters.

PERSONALITY

The Genesis of Selfhood

Like all other objects of experience, the self grows out of the matrix of indefiniteness which exists at the first perceptual level. It comes gradually into being as the process of differentiation goes on within the perceptual field. Our task, then, in this chapter will be to trace the development and form of organization of this perceptual unity, reserving for the following three chapters the discussion of the activities which are carried out in adapting to, enhancing, and defending the self.

We have learned from Piaget (page 339) and from Werner (page 266) that the visual percept of the body, the auditory percept of the voice, and the flow of sensory impulses from viscera and muscles are probably first experienced as aspects of a throbbing totality in which affect cannot be distinguished from percept. Affect, and the drive which lies behind it, serve largely to give intensity or emphasis to things cognized, but as yet the cognitive aspect is not dissected out from the whole. As figure-ground relationships begin to be defined, these experiences of seeing and hearing, and the organic and kinesthetic experiences become not only differentiated but pushed more and more into the position of figure in the perceptual field. Egocentrism in Piaget's sense, the state of sheer undifferentiatedness, yields to a state of chronic perception and concern with body, voice, and kinesthetic and visceral experience. The evidence already cited for the doctrine of perceptual development (pages 333 ff.) must suffice here for this growth of self-perception, except that there is also considerable evidence to show that the body in all its forms is at first as strange, as unfamiliar, as unorganized as are any other perceived objects. For many months, much of it is not recognized as self. A child, for example, habitually exploring with each hand and bringing to his mouth whatever is found, brings the two hands together accidentally, and now each carries the other to the mouth with the same eager glow of discovery and achievement that results when an outside object is discovered. Even in the second year of life, many parts of the body, such as the inner surface of the cheek and the small of the back, may when accidentally touched bring a sense of strangeness, an experience not fully assimilated with the self. The adult occasionally experiences a twinge or an ache which not only fails to be localized within the spatial organization of the self but somehow "does not belong" to the self. In some hypnotic subjects, for example, anesthesia is produced not by obliterating pain, but by throwing it into the category of impersonal experience—it is not *my* pain, so what of it?

Visual perception of the various parts of the body, auditory perception of the voice, and the experiences of touch, pain, striped-muscle strains, etc., are evidently differentiated out of the original matrix *before* they are articulated within a single going concern. It is only because these various components are experienced together, and in their interaction, that they come to make up a perceived whole rather than a conglomeration. Concurrently with this self-perception, however, goes the parallel perception of body forms, voices, and so on, in the environing world. Mother's voice has something in common with the child's own voice, and one is assimilated to the other; that is, transferred conditioned perceptual responses (page 355) are made from one to the other. Mother's form is seen much more clearly than one's own, because it is more completely contained within the visual field. There is, moreover, some reason to believe that early self-images are based in considerable measure upon the mother image, partly because of the huge role which this image plays in the infant's experience, and partly because it includes a face which is lacking from the child's view of his own image until he has seen it in the mirror and integrated it with the rest of his body. Mother's outline serves as an anchorage point for the slowly accumulating self-pattern. Other people contribute in accordance with the frequency and importance of their appearance to the child. The sound of his own voice is doubtless assimilated to the mother's and to that of other persons in some degree; but the kinesthetic factors and vocalizations, together with the tactual experience from mouth, lips, and tongue, presumably give vocalization a more individualized, less easily assimilated form. It is of some interest, however, that almost all accounts of the intimate experience of selfhood, whether in childhood or adulthood, feature the visual rather than the auditory. Indeed, even when the sound of the name is included, auditory materials make up a rather small portion of the materials which denote self. We have, then, a slowly forming active system that is perceived largely by analogy with the moving system that is the mother, but abetted and elaborated by other figures which, coming and going, serve as prototypes.

It may well be held that this view of the self is too "intellectualistic." On the basis of analyses of psychotic patients, Rado, for example, comes to the conclusion that the self is built up from the *primitive struggling activities* of the individual. But since we have defined the self as a thing perceived, we can use Rado's approach only so far as this struggling gives rise to *kinesthetic experiences*. This experience of struggle is indeed important. But in limiting the term self to this *object* which we slowly come to recognize, we are bound to regard the kinesthetic as a component in a total that contains many other ingredients. The action phase of selfhood will be considered in due time, and it will call for another terminology.

As a constant object of this sort is discovered, it serves as a standard in whose light other things are judged or felt, and eventually it becomes one pole in a bipolar frame of reference. In this respect it is not unlike many other constants in the field of experience which are used as standards in making judgments and as poles set up in a bipolar organization of the perceived world. There is, then, nothing in the least mysterious or even exceptional in setting up the self as *one aspect of the world perceived*. The self could not at this stage be confused with the thing doing the perceiving; this is a later quasi-philosophical way of looking at the matter.

Much of this process of perceiving is doubtless marginal from the point of view of consciousness (cf. page 349); it lies at or below threshold value. Perceptual habits in relation to the self are, like other perceptual habits, elaborately organized systems of which only a small part may be in the consciousness at all, and only a minute portion of that need be thrown into the role of figure. Expectations are built upon such percepts, so that one is shocked to find the self-picture not conforming to a standard, though he cannot say what the standard is;

in the same way, comparisons of others with the self are constantly being made, although the self-picture is largely buried in subthreshold organization.

Regarding individual variations in the early experience of the self, very little is known. We can say that variations in intelligence make for variations in the complexity of the experience involved; among imbeciles, for example, we should expect the recognition of body boundaries to be retarded. Conversely, the early acquisition of an appropriate body vocabulary seems (as in Stanley Hall's cases) to accelerate the growth of self-awareness. We owe to Horowitz some case studies of the *localization* of self in early childhood which throw considerable light on the process by which consciousness of self grows:

Joan, aged 3 years 8 months, was interviewed in the presence of her mother. Questions aimed at the discovery of the attitude of the child towards the inanimate objects about her revealed some concepts startling to the interrogator. The conversation developed somewhat as follows: "Who are you?" "*Joan.*" (The child was well known to the interviewer and the question was designed to serve as a baseline.) "Who is Joan?" "*Me.*" "Is this Joan (pointing and touching bed alongside)? Is this?" "*No.*" Touching the various objects as we proceeded, we drew such responses as: slipper-no, sweater-no, leg-no, head-no, body-yes, neck-no, etc. She seemed to localize Joan quite definitely in the abdomen and lower thorax; the back was not Joan, appendages and head were described as hers, but not her.

This experience surprised us somewhat, and four days later we were discussing it with a friend in a store when in walked a strange youngster, and we proceeded to demonstrate the phenomenon. Conversation yielded that the child's name was Lena; Lena was three years old (accuracy unchecked). Lena localized herself at first in the body. As we continued exploring, in order to check the consistency of the response, Lena appeared in her lower right jaw. She was not in the hand, arm, or leg, nor in the eye, head, nor other (left) side. Lena seemed fixed in the lower right jaw. The definiteness of this localization may be indicated by her petulant response when we touched her right cheek-bone and asked, "Is this Lena?" "*What is the matter with you? I told you three times this* (pointing to lower right jaw) *is me.*"

The following day, five days after the original exploration, a retest was made of Joan and she was found to be still in the same place, the belly and lower chest, but not in head, neck, arms, legs, nor back, nor dress, nor shoes.

Barbara, Joan's sister, at the age of two years six months, localized herself in the mouth region. The gesture indicating where Barbara is was this: hand across the mouth covering the chin and opened mouth, with the finger-tips resting on the edges of the upper incisors. A pinch on the calf of her leg hurt "my leg," but not Barbara herself.

Mona, aged four years and two months, said not "Mona" but "my leg," "my head," though she had pointed to head as "me"; later she indicated her body. After a while when asked in peek-a-boo fashion, "Where is Mona?" she tapped her head.

Doubtless the area in which the self is localized depends both on the way in which adults emphasize selfhood by touching and pointing and also upon the vital *importance* of the region from the child's point of view.

Early Canalization upon the Self

Since we have stressed that there is no perceptual whole which is not dynamically organized in terms of needs, that there is no perceived object toward which there are not directed a variety of drives serving to give the percept organization, it will be natural and easy to think of the self as a center for habitual or chronic canalization; toward the self are directed many powerful drives. By virtue of the rhythms of activity, the pleasures of tactual experience, and perhaps the esthetic satisfactions of line and color, there are early sensory satisfactions; the body image is satisfying and comes gradually to be looked upon with more and more pleasure. The primitive, undifferentiated affective life becomes focused more and more on those aspects of the world that are always safely there; frustration is never produced by their unaccountable disappearance. A prominent place in the total must, however, be given to deeper *visceral fulfillments*; these are profoundly satisfying, and to them the visual appearance of the body is *conditioned*. It is true that pain and frustration are also associated with the body image, but this gives ambivalence rather than the neutralization of opposing affects. Autistically, one maintains in the picture all that is satisfying, and self-love becomes a norm; self-love is one of the few things about which we can be reasonably sure as we compare the experiences of infancy in varying cultures.

But such canalization upon the self, and the conditioned responses which serve to enhance its value, are undergoing formation long before the self is a complete whole. Schilder's studies and the case histories of Horowitz offer some fascinating suggestions regarding the early focusing of love and pride in particular body parts. One part may be excessively loved, another excessively hated, all of one's "good qualities" being anchored in the former, one's "bad qualities" in the latter; or a single part may appear ambivalently as both good and bad.

Much of this canalization process appears to begin in very early infancy; infants may be observed to devote more and more attention to one or another body part. And such canalization may give rise to many developmental difficulties; there are snags all along the way which interfere with steady growth. In some cases stoppage or fixation is so common that we have no right to speak of a "deviation from the normal." Rather, we might attempt to classify persons in terms of the type or locus of stoppage or "snagging" which has characterized them. According to Freud and Abraham, a part of the infant's body may become the seat of such intensely satisfying and frustrating experience that experience in relation to it may serve to mold both subsequent body processes and subsequent conceptions of the self. The observations are meager and the theory overpretentious; but for all that it is a highly stimulating conception, some aspects of which have been experimentally confirmed, as we shall try to show.

Let us consider what will happen when there is interference with the infant's oral activity. Not only is the lip and mouth region important as a means of getting food into the stomach, it is also a center of direct intense satisfactions. The normal infant spends a good deal of time in mouth and lip exercise; the less time given to feeding, the more is given to these supplementary activites. David Levy separated a litter of six puppies into three groups of two each. Two nursed normally from the mother; two obtained their milk from a bottle whose rubber nipple had a very small aperture so that they had to suck a long time; two obtained it from a bottle with a large-aperture nipple so that they gulped down the contents of the bottle in a few minutes. In contrast to the other four, the last two continued to suck and bite on all sorts of things throughout the whole growth period. Because the nipple had a large aperture, they got insufficient mouth and jaw exercise in infancy; consequently they continued this activity throughout growth. Roberts has recently shown that the finger sucking of infants appears to be in inverse proportion to the total feeding time within a 24-hour cycle. The need for mouth activity must be satisfied.

Suppose now that the child who has been both adequately fed and adequately exercised in lip and mouth activity is suddenly or forcibly or painfully weaned. We should expect a sudden effort at correcting the balance by way of direct substitution in the form of lip or finger biting, or finger and thumb sucking; and a little later we should expect to find lollipops and chewing gum playing a large role. Mouth activities also become prominent, Abraham notes, in such activities as smoking, singing, and talking. If the child picks up a musical instrument we should expect him to choose, without knowing why, a mouth organ or a woodwind rather than a guitar. Even in high school and college Abraham would expect him to prefer debating to athletics, and when he comes to choose a vocation would expect him to select mouth-center activities such as preaching or teaching. The oral type is shown both in these official continuities of behavior and in an intermittent pattern of mouth-exercising activities such as drinking, chewing, and so on.

More subtle still is Abraham's derivation of a theory of behavior organized in terms of the *kind of process* which the mouth carries out. Quite aside from the utilization of the mouth, the painfully weaned child whose assimilative processes have been interfered with may become a dependent person, morbidly needing to be ministered to, trying ever afterward to recapture the blissful state of passive dependence and assimilation. The oral type is dependent because the supreme value is the dependency relationship.

One apparent corollary of Abraham's conception of body parts as related to character types (pages 745 ff.) is that the first crude self-portrait is anchored upon a schema of the self as a mouth-centered, assimilating object. Erikson, who developed this idea further, suggested that in the infant's first primitive body schematizations all processes may be regarded as "taking in" or "giving out" or "retaining"; on the basis of the child's own experience, the accent is given to one or the other. The result is Erikson's series of studies of body portrayal. As the child vaguely experiences his own contours, his own inner patterns, and in particular his avenues of contact with the outer world, he tends to express them. We have, then, in the projective play techniques an opportunity to study the form of the child's own self-delineation. The fat and the thin, the passive and the reactive, may be portrayed in the design unconsciously developed in block-building. The parallel between these efforts and the more elaborate efforts of certain professional artists is clear. A cartoon in the New Yorker shows how the fat and the angular artist put their own fatness and angularity into the subjects they paint. The individual cannot tell the story of what he sees with his eyes without at the same time telling what he feels in response to the flow of the visceral and the kinesthetic. Erikson here compares block designs with the salmon-fishing habits of the Yurok Indians of California, and shows some of the diverse ways in which life can be obsessed by such an oral-assimilative disposition. As with the American child, so with the Yurok adult, language, fantasy, and ritual constantly recapitulate the theme of "taking into the body."

ACHIEVING UNITY

We have tried to show that attitudes develop toward the parts or phases of the organism itself; the organism is a stimulus complex reported by its own receptors like other stimulus complexes. To the newborn infant the boundaries between organism and world are as unknown as are those between any two external complexes. It is hardly likely that the responses or the consciousness of the newborn or the embryo is at any time *completely* homogeneous, undifferentiated, diffuse; but it is likely that growth and experience alike tend to define patterns and to mark off objects that cling together functionally. As fast as this occurs, attitudes toward the differentiated objects can develop. The child may come to look at, enjoy, and love his own hand or foot, note and love his own voice as he does that of another. These responses are the germs of the self; they are formed, as are all other known objects, by associations of recurrent experience, and they progressively achieve a degree of unity which reflects the actual recurrence, stability, and interdependence of experiences. Since the behavior of organisms is never ideally unified, with all the components tightly integrated in response to a given situation, it is inconceivable that the self, the empirical phases of the organism's own activities, could ever achieve any such "unity" as law and moral and social intercourse would assign it. The tightness of structure varies with age, with intelligence, and with the social standardization of conduct through interdependent uniformities—"he who builds up the fire must not chastise the water for boiling." The individual has an attitude toward his own person that is comparable to his attitude toward music; it is general and also specific, varying in generality from one person to another but also varying from day to day, hour to hour, in the same person. For an empirical psychology, the ego—that is, the philosopher's homogeneous ego—is, as Nietzsche said, a grammatical illusion. The self is an empirical object more homogeneous and more stable than some others (e.g., sunset skies), less homogeneous and stable than certain others (e.g., Pike's Peak).

Some rather serious consequences follow a failure to watch the confused heterogeneity of the self-forming processes. Shrewd associationist though he is, Janet seems to need a unitary ego in the very midst of his studies of its diffuseness. Lewin, clear as crystal on the relativity of the term "organization," speaks of ego level as against aspiration level (Hoppe's terms), although the investigations of Gould and Gardner, conceived originally in such terms, find many ego levels functioning at once, in fluid and "self-contradictory" fashion. But the situation is saved for the proponents of unity by the fact that the subjects of research are in many respects and in many situations constrained to find a unity; they accept the cultural definition of selfhood, try to be consistent, strive toward external identity and inner coherence. The trend is there, though never fully realized. Language and law emphasize unity, and social privileges and responsibilities buttress the process. The organism accepts the coercion. When three-year-old Joe is called to lunch he may insist that he isn't Joe, but a rabbit; but when mother is sad that Joe has disappeared and says that since bunnies eat only bunny food, there will be no ice cream, Joe comes back. With age and greater responsibility, the individual organism is persuaded more and more to act like a unit, to phrase the multiplicity and incongruity of its wants in terms of the multiple expressions of a fixed self. Empirically, the organism's *wants*, and therefore its *attitudes*, are legion; and its awareness of these, whether vague or clear, is an awareness of a cluster of selves, spatially and temporally overlapping and fusing with one another, dropping old phases, adding new ones. The whole process is constantly guided by autistic mechanisms; some phases are accented, others half concealed. The system of interrelations, including the unified architectural wholeness itself, is in part an autistic product; for the self is after all a perceived object, and the general laws of perception, including those related to autism, apply.

What is it, then, that entertains the attitudes we have been describing? It is the tissues, specifically those involved in perceiving and valuing. Since these are necessarily properties of an incompletely organized living system, it follows that the thing that has the attitudes, i.e., the organism, has its own wild complexity and its own incomplete unity. A person's attitude toward himself would vary even if the empirical self were constant. Attitudes toward the self are complex, heterogeneous, for two reasons; the thing that is there to be seen varies somewhat with situations, and the inner tissue situations vary both locally and generally. One may wear "rose-colored glasses" while looking at the self as well as when musing on prospects for a good business year.

Since selfhood is viewed here as the result of activity, it follows that if activity is to be continuous and consistent, the self must appear more or less as a constant. The principle of homeostasis (page 32) is worth recalling here. We drew attention earlier to this property of organic systems by virtue of which each function holds the others within a certain range, so that the system as a whole is maintained. We found in motor skills and in perceptual structure a number of examples of exactly this broad principle; each component varies, but as it does so, it is involved in mutual adjustments of the remainder which prevent the first from moving beyond fixed limits. Thus the *person*, as we have used the term, is at the same time a motor skill and a perceptual structure. It is a perceptual structure so far as it is the recognized empirical self which, though its phases vary, must continue to be recognizably the same; it is a motor skill so far as acts must conduce to the presentation, the enhancement without injury, of this central picture.

Though a prominent place has been given to unity in personality, there has also been emphasis on the chronological priority of parts over wholes, and on the slow and gradual character of the orchestrating process by which one compact self is attained. There is "integration." But in accordance with the whole point of view developed on organic development (pages 62, 65), this has been found at the third, not the first level (page 66). We do not mean to beg the question whether there are, within the perceiving and valuing organism, integrative principles of which we have no empirical knowledge. Most of our knowledge of integration is recent, and we have only gone a small fraction of the way toward understanding the process. Nor do we wish to deny the possibility, suggested by James Ward, that all awareness is colored by selfhood, whether the self is empirically perceived or not. Least of all do we wish to attempt to brush aside the still unsolved philosophical question whether the process of experiencing necessitates the existence of a non-empirical experiencer, just as refraction of light logically necessitates the postulation of an invisible wave form. This mode of thinking is entertained by competent and serious thinkers. Nothing would be gained by attempting an arbitrary Gordian-knot solution of such a tangled problem. We are concerned solely with this immediate question: Should the student of personality at the present stage of research postulate a non-empirical entity distinct both from the organism and from its perceptual responses to the forms and symbols which are called self? To this limited question a negative answer seems advisable.

IDENTIFICATION

The tendency toward integrating the self-picture, for which there is plenty of evidence, is by no means automatic; the satisfactions from the possibility of dealing with functional unity must outweigh the gain from the piecemeal approach to the component parts. The habit of piecemeal perception may be prolonged when identification with a parent is made in terms of a particular body part, such as the hand or mouth, while one's other body parts are assimilated to no external standard—"I have black eyes like my daddy." We might therefore suppose that in some children the earliest materials for selfhood consist of two rather similar mouths, four rather similar hands, two rather dissimilar voices, and so on. There are a great many factors that drive toward identification; and among them identification with the parents is especially important. The process of *identification* can be understood only if the primacy and the functional independence of these early component experiences are clear. If we were willing to concede the little child a working conception of the whole self before he begins to assimilate this self-picture to the picture of other persons, the process of identification would be a secondary elaboration of the sense of selfhood, not a primary experience. If, however, a partial assimilation of the self to others is under way, and if at the same time affectively charged responses are made jointly to parts of oneself and to parts of another person, the identification process becomes a focal point in terms of which the later development of the self-picture and of selflove must be understood. The child becomes, in rather large measure, his mother, and his mother becomes himself; or, to put it more broadly, selfhood is interwoven with experiencing other individuals. As fast and as deeply as father, brother, sister make their impression upon the child, they become parts of him, too. This dependence of self upon the perception of others is a primary clue to the social nature of man and to his utter incapacity for any complete autonomy of either perception or action.

A half century ago, W. K. Clifford undertook to explain the elementary sociality of man in terms of his capacity to glimpse the thoughts of others by analogy with his own, and to attribute to others a recognition of his own thought. Man reacts not only to the behavior of others but to their thoughts, and in particular to their thoughts regarding himself. M. F. Washburn showed more recently that social psychology can be systematically viewed as a study of such "ejective consciousness." The problem is doubtless more complex than is at first evident, but the main lines of interpretation seem to follow directly from the theory of self-development already sketched. It is not that the child first develops a picture of himself that is rounded out and finished in detail, and then proceeds by fiat to create other selves to people his world, but rather that he has been engaged continuously in a process of transfer, back and forth, between self-perception and the perception of others. The mechanisms of participation (as described by Piaget) have enabled him to find selfhood in the behavior of others, and to build a rather clear picture of their states of mind by analogy with his own. The study of the kinds of people with whom he does and does not sympathize shows, as we have already seen, how limited he is in the capacity to supply a background for adult conduct. In general, the stages in the capacity for ejective consciousness are stages in the capacity both to differentiate between self and others and to note where resemblances actually lie between one's own motivation and that of others.

Thus far, then, we have self-portraiture and along with it, as we have seen, increasingly definite self-love. This primary process of self-love, which Freud called narcissism (from the story of Narcissus, who fell in love with his own image reflected in a pool), is accompanied by a number of other responses to the self, doubtless including wonder, bewilderment, disapproval, and even fear, as the image changes unexpectedly. The attitude toward the self becomes a complex of dispositions. Usually, however, satisfaction, or in some cases passionate love, is the dominant feature of the response. This love of self and the accompanying love of a parent may be regarded as the core of the problem of personality adjustment, for the beloved parent inevitably interferes with and balks one's own efforts at self-fulfillment. But in the long run, and in most individuals, affection gains ascendancy over the counterbalancing aspects.

The result is not only integration of selfhood and the beginning of elementary social adjustment, but the foundation of most of what is social in man. The earliest forms of sympathy, for example, which, as we saw earlier (page 221) depend on analogies between oneself and another, grow rapidly as one experiences more and more situations through which he sees others pass, being thereby permitted to share their experience by virtue of an analogy with his own. At this earliest phase, sympathy is indiscriminate; adults, children, pets, toys, firewood, receive sympathy, at least in our culture, in so far as they confront situations which are distressing to the child himself. The differentiation processes described earlier in connection with conditioning are effected slowly as perception marks off other objects more and more clearly. The individual has more sympathy for that which resembles himself—more for persons than monkeys, more for monkeys than spiders. This principle is complicated greatly by the growth of personal values which by no means respect the supremacy of man over beast. Thus a child may sympathize more with things that are little like himself—kittens, puppies, mice—than with big things such as grownups. Passionate sympathy for the rabbit that slips on the ice or for the toy duck that breaks its foot goes hand in hand with increasing indifference to people or animals that are recognized as parts of another world with which one has no commerce.

These are some of the mechanisms which James had in mind in his discussion of the "expansion of the self," the gradual inclusion of more and more persons, things, and even abstractions as parts of a going concern to which one is devoted. The self can become a conglomeration or an organized perceptual whole which contains many ingredients that have nothing to do with the body; both the process of confusing one's self-picture with the pictures of others and the process of primitive sympathy play a large role in this expansion. One literally does not know where the self stops.

There is no sharp line of cleavage between "sympathy" and

"empathy"; the latter term is usually applied to *putting oneself in the place* of either a living or a non-living thing. Exactly as an individual puts himself in another's place, assumes his spatial position and its appurtenances, glows with his pride, suffers in his embarrassment, so he puts himself in the place of the pillar that is too slender to support the shaft, and he judges it inappropriate; he is pulled awry by the Picasso painting which tilts the house upon its foundation. His muscles tighten as he watches the tug of war; his larynx tires and his heels rise as the soprano strains upward; even the battle of the elements can be fatiguing. It is satisfying to the little man to put himself in the shoes of the great as he listens to the dictator's speech and moves with his movements, and in the same way it is satisfying to the climber to melt into the vast ruggedness of the peak which he ascends. Empathy here is of a broadly sensory sort; the individual needs nothing more.

But such identifications entail their own frustrations. One watches the satisfaction of the diner at the next table while he himself is tediously pondering the reasons for his waiter's delay. The intense anticipatory responses which this induces belong to that class of autisms which is frustrating (page 376), for the difference between fully canalized *sensory* needs and the anticipatory phase of the *visceral* needs must be stressed. Though the roast smells good, it is irritating for the hungry man to smell it if he knows it will be another hour before it is ready. When a competitor wins the coveted loving cup, the sight of it becomes an annoyance to the loser; he longingly puts himself in the winner's place, half tastes the sweetness of success, and, in itching perception of the reality, hates him for it. It is because the individual puts himself in the other's place that the return to his own place is bitter.

Identification, however, is seldom a passive process which involves merely the disposition to view oneself as one with another person; it normally involves the enacting of the other person's role. The child dresses up to *play* pirate, not just to *be* pirate; he wants daddy's hat and cane not merely to look like daddy, but to aid in immersing himself in the daddy round of activities. It is likely, indeed, that the psychology of clothing has too often been conceived in terms of a simple narcissistic delight in one's appearance; clothing is largely a means of making real the role that is to be played in life. Flowing gowns make the role of gracious hostess easier, partly through the kinesthetic smoothing of activity, partly through the sheer associations given in social convention. Corduroy pants make the girl who is ready for hiking or boating a rougher and readier participant in the activity, more likely to tussle with her masculine counterpart—"it's natural to fight when you're wearing the pants."

This utilization of clothing in the enactment of roles that begins in later infancy remains a life long preoccupation. Especially interesting is the donning of the garb of the opposite sex—transvestitism. In the English horsewoman's need for masculine attire, not only where it serves the ease of riding but even where it hinders it, there is acceptance of the fact that the postures assumed by a rider are inconsistent with those assumed by a gracious lady; so, instead of becoming an ungracious lady, she simply becomes a pseudo-man, even to the point of wearing a derby hat. In the Naven ceremonies of the Iatmul of New Guinea (page 789), the women can glory in the achievements of a little child by arraying themselves in masculine garb; having no normal means of self-display—this pattern is entirely alien to the feminine ethos of the group—they can be triumphant only if they are pseudo-men. In these ceremonies the men, who fear the sentimental role of triumphing in the feeble achievements of a little child, can adjust themselves only by clowning; they put on the dirtiest and meanest female attire they can find and make themselves into ridiculous hags at which the village can laugh. To be laughed at in one's own capacity as a man would be unendurable; but to be laughed at in one's role as a woman is an escape, and rather a pleasant one, from an activity as unmasculine as making a fuss about a child. In the case of both sexes, then, the identifications are actively assumed for a definite purpose, and the raiment of the other sex is an organic feature of the process.

PROJECTION

From this indeterminateness of the boundaries of the self, especially in infancy but to some degree throughout life, follows the process of

[495]

projection by virtue of which experiences arising from one's own sensory processes are felt to belong to others, the motives of others are judged by analogy with one's own, and the world is peopled with individuals essentially like oneself. It is not quite enough to say that others are responded to by means of transferred conditioning, for there is a rather complex self-picture which must be understood if we are to know what is to be transferred. Nor is Piaget's conception of participation (page 340) adequate, because there is definitely an attribution to others of characteristics which are sensed within one-self. This latter process would not follow from Piaget's egocentrism; indeed, it would entail some awareness of self, some awareness of others, and an analogy between the two, and would hence belong to a later phase than the egocentric, as Piaget conceives it. (Freud's use of the term projection is discussed on page 546).

Parallel to and simultaneous with projection in this sense comes introjection: the process of experiencing within oneself what actually belongs to other perceived persons or objects. The tired soul finds the slow-moving stream restful, the turbulent torrent upsetting. The mountains are "uplifting" and sustaining in their steadfastness—"I will lift up mine eyes unto the hills, from whence cometh my help." The coward is strong in the leader's courage; the Maori warrior is great when his chief is honored. Unemployed youth in the Germany of 1933, who were nothing in the eyes of the community, could attach themselves to the Führer, serve as proud members of his "bodyguard," identify with him, feel a transfusion of his power. In this way the child, imitating his parents, takes over some of the heroic attributes which he believes belong to the adult, and obtains the assurance, the sense of power, that such a simulation permits; he is pushed forward toward maturity. From this follows the habit of looking through his parents' eyes; and this in turn leads by insensible gradations to a point of view in which he sees and judges as the parents are conceived to see and judge. We shall return to this point in the next chapter (page 515).

But the social environment plays still other roles in the building of the child's selfhood. We discussed earlier the perception of and canalization upon parts of the self, sometimes accompanied by the development of a dislike for other parts. But by the third year, as a rule, the self-picture is fairly well integrated, and this process of looking at the self through others' eyes does much to accelerate self-unification. By this process, the child may begin to anchor his perception of self in a fashion that depends less on his own direct experience than on the way in which adults see him. The first self-picture may be unlovely. If the parent and the neighborhood reinforce the caricature, it may be impossible for him ever to get out of his original perceptual habit. Similarly, if the child begins with a completely favorable self-picture and is then pushed brusquely into the competitive world of nursery school or back-alley play group, his attention may be forcibly drawn to his weaknesses, stupidities, and general inadequacies, and he may experience such shock in the process that he is unable to find his way back to the original satisfying picture. The process of shock makes self-enhancing autism impossible (cf. page 381). Since unlovely self-pictures lead to unlovely views of others because of transferred conditioned response, embitterment and cynicism are easily produced. In contrast to the belief, held by the Calvinists, that self-depreciation is compatible with the love of God, it has become evident that it is largely through a primary lovable picture of the self that loveliness can be discovered either in others or, indeed, in God. But not all of this process is completed in the period of infancy, for much of it depends upon the use of words. Selfhood depends in some measure upon the demarcation, by means of words, of what belongs to the individual. The pronouns do a good deal to define appropriate masculine and feminine traits and to show one's own relation to them. Proper names have their overtones and convey their own sense of richness and poorness, beauty and ugliness. The names and adjectives that are applied to the individual serve constantly to modify and rebuild the self-portrait. The process is continuous throughout life, but it shows diminishing returns as the picture becomes well established.

While the process of identification is beginning to form both the self-portrait and the attitude toward the self, it is also guiding the perception of the outer world in relation to the self. Since the child confronts many new affect-laden situations in the company of his parents, and since his own response to the new is so often tentative and ambivalent, the parents have a prominent part in determining how each situation is to be sensed and felt. It has, as a rule, many facets; it has some appealing aspects, some disturbing ones. But what is to be dominant, what is to serve as an anchorage point in the whole, is controlled in some degree by parental emphasis.

This is, however, only the first phase in the process of sharing the parental outlook. As the child's own self becomes distinct, identification with the parents occurs in a fuller sense than that described on page 491. Perceiving himself and his role rather clearly, he puts himself in the place of his father or mother, or both. What has at first been accepted uncritically as good or bad, reasonable or absurd, is now "autonomously" accepted. This is easy, partly because the affective bond and sheer proximity make identification with the parents feasible, partly because father and mother know about these things. Suppose the question comes up: "Is it right for a hungry boy to snitch an apple from a fruit peddler's cart?" The affective loading, the way in which the situation is perceived or conceived, is indicated by the parents; but more than this, the parental say-so provides most of the cognitive loading also, because *it is the role of the parents to know what is right.* For the little child, right and wrong are objective things like windows and wheelbarrows. How can the omnipotent parent who knows how to mend one's bicycle, how to drive a car through traffic, how to provide food, toys, and shelter, fail to know a simple thing like the right way to vote, to pronounce a word or to handle a relationship between nations (Piaget's *moral realism*)?

Whatever the self is, it becomes a center, an anchorage point, a standard of comparison, an ultimate real. Inevitably it takes its place as a supreme value. To those few for whom it does not, apathy and self-destruction offer ready invitations. To most men in most societies, the self may be full of blemishes, of sin, of incompetence, but it is the one beloved self, the lawgiver. In a fundamental sense, the self is right. My nation is right, my class is right, my family is right, and I am right. The altercation that follows an automobile collision and the account the driver gives later to his friends are hardly the primitive "rage" that Watson traces to obstructed movements. They are portraits of the artist as the right kind of person; he has been insulted by the carelessness or incompetence of another driver who did not see what the traffic situation really was. The first postulate is that I saw the situation as it was; the accident was due to the fact that the other driver did not see it as I did.

This fundamental self-rightness stems as much from narcissism as from Piaget's egocentrism, as much from the axis of reference given in the value system as from the perceptual difficulties in achieving objectivity. In other words, the central polarity of the self and the world is a means of ordering events and persons in terms of their affective acceptability. The G.I.'s are not only against the "Krauts"; they say flatly that they don't like the "frogs" either. Within their own group, the G.I. infantryman is frankly suspicious of the artillery, and the 80th Division is inclined to look down on the 81st. Within his own regiment, his own company is the in-group, another regiment the out-group; and if the truth be known, my own buddies are good guys, but those in Company B will steal your chow.

But the self is not only an aspect of all experience and a standard for all experience; it contributes to the *quality and form of all experience*. Each person, each thing, each idea is in some degree my own, in some degree external to me; and by virtue of that subtle process of interpenetration which characterizes all associations, each person, thing, or idea becomes touched with the brush of my own selfhood. I will follow the familiar, then, not only by canalization upon it, but because my feeling is already thrown about it; a view I have casually entertained may become one I am ready to fight for if, through repetition and closeness of association, it becomes intimately my own.

A reasonable objection may be offered to the thesis as it has been presented up to this point. It may be urged that it is never really the organism as a whole, but always some group of specific motor, glandular, or neural responses that is involved whenever the self is perceived or adjustment is made to it. Although this objection is sound, it can, perhaps, be met if the thesis is developed as follows: A large proportion of the individual's perceptual and motor activities are concerned rather directly with his own body. Most of the perceptual responses to interoceptive and proprioceptive situations have to do with the body; so far as they are referred to space at all, they must normally be referred to the region within the skin. Of the exteroceptive functions, moreover, a large proportion have to do with seeing and hearing *oneself*. A person cannot open his eyes without supplying the object viewed with a fringe of face, chest, hands, and arms; he cannot speak about the most impersonal thing without hearing his voice, both through the outer air and through inner bone conduction. The self is always context, even when it is not figure. As he adjusts the eyes to see or turns the head to hear, the proprioceptors serve to make the activity a self-activity. By means of experimental and clinical data, Schilder has shown the system of associations which connect these self-images with the unconscious or half-conscious schema of the physical self, the "postural model of the body."

In connection with the motor responses and their relation to selfhood, Holt has demonstrated that a large proportion of these responses consist not simply in responding locally to an outside object but in immersing the body more and more richly in the field of stimulation (cf. page 167). Each such activity is drawn into the field of self-relationships. Another large group of motor activities consists in adjusting one hand to the other in a bi-manual task, or one leg to the other in locomotion, or the various parts of the body to a single hand in executing a delicate task. To carry this still further, no matter how quickly one shifts his focus in reference to each new external event, the activity stream is ordered in terms of the expected or desired outcome of each activity for the self. One sits as spectator at the races, but one's own horse or crew is ahead or behind. There are indeed *moments* of utter indifference, as when a person watches the clouds drift, and there may even be genuine attitudes of indifference to the self. But the primary concern of life in all cultures that permit any competitiveness whatever is with the self. Even in "unselfishness" the usual self is redefined to include others. The process of identification with parents, with brothers and sisters, with playmates, friends, heroes, pets, toys, and everything that has personal value may go so far that the child's body is but a fragment of the whole. In this "expansion of the self," as James called it (page 493), there is no paradox; it is the sacrifice of the little for the sake of the much.

But is there not selflessness in another kind of situation, the contemplation of beauty? It is true that in maintaining "esthetic distance" there is a delightful sensing and motor response to the composition, quite aside from any practical concern with the objects represented. One enjoys looking at the apple in a still life but does not think of eating it; the muscles respond to the balance of the composition, but the mouth does not water. This may, not unreasonably, be urged as an instance of selflessness, and it is likely that such experiences melt into the class of experiences of detachment which we mentioned above (page 406). As a rule, however, when we respond to beauty we avidly explore the picture or move with the music; for the lover of beauty this is surely an experience in the first-person singular, with abundant reference to the self.

A large proportion of the perceptual experiences which refer to the self are, of course, only dimly conscious, just as a large proportion of the motor responses which serve the needs of the organism are executed almost automatically. Consciousness of self sweeps downward from the bright light of direct self-portraiture into activities upon which there can be no introspective report. The physiologist, however, finds no sharp breaks in the process. There are plenty of sensorimotor adjustments of which we are unaware, and there is no reason why those which refer to the body should necessarily be conscious in any greater degree than are others. The identification of the self with clear consciousness, though favored by the philosophic tradition, is no more warranted than the identification of any other observed object with clear consciousness. The self is a perceived object; when not clearly perceived, it can still be dimly perceived. And when not even dimly perceived, a set may be maintained toward it, a readiness or disposition to respond to it as to anything else which lies near at hand and to which adjustment must be made. In all perception there are elements which in themselves are unnoticed, yet make up vital parts of the total. In the same way, the self may be an unnoticed part of the continuing life picture.

Thus the more closely we look at the matter, the more probable it appears that most human adjustments are in some degree adjustments not to an external situation alone, but to a perceptual whole of which the self is a part, a self-in-situation field. This does not mean that most people are necessarily "thinking about themselves" most of the time. The amount of preoccupation with the self involves a very different question; the enormous individual differences in this regard will be considered later. We wish only to emphasize that the self is not merely one isolated chapter in a psychological book, but a phase of all or nearly all psychological events.

Our thesis is, then, that perceptual activities and motor activities are at first utterly selfless; that as one perceptual object, the body, becomes defined, other objects are related to it as context; and, similarly, that motor responses which are at first rather independent activities becomes activities oriented to or serving the self. Unconscious dispositions maintain the self-reference of our activities, and these dispositions have become associated with selfhood through a nexus of associative processes similar to those in operation elsewhere.

The thing that responds to the self is thus the organism as a whole, but some parts are more involved than others. Such a large array of perceptual and motor dispositions are drawn into closer and closer association with the self-pattern that it is hard to say just what parts of the organism do not participate significantly in the process; yet for most purposes, the pattern of response to the self is smaller and more compact than the organic response system as a whole. The response to the self may at times include almost anything in the organism's repertory; but some parts, concerned with self-enhancement and self-defense, are almost constantly at work. To these parts the next three chapters will be devoted.

After all, this situation as regards response to the self is similar to the general situation regarding all perception. We are driving in traffic, following the car of a friend who has asked us to lunch; come what may, we must keep oriented with respect to his car. Our field of vision may comprise a thousand other objects constituting immediate or potential signals for adjustment which might seem likely to overwhelm the image of his car; and they might do so, were the *set* not there to keep us in contact. We perceive the car most of the time, and when we do not we are oriented to it, ready to catch sight of it as a fender or a license plate permits. The perceptual object is small and clear, the responses to it are infinitely varied, and it controls conduct, even when it is not perceived. So it is with the self.

The general theory of self-development presented here is derived partly from scattered observations of infants, partly from the memories of adults, and partly from a backward extrapolation from the stages which can be seen rather clearly in the nursery school. These nursery-school observations are consistent in showing an anchorage of the picture of the self upon some part of the body, some attribute, or some point of special affinity between child and parent. At the same time, the self is rather unstable and, as Freudian theory requires, rather easily weakened in the face of rage and panic situations. Many a temper tantrum sweeps away a clear picture of the self, and an appeal to self-interest would be fruitless. At the same time, all the real essentials in the architecture of the self seem to be well separated by the end of infancy, roughly by the time the child is two years old.

21. The Evolution of the Self

WE HAVE not meant to imply that infancy determines the entire structure of later selfhood, but we have meant to suggest that, for the reasons defined by Schilder, self-demarcation and self-love are laid down in their essential forms in infancy and that, for the most part, subsequent elaborations follow the architectural designs that are established early. The perception of the *parts* and of their interrelations, the total going concern of the self, and the system of affects directed both to the parts and to the whole, seem to be clear when youngsters enter nursery school, broadly by two years of age. However, a series of changes occurs in the next few years; some of them appear in most children, but others are more individualized. It will be appropriate, then, to continue the genetic approach and to look briefly at some characteristic *changes in selfhood* as the individual plays his successive parts on life's stage.

Although it is commonly recognized that in our competitive society the individual's effort to achieve a distinct self is constantly stimulated by a general pressure to "make a name for himself," to "be somebody," and the like, it is not always clearly realized that *specific* details of child care contribute to the same pressure. Especially in "small" families the mother's achievement in producing a baby is thought about so long and so intensely, with such enormous emphasis upon problems and difficulties, that its completion is regarded as little short of a miracle; and every step in the baby's growth—beginning to smile, to sit up, to stand, to walk, to talk—is greeted with great excitement. Whatever mistakes are made in "training," feeding, and love-giving, these aspects of motor stimulation are almost universal. The baby is made to feel important; his achievements are exciting; he is stimulated to grow and to attempt new achievements. Constant comparing and bragging about their babies is the rule among adults who would never think of bragging so openly of their own achievements. The child's self-awareness is further stimulated by frequent comments on "looks," "handsome eyes," "perfect build," "lovely hair," "good complexion," or whatever the particular feature of the child concerned. Not uncommonly, as with Margaret in Ruth Suckow's *The Folks*, awareness that he does not fit the approved family pattern of "fair" complexion may make the child feel an outsider and lead to a withdrawal which may underlie prolonged maladjustment; this is the reverse side of the same coin.

In our culture the dynamic aspect of the self, in the sense of the motive structure that aids its development, seems to move, during infancy and early childhood, from body awareness to two other concerns, prestige and power. Experiments on competition in three- and four-year-olds have indicated the important and constantly increasing role of the effort toward applause. A large part of the quest for possessions, as contrasted with the search for immediate satisfactions, is rooted in the need to display the broadening selfhood which property brings; and a large part of the "naughtiness" pattern—interference in other children's play, the snatching of their toys, and "willful" or negativistic resistance to adult control—is a pattern of power-seeking. We might argue that the power motives gain ascendancy at the expense of prestige motivation or, perhaps more accurately, that the passive self-love which belongs to the cult of the pretty or "cute" child yields to the actively sought satisfactions from those types of prestige which power alone can bring. This is particularly true because one's contemporaries, when one is four, are much more concerned with prestige derived from power than with prestige derived from appearance. It makes little difference who is cute, but it makes a great deal of difference who can dominate the play situation.

Along with the power-self, or the development of self-assertive motives, goes the use of labels and epithets; in particular, the development of a terminology of trait names or similar abstractions—strong, naughty, smart, silly. Children are forever classifying one another by the use of good and bad names, applying to one another the nouns and adjectives which they have heard used in such a tone as to make them appropriate for praising or damning. The vocabulary of the self becomes, so to speak, less and less *visual*, and in general less and less *sensory*. It becomes more and more a language of traits. Most of the trait names that are used represent general action tendencies; and as soon as they are applied to oneself, or as soon as one finds himself applying them to others, they stimulate a trait psychology in their user. Consequently, over and above the generalities of behavior which are already there, generalities are evoked by means of labels, and behavior is made to generalize as would any conditioned response; the child lives up to the terms employed. This follows from the principles of suggestion and of transfer developed above (pages 217 ff.); and child psychiatry has empirically confirmed the fact that the appellations which become part of the self work more and more to induce behavior appropriate to them. The child forms general ideas of himself. *In short, the self becomes less and less a pure perceptual object, and more and more a conceptual trait system.*

In the elementary school the tendencies just mentioned continue and are augmented, particularly by the removal of immediate watchfulness (and domination) on the part of the parent or parent substitute. The child's presence in a group of thirty or forty children involves both some possibility of screening himself from too penetrating observation and a rapidly increasing sense of responsibility. The parents, moreover, are yielding in some degree to teachers and other adults as lawgivers; and the physical resemblance of children and parents as a basis for identification becomes less and less important, while *attributes* praiseworthy in the eyes of adults draw nearer to the center of attention. Being held responsible, as when one is a monitor or is singled out for special praise or condemnation, gives the self more and more the role of a good or bad entity, its goodness or badness being determined by its acts. Proneness to particular behaviors, such as habitual kindness or social finesse or stubbornness or lateness is recognized *as one's very own*, and in due time becomes a prominent feature of the self. The increasing sense of responsibility and autonomy does not, however, mean that the norms can be autonomously determined. With the decline of egocentrism and the increasing understanding of the points of view of others, the child identifies more fully with them. He has the feeling that the self "deserves," or is logically and rightly involved in, the patterns of approval and disapproval which at first often seemed arbitrary and magical.

To the elementary-school period must also be assigned the enormously important role played by remote standards in the form of national or religious leaders who are conceived to be like the father or the neighborhood hero, but "more so." These national heroes and their like are presented in terms of a trait psychology. The George Washington who cannot tell a lie and the honest rail-spitter Abe Lincoln are fair samples of the general western European folklore, in which national character is stereotyped in the child in large part through the inculcation of traits considered commendable. The studies of Hartshorne and May make clear how devastating a job has been done on American children by the fifth and sixth grades in the sense that many of the trait stereotypes of this sort, such as "honesty," have not been made fully clear and organically related to the child's life. Yet lip service to them constitutes a large part of moral education, and deviation from them provides a center for an inferiority feeling or self-disvaluation that operates through the adolescent period to intensify the sense of guilt arising from primary behavior deviations. We might say that the self-picture has become a vague blob of rather uncertain texture—the child is still trying to find out who he is—with such bright and shining secondary trait attributes as ideals and good qualities lying around the center, some undesirable traits further out in the periphery, and a sense of unreality pervading the whole. In his heart, the individual knows full well that this official self-picture upon which the grown-up world relies, and which he must pretend to accept, is quite different from the complicated individuality which he would see were his eyes allowed to open all the way.

Adolescent and Adult Selves

Body awareness, which during the preadolescent years has been pushed somewhat to one side in favor of an awareness of one's *status* and *traits*, surges back into prominence at puberty. One feels different inside—warm and good, but still different. The tide of new impulsions may be disconcerting. Often one's energies overflow their banks, and rapid and imperfectly balanced growth results in awkwardness. The new interest in members of the other sex may be exciting and exhilarating but it involves new competitive strains, for one must achieve status in their eyes. As the California Adolescence Study makes clear, even those who earlier have won high status with their own sex group may be the most inept in their efforts at conquering this strange new territory. One must consolidate a *new self*—both a new bodily self and a new social self. On the basis of Margaret Mead's studies of Samoa and Elmer Clark's study of the religious experiences of our own adolescents, we seem on safe ground in concluding that the transition may be relatively easy if society makes the way smooth. But because it is the last great physical and social change before maturity, it is of the utmost importance in consolidating the adult self-picture.

Many of these adolescent changes have to do with ill-defined though often intense visceral experience for which no vocabulary is ever acquired—a factor related, of course, to our system of taboos and serving to give a sense of "the unknown which terrifies" whenever marked deviations from the familiar occur. The rapidity and intensity of such changes may in some cases upset the equilibrium so seriously as to make one feel that he is no longer the same person; he is lonely for his old self. But even in the mildest cases, where the change does not penetrate the center of awareness, it constitutes a security threat. This is undoubtedly a factor in the "negative phase" of puberty, the loneliness, moodiness, and intractability studied by Bühler and Sender.

Much of the *social* transformation in early adolescence is also hard to verbalize. The adolescent is not sure *what* his status with the all-important opposite sex will be, or how the new roles will transform his old familiar roles with his own sex group. He has not yet learned how to *see* himself. Altogether, the adolescent has a problem which ranges from the disquieting to the threatening, until a new figure-ground pattern of the self is defined and verbal symbols are acquired for the more communicable aspects of the experience. The anchorage of the self upon a part of the body still holds for many in late adolescence and early adulthood, according to Horowitz' findings. His studies of self-localization in childhood (page 483) led to case studies of two young adults, one of whom centered his self-localization in the right hand, the other in the nose.

On the basis of such findings, Horowitz prepared a questionnaire on self-localization for use with a student group. The question read: "If you *had* to locate yourself at some point either within or external to your body proper, some one point that 'is you,' where would that point (or area) be?" Thirty-two of 45 male subjects gave a positive response, 13 named 3 choices (as requested); 8 named 2; 5 named 1; and 6 gave answers not readily classifiable.

FREQUENCY TABLE FOR THE DISTRIBUTION OF SELF-LOCALIZATION

Head	9	Hair on head	1
Brain	6	Throat	1
Brain back of eyes	1	Heart	6
Back of eyes	1	Chest	3
Eyes	6	Lungs	1
Between eyes	1	Shoulders	2
Above eyes	1	Hands	4
Glasses	1	Fingers	1
Face	4	Genitals	3
Profile	1	Abdominal and	
Forehead	1	genital region	1
Nose	1	Body (form)	1
Mouth	1	Body as a whole	1
Teeth	1		

UNCLASSIFIED RESPONSES

Subject No. 2. Some point intermediate between the brain and the genitals.

    4. Don't think of myself as an area but as a feeling.

  14. An invisible vantage point from which all the world could be seen; a bird.

  16. Surrounded by a group of people; making a speech; power behind the throne.

  19. Very near to my body; farther away.

  34. At my whole person; my home; my associates.

Self-localization is, however, only a phase of selfhood; the self may be pegged, so to speak, at one spot, and yet be only superficially definable through its localization. As values grow, the self-portrait becomes more and more clearly tied to them; the self is the kind of thing that pursues these values. It cannot be studied with any degree of depth unless its relation to the value system is made clear. The student group which made the self-localizations above gave the following responses to a question that related to *activities* with which the self was identified: "general striving for social good, but not very energetically"; "swimming ability"; "the symbol is a great athlete, such as I would like very much to be"; "a desire to have power, to be president"; "a person successful in academic life, recognized as an authority in history, economics, etc., and who is a truly cultured man"; "good-natured"; "I try to be a good-natured, jovial, polite sort of person"; "I identify myself with a man dressed in white who leads the crowd"; "some symbol of good looks"; "intellectual conquest, and a desire for knowledge (not a bookworm)." But these are still just fragments, islands dotting a slowly forming representation of selfhood.

Though it is hard for the adolescent to describe what is going on, the profound inner changes and the flood of new experience and feeling that mark the onset of adolescence mean the beginning of a new self that of course retains many features from the childhood pattern, yet has many new components and shows a radical transformation of the old. Many youngsters are exalted or confused, or both, by the process; and almost all "turn inward" to some degree, in adjusting to this transformation. But almost all of them carry out at the same time a dramatic flight into social reality, the discovery of a new meaning in old companionships with those of the other sex, with often the thrill of infatuation for those who were before "just friends." The adolescent must above all make good, be accepted by the real world of his contemporaries of both sexes. He must find a new basis for the respect he receives from his own sex group, for the old forms of preadolescent prowess no longer suffice; he must make good *as an adolescent*, validate himself afresh. Again, the logical opposition of extroversion and introversion does not help because the adolescent suffers from, and glories in, a flood of *both*.

This process, forcing the relative abandonment of the familiar self and the quest for a new one, involves some departure from the system of *values* associated with the earlier self. The shift does not occur because of an adolescent loss of interest in the games which were played as a ten-year-old; rather, the new adolescent self is anchored in large measure in a system of activities characteristic of its group. One has to give up the earlier activities if he is really to be no longer a child. There is definite experimentation with new selves, and with the various activities and values which are appropriate to each self. This does not mean that the self is determined in the abstract and then applied in practice; one of the things that makes a new self good or poor for the purpose is the feasibility of attaching various types of activities to it. A serious self "goes with" debating and literary activity; a jovial self with sports or the glee club. The questions raised with reference to any new activity or value are like the following: First, do you want it for itself? Second, can it be had along with the new self-portrait you are painting? Third, if it proves to be incompatible with the self you are painting, do you want it enough to endanger the self or to run into perpetual conflict? The struggle to find a new self is well shown in the California study of a boy who had difficulty in making the adolescent transition. He remained small while the others shot up in the "adolescent spurt," and he lacked the social graces and social skills which suddenly came to be emphasized in the group. Unable to win the interest and respect of girls, and an odd little runt among the boys, he strove to make the most of his earlier resources, but now they were worth little in themselves. Finally, becoming frantic for recognition, he stole automobile parts with the idea that with the car he would own he could command attention, take the girls for rides, be somebody.

One study concerned itself largely with the type of selfhood toward which the early adolescent tends, and the kind which in our culture proves most satisfying. Boys at a summer camp were observed in terms of the *cordiality given* by each one to each of the others, and in terms of the *cordiality received*. From this study it appeared that the amount of cordiality received by each boy was a stable and accurate measure of his status in the group. The "king pin" had the highest "cordiality received," for almost every one in the status hierarchy, from top to bottom, accorded him a high degree. This position of security was attained within the first few days and was maintained with no significant variations. The *cordiality given* was a completely different matter. Secure boys gave it in copious or niggardly fashion, depending on the boy they were with; their own status was in no way affected by the amount given. On the other hand, though many boys low in the status hierarchy gave high cordiality to others, this did not guarantee the cordial response at which they aimed. The struggle to make oneself accepted seemed almost completely irrelevant to the result.

Indeed, acceptance among adolescents is apparently more likely to be related to self-sufficiency—the lack of need for approval—than to the effort to be accepted. This means, in practice, that many adolescents mistakenly resort to techniques that have proved relatively satisfactory in the family situation and in many early school situations, but whose value has begun to fade, so that in the adolescent world they are not only useless but frequently damaging to individual aspirations. The essence of the adolescent struggle for selfhood is the struggle for independence from the opinions of grownups; it is rooted in large part in the need to shake off adult controls. Adults are likely to assist unwittingly in this process, for they have neither the closeness, the authority, nor the know-how to maintain the earlier parent–child relations. When one has learned to *act* and to *feel* independently of adults, both action and feeling bespeak self-sufficiency and are appealing to other adolescents who likewise cherish and admire self-sufficiency more than they do the effort of others to please them. Thus as each one discovers that he does not need the adult world, he discovers a self-sufficient pattern which others are ready to admire. Those who strive to please their contemporaries fail in the essential part of this adolescent task. On no point is childhood technique less likely to be useful to the adolescent, and, as clinic and court make clear, on no point does the pitiful effort for recognition go astray more catastrophically.

Much of this could be summarized by saying that one of the chief aims of the young adult is status, and that his picture of himself as the recipient of a certain kind and degree of status is so clearly drawn that almost every aspect of it gives a fair clue to all the rest. This is true even if his experiences in achieving status in adulthood are mixed, involving both conquests and defeats. The individual enters adulthood with a fairly well-generalized conception of his status. Many of his status aims have been to a large degree defined during adolescence by setting up a picture of himself in which the steps he has already taken are regarded as evidence of the degree of his worth. He has a certain position in scholarship or athletics, or as a promising apprentice or a member of "the gang" or a good son or daughter. When his status is higher in one sphere of activity than in another, he anchors the self at a point that permits a rather constant degree of self-esteem, and if adulthood allows him to continue using the same anchor, failure in other respects can be borne. Thus Hyman found that young adults varied widely in the relative value they attached to intellectual, social, and other achievements, anchoring the picture of the self upon the particular type of proficiency in which they conceived themselves to be noteworthy. The young accountant in the school of business, for example, disparages many of his own attributes but manages to make efficiency and accuracy so central that by clearly perceiving himself as extremely efficient and accurate he can give himself a high over-all value.

The pattern of attributes, however, whether seen by another or by oneself, has what the Gestalt psychologists call "membership character" (page 385). The young accountant's accuracy is not quite the same as that of the young engineer, nor is efficiency in business quite the same as efficiency in constructing steam engines. The specific errors avoided by being accurate or efficient will depend upon the tasks assigned in business and in engineering. The term "accuracy" as a value is not rigidly fixed; it must be seen in the light of the value organization of the individual. As we saw earlier (page 275), value has its contextual definition. This means that when the adolescent or the young adult, replacing one system of values by another, seems to retain a few old values as a nucleus, each such value must be transformed by its membership character in the new pattern. Even athletic prowess and dancing skill, which seem to carry on from ten to fifteen and from fifteen to twenty, are transformed. Prowess and skill are different conceptions when applied to childhood, youth, and adulthood. For example, the use of excessive force, when care and skill would suffice, is a common expression of the adolescent's protest against the retention of attributes once defined as those of a child. Adolescent clumsiness is not just a question of a change in the relationships between body parts such as muscles; it may be hesitation, or even a repudiation of grace, since grace is something immature which one achieved as a child. To be pretty, to be attractive, to have charm was mildly pleasant at ten—pleasanter for the girl than for the boy, but still pleasant for both. But as one enters adolescence such qualities are tepid, lack fire, for something more than grace and charm is required. Much of this is not at a verbal level. But a boy knows well enough that to be a man is not just a matter of grace or skill; and a girl knows that something more intense and vital than the naïve grace of a child is required if she is to be popular. It is better to be awkward, as one experiments with adulthood, than to run the risk of being regarded as an overgrown child. And along with anxiety as to whether one's growing body *looks* right, there is of course also the awkwardness of sheer experimentation with new postures, strides, stances, gestures.

A common difficulty which high schools and colleges encounter appears to belong largely in the same category. There is no clear reason why English literature, in which one was adept at twelve or thirteen, should be difficult at fourteen or fifteen. There is no clear reason why the child who has made mincemeat of the more difficult work in fractions or square roots should have trouble with elementary algebra or geometry. The school and college atmosphere as defined by the young people themselves leaves no doubt as to what is important and what unimportant; the very attitude of burying oneself deep in English literature or mathematics, the very attitude of taking these things too seriously, entails the risk of falling out of line with one's contemporaries. The negativism which Bühler and Sender and others

[514]

have defined as characteristic of early adolescence is frequently this exploratory rejection of one adult interest after another, until the youngster learns how to accept it without sacrificing the adolescent self while such delicate experiments are being carried out.

The whole process is, of course, far simpler if a good, clear *identification object* is at hand. Parents serve as bases for identification during the early years, and still appear to be the chief models for children at ten to twelve years of age, though with some assistance from national and local heroes. By fourteen or fifteen this is no longer possible. Parents do not know how to be "chummy" with those whom they have always enjoyed as children, and children are literally helpless to accept their parents in a new role as big brothers or sisters. Men teachers serve as norms for the adolescent boy; and the adolescent girl's "crush" on the woman teacher is testimony of the degree to which the mother has been displaced. The utility of an identification shift lies in the fact that a whole pattern of new values, with their "membership characters" already established, can be assimilated. The boy assumes the swaggering gait of the athletic coach; the girl takes on the smile and the mannerisms of the teacher to whom she is devoted. Although process is of course overdone, it is an important scaffolding in the direction of a new structure, and is on the whole more feasible than any attempt on the part of religious or other instruction to rely entirely upon models remote from the immediate social world of the adolescent.

In later adolescence and early adulthood the value syndrome again undergoes great changes. The youngster must complete the demonstration of his independence, and with the approach of genuine economic and social self-sufficiency he must adjust to the sobering recognition of responsibility. In making this adjustment, which involves the loss of one freedom for the sake of another and the strain of making a series of more or less irrevocable decisions, the chief positive satisfaction is the self-esteem that goes with acceptance of oneself as a full-fledged autonomous member of the community. The transition is aided by three factors: first, rediscovery of and emphasis on the most satisfying components in the system of selves which have long been experimented with; second, the development of specific new forms of self-enhancement and self-defense appropriate to the more mature self, sometimes as modifications of adolescent measures, sometimes as new departures; third, the supporting influence of friends and persons admired. In consolidating this particular self, the acquisition of a husband or wife can play a huge role. Consolidation, rapidly effected during the twenties, includes a system of positive and negative conditioned responses, as well as a central system of canalizations, the whole structure being more and more tightly organized as the result of steady experience in one's new roles in family, job, and neighborhood.

The swing from relative confusion to relative stability which is characteristic of early childhood of course continues during the later adolescent period and early adulthood. Emphasis on the visceral phases of selfhood gives place more and more to emphasis on the social and the verbal, and terms related to individual status and prowess tend to dominate the self-portrait. One emphasizes one's place in the group—"It takes a *slick* man, a damn fine man, to make jolly DKE." The responses to the myriad questionnaires and rating scales given to young adults suggest that the term self can be organized largely in terms of socially defined habits, especially as they cluster together in the form of socially recognized *traits*. Furthermore, point-blank questions as to what one means by the self do not produce clearly delineated self-pictures. They result in references not to organic and kinesthetic components, but to types of competence and of adjustment in which one constantly classifies and compares himself with others from his own or other social groups. Adult selfhood is only dimly and marginally a matter of the organic and the kinesthetic. To be sure, sudden or marked disorder, such as occurs in some visceral diseases and some paralyses, may give one suddenly the sense of being someone else; but such disorienting experiences are far more likely to arise from social failure or social rebuff. They are likely to accentuate self-awareness; the whole self, like an injured member, suddenly attracts attention and its visual and other sensory phases again become prominent. Social acceptability is, however,

[516]

the chief factor that determines the degree of the awareness of self, and social evaluation (such as the status concepts) is the factor that determines whether the self will be a peripheral or salient experience. If the self approximately fulfills one's expectations, it may remain a peripheral experience; if it falls shockingly short of doing so, it may become a prominent part of the landscape.

It may be argued that we are here grossly overemphasizing the social, since *physical appearance* is a major factor in social acceptability. In most modern cultures physical appearance is far more important for women than for men. Standards of living are heavily weighted with items concerned with the maintenance of physical appearance, and feminine clothes and beauty parlors rank high in importance. But the point which is likely to be forgotten is that physical appearance is to a large degree codified with respect to social status items. There is little place for elementary esthetic appeals of the sort that may be recognized in a pretty infant. Every society has a set of rules as to how the person is to be cared for and beautified, and the adequacy of the self is measured largely with reference to the adequacy of these techniques. One's acceptability or non-acceptability—that is, his status—is defined not with reference to the raw or elementary sensory appeal but with reference to the system of social sanctions which he endeavors to meet. It may be protested that raw elementary beauty or homeliness still remains a prominent value in our culture and in most cultures. Although this is possible, it is hard to know just what to do with such a principle, in view of the fact that standards of beauty vary widely even within a rather uniform culture area, and that fads make the unappealing girl of yesterday (e.g., the outdoor girl of 1880) the belle of today. There is a "common core" of beauty in terms of symmetry and of some elementary principles of line and color; and if these are seized upon and made central in the standard of beauty, they may be codified in such a way as to make up a large part of the self-portrait in those who conspicuously possess or lack them. On the whole, however, it is likely that the looking-glass self, the self that is seen visually, fades in importance as conceptions of role and status develop, and that face, hair, finger nails, and clothing are beautified partly as a means of opening the door to a status position. Many adults, in their ceaseless efforts to create for themselves an adequate, admirable, and lovable self, resort far more to cultivating behavior devices and techniques for altering their social role than to the more elementary devices of self-beautification; and in their inner autistic worlds the molding of their social virtues may be even more violent than the molding of their pictures of their physical selves.

The psychology of clothes, already mentioned in relation to the general psychology of selfhood (page 494), calls for more direct treatment in relation to this question of status. Beautification of the self is effected largely by means of clothes. And because of the greater importance of the visual factors in feminine selfhood (because the woman is the one sought rather than the primary seeker?), feminine concern with clothing is far more subtle and elaborate than is the masculine. Even here, however, sheer beauty, as it might be considered in the esthetics laboratory, proves to have a rather limited role in comparison with the capacity to meet varying standards regarding the taste or style factor, the latter being economically so regulated that relatively few can fully meet the desired standards, the great multitude being under constant pressure to imitate the forms set by their "betters." Selfhood again becomes competitive. One attempts to look upon himself as adequate in the fulfillment of a given role; selves can be classified in accordance with their status. Clothes make the man—and especially the woman—not primarily by virtue of pure art as such, but by virtue of degrees of fulfillment of a code geared to society's general prestige code. Tailors and beauty-makers generally have been the ones who have told us most eloquently that appearance is the center of social acceptability. The fact remains that as society busily classifies its members, a marked deviation from the norm is required if the garb is to be more important than *the role it symbolizes*. Primarily, people are still classified largely by their occupational status; one must dress up to his status role, and his car, home, and club are outlying portions of the status-geared self.

Selfhood undergoes systematic changes throughout life, despite the struggle of the young to be old, and of the old to be young. The self that is achieved in the prime of life is stabilized and held on to tenaciously for years, as one fights a rear-guard action against the recognition of failing powers. Christine Morgan's studies of the aged suggest that a gradual debasement of the self is one of the central miseries of the aging process. Conversely, according to her studies and those of others, if the self can continue to receive the ordinary emoluments of social recognition, the loss of physical stamina need not take away zest in living. Here again, however, we must distinguish between the mass tendency which holds for the common run of humanity and a deviating tendency which appears in a few people. Although in most persons the loss of physical vigor involves no very dramatic changes in selfhood, there are a fair number who, in the period between forty-five and sixty, undergo such abrupt and profound physical changes as to lose their ordinary grip on their picture of the self. Either the individual ceases to experience the ordinary sensations from the viscera, or he experiences new and disturbing sensations; he no longer feels himself. In involutional melancholia the changes are sometimes so profound that the patient announces that his stomach is made of lead or that he has no heart or that there is nothing between his head and his feet, or even, in the condition called "nihilistic," that neither he nor anything else exists. The extraordinary capacity of the human animal to rebuild with the most fragmentary materials is witnessed by the fact that even these patients are usually restored to health when the crisis has passed. As in Kurt Goldstein's patients who learned to adapt at a lower or simpler level of adjustment, a new pattern of visceral and kinesthetic selfhood is established and life goes on much as before.

Loss of Selfhood

Though we have spoken of the solidification or crystallization of selfhood, it is evident that the self, like any other percept, can be dissolved. Loss of selfhood may occur in a number of ways.

First, as just noted in connection with aging, but as an expression of other conditions as well, changes in organic and kinesthetic sensations may alter the bodily matrix of selfhood so that one does not recognize himself. This may occur even though a person still recalls his name and many facts about his life—he still cannot accept his identity because things do not "feel right." These experiences of loss of selfhood may appear in febrile diseases, and in neurological conditions.

Second, selfhood may merge into one's experience of the environment in such a way as to create an undifferentiated universe of experience. This has always been a matter of special interest to mystics, some of whom have found in the infinite expansion of the self an identification with the deity, whereas others maintain equally firmly that the self disappears. Among modern mystics, who are often more careful in their language than were those of other years, this contradiction still appears, and it is doubtful whether it is purely verbal. To some individuals it is apparently essential, even as the self fades away, that the term and concept of selfhood be salvaged, whereas in others the disposition to welcome the bigness and self-sufficiency of this universal experience may entail a complete willingness to get rid of the self altogether. It may fade in panic or pain or ecstasy; the moralist may storm or the mystic glow in the liberation from selfhood that follows. The pattern of self-obliteration is cultivated as a great desideratum in Buddhism, Moslem Sufism, and some phases of Christianity. The practical problem has always been to retain the value of the individual person while demolishing his selfhood. The problem is not necessarily as hopeless as it sounds, since the person may achieve an utter loss of self-awareness.

Third, loss of adult selfhood may take the form of a reconstitution of its elements, so that one discovers a new person within him. Most conversion experiences—Tolstoy's, for example—reveal this process of self-discovery. Such remade selves often contain some features of a regression to an earlier phase. Indeed, DeSanctis has suggested that most religious conversions involving self-alterations of this type are throwbacks to periods of less differentiated selfhood. It is tempting to regard mystical experiences as cases of even more extreme regression, namely, regression to the undifferentiated state of infancy;

but this leads to fatal difficulties because mystical experiences are often reported in terms of a complete and systematic ordering of the infinite parts and attributes of the universe, and not as a blur of undifferentiated totality. It would make better sense to say that along with the greatly increased sensitivity to many aspects of the universe there is a loss of the sense of contrast or opposition between the self and the world. The content of self *is*, then, the world content; one is caught up in the joy of union with the cosmos. There is apparently no reason to believe that these experiences are especially rare. Although R. M. Bucke went to some effort to collate seventy-eight cases of "cosmic consciousness" throughout all history, there seems to be a continuum from the most spectacular mystic experiences to the momentary feelings of enlightenment and loss of selfhood which are rather common. A teacher finds himself "lost" in a sea of music, no longer sitting in his seat in Carnegie Hall; a farmer tells how his "old rusty hayrick" became a transfigured thing of beauty and he himself came close to God. Again, the experience of selfhood appears to be not a special or unique psychological problem, but the usual problem of the way in which perceptual wholes are differentiated or integrated, or, under certain conditions, differentiated over again, dissolved, or annihilated.

INDIVIDUAL FACTORS IN SELFHOOD

According to our schematization up to this point, the self may be chiefly a physical object or chiefly a system of abstractions; it may be loosely articulated or well structured; it may be supremely valued or utterly loathed. To determine what will actually appear as the self in the individual case, more specific hypotheses as to the decisive contributing factors may be formulated for validation against clinical and experimental material. To pave the way, the following hypotheses are hesitatingly offered:

1. The tendency to regard oneself as a system of traits or other abstractions rather than as a physical object is highly correlated with education.

2. The tendency to structure the self with a high degree of integration is correlated with the richness of verbal symbols and with the varieties of verbal ritual which one has established.

3. The tendency to emphasize the self, rather than to accept it casually, is correlated with the degree of respect attached by the culture to distinctive individual characteristics.

4. The tendency to value rather than disvalue the self is correlated with parental approval and with success in achieving group aims.

This last point should perhaps be formulated negatively by saying that shame and feelings of unworthiness tend to be blind carry-overs from a parentally induced sense of shame or from early reactions to failure. When a worthy self already achieved has been challenged through failure, severe self-disvaluation will be manifest only in a society that has severely censured its small children or has emphasized both self and status in the small child. It is the collapse of great expectations that hurts the self.

The verification of these hypotheses may be sought in clinical, experimental, genetic, or comparative data. Although their verification will be neither easy nor swift, these hypotheses will help in focusing the material in succeeding chapters, which will be concerned largely with the way in which the self is enhanced and defended and, in particular, with the varying forms of self-enhancement and self-defense found in widely differing human groups.

22. Enhancement and Defense
of the Self

WE HAVE stressed how deep a value is attached to selfhood in our culture. This cherished possession must forever be made more adequate, more worthy; and it must forever be defended against stain and injury, whether from the acts of others or of the valuing organism. This system of self-enhancing and self-defending tendencies we may as well call the ego. We have already used "self" for the individual person as the object of his own perception; even though the terminology here is so confused that nothing we can do will avoid all difficulties, let us use "ego" to denote the system of activities organized around the self—in particular, the struggle to do everything that can be done on behalf of this self.

Chein has vividly distinguished the self from the activity patterns oriented toward it: "We have . . . a structured set of interrelated motives centering about the awareness of self. It is now suggested that *this structure is the ego.*" This set of interrelated motives must of course be socially colored. Indeed, so social are we that in order to look happily upon the self we must be sure that others accept and approve it. The need to be accepted has been phrased by J. M. Plant in terms of the distinction between the "who" and the "what." In all societies the first categorization of the self is in terms of "who" —the family to which one belongs, with all the marks of locus and status which belong to it. One can, however, do much or little with this heritage; hence he makes or does not make a "what" out of himself. To ask *who* a man is asks a question about his origin; to ask *what* he is asks a question about his achievement. Plant shows with his clinical material that in a sense one must have a vigorous "whatness" to make up for any grave defect in "whoness." The urban child of today is no longer a "who" in the sense in which the medieval or even the frontier child was, with status in his group by virtue of his family. Today the child is a contender for status even in his own group. The elementary security that is assumed to be an inalienable heritage of American children is actually found in only a small proportion of the cases in urban centers, and the patterns established by the large cities are more and more setting the pace which is emulated by smalltown life, as in *Middletown* and *Yankee City*.

To this need for status—either that given by the family or that acquired by achievement—must be added the need for *independence* that springs from the pressures, the mechanization, the impersonality of urban life. To be dependent upon routines, schedules, laws, and authorities is to lack the inner sense of spontaneity. The need for autonomy is so great that one seeks rifts in the solid wall of constraint and tries to work his fingers into them to widen them; if this fails, he attempts to create for himself a world whose order and regimentation stem from himself. He builds a scaffolding, a tentative plan for the self, that suggests the future direction in which the self-building is to continue, and he strives to create the environment in which this larger and more adequate self may function.

This enlargement of one's personal environment is assumed in many cultures, including our own, to crowd the world in which others may live, to limit the space in which the extended selves of others may find their housing. This is so much taken for granted that the term "ego" as used in western culture is regarded as axiomatically a competitive term. Egoism is set in opposition to altruism. A person is said to have "too much ego." Or the word is modified and elaborated to give us terms of opprobrium like egoistic and egotistic. Without the slightest thought about the matter, it is assumed that sheer selfhood involves all the elaborate mechanisms of self-defense, self-extension, and opposition of the self and other. It is difficult to conceive of selfhood except in terms of a commodity obeying economic laws— the more and better selfhood a person has, the less is available for others. No one can enhance or defend himself without encroaching upon the self-enhancement and self-defense of others.

This is a very extraordinary doctrine. In view of the fact that the self is in the first instance a perceptual experience analogous to that of distant mountains, strains of music, or the coolness of the wind, it is difficult to see what there is about the experience which should crowd or limit the experience of others. Indeed, the analogy between the self and other which we used in analyzing the identification process shows the mutually supporting aspects of the selfhood of two or more persons. Selfhood begins as an experience shared and mutually reinforced. Yet in our culture, the concept of competitive self-enhancement is clear in almost all normal children by the age of three or four. Terms of scorn and show-off on the one hand, and of hurt feelings and bitterness on the other, indicate that the competitive nature of selfhood has been brought all the way home. What society has managed to do is to attach to selfhood the sense of supreme value, to canalize affection powerfully upon it, and then to limit severely the self-gratifications which are available. The individual can no longer rejoice naïvely in elementary physical or social selfhood; he must compare the self continually with a standard set up within, or with an objective standard defined by the self-gratifications available to others.

That the process is primarily one that is culturally derived, not biologically inevitable, is clear from a study of the human societies in which delight in the self remains the rule throughout the growth period, with no limitation of the self-satisfactions available to other individuals. Even within a single complex society, it has sometimes been possible to arrange the social classes so that selfhood becomes a highly competitive value at one level, but a non-competitive value at another. This of course suggests the economic determination of the competitive struggle for the right to regard oneself complacently, as Veblen once put it. But, as we shall see later (page 797), the economic order is itself in some degree an expression of the self-attitude rooted very deeply in the fundamental outlook of the culture.

The Growth of Competitive Selfhood

How early the competitive habits begin depends on the goals for which one competes, and on the process by which they are pursued. Children six months old grab for things which other children hold, and Charlotte Bühler's studies show several juvenile "despots" of less than eighteen months who succeeded in achieving domination by competitive onslaughts on the "property" of younger children. For the most part, at this period the child grabs for the object in question in about the same way whether it is in another's hands or not; hence, although a formal sociological definition of competition may be satisfied, the chief psychological problems relate to the appeal of the valued object. Again, children between two and three years of age may be called "competitive," in the sense that they brag of their achievements or try to attract attention to their own exploits. In studies by Greenberg and by Leuba no clear-cut competitive effort to surpass others was in evidence until three and a half or four years of age, but this was evidently due in some degree to the difficulty the child had in comprehending the nature of the task. It seems fair to say that patterns of coping both with desired objects and with the interference which other people offer in pursuing these objects are learned at the same time and under the same conditions, so that the process of developing a way of pursuing goals involves the development of competitive techniques. This means that maturity in goal definition and in goal-seeking techniques is usually paralleled by maturity in competitive techniques.

What interests us most, however, is not whether competitiveness is learned—for it meets all the criteria for learned behavior—but the major factors which support and abet the competitive pattern. Specifically, for what things do small children compete? We could of course brush aside the question by saying that everything will depend upon the objects available and upon the presence of others who might snatch them away before they can be enjoyed. But, to refer again to Greenberg's and Leuba's studies, it becomes clear that a great deal that looks like competition for objects is in fact competition for *status*. Leuba succeeded in separating quantitatively in older children the value of a chocolate bar and the value of having one's name written on the blackboard as winner in a contest; and Symonds and Chase demonstrated, in a somewhat similar experiment with sixth-grade students, that the knowledge of one's relative standing was the equivalent (in terms of the learning curve) of several repetitions of the entire task. In a society in which the struggle for material gain, for power, and for prestige is one indissoluble whole, it may seem absurd to ask which goal actually introduces the chief competitive element into the struggle. Yet it is possible, as L. K. Frank has done, to show that the wear and tear manifest in the neuroses is largely the wear and tear of ego or prestige motivation, just as it is possible to show, in the case of war neuroses, that the simple conflict resulting from the need to escape discipline is profoundly complicated by the fact that any means of achieving safety is a way of losing *status*.

The Commercial and Industrial Revolutions and the process of advancing the frontier have created in western man, and particularly in Americans, the conception that individualism, or even self-assertion, is an elementary form of self-expression analogous to the dominance behavior of animals. The term "individualist" has come to signify one who defies the encroachments of others, seeking to assert the legitimacy of his own way. We need not trouble with these more naïve descriptions of individualism; for the most part they are mere restatements of the doctrine of the "competitive instinct," for which we have had no use. Yet the doctrine of individualism often appears in a much more subtle and appealing form: self-assertion is conceived to be the factor that gives strenuousness and vitality to life. We are told, as in William James' essay on the "moral equivalent of war," that the flaccid quest for safety will never motivate man sufficiently to make the works of peace appealing. Life is real, life is earnest, and there is no point in living except in response to a great challenge. This has usually led to the conclusion that spiritual exercises must be found in order to keep alive, in men in a mechanized society, the opportunity for strenuous advancement of oneself at the expense of others. There must be competitive sports, contests, chances for personal glory. Just as the British authors of *Mass Observation* tell us that lotteries and pugilism are necessary to feed the aggressive self-assertion of the common run of humanity, the more idealistic educators of our own land eagerly insert into modern curricula various devices for challenging youth or putting it on its mettle, in terms of individual competition.

There is a very profound truth here, well blended with a very profound error. It is surely true that it is the nature of industrial society to make uniform, and therefore to mechanize, one aspect of life after another; and it is true, as Moreno has continually made clear, that the habit of submitting to mechanization is transferred to one phase of life after another, so that nothing short of systematic "spontaneity training" is adequate as a counterpoise. On the other hand, the inference is unfortunately drawn that the process of being eager or strenuous must *ipso facto* take the form of individual competitiveness. This is a little odd in the light of a good deal of evidence to the effect that children, adolescents, and young adults in our society may compete more vigorously as members of teams than they do alone; the highest degree of strenuousness can be called out by marshaling the group with reference to some threat or some goal that concerns them collectively. This is not to deny that competitive self-assertion is, in our society, a powerful motive; but it is necessary to insist at the same time that the sense of group identification may be still more powerful. The true place of individualistic competition can be appraised only when much more sophisticated cross-cultural studies are available, so that we can see how it fares in comparison with various types of group-centered activity.

Self-Defense

The fact that the self need not stand in a competitive relation with other selves does not, however, mean that it can remain as an absolute value, never being compared with any other good thing in life. The self as an object must be compared with other things—for example, with the objects and forces of nature, and with things that are good and bad in relation to the physical needs. Even among the non-competitive Arapesh (page 809) the sense of injury to self-love may be brought occasionally to the point where one strikes out violently with black magic against attack. But a powerful factor in the continual feeding of the competitive self-valuing tendency is the primacy of the group. In the child's early struggle to make sense out of his world by virtue of the identifications which underlie his own selfhood, the group is conceived to be supremely good both in and for itself and in comparison with "out-groups" of all sorts, both human and non-human. It is impossible to defend oneself without defending the group to which he belongs. By the same token, self-valuation is carried out according to group norms. Primitive identification involves group enhancement and group defense but is at the same time organically united with the process of individual self-enhancement and self-defense.

We saw in Chapter 20 that both perception and valuation of the self are complicated processes that take a long time to crystallize. But the result of all these developments is that, like the childhood rag doll, the self, scarred and tattered as it is, becomes a deeply treasured possession; for most of humanity, at least in competitive cultures, it is probably the central value of existence. However poor, confused, and incoherent it is, it is central, and it must be defended not only against outer attacks but against a clear perception of its unloveliness. In other words, since it may be viewed as a whole in many ways, and since its separate aspects may also be viewed and valued in many ways, a dominant self-value can and does block the functioning of other attitudes.

There are two paradoxes in this process. In the first place, since one may value the self, as he sees it autistically, much more than he actually values the whole functioning personality which an unbiased observer may see, one does things that are contrary to his best interests in order to save face; he believes things about himself that keep him from getting where he wants to go. Love is blind—and self-love in particular. In the second place, this "empirical self," as William James so euphemistically called it, must be defended against what would improve or enhance it. It is primarily the thing now seen and hugged to one's bosom, and not what it might become, that is in danger. It is therefore endangered not only by slurs from others, but by every disvaluing attitude arising from one's own tissues, especially by the disvaluing attitudes that are directly associated with the setting-up of standards for a more valuable self.

It follows that self-defense is a central concept in personality study. This is of course partly an actual defense of one's skin, but it is also partly a defense against a direct or indirect disvaluation of one's self-picture by others, and partly a defense against one's own tendencies to self-disvaluation. If this is so, we may ask what it is that does the defending. It is the value tendency directed to the empirical self; for just as any physiologically dominant pattern may conquer another, so any value tendency, being at root a physiological pattern, may conquer another, weakening or blocking its expression.

But the defense of anything, from a fort to a self, may consist both of strengthening the bastions and of weakening the enemy. Let us consider first the mechanisms by which the self is made strong against attack. Since the perception and valuation of the self are like the perception and valuation of anything else, we can learn a good deal here from studies of perception in which the self is not directly involved. When perceptual fields are likely to shift, the individual discovers devices for *stabilizing* them. In the familiar studies of "reversible perspective" we "hold" the cube or the staircase against shift by means of an attitude, a determination to do so; the attitude is controllable partly by external cues, partly by cues initiated within. Thus the wanderer on a stormy night "holds" to a landmark that threatens to become lost in the chaos; the listener to modern music "holds" to the kettledrums lest he be sunk in an angry ocean of tone. One holds to and "blacks in" the edges of the self, lest it be lost. Many a nervous sufferer finds the self-boundaries fuzzy, wonders who he is. Many fear to be hypnotized, to take ether, or even to sink slowly into a dissolving drowsiness; they "fall" asleep but cannot slide down into it. One keeps the self there at all times if he can. Perhaps other fears enter here—not only fear of losing the valued self but fear that losing the polarity of the self and other might sweep all the landmarks from an uncertain path. But if the good old self had not the supreme value of providing guidance and serving as a landmark, it is doubtful whether it, rather than any other familiar object, would be so desperately needed. We may summarize the first means of self-defense by the term *autistic self-stabilization*.

The second means of strengthening the bastions is by extending the boundaries, when necessary, to include not only the familiar empirical picture but, fused with it, valued elements which make the new totality lovelier than what went before—a process of self-idealization. This doubtless happens most actively under pressure of attack; it is no casual habit, but a means of defense. Just as junior, beaten in a fight, boasts of dad's prowess, a slighted adult recalls that he is, after all, a selectman in the county's largest town. The value tendencies which have supported the self come to support a bigger and stronger self than before. The clinics, the courts, the legislative chambers give ample expression of this simple and often adequate device.

Now turning from the fortifications defending the self to the enemies which threaten it, we find that the first expedient is to rob them of their weapons. Their opinions do not matter; they lie; they make themselves ridiculous. Like the man accused of damaging the borrowed kettle, one replies that one never borrowed the kettle, that it was damaged before it was borrowed, and that it was in good shape when returned. It makes no difference who or where the enemies are. If they are within one's own skin, the quelling of such accusations is sometimes called *rationalization;* nevertheless, the essential mechanism of the autistic disposal of possible threats to self-esteem is the same whether the threat comes from without or from within.

In the preceding chapter we emphasized the process of identification as a way of extending and unifying the self. When we turn to the mechanisms of enhancement and defense, however, we encounter complications. Any person with whom the child identifies is a *heterogeneous* thing. Father and mother, brother and sister, playmate and adult hero, display strikingly different qualities, so that the self-picture based upon identification with them becomes an intricate mosaic of varicolored components. Moreover, for the perceptive child each one of these individuals becomes a complex and rather self-contradictory composite of dispositions. "What, must I become all this?" is the attitude to be expected from a literal application of the Freudian principle. In spite of the rejection of some components, the blurring or fusing of others, and a great deal of autistic magic in organizing these components, the process of achieving selfhood involves a considerable strain. In particular, there is canalization both upon a system of contradictory components and, since the self-picture differs from hour to hour, upon somewhat different totalities. The result is strain; strain which is frequently expressed and verbalized even by the two- or three-year-old; he betrays how he feels after each failure in his struggle for a new and more adequate self. Strain is especially likely to appear in his fantasies, with the result that his exploratory self-portrait is constantly varied. The real satisfaction of one type of self involves the mangling or even extinction of the other precious selves.

This is perhaps the clue to the great usefulness Lecky found in a clinical approach to the self in terms of the doctrine of "consistency." For Lecky, personality adjustment is almost entirely a question of the slow and orderly development of a consistent self-picture, the subsequent acceptance of all that integrates well with its design, and the rejection of all that proves incompatible with it. Irreconcilable pictures constitute the basis of double personalities. In general, however, the normal self shows a good deal of integration (page 487); it is not a mere synthesis. If we cannot agree in every detail with Lecky's more universalized statement, it is because some inadequacy in the effort to create such integration seems to be the rule rather than the exception. The *urge to consistency* can indeed be accepted as a primary mechanism; but if consistency were regularly achieved, neurotic tension would be evident only in moments of forced alteration in the design, whereas clinical experience makes clear that unity is hard to achieve, and that the struggle to achieve it never subsides.

It might be worth while to describe in these same terms a major source of conflict defined by the Freudians, the boy's struggle to achieve a unity of response to his family situation. The Oedipus situation is conceived to consist first in love for the mother; second, in love for the father (so far, there is no conflict); third, in the discovery that the father is an obstacle between the self and the mother, the outcome being fear and hate for the father, a wrestling with one's fear for the punishing father until some sort of resolution can be achieved. According to Freud, the love and fear components are finally paired in opposition and crystallized in the form of a type of affection that is ready to repress the profound hate component; all this operates, for the most part, at an unconscious level.

We shall now look at this situation from the somewhat simpler point of view of the struggle to achieve an adequate self-picture. All the forces which make the self lovable, as it is already seen, are reinforced by the love for the child that is displayed by the parents themselves. When, however, they deprive him of what he wants, the result is not only frustration of his wants, but a self that is less adequate because it cannot fulfill these wants; at the same time it becomes evident that the values which parents place upon the self are not what they had seemed to be. So far as the child identifies and accepts the parental point of view, the mere fact that they deny or frustrate him makes him aware of the primitive sense of inadequacy or unloveliness. Father contributes more than mother to this total distress if mother gives more affection and father withholds it, and if father is in general the more severe disciplinary agent. The painfulness of the Oedipus situation can perhaps be accounted for partly in terms of the self-problems that are inevitably defined.

Indeed, the Freudian contributions as they relate to the mechanisms of identification and self-love would suffice to explain an important aspect of the conflict without bringing in any theory of infantile sexuality. Aggression which develops toward the restricting or frustrating parent—and it is a clinical commonplace that it is often the mother rather than the father who is the frustrator and the object of the aggression—may result from injury to the self and not from the sexuality of the child. (It is not sexuality that is in doubt, but the need for primary emphasis on sex when confronting the fact of hurt feelings.) What hurts anyone—whether boy or girl—is to be pushed aside in favor of another—jealous dogs show the same mechanisms as children. Perhaps it is later, if and as fondling by the parents begins to show consistent sex preferences on their part, that a preference for the parent of the opposite sex appears; and even here it seems likely that it is enhancement or frustration of selfhood, differently induced by the behavior of father or mother, that causes much of the strain, rather than primarily sexual aims in the children themselves.

PERSONALITY

THE STRUGGLE TO CLASSIFY ONESELF

Just as the various components of the self take on a structural form, each sharing the membership character which comes from the whole, so the self as a structure compared with other structures gradually takes on a definite membership character from the group. During the second and third years, for example, the self is defined more and more clearly in terms of the group with which identification is made. Red-haired four-year-old Margaret, arranging the miniature benches to watch the tin soldiers parade, puts a row of them up in front "for the redheads." Similarly, Clark's subjects find skin color a basis for grouping, for the establishment of membership character, long before they have even the vaguest conception of "race" or "status." And throughout this whole period there is far from a passive acceptance of one's place in the group; the child strives to classify himself in the "good" group if he can find attributes that can be played up for the purpose.

As conceptualization proceeds, the simple physical bases of membership character are replaced by conceptual bases. One belongs to a certain abstractly defined social group. But since cross classification and grouping are endless, one decides where to anchor, what aspects of the self are to be emphasized. If to be socially accepted he must have a certain type of clothing or hair, a large part of his income may be spent on the appropriate techniques. If the techniques are verbal, if he must learn to say the right things, this is well worth learning. If they are still more abstractly conceptual, consisting of thinking the thoughts that make one a member of the desired group, this, too, is worth the effort. Newcomb's student group (page 892) labored patiently for four years to articulate their social ideas to the conceptions dominant in their community, and in general moved toward the goal of achieving the point of view approved by the "Bennington atmosphere," a social approach espoused by the social science teachers and the senior students. The self finally takes on the form more or less prescribed by existing social groupings. But since success is of course relative, one tries constantly to make the best of the more favorable aspects of the grouping; one anchors to the aspects of the self that are socially approved.

We confront here a serious theoretical difficulty. A person learns to see himself in a certain integrated way despite the fact that many conflicting components push him in different directions. In Newcomb's study, for example, the girl sees herself at Bennington as a liberal, the senior being more liberal than the freshman. But when she receives a letter from her Republican father in the small town in Massachusetts or meets her boy friends during Christmas vacation, she sees herself in the earlier, more familiar terms that antedate college, and she discovers a certain kaleidoscopic quality in the process of self-perception as she sees what it takes to be a real member of each group. But in each group she retains, frequently with considerable conflict, much that she acquired in the other groups. In view of all that has been said about dominance and the elimination of weaker competing systems, why are not the weaker components eliminated here? Why, in the normal adult, do conflicting self-portraits crop up from time to time, giving him a sense of spinelessness mixed with a little guilt at his inability to maintain the rigorous inflexibility of a "mature" person? The answer seems to be that canalizations have been established not only upon mutually exclusive external goals, but upon two or more incompatible selves. Since these canalizations are not extinguishable, the unconscious tension systems which underlie them cannot be dissipated. Conflict being therefore inevitable, autism would be expected to force one of the pictures to one side. This is excessively common; like Peter, one denies the other self.

But there is a still simpler device, that of avoiding both the troublesome stimulus and the second-order stimulus which stands for it. One learns consequently to keep away not only from situations which induce an unsatisfactory or conflict-producing self-portrait, but even from those that remind him of such troublemakers. Part of the process of personality crystallization is actually the environmental narrowing which results from such steadying of oneself into a definite and narrow way of life that yields a consistent self, adequate for a given community, a given job. But one can make such a narrow environment even narrower by making sure that no forces will be allowed to operate which swing him off the specified track or cost too much in terms of secondary conflicts. In the manner of the second law of thermodynamics,[1] life shakes down from multiplicity of objectives to simplicity. The integration achieved in early adulthood on a reasonably flexible basis is more and more insistently preserved as a device for keeping trouble away. Thus a student from a conservative background, who according to each of five criteria should be moving in a strongly radical direction, said flatly that he was a reader of a great deal of radical material but that he had decided, as a matter of self-defense, to read it "as literature only."

If I want something very much, but at the same time want very much not to be revealed to myself as a person who wants such a thing, I am faced with a harsh dilemma. I may go and get the thing I want overtly or autistically, then upbraid myself, then get it again, then upbraid myself again. The "weak-willed" character does just this, alternating between incomplete satisfaction and remorse. But with better "attitudinal control" (cf. page 201), a person may, when the tension appears, vigorously maintain such attitudes toward himself as will keep the temptation in the outer fringe of awareness, or even beyond it. The tension, nevertheless, continues; it cannot be reduced by fiat. The self-attitudes are seldom so homogeneous, so "single-minded," as to do a decisive job. They are likely to wink at the tempter, ogle the seductress a bit. The main self-attitudes, those involving the fear of losing the self-esteem, are horrified, and struggle to keep the self-picture good. In this push-me pull-you game, the self-approving, narcissistic attitudes have on the whole the upper hand, but there is considerable fear of defeat, fear that unlovely impulses and consequent self-disapproval will momentarily recur. This is common in neurotic anxiety, and it persists whenever or as long as the temptation and the opposing fear of self-disapproval remain in balanced opposition.[2]

---

[1] To the effect that there is a tendency to the "degradation of energy," all forms of energy tending toward heat, and heat tending toward an even distribution through space.

[2] There are many different and usually much more complicated views of this mechanism.

SELF-ENHANCEMENT; SELF-DEFENSE

Balanced opposition is, however, often precarious. When shock leads to failure in maintaining the self-picture, the shift to chaos or to a bad picture is usually abrupt and catastrophic; we have had occasion to refer to the all-or-none tendency in evaluation (pages 226, 326). Frequently a drive functions with considerable intensity if its threshold is reached, but failing this it cannot be aroused at all. Consequently, the canalizations based upon the drive follow the same all-or-none principle. Self-evaluation is no exception. Even in a competitive society most people can go about their daily affairs without "self-consciousness"; they are concerned with outer goals, the self constituting a mere background and frame of reference. But an insult, a slight, even a non-flattering picture of oneself in a mirror or a plate-glass window, or any sudden and sharp recognition of failure, may restructure the whole outlook, so that objects that previously functioned as the figure now constitute the ground, and the self, because it is now figure, becomes a complex and structured object with some of its less adequate components serving as anchorage points. If the shock is severe enough, the shift may last for years or prove irreversible.

Negative Self-Feeling; Shame

If the theory is adequate to this point, it should provide an explanation of shame. It is commonly noted that embarrassment, in the sense of averting the eyes or the whole head or attempting to block off the face from the gaze of others, appears at eight or ten months, more or less, and that ever afterward one hesitates to allow invasion of the self by the steady gaze of another; one looks away, for the other person might see too much. Infants perceive egocentrically, believing that their thoughts can be pierced through, whereas they need rather to do the piercing themselves; they need to exercise their own omnipotence. (This general tendency even the adult retains.) The first phase in shame is, then, the mild embarrassment that involves the protection of the self-picture from scrutiny. The self-picture is carried about and consolidated until the individual feels that ordinarily it will hold up pretty well against the efforts of others to penetrate or disvalue it. Any effort of others gradually to dissect or belittle it is handled with reasonable dispatch by taking counter-measures. If, however, the blow comes *suddenly*, and he finds the structure shattered, he experiences the frustration that any frustrated canalization brings. He experiences the painfulness of any inhibited drive, and at the same time the ambivalence that comes from trying to avert the gaze from the broken object and at the same time to look at it in order to do his best to repair it. Just as the infant, when tickled, tries at the same time to get more and to get less of the stimu-lation, so the badly embarrassed adult tries at the same time to over-look the situation and to look at it as hard as he can, to stare it out of countenance and somehow remake it into a situation that can be borne. The blushing and tingling which go with this ambivalence are some-what similar to the upheavals which occur in situations which make us both laugh and cry.

We are likely, as a rule, to reserve the term "shame" for cases in which moral culpability is involved; but we sometimes apply it when other serious approval and disapproval patterns are involved, especially where the shift from approval to disapproval is sharp and catastrophic. In these situations a person wants simply to hide, as if he knew that any attempt to restructure the self-picture is hopeless. Interesting in this connection is the fact that many domestic animals—cats, for example—knowing full well that disapproval is imminent, try to escape, whereas many dogs (and, according to Margaret Mead, the pigs of the Arapesh) have had enough experience with human affection and approval to make the human response of trying to bury the self as one would a bone, just as Chihuahua dogs weep real tears. To cower with the tail between the legs might be interpreted by a ruthless follower of Descartes as sheer avoidance of punishment, though even here the behavior of the tail is rather meaningless. But the behavior which we commonly call "fawning" is clearly a bid for renewed approval in the very midst of the abject response to dis-approval. Shame, then, is a collapse in the usual mechanism of ade-quate self-portraiture, and an immobilization in helplessness, with or without an appeal for the renewal of status. From this point of view, shame, despite its catastrophic consequences—for it is indeed one of the most poisonous of human experiences—is no more "instinctive" than any of the other complex motivations built around the self.

ASPIRATION LEVEL

There are always at least two selves: a self *observed* with whatever degree of realism one can muster, and a self clearly or dimly glimpsed as *something to be realized*. The interrelations of these two selves have been studied under the term "aspiration level," as contrasted and compared with "ego level."[3] A great many studies of aspiration level have been made. In Hoppe's classical experiments, for example, subjects who had completed given tasks, such as hanging rings on the hooks of a rapidly moving belt, were asked to say how well they would do on their next attempt at the same task. Such studies throw light upon the ego organization. Thus it has been shown that some people characteristically play safe by setting an aspiration level only slightly above what they have already achieved, and consequently are usually "successful"; others consistently enhance the self by setting the level so high that they can, as it were, pretend that they are superlative persons, though in fact they never achieve such a goal. In general, caught between the need to have a high standard and the need to succeed with reference to the standard announced, most people probably set the aspiration level near the upper limit of their abilities.

It has, however, been demonstrated, notably in Gould's studies, that the ego level and the aspiration level vary strikingly with the tasks imposed, so that the facet of the real or imagined self that is expressed by a given score in a given task overlaps only slightly the aspect of the self which appears in relation to another task. But there are many ways of adjusting the ego to the aspiration level; most of them, as a matter of fact, are shown in Aesop's *Fables* and the Book of Proverbs—the sour-grapes mechanism, for example, the dog-in-the-manger mechanism, and the little-frog-and-the-big-frog mechanism.

---

[3] This term is currently used to refer to what we should call self-level, but no misunderstanding seems likely.

23. Psychoanalytic Mechanisms

SO FAR, it has appeared that a fairly good job of self-enhancement and self-defense is accomplished by making firm the bulwarks of ordinary autistic self-perception (including occasional rationalization) and by autistically distorting one's enemies' slurs and threats to the self. But human resources for self-beautification and for protection against the danger of self-disparagement are rich and varied; frequently they involve more complex mechanisms, including a group of devices for resolving conflict. We owe most of our clinical knowledge of these manifold mechanisms to Freud. There is, however, no need to subject the reader to the thousand-and-first condensation and critique of Freud, for this would be quite alien to our purpose. Our purpose is not to *discuss* Freud but to use him, and to show, as best we can, how his findings fit into a psychology of self-enhancement and self-defense. We are, then, selecting hypotheses which seem useful —and will mention a few others which we think must be rejected.

A convenient avenue to the Freudian findings is offered by a defense neurosis in a child. Every evening, before going to bed, a boy performed the following ritual: He placed three chairs between his bed and the door of his room; he made a barricade. He called his mother and related to her the various things, however trivial, that he had done during the day. Upon getting into bed he turned on his side and kicked. If he failed in any of these particulars he could not sleep; he was a worried and distraught child. Although there was much else to suggest fright or a series of frights, the core of our present concern is the act of defense. Against what is he defending himself by this ritual? It was found that he had been the victim of a sexual assault. The episode had engendered feelings of terror and guilt which he had repressed, thrust from consciousness. Yet the ritual shows that he had not perfectly blacked out the experience.

The ritual is symbolic protection against the return of the intruder, for in a functional sense, if not in terms of introspection, the intruder is still likely to return. Since the unconscious is "timeless," it is necessary to prepare ever anew for a recurrent danger. But something is wanting in this statement. The chairs would not really keep the intruder out, nor would turning on his side do so. He is, again in a functional and practical sense, defending *himself* not against the intruder but against the *thought* of the situation involving himself and the intruder. As a bad boy he might be punished; he turns away in dread.

But there is still a salient feature unexplained: Why the confessional to his mother? It all looks as if the defense is not really against the intruder, but against guilt, against the sense of being naughty in his mother's eyes, against the loss of love. But it is the trivialities of the day that are recounted to mother, and he knows that these will be forgiven. The behavior cannot be construed as pressure for reinstatement, for he knows that his mother's affection has not been lost.

Then against what is he defending himself? For one thing, he is defending himself against *pangs of self-reproach*. He is old enough to have a conscience, to see his acts against the frame of reference of the adult view of sexual sinfulness; through identification with the parent, he has taken over and incorporated within himself the attitudes of condemnation of those who transgress. It is he himself who is a transgressor; the attitudes function relentlessly, making no exception. He has felt the terrible anguish of self-condemnation. He cannot allow this terrible experience to recur; he will keep it out at all costs; he will carry out the acts of barrier construction which reinforce his determination not to let this experience recur. Though most of the guilt feeling can be blocked, there is still a little left, so he will assuage the guilt tension by making his mother's approval more real, more intense within himself; knowing that mother is right (he is not really a bad boy), he will find his self-valuing attitudes reinforced. Still, just to make sure that nothing is left undone, he builds further defenses; the things that he does not dare to remember are behind; he will be an ostrich and not see them. We noted that under threats one may weaken the assailant or put up a barricade. This boy has done both; he has defended himself from guilt feelings (1) by forgetting the painful episode, (2) by constructing a symbolic barricade, (3) by averting his eyes, (4) by winning his parent's forgiveness. In therapy he shows *transference*—transferring the filial attitude to the analyst.

Using this child's difficulty as a starting point, we may attempt a free sketch of the Freudian defense mechanisms; however, we again emphasize that our purpose is not a didactic exposition of psychoanalysis but a summary and interpretation in which we select the features which appear to make sense from the general point of view of the present volume. We necessarily begin with Freud's insights into the origins of selfhood, with the first infantile drives. These are disorganized, tension-reducing trends, with no awareness and certainly with no organized self-picture. In these impulses there is no possible distinction between outer and inner world or between realistic and autistic contact with the environment. Through the process of interaction with the mother and father, the child makes distinctions between the continuous matrix of experience coming from his own body and the intermittent and not perfectly controllable experiences which are associated with these parental forms. Partly through perceptual assimilation (page 481) but largely through sheer love of the parent who ministers to his needs, the child builds up a structured perception of the mother or father and proceeds slowly to note some resemblances between each parent and himself. At this stage, of course, he simply loves both parents. He gradually assimilates self-picture and parent picture to each other. Both pictures are invested with love— for Freud the *libido*, the creative, broadly sexual, life-enhancing impulse.[1]

Conflict ensues because the parents interfere with many of the

---

[1] Freud, who wrote in German, used the neuter pronoun to describe the original raw impulse. He spoke of *das Es*, which is literally translated in English by "the it," but which translators have rendered by the Latin *id*, the third person neuter pronoun. The first person singular is similarly Latinized, so that Freud's *das Ich und das Es* becomes "the ego and the id." The ego owes its existence to id energies; it consists, in fact, of a certain fund of energy drawn from the id and crystallized in terms of self-perception and "executive functions" in realistic living.

child's impulses, yet he cannot break away because of his love for them. It is not only because he fears punishment from them; it is partly because he has taken within himself the commanding and tabooing attitudes which they exhibit. In the course of time, the attitude of self-reproach, the attitude of parental censorship which is part of the parental system of energies, becomes separable from the simple attitude of parental affection. The child has then *identified* (page 491) not only with the parents as givers of love and all good things, but with them in their role of lawgivers or disciplinary agents. When, by this process of identification, he demands from himself conformity to a standard of conduct, the *superego* is said to be making its appearance.

The individual develops within himself a moral attitude, an attitude involving right and wrong, a system of forces which, though derived from the ego, becomes somewhat detached from it and frequently demonstrates itself to be more powerful. Since the strain between ego and superego is perpetual, and since most ego functions are conscious, it is not surprising to learn that the superego (or the bulk of it) operates unconsciously; but though relegated to the unconscious sphere, it continues to exert control. Without knowing why, a person finds much in the thoughts and actions of today that is rejected as unlovely and base, ultimately because the parental norms so considered it. The moral law is, then, based upon the unconscious, and is not ordinarily accessible to clear analysis. For Immanuel Kant the two great mysteries were "the starry heavens and the moral law." The inscrutability of the moral law is indeed inevitable if, as Freud maintains, morality is removed from the domain of conscious exploration. It is not entirely clear why so much emphasis should be placed upon the *unconscious* phases of this process that the conscious aspects are forgotten, or so much upon the sexual tabus that other tabus are forgotten. Many tabus dealing with property, the proprieties, respect for authority, and general behavior are rigidly enforced in our culture; they are openly taken over, with full awareness, in the introjective processes of some two-year-olds, and can be seen to play a large role in the development of a well-defined conscience by two and a half or three years of age. It is quite true that when parental control is austere or violent, the frightened child may take over a violent self-censoring attitude, with such bitterness and such sense of conflict that we are scarcely surprised to find an unwillingness to look directly at the content and mechanisms of conscience; in such cases it becomes largely an unconscious process. And if this parental violence is directed expressly at the child's sexual curiosity or sexual play, we should expect the superego to be anchored largely upon the sexual tabu.

The three forces in the system—id, ego, and superego—may combine in any type of warfare. Although under ordinary conditions the ego and superego stand together against much that lies within the id, the dreadful delusions of unworthiness and sin, the horrible attacks upon the self which characterize many psychotic conditions, are perfect examples of what Freud calls the joining of forces by the id and superego in common attack upon the ego. In more commonplace life situations, we may phrase the conflict of ego and superego in terms of the conflict between authority and love. Parents exhibit both; they appear to the child in the role of spontaneous dispensers of affection and in the role of arbitrary lawgivers. He is bound forever after to his parents, but the feeling is never one of primitive and unreserved affection; there is about filial devotion a quality that is never the uncomplicated, spontaneous impulsion of infant to mother.

This duality in the filial attitude shows itself also in the core of the process by which the individual maintains himself in society, namely, the quality of his self-love. He may love himself as naïvely as he wishes, but he must at the same time love himself *as a parent would love him*. In other words, he must complicate his self-love by a type of self-discipline, for otherwise the conscience within him, the continuing parent symbol, would no longer approve, and the ego itself would abet the conscience in disapproving the excesses to which self-love leads. Each man's self-love has a quality given partly by his early conception of his parent's love for him. Neurotic indecision, in turn, frequently consists of an alternation between self-love and self-castigation; it is essentially a balance between two forces: (1) the early ego components, which derive from the first uncomplicated stage in ego formation, and (2) the later superego phase which exerts a restrictive control over the whole process, emphasizing unworthiness and unloveliness.

The superego, it will be noted, is considerably more rigid than the ego, just as the role of lawgiver is more narrow than that of lover. While on the one hand the ego has the advantages of fluidity, the superego has the strategic advantage of staying put and standing forever in defense of one simple normative system. It is, after all, omniscient and omnipotent at the time when it first takes articulate form; hence, owing to the "timelessness of the unconscious," it retains these valences. Moral realism (page 386), then, and the masochism (need to suffer) so often associated with it, appear to arise not from the simpler dynamics suggested by Piaget but from the compulsive need to make the identifications in which the parental role of lawgiver is carried forward through life.[2]

We have already seen (page 491) how large a role identification plays in self-awareness. In part, the individual learns what a person is, learns how a self is made, from the adult prototype. Identification, then, has begun before the self is well defined and it continues as the formative process continues; indeed, it does much toward facilitating the self-structuring process. But here it enters upon a new phase. *It becomes a wish-fulfilling, purposive mechanism; the individual enhances and defends the self by an appropriate choice of those with whom to identify.* When the self is structured and has a spatial localization, a person tends to respond, in anticipation of a new performance, as if he were on the point of achievement; as he approaches the door, his set toward opening it consists partly of a schema of himself taking the appropriate position and executing the proper movements. If mother is approaching the door, the child can be seen to do likewise. Let us differentiate this process from the identification heretofore described and call it empathy (cf. page 494). One sees it as the spectators at the football game help to push the ball over the line. One shares the motor adjustment. Since the self is a perceptual structure involving a

---

[2] A. W. Stearns found, in 150 cases of attempted suicide, that the attempt was the end phase of a long series of progressively more and more violent attacks upon the self, the first of which were simply ways of *hurting* the self.

motor disposition, both phases of identification must be considered; and both are continually manifested in the daily round of the child's life. Visual and auditory aspects come first, as they often do in the simplest learning process, but this phase presses forward into the motor, and the kinesthetic follows to complete the picture. But the full self, once formed, grows more and more distinct from the primitive self. As a well-consolidated system it may stand in the background but be ready to emerge when needed. After being "lost in" the doings of another, in sympathy with a troubled friend, or in identification with the hero of a novel, a person comes back to full selfhood, resumes his immediate tasks.

The attribution to others of feelings which belong to ourselves has been mentioned under the term "projection" (page 495). The process, however, is more complicated. Psychoanalytic literature gives evidence of a further factor, without which the term projection is not used by psychoanalysts. The individual, finding something unbearable in himself, denies its existence, but the vague or unconscious perception of the unlovely tendencies nevertheless continues. His gaze falls upon another person. The association then takes shape: these unlovely trends are the other person's. This feeling is satisfying, so he dwells upon it. It is the other person that is unlovely; I am the sort of person who repudiates unlovely things such as these. The sharp definition of the other and the self in contrast relieves the tormented soul; the individual is less annoyed by guilt because the self-deception has been partially successful. The impulse is said to be projected if it is inwardly condemned, then turned outward and placed where it does less havoc.

It would follow, if this is correct, that persons upon whom we project tend to be like ourselves. It is exactly this phase of the hypothesis that Josef Lang attempted to test. Hospitalized patients with delusions of persecution were found to cast in the role of *persecutors* the members of their families who were psychologically most like themselves (in association type). Not recognizing their own hostile wishes, they unconsciously followed the line of least resistance in "finding" a person who harbored hostile wishes. Sears has shown that students who lack insight into their own personality mechanisms assign to others the extreme "stinginess" and "disorderliness" which are really their own. Frenkel-Brunswik found the same thing among students in the Psychological Institute of Vienna. If in the same way we attribute the qualities of others to ourselves it is *introjection*.

The mechanism of *rationalization* involves the discovery of a socially acceptable or reasonable explanation for one's own conduct. The real motive is not perceived; a socially acceptable one is substituted. Some instances of rationalization doubtless involve first the mechanism of repression and an attendant effort to discover a socially acceptable basis for behavior. It seems likely, however, that in the majority of such cases a much simpler mechanism is involved, namely, the figure-ground organization of the self-picture in terms of emphasis upon the real aspects of motivation that are acceptable. Since human motives are almost always complex or, as Freud said, "over-determined," one reasonable aspect is likely to be discoverable. Suppose, for example, that in the plans of King Leopold of Belgium relative to the exploitation of the Congo area, the sheer economic motivation constituted actually 90 per cent, the love of glory and the status as an empire builder another 5 per cent, the fun of power politics 4 per cent, and all the more idealistic motives, such as education of the natives, 1 per cent. Leopold then needed only to make this last 1 per cent the anchorage point or figure, relegating to the ground the other 99 per cent. As in the theory of values (page 272), we are dealing with real motives, but with motives whose relative position varies with our way of regarding them. Rationalization seems in most cases to fall naturally within the sphere of autistic perception, recall, and thought.

Regression is the technique described by Freud, by means of which a person withdraws from a battlefield where he has encountered defeat to an area of earlier fixation. Rejected in love, one may go back to his friends of an earlier period; if rejected by them, he may go back to his dependent and filial relations with his parents. Here, however, the analysts distinguish between the return to an earlier *goal* and the much more complex process of returning to an earlier *form of organization*, a less differentiated pattern of demands. Illustrative of the former process is the return of the unhappy old man or woman to the fantasy world of earlier days, in which wants were gratified and life was satisfying. The latter process is illustrated by the return to the less differentiated organization of wants, mentioned above (pages 145 ff.) in connection with the behavior of children as a result of frustration.

It is important to emphasize the ego functions that are served in the regression process. Often it is not a sexual but an ego function that is frustrated in rejection in love, for surely it is not implied that she who has rejected the suitor is the only possible mate in the universe. As the sardonic adage has it, confirmed bachelors are those who have been made bachelors by a woman. From this point of view, it is the loss of self-fulfillment that results in the generalized rejection of the adult role in favor of a more protected childhood role; the mechanism is exactly the same as that appearing in the lonely adolescent who is "not accepted" and returns to his pre-pubertal cronies. So, too, it is not the loss of childhood goals as such, but the loss of status among other children that causes the return to earlier patterns; among children in the elementary school it is difficulty in achieving status that results in "cry-baby" or other infantile behavior. It is, then, usually the self-goal that is frustrated when regression occurs. Only when there has been profound self-frustration is it necessary entirely to recast the picture of the self and drop back to a more primitive, undifferentiated self-picture. Return to an earlier form of organization is largely a return to a more primitive self. Finally, if even this more primitive picture involves too much distress, the self may fall apart altogether and the organism return to a "pre-self" type of behavior. This is shown rather clearly for example, in Mc-Dougall's four cases of regression in war neuroses, in which soldiers went back to toddling, crawling, and baby talk.

Repression is the opposing of an unconscious impulse by an unwitting counter-pressure. It has become common to use the term *suppression* for the conscious, rather than the unconscious, rejection of ideas or impulses, although there is probably a continuum between the two. The energy required for repression and suppression comes from the ego or the superego, or from both together. In the earliest psychoanalytic cases, repression was primarily a means to protect oneself against the recurrence of a traumatic memory; but with the decreasing emphasis upon trauma, it has come to be a very general term for the unconscious blocking of impulses.

Displacement is nothing other than the transferred conditioned response (cf. page 204) under circumstances which prevent its discharge directly on the stimulating object. Kempf's monkeys, when beaten by the strongest animal in the cage, turn upon a weakling; in the same circumstances, man does likewise. Often a patient's fear of the aggressor is so great that he disbars him from the field of awareness; he may even succeed in becoming unaware of the fact that fear and hatred are at work within him. The demand for a victim may call from the storehouse of memory images a picture that may be mentally mutilated. As the savage transfixes the waxen image of his enemy, so the individual in our culture *autistically* transfixes a substitute victim; this is one form of the scapegoat phenomenon. He need not fully believe that the victim will be harmed, any more than the savage needs always to believe completely in his magic; in autistic compulsions of this sort the individual seldom either fully "believes" or fully "disbelieves." (The mechanism of *substitution*, as when one substitutes an animal for one's father in a daydream, and the closely related mechanism of *symbolization* are omitted here, as are several others frequently encountered in psychoanalysis.)

Displacement has still other phases. When for any reason a person is not allowed (by others or by himself) to love or hate a given individual, he may find a substitute to love or hate. In the case of a substitute to love, the image of the person chosen is more than a conditioned stimulus serving in his stead. In view of the distinction made above between genuine satisfiers which *canalize*, and arbitrary substitutes which merely *condition*, the image may often be sufficiently similar to the original to act as a satisfier in its own right. Even the "hugging" and the fond manipulation of images of cherished scenes or of imaginative poetic constructions may in some degree be a true substitute, a daydream or an imaginary companion that is almost—and at times fully—as good as the original. There is therefore no necessity that such imaginative processes should weaken and finally die out; one broods upon them, keeps them strong. Alexander Selkirk, after years of isolation on his distant island, is still as fervently at home in his thoughts as on the day of the shipwreck. But images, as we have seen, are manipulable just as are muscular acts, and they may be rearranged, freshly reconstituted, to give new and better satisfactions. To the normal frustrated adult or child to some degree, and to the withdrawn psychotic to an extreme degree, the world becomes patterned more and more completely in terms of needs (the mood being somber, the pictures will be drawn in terms of fear or self-reproach). The result is often a *substitute world*.

But when imaginative play moves into regions which are tabu, when the onrushing pressure of the need brings dangerously near to consciousness that which would show the thinker his own weaknesses, his guard goes up; his attention is forcibly directed to more worthy objects. He finds, then, that a guard must be kept posted at all hours, for a moment's relaxation brings the foemen within the gate. The result is that he develops, usually unconsciously, a habitual blocking device. This may be the image of himself doing something very different from the tabu act (in some cases even its opposite), or it may be some incidental thought that can hold attention and preempt the field. Thus the child, worried by his fantasy, starts to count the seconds till mother returns; the counting, if taken seriously, can engage all his available powers, for effort is required to keep the numbers straight. This device, like others discovered accidentally, persists when another similar need arises, and soon there is a full-fledged "counting mania." More often the act that arises in consciousness is one which when carried out would negate, destroy the act that is imaged. The modern compulsive hand-washer must, like Lady Macbeth, rout the "damned spot" by real or symbolic movements that remove the pollution. In Lady Macbeth's case the thought that she is a murderess cannot directly force its way to her attention, but the associated thought of bloodstained hands can do so; it is obviously not a stain or spot, but the guilt it stands for, that is compulsively rubbed off. Such behavior is neither a direct expression nor a symbolic substitute for what one wishes, but a device (discovered in stress, and usually by accident) for keeping the wish from baldly declaring itself, to one's consternation and horror.

A closely similar standard device for handling oneself in this predicament is to draw a picture of oneself doing something very different from the thing that involves temptation. The camp counselor, for example, is afraid of his impulse to beat up the unbearably cocky ten-year-old; hence he maintains before his own eyes the self-picture of a benign, ever-patient father. If holding up this picture is not sufficient to quell the opposing images, he overtly enacts the role of the patient, loving observer, lives as an impossibly patient and forgiving person; the other boys and visitors at the camp wonder how he can ever maintain his equanimity in the face of such irritations. When successfully carried out, this substitution of a divergent or contrasting response in place of the raw impulse which threatens one's favorable self-portrait constitutes the Freudian mechanism of *reaction formation*, a form of conduct ultimately motivated by tendencies far different from—and, indeed, usually opposed to—those that appear.[3]

SECONDARY AND TERTIARY WAYS OF EVALUATING THE SELF

So far we have considered attitudes of self-evaluation in terms of the sensory and activity satisfactions involved in the perception of the self. There is, however, a secondary system of evaluating tendencies, because the self is the object upon which the organism depends in planning the fulfillment of its needs. Just as one kicks himself when he realizes a lost opportunity, so he applauds himself if, like little Jack Horner, he has pulled out a plum. Each object conveys to the self not only a primary satisfaction or frustration, but also a secondary value or frustrating experience. There can be little doubt that, at

---

[3] Another profoundly important mechanism, *compensation*, will be considered in the next chapter.

least in our culture, self-love or vanity owes a great deal to this secondary evaluation process. But the primary and the secondary valuations are fused so completely that a dissection to discover the line of cleavage between them would be fruitless.

As both Horney and Maslow have shown, there is still another evaluative tendency which we may call the "tertiary" evaluation of the self. When the self has failed to be lovable, in either its primary or its secondary capacity, it may be redefined so as to take on a form even more autistic than usual, and be thrown upon the screen of experience in a much more prominent position than the one it previously held. When we become morbidly self-conscious—the self being not merely the steady background but the prominent center of all experience—the self sticks out like a sore thumb and projects itself into everything. From this Horney concludes that narcissism, and self-concern generally, are the results of neurotic frustration. This latter statement seems extreme, since, for all the reasons stated above, there must be powerful canalization upon the self if we are to function in our society. But we can well agree with her that the thrusting of the self into a position of special prominence, and the attachment of a morbidly intense value to it, do constitute a mechanism of defense fully as striking as any of those recognized by Freud.

The Freudian dynamics have, then, been considered primarily as dynamics of a conflict between the selves, dynamics by which a worthy self is kept dominant at the expense of an unworthy one. A considerable part of the complete theory of tensions and conflict, as developed by modern psychiatry, could perhaps be rather simply stated in terms of a conflict between perceptual systems, especially self-perceptual systems. Of course, if percepts are regarded as passive things, like reflections in mirrors, they will conflict only in the most formal sense. But if, as we have tried to maintain, life is in large measure the *effort* to support a self-portrait or a group of such portraits, the major aspect of conflict, at least in most persons, may be the difficulty of maintaining a desirable picture against the pressure from undesirable ones, and the parallel difficulty of deciding between two desirable ones. These two types of perceptual conflict are reminiscent of two types of neurotic patterns which students of experimental neurosis have defined: the differentiation neuroses and the "hopeless situation" neuroses (page 311). This does not mean that the ego is a more primary concept than tension, but rather that the tensions which at the level of rat or sheep or dog relate largely to food and pain are likely in man to relate to alternative self-pictures. From this it follows that the physiological wear and tear which these two types of conflict entail—this is the chief concern of psychosomatic medicine—appears to be largely a problem of ego organization. Although several hints in this direction have already been given, it may be helpful to state, simply and without equivocation, that the psychosomatic problem is partly one of conflict in maintaining an acceptable self. This *might* be expressed in the hypothesis that the whole organism is sick when problems of the self are basically insoluble. But since in a first formulation simplicity is more important than absolute accuracy, it will be well to content ourselves with the simple hypothesis that most serious personality trouble is ego trouble.

It would be tedious to review all the quantitative personality studies which might make more complete sense if looked at in this way, so a single one has been selected. Howells' study of persistence is a good example of the measurement of an "x response in a y situation," as described on pages 141 ff. The persistence measured in this experiment is the endurance of pain while the experimenter looks on. Eight situations are presented, such as "edged instrument pressed against thumb," "holding hand over hot coils," etc. Each situation becomes more grueling until the subject says stop; hence the time that elapses until the word is given measures the amount of punishment. The raw correlation of endurance in four of these situations with endurance in the other four is about .80, which gives a reliability coefficient of .90 for the eight. All eight tests involve the acceptance of pain for the sake of *making an impression upon the experimenter* and hence of seeing oneself favorably. There is no way of telling to what extent the scores express the intensity of the physiological pain mechanisms (for example, one person may feel less pain than another in response to the same stimulus) and to what extent they express the sheer need to appear heroic; but we can be certain that persistence as represented here is not what we have called a simple physiological trait like tissue lag or autonomic threshold; it is "courage" in a specific authority-laden situation.

This is worth keeping in mind when the persistence scores are combined with intelligence test scores to determine the multiple correlation with college grades. While grades alone correlate .51 with intelligence tests, the multiple correlation, when intelligence and persistence are combined, is .64. "Making an impression," especially upon the teacher, is decidedly what a person does when he achieves grades. Given a certain intellectual level, he can utilize his capacities to greater or smaller advantage, depending upon the social motivation. Of course, there is much more than this in the total grade situation, and .57 is still meager; the essential thing, however, is that the persistence test apparently grasps part of the quality that is expressed by the phrase, the "urge to do well in the eyes of another." In other words, it provides a genuine measure of an important ego mechanism, the mechanism for enhancing and defending the self. A large proportion of our personality tests are tests of the ways in which one habitually sees the self and, in particular, of the ways in which one has learned to enhance and defend it. Tests of neurotic tendency, ascendance, and dominance feelings are clearly in this category, and many others may well belong here though not so intended by their authors.

Love and Aggression in Relation to the Self

A few more words may be needed to justify the notion that all these defense mechanisms are essentially *self-oriented*. Are they not direct derivatives of love and aggression, and hence independent of the self? Let us consider another of Freud's contributions, the concept of love and aggression.

It has often been asked why, in so complex a world, Freud should have seen fit to put love almost everywhere. We commented earlier on the need in 1895 for emphasis upon the sexual factor, for the

public and the medical profession feared to face it. In a more philosophical sense, however, particularly as it relates to the ego, there
was everything in western culture to drive Freud toward a broad
recognition of the role of love. Just as in the *Republic* Plato found that
only Eros held life together and gave it meaning, so to the deeply
philosophical impulse within Freud, the only really adequate picture
of life was in terms of a creative impulse which literally pervaded
every process within the living being.

Love has its "free valences," as the chemist would say. Just as the
puppy or kitten makes contact with everything that does not injure
it, and shows a dozen positive outgoing responses for one withdrawing response, so the child is primarily "positive"; he reaches
out to, snuggles up against, immerses himself in nearly everything
with which he is free to make contact. As soon as anything clearly
recognizable as *love* (in the sense of a strong personal attachment)
appears, it begins to serve as a powerful dynamic in living. Unless
he is starved or frustrated, the child lives his life in terms of the
people, the things, and the activities he loves. Such a torrent of
loving cannot remain undirected; the persons and things and activities which satisfy the love impulse are *canalized*, and those that do
not are crowded out, ignored. The child needs canalization objects,
and if life is reasonably rich, he finds an abundance of them. Long
before the advent of the lawgiver, and long indeed before the appearance of the superego, life has been structured in terms of a satisfying
system of love objects. Love has been exercised, strengthened,
articulated; the real world is made up largely of love objects. Autisms
have given the loved objects positions of anchorage in the figure-
ground relations of the world, and everything is set to make human
nature the continuing fulfillment of an affectional system.

But in every human society *some* of the love becomes attached to the
self, and in prestige-centered societies a great deal of it does so. It is
self-love that seems to drive the engines we have considered in these
last few dozen pages. Love may indeed be attached to material objects
(we speak here primarily of sensory drives; page 112), but it leads to
few battles unless these objects become self-enhancing. Though the

love of woman has been thought to be the chief motive in western man, it is seldom the kind of love that demands no return. The normal lover needs to be loved and to *know* very clearly that he is loved; he needs to share fully in the process by which his own image is bathed in love. And though love that is not oriented toward the self can be found, it is to be noted that it *does not require the mechanisms of defense;* all the way from "id" love to cosmic love, it knows its aim, needs neither apology nor disguise, nor any type of outside help. On this point Goethe's Faust and Paul of Tarsus understand each other perfectly; Faust's quest of the "eternal feminine" and Paul's love which "vaunteth not itself" ask no reward or payment in ego terms. Love directed outward causes no conflict; it is a pretty safe general rule that it is self-love that winds the neurotic windlass ever tighter.

But if not love, can perhaps *aggression*, instead, set going the mechanism of defense in a creature without selfhood? To make observed motive patterns into entities is always dangerous, especially when very different action patterns are grouped together under a common name because they have some end result in common. These dangers are especially serious in the case of aggression as an entity. One person may injure another by accident, or by the literal enforcement of rules, or to prevent specific behavior, or to achieve power, or to cause pain, or for a dozen other reasons (in therapy, to make him well). Although we cannot consider all the categories, there are at least four types of behavior dynamics that must be discussed before we shall be in a position to evaluate the concept of an aggressive impulse which may give rise to mechanisms of a psychoanalytic type.

First, there is sheer activity, the primitive push and pull of the muscles, the ongoing tension system itself. This may and frequently does lead to sudden pressure upon the world outside. From it may develop canalizations of the activity drives, tendencies to push harder and longer; and from it may also develop the compensatory effort that is made when pressure is applied to our own bodies.

Second, there is the rage pattern, including the impulse to strike. This may well merge at one end with the need for sheer activity; but as rage becomes more violent it can usually be resolved only through attack upon an outer object and the destruction or removal of that object. From the rage impulse there therefore develops a primitive type of "retribution." The rage mechanism must also be understood if substitute or deflected aggression is to be understood. When the individual cannot get at the interfering outside object—indeed in some cases he may not even know what is causing the interference —he may "satisfy the drive" by pushing or smashing another object. If he is old enough to recognize the cause of his frustration, the object attacked will usually be similar to the cause; but any object, animate or inanimate, will serve. The need for aggressive expression may be reinforced circularly through use (page 319); and in certain cases of sexual deviation, the sexual and the rage impulses may spill over physiologically into each other's systems (page 423) so that the sexual situation arouses an impulse to violence or the violence situation arouses a sexual impulse. Such energies may also spill over into the self-love system so that even as an aggressor one becomes a "martyr" standing for the right. And of course throughout all such responses the aggression may be deflected to one's own person, to initiate the familiar "masochistic" pattern (page 545).

Third, aggressive conduct may develop from considerations of gain. He who is moving toward a desired goal may push or fight against obstacles; he may incidentally work up a hatred for the obstacles or simply brush them aside as best he can, with no affect except that which is devoted to the goal object. The gain motives may be complicated by the prestige satisfactions and the love won through success (page 243), by the badges of security which protect against future dangers, and by the acquired protection against later attack.

Fourth, what passes for aggression may be self-expression, arising from the fact that in most societies satisfaction with the self comes from *power* (page 244). A person works his way forward against obstacles until he has achieved power; having achieved it, he must use it to gain still more power. Veblen pointed out long ago that predatory behavior in preadolescent boys comes largely from the double role assigned to masculinity in most cultures. One "asserts" one's masculinity, and achieves the prestige associated with it, by going further than the others in sheer violence, or wantonness, as in the destruction characteristic of old-time Hallowe'ens. For it is in destruction, as in the potlatch of the Kwakiutl Indians of the Northwest, that one shows the sheer exuberance of his animal spirits and his freedom from the narrow pinch-penny attitudes of constructiveness and thrift which for ordinary, i.e., non-predatory people, mark the essence of "being good." The preadolescent, then, sets for himself the impossible task of winning glory by a technique that is tabu in the eyes of the adult males whom he emulates. The aggressiveness of the delinquent is not just protest against restrictions or crowded streets or a poor biological environment; it is not just exuberance or getting even or showing off. It is to some degree the product of the elemental recognition that power can be achieved only by cutting loose from the power systems established by others, and by setting up, arbitrarily or capriciously a limited power system of one's own. The robbing of a shop and happy participation in a club or junior republic may have a great deal in common psychologically.

Although an even larger array of sources of aggression has recently been listed by Schreier, for our present purposes these four will suffice. This is one of the instances in which Freudian motivation psychology (concerned with aggression as an *entity*) has dealt with a somewhat more abstract level of motivation than we can profitably use. Even though the various impulses melt somewhat into one another, they are for most purposes distinct; and when it comes to a study of individual differences in aggressive patterns, it is necessary to define what specific types of impulsions are at work, whence they spring, and how they are implemented. Even when trying to keep it out, we have found the self playing a role in these aggressive processes, especially in the fourth type. And when the self is *not* involved, e.g., in the primitive "smash-bust" type of aggression, there has been no trace of the "mechanisms of defense." These mechanisms of defense do not, then, appear to derive directly from love and aggression; they seem to be mechanisms of *self*-enhancement and *self*-defense.

The opposition of ego tendencies within the individual *need* not, however, lead to defense mechanisms; two or more incompatible roles may be worked out, each to be enacted in its own specific situation. Social usage may give expression to such tendencies by providing a system of situations which allow a place for each role, and the activities of each individual may lead to the definition of appropriate counterroles for one's associates. This is the fruitful concept developed by Gregory Bateson, to be analyzed more fully in Chapter 35. The most important thing about this concept as it relates to our present problem is the conclusion as to the nature of *shifts* in the pattern of the self. The transition from one self to another self is effected abruptly, not gradually. One does not drift into another; there are, rather, a finite number of mutually exclusive selves that follow in temporal sequence. Growing up in the culture, the individual learns what these various selves are, how they are to be acquired and developed, what they cost, how they can be preserved from damage, and how they can be enhanced, beautified, and glorified. Looking through Bateson's eyes at various other cultures, we may be quite sure that all recorded cultures offer these handfuls or bunches of selves, and that the more differentiated societies, such as the industrial, usually offer a richer variety than the more primitive ones. Of course, speaking literally, we should need to admit that some of the properties of selfhood are carried over from one role to another—some of the organic and kinesthetic features and other aspects of body awareness, for example—and since we are not dealing with multiple personality in the true sense, it would be grotesque to insist upon even relative *amnesia* for other roles. Even so, however, it is of major interest to personality study to be able to conceive the dependence of personality on context in terms of *shifts in selves*, shifts in the fundamental perceptual patterns which derive from different social contexts of individual functioning.

We are reminded here of Ralph Linton's clear demonstration that it is not to the culture as a whole, but to specific roles that the cultural phase of personality owes it origin. Roles in terms of age, sex, occupation, etc., are assigned to the child, and through such serially enacted roles, as through a tube, he makes his way to old age. Personality is in considerable degree a matter of role behavior; even more, however, it is a matter of role perception and of self-perception in the light of the role. Bateson's contribution enables us to see more clearly the complexity of roles to be enacted by one person within a given period of his life, and also the dependence of each person's roles upon those enacted by others, the interdependence of complex role patterns by virtue of which the individual's self-portrait varies both with tasks and with the fulfillment of tasks by others.

"The Ego Is a Grammatical Illusion"

As we come to the conclusion of this evaluation, it may be wise to pause and allow a hostile critic an opportunity to formulate a difficulty which has undoubtedly been taking shape in the minds of many readers. A picture of a thing is, after all, something like the thing portrayed. Ordinary human beings, not concerned with abstractionism or surrealism of any sort, must keep the picture of the self in some sort of functional relation with the organism as a whole. There may be a good deal of distortion, but most people succeed in handling life with reference to their own individuality without noticeable confusion. In a rough, broad, practical sense, the self that one observes is the person as a whole. To say that one does something to enhance the self sounds like a rather "fancy" circumlocution, a psychologist's way of saying that one does something because he wants to do it. The mechanisms of defense are not simply mechanisms for defending the self-picture, but mechanisms for defending the organism. This is the type of objection to ego theory which Nietzsche first formulated when he said "The ego is a grammatical illusion." Everything that is done for the sake of the self would still be done for the *individual*, if there were no "self." To say that the self is a primary value is almost a way of saying that one values what he values; to say that the self is a secondary value, a thing perceived as helping the individual to obtain what he wants, sounds like a rarefied and indirect way of recognizing that any person of ordinary intelligence learns something about his own weaknesses and learns to rejoice in his own abilities.

It is exactly this type of objection with which the more serious study of adult maladjustments on the one hand, and cross-cultural studies of the organization of the self on the other hand, must deal. It is exactly on the grounds advanced by the critic that the issue should be fought out. Our only answer is that as far as neurosis is concerned, the vast bulk of clinical data indicates that it is *not* in the realm of the ordinary run of wants that the conflict is staged, but that neurotic conflict is quite literally a question of keeping a perennially beautiful self-picture before the eyes. It is because the *picture* rather than the person is besmirched or mutilated that neurotic breakdown occurs. Subject to increasing complications as we proceed to cross-cultural comparisons (Chapters 32–37), we offer the further hypothesis here that the fundamental demands are not very different from one society to another, but that the ways of schematizing a worthy self differ profoundly. Hence both the neurotic and the normal personality types in different cultures are modes of self-perception and self-evaluation which arise from the specific qualities narcissistically adored in one society or another, and from the techniques of self-enhancement and self-defense stylized and ingrained in each generation of children. The ego is indeed a grammatical illusion because of the tendency to confuse three things: (1) the self, (2) the self-enhancing and self-defending mechanisms, and (3) the whole organism of which the first two are aspects.

But there is no need to assert that the self is at the heart of *all* personality problems or of *all* maladjustments. From the emphasis given to the ego, and especially to the hypothesis that all canalizations tend in time to be colored by the character of selfhood, it might be maintained that *all* conflict is conflict among methods of preserving the self. This would be unwarranted. There is much conflict of impulse, of motor tendency, where perception is not involved. We earlier emphasized conflict engendered by opposed perceptual habits, as in figure-ground reversals (page 370), by opposed canalizations (page 300), and by opposed conditionings (page 230). Opposed autisms, when demonstrably of dynamic importance in supporting opposed perceptual patterns, are sometimes primitive expressions of drives in which the ego is not involved. A figure-ground situation, say a still-life painting with fruit in the foreground, might well be structured so that for the hungry child the fruit was thrown into sharp relief, whereas for the satiated child it might be subordinated by the dynamics of a genuine esthetic gratification; the hungry child trying to enjoy the painting as a painting is in a state of real conflict. The Morgan-Murray pictures (page 670) apparently induce varying figure-ground patterns in precisely this way. Here is conflict at a "subego" level.

These non-self-oriented mechanisms seem definitely of secondary importance in the cardinal personality problems of men and women in our culture. Most of life's problems and difficulties are self-problems. We soberly recognize the primacy of these deeply ingrained mechanisms when we adopt as a standard of conduct: "Thou shalt love thy neighbor as thyself."

Individual Proneness to Using Each Mechanism

It is probable that all the mechanisms described in this chapter are at times used by everyone, but it is equally probable that each of us has a predilection for one rather than another, that degrees of proneness in using them make up a very important and fairly stable aspect of personality. There may well be constitutional predispositions in one direction rather than another, since these are obviously learned mechanisms and we have found that the constitution influences the direction taken by learning, the proneness to learn one thing rather than another. In any event, however the tendencies begin, they tend to transfer and become consolidated in a wide variety of situations, as is the general nature of habits. There is little research along these lines, but one experiment is of great interest. Preliminary data having strongly suggested that there is a relation between (1) tendency to repression, (2) hypnotizability, and (3) tendency to impunitiveness (acceptance of frustrating situations without aggression toward others or the self), Rosenzweig and Sarason made experimental measurements of these three variables. Their subjects were given jigsaw puzzles and were interrupted while solving them; later they had to recall as many as they could. Repression was regarded as appearing in a tendency to recall successful more frequently than unsuccessful attempts.[4] As thus measured, it correlated substantially with hypnotizability and with impunitiveness. Individuals who repress have "managed" the situation; they tend to be people who can accept both hypnosis, with its loss of self-assertion, and frustration without the impulse to retaliate. Those who do not repress so easily tend perhaps to "fight" hypnosis and repression. Such quests regarding the nature and extent of generalized proneness to the various psychoanalytic mechanisms offer a great deal to an understanding of the meaning of the mechanisms themselves and of the value of psychoanalytic mechanisms in the study of personality.

---

[4] Here, and elsewhere in the entire field of Freudian mechanisms, research has tended to generalize the meaning of terms. In Freud's writings repression relates to traumatic events. How far we may properly go in using terms for related but not identical processes will be clear only when we know how far the basic psychology of everyday life is identical with that of Freudian clinical findings.

24. Compensation for Inferiority

WHEN the heart valves partially fail, the heart muscle grows thick; it compensates. When a lung or a kidney fails, the other lung or kidney may assume extra labor. Compensation is not only physiological, it is psychological. The man who has lost an eye develops unusual monocular skills. Dwarfs, said Francis Bacon, are "exceeding bold." It is from the fact of "psychical compensation" for an organ inferiority (already recognized by Freud in the case of sex organ defects) that the psychology of Alfred Adler takes its start.

Adler was a member of Freud's little "seminar" that met in Vienna early in the present century. Freud accepted Adler's emphasis on psychical compensation and regarded it as a significant contribution to the theory of the ego. But Adler insisted less and less on "organ inferiority" and more and more on inferiority in general physique, attractiveness, intelligence, or economic or social status; less and less on actual inferiority, more and more on the sense of inferiority. In time the root conception became simply the thesis that man is born weak, ignorant, clumsy, and helpless, and that in his misery he struggles for power. This thesis was judged alien to psychoanalysis, and Adler was asked to leave the seminar.

Personal bitterness prevented, during the lifetime of the two men, any serious and sustained effort by them or their followers to ascertain critically the points of similarity between the two systems, or to use their clinical findings in constructing a non-sectarian view of personality development. We have seen, however, that the Freudian findings can be brought into organic relation to the general body of knowledge regarding conflict of motives, and that many of the theoretical formulations are easily harmonized with hypotheses which appear sound and useful in the light of other data, in particular with hypotheses regarding the self. The same is true of Adler's clinical findings and, with some restatement, of his central theses as well.

Indeed, his findings and theses appear to fall perfectly into place in a psychology of the self such as has been sketched in the preceding two chapters. In the case of Freud we felt that it was better to go directly to the heart of what could be used, rather than to subject the reader to still another systematic critique of psychoanalysis. This is also true of Adler—he will be used, not dissected. There was a time when a new comparison of the evolution of Freud's, Jung's, and Adler's systems, with a fine eye for distinctions, served a purpose; moreover, in the first alignment of the systems for comparison, there had to be definite boundaries. At present, however, we are not comparing these three men but are attempting simply to use them in an enterprise of our own.

TYPES OF COMPENSATION

Compensation is a widespread biological principle, ranging from the simplest level of chemical or postural balance to the most complex expressions of social statics and dynamics. We have seen how tensions may fail to gain expression, their energy being directed to a new goal (page 199); this is the dominance principle. But on the contrary they may gain in strength as they are blocked, in a way that is reminiscent of Newton's third law ("to every action there is an equal and opposite reaction"). The resulting motive force is proportioned to the force of the thrust that has to be overcome. The ramifications of this principle of compensation are fraught with implications for personality.

Compensation may occur in the physiological domain, as in the compensatory tensions—and sense of effort—in the external eye muscles when congenital muscular imbalance is present. In such instances it takes place within the tissues that are primarily involved. Compensation may also occur in another part of the body, as in the blind man's compensatory development of great skill in the utilization of the finger tips. The supreme organ of compensation, however, is the central nervous system. Simply because frustration involves resilience, struggle, and renewed pressure toward adjustment, the physical basis of the learning process is the seat of most of the important compensations of man—another way of saying that the central nervous system must carry the strain imposed by the compensation.

In man, whether the cause is organic, intellectual, or social, the chief compensation takes place when the frustration, instead of being segmental, involves the goals of the organism as a whole; in other words, the really critical compensations are ego problems. Whatever in the environment threatens the self or robs it of its defenses or its means of enhancement, leads to a compensatory effort of the system as a whole, and not merely of its segments or parts. There is a perpetual struggle to make the actual self as much as possible like the ideal self, a self which has been enhanced and freed of its limitations to the highest degree imaginable.

It follows that inferiority feelings are universal stigmata of human civilization. No society has the power to give absolute security, to protect the child—or the adult—completely against the loss of love. Few societies protect those in the declining years of life from the loss of importance in the group that is their usual lot. No society, however rigid its structure, can withhold or bestow prestige according to an ideal or prearranged system; much depends upon accident—"time and chance happeneth to them all." It is nevertheless true that inferiority feelings differ in both quality and intensity with varying cultural demands, especially with the curtailment of the amount of prestige that is available, and with the salience of the prestige drive among the socialized drives of the group.

It is likewise true that subcultural groups vary in the incidence of neurotic inferiority feelings; these may be more characteristic of the business than of the working class, and of urban than of rural communities. During the First World War, nervous crack-ups of officers in the British army usually took a neurasthenic form based on threats to individual prestige standards or fear of inability to discharge a duty successfully, whereas crack-ups among the enlisted men were largely in terms of hysteria, involving the struggle to cope with fear in its simple form. It is doubtful whether anything strictly comparable to this occurs in civilian life, although the "nervous breakdown" of business or professional men is usually more neurasthenic than hysterical.

We may say that individual families differ strikingly in their prestige demands on their children. Some demand the impossible of the first-born; some drive the youngest to emulate the achievements of the older children; some put an impossible strain on boys and not on girls, or vice versa. Some families in almost every cultural group insist on the competitive advancement of every member of the family, whereas others are supremely indifferent to what other families think.

Although all such tensions involve strain at the time of the compensatory effort, the enduring consequences are more serious still. Nervousness, or even instability, may result partly from the fact that complete compensation can never be achieved; the struggle must go on and on. Such strain, in the form of continuous rather than fluctuating drives, allows no respite. If prestige came and went like the seasons, people might develop the alternating stress and repose to which Veblen and Hocking give so much attention. But unfortunately it is the character of many human societies to define status in long-time terms. The Comanche Indians represent the ideally exceptional situation, the sort of thing that Veblen had in mind—violent struggle for military prestige, followed by a period of peace during which there is no effort to continue the day-by-day "validation" of an individual's military position. In many primitive and advanced cultures, however, prestige must be maintained daily by appropriate conduct. It may be lost through a casual digression from the norm. Though a man may not lose his caste or his family, he may lose his *place* within the caste or family group because of failure to embody the virtues (such as business acumen) upon which the group insists; in less stable societies with high vertical mobility, failure may bring the loss of *all* status. "Nervous breakdown" may result from a long period of compensatory struggle as the defense of the threatened self becomes increasingly more difficult; one strives to prove himself equal to a series of mounting threats, until the nervous system, unable to stand the continuous strain, begins to show functional disorders or even the overt organic manifestations of depletion. The nervous breakdown in the business man or the frustrated lover is no simple and direct expression of frustration as such. Failure brings collapse because life has been structured in terms of self-enhancement and because the struggle to earn a favorable view of the self has been unremitting. There is, then, always a base of continuous and general strain upon which the local strain of a specific business or social situation is superposed.

The competitive structure of society is of course the ultimate source of these individual catastrophes. Lawrence K. Frank's paper, "The Cost of Competition," shows that the economic waste of people's working to defeat one another constitutes but a small fraction of the vast cost to the organism in its struggle to excel, under terms which make excellence, as socially defined, the achievement of the few, and for those few, only in limited areas and for limited times. If this way of reasoning is correct, neurosis should be the general characteristic of man under industrialism, a point suspected by many Freudians and, in particular, by that branch of the Freudian school (Horney and her associates) that has learned most from Adler. Before proceeding further, it may be worth while to look at three classical examples of the Adler principles, examples of supreme compensation for inferiority.

Whether Demosthenes overcame stammering by putting pebbles in his mouth we do not know. We do know, however, that he was the spoiled child of a doting mother who dressed him gaudily and got the archons to excuse him from military exercises; and we know that his father, having been swindled out of a fortune, could be posthumously revenged only through the power of the law. Here, then, was a career which would make the boy the savior and bulwark of the family; he must become a barrister and through his eloquence overwhelm the court. Fop and sissy that he was, he dreamed vitally of conquest and power, and mastered the orator's art. But Philip of Macedon intervened. Athens was about to be attacked. There was a place for the exhorter of men. When other orators pleaded for recruits, the audience clapped; when Demosthenes spoke, they roared, "We will march against Philip; we will conquer or die." The savagery of his verbal onslaught was such that the word "philippic" has come into our language as a synonym for eloquent fury. The stripling excused from military exercises had in a literal sense become a military hero.

Lord Byron's father was a rake, his mother an impulsive woman who found it difficult to give her child security. Infantile paralysis affected his legs. His persistence and vigorous exercise made him an athlete. Indeed, on a journey to Greece, he found time to be Leander, to swim the Hellespont. The foot and the hand, the extremities and the brain, were playing their part in the compensation. His published verse was powerful, and a hero-worshiping audience resonated to it. But there was criticism of his personal conduct. Well, then, there was another way to rise above them; he could affront them, violate their standards, overwhelm them with a god's mockery. The Italian episode which followed began with a series of heartless affairs, with as much self-torture as scorn of his enemies. No one with an eye to Byron's pitiful frustration could possibly call all of this free love; it was neither love nor free. Yet through all this period he worked hard, turning out a series of magnificent and immortal poems. He died participating in the struggle of Greece to regain her independence. According to Adler, the effort toward compensation may eventuate in genius, in neurosis, or in degeneracy. In Byron all three were realized at different times.

As a boy, Theodore Roosevelt, an asthmatic and a weakling, traveled in a stagecoach with other boys. They jeered at him. When he tried to fight, they held his hands and hooted. His father understood; he fitted up a gymnasium for Teddy, who developed muscle and skill. At Harvard he mastered literary form, but he went forth intent less upon expression than upon action. He knew only dimly what he wanted. Three worlds of power were open to him; in the modern state the overt vehicles of force are the police, the military, and the world of political domination. He became police commissioner of New York, and soon thereafter governor. In both he was strong, with a touch of turbulence. Ill health, however, recurred. It was not enough to go west, rest, build up; he must ride the hardest mounts, organize his Rough Riders. When the Spanish-American War offered them the opportunity for active service, it was he who led them at the storming of San Juan Hill. He must wear his Rough Rider's uniform to the Republican National Convention, where he won the vice-presidential nomination. As President, he became the celebrated exponent of the "Big Stick," finding time in avocational hours to attack an assortment of "nature-fakers" and other candidates for his "Ananias Club." When at last political power fell away, he must shoot in Africa; upon his return he opened the guns upon President Taft. His last great appearance in the public eye was when he tried to lead a division in France during World War I.

In these and countless other agitated souls, weakness has led to power. It has, however, led to much else besides. As we suggested earlier, our own culture indissolubly links gain, power, and prestige; and the quest for one is often a quest for another, or indeed for all three at once. The struggle of the weak is usually the struggle of those without status. Its successful outcome is attended by prestige as well as by power, and often by gain and other advantages in addition.

If we examine carefully the three cases just presented, we see how rich, how interfused, their goals were. Demosthenes' prestige became greater, and today remains greater than that of Philip, whose phalanx swallowed the little Athenian city-state. Byron's exhibition of power in swimming the Hellespont was plainly a gesture which also gave him status, and his magnificent words gave him power only in the sense that they gave him an admiring public. The frantic Italian episode was an effort to persuade himself that another kind of power (the fancied assumption of great masculinity) was really his. But all of these left him hungry for simple acceptance, for regard for himself as a person, which no one knew how to build within him. His fundamental sickness was lack of self-acceptance, self-love, status, and prestige in his own eyes. Were it not for this, the admiring majority who loved his verse would have sufficed; a few angry critics would have meant nothing. The trouble was that his inner response to himself was rejection, and those who rejected him fed that scorn of self which consumed him throughout his life. There was no quest for power as such; there was a never-satisfied quest for serenity in contemplating himself. T.R.'s story presents a better case for the hypothesis that the will to power is the only drive; but it bears analysis no better. Not asthma alone, but the boys' taunts, forced the compensation. A police commissioner has power but little prestige; hence the position could not hold him long. The illness that drove him to the West led to bold horsemanship, but he surrounded himself with those who hailed and magnified such exploits. In pioneer America, power was necessarily a central source of prestige; in Wyoming particularly, power against mountains and broncos took the place of power over investments manifest in the eastern prototypes of the Gilded Age. It was power, but it was also prestige, that led to his voyages of discovery in South America and his animal collections for the New York Zoological Society; it was vanity that led to the name-calling, the "I'm right and you're wrong" of his controversy with the naturalists. Thus even when we deliberately select three hero patterns for analysis, the heroic quest for power proves to be largely the vehicle which carries one into the white light of admiration, and the echoing and happy admiration of the self.

In daily living, for every heroic goal there are a hundred other ordinary prestige goals. Even orators, poets, and Presidents seek admiration; clerks, switchmen, lumberjacks want to be known everywhere as "good men." The woman wants to be a good wife. The tiny child who can hardly talk is as much interested in his admiring audience as in the somersault he can turn. Flattery and fishing are the universal coin of communication; one seeks forever to appear well. Sometimes the approval of anyone and everyone is important, as when one tips well for the sake of the waiter who will find the quarter after one has left the restaurant; but sometimes it is only the approval of one's wife or one's father that matters. In both cases, however, according to the present hypothesis, the primary goal, without which the satisfaction is abortive, is the impact of all this upon the individual's own view of himself. Other events and the opinions of others are valued as signals, indicators, validators of a final self-approval.

THE PERSONAL HISTORY OF COMPENSATION

In these three cases it was clear that the sense of inferiority was already acute in childhood. Let us turn, then, to the first manifestations of inferiority and the first efforts to compensate for it. We

[571]

should expect, in the development of the individual child, to find a series of stages and a series of transition points in the exhibition of compensatory behavior. Most of the compensations of infancy do in fact appear when the child's wants surpass his physical skills, and he ambitiously gets himself into situations from which he has insufficient knowledge and skill to extricate himself. The compensations of the second and third years of life seem to consist almost entirely of protest and struggle against the parental restrictions imposed upon the great new powers and self-satisfactions that are brought by the ability to walk and talk. The child has become a threat to his parents' possessions and to their leisure, but he can scarcely retrench during a period of such rapidly expanding selfhood. By four or thereabouts, he has taken these restrictions in his stride in most matters, and the struggle to cope with children of his own age or a little older has become his chief concern.

Developing the implications of Adler's approach, let us imagine three six-year-old children, observed since infancy, to be compared with the three adults mentioned above. In the case of the first, the father was away most of the time; the mother was ill and burdened with the care of two younger children. The six-year-old had at various times tried all the devices there are for getting ahead. Mother was too ill to pay any great attention unless there was a strong demand and a strong will to see it through; she had no defense against her child's sheer vigor of self-assertion, either in relation to her own needs or in the protection of the younger children. Domineering was the pattern which this six-year-old had established as the one that worked. In the second family, both parents were petulant, easily irritated, ready to punish. The six-year-old's *direct* self-assertion against them and against a big brother had monotonously failed. Inert, apathetic withdrawal also got him nowhere; he was not even noticed. But the parents had no nerves to withstand whining and wheedling. The whine-and-wheedle method found the weak spot in the wall; it worked so well that it became the *modus vivendi*. In the third family a gentle and intelligent mother, abetted by a maternal-hearted big sister, had been disturbed and disapproving in the face of aggressions both overt and verbal; but they were sorry for a little girl who needed so much and was so dear, so they paved her life with attentions and with solutions of her problems before she had a chance to meet them. Each of these three children brought to school the way of behavior which his own immediate necessity had imprinted upon him. He transferred to the teacher what he had learned in relation to his mother; he transferred to the other children in school what he had learned in relation to brother or sister. As long as these methods worked, these children continued to use them. Such findings are in line with Adler's whole approach.

It was Adler's hypothesis that these and other familiar types develop early and become very stable. During the elementary-school period the technique of aggression is at a premium with boys in our culture—at least until each boy has validated himself in the eyes of the others and won some degree of in-group feeling; a good deal of the pressure against outer restrictions takes the form of a struggle against adult authority. Among preadolescent girls there is conspicuously less person-to-person struggle, and also much less struggle of the group against the adult world—or it takes a more subtle and less readily observable form. The picture changes somewhat with puberty. We referred above to the activity level and to metabolic requirements (page 130), and to the kinetic qualities associated with the endocrines (page 97); here it is of interest that during earlier puberty, when the activity level of girls is above that of boys, girls equal or surpass boys in competitive potentialities. All this suggests that the general fund of energy available to the individual, as well as the social pressure applied to him, must be considered before the vigor of individual compensation can be appraised.

But it is insufficient to speak of competition globally and of compensation in general. For every age and for both sexes there are normal, legitimized outlets of compensatory energy; a person learns to compensate in accordance with an approved technique. As he passes from one developmental level to another, the old techniques frequently fail to serve. Take a ten-year-old boy, markedly successful in sports and other boyish activities, who discovers in early puberty

[573]

that he is falling behind in the growth spurt which his fellows show; he is a "runt." Though still athletic, he has lost his position of preeminence. As the boys become interested in girls, he remains "a child" and is regarded with disdain by both boys and girls. He goes on using the same compensatory tactics with reference to his small stature which he found useful a few years earlier—he is still bold, athletic, mechanically-minded, an all-round competent person. But these compensations are worthless when the club room and the social life of the fourteen-year-old make their imperative demands. Those who have any type of disability need not only compensation *in general* but a *specific* type of it. Woe to those whose compensations are anchored at one developmental level and incapable of adjustment to others—the "cute" child when the cuteness drops away! As we shall see, a new kind of compensation is often attempted when the primary one fails.

The compensations which develop in exploratory fashion during the high-school years may be set down rather arbitrarily as athletic, social, and intellectual, each of the three being cognate with the other two, and all involving an effort to make good in one sphere to mask relative deficiencies in others. Perrin measured some of these aspects of the compensatory effort in university students. It is true that intellectual effort is in some measure compensatory, but it is equally true that social and athletic skills are developed when they can serve as screens for limitations in other fields. Every type of interest, moreover, has its initial seed in a genuine need; compensation is usually not the source but a basis for elaborating and developing an interest that is already undergoing cultivation.

Deriving from the current preoccupation with individual competition, there is a large experimental literature on the "pecking orders," the "dominance relationships" observed to develop among animals as among men. Through conflict or intimidation the strong or the bold find their way to the top. Bühler's studies of children's groups show that individual and age factors lead quickly to the establishment of roles of dominance and subordination, or despot and slave. But when control is maintained by less obvious techniques, the long and complex process by which the final positions of dominance are achieved has frequently been overlooked. Since status roles are achieved, as a rule, through a long process of trial and error, the end results, like those in all learned behavior, show a great variety of qualitative manifestations. All the status roles are, so to speak, "played for" by all the members of the group, so that a visible degree of success in one or more roles is achieved by nearly everyone; some individuals gain preeminence in several of them. Since such roles usually overlap considerably, the individuals who achieve the highest status in one significant role thereby attain sufficient prestige and power to *generalize their behavior* and hence to become all-round dominators or leaders.

Domination and subordination consequently appear to be rather highly generalized, and this is indeed the case for the measures of ascendance-submission and for the observed patterns of aggression and leadership in childhood, adolescence, and early adulthood. There are, of course, non-aggressive types of dominance, but in general the various manifestations of this quality are apparently quantitatively interrelated. The only possible basis for this interrelation, in view of the specific character of compensations for specific defects, is the mechanism of transfer and generalization; one carries over dominant attitudes to new situations and applies them wherever they will work. Strength, speed, and skill as primitive organic attributes are important as expressions of mastery only so far as they serve as a substrate that permits relevant *learning and transfer processes* to occur, thus enabling mastery of a wider and wider range of social situations. Many other forms of competition, such as the social and intellectual, are more important in our society. It is common to see the huge, strapping, athletic college student displaying the most pitiful of inferiority feelings because, though completely successful at a physical level, he moves in a society which values the social and intellectual skills that he has been unable to acquire.[1]

Maslow has offered some very pertinent data on the generalization

[1] In *The Road Back*, Remarque describes how the simple exuberant acceptance of *prowess* among soldiers was insidiously replaced by *scholastic* standards when the men returned to university life.

and the generality of dominance feelings. In the individual whose dominance feelings are well developed, he says, confidence, security, prestige, and a feeling that the self is adequate are especially prominent. We might suggest that the one thing really important here is the awareness of one's competence to meet the threats to the self, or, as Veblen put it so perfectly, "the degree of complacency" with which the individual may properly be regarded by himself and by others. From the point of view developed here, the eighteen attributes listed by Maslow are secondary or symptomatic aspects of this complacency; the nucleus is self-confidence, a feeling that the tools for the service of the self are adequate. By and large, such self-confidence should be closely related to actual success in making a place for oneself in society.

Yet if we look more closely at the phenomena of ordinary dominance by some people over others, we find much that squares poorly with the conception of generalized dominance just presented. Do not insecure or even frightened people dominate others and thereby achieve some degree of dominance feeling? Do not hypertrophied mastery motives appear in those whose self-attitude is far indeed from one of complacency? Does not savage or sadistic aggression appear as an expression of a pathological drive to dominate in people who are so insecure that they show the minimum degree of self-satisfaction or complacency?

The paradox is actually not difficult to resolve. The first step is to consider the person with strong dominance feelings. Compensations have developed early on a stable basis. They have been perceived and generalized in relation to more and more situations, and their fortunate possessor has a reasonable basis for feeling that he can successfully meet more situations like them. But he may confront a completely new situation. Consider, for example, the competent student faced by a strange type of examination with which he cannot cope, or the competent athlete up against an utterly new form of tactics on the field; a child-like explosion of insecurity may occur. Typically, the dominance feeling is a happy knowledge of oneself in relation to situations of a sort in which one has been competent, but it is not proof against *all* assaults.

Next consider the man whose compensations have never been

satisfactory; suppose that status and power have not been achieved by the means of compensation available to him. The time comes when, through the blundering process of trial and error, he discovers that by actually hurting, browbeating, or terrifying others he can intimidate them into a position of subservience and awe. The kind of prestige that comes from "being nice" cannot of course be achieved this way, but the kind that comes from "being strong" can thus be bought. If there is not too much identification with others, not too much fellow-feeling, a person can hack himself into a position of mastery. But because he is frightened, uncertain whether the trick will work, he goes at the task with a fury and a violence which the strong and assured never use. A frightened despot may develop not true dominance feelings, as described by Maslow, but a very different feeling, an abnormally intense mastery motive. We should expect, then, following Adler as well as Maslow, that mastery motives might often appear with special distinctiveness among the weakest, the least self-sufficient members of the social group.

Even the excesses and the paradoxes appear to fit rather well the conception that dominant behavior and dominance feelings are both the products of learning in a competitive social setting, the main drive at work throughout being the struggle to find a way of looking serenely upon the self. It is true that to the very young—and to the adult with the mental age of a child—sheer physical victory regardless of self-attitude is an adequate goal, and it is also true that the more extremely autistic may view themselves as adequate without a compensatory thrust against their neighbor's status; but the common run of mortals in a competitive society can achieve the glorious sense of personal adequacy only by securing a *place*, a *name*, a *status* in their group.

THE STYLE OF LIFE

Such *generality* as we have described is fundamental to Adler's thesis; the basic compensation must be highly generalized if it is to serve effectively in all of life's situations. The "style of life" is Adler's phrase for the individual's central, unitary, indivisible, strivi.ng process. In response to the specific pattern of inferiority feelings experienced by a child in a specific home situation, one unitary way of coping with the problem is discovered; one fundamental attitude is developed; one basic form of striving, *one mode of compensation*, is achieved. This conception of Adler's is the greatest effort at unity in the definition of personality which we have thus far encountered.

The idea is certainly highly fruitful, but there are two difficulties: (1) The generality is less than one hundred per cent in reality, and (2) the generality that we observe is obtained not all at once, but slowly. Quantitative studies give evidence of considerable generality as expressed statistically in terms of correlations. Nevertheless, we should expect that both the subject's and the clinician's appraisal of unity of character would be more extreme than is warranted by the facts, because they have the verbal tools with which to look for such relations and can therefore discover them autistically even where they are not. Actually, the degree of generality falls short of warranting any theory of complete unity. Moreover, instead of achieving such generality as there is with one fell swoop in early infancy, the individual apparently achieves it only slowly and haltingly. Throughout childhood, not only is there a general security level, but there are also *areas of security* so well defined that the little child may change, chameleon-like, from shy to resolute as he moves from the strangeness of his first day at nursery school to the familiarity of his old neighborhood situation. However, this is not true of all individuals; as Eugene Lerner used to say, some, even as two-year-olds, are not chameleons but "beavers." Similarly, in the first grade or in the freshmen year at college or indeed in the first business position, some people find themselves unable, in the new situation, to generalize the techniques upon which the sense of adequacy has been based; or a somewhat variable and fluid pattern of secondary techniques may be superposed upon the basic life technique. The kind of unity that Adler describes here *does* exist, but it does not take account of the full biosocial unity that has been developing in a complex environment. As. L. J. Stone puts it, "A mode of acting developed 'in the face of' cannot be as general as something coming essentially 'from the core of' the person."

In spite of all these limitations, the emphasis on unity is wholesome and fundamentally useful. The style of life is the final pinnacle in the Adlerian architecture, the last construction for the interpretation of personality and the life history. If personality is as highly stylized, as dependable, as unitary as this, its theme may be caught, its trends predicted, its aberrations reduced to order. For Adler there were two fundamental styles of life. Western culture is shot through and through with an ambivalence that puts its mark on every growing person: Get ahead; don't be forward. Climb to the top; don't climb over others. Heaven helps them that help themselves; he that saveth his life shall lose it. The child must confront these contradictory goals and see them through in the family situation; he must see them through at school; he must see them through in the economic world.

This issue is of the sort which we discussed in relation to the adjustment of action tendencies (cf. page 196); it is the old problem of dominance (in the biological sense), alternation, or compromise, for a genuine "integration" of contradictories makes no more sense in biology than in logic. The result for human personality types (if we may use the concept of types as constructs to guide our thinking) is simple; each personality becomes centered in one or the other of two possible modes or themes that recur endlessly. The slogan for the one is "Through strength I conquer"; for the other, "Through weakness I conquer." Whether the ultimate objective of any activity be gain, power, prestige, or something else, or any combination of them all, the first road to this objective is a power road. If this road is blocked, there is another that may still lead to our destination: we may be gentle, opposing no one; we may make people like us, speak fair words, bid for sympathy. Others as weak as we are will join with us, and some who are strong may protect us. At the root of childhood personality—for all moralisms are utterly irrelevant to the issue—is the choice between these two life themes, the direct and the indirect approach to the good things.

There are of course vacillations, deviations, blockings when the two tendencies are balanced; nor does the style of life become so rigid as to be used unaltered regardless of changed situations which would rob it of its meaning. Macduff can sob; Uriah Heep can roar. But the decision between the two tendencies, made slowly through the months and years of experimenting with life and with the ways of one's fellows, must tend, like all products of trial-and-error learning, to become more and more definite, quasi-mechanical. We have finally acquired our own clear pattern and have at the same time learned our comrade's ways so well that in similar quasi-mechanical fashion we expect from him what is "typical."

The types thus constituted, with as many subtypes as are recognizable and useful in prediction, are types not of goals but of methods toward these goals. They may be money, or a woman's love, or a place of honor. Whatever the goal, the technique is what marks off the aggressive from the submissive, the active from the passive competitor. It is for this reason that personalities are classified not with respect to their aims but with respect to their styles of life. The style is conceived to be a unified, persistent, all-encompassing attitude; a way of seeing, of feeling, and of acting; a leitmotif around which the changing impulses are ordered. Such a classification cuts across a classification in terms of life values (cf. page 283), but it has much in common with the Freud-Abraham typology (cf. page 485).

Thus far it might appear that the style of life once achieved by means of compensation in early childhood remains as a fixed expression of character, so firmly anchored in the individual's life process that he cannot cast it off. But since anything that can be learned through such trial-and-error and conditioning processes can likewise be unlearned, we should expect this entire process to be reversible, at least in some degree. We should expect to find children with strong dominance feelings becoming less secure when their techniques for dominance fail, and we should expect to find shy children becoming ascendant if they can be taught techniques for mastering situations and other children. In the same way we should expect self-respect or self-sufficiency to be rapidly modified during the elementary-school period, with the greatest fluidity or modifiability appearing in the sensitive period of early adolescence. In support of this view, the California Adolescence Study offers cogent evidence that changes both in outer status and in inner dominance feelings may take place with great rapidity during a year or two of critical change (cf. page 514).

Adler was thoroughly alive to this issue of the remaking of the style of life. One of the most ingenious aspects of his theory relates to what happens when a basic life style, thoroughly adequate to the individual's needs, meets a later situation which refuses to yield to it. The individual has learned to handle frustration by means of his ever-present compensation; but now *the compensatory mechanism is itself frustrated.* It follows from all the preceding theory that he must resort again to infantile efforts, must regress to the chaotic trial-and-error behavior of his earlier years; the study by Barker, Dembo, and Lewin (page 145) makes clear that this may indeed happen. But the individual is still capable of learning. Despite Maier's hypothesis that frustration behavior is basically different from drive behavior, the exploratory process recommences; and since the new situation is by definition radically different from the old, *a new style of life* is forged— at least in the normal person.

What will happen if all the exploratory steps taken to find a new style of life eventuate in similar catastrophic failure, if all the doors prove to be locked? The sense of failure will force itself upon the individual, suffuse with its color his whole portrait of himself; the one aspect of experience from which we ordinarily avert our eyes, the fact that we are failures, is the one thing that is clear. In consequence, the *secondary inferiority feeling* arises. This is far more serious than the primary feeling. For it is the nature of all of us to develop primary inferiority feelings, and the good fortune of most of us to develop successful compensations leading to a stable style of life; but the secondary inferiority feeling which befalls those whose technique drops apart in their hands forces the individual to restructure his picture of himself in terms of the awareness of failure and of a conscious sense of inferiority. Of course our compensations fail all of us occasionally and to a limited degree, because no first compensations work perfectly in all situations. But if we are to understand neurosis, it seems fair to agree with Adler that there is need for the specific study of the extreme, yet common, reaction in which the first compensations collapse completely, and the individual starts all over again with inferiority and an effort to compensate for it.

There is only one possible outcome in this situation. Since life continues to be a struggle, and since, in our culture, to be pitiful and frustrated is a means of securing a modicum of prestige as a sufferer, a person worthy of pity, the sufferer discovers by trial and error (or by imitation, etc.; cf. page 221) that this is the one device still ready to his hand. He becomes almost a walking inferiority feeling; he inserts his sense of inadequacy into his conversation on every occasion. Not only does he fish for compliments and reassurance; he belabors his listeners with the story of his failures, as if to make sure that no one could escape from such a plight any more successfully than he. The process tends to snowball in such a fashion as to consume his every energy. As in the principle of physiological dominance (page 200), competing tendencies are swallowed up and every phase of life is colored with the sense of helplessness. This is in fact what is seen in many cases of depression and involutional melancholia. To some degree, the technique actually works; the environment can to some extent be dominated by this device. Many a neurotic patient succeeds in constructing a world subject to his sham domination. The process is never self-correcting, because the need is so imperious; every hour demands that the technique be used afresh. In the meantime life becomes narrowed; new situations which might liberate new energies are avoided; barriers are built up against any possible interfering process. The individual has thus brought himself to a dead center of fixity, or rigidity, and there is within his power no device for working himself away from it again.

The *therapy* of inferiority feelings must be considered with reference both to the general pathology just described and to the patient's own predicament. The problem is essentially situational. Since the patient has worked himself to a dead center, new energy must be introduced at the proper angle by an intelligent outside force. Specific steps must be outlined which are pertinent to the specific kinds of secondary inferiority feelings expressed. These may be defined as (1) the discovery of the remaining security areas, (2) the inculcation of social feeling, (3) the unmasking of poses.

Security areas may be easily discovered in the nervous child, but the process may be very difficult in the confirmed adult neurotic. In theory, such areas always exist, no matter how perfect the mask; and when discovered they can be broadened and redefined, so that the patient can undertake more and more each day, and find more and more real satisfaction in his actual achievements. Though the concept of transference is not used in Adler's therapy, the physician himself may through reassurance provide a social, conversational area of security, teaching the patient how to extend this area first with his intimates and then with strangers. Thus reassurance given a small child in a situation which makes him feel shy or inadequate may feature the phases of a situation in which he feels adequate; robbing a specific threatening situation of its terrors (cf. page 530) tends to result in more generalized reassurance. Learning to master rather than retreat might become cumulatively a life technique.

Social feeling is almost equivalent to identification, as was said above (page 577). Although the nervous sufferer has long since given up all effort except the attempt to assuage his own distress, he still possesses potential social dispositions, such as those he entertained as a child in relation to his parents. Even if identification with his parents was originally based chiefly upon the will to power, it had also its tender phases; and tenderness may develop rapidly as he recognizes that we are all caught in more or less the same predicament and that we might, as well as not, help each other out of it. Identification with the psychiatrist, and through him with others who are striving to help people, may turn the power drive in the direction of the kind of domination which active helpfulness entails; self-expression, domination, affection may be so fused as to make it futile to try to disentangle them.

A considerable portion of the therapy, however, involves a direct effort to gain insight for the patient by confronting him with the techniques by which he has sought to deceive both himself and others. In a sympathetic but straightforward way, the psychiatrist explains the poses, the shams, the indirections which make up a neurotic's life; he points out that genuine mastery cannot be achieved by any of the gestures toward invalidism which the patient has used, and that true self-realization lies only in social participation.

The therapy is simple—often much too simple. While we might say that the behavioristic and psychoanalytic approaches incline to see personality as a structure made from many components—to see the trees rather than the forest—Adler's approach, like that of Gestalt psychology, is much more likely to see the forest than the trees. We see in a flash the massive trend of a single life style. This may lead to arbitrary, oversharp diagnosis and to short cuts in which individuals are classed together on the basis of surface manifestations, hidden elements being either ignored or approached through intuition rather than observation. It is of some interest here that whereas many practitioners have rejected the psychoanalytic theories, few who have once learned it have rejected the psychoanalytic *method* and the enormous value of the rich material it discloses; Adler's theories, on the other hand, have crept into both our psychiatry and our folklore, though he left no ordered account of the therapeutic methods which he regarded as essential.

It must be recognized that this therapy shares one weakness with the psychoanalytic system, namely, the polarization in the doctor-patient relation. The psychiatrist puts the patient on the spot; he is "in the right," the patient is "in the wrong." Nevertheless, during the last years of his life Adler began to use social forms of therapy, particularly in the public schools of Vienna. This method transcended therapy and became social reeducation. The humanitarian impulse, becoming ever stronger as Adler grew older and as he participated in the work of the Social Democratic movement in Vienna, came close indeed to what in the United States would be called progressive education, especially where it overlaps the "group work" movement as a modern social-work technique.

It is hardly surprising to discover, in view of this social emphasis, that the social philosophy of the last years of "individual psychology" in Europe inclined not only to democracy but to Marxism and to revolutionary thinking generally. Nor is it surprising to learn that many people, convinced by the difficulty of the times that the individual has no real escape from the encrusted barriers of the economic system, became mystics. Philosophical materialism and mysticism similarly gained ground in Greece after the collapse of the city-state. They will perhaps always appear when the primary values of life are profoundly frustrated, for under such conditions the individual feels the need to escape either into an un-social world or into a completely remade social world.

POSITIONAL PSYCHOLOGY

Though all human beings are born into specific positions in families—first-born, last-born, only child, etc.—and though a few of the Freudians realized the importance of order of birth in personality formation, it remained for Adler to conceive the importance of birth order as a factor to be fully and systematically explored.

In beginning a study of "positional psychology," we must ask what one *finds* when he is born, and what role he must play in that situation. The first role the new born must play is that of newcomer in the family. He may be well or ill cast for it, and he may receive good or indifferent "support" from the parents. The first-born child conveys to his parents a bundle of meanings which precipitate upon himself an avalanche of meaningful responses. He is a consummation, a physical symbol of the family; a replica or reminiscence of the parent; something to admire, hold, and photograph; a token of the future, something that will one day bring pride or grief; a responsibility, a hostage, a barrier to much that without him the parents were able to do; a comfort and companion to the mother when the father is away. "Does he have a family?" "He just has a wife, no children."

Much has been written about the newcomer's gift of bringing estranged parents together, but very little about his capacity to divide and conquer. Until he came, marriage was simply marriage; the two existed for each other. Now they must exist for him. The mother's energy, time, strength, even her feeling, are drawn mostly into his care; the father's economic responsibility takes on a grimmer character. In addition to all this, which any child can do to a pair of adults, there are special influences dependent on sex; there is the father's identification, pride, responsibility for his son, and the mother's identification, closeness, ambivalence (in a world of sex inequalities) in relation to her daughter.

After the flush of excitement, pride, and responsibility, the parents settle down into their new stride. From the baby's own "point of view"—as fast as he acquires one—he is little, helpless, ignorant; these big hulks go and come as they please, make the rules, administer the "sanctions." But retaliation is possible. The baby can kick and scream, he can be cute and winsome; he holds plenty of aces. He controls much of what father does, and nearly all of what mother does. His rule is capricious but despotic. It is a constitutional monarchy, to be sure; he can be controlled by parliamentary methods. But he cannot abdicate; and though he can be ignored at times, his powers cannot be clipped below a very clear—and large—grant. As he grows, he learns how to rule more effectively, more powerfully; he learns the weaknesses of this parliamentary control, especially on all points on which parliament is divided. He learns how his weakness, as well as his strength, can command the field. But not only does he learn the sense of power; the self is undergoing development, and he learns to note his own worth. His parents evidently find him important, a supreme value. Since they know all about things, they are probably right, so he concludes very reasonably that he must be very, very valuable.

The simple consequence of all this is that nearly every personality in western civilization shows the residues and the directional thrusts which this first central experience in life has imposed. The individual has been king, even though it was when he was weak and ignorant. But he has grown stronger and wiser, and has thrown off all the special characteristics which made the regal role possible. However, the fact remains that he learned the feeling and the art of kingship. There are all kinds of kings and all kinds of realms. As we suggested earlier, it is the diversity of the realms, and the resulting types of kingship which one has learned to exercise, that give the first clue to personality differences.

With the gentlest of warnings, perhaps (but even the gentlest are rude enough), the child awakens to a great tragedy against which he can have no defense. Another king is on the way. Mother goes off to her room for long periods; finally she is "confined"; he cannot see her. When she comes back there is a small stranger with her. She is absorbed in him. There are intimate times when the child must stay on one side of a door when she and the stranger are together on the other side. The child cannot even get complete answers to his bewildered questions. The first losses are in the ego realm (someone else is now the supreme value), rather than in the power realm. The child vaguely grasps that he is not the world center. But the power losses follow quickly, and other losses too; people have less time, less energy for play with a two-year-old; he must keep quiet while little brother sleeps; mother isn't feeling very well yet.

Sometimes the child is blocked, thrown on dead center, by this experience. He may develop the full-fledged secondary inferiority feeling already described (page 581). But if he is still very plastic, exploratory, he is much more likely to be simply bewildered and miserable, and to begin a new series of compensatory efforts. Except in the moments that the parent can spare to play with or to reassure him, he lives in the realms of personal and solitary play which he has already developed, especially the play with his own body and the dear familiar toys which are now all the dearer. For most children in this predicament, it is still too early for imaginary companions, but it is not too early for fragmentary daydreams. Since the sense of blocking is quickened when the rival is in range of eye or ear, the result may be the tension of stammering, or, since the child is now old enough to use directed attack (cf. page 557), it may be expressed directly in assault and battery.

The aspect of the situation on which our interest focuses is the necessity of remaking one's style of life, often at a time when the first flush of satisfaction with the self (cf. two-year-old mastery of language and locomotion skills, and two-year-old negativism, page 218) means that any redirection of life is a renunciation. Even though the child may steer clear of a neurotic solution, the problem is difficult. If the first style was that of the conquering hero, the conquering darling, the sorrows of dethronement are made more bitter by the evident disapproval, the loss of status, which accompanies his every effort at reinstatement. "He's jealous of his little brother," say the parents; "why, instead of being proud of him, he's as mean as he can be!" If the conquering-hero style is to be maintained against this, audacity is needed, and a fine coating of indifference to the opinions of mankind. Otherwise the only new avenue of escape from the predicament is to be a sad, lonely little child, or to have stomach-aches, headaches, or allergies. Depending on sex standards, the child's sex is important in determining the pattern adopted.

These behaviors bring attention, self-enhancement. They are not "purposive" at first; they are spill-overs from a state of strain, and they gradually recur more uniformly in time of crisis, in a manner suggesting the usual trial-and-error sequences. This new style of life, whatever it is, will remain as long as it serves the need; often enough it is entrenched for the entire growth period, and has a direct effect upon the choice of activities and playmates. The longer it is entrenched, the more clearly it becomes part of the self—one "can't fancy oneself" arguing back, or not arguing back, as the case may be. The habits thus established will persist as long as they work. And if one remains big brother or sister in a household which adores little brother or sister, they are likely to become fully ingrained. This suggests the generalization that *personality is largely a reaction to the competitive situation first encountered in the family.*

The newcomer in the family knows little about all this until long after he has worked out his own first great "style." His situation is like that originally encountered by the first child, but instead of two people to control there are three. Direct control over the older sibling is of course a possibility, and one that is often seized in later years if brawn or brain permits; but all the first techniques are part of the craft of weakness. If that big fellow takes your toys, your tears will bring healing intervention. In time he learns the boundaries of your absolute domain; and in every case in which you are too little or too weak to stand on an equal footing, he also learns the extent of your relative or, as we have called it, constitutional monarchy. If you are a girl, you may more easily win parental approval conjointly with the tactical victory. Again, the resulting styles are habit patterns which gain cumulative strength, snowball into mountains. The third-born child initiates a sequence somewhat like that precipitated by the second. Perhaps a new child means less excitement now; but the domain to be controlled is still larger. Dethronement by the third child may be more difficult for the middle child to bear than it was for the first-born when he found himself dethroned by the second, because the oldest and youngest both have a special advantage due to birth, whereas the middle child alone has none. To the last-born children, with the rich experience of unsurrendered sovereignty, the neighborhood and school may later bring difficulties. But the youngest child has learned in the family some of the ways of coping with competition, especially those which pivot upon the ways of babyhood. He is forever the baby of the family, especially to the mother, nostalgic for the experience of mothering as it fades away. The youngest must be kept young. The only child is the first and the last; he is never dethroned. The dethronement experience that he is bound to undergo in neighborhood play or at school is perhaps that much the harder; for him the family will always be a very special asylum, the outer world always a little harsh. He feels a special need to find in the outer world substitute fathers and mothers, people to idealize and people to trust.

A composite photograph of many of Adler's positional types may be attempted in the story of "little mother" (she is literally a composite; she will be found in no case history document). Mary was a six-year-old, the darling of her parents. She was mature beyond her years, understood the care of the two little brothers, saw through mother's eyes, kept the youngsters quiet when daddy was resting. Late in the autumn mother complained of headaches; she went to a hospital for a few days, but she did not come back. There was mourning, and daddy was broken. Little mother never faltered; it was her own courage and devotion that carried father through the anguish and kept the home a home. Eighteen months later her father remarried. The new mother was sweet, devoted to the children. But she did not understand. When Mary took her brothers out for a walk, the new mother called after her, "Come back and get their wraps, dear; it's cold." *How absurd; nobody but a dope would think it's cold in May; she doesn't know I've been taking care of them for years and years.* The following week, with her own spending money, Mary bought them ice-cream cones; it was so hot. The new mother smiled worriedly: "It was sweet of you, but they have had too much ice cream lately." Tensions mounted steadily; there were sobs and wet pillows, and a series of nightmares. Often in the mornings there was blood on "little mother's" palms where the nails had cut as her hands clenched in agonized convulsions. Two weeks later came screams from the next room; father rushed in and found welts across the younger boy's face and Mary about to slap again. A child welfare clinic saw Mary, the little mother who had become a raging "sadist." It was all pitifully simple. Her *whole self* was little mother; it was her life, it was as little mother that she was adequate, worthy, lovable. When the new mother took away the role, she took away the whole basis of *worth*, and nothing but convulsed and vibrating frustration was left.

But it is time to return to the normal, the everyday, the humdrum. If Adler's approach applies to the epic of the neuroses, it applies also to the common prose of daily living. Everything that appears picturesquely in the Adler case studies appears just as clearly to the discerning eye in almost any daily fragment of normal behavior. To summarize the picture sketched thus far, we may ask the meaning, in Adler's terms, of a very common artless remark: "I never could do math." This slogan of the high-school and college student is a compact summary of most of the mechanisms that have been described. We begin with the first person singular. The statement has interest and importance because of the person who is talking. If John or Mary can't do math, the response is "So what?" But if *I* can't do math, it is news; it is on this basis that one ventures to make the petulant assertion and to demand the attention of the listener. Second, it is clear from the word "never" that this special disability has been there from the beginning of time. No total depravity or moral lassitude is involved. The situation is like that of the blind man whom the law requires to see, or the dwarf whom the law requires to behave like a giant; it is unfair. The fact that one *never* could do math is surely evidence that it was fate and nothing else that decreed the situation. Third, the word "could" again makes it plain, but more subtly, that the situation involves no act of will, nothing that any heroic volition could have evaded. So put the blame upon those who are so stupid or depraved as to demand, in their cruelty, things which are contrary to the ultimate laws of nature. Fourth, it is clear that math is the difficulty; the difficulty is not generalized. It is implied that I am good at English, history, French, economics, psychology. Math is the thing that sticks out like a sore thumb; it shows the region of special frustration and, by contrast, the laudable achievements in other spheres. The speaker is not concerned with a general disability; on the contrary, he is a good student—this is clear—who was confronted by a single obstacle. There is, moreover, an implication, in the way in which the words are put together, that this foreign body in an otherwise healthy organism of academic achievement is frustrating the life of an otherwise effective and happy individual, and hence constitutes a sort of offense against decency and good sense.

On the surface, the innocent little statement sounds like the sorry excuse of a pathetic and self-pitying person. At second glance, it looks like a factual statement offered as an excuse. At a third and perhaps more penetrating level of analysis, it seems to be a technique of self-enhancement, fraught with very considerable poignancy and subtlety, that is by no means inferior to the shy techniques of self-enhancement which we encounter in the Pueblo Indians (page 806).

INTEGRATION OF ADLER'S FINDINGS WITH THE FINDINGS OF OTHERS

The main facts about inferiority feelings and their compensation have been noted many times by those who have worked clinically with disturbed human beings; most of them, indeed, have been observed by every intelligent human being regardless of his contact with the learned world in general or with psychology in particular.

Ordinary parents see these mechanisms in show-off children, and vice versa. The Adlerian material, like the Freudian, makes sense at the empirical level. The data fall into natural groups; they have the ring of genuineness and their collective pattern makes sense. Our problem, then, is not the sifting of the *findings*; it is rather their integration with the interpretations to which we feel we have already been driven. Actually this integration is far from difficult. In contrast with the bitter acrimony of Freudians and Adlerians, their materials, when juxtaposed, show a surprising similarity. And just as we have found it possible to integrate Freud with the earlier experimental materials, so it is easy to show the way in which Adler's theoretical scheme articulates with data accumulated by others. In the case of Freud, we tried to show that most of the theoretical contributions which have had enduring life relate to the nature of the ego, its conscious and unconscious structure, its dynamics, and its tendency to breed conflicts. Suppose we attempt the same thing regarding Adler's findings.

The simpler physiological types of compensation are of small importance in relation to Adler's basic schema. What is important is the misery of the slighted person; in its more extreme form it is the injured self, the shamed, humiliated, beaten, embittered member of the community, whose self-respect, whose status, whose sense of his own worth has been challenged so vigorously from without that he has learned to challenge it himself. If there were no ego, there could be no inferiority feelings; or if on the other hand the ego were adequate, there would be none. The self-picture which the individual tries to maintain in unblemished form forever needs enhancement and defense. The mechanisms of compensation are purely those of self-enhancement and defense.

Unwilling to talk about an ego, unwilling to raise questions about basic drives or the learning process, Adler classed all the complicated mechanisms of self-defense and self-enhancement under the narrow term compensation. The result, while of considerable practical value for many patients, confused the efforts at theoretical clarity. The individual does not struggle to enhance the ego on Monday, Wednesday, and Friday, and to compensate for inferiority on Tuesday,

Thursday, and Saturday; the mechanisms are the same but they have other names.

It is consequently possible to do a somewhat better cross-cultural job with Freud's system than with Adler's. It would be hard to explain why the Arapesh compensates so little and the Comanche Indian so much. But if differences in ego development and organization are made clear in cultural studies, it is easy to see why the Arapesh need strive but little to enhance the self, whereas the Comanche have to strive so unremittingly. Whatever in the social situation modifies the self and the devices for self-enhancement and self-defense modifies all the patterns about which Adler has spoken.

We may say then, quite simply, that the terminology already used can well remain in force, and that the Adlerian terminology may be properly demobilized except for biographical and historical studies. Nevertheless, the mass of data relative to the problems of the ego that has come to us from Adler and his school is tremendously rich; we shall remain forever indebted for the ruthlessness and simplicity with which such problems were described in an era when Adler was generally ridiculed by the analysts and ignored by "hard-headed" medical men. Adler did as much as any individual to make clear that ego problems are as central as sex or any other problems—indeed, that for most civilized men they are the most burning problems of all. The fact that he hit upon an unfortunate nomenclature will in time mean less and less; the fact that he hit upon a universal and compelling dynamic of human behavior will in time mean more and more.

25. Extroversion-Introversion

AT THE turn of the century, when Freud's reputation spread far and wide as a result of his *Interpretation of Dreams*, a number of the psychiatrists of the German-speaking world became willing to listen to theories pertaining to the unconscious. Among these was the Zurich psychiatrist, C. G. Jung. His response appears to have been wholehearted, his application of the new material avid. He introduced a number of experimental methods into the study of psychoanalytic dynamics and wrote an epoch-making psychoanalytic study on the theory of dementia praecox. But in 1911 a series of issues led to a breach between Freud and Jung, an important difference being the definition of the libido. Although we shall not go into the controversies that followed, we must discuss one aspect of Jung's libido theory which has led to a huge amount of significant personality research.

Noting that some people live within themselves and others only in their converse with other people, Jung was led to postulate two great types characterized by the *inward* or the *outward* turning of the libido, by preoccupation with the world of the self or by preoccupation with social reality. The thumbnail sketches given on page 568 to illustrate the Adlerian approach could be paralleled by examples of extroversion and introversion in terms of such personalities as Theodore Roosevelt and Woodrow Wilson. The sketch of Theodore Roosevelt would emphasize not the asthma and the humiliating experiences as a boy, but the temperament that led to vigorous identification with his active and successful father; it would note that skill in boxing led to an extension of social aggression in many situations, and would stress the social participation and leadership in college and in political and military positions involving contact with all sorts of people and the capacity to win their loyalty. The "big stick," the Ananias Club, the African big-game hunting trip are examples not so much of the quest for power as of the quest to make his personality omnipresent, to escape from himself into a seething multitude of new experiences. In the case of Woodrow Wilson, the emphasis would lie upon his constant need to define social experience in abstract and contemplative terms, his need to fulfill a clearly defined inner picture of selfhood, his inability to rub elbows with the common man, and an incapacity to understand the needs, the feelings, the thoughts of others.

The types may be obvious or obscure; there are indeed many sub-types to be disentangled, and, Jung says, their proper placement may take months of the analyst's time. It is important to realize that it is the direction of the libido, not the activity arising from it, that distinguishes the extrovert from the introvert; thus many an engineer who is fascinated by wheels or air pressures may be an "objective introvert" to whom not the work done by his engine but its inherent fascination is satisfying. As a matter of fact, Jung's concept is difficult to adapt to the ordinary procedures of psychology, so much so that it is best to stress at once that for him the determination of intro-version-extroversion is a complex analytical task which overlaps, to an unknown but probably only a slight degree, the procedures currently used with large populations whose individual members are not well known to the experimenter.

Two points are involved, nevertheless, which in the form considered here are very simple. As with Freud and Adler, we are interested not in pure exposition, but in putting Jung to work; hence we shall freely use and recast his ideas. The first point is Jung's theory that motivation is general before it becomes specific (cf. the data in Chapters 3–7). The term libido designates for Jung the entire system of energies apparent in the living organism, the life energy available to the person; specific drives, such as the nutritive, sexual, or maternal, are developed later on as the tissues themselves develop. Second, the fund of life energy may be turned in the direction of outer response and be discharged upon the outer world, or it may be inwardly disposed, discharged within. This is not far from the concept of energy

discharge as taking an outer or an inner direction, which we quoted
earlier from H. E. Jones (page 82; cf. also Marston, page 603).
This does not, of course, do justice to the complexities of Jung's
theory of the libido, but it does bring out the essential point which
we wish to stress here, the fact that a person's life may be devoted
chiefly to interaction with the outer environment (largely through
the mediation of the exteroceptors and striped muscles), or primarily
to cerebral or autonomic processes (making large use of the inter-
oceptors and unstriped muscles). Among the problems raised by
this approach are (1) the dynamics of this outer or inner disposition
of energies, and (2) the question whether human beings can be fruit-
fully classified in terms of this energy disposition—extroverted,
turned out; and introverted, turned in. Both problems might be conceived as aspects of the balance of the *self* and *non-self* or the *ego* and
alter as it manifests itself in the individual's life. This is not to assume
that self-love is the *only* motive that can lead to preoccupation with
one's inner world; a person may have a problem to solve, or he may
be under the influence of opium. Nor does it assume that love of the
outer world is the *only* motive that leads to activity in relation to it;
the individual may need to have commerce with it to satisfy his
inner needs. But if introversion and extroversion be defined as preoccupation with the inner and outer worlds respectively, and if it be
granted that love, in the broad sense of *positive response*, plays a large
part in determining this preoccupation, the concepts will be well
worth exploring.

The exploration, however, must begin cautiously. Canalization
upon the self does not necessarily involve unreadiness to canalize
upon other objects. He who loves himself may love all men, and he
who loves himself very little may be incapable of love for others;
an increase in self-regard may lead to an increasing love of others.
Indeed, we have noted (page 497) that attitudes toward the self and
the non-self seem in general to be correlated positively rather than
negatively. It is not he who is in love with his environment who slights
or despises himself. Just as in one study it appeared that those who
feared death most were those who had the least to live for, so positive

attitudes toward what lies within the self go hand in hand with positive attitudes toward all that lies beyond it. The existence of a *generalized* attitude of affirmation—the "yea to life," as Nietzsche expressed it—puts an end to the conception of a fixed quantity, or fund, of the capacity to respond, which must be used outwardly or inwardly. He who has the gift of response is able to use it either inwardly or outwardly. The very fact that a person values the self may mean that he thereby values the work of others more highly; conversely, the collapse of self-regard may involve not readier sacrifices, but apathy in responding to all such appeals. To put the matter more broadly, there is no necessary compensatory role by which a surplus of affect for any one component in one's world automatically robs another component. There may well be a general tendency for each to increase in value with the rest. The problem of this adjustment of values should not be prejudged. We may find that the individual discovers a means of maintaining a balance between the *self* and *other*, or a characteristic way of losing it; but it does not follow that introversion implies the want of extroversion, or vice versa.

This has immediate implications in personality research, especially with small children whose behavior is not necessarily analyzed in terms of pairs of opposite traits as seen from the adult point of view. Studies of the relations of "desirable" and "undesirable" traits afford a striking example. The demonstration that "desirable" qualities are positively intercorrelated provides the background for such a problem. Intelligence, for example, is correlated with honesty, with generosity, and with persistence. Studies of gifted children generally indicate that even such factors as height, weight, and health are positively correlated with intelligence—the favored organism "has everything." In the light of such evidence, it is very natural to study the interrelations of "bad" qualities. These also turn out to be intercorrelated. Esther Berne, however, had the perseverance and the sense of humor to go beyond this rather Zoroastrian dualism of good and bad; accordingly she proceeded to correlate "good" qualities with "bad," and discovered positive intercorrelations. The reason for all this has become clear in later studies. Whatever involves *outgoing* response appears in all the specific facets of behavior. The more the child tends to *do things*, the more he tends to do *all* the things there are to be done. The most relevant dimension is the activity dimension—children who are active are aggressive, cooperative, sympathetic. L. B. Murphy found aggression and cooperation to be positively and substantially correlated. The fact that children have resources for living means that they live more richly in their environment. But they also live more richly in themselves. Thus Munroe and Levy were able to show that children living in a favored environment have a richer fantasy life than those in a poorer environment. The rule, as Thorndike would say, is not compensation but correlation.

This is doubtless partly due to intercorrelation in the positive hereditary assets (through assortative mating, etc.), and it is likewise partly due to the positive intercorrelation of the various "advantages" which children may derive from favored homes. But it is partly a matter of transfer—especially transfer of attitudes of confidence and hence of participation—from one situation to another. There is more of this transfer in early life than later because the self is less sharply defined; there is less functional difference for the small child between what is outer and what is inner. Although an adult traumatized by his environment can withdraw "into the self," a child playing in a sandbox cannot do quite the same thing; he may keep out of the way of other youngsters with whom he cannot cope, but the self into which he withdraws is still in large part a self of action, of observation, of physical contact with the environment.

There is still another reason for this transfer from self-attitude to attitude directed to the outer world. So far as the individual's contact with the outer world brings *good* results, he feels inwardly like a *good* person—like little Jack Horner. At the same time the more adequate and satisfying his inner existence, the greater the tide of energy supporting outward activity. He who freezes and does nothing does not thereby develop a rich inner world. Even when the person is frustrated in his outer life and withdraws into his own inner activities, these activities are likely to be modeled on earlier external experience, fantasies relating to the outer world. When the outer world has left a deep enough joy in the heart, there is some satisfaction even in the pale reliving. It is not the outwardly frustrated individual who discovers the greatest riches in his own world of fantasy or creation; it is a Shelley, a Wordsworth, a Goethe, rich in the outer world of persons and beautiful things, whose *inner* world is most deeply rewarding.

In the face of correlations such as these, the theory of outward versus inward turning of the libido has to be recast. Indeed, the concept of self-love as a sort of logical opposite to the love of others is in conflict with the elementary fact that as the self expands, the world to be loved expands. There is little to add today to what William James wrote in 1890 regarding the expansion of the self, but there is much to confirm the soundness of his definition of the elementary conditions of mental health. Selfhood, having begun as a physical object such as the tip of the nose (page 483) or the sound of one's own voice, has spread out to engulf a vast visual, auditory, tactual, kinesthetic, organic network of experiences. Traditionally, the moralists have been troubled with the question how one ever emerges from this network of selfhood. The boundary which has been implicitly set up between self and not-self is, however, a figment of the philosopher's imagination. The child does not even know whether the hand or voice belonging to his father or mother is inside or outside the self; nor, as he identifies with their purpose, does he know what it is they want and what it is he wants. The to-and-fro movement of the self and non-self is such that the feelings and purposes of others constitute a large part of the normal self; indeed, the incapacity for this expansion of the self is a good indicator of a schizoid trend. There is therefore no intelligible problem of drawing a line to mark a fixed boundary. The clothes, the furs, the ring, the hair-do, the pet, the favorite book, the summer place, the club, the political party— these represent perhaps levels of diminishing intensity of selfhood, but they all have a place in the self. For the mystic, the poet, the star-lover, the self may quite literally comprise the universe. The ultimate test of this self quality probably lies in the hurt feelings which are aroused by derogatory remarks. "Love me, love my dog." "Who steals my purse steals trash." Who prefers the Milky Way to my Pleiades, his geraniums to my delphiniums, insults my sensibilities.

The self may spread far out or extend only a little way, but it must include a great deal more than one's own anatomy or personal memories if it is to be a functional component in social living. Instead of believing with Hobbes that one seeks what will benefit the little volume enclosed within the skin, it is becoming a commonplace of all clinical and educational work that generosity is much more "natural," much "easier," much more "normal," than exclusive concern with one's own protoplasm. Social feeling requires far less pressure for its inculcation than does the rigidly or narrowly defined attitude of looking out for the self. It is, of course, true that the gradient of self-feeling falls off rapidly as family and associates are left behind, as one reaches out to those with whom there is no direct contact. But both the distance to which the self spreads out into space and the intensity of the wave which carries it forward depend very largely upon the warmth and fulfillment found in one's first experiences with family and neighborhood. It is the meager, shallow, unsatisfying self that in general proves incapable of any considerable extension. It is perfectly feasible to study this interdependence of extroversion and introversion in the same individual and to note how the development of either one of them influences the development of the other.

THE EARLY GROWTH OF INTROVERSION-EXTROVERSION

But though introversion and extroversion do not prove to be incompatible, each is a real and fascinating problem in itself. How do they arise? Beginning with introversion, what factors in one individual's life make the inner world an object of special preoccupation to a degree greater than that characteristic of other mortals? Several factors are too obvious to overlook. Individual differences in the degree of positive response to the self would be expected first of all as a result of the sheer vitality, the sheer richness of experience, and the sheer esthetic adequacy of the individual as molded by the esthetic norms of the group. According to the cultural norm, a pretty child should love herself the more, and as the self becomes more and more a conceptual thing (cf. page 506) this love would lead to introversion. Second, identification with parents who love or hate the child may lead him to love or hate himself, so far as he assimilates their point of view. Third, the adequacy of the self as a primary tool toward the achievement of one's life goals should make the individual love (or hate) himself, just as the musician loves (or despises) the instrument in terms of its adequacy in relation to his musical design; one may love himself as a *means* to all good things.

In the same way, individual differences in extroversion due to differences in the purely personal value of the external world should be expected to be widely manifest. Some people find the external world, as a sensory or meaningful whole, more satisfying than do others (esthetic and intellectual factors operating in one's first contact with environment play a part). Thus it is not enough to say that religious orders such as the Franciscans reject the world, for some follow St. Francis in loving the creatures of field and stream and "our brother the sun," as well as their fellow human beings, whereas others look upon the entire outer world as an obstacle which keeps the soul from God. Among the Hindu philosophers who regard the outer world as an illusion, some see in it a dead and static façade devoid of meaning, but others poetically find in it a symbolic representation of the great unseen reality. Moreover, identification with the parents who direct the child to the outer social reality enhances the values already discovered there. Finally, the individual may come to love the outer world, and in particular the people in it, as a *means* to his own living. These factors are symmetrical with those suggested above as contributory to introversion. They are based neither upon sheer heredity nor upon learning as such, but upon early biosocial interactions.

Although in consequence of all these factors introvert and extrovert tendencies are formed in early infancy (each child developing some of both), there is reason to believe that some very important mechanisms for adjusting self-love to love of the outer world come vigorously into play in that period of early speech and locomotion in which the child discovers himself as an entity sharply distinct from his parents, capable of disagreeing with them, flouting their intentions, and making of himself an autonomous social unit. This, as we have said (page 217), is the period when negativism first appears. This negativism is not necessarily due to an increase of narcissism—there has been plenty of this all along. It may be primarily kinetic, the mere reinforcement of self-sustained activity when outer obstacles are encountered. It has in it much of the *fear of being overwhelmed*, as when an infant holds his hand before his eyes, the fingers somewhat apart, so that he can see you although you can barely see his eyes. But there is something more than a fear of being *physically* overwhelmed; there appears to be a fear of being looked into (cf. page 537). The period in which speech first comes rapidly marks the consolidation of the self. During this process one must keep a certain amount of self-valuation, of self-preoccupation, continually in operation; there must be no complete loss of self-awareness, no complete yielding of the self to capture by the outer world. As Freud pointed out, panic may in the same way involve the loss of self, and hence the fear of fear; panic is unutterably terrifying because what is involved is the possibility that the self may be dissolved. This is apparently the basis of the widespread fear of losing consciousness as in fainting, being hypnotized, or undergoing general anesthesia; and this fear is entirely aside from the death fears which may be commingled.[1]

All of this suggests that though in early infancy there may well be a strong positive, rather than a negative, response to both self and

[1] Another generalized fear appears with the loss of the childhood self as one enters puberty; the old familiar self is overwhelmed by physiological growth and transformation and by the social redefinition of the self in terms of the beginning of adult manhood and womanhood (page 508). Starbuck's manuscripts on the religious experience of early adolescents, and the diaries of early adolescents published by Stern and by Bühler, indicate in a literal sense that the old self is being lost and that a new one must be found (cf. page 510).

non-self, the nature of social pressures, especially interference from adults or other children in the form of discipline, ridicule, nagging, etc., is such as to make the child fight for his life—or rather for his self. And since children differ in self-confidence and in the arts of self-defense, we should expect them to vary tremendously with respect to their success in this duel with society. As measured, then, extroversion may prove to consist primarily of the *capacity to retain self-confidence* despite social onslaughts upon it, rather than being determined by the simple combination of the three factors mentioned on page 601. If so, we should expect to obtain a wide scattering of extroversion scores. They will probably be essentially scores on self-confidence. Most studies of extroversion-introversion have disregarded the possibility that the two tendencies may be *positively correlated*, and have been concerned simply with their *relative strength*. This is a problem important in its own right, and a few examples will be given.

The method of measurement is well illustrated by Marston's study. Children who had been rated by their teachers on a 20-item scale were subjected to six experimental situations. In the first the child was led by an attendant to a room; the attendant left the room after removing a screen behind which the experimenter sat, playing with a "teeter-tauter." He did not look up at the child. If the child advanced toward him in 60 seconds he was given a score of 5 (maximum extroversion). If the child did not advance in 60 seconds, the experimenter looked up at him, then resumed his play with the toy. If the child still held back, the experimenter looked up and smiled. If there was still no response, the experimenter continued playing another 30 seconds, looked up, and said, "Do you like to teeter-tauter?" The ice, so to speak, is melting by perceptible stages, and the child's sociality is measured by the promptness and extent of his willingness to risk a rebuff. The child who fled or who would play only after much urging was scored 0, with intermediate degrees of extroversion scored 4, 3, 2, or 1. The results of the six experiments agree fairly well both with one another and with the teacher's ratings. There is, then, a recognizable strand of tendencies that runs through a wide variety of behaviors;

extroversion, like the majority of social habits, is rather well *generalized* (page 204). Very likely it is a generalized attitude of self-sufficiency.

This degree of generalization does not, however, mean immutability. Self-confidence may be shattered by one great blow or by a series of small ones, and though the process is slow, it can be built up, as is shown by an experiment by L. M. Jack. From a group of eighteen nursery-school children who had been rated on "ascendance" by teachers who knew them well, the five most ascendant and the five least ascendant were chosen. The latter were given intensive training over a six-week period in three playtime activities: telling a story, making mosaic designs, assembling a picture puzzle. When these five non-ascendant children were paired with various ascendant children in situations calling for prowess in these skills, four of them became ascendant; and Page's study, with larger groups, confirmed the findings as to the effects of training. Although unfortunately we have little information as to the *generalization* of the ascendance thus built up, it is a common observation that in children prowess means confidence not only in the task at hand but in others; this is the apparent basis for generalized self-sufficiency.

Newcomb similarly looked for an answer regarding the degree of generality of extrovert and introvert tendencies among preadolescent boys. Boys at a summer camp were rated by their counselors each evening on items such as these:

Did he speak before the group at campfire?
  1. Made a speech or told a story.
  2. Answered request for reports.
  3. Answered questions, or took part in discussion.
  4. Told another something to say for him.

Three kinds of consistency were studied in the responses. (1) The day-by-day "specific behavior consistency," such as consistent speech-making, was rather marked, but it was no higher than (2) "trait consistency," the day-by-day consistency in general traits like resistance to authority. For example, the information that Joe refused to come out of the water on Monday would have some predictive value in relation to the likelihood of his coming out on Tuesday, but the predictive value here would be no greater than it would be in relation to his willingness to leave the tennis court or to clean up around his bunk. So far, we have evidence of two closely related types of generalization in extrovert-introvert tendencies. (3) The well-defined traits that thus appeared were only slightly interrelated. There was an interdependence of these traits somewhat above what could be attributed to chance, indicating *some* generalized extroversion-introversion, but the degree of generalization was not great.

The generality of extrovert-introvert tendencies among adolescents and adults has usually been studied by means of ratings and paper-and-pencil tests, in which a series of behavior situations is defined, each of them offering an opportunity to react upon the outer world or upon oneself. The questionnaire or rating scale may contain items dealing with interests or with the sense of security in society or with the self. The same items may be used for self-ratings and for the rating of others. Thus in the Heidbreder investigation 200 students filled out the form for themselves, and each was rated by two close associates. The results showed that there was a factor or a group of factors running through the items that was recognized by the individual and by others. The data from these 200 students yielded a normal distribution, few extreme extroverts and few extreme introverts being found. Even in the absence of bimodality, the generality of individual response is evidence both for the reality of Jung's introversion and extroversion and against the sharp separation of the types, if in fact the Jung types could be equated with the types conceived to lie embedded in these reaction patterns.

Evidence of generality there certainly is. Perhaps, in view of our analysis, self-confidence is the generalized response that plays the largest part. But we saw above that there are at least three pairs of tendencies that may lead one to respond in an extroverted or an introverted way. Because of this heterogeneity of the underlying factors, we may well hesitate as to the exact meaning of the scores from these ratings and questionnaires. Furthermore, the issue is even more complicated here than it was in the case of the infant (page 601); for in the adult, both the delight in others' faces and voices and in tactual contacts with other persons (cf. page 484) who accept one, and the delight in oneself, have become the means of self-enhancement for various activities which can or cannot be carried on alone. Aside from the simple pleasure in group participation as such, there are many activities that are practically impossible for the isolated person (the "two-man saw" situation), so that one who enjoys these situations necessarily appears extroverted; on the other hand, the sheer richness of imagery or the pleasure of thinking (autistically or otherwise) or other activities for which no partner is needed may be so satisfying that one who enjoys them is necessarily classed as an introvert. Moreover, most opportunities to win approval and prestige arise in group activities, as do also opportunities for conspicuous failure, disapproval, and ego wounds. All these factors would be associated with introversion-extroversion scores on any test or rating scale.

Experience with college students has made it obvious that the last-mentioned factor is usually most important, and that practically everyone is strongly extrovert in the sense of *wanting* these types of social recognition; people differ, not in their desire for it but in their ability to obtain it. Most of those who make high introversion scores seem, when closely studied, to be not people who lack an interest in society, but people who have been frightened by social rebuffs. They are far indeed from the Jungian group who find happiness in solitude: the dreamers, readers, artists; on the contrary, they are shy, traumatized, hungry for companionship which they would win if they knew how. The confusion of "willing" and "unwilling" introversion would in itself be enough to invalidate the notion that we are dealing here with a single entity.

The statistical results are enigmatic; they may appear as easily with a complex nexus of factors as with one. More refined statistical studies have in fact yielded evidence that the scores result from several uncorrelated *clusters* of items, as we suggested above. It would be helpful to regard the introversion-extroversion scores as the product of various attitudes toward the self and toward social contacts, the adequacy of the self-picture being a central component. Indeed, we noted earlier a high degree of generalization of the attitude toward the self. Marston's and Berne's studies reveal this generalization at a high level between two and four years of age,[2] and Pallister's work with college students (page 213) suggests that the self-attitude has reached an even higher degree of generalization. But though transfer from real adequacy in one situation to real adequacy in another is doubtless the primary factor at work, there is considerable reorganization of the self-picture through autism and through psychoanalytic mechanisms as well, and there is a good deal of adjustment of parts to one another, a great deal depending on the phase of the self that serves as the anchor. The self-assured extrovert may be a relative failure who views himself favorably; the socially rebuffed introvert may see only his failures.

Social situations may evoke from the members of a large group a complete continuum of habitual self-attitudes ranging from the most confident to the most diffident, and, indeed, appearing in the form of a normal distribution. But when social stimulation is intense and severe, the issue ordinarily is of the all-or-none type—some can take it, some cannot. Bimodality, and in some cases complete discontinuity, in self-attitudes appear when the issue involves real threats to the self. In a large-scale investigation at Minneapolis with adolescent and young adult groups, the generalization was made that attitudes dealing with remote issues not concerning the self are normally distributed, whereas those presenting a critical issue to the self are bimodally distributed. This principle is brought out in several other studies, as we shall see later.

The reason apparently lies in the nature of the threshold. The stimulus situation will typically be threatening enough to evoke self-defense or, falling just short of that, it will evoke positive or accepting attitudes. In measuring the tendency to self-defense, we are likely to find the stimulus above the threshold for some, below the threshold for others, and at the threshold for only a few. Thus in a series of situations, each specific situation that involves potential

---

[2] A factor-analysis by Williams confirms the generality which appears in a first glance at the data; there is an "approach" factor and an "ascendance" factor

threat will be reacted to defensively by a large group, acceptingly by another large group, and neutrally by a few. Since this will be true of every other item on the scale, and since the items will of course be intercorrelated if they are used to make up a scale, the result will be the tendency to a bimodal distribution just mentioned. The measures of self-attitude do not give a normal curve as they would if the items were independent. Generality goes hand in hand with bimodality; it is in fact likely, though not yet proved, that all the more profound self-attitudes are of this bimodal sort, the more casual ones being more normally distributed.

We are referring here to the large core of self-attitudes which the individual has lived with for a long time. Doubtless, however, there are outlying regions of self-attitudes relating to recent experiences or to infrequently experienced situations, which may be poorly assimilated either to one another or to the central core. In this case specificity rather than generality appears. A chart on which selfhood is represented in a two-dimensional diagram in the manner of Burks and Jones will show a central unity and scattered "independent" traits at the periphery. This is in complete agreement with what was said earlier about the aspiration level, in which we know—from Gould's study, for example—that the main core of generality is supplemented by a number of peripheral cases of specificity. (See page 609.)

All these studies may make us prone to conclude that within the first few years the self-attitude has generalized almost as much as it can, and that from such self-confidence a trend to a given degree of outgoing response has been derived. There is, however, at least one notable exception. In certain types of defeat, the result is not transfer of the hesitant attitude from outer to inner situations, a sheer carry-over of disvaluing tendencies so as to disvalue the self; on the contrary, the individual may fall back on early, familiar, self-trusting tendencies, thus finding inner shelter from further wounds. He who finds life's goals difficult to achieve may develop, as Horney points out, an active narcissism, a need to cling to the self as something which at least is securely held—"a poor thing, but mine own." Although, as we saw, this is not universal, it does occur. One may hug the good old self and discover in it all sorts of virtues never previously suspected.

Peter, aged four, brought up by a nurse who kept him in his stroller almost continuously (not letting him touch the floor) because this made him less of a bother, showed in nursery school an almost

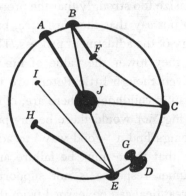

Integration, partial integration, and dissociation in personality: A, The act is fully expressive of the central core of personality, J. B and C, Dissimilar overt acts (i.e., far apart on the surface of the sphere) are nevertheless fully congruent, since they both depend upon J and a common source, F, not closely bound to J. B is more dependent than C upon F, and more dependent upon F than upon J. C is equally dependent upon J and F. D, An act depending upon a source G having almost no relationship to J (e.g., a habit). E, The act is similar to D in overt expression (i.e., close to D on the surface of the sphere), but not congruent with D because it derives from different sources. It is more dependent upon H than upon J, and more dependent upon J than upon I.

complete and literal inward turning of the sort described by Jung. He cultivated a preposterously rich fantasy world, and made such little contact with the outer world that when tested by a conscientious expert at a great university clinic he had an I.Q. of only 65. As intelligent therapy made the outer world less and less dangerous to him, and as he discovered more and more possible values in it, his preoccupation with himself diminished, and his I.Q. rose balloon-fashion month after month, until now, when Peter is ten years old, it is 145. Peter's case exemplifies almost literally Jung's notion of the mutual exclusion of extroverted and introverted responses. In schizophrenia this is excessively common.

We cannot emphasize too strongly that the processes just described are morbid. We do not say that they are rare, but rather that they represent a pathology of the adjustment process. They need not occur; but when they do, they lower the value of life and interfere with functional health. Even though little Peters are tragically common, they are not the norm of childhood. There are, of course, other types of morbid withdrawing, nor would there be any point in maintaining that most human beings find a "good way" to adjust; however, the cardinal assumption that there must be failure and a compensatory cultivation of the inner response is not supported by an over-all view. Although a great deal can be learned from the morbid as to the nature of personality dynamics, other principles besides those just discussed do exist.

It should in particular be stressed that in these morbid cases there are gross difficulties in the identification process and in ejective consciousness. It is the unfeeling nurse who has no contact with Peter who serves as his only available identification object, and she is excessively poor in this role. Many morbidly withdrawn personalities are probably deficient in identification objects. The fact that this process is so vital and so central in early childhood serves to throw further light on the relation of the self-attitude to the attitude toward others.

Since social frustration *may* nevertheless lead to a compensatory habit of seeking satisfaction in the self, the question naturally arises as to whether it is the *whole* self or only a satisfactory *aspect* of the self that is thus inwardly cultivated? The answer apparently is that the various attitudes toward the self become consolidated rather rapidly, so that by mid-adolescence (a period for which there are many case studies and questionnaires) the self-attitude is rather homogeneous. As far as we know, the self is responded to as a whole whether it is (1) a good thing along with other good things, (2) a poor thing which other people reject, or (3) a good thing which one cherishes inwardly because the outer world rejects it.

Here we run full tilt into an apparent difficulty. If the self-attitude is so well generalized, how can we speak of heterogeneity of tendencies entering into introversion-extroversion? Do not the factor analysts make it plain that several distinct tendencies must be included under a catchall term like this? The answer here seems to be as follows: What is generalized is the self-attitude proper, and the sheer appeals of outer and inner *activities* as such are to some degree independent of the attitude toward the self. Most personality questionnaires emphasize the self-attitude, but at the same time certain other elementary values and interests are introduced which, in the light of factor analysis, appear to be measures of canalizations and interests that are essentially independent of the self.

The Modifiability of Adult Extroversion-Introversion

We have protested against the assumption that introversion is consistently due to a *primary satisfaction* with inner activities; on the contrary, we hold that most of what is *called* introversion is purely a retreat from social rebuff, and that the self-attitude, as it is ordinarily studied, is primarily the degree of self-satisfaction that has become crystallized as the result of being accepted or rejected and, by identification, of adjusting one's self-portrait to this circumstance. If this is true, "introversion," as the term is currently used (to mean essentially low self-confidence, especially in social situations) is *modifiable*.

Reference was made earlier (page 604) to Jack's study of the modifiability of ascendance in nursery-school children. Diamond's study of the changeability of extrovert-introvert patterns among young adults is more thoroughgoing. His problem concerned the factors responsible for shifts, during a three-year period, in the introvert or extrovert direction. A self-rating schedule relating to such shifts was administered to some hundreds of young adults, and each subject was also rated independently by two close associates. Although the correlation of .72 between the self-rating and the ratings by acquaintances was not high enough for individual predictions, it was adequate for group predictive purposes.

First as to the relation of such shifts to personal outlook. The students were asked to indicate their political preferences and also to respond to a social attitudes questionnaire. The result showed that students with conservative attitudes were distributed normally in terms of degree of change in introvert-extrovert trends (a few becoming much more introverted, a few much more extroverted, and many changing only slightly), but that students with socialist and communist opinions were distributed bimodally, many moving in the extrovert direction and many in the introvert direction, only few remaining essentially unchanged. This bimodality was apparently due to the social conflict which the espousal of unpopular opinions involved. Some students were "finding themselves," others were "retreating" from social tensions and social disapproval.

The schedule was then administered to about 140 members of the Communist party and of the Young People's Communist League—individuals who were required to do many hours of party work each week, and hence had to develop a rather complete integration between belief and conduct or else drop out. The distribution curve for this latter group (in terms of change in extroversion-introversion over a period of three years) showed that the *entire* population lay to the right of the mid-point of the scale; in other words, every one of the 140 subjects had moved during three years in the extrovert direction.

This result may in part be explained on the grounds that no one would be admitted into these Communist organizations if he showed signs of faltering or holding back, or if he were incapable of active work. However, as autobiographical material makes clear, a large part of the shift is due to the rapid increase in self-confidence which resulted from working with others toward the aim which all approved, caring more and more about the goal and less and less about one's personal attainments. It is reasonable to conclude, as Diamond does, that these dimensions of personality are approached more easily through changing group contacts than through individual therapy.

He goes on to comment appropriately on the history of introversion in European society. Social withdrawal—meaningless in a rigid caste system where the individual has to be fully accepted as a member of a group and has to respond outwardly to others in his group—became, he believes, more and more a reality in Europe and America during the Commercial and Industrial Revolutions, when a person had to *make his own way*, taking nothing for granted and being capable of failure at any point; failure and rebuff led to a turning inward. The less the security in the social structure, the less the inner security in the individual, the greater the proneness to introversion when outer contacts prove unsuccessful.

The Need for Introverts and Extroverts

Finally, we must ask whether extroversion and introversion (in the sense of withdrawal from social contact) are equally normal. What is the role of each in a society such as ours? For what tasks are introverts needed and for what tasks are extroverts needed? This implies an emphasis on relative rather than absolute amounts of each of these tendencies. At a superficial level, the answer is easy. A single typical example of the huge advantage of extrovert tendencies in our own society is provided by a study of a midwestern college group who were given both intelligence tests and introversion-extroversion tests near graduation. The earnings of these students five years after leaving college were found not to be correlated with the previously established intelligence levels, but to be substantially correlated with extroversion scores. It might at first appear that extroverts alone are wanted and are happy.

But a closer look at our crazy-quilt society might lead to the conclusion that the decline of introspective interests, our increasing reliance upon science and upon objectivity, and even the psychoanalytic distrust of self-observation, have tended to make us struggle for social sanity and health in interpersonal living, and to run away from a clear definition of the elementary conditions of inner living that are really satisfying and make for happiness. Among psychologists there is considerably less straightforward self-analysis than there was in the era of William James or the Wundtian introspective psychologists. Introspection has been replaced to some degree by the "stream of consciousness" type of literature as represented, for example, by James Joyce and by stream-of-consciousness movies, and by a series of currents in art such as that initiated by Dali, in which an attempt is made to get at the subjectivity rather than the objectivity of the world with which the representative arts deal. The rather paradoxical result has been that the honest and systematic study of the basic conditions of inner serenity and joy has been allocated to the artists, the term being used broadly; and they have in fact done most to elaborate and enrich the problem. But science, which is always needed to evaluate or to act as a balance wheel, has retreated more and more from the task. Hence, our desperate need for introverts to teach us how to live in a world which threatens us with its vast impersonality is being met almost exclusively by the arts. At least, it is being satisfied for a certain stratum of the elite. It cannot be said that the need of common men for self-understanding is being met by the arts any better than it is by science. In spite of many efforts to make contact with the common man, abstractionism and other types of remoteness, ultra-subtlety, and intellectual isolationism have been the rule. Society's primary need for introverts is for those who are capable of plumbing the real depths within the self as it takes shape in industrial society, and at the same time conveying to others what they have found.

To say at the same time that extroverts are desperately needed will mean little if we refer to current clichés regarding the need for better salesmen and business organizers, but much if we remember that what has gone by the name of extroversion in industrial society in recent decades has involved the sacrifice of depth for the sake of extensity. Even our progressive nursery and elementary schools have tended to encourage the rapid accumulation of superficial social contacts and social victories. If it is as "natural" or "normal" to demand intensity as to demand mere volume of acquaintances, our society can hardly be regarded as doing a good job in the cultivation of extroverts. Indeed, the anxieties and inferiority feelings which writers like Horney attribute to the masses of industrialized people suggest that a few really well-appointed extroverts, taking heroic joy in their extroversion and boldly boasting of their achievement through the arts, might make the current cult of "social adjustment" look rather sick.

The Self as Believer and Doer

At the end of this series of chapters dealing with the self and its troubles, a word is needed about a very simple and much neglected aspect of the self, an aspect connected with what we may call the casual normal solution of the problem of extroversion-introversion achieved by casual normal people. Partly because we live in a society which emphasizes the struggle for status, and partly because those who come to psychiatrists have usually been signally unsuccessful in finding satisfaction in their picture of the self, there has been a general tendency to think that the self is uniformly and by nature a source of woe. But this is a very eccentric conclusion. Societies differ hugely, and individuals within each society differ hugely, in the satisfactions and frustrations which come from selfhood. Even in our own competitive and at present extremely confused society there are people on every hand who are absorbed in the roles and meanings of normal family life, in the daily cycle of satisfying tasks, in the casual recreations of leisure hours. Garage mechanics may be jealous of their status when it is challenged, but be primarily concerned on the job with a genuine interest in solving one problem after another; housewives may be aware of the Joneses in greater or lesser degree, but be primarily concerned with the health and happiness of husbands and children. Gardens, movies, dances, baseball, church, week-end trips, have a pulling power for many people that carries them through the cycle of the years with the sense of positive living; illness and joblessness are the stark interruptions which punctuate the flowing existence of a hundred interrelated positive values. And all these things— trivial or serious—in which people believe and for which they live involve the self just as profoundly, if not as dramatically, as does the tension of recognition and status. The self is what is involved, enmeshed, in all these positive values; it is a good self, a casual self, a self that is related to immediate realities and not alone to comparison with others and hence to competition. It therefore brings the satisfactions of both extroversion and introversion. The generation that followed the First World War has been steadily carrying on a battle against "stuffed-shirt" values. Increased simplicity and appreciation of the functional values in clothes, furniture, and housing are part of this shift, along with the drive for greater simplicity in language and scorn of the flowery terminology of a more pretentious age. The struggle is carried on by means of cartoons like William Steig's "About People," in which various kinds of masks and false fronts are a major concern of the artist.

Progressive education, too, with its central value that of freeing the individual child for genuine experience and creative living, has proceeded to offer the same emphasis by both positive and negative steps. Positively, it attempts to recognize the individual growth pattern of each child, and to permit him to learn and develop academically, as well as in other ways, at his own pace; in general, it tries to stimulate children to value their own ideas and plans and to work out their own projects. Along with this goes an emphasis on learning to live and work with others of their age. Negatively, it throws out the trappings of competitive education—the marks, honors, and external rewards which often tend to stimulate a false effort at "good records" whether the good records are accompanied by good development or not. Thus it aims at stimulating an awareness of the self as an experiencing, creative person rather than as an individual with a certain status. There is nothing inevitable about the frustrated self which we have mentioned and given attention to in the past few chapters. The perspective of the next few chapters will perhaps make clearer why the psychiatric data from an industrial society so heavily stress the problem of the self in difficulty.

Part Five

WHOLENESS

26. Personality Structure

THROUGH all the centuries since the Middle Ages man has learned by experiment and mathematics how to analyze, how to cleave and whittle, how to sort things into their elementary parts and classify each in its proper box. Having done a good job at analysis, he found, as a rule, that he could make some headway at synthesis—he could often put the clock together again. But he was troubled by the fact that sometimes he seemed to have lost the clue to the structural whole, for he found parts which somehow did not fit into the pattern; and sometimes he found, to his dismay, that a part he placed in the wrong position worked in a different way from the way it had worked before. Accordingly it became necessary for him to look more closely at wholes as wholes—*to study structure.* This is where we find ourselves now in our effort to understand personality.

Throughout our study of development, we advanced the hypothesis that there are three developmental stages in the organization of tissue systems, and we offered evidence for its validation. The stages comprise (1) a homogeneous, undifferentiated, global mass; (2) a differentiation, a cleavage between qualitatively distinct parts or ingredients; and (3) the establishment of functional relations between the differentiated parts so as to constitute a system. In the discussion of embryonic and neo-natal growth (pages 63 ff.), the work of Coghill, Bühler, and Shirley gave us evidence of orderly progress through these stages; again in the study of perception (pages 333 ff.), we found such stages both in the individual's basic perceptual disposition and in each new type of perceptual contact with the world.

We have now come to a test of this hypothesis as it relates to the development of individual personality as a whole. We should expect, if the hypothesis is sound, that human personality would pass through global, differentiated, and organized phases, and that each individual personality would betray its identity not only in its content at each stage, but in the manner in which differentiation goes on and in the form and ultimate dynamic of its integration. Moreover, we should expect to find that within each differentiated part a similar progression might well be manifest; each part might at first be homogeneous, then differentiated, then integrated.

If so, we must begin by considering qualities at the first stage, i.e., global dispositions. We might expect that certain attributes would characterize all the cells of one person's body, in comparison with those of another. And persisting within all the major portions of the body as they become differentiated, we should look for certain *global qualities*, such as the speed of conduction within the nervous system, the various metabolic rates, the rhythms, the thresholds, the latent times and after discharges of groups of tissues. Each of these would reveal some primordial personal quality that pervades the whole organism, or a significantly large portion of it, and endures through life. Even if we were prepared to relinquish our emphasis upon the *constitutional* qualities, the biocultural *interactions* which we have stressed would still presumably give the individual some global qualities of the type described, that would manifest themselves through all the vagaries of individual conditionings. We should expect to find all-round motor dispositions, such as strength, endurance, skill, speed; sensory dispositions, such as acuity and imagery; affective dispositions, such as shallowness or intensity, evenness or volatility; and that general intelligence which Spearman and many others have pointed out. These general or global factors would never completely dominate the picture; indeed, they might at times be so faint as to be distinguished only with difficulty. Often, however, they would stand out clearly enough to be detected and measured; and in certain situations they would be dominant. Under acute stress, for example, when a return to an earlier phase might be expected and when well-organized or integrated acts are lost, we might confront a resurgence of older, *more general* dispositions.

We have constantly referred to the transfer or generalization of conditionings and canalizations. In the light of the present analysis, individual proneness to such transfer appears to be in some measure a matter of global dispositions. The individual can hardly transfer a conditioning if the global readiness of his response is low. To use a very simple example, the transfer of a conditioned fear to new conditioning stimuli is partly a question of the person's timidity. A basic lethargy will act, as does a momentary drug effect, to cause difficulty of transfer, whereas, as Lewin has shown, a perseverative trend may affect the ease of transfer. Gestalt psychology has taught us to think in terms of the individual idiom which plays a predisposing part in each new habit.

Indeed, if the global qualities are what they seem to be, they must enter into every new response. They express themselves in the manner in which differentiated responses originally appear, and in the way in which the differentiated responses ultimately achieve integration. This is an apparent explanation of "intersensory" effects —a sound may make a light seem brighter, and may increase the tendency to experience "apparent movement." In view of such findings, each specific sense perception appears to be superposed upon a primitive intersensory quality which represents the individual's characteristic form of interaction between sensory modalities. Intersensory experience reminds us again that many undifferentiated tendencies remain even in the highly integrated organism. And the individual differences which appear in the magnitude of intersensory phenomena—for proneness to such phenomena is in some degree generalized—suggest that the amorphous, undifferentiated part is larger in some individuals than in others.

Differentiated attributes depend, then, to some extent upon global attributes. As differentiation goes on and recognizable parts emerge, we should expect the parts to bear some formal relation to one another, both because they are all traceable to the same global matrix and because, existing in the same organism, they are acted upon constantly by many of the same inner and outer stimuli. Traits which seem to be independent habits, such as the speed and style of the movements made with the right hand and the left foot, tend to correlate substantially. As Allport and Vernon observe, many different tasks "correspond," i.e., show quantitative relations of a functional type; the more there is of one, the more there is of the other. It is often because a certain global quality predisposes to them all that correspondence in personal characteristics appears; strength and endurance, for example, enter into many correlated skills. This is evident also in June Downey's pioneer studies of "postural generalizations" and in Werner Wolff's recent work showing the ease with which extremely complex movements, such as those in walking, may be identified when the more primitive global attributes are known.

All this makes sense from a biological standpoint. In our earlier reference to embryonic development (page 53) we saw the biochemical interdependence of tissues and noted that each group of cells is part of the environment of every other group. Vitality and disease, high and low energy gradients should naturally involve a simple spreading of any tissue tendency that is present anywhere; in fact, we find ourselves forced back to the one-cell stage, the global qualities of which manifest themselves step by step in the many cells of a later period. Not only the influence of differentiated cells upon another cell, but the fact that all the cells are derived from a common ancestry, constitutes a major clue to the phenomena of correspondence.

Comparison of movements executed with the right and left hands leads us not only into an analysis of tissue similarities in muscle, nerve, and bone, by which the right-hand functions are bound closely to the left-hand functions, but also into a study of the conditioning of each hand to the movements of its counterpart and to outer stimuli. Although never given formal drill, the left hand has taken over many dispositions of the right. The fact that writing done by the left hand has tendencies characteristic of that done by the right hand, and that even foot- or hip-writing is identifiable as to source, does not in itself *prove* the existence of a constitutional kinetic disposition. Observation of the small child's first efforts at cursive writing often shows the tongue or the whole head moving to the right in company with the hand, just as most motor acts are at first massive rather than purely local (cf. page 63); and in each one of us, in all probability, the entire body has participated in acquiring a skill intended to be taught a single member. Tension patterns involved in a coordinated local pattern are to some degree accompanied by slight corresponding tension patterns in a distant part. Some of Luria's techniques (page 312) rely upon this concurrent systematic spread of patterned excitation. It is not surprising that outer resemblances between contraction patterns in the right and left hands are demonstrable, or that the degree of resemblance should vary with the functional movement similarities between limbs, the left hand resembling the right hand more than the right foot does the right hand.

Correspondence of traits may thus be due to the sheer generality of an organic disposition, to conditioning, or to both factors. The existence of intercorrelations between functions can tell us nothing directly about the *origin* of their functional dependence, or about the inner conditions by which they are sustained. Some of the experimentally demonstrated correspondences—in speed, for example (page 134)—appear to be equivalent manifestations of the same fundamental organic conditions; some are affective responses generalized to similar situations (e.g., fears generalized to all social situations); and some are an expression of different means used to achieve a given end. For when several means to a goal must be used serially or concurrently, each must be physiologically compatible with the others, and when so used must not interfere with another behavior pattern being employed for the same purpose. This particular type of integration is, however, very loose indeed. The traits are allowed to function together as long as each serves the goal in a given behavior context, but the content of the behavior is usually a mere combination of dispositions which are not at open war with one another. Thus correspondence as such reveals little about the developmental level. It may derive from diffuse, general, undifferentiated tendencies, or from differentiated and generalized tendencies, or from parallel integrated habits.

But when we say that correspondence may arise at any of the three stages, we must remember that the concept of the three stages is still a hypothesis, not a fact; even if we accept it as fact, its universal pertinence still remains to be established. Though generalized tendencies always appear to be global traits, they may actually be the products of transfer or integrated pattern; close observation is required to determine this. It is not likely that any Stage 2 or Stage 3 response is ever so completely generalized as to duplicate a Stage 1 global response trait; but the data are often not clear, and premature inflexibility in using such a scheme would spoil it.

THE ALLPORT-VERNON EXPERIMENTS

It is in this context, the Gestalt concept of stages, that the experiments of Allport and Vernon seem to fit best. Their measures of sheer speed are apparently clear examples of Stage 1 global traits. Here, however, our chief interest concerns more complex matters. One man gesticulates freely, writes large and draws large; when a cleat is attached to his shoe for drawing in a sandbox, again he draws "in the large." When rating himself, he uses long strokes for the check marks. Another man is contractile rather than expansive; the hands are held close, the handwriting and drawing are small, the self-rating checks are short.

Working with 25 young male adults in the Harvard Laboratory, Allport and Vernon were able to establish a considerable degree of correspondence between many simple measures of expression, indicating high degrees of generality. The data show, for example, some substantial correlations between a number of separate measures and this general factor of *area*, i.e., the tendency to use more or less space when making manual, postural, or gestural response. The area factor is demonstrated; the degree of "space-filling" tendency is a generalized expression of the individual that varies sharply from one man to another. The Allport-Vernon data indicate something—perhaps kinetic, perhaps affective—in the markedly space-filling individual that causes him to spread out more than his fellow does when he makes an expressive movement.

The area factor has been independently confirmed by Eisenberg, who obtained evidence that the Allport-Vernon measures are reasonably reliable and that they are meaningfully related to the personalities investigated. Eisenberg, however, was able to go further. He administered to a group of undergraduate students a "social personality inventory" that permitted the individual to report his own feelings of dominance (very similar to self-confidence or security) in a variety of social situations. Selecting the most assured and the most diffident subjects, Eisenberg made individual laboratory appointments, tested these students for the area factor, and while securing the quantitative data had a large number of qualitative observations made by a second observer who was watching through a one-way screen. The assured individuals (as judged from the questionnaires) took up much more space than the diffident; moreover, they behaved like assured people. They frequently came late and made no apology; they did not knock, but entered freely and often asked casually about the experiment, criticized it as it proceeded, and slouched in their seats; the less assured students usually came early, knocked, asked deferential questions, sat up straight, etc. The results suggest that the area factor indicates that those who are secure are, as the common expression has it, *expansive*. The insecure are contractile; they take up little space. But this does not mean that social confidence or timidity is the *only* basis for the area factor. As far as the data go, they indicate a generalized social confidence or fear that reaches through the various expressive measures and causes them to correspond. (Efrón's data on page 306 tell a similar story.)

The same approach to the area factor has been used by those who have worked with children's drawings; they have repeatedly found that sweeping strokes or the massing of color over a large area is characteristic of self-assurance, whereas the shy child confines himself to one corner of the paper (like Kipling's Chuchundra, the "timid man" who never ventured "into the middle of the room").

All the evidence cited thus far relates to the space-filling tendency in *social* situations. It looks, therefore, like a generalized conditioned response; there is no reason to think that it would affect space-filling tendencies in impersonal, mechanical, solitary activities. It does not qualify at Stage 1, the global level. Indeed, most second-level traits—specific reaction tendencies that are localized within the organic system—appear as a result of this conditioning and transfer. Such traits appear to be rather well *generalized*; indeed, this must be the case if they warrant our calling them traits rather than just habits.

Most behavior traits that have been experimentally studied are clear examples of Stage 2 patterns of generalized conditioning. Thus "generosity," "timidity," "persistence," "confidence," when once established, tend to transfer, to spread to new situations; other, more complex traits, like "tact" seem to be organized composites of a number of different conditionings. Personality terms ending in *-ness*, *-tion*, *-ity*, etc., are almost without exception tributes to generalized conditioned responses. As usual, the organic make-up plays an important role in predisposing toward or away from the acquisition of the conditioned response, but so far as the traits can be pigeonholed under the accepted headings of personality formation, conditioning must serve. In almost all studies of personal traits in which paper-and-pencil methods are used, we find ourselves confronting chiefly the generalized conditioned responses of the subjects. They show themselves consistently neurotic, or ascendant, or extroverted, or dominant, or self-sufficient by virtue of the consistency of their transfer of such behavior to wider and wider social contexts. Even when their actual behavior is not thus generalized, their image of themselves as possessing such tendencies is usually defined well enough to yield the desired reliabilities; moreover, their tenacious grip on this image probably increases the generality of response through the years.

Over and above correspondence, as it reveals itself through simple quantitative correlations, Allport and Vernon speak of *congruence*, the integration of behaviors in terms of the goal they serve. Knowing the goal pursued by an individual, we know that all that he thinks, does, and says will express phases preparatory to its achievement. Although it would be ridiculous to expect these phases to show any foreordained quantitative relation, congruence, the expression of integration, will appear. Handwriting areas and areas of foot squares correlate substantially, and hence they may be said to give corresponding expressions of the area factor; but there are many acts which clearly belong together functionally, although no direct quantitative correspondence is involved. The alert business executive whose ideal is "efficiency" paces slowly to and fro as he thinks, but walks rapidly when his decision has once been made. Slow motion is more conducive to efficient thought than is rapid motion, and rapid motion is more efficient than slow motion in keeping an appointment; thus although these two forms of behavior give no corresponding scores, they are still compatible because they are expressions of the same purpose. For Allport and Vernon the major problem is to discover the individual's purpose; all the acts which serve this purpose are treated as congruent.

This logic evidently applies to both simultaneous and successive acts. To bend at the waist and alternately push down the feet is congruent if I wish to ride a bicycle; to alternate between moving my right hand and sitting motionless over the board is congruent if I wish to play chess. Congruent acts, then, may be phases of a complex organized act. This conception refers both to the discreteness of the steps followed in carrying out goal activities, such as the preparatory and consummatory responses of hunting-catching-killing-eating-digesting, and also to the diversity of the simultaneous expressions of a single goal-directed act. Traits appearing at Stage 2, when integrated with others at Stage 3, have such membership character that they can no longer be understood at all outside of their full personality contexts.

Though all these ideas, taken separately, are exceedingly familiar, the Allport-Vernon formulation nevertheless constitutes an important contribution to the study of personality organization. It suggests that unless we are constantly on guard, measures which miss the true basis of interrelatedness—e.g., measures of cross-sections taken at different phases of an act—may be non-comparable from one person to another. Consider the childhood sequence—solitary play, parallel play, cooperative play. One child may be reliably measured and placed at two sigma below the mean in extroversion; another child who has become *habituated* to the situation may be one sigma above the mean. However, when the degree of habituation is controlled, the first child may appear more extroverted than the second, in the same "objective situation." Students of most psychological functions have long since learned to control practice—habituation—effects; but not so the students of personality.

Another signal value in the concept of congruence is the distinction between traits expressive of a general psychological system and those induced by the pressure of a specific goal tendency. Some of the staccato phases of leg, trunk, and arm movement in walking may arise from the fundamental construction and kinetics of the body, some from social tensions (cf. page 306), and some from a conscious or unconscious desire to impersonate a staccato model. The "corresponding" measures discernible in a statistical population might often prove to be more expressive of *general trend* (e.g., awkwardness of trunk being embryologically related to awkwardness of legs), whereas the "congruent" measures might be expressive of the local and particular goals of individual persons. The fact that the goals are often grasped intuitively by the observer seems to mean that familiarity with human goals and the means used in achieving them makes it possible for one to infer for a person expressive patterns which are nonetheless real despite the difficulty in identifying them and verifying them statistically in a large population (cf. page 609).

From our present point of view, congruence means simply that we have passed beyond Stage 2, the stage of differentiation, and have achieved the type of functional unity of the organism described as Stage 3. A genuine integration or Gestalt maintains at a cross section in time, and over a time span, something far more important than "harmonious interrelationships" within a bodily system. It involves the wholeness of the entire pattern of life. One might say that as Peary approached the North Pole, he showed within him many "harmonious" physiological systems; his adjustments to the cold, to the stars, to his scientific apparatus were all harmonious adjustments of systems. Everything, however, was subordinated to the maintenance of the direction north, until the Pole was reached. It was quite literally in Peary's personality at that time to struggle until he arrived at the Pole. Congruence is not merely a question of harmony of parts; it is a question of the magnitude of the living unit with which we are working. The term would best be reserved for full-fledged Stage 3 phenomena in which the apex of the hierarchy is reached, the various aspects being interrelated in the achievement of a central value.[1]

Each aspect of such a hierarchical system presumably has its own membership character within the system; and each system doubtless partakes, as a whole, somewhat of the character of the larger total within which it functions. We are led to the notion of the coexistence of many systems within the individual, each system to some extent being related to all the others both by some degree of similarity arising from a common origin, and also by the responses which each elicits from the others. The degree of dependence or independence of the various systems varies widely. The general theory of development which we have followed suggests that very early in life all the systems are rather closely interrelated, largely through the common quality of the Stage 1 matrix from which they emerge, and that though this matrix persists through the three stages, the more sharply differentiated systems have much less in common. This appears in studies of mental organization at different levels; as noted earlier (page 212), mental abilities become progressively differentiated with age.

The discussion of the problem in terms of age levels, however, does not do full justice to it, for each individual undergoes his own differentiation at his own rate and in his own way. Moreover, the very systems that are loosely integrated in one person may be tightly integrated in another. Here, as Hollingworth showed, the study of

---

[1] Integration may also be involved if another condition is satisfied, namely, the establishment of a group of values in relation to a single object, as in McDougall's "sentiments," which are clusters of affective dispositions formed in relation to a person, a thing, or an idea. Patriotism, for example, may involve many distinct responses held together in a unified cluster. An appetizing dish at Kelly's, however, or a brand of securities at Lloyd's may have many appeals for the gourmet or the investor. These appeals usually prove to function first of all by *summation*. As the dish loses its savor, or its moisture, its appeal dwindles, each component appearing to act additively, and its loss subtractively, till one goes elsewhere to lunch; as the securities decline in their safety or their interest rate or their chances of tax exemption or their soundness or their likelihood of being called in, one switches his capital elsewhere. Many a cherished object or person is attractive because of a diversity of rather independent appeals. But let one begin to *compare* and *interrelate* the appeals, and they soon take on *structure*.

the interdependence of traits within the individual, is one way to make clear not only the individuality or idiosyncrasy of the specific capacities and traits, but also the individuality or idiosyncrasy of the interrelations between them. In some people there are compact, tight interrelations of functions which are altogether wanting in others.

The value of keeping in mind this question of stages or levels is well brought out in the study of speed, or rate of performance, already mentioned as revealing correspondence in Allport and Vernon's work. In the case of speed, as in many other instances, language has a single name for a trait which upon closer analysis reveals three kinds of phenomena. (1) There is good evidence for a physiological speed factor. For example, there is the rather rigid and unalterable speed of embryological development (page 82), varying from species to species and from individual to individual. There is the well-defined group factor of speed in verbal tests, there is evidence that this group factor is in large measure a physiological unit that correlates substantially with reflex speed (page 134). This may be a Stage 1 type of speed, a property of the organism as a whole. (2) Speed of writing, speed of talking, speed of drawing (not carried to the individual's physiological limit) constitute habits which need not be positively correlated or even directly related; they may represent specific adaptation to different kinds of problems. They are second-level traits. (3) When Klineberg tested white and Yakima Indian boys, the latter tended to move more slowly and more accurately. The competitive culture of the white has evidently made a rather central value of accomplishment (quantitatively considered), and speed is an expression of the resulting architectural pattern of personality. It is so much a part of the whole that it can be safely studied only as a Stage 3 trait. A systematic study of "speed" in human behavior might easily confuse the three senses in which the term is used.

Clinical study of personality will, as a rule, greatly influence the level at which a trait is put. A broad tendency to irrational fears, for example, is a perennial problem in both adults and children, but such fears may belong at any one of the three levels. For example: (1) Are we dealing with constitutionally low thresholds? Or with the sequelae of disease? In either case, this may be a pervasive Stage 1 trait, and medical aid may be necessary, especially in the matter of rest, regimen, nutrition; even so, it may yield only slightly to attack. (2) Are we dealing with the specific consequences of conditioning experiences, and with these alone? If so, M. C. Jones' experiments (page 196) and others like them may show how to eliminate them by reconditioning. (3) Are we dealing with fears which protect the individual against still greater agonies (cf. page 541); or with fears reflecting the profound insecurity of the whole personality, so that one *pictures himself as timid* and would fight against the removal of the timidity as he would for self-preservation; or with fears that are used to enhance prestige or to win attention or pity? With fears belonging to these last categories we shall have no success with either medical or reconditioning procedures; we shall have to proceed architecturally, understanding the structure before we try to deal with the individual stones in the building.

In utilizing this tentative hypothesis as to stages in trait development it would be a serious mistake to assume that movement is *always* in one direction. Pathology can often reverse the process; and as we saw in the Barker, Dembo, and Lewin experiment, even ordinary frustration can do so. But we must go further, for there are plenty of life situations in which the ordinary normal processes of acquiring and using habits manifest the same principle; an example is the way in which the organized total personality "uses" some of its component parts.

TRAITS AS TOOLS

When a trait has arisen in the service of a need, it becomes a free instrumentality to which the individual resorts in other need situations. No matter how local, temporal, and specific the original habit or habit complex may be, it may crop out when he finds himself in a new environment. The animal or child who is acquiring various skills in a problem box resorts to its use in quite different situations. Traits may come to expression when tension is high, and sometimes they definitely *work* and become consolidated despite their being grafted or transplanted from completely different contexts. It is as if an adult, having learned a few words of Spanish, tried them on a Greek friend who also, by an odd chance, had learned a few words of Spanish. A trait may indeed prove to be a very serviceable, all-round instrument to have in one's behavioral kit. In other words, traits can be used as tools. A hammer is made to drive nails, but a person can also straighten wire or crack nuts with it. Various forms of hesitant speech may originally arise from the need to find the right word; they may persist as a means of showing deference to others or the mark of a don't-hit-me-for-I'm-sure-you-know-better-than-I type of man. The areal traits described by Allport and Vernon certainly look like generalized tools of this sort. The ingrained ways of accomplishing all kinds of expansive and retractive purposes (going out or staying in) permeate even the simplest skilled act. At this point our hierarchical concept of levels must be used in reverse; that is, a trait employed in this sense as a tool is of course a second-level trait but it is used by the organized personality as a whole, and since its use is determined by the whole, it is chronologically and logically a sequel to the third-level aspect of personality. It is only from the point of view of the completed architectural whole that the origin and utilization of second-level traits can be made clear.

We have already encroached upon personality style—a problem as old as Aristotle's *Art of Poetry*, and one that has been abundantly and competently analyzed by critics of art and literature. We seem to have raised two questions without sharply disentangling them: the problem of body dynamics and the problem of attitudes toward the environment. Let us look at them more analytically.

On the one hand, there is the problem of the elementary statics and dynamics of body interrelationships, e.g., the way in which the muscles are inserted, the relation of the body's center of gravity to the length of the upper and lower leg and to the length of the foot. Such questions have to do with the geometry and mechanics of all movements of the body, and with the adequacy of the striped-muscle system to maintain and direct dynamic equilibrium. Here we are dealing with the elementary constitutional attributes from which not only speed and strength but the qualities of style emerge. Style has been observed and measured in the locomotion and prehension of infants, and its study in the earliest crayon and pencil sketches of children suggests that these primitive qualities of the body play a considerable role in the expressive pattern.

On the other hand, there is the problem of attitudes. For by the time a child is old enough to wield a pencil or, indeed, old enough to walk, he has built up a group of *attitudes* toward other persons, toward objects, toward space, and toward himself, all four of which demonstrably influence the poise, the rhythm, and the style of his locomotor and representative acts. Just as attitudes show themselves in drawings (see page 683), so the posture, stance, and locomotor movements of the shy child are easily differentiated from those of the socially confident child, even when both children are approaching the same object or pursuing the same activity. It was on the basis of these socially ingrained types of bodily activity that Krout was able to develop the concept of "autistic gesture," and that Efrón, from his photographs of Italian and Jewish immigrants, was able to show the social history of the individual expressed in the medium of gesture and posture. From the major gesture of the arms and hands, sweeping or retreating in form, one can push inward to the minor or local gesture—the quiver of the finger, the drooping of the eyelid, the rippling or stifled quality of the laughter.

These various aspects of style, whether they concern kinetics or attitude, are all interrelated; they all betray membership character. The interrelations are doubtless due partly to the global Stage 1 qualities which flow through all structured attributes; partly to cross conditioning, or the transfer of training from one member to another; partly to the fact that common pressures have acted similarly upon a wide variety of expressive mechanisms; and partly to the fact that all of them express a major value. Though there is abundant evidence that each type of expression, such as posture, gait, and voice, is connected with every other type of expression, we do not yet know which of these sources, or what combination of them, should be emphasized in the study of this interdependence.

A Definition of "Organization"

The terms "organization" and "structure" are used a great deal today in reference to personality. They very properly point to the interrelatedness of organic responses and to the dangers inherent in what the biologist calls "isolation experiments," but all too often they are left undefined. For our purpose we shall need to consider several possible meanings of the word "organization" ("structure" will occasionally be used as an equivalent, for variety's sake only), and to show their relation to the Stage 2 and Stage 3 traits already discussed. (It will be remembered that from the present point of view *all* traits express drives, are drive manifestations taking specific directions; cf. page 194.)

1. First there is the concept that some traits result directly from other traits. (The former may be thought of as dependent variables, the magnitude of their manifestation being directly traced to the magnitude of the primary or independent variables.) Under this head falls the Freudian concept of reaction formation (as when neatness arises from love of dirt); the derived trait is present in whatever strength is required for it to act as an adequate repressant of the repressed trait. Here likewise belongs the Adlerian concept of compensation, when it is proportional to the sensed inferiority. Trait T_1 results from the presence of trait T. When two or more traits derive

$$T \longrightarrow T_1$$

from one original trait, the logic of the situation remains unchanged.

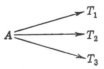

This is exemplified by the Freudian concept of character structure (pages 485 ff.); for example, painful weaning leads to a variety of mouth-centered traits.

2. The concept of convergence, or overdetermination, postulates that the strength of any given trait depends upon the joint strength of two other traits, whether the two latter ones are correlated or not; two factors A and B converge upon trait T as a final common path. An example is the derivation of a given fantasy tendency (as in

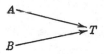

the Thematic Apperception Test) from two or more needs; thus the intensity of the desire to be accepted as a hero might derive from a strong narcissistic factor and also from a strong father identification. This conception of traits as derived from two or more other traits has been symbolized in the figure borrowed from Burks and Jones (page 609.) Compare also the figure on page 636.

3. Fundamental in the study of organization is the concept of traits as being due to conflict. This concept specifies, as in the Oedipus complex, two or more impulses leading toward behavior that is antithetical in result; e.g., the behavior arising from one impulse will frustrate the other impulse. Another case in point is the Adlerian concept of the collapse of the style of life, in which the individual is required both to rebuild and at the same time to raze the structure

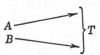

so as to start anew on the same ground. In such instances no "solution" is feasible, and the problem is by-passed by one or another

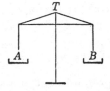

method of compromise or evasion, as noted on page 311.

4. All concepts of organization make some use of the idea of a balance in which potentially conflicting forces are bound in the form

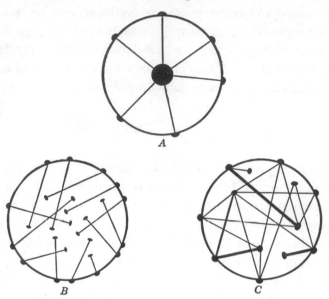

In the diagrams, dispositions or behavior tendencies are represented within the circle, and overt behavior on the circumference. In A, all overt behavior of an individual is determined by the personality as a whole, responding to specific external or internal stimuli. In B, the various patterns of overt behavior are independent events arising from independent internal sources occurring at various degrees of profoundness (i.e., some are much more basic and permanent than others). The behavior patterns and their sources, however, can be classified according to similarity (emotional, social, etc.), as indicated by their arrangements within the circle and on the circumference. In C, behavior is determined by a number of discrete tendencies or "factors" of varying profoundness. That some of these contribute more than others to specific items of behavior is indicated by the varying widths of lines.

of chronic suspense; this is reminiscent of a scalepan in which exactly countervailing forces are put. The Rorschach test deals directly with this concept, as in the notion of an *ambi-equal* trait in an individual who is nicely balanced between extratensive and introversive trends, neither obliterating the other. In the same way, tendencies to the whole and detail are conceived to exist in some degree of balance.

5. A related type of balance is seen in a group of responses that is regarded as organized when each of them limits the range of variability which can appear in the others. Homeostasis is a good example; the body temperature and the pH of the blood are held within narrow limits by other bodily processes. Although we do not always know enough to be able to name all the components in an organized system or to tell how they work, we do know that some components are restricted in variability by the functioning of the others. A good example at a higher level of complexity is VTE behavior (page 297), in which each of two stimuli limits the response to the other; another example is the perceptual constancies (page 355), and still another is the anxiety-temptation balance (page 301). The maintenance of the picture of the self also involves balance. Like any other picture, it is recognizable only as long as certain rough *proportions* are maintained; each phase of it is acceptable only if other phases remain within limits. For many people, too many successes, too many failures, too many illnesses, too many good times, too much fat, too much money, tend to make the picture uncomfortable and strange, and the individual endeavors to restore it—"I feel like myself again," he says after an aberration. This is not meant to imply that such systems are, like homeostasis, *necessary for life;* under certain stresses, they may collapse. But as long as they do exist—and for most normal persons they not only exist but stand up rather well in the face of disturbance —they are conveniently and properly referred to in terms of organization. In all probability, personality organization depends in large measure upon a *perceptual* system based on the fact that the self-attitude is necessarily a matter of the valuation of a perceived whole whose parts cannot change too much without destroying the value of the whole.

6. Closely related to balance is the idea of "reversible reaction," as it is developed in chemistry. Here the balance is not static; rather

it consists of a tendency for two forces to alternate, as one or the other is reinforced, neither being able to preempt the field. The early

$$T_1 \left| \; \underset{\longleftarrow}{\overset{\longrightarrow}{\rule{2cm}{0pt}}} \; \right| T_2$$

life history of individuals who have made unsuccessful attempts to rebel against parental domination support this concept.

7. There are, however, cases in which no form of balance is feasible, whether in static or dynamic form; as in physics, imbalance leads to a reorganization in the form of a new equilibrium. This is exemplified by a chair which, when pushed beyond a certain point, fails to come back to its first position and instead falls backward to the floor, reaching a different level and form of equilibrium. A more dynamic example is failure to resist disease bacteria, which may lead to a chronic adaptation of host and parasite at a definitely reduced health level. We are concerned here with the all-or-none transition from one form of organization to another.

8. Considerable use is also made of the interdependence of two or more characteristics, in a Gestalt sense. We cannot use the piece-by-piece description of traits, because it is impossible to delimit any of the interdependent traits except as aspects of a larger field. The courage and patience of a parent in caring for a very sick child are interdependent, as are *B* and *E* (we use here a figure like the one used on page 93).

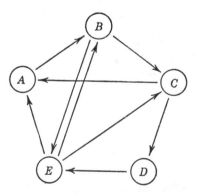

9. This leads to the more complex instances of interdependence in

which a complete system permits no specification of any local proper-ties whatever, except as aspects of the whole. In relation to such systems, emphasis is usually placed upon relatively fluid or constantly altering modes of equilibrium. The courage of the sick child's mother is an aspect of her entire personality that is focused upon one supremely important goal.

10. Such a system, however, is not homogeneous. The dominance or relative focusing of energy at one rather than another point pro-vides a basis for anchorage (page 346), as developed by the Gestalt studies of perception. Most of the matching methods (for example, those used by Arnheim and Wolff) clearly match not in terms of the entire personality (whatever that may be) but in terms of an anchorage point characteristic of two or more modes of expression; such a point is likely to be a structural outline that appears in two or more areas of activity. Heavy lines represent salient, emphasized relationships.

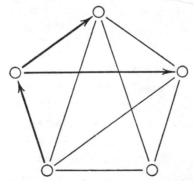

11. We come at last to structure as a specification of an archi-tectural whole, in which both second- and third-level characteristics are defined, and in which three-dimensional form is conceived to be the true analogue to personality structure, exactly as when one dif-ferentiates between cubes, pyramids, and cones. One supplement, however, must always be added to our geometrical figure. The princi-ple of membership character must be applied not only in relation to the various second-level characteristics around the base of the pyramid or cone, but also in relation to the form of dependence between the traits at the apex and those on the base line. As a rule, at least under

conditions specified in our culture, the apex proves to be the attitude toward the self. This is not to say that most people consciously pur-

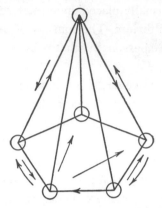

sue with a high degree of consistency goals that are conceived solely as a means of enhancing or defending the self; but under the conditions imposed by ego competition, such as those described earlier, almost all motives of any degree of sophistication and complexity become aspects of a deeply ingrained self-enhancing or self-defending style of living. The degree of organization, of interdependence, of focusing involved in these last three concepts need not be identical for all members of a group, or even for an individual from one hour to another. The tightness of the structure varies with age, genetic disposition, and the stresses and strains of individual living. But when true interdependence of second- and third-level traits is demonstrated, we may properly speak of architectural wholeness. Finally, we should stress the fact that the architectural whole is in constant motion, with areas of relative stability, but with a capacity for internal reorganization as well as free adaptation to new situations. The time dimension, which indicates certain shifts in pattern, cannot be effectively represented here.

Many will feel that the foregoing, despite its discussion of the properties of structure, implies too much attention to component parts; it may be considered "atomistic." But in the passage from the global phenomena at Stage 1 to Stages 2 and 3, we have need of conceptual elements, and of simple and conceptualizable relations between them. Moreover, clear conceptual components of personality structure are needed. They are not far to seek; we have encountered them at every point. From the present point of view *the ultimate elements in personality structure are the needs or tensions, and they are interrelated by means of the functional connections between regions which permit the spread of these tensions.* The result is a *tension system* whose lawful structure is expressed in terms of the relative strengths of tensions and the relative rigidity of barriers to their diffusion. Our hypothesis therefore claims that *the organism's tension system is organized*, in the sense that each event is limited and controlled by the relations between elements, as in homeostasis. There is organization at every moment in time, in the form of a "static" system. There is also temporal or dynamic organization, each tension or group of tensions initiating changes which eventually bring the organism to a new balance, or restore it to the first. Of special importance is Weiss' concept of the *development of a system that retains its organization.* This may be achieved through the gradual complication of individual parts, the over-all relation between the parts remaining unchanged. Such phases of personality development as "kinetics," "style," "individual rhythm," etc., are of this type. The organism is a physiological gradient system. Jacobson's relaxation experiments indicate that muscular tension in one region spreads gradient-fashion to other muscle groups; similarly, the reduction of tension in one region spreads until the tension is reduced in the functionally correlated muscle groups, the process in all probability continuing until most or all of the muscle groups are involved. Considerable other evidence tends to the same direction;[2] and the principle holds for neural and biochemical tensions as well (cf. page 120).

---

[2] This concept of three levels and of interrelatedness at the third level should apply in the case of body form as well as of psychological function. It is characteristic of modern studies of biotypes to conceive relations not between narrow and specific bodily traits on the one hand, and narrow specific psychological traits on the other, but between bodily and psychological systems. The conceptual clarity with which this is done varies a good deal from one piece of research to another. In the method developed by Sheldon, Stevens, and Tucker, mentioned briefly on page 59, biotypes are considered in terms of numerical scores on each of three fundamental bodily components, here and there stated to be interrelated in a complex total; on the psychological side the dispositions described are frequently complex, third level dispositions.

At several points we have been unable to follow literally the Gestaltist's insistence that interdependence is found on every hand. The study of such personality difficulties as conflicts force vividly upon us the question of the *degree of autonomy* which can exist within the living total, a problem reminiscent of that concerning degrees of dissociation raised in Chapter 13. Since the organism is full of opposed tendencies, there must obviously be a considerable measure of dissociation if genuine conflict is not to appear. Here the occasional claim that conflict is an artifact, or that wholeness is the single ultimate reality, has no meaning. Conflict is too potent to be glossed over. On the other hand, the fact that there *is* conflict is evidence of wholeness of a sort, for instead of functioning at two levels and developing two completely independent spheres of activity, the individual's picture of the self forbids even the temporary mutilation of the image. The fact that memory is long and goals persistent means that some compromise, some gesture in the direction of wholeness, must constantly be made. On this point the Rorschach approach seems considerably sounder than that of the orthodox Gestalt psychology, for here we recognize all degrees of the capacity for organization— *Gestaltungskraft*. Organizing power, highly correlated with intelligence as measured by standard tests, appears in the tendency to use appropriately much interrelated material, especially in the tendency to use wholes that are sound and genuine rather than forced resemblances to the objects named. In the same way, the concept of creativity or originality has been used by Rorschach examiners on the assumption that an individual may reveal any degree of scatteredness or integration, any degree of independence or interdependence among the objects of his thought and fantasy. It is hard to see how the concept of three stages as developed here could be used at all with-

---

We could wish that an attempt had been made to separate the psychological dispositions into categories defining their complexity, and that it were clear whether specific mechanisms, such as shyness or fondness for ice cream, are to be conceived as narrowly related to specific bodily dimensions or as the expressions of total bodily organization. If, as seems likely, some positive relation of biotype and psychological type remain after a thorough retesting and reevaluation of this study, we shall still need to find out whether such interrelations depend upon relatively simple Stage 2 relationships, of which there is an abundance, or whether a considerable number of them are actually expressions of structure in a true third-level sense.

out the parallel assumption that there are all degrees of organized-ness. The experiments of Heinz Werner (page 266) and of Barker, Dembo, and Lewin (page 145) seemingly indicate that increasing differentiation, and at times the loss of it, are both formal aspects of individual living. Medical research has long since made clear that *some* biochemical reactions in the body *are* isolable, for what is found *in vitro* is also found *in vivo*, and that other reactions are so much influenced by the context that the laws *in vitro* do not hold *in vivo*. It is a question, again, of Stage 2 versus Stage 3.

If so, the implication follows that any given personality has its own characteristic degree of tightness of structure. Constitutional factors, such as those having to do with intelligence, would play a part; the tendency to dissociation studied in Chapter 13 would play a part; the developmental level would obviously play a part; and sheer vitality or energy would probably be as important as any of the other factors. Few concepts are more important in clarifying the idea of personality research than the degree of autonomy or inde-pendence of the component phases. Although statistical devices such as factor analysis are suitable for testing broad dispositions and the form of their relations to other dispositions, such techniques are not at present capable of indicating to what degree the factors defined function in each person as autonomous units, and to what degree they fuse with other tendencies. For personality study as it exists today, the primary emphasis must be given to the degree of autonomy actually existing in each disposition. Hence our emphasis upon methodology and the theory of levels.

EMERGENCE

An attempt has been made throughout to show that Stage 2 dis-positions frequently arise from Stage 1 dispositions by virtue of specific local modes of interaction with the environment, and that Stage 3 dispositions arise from interactions of the Stage 2 components with one another and with phases of the environment. Stage 3 reveals new phases of personality, real and extremely important aspects that are in no way predictable from the original Stage 1 dispositions; for it is only through interaction with a specific environment that dispositions at the first two levels are capable of yielding a Stage 3 result. Personalities function to a large degree at the second and third levels; or rather, they function most of the time in a manner reflecting the combination of responses at these two levels. Now for the critical question: Does Stage 3 really contain anything *new?* Is it not simply the inevitable product of specific Stage 2 components interacting with specific outer situations? The answer will be facilitated by C. D. Broad's way of phrasing the issue (cf. page 35). If the organism's physical forces reach a certain level of complexity, and if completely new *functions* are attained that differ from all those observed at the level of the non-living, but no new *substance* is added, the process may be called "emergent vitalism."[3]

The position taken here is not identical with either of these, although it is much nearer to emergent than to substantive vitalism. We have tried to show that first-, second-, and third-level activity is present in every organism, including the unicellular. Indeed, the general laws of development, as formulated by Spencer, are conceived to exist as attributes of all matter and as very conspicuous aspects of living matter, so that they will inevitably be present as any individual personality grows. In this sense, the second and third stages are fulfillments of what is biologically predestined. But it is the physical, not the disembodied, character of atoms and molecules, it is the physical structure of the stuff out of which the universe is made, whether appearing in non-living or in living systems, that appears to be responsible for the particular developmental laws of which Spencer made use. As systems become more complex, they exhibit *new functions.*

A similar answer may be given to the question of indeterminism. The question is best phrased in terms of James' alternatives relating to "hard" and "soft" determinism. We follow here the principle of

---

[3] Gestalt psychology seems at times to espouse exactly this type of principle. Integral responses are unpredictable from elemental responses, yet they are organically continuous with them; there is no substance, only a new level of complication. At other times Gestalt psychology insists in almost Platonic terms that forms or modes of organization are primary, i.e., independent of specific matter, merely happening now and then to appear embodied in concrete physical forms.

"soft" determinism—determinism from the inner nature of life, not from external pressures alone. There may of course be a sort of "arbitrary spontaneity," a certain complete indeterminism, in all organic events; but if so, the process is not discoverable by present-day methods. When complete indeterminism is reported, as in some types of atomic behavior, the physicist simply describes mathematically the region within which prediction can be made, displaying no hesitation whatever in acknowledging a "principle of uncertainty." With our much more limited knowledge of biological and psychological laws, it might be wise to accept the same principle and give indeterminism wide berth. But this has nothing to do with the philosophical question of free will; it simply states the range of prediction which follows the general principle of "soft" determinism.

In actual practice in personality studies, however, indeterminism is not a major issue. The chief issue concerns the concept of pressures from without and pressures from within. If we say that a child born in difficult circumstances is destined for a neurotic or a delinquent career, we are speaking in terms of "hard" determinism; we are assuming that environmental forces can yield only a single result. If, on the other hand, we say that in the complex interactions which are bound to develop, he will slowly develop a relative autonomy, a participation in the causal sequence, based on the influence of his own complex make-up on his conduct, we are espousing the doctrine of "soft" determinism.

It may well be that Bergson is right in arguing that neither determinism in any of its forms, nor the free-will doctrine in any of its forms, will prove adequate to deal with spontaneity and creativity. But as science and philosophy stand today, we cannot evade the question whether prediction is possible or not. We would say that it is in general possible to a far greater degree than was the case a generation ago. As matters stand now, we must on the one hand use the physicist's principle of uncertainty, considerably extended; and on the other hand we must adopt the principle of "soft" determinism —the participation of the person as cause—as one of the most valuable working concepts available.

27. The Recognition of Personality Structure

MAX WERTHEIMER used to ask a group of friends to gather around the piano while he played a series of compositions revealing the individuality of each person present. Each one would then indicate privately the name of the individual described by the composition. Although the results, as is true of earlier and later studies by the same method, are incapable at present of an exact quantitative summary, they are considerably better than those obtained in random matching. And it is of interest that Wertheimer's subjects, like many others, often insisted that the global impression of character was to be more relied upon than any attempt at analysis. To conclude that this must be Herr Schmidt because of the heavy tread is a poor method; the response should be made at the non-analytic, global, "intuitive" level. As Wertheimer liked to put it, the essence of personality is cast not in a single tone or in a single melodic line, but in the wholeness of the musical conception. As he saw it, the *radix* or root of the personality was independent of specific modality; it was intersensory (page 334). The type of organization was a matter of pure (intersensory) form, but was capable of embodiment in any one of several modalities.

Powers' study of handwriting illustrates the strengths and weaknesses of most investigations of expressive patterns in which this type of matching method is used. A large group of Dartmouth freshmen were required to read ten short paragraphs describing the personalities of ten young male adults. The students were also given ten short handwriting samples, the verbal content being the same in all. Their task was to divine which of the ten persons had written each of the ten samples. The results showed great variability in success, both with respect to the individual judgments and with respect to the ten personalities which had to be matched. On a chance or random basis, we should expect one correct matching in ten. The average was 1.7 correct matchings, which is out of the chance category statistically, though still poor in absolute terms. Some individual judges did very well, others very poorly; and while some of the handwritings were matched correctly by the majority of the freshmen, others were spotted by almost no one, so that the result in these cases was worse than chance expectation. This variation in matching seems to be due to the fact that certain stereotypes based on experience with people and their handwriting operate as the matching is being done. Some of the stereotypes contain a good deal of truth, others none. If a man writes a "non-characteristic" hand he may be consistently classified wrongly. In this study, the freshmen were supplemented by hand-writing experts. Of seventeen experts, seven made three or more correct matchings. Their average performance was considerably better than that of the students.

Strang was able in the same way to express personality by non-representative sketches, the lines and surfaces of which conveyed individuality to those who knew the people symbolized. A number of other art forms have been used for the same purpose; in fact, there have been many attempts to evaluate what can be done by way of character analysis through responses to voice, stance, posture, way of walking, handwriting, drawing, and painting. From the wide success of these studies it would certainly seem that the statics and dynamics of the body reveal themselves in the balance and flow of *all* expressive activity, including of course the symbolic and the representative arts. There is much to confirm the Gestalt thesis that structure or inter-relatedness is observed directly, not merely inferred after individual items have been noted. This, if consistently true, reminds us of Wertheimer's view that subjects interpret facial expression better when allowing multiple cues to act in terms of their own balance than when heavily accenting one of them; the latter procedure might throw the balance off, destroy the proportions. Moreover, on purely statistical grounds it must be noted that if each cue is slightly more likely to aid than to impair correct interpretation, the use of several cues (as in ordinary multiple correlation situations) should give better results than the exclusive use of one.

But any generalization about the *universal* superiority of non-analytic methods can hardly go unchallenged. In some judgments of the face, the reverse is the case. Strang's study, mentioned above, was very revealing. One of her formal symbolic sketches showed brightness and fury bursting all over the landscape, a sort of Northern Lights effect. Every person who undertook to make the matchings identified this particular sketch, correctly, with ZTF. The procedure was simple. The brilliant chaotic shafts of light in all directions, commanding the beholder's attention but leaving him with a certain doubt as to the direction and final import of the display, led to the analytical question, "Who has spectacular but unfocused brilliance?" The answer was obvious to all who knew the group. Thus, in this case, the procedure was purely analytical. But even when a judgment appears to involve no analysis, some analysis is probably made through subliminal cues (page 655), and some of it probably uses conscious but non-verbal devices about which later testimony is notoriously unreliable. Wolff's well-reported experiments (page 622) give evidence of a great deal of analysis, and of all levels of skill in integrating the discrete features. Moreover, since integration never involves absolute equality of weight of the various components, we should expect to find clear evidence of dominance, of anchorage, and of figure-ground relations in the total structure.

Another example of the effective evaluation of personality from expressive style is provided by children's paintings. Some of the salient emotional characteristics of children are likely to appear in their choice of color; for a particular child working at an easel for a certain length of time, the use of color may properly be the anchorage point around which the experimenter organizes the personality interpretation. But it is entirely conceivable that another day the same child may be more profoundly concerned with problems in the utilization of space. As the child's emphasis varies, the perceptive interpreter will be able to define the limits within which these variations are contained, and these limits offer important clues to his personality.

It is, however, reasonable to expect different perceptual anchorage points, different forms of attack, for different individuals. This is one of the perennial problems of the personality analyst who attempts to be systematic in his approach to all aspects of expression. The anchorage points in expression are evidently derived largely from the individual's value system; the major values, as canalized drives (page 182), provide anchorage for all goal-seeking behavior. We should therefore expect the dominant value and the organized system of values surrounding it to be reflected to some degree in the aspects of expression that are most dominant, and in the minor expressive patterns surrounding the central one. Although it is still too early to be sure, a comparison of the Allport-Vernon and the Werner Wolff data indicate that this is the case.

But with all due recognition of parts, there is also a place for the recognition of *structure*. We noted earlier (page 334) the intersensory effects, the influence of one sensory modality upon another. This interdependence of sensory experience, through dynamic relations that are not in themselves sensory, suggests structural properties of organized interrelatedness within the individual. The field of expressive movement, revealing structural properties independent of specific modality, as in the matching techniques, appears to exemplify the same thing. The matching of handwriting samples with photographs showing locomotion, with profiles, with the voice, and with many other types of personality expression may bring out not only common *values*, but common spatial, temporal, and other structural properties. There may, for example, be something in the emotional warmth, the dead-pan monotony, or the cadence of the voice, even when uttering impersonal, routine prose, that permits one to match it with the temporal flow, the rise and fall, of the handwriting.

But we must be cautious in attributing the success of matching solely to the existence of structured patterns of organization. A very strong or tough or active individual—these characteristics lie for the most part at the first level—may show his strength or toughness in a booming voice, tight muscles, heavy tread, etc., so that no real structure, but only generality of response, is involved. In the same way, specific habits at Stage 2—for example, rhythms or irregularities of rhythm in one type of expression—may appear in other types of expression simply because some of the same muscles and the same ways of using them are involved. Nevertheless, such studies as we now have suggest that a large part of the unity which transcends specific areas of expression is dependent upon a true *interstimulation* of parts, the stimulus value that one bodily activity has for another part of the body. Thus, if the right arm swings forward as the left leg advances, the left arm and the right leg are thrown into appropriate types of response. If one handles a pencil in a particular way with the right hand, while the left hand presses down upon the paper, the arms and the trunk must participate in supporting the activity. In this sense an exceptionally heavy attack on the process of writing, as when writing a letter of protest, alters the tension pattern in the legs. Moreover, as the words tumble out geyser-fashion, the posture is affected not alone by a sheer increase in muscle tension, but by an overheavy accentuation of the writer's mannerisms; there is considerably less flexibility and richness of background than would appear under conditions of lower intensity in the primary focus of activity. Hence some generalized aspects of expressive organization are to be expected from what we know about personality at both the first and second levels.

Again, however, there is no warrant for insisting that *all* successful matching springs from third-level or architectural traits. Moreover, since the matchings thus far achieved are better than chance matchings but not as a rule brilliant, we may be fairly sure that successful identification of third-level traits is difficult. This may be due to technical imperfections, or to the large amount of Stage 2 material, i.e., the large amount of specific segmental behavior, to which people respond; this material is less useful than Stage 3 material in matching.

The fractionation of patterned wholes may destroy the observer's capacity to derive a personal meaning from the separate bits of expression. Fragments of photographs, no matter how numerous, do not necessarily reveal a complete personality; fragments of handwriting cut up into little bits leave most observers helpless. However, a long series of independent investigations shows that in general expressive wholes, when presented as wholes, can tell a recognizable personality story without any assistance from words. This does not of course mean that in interpreting them the analytic method is never used; on the contrary, the observer may pass from Stage 2 to Stage 3 as he makes his judgment. Stage 3 will be necessary if a statistical study of the components is undertaken. But frequently the parts will be seen at Stage 2 before the interrelations become clear, and judgments may be made either at this stage or at Stage 3 without explicit recognition of what is being done. The judge responding to traits at all three stages is also a personality, and as such reacts at all three stages.

It must of course be stressed that behind such local variations (e.g., smiling mouths) there is an individuality in the *pattern* (third-level organization) of each person's facial musculature which transcends the variable expressions with which varying stimuli are responded to. This relative constancy of "personal idiom" is found in every mode of expression. It is for this reason that the vocal portrayal of personality is feasible despite variations in what is said; it is for this reason that handwriting analysis has made rapid progress despite wide variations in what is written; and it is for this reason that even the photograph of the hands used by Wolff can catch some of the qualities of muscle tone, incipient rhythm, etc., which flow distinctively from specific personality qualities. Although the third-level study of personality is especially needed, it must be conceded that as these methods are currently used, the observer or experimenter usually responds simultaneously at all three levels; he responds to global or pervasive attributes, to differentiated traits, and to integrated wholes without being very explicit as to what he is doing.

The way in which the small child reproduces in action his experience with faces or postures or the flow of speech, with all its individuality, shows clearly that he has grasped systems of relations as well as elementary particles; he is able, without need of verbalization, to catch and reproduce the structural qualities of persons as wholes. This is a Stage 3 type of response. The response to movement qualities suggests that kinesthetic impressions are given organized form just as are the visual and auditory; they are not received piecemeal and then integrated. The interrelations between the components are clear. The spatial and temporal values manifest in the flow of such sensations appear in the child's posture. Kinetic qualities such as rhythm and grace are manifest in the even distribution of energy, as contrasted with jerkiness or a staccato quality. A rigid, constrained, or inhibited pattern is equally evident in the manner of walking or standing or sitting, in the way in which the head is held, and especially in the facial expression and gesture which accompany speech.

It must not be assumed that individuality is always recognizable from expressive movements. People differ in their degree of identifiability, partly because of the continuity of most kinds of expression from one extreme to the other in a social group. He who is near the middle of the distribution curve in any measurable characteristic at Stage 1 or 2 is hard to individualize; and since many of the characteristics are intercorrelated and partake of one another because of membership character, the person who is non-distinctive in one characteristic is likely to be non-distinctive in a whole series of them. A further difficulty is the varying degree of isolation of the parts. The fact that membership character is high in one case and low in another means that all types of identification based upon sharp definition of component parts are inevitably handicapped as membership character increases. In the same way, the people easiest to spot on Rorschach tests are those who have two or three sharp idiosyncrasies—in other words, those in whom distinctive functional parts can be isolated relatively easily.

A third factor that makes for difficulty is the variation in thresholds among the observers. Discriminations (of attributes at any one of the three levels) that are easy for one observer, because of his general endowment or his special practice in making comparisons, may be below threshold for another; the globality of a characteristic is frequently sheerly a matter of the poor resolving power of the lens—the perceptiveness—through which the observation is made.

JUDGMENTS OF PERSONALITY

"Judging personality"—a more explicit process of "recognizing" personality, already described—usually involves the utilization of evidence from all three developmental stages; in fact, the judge himself responds at all three stages. Some personality judgments are made by conscious or unconscious response to Stage 1 tendencies. When a trait is actually at this level, the observer who has noted it and assumes its presence in other situations is likely to be unusually successful, and his judgments have high reliability and validity.

Most judgments carried out by existing methods are made at Stage 2 (the responses of the judge and of the person being judged are both at this level). People have been observed in specific situations to act honestly or dishonestly, courageously or timidly, etc. Honesty, courage, and the like, are usually evaluated by observing actual behavior and applying certain implicit assumptions regarding probable transfer to other situations. Just as one who has learned to write with a pencil is presumed to be able to write with chalk on the blackboard, or even with his toes in the sand, so one who has exhibited emotional behavior in one situation is assumed to be likely to exhibit it in others, and so on. The larger the *number* and the greater the *variety* of the situations in which a specific conduct has been observed (e.g., the more samples of honesty or courage observed, and the more varied their contexts), the higher the reliability and validity of the judgments. This is a way of saying that transferred conditioned responses are operative to a high degree in the judge as well as in the person judged. Although naïve transfer on the part of the judge will lead to poor judgments (because the transfer may for some good reason fail to appear in the subject judged), a cautious and analytical study of the subject's probable transfer or lack of it often permits judgments with reliabilities of .90 or better.

There appear to be five kinds of judgments based on transfer; we may classify them under (1) stereotypes; (2) marginal cues; (3) subliminal cues; (4) multiple cues; (5) identification.

1. Naïve transfer of the sort just mentioned is the basis for the ways of thinking to which Walter Lippmann refers as *stereotypes*—the "pictures in our heads" which make it possible to regard all Russians, all Chinese, all Rotarians, as carbon copies of those whom we have known or about whom we have read. *Something* real is, of course,

shared by the persons bracketed together; they must all have the definite attributes which go with being Russians, or Chinese, or Rotarians. An introductory psychology of personality could be written in terms of stereotypes emphasizing what members of various groups have in common; in fact, many of the most respectable and time-honored systems of characterology are essentially in this class.

A somewhat more sophisticated use of stereotypes is made when we expressly define through deductive reasoning the group of characteristics that "ought to be present" when a given quality is present. The stereotyped pictures given us by Theophrastus—which show for example the fawning "flatterer" in all his loathsome yet ridiculous antics—portray people in whom an attribute has been observed and its consequences deduced. His efforts were relatively successful, because there really is a certain degree of forced interdependence among the attributes described. But all such procedures beg the question as to the *degree* of interdependence. This must depend upon the degree to which they derive from Stage 1 characteristics, the degree to which they represent transfer at Stage 2, and the degree to which they represent interdependence at Stage 3.

Stereotypes may thus assist judgment in three types of situations: (a) They are useful in cases in which a physiological disposition forces all who possess it to behave in a predictable way; this is exemplified in many types of mental defectives, in the deformed, in the prematurely born, and in spastics. (b) Stereotypes are useful at Stage 2 when it has been demonstrated that specific conditions do in fact lead to generalization in particular ways; for example, when racial attitudes have been shown to reach a level of generalization that permits us to predict the specific attitudes of those known to respond in a specific way in specific situations. (c) Stereotypes are useful when it has been demonstrated that certain Stage 2 dispositions necessarily must organize themselves in particular ways at Stage 3 because there are no other ways in which the environment can be met. In these three kinds of situations the stereotype is simply the use of a *valid* generalization.

But the conditions which warrant the use of stereotypes in these categories are rarely fulfilled. As contrasted with the various ways in which personality may legitimately be typed (see pages 734 ff.), the stereotype or symbolic short cut based upon a single attribute has been misleading most of the time. Though it does have certain values as an exploratory technique in attempts to work out some of the simpler personality dynamics at all three levels, it is usually a blind guide. Hence it is important to know both when we are using a stereotype and where its specific pitfalls lie.

Before dismissing the question of stereotypes, we should add that individual judges differ greatly in their capacity to make effective use of them and to resist false cues. Some of the judges in stereotype experiments are able to discern the probable area in which a stereotype would be helpful, and to use it in that area but no further. Personnel workers and physicians often make diagnoses in terms of stereotypes; they work by analogy, within a frame of reference determined by age, sex, and class. But their experience is usually confined to one subculture, so they may be extremely naïve with reference to the feasible limits of such transfer. Northerners make grotesque errors in evaluating Southerners, and vice versa; a gesture, a nod of the head, may have different meaning in the two areas. The Japanese waiter may smile as he sees the soup he has spilled on a lady's dress, and those nearby may be incensed at his "making light" of his clumsiness; they forget, however, that for the Japanese the smile is a traditional way of saying, "See how clumsy, how ridiculous I am."

2. Assessments of other persons are made not only in the light of salient behavior, but in the light of all sorts of little things which only *marginally* impress us. As we respond to the major features of behavior, we respond also to facial expression, gesture and posture, breathing, the blanching or flushing of the skin; we transfer from previous experience a host of stereotypes, long-standing conditioned responses to such features. These cues to which we respond *without* being explicitly aware of them may be called secondary, rather than marginal, cues.

3. In conjunction with these marginal cues arises the problem of *subliminal cues*. The word "limen" here denotes the point at which a stimulus attains the capacity to evoke a conscious response. It is one

thing to be unconscious of secondary cues because we are attending to something else, and a very different thing to be incapable of becoming aware of them because they are below the sensory limen. The latter cases present a subtle and difficult problem. Street sounds may strike our ear and even influence our respiratory rate without our actually hearing them; similarly, much that a friend does as he talks to us is subliminal for us.[1] It is likely that we judge one another not only by virtue of transfer from ordinary non-attended-to cues, but by virtue of cues that are so slight that they *could not* be attended to.

4. Major importance must be attached to *multiple cues*. Here two or more indicators are used jointly, though we may be aware of only one, or none. Sometimes multiple cues stand in a purely additive relationship; thus in judging a man as an anxious person, we may be influenced by his pallor, the clenching of his hands, his averted eyes, his irregular breathing, etc. But there are other cases in which the relation is not additive but integral; a number of expressive signs are perceived in such a way as to arouse an organized Gestalt response on the part of the observer. An indicator which by itself may mean anxiety may in its context mean simply excitement or eagerness. A response which by itself may mean aggressiveness may in another context mean dogged persistence. People who make accurate rapid-fire judgments often do so by using multiple cues in their integral form. Such integral judgments may, like other kinds of judgments, be right or wrong. As L. J. Stone points out, *learning to observe* depends largely on learning to discover *to what cues one is responding and how one is interpreting them.*

5. This might seem to be the whole story of "intuition." But there still remains a large and important factor which the psychoanalysts have stressed, the factor of unconscious *identification.* How well do we judge a person belonging to our own group? Or belonging to a group with which we have dealt a long time, but that comes from "the other side of the tracks?" Or belonging to a totally unfamiliar group? There

---

[1] While studying reaction time, T. N. Jenkins devised a cylinder which could be slipped into the outer passage of the ear. Inside the cylinder was a wire which could be made to hum whenever it was put into an electric circuit. Although its hum was too low for anyone to hear it, *his subject learned to respond to it.* But cf. footnote, page 233.

is considerable evidence to show that we must stand in another person's shoes and look through his eyes if we are to achieve a really sage evaluation. From childhood onward, we have developed a sense of affinity with others, based ultimately on the fact of our relation with our parents, with whom we identified in the first place. Something in the person we are judging brings out, for example, a response first experienced in relation to our mother. There are also many secondary identifications that are based on closeness to brother and sister and to neighbors. We gradually make contact through these identifications with the frames of reference of other persons. The way to achieve any frame of reference, as the dramatist and novelist have shown, is to attain enough identification to permit us to pick out as landmarks in our life the same landmarks the characters used. Thus we recognize the greatness of Thackeray and Dickens not because of their literary devices, but because they taught us to identify with the Becky Sharps and the David Copperfields. The more complex the process of interpretation, which in its use of integral cues frequently involves unconscious identification, the more likely is the result to be an intuitive total worth reporting. (One can, however, identify to such a degree that one *loses* insight, as we shall see later.)

But do we not thus turn our backs on scientific method, which tries to select variables and measure them one at a time? The answer may lie in whether we are making real use of the concept of the three levels of personality. The difficulty will disappear if we ask at what level each trait appears in the person studied. When dealing with global dispositions, we need no complex intuitions; we need clear-cut scientific observations and measurements. If, for example, we wish to gauge the speed of response, we shall do well to measure with a stop watch or a chronoscope. Whenever first-level traits are involved, the task is to standardize an objective procedure. When working with second-level characteristics, the task is to ascertain how broad the area of the differentiated trait actually is, to see how specific and how general the trait is, to determine how far it pervades the personality. Though this is again a rather narrow and objective question that can usually be answered experimentally, it requires us to keep an eye on membership character. If we work at the third level, dealing with integrated traits, we shall need to be sensitive to many structural possibilities; we shall need to move back and forth, up and down the ladder, viewing at the first, the second, the third level and back again, and using what we learn at all three; for integral traits are emergent products of the specific components of the system.

An illustration of the way in which we must work is seen in an experiment by F. H. Allport involving interpretation of pictures displaying emotion. The task of the students who looked at the pictures was to state what emotion was portrayed in each. Allport found that many of his subjects could intuitively identify laughter or pain or fear. But when they were required to practice to improve their scores, these intuitive judges improved only to a small degree; they were about as good at the beginning as they ever could become. However, the students who did poorly at first could benefit from practice by working analytically, noting the shape of the mouth and the little vertical lines beside it, how wide open the eyes were, and so on. While the intuitive judges found it difficult to go down the ladder and find the more elementary components, those who began with an atomic analysis could rapidly learn to integrate. The shrewd judge of personality, we may infer, is usually a person who can use all three levels and knows when to use each one; in other words, he can, under pressure, make a global judgment, but he knows also under what conditions a genetic and more detailed analysis must be made.

In applying one of the many "systems of character analysis," one person frequently seems to obtain good results, whereas another is a dismal failure. That the system may in itself be almost or completely worthless, but permit the experienced eye to anchor upon the real essentials, is suggested by a story told by F. B. Knight. While a student at Columbia, Knight determined to "show up" a well-known character analyst in New York. When he went to see her, he told her that he was a plumber and that he felt he had missed his calling. "Young man," she said, "if I had just one guess, I would say that you are a graduate student at Columbia University." People who "size up character" do so on the basis of their experience, picking up all the cues available, regardless of whether they are codified into a "system" or not.

In the light of all this, what does the process of learning to judge personality consist of? It appears to consist in the first place of train- ing oneself to recognize behavior traits, and the modes of interrela- tions between these traits in various common forms of personality architecture; in particular, of training in the rapid integration of multi - ple cues. That is what *experience* in judging people usually means. Experience in judging comprises training both in the piecemeal judg - ing of separate, diverse characteristics and in the integration of these characteristics.

But beyond this there is a further point which psychiatry has taught should be emphasized. In view of the huge importance of identification with other people, one might get more "training" from a class in tapdancing, or from hearing *Tristan und Isolde*, than from courses in personnel work. The best judge of personality is not neces- sarily the individual who is most sophisticated in using personnel devices. To have subtlety, range, depth of human identification, may be much more important than a panoply of narrow skills. What trans- fers best, as we have tried to point out (page 655), is broad experience. This does not mean that by doing psychiatric social work in New York a person can be a howling success on a Texas ranch; there are cul- tural difficulties. But if he has the skills required for social work in New York, it will show itself in his discovery of appropriate areas to which transfers can be made and the means of effecting it. The en- richment of one's experience is the chief means by which the capacity to judge people is ultimately developed.

In judging *oneself*, the first problem is *insight*, an objective integral view. Can insight be achieved simply by applying all the rules that have just been laid down? Hardly. Self-understanding may well be more difficult than the understanding of others. The rubrics which guide an individual in learning to judge others are not necessarily useful in judging himself. He struggles autistically *against* the use of many of the available cues. The answer is usually the one which John Levy once gave: Insight can seldom be increased directly by a hammer-and-tongs method; rather, as a person works with his deeper problems, with the network of his motives, and discovers what he really wants, he finds that he has achieved insight. Insight comes as a late cognitive expression of the readjustment of the motive pattern. That is one reason why psychiatric social workers have for a long time been convinced that the first step in understanding delinquent boys or drunken fathers or confused and frightened mothers is to undergo their own psychoanalysis, or in some other way to work through their own deep-level problems. One needs to understand his own identifications. Some light is thrown upon this problem by the paradoxical case of the mother who identifies herself so completely with her child that she cannot understand him. Here we are reminded of Werner Wolff's studies, in which the subject finds it harder to recognize his own expressive patterns than those of others. Perhaps a person can understand himself best by "working through" his understanding of those with whom he identifies, especially by noting where his *predictions* of their behavior go awry.

In a study of organization, a few words should be said about the traditional and still vital view that the real unity of personality is a matter for the arts, not the sciences, to grasp. The five ways of interpreting personality listed above, especially the process of unconscious identification, have of course always been employed—implicitly or explicitly—by those who use the concept of personality structure in the arts. The audience must be responsive to the subtle as well as to the salient aspects of individuality, and must make constant use of multiple, and perhaps also subliminal, cues. But it must above all be able to identify with the major characters if they are to be understood. Hence, we may ask whether there is in fact any great difference between the approach to personality structure in the arts and the corresponding approach from the standpoint of science, and whether, when the two disagree, the artistic may not be the more comprehensive and adequate.

The answer appears to be that art and science abstract from the concrete reality of personality in quite different ways; some overlap is involved, but there are large areas which do not overlap. Art selects, as a rule, what is or can be *structured*. But William Stern used to emphasize that personality exists in every degree of order and disorder, in every kind of form and formlessness, in structure as clear as crystal and in misty insubstantiality. As he put it, personality is Gestalt and it is also ungestalt. There is forced order, order that is arbitrarily imposed, and there is chaos, chaos that is refractory to this forcing and remains forever chaos. Personality is not always a tightly structured architectural whole in which no stone ever becomes displaced. It achieves its integration slowly and incompletely; all normal people have many loose ends. It can seldom be safely viewed as focused forever at one point. The frame of reference varies; what is central depends partly on the task of the moment. Personality has many centers, and a shifting system of relationships between the centers. The business of the artist as artist is to find order wherever he can find it and to create it wherever he can create it, neglecting chaos wherever he can. From the time of Theophrastus, every artist— especially the dramatist, the novelist, and the biographer—has been desirous of imposing unity upon personality. Occasionally a biographer will give us, as Boswell did, the rich ungestalt and chaos of his subject; more often, however, we encounter artists like Emil Ludwig, who coin a phrase to epitomize the whole of a personality. The essence of Leonardo, Ludwig says, was to put questions to nature. But this is not his *essence*; it is a *facet* of the man, and only a facet. Character does not reduce itself to a formula and personality cannot be described in a phrase, however brilliant; art seeks a simplicity and an order which belie the complex totality. Thus the work of the artist can and does greatly enrich the work of the scientist, and vice versa, but their tasks are not the same. The work of science often goes off in a direction far different from that with which the arts are concerned. Science selects in order to define abstract and general laws. Art—usually, at least—selects in order to produce esthetic unity in a concrete embodiment; it must emphasize the attributes that help to portray its intended pattern and neglect others.

Is there, then, a possible unification of the two? One attempted answer is seen in abstractionism in art; another, in the use of arts in medical practice and in rehabilitation; another, in the use of projective methods with children. There are indeed probably dozens of ways in which the joint application of the arts and sciences may reveal an overlap between the things selected by the two. (A typical "curve of learning" abstracts from nature in precisely the form of many a Greek vase; the two acts of abstraction here coincide.) Many who work as artists with material which can also be approached through the sciences—most therapists are fair examples—may be unable to tell which aspects of their work are artistic in the sense of creating, and which scientific in the sense of discovering principles. The artist may select and organize for his own artistic purpose, and yet find later that his selection is the one that science would have made. But despite this overlap, the purposes of art and of science are so fundamentally different that every artistic effort to grasp the unity of the person must be critically considered when our purpose is that of science. We may find that the artist has exaggerated the features of the outline that serve the purpose of art, and at the same time has neglected many of the complexities—phases that reduce to no simple order—upon which more complete and adequate science would lay stress.

28. Projective Methods
with Adults

THE "recognition of structure" leads at once into the more systematic experimental methods of exploring and comparing the personality structures of individuals; these "projective methods" will constitute our problem through two chapters. But in introduction, it seems appropriate to give a few paragraphs to the way in which our theory of personality structure, with its conception of levels and of architecture, influences our efforts to define what the projective methods can achieve in assessing personality traits and their interrelations.

Some of the physiological tests, such as those relating to general intensity and duration of response (cf. pages 152 ff.), may be placed at the first developmental level. Tests of muscle tension and endocrine function stand midway between Stage 1 and Stage 2, for general organismic dispositions are involved, but local and specific dispositions are superimposed upon them. Tests dealing with canalizations and conditionings and their transfer are usually at Stage 2; on page 626 we noted traits which seem to be essentially generalized conditioned responses.

In many situations, however, traits based on wide transfer coexist with others based on narrow transfer, and here we are in danger of being led into an argument as to whether personality is "general" or "specific." An example of data which show high specificity if regarded in one way, high generality if regarded in another, is the Bogardus Social Distance Test, with seven classifications of social distance, or nearness; one accepts a group in terms of "close kinship by marriage" or at the other extreme takes steps to exclude it from one's country. It would ordinarily be assumed that acceptance of the various social groups would certainly be specific; to accept Danes to close kinship by marriage does not conflict with rejecting Portuguese. However, when we cut a list of 21 groups in two, and compare 11 against 10 (i.e. if on the basis of the total social distance expressed in the first part of the list, we predict the total amount of social distance or prejudice in the last part), we obtain a correlation of .95 to .97 between the parts. There is much specificity to individual groups, but there is enough overlap to give high generalization if we use all the data from the entire list in this way.

Personality is thus both specific and general (page 134). Most of the names assigned to behavior dispositions represent recurrent and recognizable aspects of conduct, so that different samples of these dispositions intercorrelate; and at the same time most traits which have names overlap with other traits which have names. The overlap is large between such traits as cooperation and loyalty, and very small between cooperation and sense of humor; but there is always some overlap between situations and some absence of overlap, so every trait appears somewhat generalized, somewhat specific. Symonds' data show the generalized trait of *tact*, but tact varies somewhat with situations. This corresponds to the fact that situations resemble one another, and that responses to them must in some degree resemble one another. Traits do not exist inside a person's skin. Traits are functional descriptions of relations between individuals and situations and as such they overlap with other functional descriptions. "Trait names are little labels which seldom fit a personality very well and have to be pasted on so that they overlap." (L. J. Stone.)

Midway between Stages 2 and 3 lies the vast array of personality traits in which interrelations of two or more systems of transferred conditioned responses are involved, with problems of generality of the conditioned response being interwoven with problems of personality structure in the true sense. There are relatively few personality tests which hit the organism squarely at the third level, the level of organization as such. A good many of them aim to do so; but since the organism is capable of functioning simultaneously at Stages 2 and 3, and since the method of analysis usually takes the form of intensive attack on specific units or aspects of the whole, Stage 2 is nearly always represented even in the holistic measures.

An example of a personality study reaching all three levels is the Rosenzweig Picture Frustration Test (page 318), in which individual frustration-tolerance appears to be an expression of global organic tendencies, of specific techniques for coping with specific tensions, and of ways of integrating such techniques. But tests are seldom conceived in terms of a specific theory as to developmental dynamics; they seldom concern the origins of dispositions at a given time. Frustration-tolerance tests, for example, deal with the person as he is today, not with genetic or developmental considerations. The same is true of most tests of complex personality functions, and it holds conspicuously for almost all the behavior tests. Personality measures are often competent to give a cross-section picture of traits and their interrelations, but they must be repeated from time to time if the continuity and evolution of individual functions (the total activity stream; cf. page 260) is to be clarified. Wordsworth showed amazing continuity in poetic power until he was thirty-seven; then somehow he rapidly "went dry."

Even so, there are a number of measures in which there is enough of the third-level approach to suggest what the first and second levels in the same person may have been; we can thus guess to some degree the developmental history of the prestructural whole. Moreover, working with a group whose members are at different phases in a common developmental sequence enables us to observe the development of stages. A fruitful field for such studies is the analysis of general bodily kinetics, particularly posture and gesture. The study of children and adults in culturally differentiated groups may show the stages through which cultural interaction has crystallized the mode of manual or postural expression. Thus Mead's and Bateson's Balinese children have by the end of infancy much of the Balinese "grace." At the same time we may study the nature of the cultural pressures at work upon the raw biological dispositions; specifically, at Stage 2, the processes by which the thresholds for specific conditioned responses influence the acquisition of additional conditionings along the lines predicted by the theory of dominance (cf. page 199). Also at this stage there are studies of energy distribution and perseveration which show some degree of intensification of organic dispositions in the areas in which there has been special opportunity for their exercise; for example, the person who responds quickly by virtue of physiological speed responds especially quickly in the specific manual movements in which he has been trained. Similarly, emotional explosions, while to some degree based on constitutionally low thresholds, may be shown to be particularly violent in the areas where culture has consistently legitimized them.

At the third level there are studies of such traits as creativity and self-control which clearly involve the interdependence or architectural wholeness of various dispositions, and studies of the integrating role of values (e.g., the Allport-Vernon studies mentioned above). Most studies of value are couched in third-level terms, because the self becomes involved in the process (cf. page 187), and this involves the integration of many specific habits. Studies of value are to be assigned to the third level almost as consistently as studies of simple conditioning are to be assigned to the second. From this follows the fact, well defined by G. W. Allport, that even the traits which are most specific —even unrelated in the statistical sense—often spring from a well-unified core of personal *value* (cf. page 626). Many traits belong to Stage 2 as measured traits, but to Stage 3 as aspects of a complete person.

We have emphasized the importance of personality approaches at the third level, the delineation of structure, even though tests as they exist today are not completely satisfying in this respect. But suppose it be objected that the third-level approach depends entirely upon the reliability and validity of second-level studies—we can hardly see the total personality organization clearly if the components are indistinct. There is a reply to this objection which, in spite of its paradoxical form, seems to give special cogency to the Gestalt approach. (1) The personality structure, or personality Gestalt, may well be at times more invariant than any of its parts (cf. page 649). (2) Personalities, moreover, may differ from early childhood in the tightness of their integration; the *degree of structuring* may be a true third-level trait.

In the light of recent observations it is quite likely, for example, that a child with a closely knit personality structure will learn almost everything in highly integrated fashion, grasping and assimilating complexities in terms of both perception and action, with a deftness of touch rarely seen in another child even after long experience in comparable situations. Studies of childhood language and other skills have often disclosed such patterns as these; one child learns to talk in phrase or sentence units, another a word at a time. In a Gestalt type of child the complex skills—let us say the roller-skating skills of McGraw's nineteen-months-old experimental twin—may be acquired, or dropped, in a Gestaltish way. As interests change, other complex activities may emerge which have little in common with the first, in terms of either form or content; yet each is attacked with the same complex of techniques involving simultaneous use of all three levels and exemplifying an abundant organizing power. We may be able to say, then, that it is characteristic of such a personality to proceed integrally rather than partially. Similarly, there are children who attack each new problem piecemeal, putting the parts together into a jerry-built structure, and with each act of trial and error knocking down and reassembling until they have a habit pattern that will work. Some complex personality dimension is involved in the difference between these children, not just specific contents or specific modes of transfer. Unfortunately, the term "personality structure" is often used by psychoanalysts and other clinical workers to mean the mere mode of aggregation of a series of specific cathexes or mechanisms of defense. From the point of view developed here, some of the main outlines of the personality might well be the same if the cathexes and the defense mechanisms were entirely different; e.g., a person might be well balanced without our needing to say *what* tendencies are balanced.

Again, this does not mean that organization can be conceived at the third level exclusively, or that the first two phases can be ignored either by the child or by those who study him. It does mean, however, that the concept of personality structure will not work well if the components are regarded as the only factors which contribute to the mode of organization. The mode of organization may be intrinsic in the way the organism is made—indeed, it may well be present in neonatal or even in prenatal development. But there is no need to insist that this dimension is due solely to constitutional factors. Social fears or sheer exuberance, for example, may make integration difficult and consequently fragment the person. Capacity for integration is probably derived, like everything else, from a nature-nurture whole.

However it arises, structure expresses itself through *measurements*, no matter how much the experimenter may wish to avoid this. The impression has got abroad that there is an antithesis between personality measurement and an approach in terms of structure. Yet measurement supports rather than negates the emphasis upon wholeness. When concerned with structure, we wish, of course, to observe structural relations long and carefully before we attempt to decide what is to be measured, and in what way. How far we can go with measurement is always an empirical question. We are between Scylla and Charybdis; for the people who love to analyze and measure, who give us the beautiful factorial analyses of "persistence," "radicalism," etc., are seldom interested in specifying the mode of articulation between traits—mostly the measurers get stuck in measuring— and the structuralists are too enamored of relationships to bother with *precise* measurements, however quantitative their statements may be implicitly.

From the present point of view, the measurement of personality will be most fruitful when concerned with complex processes, when it attempts to catch the whole integrated personality at each of its levels. But experience has shown that personality is often more easily approached at this higher level where integration occurs through perceptual, imaginative, and volitional rather than motor tasks; thus the way a person looks at the world is a more adequate preliminary clue than anything he does. This is a primary reason why clinics have found that they need perceptual tests. Serious sampling errors are always encountered if personality is judged from a small number of behavior instances; by working at higher levels we obtain at one stroke so many expressions of personality dispositions and of their interrelations that reliability is almost guaranteed. Because outer expression is more variable than inner organization, the consistency of personality is higher with reference to the way one sees than with reference to the way one does. The clearest, most uniform, and most consistent view of an individual personality appears to be embodied in what the world means to the person. As L. K. Frank says, we seek the private world of the individual; we wish to know in what world he lives and how he sees the everyday situations which other people see in other ways.

Sometimes we get at this world of the individual's by putting a stark, clear, objective situation before him and finding out what he sees in it. But this is a cumbersome method, for the more clear-cut the situation the smaller the individual differences in perceiving it. Even a very hungry man, daydreaming of sugar buns, will call a doorknob a doorknob. There is always a struggle between cognitive processes, those that have to do with what is there, and those that represent wishful factors; but to study the wishful factors to advantage we must dull or confuse the sharply cognitive situation to some extent. A properly prepared test will bring out both cognitive and drive factors and permit us to observe their interaction.

The term *projective methods* has come into general use in recent years to denote the devices that enable the subject to project himself into a planned situation. He sees in it what he personally is disposed to see, or does with it what he is personally disposed to do. We are interested primarily not in the quantity of production, as in an educational test, but in what he indirectly tells us about himself through his manner of confronting the task. All psychological methods involve some projection in the sense that a person reveals himself in whatever he does. One may put little, or much, of oneself into a production; thus the carpenter projects himself when he makes a doorsill, and to a much greater extent when he makes a boat. The Allport-Vernon methods are in some degree projective, the graphological methods still more so, and the interpretation of ink blots perhaps most projective of all. There is a continuum of self-expression or self-projection, from the slight reflection of individuality in the rapid-fire mechanical utterance of the "opposites" to words like black or heavy, up to the identification of oneself with a character in a stage production. Since there is a continuum, the definition is for convenience only. We shall include under projection all those methods in which the individual has full opportunity to live empathically, that is, in terms of identification with the material presented to him. But we agree that there is *some degree* of empathic self-realization in a much wider variety of methods than we shall describe; that some individuals realize themselves empathically in some materials which are handled rather mechanically by others; and that a method may be exceedingly projective for a person today, but only slightly so tomorrow.

THE THEMATIC APPERCEPTION TEST

Fantasy tests have been used in an exploratory way for decades. Many of them have been developed in the Harvard Psychological Clinic during the last twenty years. The Thematic Apperception Test, the one which has been most systematically developed there, has been used for some years not only at that Clinic, but also in psychiatric practice, notably in the Worcester State Hospital. Consequently there is abundant information regarding its uses with both normal and abnormal personalities.

A "thema" is an expression of a need that occurs in response to the "press" of the environmental situation; it is thus a unified expression of need and press. Apperception is perception in terms of one's whole background of experience. The Thematic Apperception Test (T.A.T.) is consequently concerned with the world as perceived, and is an expression of the effects of both needs and presses. The primary psychological framework is Murray's list of needs which are shown in the responses to a series of pictures; the needs are as follows:

1. Aggression	6. Achievement
2. Succorance	7. Dominance
3. Acquisition	8. Nurturance
4. Affiliation	9. Deference
5. Cognizance	10. Inviolacy

11. Recognition	21. Retention
12. Excitance	22. Sex
13. Exhibition	23. Blame escape
14. Exposition	24. Blame avoidance
15. Harm avoidance	25. Autonomy
16. Construction	26. Variance
17. Abasement	27. Rejection
18. Order	28. Seclusion
19. Passivity	29. Sentience
20. Play	

The T.A.T., in the form that is best known, is a test for adults. The pictures used are chosen on the basis of clinical experience as to the wide *diversity of interpretations given.* There are ten pictures for men only, ten for women only, and ten for both men and women. These pictures are presented one at a time; the subject is asked to make up a story about each one. He is allowed all the time he wants; all his responses are taken down verbatim. The test can be administered to a group by means of slides, but the individual method is ordinarily used and is much to be preferred.

To illustrate, one picture shows a boy looking at a violin on the table before him. The story the subject makes up may deal with the boy's longing to become a great musician, or his sense of frustration, or his resentment at having to practice, or a thought stimulated by what he has just played. Through the series the subject tends to *identify* usually with a character of his own age and sex, and less frequently with other persons in the pictures. Since there are twenty cards in all for each subject, the investigator is able to secure a fair sampling of the capacities for identification. The degree of personal involvement also varies; thus the subject may identify with a number of characters, but his story about one of them may indicate more personal involvement than do the others. This should tell something about the conception of the self and the aspects of it which are most cherished. The general feeling tone of the individual—joy, anxiety, anger—is also likely to express itself quickly; the affective level often runs fairly consistently through the twenty cards. The relative intensity of the needs listed by Murray can be gauged by the test. The T.A.T. permits, then, among other things, the gathering of data about the identifications, the affective level, and the relative strengths of the various needs of the individual. It provides a direct introduction to individual autisms, individual projections. And since unconscious needs receive considerable attention, the test serves the purposes of psychoanalytic free association. The *repetition* of themas is of special importance.

If we ask about the value of the test as a clue to personality, the first reply is that we can thus obtain a view of the person's specific fears and specific wishes, while free of the social tension which the psychiatric interview presents. Anyone can "make up a story"; the subject is not giving a "right" or "wrong" answer, and is not on the spot. Second, since the pictures have been used with many subjects, interindividual comparisons can be made. With some persons a long time is required before an interview gives much more than superficial material, i.e., before the deeper wishes of the individual are recognized, whereas with the T.A.T. it may be possible for him to betray his deep wishes without consciously focusing on them. Its very formlessness, the fact that the subject does not realize that it can be scored or evaluated, eliminates much of the tenseness usual in the test situation. The test may be regarded clinically as a first form of life history and as an indicator of present needs, and as such it is extremely valuable.

Using the T.A.T., Balken and Masserman were able to show that the responses of clinical groups of patients were characteristic of the specific tensions which made up the cores of their maladies. Words referring to worries appeared frequently in the records of obsessive-compulsive patients. Their conversion-hysteria cases showed almost no reference to worry whatever, a fact that fits the general hypothesis that the somatic manifestations of hysteria constitute a sufficient outlet for the tension (and sufficient assuagement of guilt; cf. page 541). A conversion hysteric is not worried, and his T.A.T. responses are as predicted. It has frequently been suggested (as by Stanley Cobb) that psychosomatic cases may be separated into two broad categories; in one of them a conflict situation gives rise to physical upsets (such as skin allergies) without anxiety, and in the second the tension is expressed cerebrally, psychically, so that there is an abundance of overwrought, anxious, often guilt-directed fantasy.[1] The T.A.T. used in this way gives promise as an objective device for clinical differentiation.

Group comparisons can, then, be made successfully. The question next arises whether the T.A.T. enables us to discern the full individuality of a person, in the sense that his performance is distinctively different from that of others, permitting us to select his record as the only one congruent with his personality. This is done with the matching method; e.g., T.A.T. responses can be matched with dreams and daydreams. The present evidence indicates that success in matching stories with case histories is high (i.e., knowing the case history, we can determine the stories which a given individual made up), and also that stories can be successfully matched against other types of expression, such as the Rorschach.

The Rorschach Method

Ink blots began to be used in the '90's as a clue to personality; in them each individual saw different things. Around 1911, after some preliminary experimentation, Herman Rorschach, a Swiss psychiatrist and psychoanalyst, began a much more intensive and systematic study. In the early stages he tried an enormous number of different ink blots, varied their method of preparation, and tested a large number of persons. The Rorschach method was not invented in the armchair; it was a practical psychiatrist's tool for a difficult tech-

---

[1] It may be suggested that in the latter group the fantasy is ordinarily built around the self, around the individual's own inadequacy and his own guilt. In the first category, the fantasy may deal as a rule with needs more primitive than those relating to the self; consequently we should expect a lower order of integration and much less perseveration. If primitive needs lead to action, they are less likely to appear in fantasy. The diary kept by the Belgian psychologist Varendonck while in the trenches during the First World War showed that his day dreams in this period of anxiety and discomfort stemmed, as the Freudian data suggested, from needs which had no opportunity for expression, the more patent needs for safety, food, and protection from cold, being so perfectly integrated with *overt behavior* appropriate to the soldier that almost no fantasy of this type appeared.

nical job. Since it was constantly applied to clinical material of many types, it underwent continuous revision.

Rorschach was convinced that the main outlines of psychoanalytic theory, heretofore based largely on findings from free association in the analytic interview (and on Jung's free-association test), could be applied in a study of unconscious factors in perception, and that many other dynamic factors could be revealed in a perception test. He noted that a person may be unaware of what he reveals by what he sees; for the material actually reported is conscious material, and the things reported are objectively there in the perceptual field and not sheer products of the imagination. Whereas the T.A.T. makes possible a combined study of perception and imagination, the Rorschach as a rule deals primarily with perception rather than with fantasy.

Roughly, the administration of the Rorschach test consists simply in presenting ten cards, each bearing a complex blot pattern in a standard order, and asking the subject to report what he sees in them. The exact wording of the instructions is not considered important; but it is important to establish a set so that the subject may find real meaningful things in the blots, not feeling that he must describe them simply in terms of meaningless ink spots.

The scoring of the test requires three columns. Each response is first scored with respect to the way in which it makes use of spatial attitudes; it may be the response to the whole card, to a large detail, to a small detail, or to the white spaces between the blots. The response is then scored in terms of its use of the form or shape of the blot in finding a meaningful object, or the effect of the color which appears in some of the blots, or its attribution of movement to perceived human figures, or integrations of these determinants. Finally it is scored with reference to its sheer content—animal, human detail, botany, etc. The three columns are so totaled that the ratio of whole to large detail, of form to color, etc., can be seen at once.

In general, the use of form represents objectivity, a disciplined recognition of fact. The affective life of the individual is revealed primarily through color; the person with an outgoing emotional disposition piles up a considerable color score. To use both form and color indicates integration of objective and emotional tendencies. To give numerous form-color responses (form being the primary determinant, and color the secondary) indicates control, but control with some appreciation of affective realities; to give numerous color-form responses, color being dominant, is likely to mean loss of control through dominating affect. A person with a rich inner life typically has a high human movement score. A richly intuitive, subtle, responsive person, the very gifted or artistic, typically gives many responses of both color and human movement; the pedant gives neither. If there is a great deal of human movement and little or no color response, the likelihood is that the individual has a rich inner response but little affective response to the outer world; Rorschach called such a person introversive. If the individual has a great deal of color response but gives rather little of himself, the human movement responses being few, it indicates a high degree of dependence on the outer world, a disposition that Rorschach called extratensive.

The validation of the Rorschach can be gauged in terms of matching blind Rorschach interpretations against independent personality sketches, or in terms of predicting behavior. But as a general rule, Rorschach workers are inclined to be rather restive at the mention of validation through matching. Validation, they agree, is necessary; Rorschach used an essentially similar method, the "blind diagnosis" of records transmitted to him. The matching does indicate validity, but this is only the first step in the long-range utilization of the test. Perception, being a highly integrated act, should be expected to reveal what goes on in life better than samples of segmental behavior; the advantage lies not in using perception rather than behavior, but in looking for integrated rather than segmental units. For this reason the Rorschach should predict specific future behavior better than does the study of past specific behavior, except when the new behavior is essentially a repetition of the old. In order to show *how* and *why* it can predict, we need to be more specific as to the procedure. This test differs widely from the many personality tests that are not explicit regarding either the level at which they attack the personality, or the sense in which the concept of structure is to be applied. In contrast to the frequent vagueness on these points, the Rorschach method offers a full-fledged approach to the unity of personality; its systematic quest for wholeness in approaching all three levels is striking. This can best be brought out by emphasizing what the Rorschach examination means in terms of the measurement of various kinds of personality traits. It is indeed necessary to mark out within the personality certain functional units in order to measure them. Just as during an operation upon the heart that organ is lifted from its position though not separated organically from its connections with the body, so the psychological trait is seen in and by itself, but also in its larger context. When the Rorschach method undertakes to measure traits, it follows this rule. Consequently its second-level approach can be supplemented by shifting the emphasis to first- or third-level traits when desired.

Suppose we wish to measure a broad tendency such as "originality."[2] The normal adult is likely to make from ten or fifteen up to fifty or sixty responses to the ten Rorschach cards; every response gives information both on "originality" and on thirty or forty other "traits" in which we may be interested. Tables prepared by Beck show how often each sort of response appears in a given cultural group. "Angel" and "automobile" are infrequent responses to Card I seen as a whole; "bat" and "mask" are, on the other hand, very banal. From the entire series of responses, an over-all score on originality can be secured and compared with the tendency to give popular answers (those given by 5 per cent or more of the subjects responding). Originality, then, can be measured. But it is still originality in only one sense, the sense of seeing unusual possibilities in the ink blots. However, we wish to secure a broader view of originality vs. banality, so we look for human details such as eye, ear, etc. Even more revealing are the animal details;[3] their multiplicity, to the exclusion of many

---

[2] This is chosen as an example of a trait which can also be reliably measured by the ordinary method of rating. Kate Gordon asked her subjects to draw anything they wanted to, and showed that group judgments as to originality of the product had very satisfactory reliabilities.

[3] Why is it that the banal mind usually gives a large number of animals or animal details—claws, feathers, horns, etc.? Let us compare animal shapes with cloud shapes. Although there are any number of shapes of clouds, there are no *names* for these different

more interesting possibilities, is a clue to commonplaceness, to lack of originality. We also notice the way in which normal and small details are used. The subject may give an extraordinary number of quasi-original responses to tiny details, for in responding to such details he often makes a frantic effort to appear as original as possible. We can thus see at what *cost* the individual achieves his originality; we note, for example, the strain which is expressed in various types of anxiety in other parts of the test. Originality and banality, then, are not judged from single clues; various kinds of evidence are integrated.

Anxiety is another trait that is frequently shown in responding to the Rorschach. But there are several kinds of anxiety. Since in Rorschach experience response to color is an indicator of affectivity, we might expect the *tendency to be overwhelmed* by the environment to take the form of extreme accent on the color aspect of the cards. In hysteria, in severe manic attacks, and in several other disorders involving affectivity, color responses increase. This will be intelligible if we illustrate from the psychology of the manic attack. Just as there is such a thing as flight from reality, so there is flight *into* reality when the individual is afraid of what may be found in himself. In the manic attack, the patient appears to be trying to screen from himself the realities of his inner life. Abundant color response in the Rorschach does in fact often indicate flight into reality; color-form responses (in which color plays a larger role than form) dominate form-color responses, and there is much use of pure color (in which form is disregarded altogether). Color shock is another sign of anxiety. A person may be struck by color in such a way as to be thrown off his base. When a color card follows a black-and-white card, color shock is shown in the delay in response time, and also in the inability to use the color, even when the examiner shows how it can be used. A

shapes. But animal names are plentiful. Such names as leopard, mouse, and spider provide a possible funnel through which impressions flow on to the Rorschach record. If we had names for all sorts of complicated irregularly shaped clouds, we would of course take "cloud-seeing" attitudes toward the cards and give these names in response to them. It is characteristic that Hamlet, as he points to the clouds, tells Polonius that they look like animals; one would not commonly compare animals to clouds. We take hold of the significant things that have *names*.

third series of anxiety indicators is the shading responses, which Rorschach did not live to investigate fully. Some of the cards have a mottled effect produced by deep grays interlarded with lighter grays which frequently give the effect of a texture; in other cases the effect of the varying shading is a vista with a three-dimensional instead of a two-dimensional outlook. Shading response, especially in the form of texture response, appears to be a common anxiety symptom. And just as we speak of color shock, we may speak of shading shock; as the individual passes from a card that contains no prominently contrasting grays to one that has them, he shows delay in response and he uses anxiety-laden concepts. Since the examiner is interested not only in the level but in the specific form of anxiety, he notes the use of small detail and the "contents," i.e., the kinds of things designated, by which the subject may quickly betray the specific things about which he is anxious. A color response to red in terms of blood or fire may indicate a generalized or specific anxiety. Color and shading responses often reveal specific death fears, or ego fears, or sex fears, which dominate the patient's outlook. The point to be stressed here is that no single indicator is ever relied upon exclusively; a specific trait like originality or anxiety is approached through many cues.

We are now ready to consider two broad ways in which the Rorschach examiner may use the concept of personality structure; one involves primarily a study of the quantitative relations of Stage 2 traits in the total pattern, the other calls for a more intimate view of architectural attributes. Let us look now at the first of these.

One of the major uses of the Rorschach findings is in estimating the amount of psychological trouble the individual is experiencing, or, stated the other way around, in gaining an over-all view of his adjustment level. This estimate is made by referring to all the indicators of maladjustment. It has been found that the list of such indicators need not comprise more than about 25 items. Munroe's check list may be summarized as follows. Entries are of four types: plus, minus, letter, and check; and the sum of all entries is the adjustment score percentage.

"1. Refusal (√). Failure to make any response to one or more cards (as many as three checks may be made in certain specified cases).

"2. W (+, −, V, B). Percentage of responses using the blot as a whole; quality of such responses. A plus entry is made if the percentage is over 60, a minus if under 15. A vague or bad whole response is scored V or B.

"3. Dd (+). Responses using small or rare details. One to three plus entries may be made, depending on the quantity of detail and on the tendency to stereotypes.

"4. S (+). Excessive use of white spaces, i.e., reversal of figure and ground.

"5. Suc (r, 1). Succession of responses according to their location: whole, usual detail, unusual detail, tiny detail. Extreme regularity in succession is scored 'r' (rigid). Extreme lack of regularity is scored 'l' (loose) or actual disorganization ('ll').

"6. P, Com (−). Popular (i.e., *very* frequently given) and common responses. One to three minus entries may be given when these are few or entirely absent.

"7. O (+, B). Original responses (given by less than one subject in 100). One to three plus entries are made when over 50 per cent of the responses are original. B is entered for bizarre originals.

"8. At, Sex (+). Anatomy and sex responses. One to three plus entries are given for excessive number or poor quality.

"9. Range (+, −). Excessively wide and scattered range of content. Catalogues (types of things seen). One to three minus entries are given for limited range (i.e., stereotyping).

"10. F% (+, −). Percentage of responses using only the shape or form of the blot. One to three plus entries are given for those over 50 per cent, one minus entry for a very low percentage, and a second minus if there is no integration of form with responses indicating emotional elements.

"11. F (V, B, E). Vague, bad, or overexact forms; one or more entries of each letter may be made.

"12–16. Shading area. Response to shading scored in various ways, depending on how shading is used. Response to shading, form being completely ignored, receives a plus. Shading shock, the interruption or distortion of the flow of responses in consequence of the perception of shading, receives plus or minus entries depending upon the form it takes.

"17–20. Movement area. Excessively frequent perception of human movement calls for plus entries; its absence, for minus entries. Inaccuracy, and restriction of movement, are penalized by appropriate letters. Excessive animal movements or movements of inanimate things are scored plus. Total movement, the sum of all types of movement response indicating reactions determined by inner strivings, is scored plus or minus when it is excessively large or small.

"21–25. Color area. One to three minus entries for absence of form-color response, where form and color are both used, with form predominating. Excessive color-form (where color dominates) over form-color calls for one to three plus entries. More than one pure color response (form being ignored) brings a penalty. Total color, the sum of color, color-form, and form-color, is penalized when the number of such responses is excessively large or small.

"26. Color: movement. The ratio of total color responses to total movement responses is penalized when extremely high or low."

Attention must be given not only to scores for specific tendencies

THE RORSCHACH ADJUSTMENT RATING IN RELATION TO ACADEMIC STANDING
AFTER ONE YEAR

Academic Standing	Adjustment Rating from Inspection Rorschach								Total	
	A (Adequately Adjusted)		B (Slight Problem)		C (Moderate Problem)		D (Severe Problem)			
	N	%	N	%	N	%	N	%	N	%
Superior..........	14	18.2	14	12.9	6	7.1	6	7.6	40	11.5
Satisfactory.......	52	67.6	76	70.4	34	40.4	24	30.3	186	53.4
Low average......	9	11.6	18	16.7	32	38.1	27	34.2	86	24.8
Failing...........	2	2.6	0	0	12	14.4	22	27.9	36	10.3
	77	100.0	108	100.0	84	100.0	79	100.0	348	100.0

χ^2 81.98   C = .43 (corrected, .49)

—indicating, for example, a tendency to color or to color-form, or a tendency to human movement responses without color—but also to certain ratios. Especially important is the color: movement ratio. The ratio of emotional responses, as shown in color, to empathic response, as shown in movement, immediately suggests a kind of balance required for social adjustment. Although we are dealing with interrelation or structure, the reader will notice that even here, with our attention focused on a long list of discrete danger signs, there is some use of third-level concepts. These signs, having been worked out through years of clinical experience, make it possible to grade people in terms of the sheer *number* of danger signs. This may seem a crude substitute for a Rorschach interpretation. But, as the table shows, Munroe, in a blind analysis of Inspection Rorschach records derived from a Group Rorschach[4] given to students just before entering college, was able to predict rather well the general level of academic success. Indeed, it predicted college achievement better than did the intelligence test, except in the case of the intellectually superior quarter of the group.

Whether this predictive power, as shown in Munroe's experiment, is due entirely to the summation of specific (relatively independent) weaknesses whose combined weight dragged the person down, or is due in some degree to a pervasive and general weakness that expresses itself through all the individual signs, can be judged only in the light of the internal consistency, e.g., the split-half reliability of the scores for the various signs. But since there is considerable evidence of *both* types of interrelations of scores, Munroe felt that a split-half correla-

---

[4] In the group Rorschach the plates are presented in the form of slides; on a small chart showing the Rorschach cards the subject indicates what he sees in the slides. This method has at least two difficulties: first, group pressure (for a person does not necessarily see in the same way when many are responding at once), and second, the uniformity of time allowance despite the varying lengths of time required by the subjects. Nevertheless, the group test has been widely used. More recently there has been an attempt to use the test in multiple-choice form; the subject must indicate, from a long list of suggested responses, which ones seem appropriate. From data now available it appears that the multiple-choice Rorschach is much less successful than the forms which permit free response. The individual Rorschach method is still the only one if personality diagnosis in the full sense is intended. Typically an hour or so is required to administer it, and a whole day may well be necessary to score, study, analyze in terms of all observable interrelations, and work out in terms of a blind diagnosis.

tion would be meaningless. The point is that we encounter here *both* Stage 1 and Stage 2 aspects of personality. It should be noted that many Rorschach workers would call Munroe's approach "atomistic" and would demand a heavy emphasis on interdependence (Stage 3 approach). This is not our own point of view; we believe in the need for an approach *at all three levels*.

The educational use is only one of the many uses of the Rorschach. Numerous attempts are now being made to relate Rorschach data to findings on brain disease and on physiological adequacy. Thus it has been possible to predict rather well from the Rorschach which individuals will incur the greatest functional impairment in a specific damaging situation. Piotrowski was able to predict the reaction of schizophrenics to insulin shock; and Hertzman and his collaborators predicted rather closely how men would hold up under oxygen deprivation, and demonstrated significant and consistent shifts in responses under low-oxygen conditions. The tie-up with medicine has thus become close. At the same time, Oberholzer has brilliantly shown that Rorschach records of the members of a primitive community (Alor, in the Dutch East Indies) permit an accurate description of their culture and outlook upon life.

This brings us to the use of the Rorschach as an approach to Stage 3 problems, those concerned with the hierarchical organization of the personality structure as a whole. The Rorschach catches phases of the individual life at many points and can be interpreted in different ways according to the context; a good examiner will make the most of such contexts. Bits that are revealed as life is cross-sectioned may mean different things at different moments, and in such cases the examiner resorts to intuition. He asks himself what the specific detail might reasonably mean, in the light of the picture of the personality as a whole. This is sometimes misunderstood to mean that occasionally a Rorschach interpretation can be made without scoring. This is a misconception. No Rorschach interpretation worthy of the name can be made without scoring; scoring is an integral part of the method, and intuitive or interpretive approaches normally are used after, not before, the scoring. As currently used clinically, the individual Rorschach (rather than the group Rorschach) in its classical form is usually interpreted, after scoring and careful study, in terms of an intuitive conception of the total personality that has such a structure as will make intelligible all the responses and all the interrelations observed between them.

The final question as to the degree to which the Rorschach reveals permanent as contrasted with temporary personality dispositions is not as yet answerable; there are not enough long-range retests. Schachtel, who has studied Rorschach patterns in some children during the period of growth from two to seven years of age, finds considerable continuity along with the growth changes; Piotrowski and others have found continuities which run through the normal and psychotic periods of the same individual. But a systematic study of Rorschach changes throughout the growth period has not yet been made available; few studies have been published dealing consecutively with the same individual. On the other hand, the method indicates clearly the influence of marked disturbance, whether mental or physical. If the brain is affected by poison or a tumor, the effects are shown in the Rorschach; as one goes through the changes of adolescence the Rorschach likewise changes. We should expect that the Rorschach would have to change systematically throughout life as the personality changes.

Drawing and Painting

Although the journals have been full of reports of Rorschach findings, with studies of fantasy by means of the Thematic Apperception and other tests running a close second, there is an odd discrepancy between the large amount of work being done with graphic expression and its representation in these journals. The absence of systematic published reports forces an author to be extremely cautious in describing and evaluating; on the other hand, this very absence entitles the reader to demand some account of what such devices are attempting to do. We shall limit ourselves here to an elementary account of what is being done with free drawing and brush-painting (finger-painting is noted on page 702).

The problem of drawing can best be visualized by considering first the Draw-a-Man Test devised by Goodenough. The original intent was to score such productions in terms of mental age, and the test proved to be serviceable in this respect. Students of projection, however, soon realized that the child's conception of what a man is—his understanding of freedom and power, for example, as exhibited in posture, gesture, and facial expression—can make itself known as soon as the sheer problem of making a recognizable man has been solved. It also became clear that, along with his understanding of what sort of thing a man is, there is some revelation of the kind of men the child admires or fears; it is relatively easy, for instance, to distinguish the admired "superman" type of figure from the dreaded thug types with which every child is already familiar from the comics. From here it is not far to the study of the child's identifications. His own conception of himself with respect to size, build, etc., may be assimilated to that of the man portrayed, and his own attributes may be injected bodily into the representation of a person fundamentally quite different from himself.

If, now, we think of the adolescent and the adult as similarly faced with the task of drawing a man, we find that the only problem is to make the task seem natural—a "grown-up" task. Although this is hard to standardize, still, if a drawing is requested in a context of other tests, with emphasis upon the fact that artistic ability makes no difference, one can usually obtain from an adult at least as much as he can from a child. What follows is a free impressionistic account of some of the things done with adult drawings by specialists in the method.

Although with the Rorschach the interest in content comes last, in the case of free drawings content comes first. Here we are interested in the *kind* of man drawn. If there is time, the male subject is asked to draw first a man and then a woman, and the female subject draws first a woman and then a man. Usually the man or woman that the subject undertakes to draw is normal or acceptable; if, however, he draws a caricature, this also has significance. The figure is nearly always drawn full length; if only a head is drawn, a full-length picture is specifically requested. All the factors mentioned which relate to the utilization of space are in evidence here. We are interested in what the posture displays in terms of confidence and self-reliance, in free or constrained stance, in free or constrained swing of gestures, in the outgoing or cramped approach to the environment, in the general activity of the arms and hands. The age of the person drawn is important in showing the standard established. Typically, the man drawn by the young subject is several years older than he is; the older subject draws a rather idealized young adult figure. Clothing is important in relation to esthetic values, and even more in relation to the social status which it symbolizes. Secondary sex characteristics, such as mustache, the ratio of shoulder width to hip width, etc., are of interest; and, as in the Erikson experiments mentioned earlier (page 487), the body contour portrayed is usually idealized.

But it is not only the content which is important; all the factors of style mentioned in connection with the Allport-Vernon experiments appear here—smoothness or jerkiness, symmetry or a studied avoidance of it, heavy point pressure, and congruence of movements expressive of attitude. We have here, as before, the joint operation of two primary variables: (1) the kinetic qualities related to sheer neuromuscular dispositions, and (2) the unwitting portrayal of freedom or constriction in relation to the environment.

It is true that these factors of content on the one hand and of style on the other, even when abundantly enriched by psychoanalytic studies of symbolism in either or both, leave us far short of a complete personality sketch as such. Even the Rorschach, as noted above, is not really a test of the whole personality, and it must be granted that the free drawing method is much less adequate for the task. Frequently, however, one can obtain from each of the projective methods some vivid insight, so that each method becomes a useful tool in an integrated personality appraisal. If it could actually be demonstrated that some one of these methods used in isolation produces a rather complete personality picture, it would still be necessary to find common factors which connect this brief and limited sample of the total individual life with the vast reaches that lie beyond it. With due recognition of the value of every emphasis upon integration, the

fact remains that methods such as these can "spot" the individual—
can tell which member of a group, for example, has drawn a picture
by seizing upon a few salient characteristics—but fall far short of a
systematic representation of the personality as a whole.

What has been done with free brush-painting does seem to promise
even more than has been accomplished by the drawing method.
Waehner's work seems to include most of what the drawing method
can reveal, a fair fraction of what the Rorschach method has yielded,
and several other things besides. Her data are not yet sharply quantitative, nor have they been confirmed by completely independent
workers, but the consistency of her reported findings warrants close
attention.

Waehner asked fifty-five college girls to paint a subject of their
own choice, and then a series of assigned subjects, including a self-
portrait (without mirror). The size of paper, kind of brush, and the
colors to be used were decided by each individual. Each girl worked
at her own tempo in a large room which contained the easels and
other materials. Being profoundly influenced on the one hand by
psychoanalytic theory, and on the other by Rorschach practice,
Waehner proceeded to emphasize content, form, and style, and to
develop systematic methods for observing some thirty different
attributes of production. The table on page 687 gives a representative idea of the objective factors in the painting that were selected
for checking and scoring through the series of pictures.

From this check list it was possible to gauge the level of intelligence
from such factors as sharp or clear form and evidences of abstract
thinking and of clear observation. Emotional balance is determined in
terms of variety of colors chosen, the use of vivid colors and shading,
the combination of curved and straight lines. Compulsion appears in
rigidity, uniform rhythm, rigid contours, and the tendency to make
organic forms geometrical; passivity, in low color variety, no color,
etc. Aggression is evident in short little strokes, few curved forms,
and many sharp edges; introversion in a high percentage of vivid
details in silhouette, with a preference for linear expression, many
curved forms, and few if any edges. Superior originality is indicated
by unusual formats, and schizoid tendencies by such trends as unusual

formats and perspectives, a high percentage of black, and avoidance of colors. It must be stressed that these are only a few of the many indications representative of each trend; Waehner's aim was to keep the procedure flexible and to weigh the total evidence for each conclusion rather than attempt a rigid and mechanical scoring. The

Factors of Control Small Sizes	Extratensive Factors Large Sizes
Di (distance from margin) emphasis of margin	Ng (neglect of margin)
Small form elements	Large form elements
Emphasis on center and centripetal distribution	Centrifugal distribution
Narrow distribution	Scattered wide distribution
Many curves or curved forms	Sharp edges
Preference for lines	Preference for spots
Colors separated carefully	Smearing
Clear sharp forms	Vague forms
Lack of color, avoidance of colors, low color variety	High color variety
Palc and dark color scale	Glaring color scale
Preference for black	Preference for red and yellow
Form variety greater than color variety	Color variety to form variety greater than 5:4 per picture

reader will recall evidence presented earlier that the method of accumulating considerable material and suspending judgment until the total impression is clear actually makes for higher reliability in many situations than a mere summation of piecemeal items which give a misleading appearance of objectivity.

The method Waehner used in putting all these recorded impressions to work involved going through each picture systematically and scoring it with the aid of the check list reproduced above, developing, as she did so, a preliminary interpretation or "hunch," and then going through the material again to test the adequacy of this hypothesis. She gave emphasis to the total configuration, looked for significant deviations from the general adjustment rating which she had given the whole performance, and noted both chronological sequences through the paintings and evidence of steadiness or vacillation in attitudes. In general, the Rorschach conception of balance between form and color, and also of the integration of form with color, is stressed heavily, human movement being considered particularly in relation to smooth versus staccato execution.

The result of the entire procedure was a character sketch for each of these girls, to be used for matching purposes. Teachers who knew the students well enough for the purpose were used for the matching; each teacher was given from four to six personality sketches prepared by Waehner, and had to indicate which girl fitted each sketch. A total of 116 matching judgments were made, covering 41 of the girls. (Fourteen could not be matched because of illness of teachers and other reasons.) Of these 116 matchings, 103 were correct. Blind Rorschach interpretations of the same girls, made by Munroe at the same time, agreed in 87 per cent of the cases. Waehner's method is, then, sufficiently valid to warrant high hopes for its development. It overlaps enough with the Rorschach and other well-tried methods to permit considerable confidence as to its soundness of approach. It does, however, share with projective methods in general the difficulty of isolating sound from unsound components. Matching is done as a whole; hence it is impossible to determine, so far as features can be isolated, which ones lead to a sound judgment and which are misleading. If it is maintained that the interdependent aspects of the method forbid any analysis of separate components, it is hard to see how it can be further developed. Actually, Waehner's procedure shows quite clearly that her method involves, in studying each painting, all three levels of approach—the global, the differentiated, and the integrated. Insofar as we are dealing with Stage 2—and, by implication, with the various types of integration of Stage 2 material at Stage 3—there is nothing to prevent rapid progress in the detection of good and poor leads, and the development of weighting techniques to make the best use of the leads that prove to be good.

GRAPHOLOGY

While handwriting interpretation is by far the oldest of the projective techniques, it is still difficult to evaluate. It will be recalled that the matching of handwriting samples with personality sketches is possible to a degree surpassing chance, even with complete novices, and that handwriting experts can match handwritings and character sketches far beyond the chance level (page 647). To tell how they do it, however, is not simple. In fact, to judge by the many systems of handwriting analysis now in vogue, and by the very different things the experts say about their methods, it seems likely that there are many techniques, good, bad, and indifferent, overlapping and intersecting.

The beginnings of the modern approach are regarded as having been made by Klages, who demonstrated at the opening of the present century that the simplest motor impulse involves more than a response to a stimulus, that it consists rather of a joint expression of the momentary requirements and the inner personality as a whole. It was Klages who pointed out that no two individuals, even when copying the same model, can carry out the same movements, and that factors of organizing power and of deep-level dynamics enter into the entire world of expression. He and his pupils have amassed enormous quantities of material using dynamic principles, and some of them have tried to make clear in some detail just how they proceed. In general their work inclines to the didactic rather than the clearly empirical. For example, a well-defined character like Mussolini is often presented, and then a handwriting sample is shown, attention being drawn to such and such traits manifest in the formation of the letters, the slope of the lines, the utilization of space, etc. Blind interpretations and validations have seldom been published. Even when blind matchings are successfully made and the matching is objectively validated, it is difficult to determine which of the many indicators are organized in the interpreter's mind.

Much of the theory of expression offered by contemporary graphologists makes sense and is eminently reasonable. The problem of validation, however, usually reduces to this: Suppose there is a correlation between a particular attribute of handwriting on the one hand and particular personality aspects on the other. Are we speaking of a correlation of .90 or of .10? Certainly smearing and messiness, untidiness and confusion, ought to show some relation greater than zero with similar tendencies of everyday life. Certainly a rigid, mechanical script ought to be related to some extent with rigidity and mechanical stereotyping in daily living habits. But is the relation slight, or indirect, or superficial? And if it is deeper, just how deep is it, and how constantly does it permit prediction? We can learn from the texts on graphology how to interpret signs and how to arrive intuitively at a combination of signs, and this is all sound and good as far as it goes; but to what degree must we, in following the directions, make use of all sorts of intuitive procedures that are not "nominated in the bond," and to what extent are we drawn into unwitting emphasis on features that appeal to us as an individual judge, and slight the remainder of the instructions? We know what the intuitive method is, for we see it in personnel work and in the grading of term papers; however, we have no special reason to be proud of it. To be sure, it is better than a chance method, but how much better depends on a hundred circumstances. These points are stressed because of a rather general tendency to confuse a highly sophisticated quantitative and qualitative procedure, such as is used in some projective methods, with a method which still has a long way to go before approaching this status.

With these reservations, a few suggestions will be made regarding some of the clear and useful statements made by graphologists about how they make their successful matchings or interpretations. (1) They often make considerable use of the space factor in the way that has been mentioned several times: The tendency to fill up space is a highly generalized personality trait, and there is a form of expansiveness and contractility in handwriting. (2) Other factors noted by Allport and Vernon under the term "emphasis" are also rather well defined; these make up one aspect of a large dimension which we may call the dimension of rhythm. This comprises a temporal aspect of style, which in turn has many components, including variations in speed and temporal variations in intensity. We may be interested in the variability from maximum to minimum pressure, and in the evenness or unevenness of the temporal distribution of the points of extreme emphasis. (3) Another variable is style, in the large sense, in which the esthetic qualities of the script—symmetry, evenness or unevenness of slope, and so on—are considered as well as the mechanics of its production. Here we should expect transfer from the rhythmic and esthetic approach to life to carry into the area of manual expression in all its forms. It would be very hard for the smooth-flowing, gracious, and well-ordered individual not to carry over some of these factors into his visual space and into the motor space of his manual activity. (4) Another dimension may be characterized by concern for social appearance; here we are concerned less with sheer esthetic properties as such than with the way in which others will look upon the product. Factors of orderliness, or concern with correctness in the sense of etiquette, as contrasted with messiness, sloppiness, and confusion, may reflect both the quantity and the quality of the person's need to impress favorably those who read his script. Thus such formal attributes of his handwriting may tell a good deal about the way in which the individual confronts an approving or a disapproving environment. (5) This leads to the matter of attitude toward the self. This is, of course, closely related to the need for approval; but it can be more directly examined in such factors as the way in which one writes his name or the words "I" or "me," in his tendency to extend or contract these words as compared with other words in the text. This may be significant even when the uniformity of the text from one subject to another permits no comparison with regard to content. It should, however, be noted in this connection that, for the most part, graphologists use free samples which were written earlier when the individual was entirely unaware that any such study would be made; hence the experts are free to make considerable use of the content of the letter or other document. The five points listed are, of course, only a few samples of the dimensions actually used.

These factors, particularly the attitude toward society and toward self, can be analyzed even more finely. By an admirably sustained method of analysis, Saudek has been able to show that some fifteen or twenty different criteria may all be brought to bear on a single trait. For example, with the trait of honesty vs. deceitfulness, he has been able to show that there are many ways of claiming to be what one is not, and many types of evidence of sheer inability to be simple and forthright, and that a combination of four or more of these evidences of indirection and disingenuousness agrees closely with the actual experiences of business establishments as to the honesty or dishonesty of the employee studied. Since Saudek is highly explicit as to how these evidences of deceitfulness are to be recognized and used, it would not be fair to argue that he, like some others, is proceeding without clear knowledge of what he is doing. Yet even here we are left somewhat in a quandary by his reiterated statement that no one criterion means anything by itself. A combination of four or more out of a dozen unfavorable signs warrants reaching a conclusion of dishonesty. How much dishonesty we do not know, but apparently enough to produce a bad record in business. This type of work is decidedly suggestive; we need more of it in published form.

An over-all assessment of graphology as it is practiced today must deal not with the exceptional but with the usual technique. This technique today consists for the most part of applying the formal criteria set by some one school—for example, that of Klages—then working back and forth through the material to get a sharper and sharper picture, more or less as in Waehner's method described above, and finally drawing a personality interpretation which the graphologist hopes will be recognizable and acceptable. It is therefore not possible to determine as clearly as we can with Waehner's procedure, just which criteria were used and how they were used; above all, it is not clear how much the graphologist puts into the interpretation without knowing that he has done so, or what factors govern the whole process.

In the language which has been used in this book, the graphologist is working at all three levels. (1) There are certain global attributes which impress him, to which he may make an undifferentiated response. (2) Depending on the particular system he follows, he spots certain characteristics which recur and which to him mean certain traits. (Many graphologists say that they do not believe in any one-to-one correspondence between particular handwriting attributes and particular traits, but in reality most of the systems rely on such correspondences.) (3) Having this specific material regarding defined attributes in the scripts, he then proceeds to what we would call a third-level, or integrative, approach, and specifies what type of person this must be to possess this characteristic integration. And this, of course, is exactly what he must do if an effective result is to be obtained. The trouble is the lack of validation of the second-level technique, since without such validation no amount of ingenuity can lead to sound integrations. Let it be said again that graphological matchings reported by Powers (page 646) were good when done by experts; furthermore in conjunction with Waehner's studies, Lewinson, using the same subjects, was able in most instances to match character sketches effectively with those resulting from the painting and Rorschach procedures.

But while the Rorschach procedure is rather clear at all three levels, notably at the second where objective methods are used, and Waehner's free-painting method is aimed at the achievement of such objectivity, handwriting analysis at present awaits the fuller specification of method, for it now works for the most part without the full benefit of the objective criteria generally regarded as necessary for the soundest research and clinical practice. It would be so easy to develop, from Lewinson's and Zubin's suggestions for an objective method (working objectively and quantitatively with the problem of rhythm), a procedure as well defined as the Rorschach. Oddly enough, apparently no one is actively prosecuting this task.

The validity of handwriting evaluations through matching is apparently not as high as that given by the Rorschach. But the level of validity is not the important question at the moment. If sound methods are mixed with unsound ones, the relative weight of the two is of small significance compared with an intensive study of how sound judgments are made and the ways in which they can be extended. Hence there is no very profitable inclusive question as to "how good" a typical handwriting diagnosis is. This will depend on the opportunity offered for sound methods; it will depend on the particular expert who is analyzing the particular handwriting; it will depend on the particular qualities that are to be emphasized and followed up; it will even depend to some extent upon the frame of reference—clinical or purely scientific—within which the work is done. What is needed today is clarification of the specific tasks done by the expert, the discovery of his areas of greatest success and greatest failure; and above all, determination of the direction in which research can most profitably proceed. Especially important is the discovery of the extent to which the successful graphologist does each of four things: (1) specifies second-level details such as point pressure, length of the t-bar, etc.; (2) makes an explicit study of structure as such; (3) applies the Gestalt concept of membership character, and looks for the meaning of each attribute in terms of the whole; (4) tends to proceed globally by sheer "hunch" or intuition, being unable to tell to what degree he uses each detail, or membership character. Perhaps we shall find that those who use the second and third methods are the best architects and put up the best building.

COMPARISON AND INTEGRATION OF PROJECTIVE METHODS

Though we cannot do justice to any of these modern methods of approaching personality as a whole, an example from the work of a recent conference will demonstrate the simultaneous approach through (1) clinical history, (2) the Rorschach, (3) free drawing, and (4) handwriting analysis. Each procedure was followed through to its conclusion without consultation with the investigators working with the other methods. An integrative interpretation was reached later; however, it is the independent work prior to consultation that is stressed here. (In the Rorschach, the same individual administered and interpreted the test, but she was limited to what she could observe at the time of testing; in the handwriting analysis, the graphologist never saw the person and had no information except age and sex; in the drawing procedure, the examiner knew nothing, not even the subject's age or sex.)

The clinical history showed a man of 45, a radio announcer, who throughout his life had been dominated by the father image. (a) *Rather withdrawn*, (b) he had *tried to make contact with the world*, and (c) had *gloried in the vast audiences to which he spoke*; actually, he had no warm friendships. A period of alcoholism had been followed by three or four years of sobriety, then several months of acute alcoholism. He is fundamentally (d) *unable to accept himself*. Important in the picture is (e) *weak sex interest*; clinically he is hormone-defective.

The above five traits are indicated in the following records by the same letters:

According to the Rorschach findings, he has "forced intellectual ambitions"; is (a) *egocentric and suspicious* with a (d) *rigid picture of himself*; has no knowledge of his own emotions; resorts to conventional adaptive tricks.

The handwriting sample is reported to (e) *"lack the masculine component"*; he is (a) *incapable of the feeling of partnership*; he (c) *uses people to cover his own inner emptiness*; he seeks a sham security. He has no anchorages. He is unaware of his conflict. This is not a neurosis, but a hysteroid personality. The illusionistic, swollen script is simple and matter of fact in form; there is "much-to-do," but his "soul is not in it."

His drawings of a man and woman show inferiority, compensations, superficiality, (d) *self-protectiveness*, (e) *psychosexual immaturity*. He has a strong nostalgia for the narcissistic peak of his early adulthood; he makes an effort to put up a front of competence, and alcohol aids this effort.

It would be pointless here to attempt a "box score" of the agreement among these interpretations. What was done in the comparison mentioned above was to pool available impressions and work out a more complete, though still tentative, clinical picture. The research problem is not *merely* the familiar one of determining exactly how good each method can be, but of finding how it can help, when integrated with other methods, in a full-bodied clinical evaluation of personality. Illustrative of what can be done here is the study of the personalities of young adults by the simultaneous use of the Rorschach, handwriting, and brush-painting methods; the following is an example. This particular woman student is first described by her teachers. (In the following, *Ror* refers to Rorschach findings, *Art* to findings from the painting technique, and *Gra* to the graphological findings.)

Academic Work and Intellectual Characteristics. This case was a very talented art student. Her teacher felt that she was "deficient in her observation of nature" and sometimes tended toward a "well-behaved 'modern' solution in form and a purely esthetic arrangement of color," but he never questioned the brilliance of her achievement or the industry and feeling with which she worked. Her other courses were less satisfactory. In one rather factual course she confined herself to facts, and, while she was passed without question, the teacher complained of her failure to see the implications of her reading. Her approach was too "literal, her imagination too severely controlled." The girl herself was bored by the course and did not continue this type of study another year. In the courses of her election, however, affording scope for her philosophical and literary concerns, she was not successful; indeed, she came close to downright failure. Once or twice she reproduced the sense of her reading of a book rather well by writing a poem about it, but in prose or discussion she expressed herself in such vague generalities that it was difficult to tell what she had learned or was thinking—if anything. A teacher describes one paper as follows: "She made one large statement after another (some of which were very good), and each one might have been the beginning of a paper. Her series of ideas remained disconnected and left no general impression." Her teachers all agreed that she did not come to grips with her materials, that she remained detached, smug, and pretentious, or injected too much of her own feeling into what she reported of authors read. She was never able to support her opinions with evidence or even make quite clear what her opinion was. A teacher writes: "The ideas which move her strongly live a wraithlike existence in her mind. She does not have the courage to limit her judgments and make them more concrete." She left college early in her third year because she was needed at home.

Personality and Background.   As a person, teachers found her scrupulously polite and superficially friendly, but never spontaneous and outgoing. Some felt that she was overcomplacent, vain, too well satisfied with herself, and that she needed a direct challenge. Others felt that her pretentiousness and aloof poise were a thin disguise for insecurity. Actually she reacted to direct criticism of her smugness and detachment and to the possibility of failure with very great emotional distress. She dropped her contact with the teachers who had ventured a direct challenge as soon as the college allowed her to do so.

She was not spontaneous with her contemporaries either. Her manner of dress was stylish rather than collegiate, and she led a somewhat showy social life away from the college. She was not liked at first but, as time went on, came to be accepted and even respected—apparently largely for her artistic ability and the same almost out-of-character efficiency she had shown in her one "practical" course. After this she took somewhat more interest in college affairs.

Information about her childhood and home background is meager. She never spoke of her childhood, and it is hard to imagine her as a child. Some years ago she had one or two frank phobias, now overcome. Her family is one of great wealth and prominence, but has a reputation for being "erratic." A brother suffers from a severe constitutional neurological disorder which the family·handles by a policy of concealment. Apparently the humble beginnings of the father are also shrouded in darkness so far as possible. On several occasions the girl was called home because of the condition of the brother, but at no point did she confide to anyone the nature of his illness. Comments from people who know the family indicate important emotional strain, which the very absence of comment from the girl confirms.

The psychologist may feel some confidence in assuming that the extreme detachment and rigid "front" of this girl, her inability to handle ideas of moment to her except in the most abstract verbal disguise and in art, her vanity and smugness, are a protection against an inner disturbance. Most of her teachers accepted this interpretation. Several teachers held, however, that she had been spoiled by too much wealth, too much praise for her talent, too artificial a home atmosphere, and that the problem was really one of excessive complacency rather than insecurity.

Test Results: *Academic Work and Intellectual Characteristics.* All three tests emphasize the girl's artistic gift, although in the *Ror* and *Gra* no external clues were available. The *Ror* even suggests correctly the form of her gift: "She should show talent for abstract art, is likely to prefer this manner to representation. In writing would do better in poetry or some other mode of direct conveyance of mood and idea than in a human-interest story with plot and characterization or in careful exposition."

Ror and *Gra* see the dynamic significance of her art in similar terms. *Ror*: "This creative expression is of paramount importance . . . in giving her security and a way of handling her emotional disquietude . . . It is not likely, however, to foster her adjustment in human and social terms." *Gra*: "Artistic activity is an advantage and a pitfall . . . . It is an outlet for creative capacities . . . and an excuse to neglect the development of other aspects of her personality . . . . It has prevented direct emotional contact with people." *Art* is not so explicit on this point, but the following statement probably points in the same direction: "Creative in a rather introversive way . . . complicated inner life and not interested in outer world."

All three tests consider her intelligent and all mention a leaning toward theoretical thinking. *Ror* and *Gra* comment upon an emphasis on "essential" meanings to the neglect of detail, a somewhat superficial mental functioning, and a predilection for overpersonal, overemotional vague concepts. *Ror* mentions "something like a positive determination not to look too closely at concrete detail" and suggests that the philosophizing trend, like her art, represents both an "expression of her inner problems and an effort to give them an integration she is unable to achieve in actual living." *Gra* remarks that "she is too much absorbed by her own viewpoints and those she has identified herself with to establish contact with divergent ideas. . . . She does not go to the depth of a problem or she confuses it by injecting some of her vague personal conceptions . . . might gloss over skillfully the omission of details which are necessary." Yet both *Ror* and *Gra* observe that she *can* think clearly and is well able to use detail and factual evidence when she will. Thus both of these tests describe rather well the type of mind she showed in her college work, though both tests were too optimistic about her ability to meet academic requirements. The *Ror* comments that "since she seems to know *when* she deviates from common observation and logic, it is to be hoped that she will learn how to integrate these pedestrian matters better with her more personalized concepts."

On this point *Art* was even more in error. Mentioning theoretical thinking, *Art* adds that "her energy takes the form of initiative and endurance in mental activities. Procedure of working rather planful, not superficial, but elaborating a good deal without becoming minutious. I would expect a good academic success." (It seems possible that a test technique based on performance in the field of the girl's greatest gift and achievement might well overestimate her planfulness and initiative. These qualities are well and successfully practiced in her art work. The deeper emotional trends are correctly seen by *Art* in spite of her special training.) Both *Gra* and *Art* mention manual dexterity, an item definitely confirmed by the case history.

Personality. All tests draw a picture of attempted rational control, restraint, sophisticated and conventional manners covering up clearly evident emotional problems. The underlying emotional problems are somewhat differently stated, at least in emphasis, and the picture drawn by the *Ror* is the most alarming of the three. *Gra* mentions emotional immaturity and self-importance without self-confidence; *Art*, aggression and vanity; *Ror* speaks of grandiose ambition and lack of inner maturity, but stresses chiefly anxiety and an explosive, moody, chaotic character structure beneath the veneer of rational poise. *Ror* does not sufficiently *emphasize* the veneer which was the chief characteristic observable in·her behavior.

Gra and *Art* both explicitly describe her as narcissistic, "apart," affected, and vain. While the *Ror* analysis does not use these words or even a paraphrase of them, the description is implicit in the character structure suggested. *Gra* specifically mentions attention to her external appearance and good taste in dress. Whether her striking costumes could be considered good taste on the campus is somewhat doubtful, but they were tasteful enough in themselves and certainly received her attention. *Gra* also says that "she is erratic rather than spontaneous and impresses people who are fascinated by her vacillating and apparently interesting form." Perhaps her eccentricity of dress should be seen under this heading.

All three tests emphasize her aloofness from warm contacts with people. *Gra*: "fastidious in emotional contacts . . . keeps people at a distance." *Art*: "Good relations with a few congenial people . . . resistance to relations with others." *Ror*: "Relations with people are thin, likely to be based more on community of interest than on personal warmth."

The emphasis on introversiveness and a complicated inner life in *Art* is perhaps paralleled by the self-awareness and thoughtful effort to handle her problems in larger terms described by the *Ror*. She is certainly self-centered and narcissistic according to all tests. An impressive feature of her Rorschach protocol, however, was a total lack of M, the chief indicator of a rich inner life. Hence the *Ror* statement of a lack of inner maturity. It is interesting that *Gra* describes her as a "visual type" and speaks of a "lack of actual substance."

Dynamics. The three tests seem in general to offer much the same view of the emotional dynamics of this personality—an inner disturbance of a narcissistic nature handled by artistic expression and unspontaneous rational control. Observation of the girl in college seems to justify this view. Although she presented no very severe emotional problems at the college, the very striking detachment of her manner and her persistent inability to come to grips with her academic materials at a level commensurate with her intelligence seems to warrant the rather serious estimate of her difficulties made by the *Ror*. The possibility of actual breakdown mentioned by the *Ror* was not fulfilled (and was indeed stated only as a possibility), but the degree of maladjustment was probably somewhat greater than that implied in the other tests. On the other hand, *Gra* cited more clearly the danger of a "stereotypization of her performances," seen in her elaborate artificial social life and even in the fear of her art teacher at times that she might fall into "mere decoration, aping the modern vein." *Art* offered a telling analysis of the conditions under which she might become "very disturbed," i.e., "if an accumulation of aggression coincides with an experience injuring her vanity." Something like this happened in the courses where she was directly criticized. The girl remarked to her adviser at this time that she "felt there was something wrong . . . that she felt helpless and up against a mountain she couldn't get around"—and showed so much distress generally that her request to change courses was ultimately granted. It is interesting to observe that she handled without upset another more severe emotional situation which did *not* involve her vanity—the critical illness of her brother.

On the whole, then, the three tests showed good agreement with each other and with clinical observation in this case, and few discrepancies. Each test brought up some items which were at least understated by the others. The three together give an orientation and confidence to the clinical judgment which could hardly be achieved otherwise with the limited facilities for observation and interview available in the academic situation.

It seems clear enough that each of these methods has "much to learn" from the others. There are also many other valuable projective methods (cf. pages 347 and 368) to which we can do no justice here; our aim is to suggest possibilities, not to catalogue finalities.

29. Projective Methods with Children

OUR study of projective methods with adults emphasized personality structure, its appraisal and measurement. But what of the child, who manifestly is at first much less complexly organized; who indeed *achieves* a stable and recognizable personality structure as we watch him growing and learning? Can personality structure be meaningfully studied in the earliest years? Yes, for even the newborn have their own kind of structure; maturation has yielded some specific action patterns, and differentiated responses rapidly become interrelated. As social interaction goes on hand in hand with growth, structural properties appear and demand more and more attention. Indeed, if we are to make full use of the genetic approach to adult personality structure, we must be ready with methods for studying personality structure of every sort that is recognizable in the little child.

Most of the projective approaches to personality structure in childhood have taken a somewhat different direction from those used with adults, first, because we ordinarily wish to see children in a relatively unconstrained rather than in a formal test situation, and second, because children are in fact less "structured" than adults. In practice it is easy and natural to do what is rather hard to do with the adult, namely, to study all three developmental levels at once and to be able to see rather clearly how they interact.

It is at this point that the fantasy and thought of little children are of special value in understanding the development of structure, particularly in those instances in which the cultural milieu of the child has been well explored. Studies of thought and fantasy in nursery-school children indicate some of the ways in which need patterns may weave completely different imaginative sequences from the same materials. If we have a long enough time-sample for the individual, we may find verification of William Stern's "personalistic" principle, that what one perceives, if fully known, becomes the expression of oneself. Valuable here are the many techniques which present a possibility of projecting one's own outlook upon standard objective material (page 669). We shall chiefly consider the projections of small children and secondarily raise some questions as to the significance of the projective methods for the study of older children. In what follows, therefore, the subject is a child between two and five years of age.

There are many suitable "unstructured" materials: clay, paste, dough, mud, cold cream, finger paints. When there is sufficient motor dexterity for the child to control the material, crayons, brush paints, pens, and pencils may be used; the form created with these "semi-structured" materials is not greatly limited by any predetermination of space or time relations. Blocks, mosaic pieces, and beads set some limits, but still leave great scope for individual interpretative activity; incomplete pictures can be filled out in various ways. The Skinner phonograph record (page 347) presents a flowing sequence of ambiguous sounds in which the subject can "hear words." Even simple cloud pictures or ink blots can be seen in a variety of ways. Under "well-structured" materials must be included stories which the child is told and which he retells in his own way, and dolls, toys, and small replicas of objects encountered daily, especially the many sets of "miniature life toys"—dolls, toy animals, doll houses with furniture, etc.—that are used with nursery-school children. The child is given no instruction except to do what he likes with them. He proceeds to mirror in his own way his conception of family, home, neighborhood, and world. Much of his behavior is a portrayal of actual reality, and much of it involves perfectly self-conscious make-believe; but much of it lies between these two extremes, and makes clear his own egocentric and autistic point of view. He sees his father and mother, his teacher, his dog, himself, in terms of wishes and fears which are either directly verbalized or indirectly portrayed in his accompanying or subsequent conduct. Even these structured materials may be used by the child as if they were unstructured, the chair being treated as a horse, a cannon, or a building stone. But in general the individual objects direct the flow of perception, association, and manipulation; and any free fantasy which might tend to arise from a single ambiguous object is likely to be overwhelmed to some degree by the atmosphere of reality of the entire set of materials.

With any of the projective methods we may look for five kinds of personality attributes: kinetics, style, values, creativeness, and mental content. By "kinetics" we mean speed, strength, motor perseveration, general muscle tonus, and every property of action that is observable and at least potentially measurable on a linear scale representing a physical dimension of activity. By "style" we mean the more complex interrelation of movements, those not measurable on a linear scale; the pattern of oscillation between work and relaxation, the tendency to one emphasis or another, to grace or to awkwardness—in other words, all the time-space patterns which the movements describe. "Values" are directly revealed in the delight shown at contact with specific materials or in specific types of activities in which they are used. By "creativeness" is meant the richness, complexity, and originality of the resulting product.

In revealing "mental content" the projective methods may achieve several distinct things. They may directly reveal preoccupation, as when a lonely child turns the soldiers and nurses into his friends, or a dirt-fearing child's play with housekeeping toys is monotonously concerned with cleaning and dusting, with such verbalization as "it's dirty; I can't get it clean." They may provide outlets for pent-up affective trends, as when the toys are regularly smashed by a child whose trends toward aggression are ordinarily blocked. They may reveal perceptual or thought structures, as when a well-dressed Negro doll can be seen and thought of *only* as a menial servant, or when the child's own parents appear in his play only as *tools* with which to gain candy or circuses. The content may be not only directly but indirectly revealing of the child's wants. He may turn the pillow of the toy bed into a dog and play with this dog for a half-hour; he may give the pet all the privileges (e.g., of making noise) which he himself has been denied. A much deeper level of interpretation may be invoked. A small boy whom Erikson studied was constantly admonished not to be too active and excitable when with Grandmother, because she suffered from heart disease and could not stand it. She actually did die partly because of an altercation with him. The boy's play construction thereafter appeared to refer to the return of the dead and their power to work revengefully on the living. The "house" which he had built from blocks had had an odd gap in the corner; this gap not only was filled up but was given a double and then a triple closure, his comments suggesting fear of the grandmother's return.

Such studies as these reveal the personality of the child in the form and content of his imagination; the fantasy arises from a complex tension pattern, and as it emerges it is brought into ever closer relation to his satisfactions and frustrations. To a limited degree the projective methods are also suitable for group studies of the thought process in relation to age, mental age, general tempo, and habitual activity patterns, but this is secondary. The fundamental aim of most projective methods is to study fantasy patterns as related to need patterns; but if our concept of needs has been soundly developed, we may penetrate the fundamental properties of individual organization.

The integration of contributions from various projective methods with the month-by-month observations of a child's development will be illustrated by the following personality study, which began when the boy was two years old and ended when he was seven:

In the spring of 1938, at the age of 2¾ to 3 years, according to the notes by his teacher, Colin was active, concentrated, definite, focused, purposeful in motor behavior. He entered spontaneously into group play, also played happily alone. He showed unusual courtesy, was protective toward a younger girl, and helped others in routines. He was creative, enthusiastic, and enjoyed different kinds of play; he alternated play with sand and energetic play on the ladder and the swing. Indoors he built elaborate, thoughtfully planned buildings. He sang well and spontaneously. With adults he was trusting, frank, mature; he expected warmth, direction, sometimes reassurance, and some help.

In a group of experiments involving free play with toys during this same period, he appeared to be secure, loving, relying on his mother's devotion and protection: "Mommy will come and get me." Mommy tells him he is "a nice boy." In the balloon experiment by L. J. Stone there is enormous fun and enjoyment, intense and varied, gay and active, covering much ground. There were also tentative evidences of anxiety about spanking in his response to pictures; Patsy, his older sister, was bad, but Colin was not bad. There were also many evidences of great aggression, capacity for resistance, and strong ego feelings. In the dough experiment he grabbed, squeezed, pounded, and remarked, "I pull Mommy's hair at home." He dug a hole and chopped down a tower, in contrast to other children who made a pie or cake. In Lerner's exploratory sessions, Colin's car went "all over the mountain"—a highly individual image for a child of this age. "I shoot you, shoot duck, shoot door, shoot truck, shoot telephone" introduced another idiosyncratic pattern of elaborating a central theme with many variations. In this situation and in the medical examination, he resisted suggestions from the adult, stuck to his own idea, shut out the adult at times. Other images related to ego patterns appeared in the balloon experiment when he tossed the balloons as high as possible, up to the sky; L. J. Stone commented that the prevailing valence was up and up. In Lerner's experiments, later called Ego-Blocking tests, Colin at will could give way to, disregard, resist, or command the experimenter. Following frustration he became impatient and aggressive.

In the spring of 1939 as Colin reached the age of 4 the aggression noted in the fall continued with crescendo; it was not only directed toward children, but he resisted authority in "must" situations such as going to school, leaving school, taking off clothes, putting away toys; he was "definitely obstructive" to school routines and activities. At the same time, his imaginative and dramatic play increased with comparable crescendo. He was an old, old man on a hill, a grandfather, a grocery man, a chimney man, a lumber man, a repair truck man, a postman, an engineer, a "watcher" in a play of Indians sleeping around a campfire. He painted "my blue moon," "my green sky," commented on the "rusty snow," drew "the first day of spring."

Among the projective experiments, he came of his own accord to four sessions of free play with Miniature Life Toys, in which the following themes were predominant: home, toilet, fixing the girl-doll's "tinkler," Santa; a "big black cat" was a focus of fear and he "killed" it. Cars, a doctor-daddy role, gas station, fixing a car, caring for a sick baby and comments on night with the baby crying, the owl hooting, the rain coming down, and bedtime as aspects of night, were also in the first session. "I want," "Bop-bop-bop" aggression, reciprocity and giving (toys for you), destruction (I'll break this), anxiety, protection (in the house), defensive hostility and justified aggression, curiosity, guilt, power over the adult, were themes of child-experimenter relationships. In the next session, an aggressive dog, a nurturing mother, night and dark, mother with babies, garage play with a gas man and fixing the front bumper, the back bumper, and putting on chains, shopping with a book for the gas man to write in, getting shoes for his little girl, visiting the baggage man's house, fixing the broken car where the oil drips out, were the chief themes. In the next session many of these were repeated, but with more concern about fixing broken things, and an extended identification with an authoritative doctor (she'd go to bed for me! stop them crying— spank them!), a father who cuddles, mother who reads stories, gives breakfast, and puts children to bed, but who doesn't like her old baby any more cause she got a new baby; and a baby that got out of bed, beat people up, didn't want to come home, didn't want hair washed, or breakfast, didn't like mother or daddy or nobody. At the end of the session Colin said in answer to a question from the experimenter that he likes father best now.

Throughout these sessions there is much spontaneous laughter, squeals of delight, singing, growling, original verbalizing, and a coy responsive attitude toward the experimenter. Play sequences revealed an inner rhythm of ideas in which emotionally toned themes such as toileting and the girl's lack of a "tinkler," ideas of aggression, the anxiety-provoking "old black cat," and the doctor-daddy alternate with relatively unemotional ideas. Also there is a tendency toward repetition of phrases or ideas with variations and nuances, giving an effect of both a certain stereotypy and a certain fluid quality in his talk. In the Sensory Toys experiment he showed the most comprehensive capacity to enjoy every type of stimulation, tactual, visual, auditory, with free spontaneous abandon and sensory pleasure.

In Lerner's Ego-Blocking experiments of this period, there is again very definite aggressive assertiveness, vehement object aggression (hitting the couch and the table), gay, bold, determined forcing of the experimenter to give him what he wants, increasing resistance after deprivations; he assumed the superior daddy role against Lerner's inferior big-brother role (daddy goes to work and makes people well). He switched to a sandman role and made Lerner "the little boy." He did not drink in the "artificial emotional feeding." Lerner suggested that he might feel crowded in respect to self-assertion at home, but had plenty of love.

In October, as he approached the age of 4½, however, he was again extremely aggressive. Along with this were evidences of marked anxiety; he sobbed at his mother's departure, was afraid of the Fireman Music in the music period, bit his nails, and showed considerable concern with death. His play continued to be varied and imaginative; he built a Grand Central Station, Park Avenue, a train to New York, a lumber freight yard in the west, in

Wyoming, Jack Frost's house, the Meadow Brook Dairy Company. He assumed the roles of captain, a moving-van man, and "Mr. Bob Important." Doctors, ambulances, hospitals, dead birds, birds of prey, and "the old black cat" also figured in nursery-school play, thus bringing into the school group fears previously clarified in the projective sessions. He also told an excellent story of "The George Family," full of family security and togetherness.

In Miniature Life Toys during this period, he was more conciliatory toward the adult: "You tell me what I'd better get," "I think you'd better get," were characteristic phrases instead of "I want" or the previous threats. He was still busy with themes of fixing, the doctor role, "the old black cat" prowling in the night, and other creatures of prey such as owls, hawks and eagles. Against these threatening creatures he had his defense: "I could even KILL a hawk . . . yes and carry it home and have it for luncheon . . . I'd have a gun, a really fire gun." Following this expression of defensive aggression he was occupied with a constructive activity of making a car out of materials in the toy box.

In Ego-Blocking experiments in this period Lerner commented that Colin was even more clear-cut, concise, and poised, but that along with this went a new slight indirection that "apparently is the price of socialization even for" Colin. Greater self-awareness takes the place of the previous direct egocentric self-assertion and he seemed to be aware of the fact that a graceful compromise makes for a more socialized being.

In the spring of 1940, as Colin approached 5 years, a focused ambition came into expression in the form of *making big things*; a grandfather's clock, a giant book, a palm tree, a *big* trylon and perisphere. He became an inventor and claimed, "I know how to do things; I'm growing a terribly long beard." By May this became a God-fantasy: "I'm making a big snake . . . snake says I'm being made by God on his operating table. . . . I'm God. I'm making big snakes. . . . I make the world!" This new culmination of his feeling about bigness which has been variously reflected in projective sessions from the age of 2, was accompanied by a new happiness in school. His teacher reported that he was in high spirits, his old jouncy gait returned, he made delightful overtures to adults and children, worked with zest. He painted organized pictures; a picture with the sun in the day and the moon in the night separated by a yellow line; another picture of the day and night and the dawn in between. When asked why he was so cheerful he said, "Oh, because I make such good buildings and things." He was now critical of other bad boys who were aggressive, and became less able to handle aggression toward him of other children. He reported a dream that there was a little boy and he was swallowed by a whale and a walrus at the same time; he drew a picture of a sea monster he saw in a dream. Affection toward animals, growing things, little children, tender pattings and lovings were part of him this spring.

In the Cold Cream experiment he presents an image that condenses this new development of repression of aggression along with his great ambition and an element of passivity. He paints a "covered Bee with 1000 eyes, looking at 1000 people." In the experiment he joyfully took out the whole contents of the jar and plastered himself. "I'm turning myself into a new style," and he covered his face, hair, and arms to make himself a white clown. In the Miniature Life Toys he was presented with some "wild animals" which he promptly classified into a "wild" group and an "unwild" group, then made a 17-mile-long parade, a circus train; made the snake bite himself. Then the snake bit the experimenter, ate up every animal, whipped the lion, crawled up the mountain. But Colin remarked "He didn't hurt you—he isn't poisonous," by way of reconciliation.

In kindergarten the following year his teacher commented on his wealth of ideas; his individualism (you need a Colin-period of music); his aggression to other children which put them in awe of him although some of them were able to prevent him from taking what he wanted and going on his way; his enjoyment of one of the youngest; his insatiable curiosity to find out how things are made coupled with his destructiveness of objects; his great interest in science, his love of music and all aesthetic experiences. In a follow-up Miniature Life Toys session, he used the snake aggressively, was concerned about the alligator's broken tail, expressed enormous satisfaction in his new achievement of riding a "big bike," played out a conflict between the train and the fire-truck which suggested a projection of conflict between social convention (train) and his aggression (fire engine). The fire engine transcended normal limits by going off the runway into the air like an airplane going up. In the end the "track is busted" so the train itself goes off. With the soldier box he played with the cannon in a typical conventionalized aggressive fashion. He was less interested in the toys than formerly and they seemed to meet no need to express his fantasy as had been true earlier. While his teacher in kindergarten thought of him as active, he seemed to LBM to lack the vivid enthusiasm and responsiveness of his preschool years, to be subdued in his general attitude.

In first grade he made rapid progress in reading, continued to love music, was respected by the children, able to put across his own ideas; but he was self-absorbed for long periods and often uncooperative with school procedures, according to his new teacher. If he was not interested, he refused to do what was expected. His old fantasy themes continued, but expressed now for the group in a story containing a hawk, another story about tribes of Indians who shot thousands of deer. He painted a very objective picture of a bombing episode and another picture of creatures beneath the ground.

In second grade he has become more socialized, is not aggressive in the schoolroom and generally accepts the routines of life although he continues to choose his own time to cooperate, sometimes not working up to capacity if he is not interested. When he is interested and the task is his own, his work is mature and integrated. In his last story a sly fox caught an owl, kept it in prison, gave it a mouse for dessert on Sunday when the owl had been good—the first time the concept of "being good" appears in the records of Colin's thoughts.

The projective methods that utilize structured materials, such as miniature life toys, tempt us to make use of various ways of classifying children into types. But at least for the present such typing is dangerous. Suppose, for example, that we are interested in the distinction between children who mimic the world about them and those who run away from it. The distinction is often clear and consistent; but the need to mimic life situations, whether agreeable or disagreeable ones, is usually an expression of other needs, particularly the need to do something sensible and acceptable, the need to see something which one can recognize as familiar, the need to make things come out in an orderly, non-disturbing fashion, the need to cover up a distressing memory, etc. On the other hand, the need to get away from one's daily cycle of activities may reduce to the need for exploration and novelty, the need to attract adult attention through the production of the unusual, the need to picture to oneself the probable consequences of a new course of action, and so on. Thus the dichotomy does not represent a basic cleavage in terms of two fundamental personality types. Beneath all the overtly similar behaviors, there are complex and varying individual need patterns.

Similarly, we may be interested in the differences that appear between two groups of children; for example, some children using such materials act as they do in free play (being equally aggressive, for instance, in both), whereas other children make up for lost time, showing in the projective techniques the tendencies that have been most completely concealed in free play. This attempt at classification leads to a study of the actual atmosphere of the test situation, the degree to which the examiner sets free tendencies which the parent or teacher cannot liberate, the special influence on the child of being told to do as he likes, the fact that the material is small and can be easily managed, the fact that he is not reproved for doing what in life would incur adult sanctions. The test situation has a meaning for each child in terms of a complex of similarities and differences between the play materials and the materials of daily living.

From such a point of view it means little, therefore, to say that a projective technique is "validated" against "real behavior." All behavior is real behavior, in the sense that it has meaning for the child and for our understanding of him. His behavior with the toys may spring from the same motivations that arise in free play, or from very different motivations; correlations may well range from 1.00 to − 1.00. As we said earlier, the projective methods may bring out, quickly and easily, various need and fantasy patterns which often take much longer to be observed (and which indeed may never be observed) in "life situations," however wise and sensitive the observer may be. The test behavior is specific to the situation in the same sense that all behavior is specific to the situation; there is always some transfer from situation to situation, but the transfer is never one hundred per cent. Projective methods never seek simply to duplicate what other observational procedures provide. In the same way, undiscovered methods of personality diagnosis may well open other avenues to the needs and fantasy equipment of the child.

Colin's complete record contained repeated instances in which projective sessions nicely anticipated behavior which emerged only later in group relationships. For instance, his earliest group behavior was predominantly friendly and affectionate; projective methods revealed the presence of strong aggressive needs, which were subsequently expressed in violence in the group. Later, while he was still very direct and difficult in the group, projective methods showed an emerging indirection, tact, and social awareness that were later apparent in his group behavior. On the whole, the relation between behavior in projective situations and in group play is quite close in Colin's case, but other illustrations could be given in which a child with little or no contact with children or materials in the group situation reveals in detail the fears, hostility, and frustrations which underlie his social inhibition.

The projective methods, by placing the individual in a play situation, elicit expressions which are often directly confirmatory of hypotheses that have been raised but cannot be securely substantiated by other clinical or experimental procedures. Moreover, these methods give rise to hypotheses which can be tested by other observational methods. This occurs constantly, for the procedure allows time for individual observations and consequently may reveal trends and capacities which no casual observation, and no experiment planned in detail for the needs of a large group, would be likely to detect; a wish, a terror, a prestige need may force itself into fullblown expression. By confronting the subject with a relatively new situation, with planned material and a planned method of observing and recording, the investigator may elicit new trends which no spontaneous situation has elicited previously, and therefore directly generate hypotheses as to personality which other experiments and observations may in time be able to validate. In practice, these two values of projective methods are overschematic. These methods are devices for developing rapport, especially with small children, for the stimulation of fantasy and creativeness in a planned situation which permits individual comparisons, and for the systematic study of transfer to and from experimental responses and life responses. There is also a huge place for projective methods in therapy—as in David Levy's classical studies of children's use of dolls in the *release* of pent-up aggression. But the present volume can unfortunately do no justice to the problem of therapy.

No one projective method can possibly reveal the whole personality; the various methods supplement one another. The accompanying table suggests roughly the possible interrelations between several of these methods as seen by the writer, primarily the ways in which perceptual and motor tests are related. It of course embodies only one person's impressions of the present usefulness of methods which in reality lead to different results with different workers and which, because of the rapid developments in the field, are constantly changing.

"+" means *usefulness*; ++, exceptional usefulness.

	Storytelling	Miniature Life Toys	Rorschach	Thematic Apperception Test	Drawing	Finger-Painting	Brush-Painting	Handwriting
Kinetics		++			++	++	++	+
Style	+	++	+	+	++	++	++	++
Values	+	++	+	++	+	+	+	+
Creativeness	+	++	++	++	+	+	++	
Mental content	+	++	+	++	+	+	++	
Perceptual dynamics	+	+	++	+	+		+	
Psychoanalytic mechanisms	+	+	+	++	+	+	+	+

Lest the reader secure the impression that the "projective methods" are a fixed set of standard procedures, we emphasize the fact that a large part of what the child does in his play, his dreams, his school work, or his contacts with his family has great projective value and if studied systematically can lead to a projective procedure. For example, one of the oldest projective problems is the study of those perennial fantasies, imaginary companions. In our culture, at least one normal child in five apparently lives for some months with these self-realizing companions, human, animal, or of a mythical genus. Frequently the companion is like the child himself, receives all of his own projections (the child attributes his own traits to the companion; cf. page 546), and in turn provides material for introjections (the child attributes the companion's traits to himself; cf. page 547). Frequently the projection leads to the scapegoat device, the companion being naughty and getting the blame for all the child's misdeeds. Similarly, the companion may carry out numerous bold adventures of the "superman" variety, which permit the child to expand his area of expression, power, and prestige. We should judge, then, that there could be no better index to the personality in childhood than a study of the character and activities of the imaginary companions upon whom children are able to make an articulate report or about whom other projective methods can tell us when the child is reluctant to talk about them.

Projective methods with children thus represent all the phases from the exploratory to the formal test situation, depending on their purpose. And they are in all stages of development; indeed, the researcher who uses them passes, as does the child, through the three levels of general impression, differentiation, and articulate formulation of his quest for structure.

30. Continuity

EVERY study of personality evokes assumptions about continuity: short-range continuity, as in predicting, from yesterday's performance, how father will respond to junior's temper tantrums tonight; long-range continuity, as in predicting that the girl of today will make a good wife and mother over the years. Every educational and psychiatric effort, on the other hand, assumes some limits to continuity, accepts the possibility of flexibility, believes in the alterability of both surface and deep-level characteristics. All through this study we have had to make implicit, and at times explicit, references to continuity. But now that the question of structure has been considered, we must look more steadily at the problem of continuity. What kinds of continuity are there? Where do they come from? How rigid and unalterable are they? What can be done about them? In what degree is personality a thing of today, and in what degree is it a thing of a lifetime?

Despite all the vicissitudes of life there is continuity. Corresponding to the persistence of the fingerprint, the birthmark, the pattern of hair and dentition, is the individual cast of personality, something that enters into and persists through every situational adjustment. It is our task to define the sources of such continuity, not claiming too much for them, but also not claiming too little. Accordingly, we state our working hypotheses:

There are, first, the physiological dispositions that arise from genetic and embryological dispositions—strength and endurance; the attributes of limb and finger that affect skill; neural and biochemical plasticity; and also temperamental plasticity, to which Chapter 4 gave so much attention.

Second come the early canalizations, cathexes, which according to our thesis are irreversible, and the matrix from which later, more specific canalizations arise—the lifetime tastes and enthusiasms, predilections, areas of intimate at-homeness. These may be masked, and the values which emanate from them may be perpetually thwarted; but personality is rooted in them. Their stability means that any change is an effort. They have taken on a deep and intimate self-quality.

Third, there are the deeply ingrained, perennially reinforced conditioned responses which stand at or near the apex of the hierarchically organized system of symbols, the habits which not only embody "second nature" but constitute the central skills, arts, ways of living upon which social reciprocity and personal responsibility so largely depend.

Fourth, there are the deeply ingrained habits of perception. Based partly on the canalizations that give them anchorage, partly on the conditioned symbol system, these habits serve to structure the world, to give it meaning and stability, and to give the self meaning and stability in relation to it. Indeed, the self-picture has all the strength of other perceptual stereotypes, and in addition serves as the chart by which the individual navigates. If it is lost, he can make only impulsive runs in fair weather; the ship drifts helplessly whenever storms arise.

We start, then, with the assumption that there are personality constants. These traits may be approximately *fixed* for life, as is apparently the case with such variables as the speed of developmental processes within the cell; they may be *relatively* constant, as the rate of ossification seems to be; or they may be constant at one time of life, inconstant at another, as is often true of the basic metabolic rate. It should be stressed that raw scores of the sort ordinarily obtained are insufficient for testing any of these possibilities. For the term "constant" may be appropriate to a specific attribute or bodily function which expresses itself only indirectly; and in measuring the attributes that are directly observable the fluctuations observed may arise from extraneous variables such as climate, or even room temperature, that conceal a fundamental "invariant" underneath.

Despite the difficulties, however, the issue seems important enough to warrant a systematic testing of the assumption just offered, that there are true personality constants, true invariants. It must at the same time be admitted that none of the many invariants of which we now have some knowledge have been clearly established. The constancy of the I.Q. now appears to have in it much of artifact as well as considerable biological reality (cf. page 212), and the constants in social responsiveness, such as stability of interests over periods of decades, are very likely genuine constants only within highly constant surrounding circumstances, being subject to abrupt change when the environment is altered. To be sure, as we shall see in the discussion of field theory in Chapter 39, it is reasonable to define personality as an interaction between organism and environment; and in this sense the postulation of personality constants, such as the professional man's interest in the problems of his profession, may be justified. But even there we shall try to show that the degree of constancy in such field measures is not sufficient to warrant the notion of invariance as it is ordinarily used in science. There are of course many studies that show that individuals behave in more or less the same way in varying social contexts.

Organic Continuity

Let us first try to narrow the question specifically to one of organic continuity, the continuity in organic response throughout the life span. Here the guiding clue is the gene pattern with which the individual is once and for all endowed. The genes do not do their work all in an instant and then retire from the scene; on the contrary, individual protoplasm carries its gene pattern throughout its existence. In this sense there is the continuity of physical endowment and of all the various "inherited" dispositions which we discussed in Chapter 3. Factors such as strength, speed, and resistance to disease stand up rather well from this point of view. There appears to be some degree of lifetime continuity in neurocirculatory and endocrine function. Body types, as defined by Sheldon and his collaborators, apparently are based in large measure upon developmental continuities, and direct evidence of such anatomical and physiological continuities is given by Todd, by the California Adolescence Study, and by other research. Even such temperamental dispositions as cyclothymia may dog a person throughout his life; they appear to run in families to a degree that warrants emphasis upon a genetic contribution.

Continuity from year to year in motor adequacies and inadequacies is rather well defined by retest data, despite the functional imbalances and early atrophies that are sometimes present. Continuity in intellectual adequacy can be roughly defined by reference to the relative constancy of performance of the various grades of mental defectives and, with many reservations, by reference to the intelligence test continuities found in most environments. The data of Bayley and of Driscoll, though showing wide year-by-year variations and relatively low correlations of performance over periods of five or more years, do indicate some stability in competence levels in spite of considerable variations in opportunity and incentives.

The factor most difficult to evaluate is that which appears when very different types of outer behavior, appearing at different levels, indicate the presence of the same continuing dispositions. Surely the resemblance between the ability to repeat digits backwards and the ability to work out a very good plan for finding a purse lost in a field is superficially slight; yet it is a fact that something expressing itself in terms of superior achievement may take one form and earn one unit of credit at a certain age level, take another form and earn another unit of credit later on. Though intelligence is not "homogeneous," we can say that a specific intellectual performance at the age of five permits some prediction of a certain type of intellectual performance *on a very different kind of test* at the age of fifteen. There is, then, some biological continuity, though there need be no observed functional continuity.

Even more striking is Mary Shirley's observation of *changing behavior* pointing to *fundamental continuity* in twenty-five children during the first two years of life. When she worked out the relations between performance at each month's level and performance at the next succeeding month's level, Shirley found a striking continuity in the tendency to do the "unpredictable," that which the schedule failed to provide for. The specific thing that is done will, to the astonishment of the experimenter, of course differ from month to month, so that there is no continuity in sheer content. Yet in this instance we can see in some slight degree what makes for the continuity. There is energy, eagerness, activity—something which constantly leads to a spilling over of behavior into the unconstrained or the unobvious. Though sheer complexity of response, related in some way to intelligence, may be involved, the best guess would be made in terms of interest or exuberance based upon intensity of sensory or activitiy drives, or upon low thresholds for affective response (page 73).

It would be interesting to know whether continuities of these elementary types appear not only month by month, but year by year. Case material, such as Gesell and Thompson's study of a pair of identical twins, seems to indicate a rather high degree of continuity; and Barbara Burks' comparison of identical twins reared in very different environments makes it appear likely that a genetic basis can be found for a large part of this long-range temperamental constancy.

It should be admitted, however, that the demonstration of such temperamental constants would still leave us in the dark not only as to the nature of the gene complex involved, but even concerning the psychological roots of the observed behavior. In the case of a relatively simple physiological type of expression such as exuberance or joyful response, we might be dealing with sheer *thresholds* for certain kinds of external stimulation, or with general intensity levels of response (page 75), or with the highest level to which response can be driven (page 140), or with the duration of a response once brought to expression, or with long-time or short-time cycles of expression. Work with animals does not encourage the belief in simple and easy solutions of problems of disposition (page 141).

CONTINUITY THROUGH CANALIZATION AND CONDITIONING

It is not too much to assert, however, that there are types of continuities regarding whose existence and basis we have much better grounds for certainty. First among these are the (perhaps unextinguishable) canalization or cathexis responses which, as we sought to show in Chapter 8, appear to be established in the opening months of life, becoming deeply ingrained before and during the development of the self, and being interwoven in some degree with one another. Object canalizations and self-canalizations become fused and are then subjected to verbal conditioning of a type which appears to be extremely resistive to extinction. The result of all this is apparently the ingraining within the person of a very stable, albeit complex, value system during the period of active language acquisition; this system is highly consolidated by the time he is six or eight years of age, is subject to some confusion and redefinition in early adolescence, but usually preserves the essential architectural form which it received in early childhood. Despite the great flexibility of ordinary conditioning patterns, the value system appears to remain stable even when profound readjustments in living are required. Notwithstanding the great emphasis placed upon human plasticity by most clinical workers, it is of interest that the Freudian system gives such value responses almost absolute fixity in terms of the doctrine of the "timelessness of the unconscious" (cf. page 545), and that Adler saw fit to attribute to the "style of life" a degree of fixity which led him to regard as neurotic any person whose first style of life was overthrown (page 581).

Along with the canalizations, other likely candidates for relative permanence in the personality structure are the *dominant conditioned responses*, deriving either from the first period of ego organization (later infancy), or from early adolescence, or from the period of final achievement of an adult self. Of these dominant conditioned responses, the symbolic, especially the verbal, must be given heavy emphasis. The material discussed in Chapter 20 (especially pages 487–491) regarding the symbolic machinery of self-reference warrants the belief that, by their early twenties, most individuals have stylized the schema of the self rather finely; a person resists changes in selfhood as he would mortal disease. *Interests* also behave like dominant conditionings (page 283). Data on the continuity of interests, which show a rather high degree of instability during the second decade of life, indicate that in the young adult this set of symbols has taken on (within the ordinary rather constant environment) almost the fixity —even the rigidity—of the fundamental language habits themselves.

This fixity of the self and of personal interests is intelligible in terms of the concept of overlearning. A task overlearned—practiced beyond the level of proficiency required at the time—does not readily extinguish. The language skills, for example, including typing and telegraphy skills, reach a certain level of proficiency which is highly resistive to the effects of disuse; although they may eventually grow rusty, they can be brought back to their original level with an almost infinitesimal amount of "refresher" practice. Interests—in work, in hobbies, in games, in books—are overlearned responses in this sense, and they stick, consequently they play a huge role in personality consolidation.

The concept of overlearning is important for personality theory and practice because personality changes which at first sight seem profound are notoriously difficult to evaluate unless the earlier habit system is known. Pertinent here are the data of Sheldon and Eleanor Glueck, showing that the work habits of teen-agers may have an important influence on the pattern of behavior ten years later, even though there has been an intervening period of life in a reformatory in which the work supervision has differed widely from that which prevailed during pre-institutional life. Moreover, countless clinical examples show how important the overlearned habits can be, though a period of good adjustment at the conscious and behavior level permits no confident prediction unless almost the whole life history of the personality, especially its ingrained, overlearned habits, is known. Trends masked by present patterns may be touched off by appropriate, often unforeseen, stimulation, such as encounters with old associates—or old dreams. Here again the overlearned habits that are most important are those involving attitude toward life; motor habits are supported by such continuing attitudes (cf. page 628).

By this no implication is intended that such habits operate with full autonomy, independently of goals and of the self. They are typically the products of older goals which have been renounced; but when an old goal finds a well-organized habit system at its service, it can swing the individual along, protesting, as he goes, that he does not want to go. Something has "got into him." There is indeed continuity here both in the goals and in the means, but continuity of a part, defying the remainder. The same capacity of overlearned habits to dominate behavior even at the expense of the self may at times serve an important therapeutic purpose. An old skill in which there is pride may be the nucleus of the restoration of self-respect. When habits are so adequate that the execution of a skilled performance gives profound ego satisfaction, they may revitalize and reactivate goals which by themselves have shown relatively little continuity.

Continuity of goals involves the progressive discovery of more and more *means* to these goals, and consequently the adjustment of these means to one another. If a person wishes to be generous, he discovers the relation of words, acts, and even thoughts, to this goal; the result is what the spectator calls "consistency." As R. B. Cattell has emphasized, habit systems are frequently made up of heterogeneous components allied in their service of a goal. This appears to make possible the investigation of the progressive steps in the interrelation of such habits until they have become a compact, integrated group, serving more perfectly the purpose of continuity through the fact that many activities, appropriate to widely varying situations, mediate continuously the approach to the single goal.

The Character Education Inquiry of Hartshorne and May is of special interest in connection with the continuity of habit patterns in childhood. Their study of children in grades five to eight shows the consistency with which dominant patterns of honest behavior were developed, year by year, by children in favored circumstances, and the consistency with which dishonest patterns developed during the same period in children in unfavored circumstances. Starting from a theoretical common point in the kindergarten, the two groups consistently diverge. Horowitz' data likewise indicate that there is not only a consistent and progressive development of social attitude, but a steady increase in the *interrelations* of attitudes which appear in more or less the same situation.

So much for continuities through canalization and conditioning. In view of the intimate relations of motor and perceptual responses, we should expect the perceptual habits likewise to develop in consistent fashion, to move in one relatively clear direction, so as to present, in terms of the life history, a degree of continuity of perceptual habit comparable to that presented by motor habits. On this point there is rather little direct evidence. The background information regarding *general* tendencies in perceptual development is fairly clear —for example, general growth curves of perceptual skills for the childhood, pre-adolescent, and early adolescent periods, and Piaget's data on stages in cognitive processes (cf. also pages 333 ff.). Against this background there are odds and ends of information as to *personal* continuities, such as the Rorschach material indicating considerable stability in perceptual patterns—e.g., the balance of wholes and details and of color and movement—over a number of years. Here there is increasing definiteness of personality structure from year to year during childhood, and a rather high degree of stability (retest reliability) in adult responses.

Continuity of Structure

Since each of the main functions thus far described presents some degree of continuity both during the growth period and during adulthood, we might expect to find a considerable degree of continuity in the *total pattern* of individuality, and to see it revealing itself in all sorts of subtle forms—though we can never hope to grasp them all. Some aspects of this continuity would be reducible to a fundamental continuity due to the action of genes, others to cross conditioning and other types of interrelations between habit systems, and still others to perceptual organization. But direct studies of this continuity over long periods of time are shockingly few in number. To mention a few examples of those available: The Harvard Growth Study has supplied numerous (largely unpublished) year-by-year scores on tests; the Grant Study (also at Harvard) has recently begun an intensive longitudinal study of normal young men; the Cambridge-

Somerville Youth Study recorded clusters of traits shown year by year by delinquent boys (these data are largely unpublished); masses of data (largely unpublished) of almost every conceivable sort were gathered from a hundred boys and a hundred girls studied during the age period ten to sixteen by the California Adolescence Study; and J. W. Macfarlane's intensive study of personality development in a large urban group covers the period from before birth to the present (the subjects are in their late teens at this writing; the data cannot be published until the study is completed). Some of these longitudinal studies may begin to be published within a few years. Until they do, it may as well be admitted that the best information actually available on over-all personality continuity is that obtained from the more careful biographies and autobiographies. But although these sources reveal countless fascinating evidences of all sorts of continuities, both crude and subtle, both manifest and veiled, they are ill equipped to disclose the fundamental *laws* which underlie personality continuity.

In the meantime, we do have a certain type of research which comes rather close to what we need in clarifying continuity; this is a study of the *sequels* which appear in the life history when *one* profoundly releasing or traumatizing experience is traced in its implications. It may happen that a single episode, such as that of the "locomotive God," pervades life, saturates it in ever more complex ways. Though an episode can never serve as the sole clue to the whole personality, such studies cover a much larger segment of life than does the study of the continuity of a single habit by itself. Biographical studies of infantile satisfactions and frustrations and their sequelae are numerous. Studies of the influence of infantile frustrations upon subsequent drive and behavior structure (page 485) suggest a certain transfer and generalization which, together with cross conditioning, undoubtedly predispose to a genuine "personality constellation" in the adult, whether animal or man; studies of human beings seem at this point to support the Freudians in their conviction regarding the permanent importance of such early damage to the drive system. We still do not know how much should be attributed to specific frustration or trauma, and how much should be attributed to those constitutionally low thresholds which apparently make a trauma play so large a part. But at least we may say that continuity is no longer merely the continuity of an item; it soon becomes the continuity of a system.

Similarly, the sympathy behavior of nursery-school children, and the aggressive behavior both of this group and of children in the elementary school, appear to represent clusters or organized structures rather than "traits" in the strict sense (cf. page 638). In both instances there is evidence that the most profound need satisfactions (especially ego satisfactions and satisfactions from effective self-defense) lead to a process of consolidation and increasing rigidity which is, to say the least, much more common and typical than is the dissolution or decay of such patterns.

In pattern continuity symbols appear to have a huge part. What seems to happen in many cases is that the structure, or pattern, is given a name which has high continuity; or that the cluster is fused with the self-image which, as we saw, has high continuity; or that both processes occur, each reinforcing the other. In the next chapter we shall try to show why discontinuity, both in temporal terms and in the sense of dissociation, may also occur. But in the light of present evidence, integration and continuity are apparently much more typical of normal personality. And the most important single factor in stabilizing this organization, in such a way as to provide continuity and to weld more tightly the components that tend to become interrelated, appears to be the self-picture operating in a central position and serving to give unity to the diverse components with which it is connected. Much that resembles physiological continuity— as in psychosomatic disorder, for example—seems more likely to be continuity in the self-portrait (including its unconscious aspects) which produces continuous physical consequences. The same principle applies to the entire realm of habits of whatever sort: word habits, mannerisms, social habits, etc. For example, we noted in an earlier chapter that the sheer utilization of space derives not alone from kinetic or kinesthetic factors, but ultimately from self-attitude; if the self-attitude remains stable year by year, the expressive pattern will remain so. It is likely that continuity in motor performance over a span of time, e.g., in ways of attacking and pursuing a task, is more a matter of continuity of self-images than of the physiological disposition to initial spurt, warming up, work cycle, end spurt, or any other phenomenon of the classical "curve of work" as such.

Though we have been chiefly concerned with individuality in the continuities which we can observe, there is a paradoxical though fundamental relation between this individuality of pattern and the sharing of a *general* developmental destiny. There is often more continuity of destiny (this term including the individual's own goal, and his dispositions to pursue it) than is evident to one who is focusing month by month, year by year, upon the individual. Just as twenty rangers lost in a forest after "fanning out" to hunt for a spring may use compass, bark, and sun in twenty different ways—each at a given moment pursuing his own direction around a gulley or fallen tree, but all arriving ultimately at the appointed clearing—so twenty children following utterly different momentary trends may arrive at a common destination as responsible adult members of the community. L. K. Frank uses another image to suggest the relationships. Integrating a host of clinical impressions and many scattered experimental studies, he has formulated a concept of continuity in terms of an essentially common destiny for travelers who use many different routes and many different modes of locomotion. He suggests that we think of a number of people who are leaving New York for Chicago on a given day. Some will go by plane, some by train, some by bus, some will drive; a few will use slower means of transportation; some will make longer or shorter stopovers; some may have accidents and may have to remain in a hospital at one place or another on the way. Some will change their destination in the midst of the trip. By and large, however, most of them will reach Chicago. We might in the same fashion think of a group of children of the same age, each developing at his own rate and in his own way, with growth spurts and retardations, with illnesses and frustrations, and with periods of high consummation; some reaching puberty much earlier than others; all differing hugely from one another at any given point in the process; yet all somehow becoming adults and as members of the community having much more in common than they have exclusively to themselves.

Frank's figure of speech is even more subtle and complex than is evident at first sight. With maturation and differentiation of function, each child's specific trends and areas of competence become more distinctive, and the centrifugal tendencies that drive children apart appear to predominate. For example, in E. B. Greene's curves for perceptual and motor skills, not only is there good evidence that each function has its own growth curve, but there is the great variability of individual growth rates in each function. How can centripetal integrating forces compete with such increasing differences from child to child? The answer lies partly in the fact that there is more convergence in many functions (e.g., the endocrine functions); older children may differ less than younger ones. But equally important is the fact that the complex skills necessary for social functioning become finely integrated in a unity tight enough to make one person, in respect to many tasks, more or less interchangeable with another (however much the individualist may dislike it). In most jobs, for example, there are a large number of more or less interchangeable people with the required skills. Even at the highest level, it is dangerous in our society to be "too good for one's job," i.e., to pose as irreplaceable. Indeed, for most of the tasks of an industrial society the training process aims to make us interchangeable parts—and to a surprising degree does so.

This does not mean that a *whole man* is interchangeable with another; but the man in his role—be it factory operative or bus driver —is trained until he is thus interchangeable; and often, as in the Ozark hillbilly or the Maine lobsterman, the "training" makes for interchangeability in far more respects than are denoted by the job itself. Of course the equivalence of man for man is relative, and of course (as we have constantly stressed) each functioning pattern of behavior has its membership in a distinct individuality; yet, for all that, the continuities in individual personality growth are reconcilable with an essential unity of goal as socially defined, and with a high degree of common outlook and common capacity for shared living. The result of such sharing of goals and of behavior directed toward them is that the student of personality continuity tends to overlook the enormous diversification present in the formative period, and is tempted also to forget those types of individual continuity in the adult which are relatively unrelated to socially shared goals. We are often concerned only with the life continuities that are manifest in the stable and stylized end products known as class differences, occupational differences, or various kinds of subcultural differences. These types of social differences will be considered in Chapters 32–37. The social molding of personality, however, is intelligible only when the problem of individual continuity is clearly grasped.

A broad base for personal continuity has apparently been found, a base consisting of biological individuality, early canalizations and conditionings, ingrained perceptual habits, and a well-organized and rather stable structural whole. But personality does change, in matters both large and small. The growing and aging processes, the conditioning and canalizing and restructuring processes are forever at work. A critical question thus presents itself: Do personalities typically undergo their changes gradually or suddenly? So far as we are dealing with the determination of the whole by a large number of more or less independent parts, we should expect gradualness, for the parts will not all change at once. But so far as we are dealing with relatively few parts, or with the tight interlocking of parts, we should expect that the disappearance of a single component would work havoc with the whole, so as to force the appearance of a new whole. We have already given one example of the latter, namely, the sudden collapse of one's habitual attitude toward the self and the sudden appearance of another attitude when an above-threshold threat is presented (page 581). It should be admitted that the personality is a good deal more complex and more stable than the self (in the sense in which we have used the term). Yet the sudden onset of neurosis or even psychosis, and the rather frequent occurrence of "radical" changes or abrupt decisions, suggest that the rapidly changing self can sometimes swing the whole personality organization from one center of equilibrium to another. Studies of configural conditioning (page 232) are also ready with examples of all-or-none mechanisms of this sort in organized response. The fact that personality is very highly organized, and that some of its components, such as attitude toward the self, are both highly organized and at the same time central in determining what the still larger wholes do, should lead us to expect that a true transformation of the personality, in all but its most primitive physiological bases, may be fairly common.

Commoner still will be sudden change in a large component in the personality system that leaves the other loosely related phases of the system to tag along and catch up, integrating with the remainder at a later time. There is nothing to prevent this radical transformation of certain important components, such as dominant conditionings to one's role in society. This, indeed, is what many clinical and biographical studies of early adulthood reveal. According to our thesis, the fundamental canalizations do not extinguish; yet their figure-ground relations can change, and important new canalizations can always be formed. Gradualness and suddenness are, then, equally natural expressions of individuality.

In spite of all this, we cling to the evidence that there is a good deal of continuity both in the sense of *stability* and in the sense of consistent *direction in the growth process*. But a subtle and trenchant difficulty arises. Is behavioral continuity, as we observe it, perhaps largely an artifact due to the limitations of our analysis? Some years ago Shirley asked whether growth is "continuous or saltatory." The question is profound. Smooth growth curves for groups may result from many discrete steps in individuals. If we knew the saltatory phases of growth, we might prepare the individual for the jump that comes next. We know that learning, too, has many plateaus—periods in which superficially there appears to be no progress, but in which small discrete steps are being taken that will suddenly be integrated later. A superficial appearance of continuous growth can be given by the accumulation and interaction of a large number of actually saltatory growth processes.

In the same way, there may seem to be a period of arrested development that is suddenly terminated by a fresh spurt. In view of the widespread importance of the all-or-none principle and the all-or-none phenomena which are constantly manifest in embryonic and later growth, it is possible that every phase of personality appears by virtue of saltatory contributions. In the language of the present study, many of these are transitions from Stage 1 to Stage 2; they represent sudden differentations from an original matrix. And it is highly probable that the transition from Stage 2 to Stage 3 likewise involves sudden integrations of two or more second-level components.[1] Embryonic and later changes often appear full-fledged and all at once, although the contributing factors are many, and relatively independent. If enough of them are present, the individual contribution of each such change may be masked and we may falsely conclude that a slow unanalyzable mass effect is at work.

There are a few instances in which this last-named process means in practice a number of specific all-or-none changes of the *entire personality structure*. The classical example is, of course, religious conversion. It is true that what is usually meant is not literally a change in the entire personality structure, but (as in the case of Tolstoy) a change in a central aspect of the personality, to which eventually all the other phases adapt. Even so, the case is good enough; and for rough practical purposes it may be said that total personality change does at times take the dramatic, lightning-like form. If asked what is responsible for such an avalanche of change, we can do no

---

[1] A suggestion made long ago in Paul's historical studies of language is useful here. Changes during the historical period, e.g., within the Indo-European group of languages, have arisen by virtue of both continuous and saltatory changes. For example, in uttering *t* or *d* the tongue may slowly "recede" in the course of centuries, so that the *t* and *d* of a modern language may be produced by means of contact with the base of the upper teeth at a point considerably farther back than was the case a millennium ago. There are a good many evidences of very slow shifts of this sort. At the same time Paul shows that many linguistic changes could not conceivably have arisen from such continuous change. One consonant may be replaced by another in cases in which the vocal and labial apparatus for the production of the two is entirely different. One whole pattern is completely replaced by the other whole pattern. Here the historical continuity, such as it is, takes the form of a *slowly increasing number of individual persons* who make the shift; each person makes the shift on an all-or-none basis. When generations are compared, a larger number of children in one generation than in another deviate from the traditional standard in the specific way involved. It is likely that the personality changes which seem to be continuous are analogous to this second type of change described by Paul. More and more components of the personality fall in step with an established trend, but each individual component appears suddenly.

better than remark, as did James,[2] "We fall back on the hackneyed symbolism of a mechanical equilibrium." Usually a central component in the attitude toward the self drops out and a competing one has the field to itself; the entire interrelated system anchored upon the old must shift, and the new system must rapidly organize itself, as a see-saw shifts in consequence of a slight change in the weights. Much more common is gradualness of the shift, because there are enormously more complex, tightly bound interrelations than there are free components. Those near the center of the structure are, moreover, among the most stable, for the reasons discussed in Chapter 26 (pages 640 ff.).

By virtue of all the factors suggested thus far, the inner dynamics become more and more stable. The self, the symbolic system, and the value system, each related to the other, take on a degree of fixity—or even rigidity—which will resist environmental pressure, or, to speak more accurately, will require each environmental pressure to operate on the individual in a more or less prearranged way. The individual selects from the stimulus field what is appropriate to the value system, the symbolic system, and especially the self system; and he develops means of making himself impervious to disturbing or unassimilable features of the environment. A sort of gyroscopic stability develops. It will then mean little to say that one "responds to the environment." In very rare cases, stimulation may be severe enough to break up the gyroscopic adjustment pattern, so that a fundamentally new pattern is formed which is only in a small degree predictable from the old. But as long as we stay within manageable limits, the organism will make of its environment something relevant to itself, just as the body will make of the thousands of different foods the particular kinds of protoplasm which that body characteristically makes. The exceptions to the principle in the physical and psychological fields seem rather similar. If the food lacks essential vitamins or minerals, or if extreme dietetic imbalances are present, there will be adaptive difficulties. In the same way, some environments impose such extreme strain that continuity of personal adaptation is impossible.

---

[2] *Varieties of Religious Experience*, p. 197.

It is true that all adaptation involves some strain, and that invisible strains of varying degree are always involved. But human societies, developing as organs of personal interaction, have for the most part defined personal environments which—at least in peace—put somewhat less severe strain upon us than would be the case in unregulated chaos, so that even among the impoverished and frustrated a rather high degree of personality selectivity and personal continuity results.

We should confess that we know only little about the saltatory processes underlying our manifestation of personal continuity. But they appear to proceed in an orderly, often unidirectional way that is reminiscent of the unfolding processes manifest in the structural changes of the embryo. At this writing they seem to enrich and complicate the study of personal continuity, while at the same time they support the main concept. Such a concept would appear to lead ultimately to another kind of continuity—a continuity of predictable though discrete steps, whose nature and timing will ultimately fit into a clear longitudinal conception. Continuity may prove to be embodied less in the smooth onward flow of a trend than in the inherent tendency of a function, in its context of other functions, to jump to a new level or to a qualitatively distinct form of expression (cf. emergence, page 643). Continuity would then prove to be a *diversity of discrete steps*, each of which is part of an intelligible, continuous trend on the part of the organism.

But the sudden appearance of a new trait could never depend on the realization of a *single* favoring circumstance. The "favorable situation for the saltation" is a context, a state of interdependent predisposing conditions. And seldom do we understand the nature of their interdependence well enough to predict the emergent result in the form of sudden change. Just as even the metallurgist, confronted with problems much simpler than ours, cannot predict the fusion temperature if the newly discovered alloy contains too many different ingredients, so we shall have to be content at present with groping, uncertain predictions.

Yet the whole may prove, as in countless physical and biological examples, much more stable than the component parts. As S. J.

Holmes has shown, the very nature of an organism involves a system of checks and balances which provide orderly change *up to a point*, and prevent its passing that point. Each part tends to move, anarchically, out of the system, yet is caught, restrained, made to serve within it. Even the mechanism of saltatory change is included within this kind of functioning whole. For the saltations are not random; there is provision for them; they realize the system's potentialities to consummate its trends. Personality seems in all these respects essentially like the much simpler biological systems described by Holmes. It has some continuity of parts; new parts arise (often in saltatory fashion) through interaction with the environment; and occasionally a sudden and radical transformation occurs. But in the long run, stability and rather narrowly restricted change are the rule; and complexity of organization, though a mark of fragility, may also mean that the whole is less changeable than the parts. If the threat to wholeness is profound, escape through regression, fugue, explosion, or conversion is possible, the individual striving to keep as much of the original structure as possible.

It is extraordinary how much material our civilization has gathered regarding lifetime continuity among the mentally shipwrecked, and how little regarding those who have reached port. One outstanding study should, however, be cited in relation to the continuity of normal personality—the material gathered by Bühler and Frenkel. This material presents studies of individual men and women in whose life histories the waxing and waning of artistic and creative powers is carefully traced. There are two types of evidence as to the long-term personality dispositions which underlie these developmental processes. First, there is evidence that each form of creativeness—in music, in the fine arts, in science, in statecraft, etc.—shows in broad outlines its own more or less characteristic ascent (to a high plateau) and descent, along with the unpredictables which appear in everything human. The data from several national groups show enough consistency in the nature of the curves for various types of achievement to suggest very tentatively that there are empirical continuities both in level of performance and in rate of ascent or descent. Second, there is evidence as to the *individual* factors, constitutional and environmental, which express themselves in a particularly early ascent (as in the "infant prodigy") or a particularly prolonged resistance to senescent decline (for example, Verdi wrote *Falstaff* when nearly ninety). Such factors do not, of course, establish continuity with the rigor we demanded earlier, since in all such cases the degree of environmental continuity is only vaguely specified. It is likely that all growth, indeed all life, may reveal much more of the saltatory tendency than appears on the surface. Yet through all the saltations the original Stage 1 attributes and the well-differentiated second-level attributes help to call the tune, and continuity reappears in the midst of discontinuity.

31. Discontinuity and Typology

WE WERE concerned in the preceding chapter with temporal continuity, with the devices by which recognizable individuality may be maintained under ever-varying external conditions. But continuity of another sort is equally striking: the continuity from person to person in terms of the fundamental *similarity* of the individual to other individuals with respect to many traits. Most attributes permit us to arrange individuals on a quantitative or qualitative continuum. For each person with a given level of intelligence, there are others a little brighter or a little duller; for each person with a given degree of ambition, there are some a little more, and others a little less, ambitious. When measurement is impossible, the traits used in research or clinical practice can for the most part be arranged in qualitative series, like the qualitative series of the spectrum, one person being placed between two others just as if a quantitative determination could be made. From this point of view, it would seem likely that people can be arranged in continua with respect to two or three traits at a time, and that this can be done more easily if the traits are correlated. Indeed, people might be arranged in continua having many dimensions, just as plants or shells are arranged for a natural history exhibit, on the basis of the complex structural relations of many parts. This approach to personality continua is, however, almost unexplored.

The study of individual traits show that continuity is apparently

A   B

the general rule. If the amount of a trait is entered on the x-axis, and the number of people possessing that amount of the trait are entered on the *y*-axis, we ordinarily obtain normal (*A*) or at any rate only moderately skewed (*B*) distributions. There is no break as there

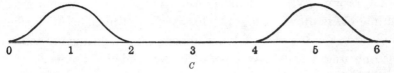

c

would be if each person had either four or more units of the trait or less than three units (*C*). There is no value in speaking of *types* if immediately after we mark them off we have to admit that they merge imperceptibly into one another.

The important question, therefore, is whether there are specifiable *gaps* between persons in terms of determinations of single traits, and if so, why. Usually there are no such gaps; however, there are exceptions. Our problem in this chapter is to look at the exceptions and to determine under what conditions they occur—in other words, under what conditions breaks or gaps occur in distributions. This may lead us to a feasible basis for specifying non-overlapping personality types. So far as discontinuities appear, we may find it convenient to group people in terms of their possessing *more than* or *less than* a particular amount of any given attribute, where this specified amount indicates a point of fundamental cleavage in the distribution; we may similarly define gaps in a qualitative series. Later we shall consider discontinuities in structural pattern.

Much of the present-day utilization of theories of discontinuity is closely related to similar theories which have been developed in the physical sciences. The Newtonian view of the world was predicated on continuity. Matter, space, time, and the force of gravity were regarded as infinitely divisible. These conceptions were later supplemented by many other expressions of belief in continuity, notably by the theories of the conservation of mass and the conservation of energy. Another way of thinking developed during the nineteenth century as a result of the formulation of the atomic theory and the periodic table of the elements in chemistry, with their suggestion that nature is organized in discrete steps. Each of the 92 elements was where it "ought to be" on the basis of its atomic weight, and it was held that there could be no elements whose atomic weights were *intermediate* between any two in the periodic table. This followed from the discovery that the amount of any given element entering into a compound must be a multiple of its atomic weight. This fact constituted a fundamental justification for the idea of types—there were fundamental units of which no fragmentation was possible. Nor did the discovery of the divisibility of the atom and the nature of atomic organization shatter this way of thinking. When we specify today the finite number of planetary and nuclear electrons in a given atom, and the greater number of electrons in another atom, we recognize that the two elements stand in a discontinuous, not in a continuous, relation. Each is, in fact, a fundamental mode of organization, and there are no modes of organization between two such atomic patterns. The gene is a philosophical analogue to the atom. Even when the chromosome is fractionated (as in "crossing over"), the gene remains whole; it is an ideal building stone and it provides ample basis for discontinuity.

BIOTYPES

Looking first at the biological phase of the problem, we note that certain genes are responsible for critical differences in total personality organization. The gene cannot be split; the individual either receives it or fails to receive it (page 40). Several pathological conditions, both somatic and psychological, are clearly Mendelian (page 50)—for example, the rare type of mental defect mentioned on page 61. Particularly clear and significant are the sex-linked characteristics, in which the individual receives all of the disposition, or none of it, depending upon his sex. It is true that most such cases are complicated by the interacting influence of other genes, and by uncontrolled environmental impacts on a given developmental tendency. But the principle is clear, none the less. Even where there are two (or more) genes at work, as in some forms of pigmentation, the steps are clearly defined, so that individuals of type A will have none; those of type B will have a specific small degree; those of type C, a specific large degree, etc.

The actual distribution curves derived from the operation of such all-or-none genetic dispositions are likely to be bimodal rather than discontinuous. The distribution curves in the accompanying figure

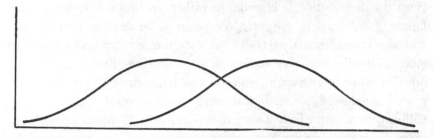

represent two populations that differ sharply, but still overlap. Such distributions are common. Many factors may cause bimodality based on two overlapping normal distributions; an example is the stature of men and of women, in which there is a mean difference of four inches, with very considerable overlap. It is quite likely that some of the psychological sex differences are distributed more or less similarly (cf. page 106).

Such discontinuities as the foregoing are evident from birth onward. But discontinuities between persons may result from specific all-or-none factors acting on some but not on others, at almost any point in the developmental process, so that what was at first a continuous

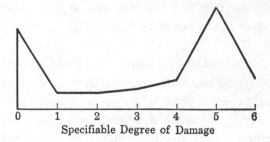

Specifiable Degree of Damage

distribution gives rise to two groups—those who have and those who have not been acted upon by the specific factor. Some developmental hazards and childhood diseases are in this class; they may do profound damage, or do no damage at all. Even if the damage is variable in *amount*, the smallest visible amount may be quite large; and in such a case we should be justified in speaking of "observed" discontinuity. The distribution curve might look like that shown in the accompanying figure (if there are seven specific degrees of damage including zero). Here the distribution is bimodal in rather an unusual sense, as the figure is designed to suggest. We seem to be dealing actually not with single unidimensional traits but with the development of two or more mutually exclusive modes of organization. For if the bodily capacity to resist disease is equal to the demands, we have one integrated mode of physiological and psychological organization; failing this, we may have a very different mode. Goldstein's work on brain injuries suggests the presence of this all-or-none principle in the capacity to adapt to trauma, and the same thing is apparently true with regard to a variety of developmental hazards such as childhood diseases; in the case of the disease, the issue is frequently whether the body can resist adequately or not, the outcome being either grave damage or none at all.

But if we try to determine why the discontinuity appears, we regularly find that the supposed "disturbing" or "complicating" variables which are responsible for bimodality are really aspects of an interacting system, and that the manner of their organization is vastly important in determining the value of the primary variable with which we are concerned. The discontinuity is not capricious; it results from the fact that between two stable, viable modes of organization *there is and can be no intermediate stable, viable mode of organization.*

However, the individual is a more or less integrated system, and the question of typing him is not necessarily to be conceived in terms of one trait, but rather in terms of a system of interrelated or component aspects. Typing in terms of several aspects may well call for a different approach. Many things encountered in everyday living—chairs, automobiles, trees, cats—behave as organized patterns and are easily grasped and typed. But if we were concerned with only one dimension, e.g., length, or weight, or color, dogs would melt into cats. The type is based not on one dimension, but on a recognizable pattern. The pattern, moreover, is a stable, coherent system, so that though it is pushed here or there, it comes to rest in its familiar form; such an organization is homeostatic. But when the balance is profoundly disturbed, the whole person may be different thereafter, organized in a different way. This is evident in the psychoneuroses and in psychoses; we are dealing not with a change in one trait but with a completely different pattern of equilibrium. A type is one of the possible forms of stable equilibrium. Certain groups of traits that cohere and are capable of achieving a dynamic unity constitute types.

A closely related biological typology is the concept of clinical types developed in medicine. Hyperthyroidism, pulmonary tuberculosis, and nephritis are not points on any imaginable distribution curve, no matter how many dimensions are considered. They are meaningful biological patterns. Whether an original "cause"—e.g., the Koch bacillus in tuberculosis—can be specified is of course important etiologically, but not in reference to the fundamental concept of a clinical pattern. We all harbor Koch bacilli, but some of us are predisposed to poor resistance to this bacillus by virtue of our *organic system as a whole*. Moreover, the prognosis in tuberculosis is made in terms of a very complex notion of clinical type; the physician is dealing with a group of interrelated symptoms, some of which point more or less directly to the operation of a central pathological condition, some of which are quite literally interdependent expressions of one another. These clinical types of interdependent traits that constitute discontinuous systems are often held to offer a close parallel to personality types. Putting aside the suggestion that such aggregates are merely statistical profiles or clusters of traits, we must emphasize that it is the dynamic interdependence, the impossibility of isolating the attributes, that is central to the whole idea. As Klüver has stated it, it is not the adventitious but the necessary systematic linkages between attributes which make up the type. An ideal type is a mode of organization that is present in all-or-none form. If it be argued that such modes grade imperceptibly into other modes, there are two replies: (1) that the intermediate modes of organization are unstable and non-viable (like certain chemical elements which appear only at high temperatures), and (2) that when intermediate modes are demonstrated it is better not to use the term "type," but to reserve it for discontinuities.

On the other hand, we must admit that it is common to find ideal or pure types exhibiting true discontinuity in respect to some central and fundamental characteristic, yet nevertheless mingled with or surrounded by a number of other characteristics less tightly bound to the central core and exhibiting no discontinity from one person to another. We have, then, in practice, ideal types which are so heavily loaded down with "impurities," or non-necessary secondary characteristics, that a statistical demonstration of discontinuity is impeded. For example, according to the current theory, cycloid and schizoid personalities may perhaps be regarded as ideal types in the clinical sense, but they are so heavily freighted with traumatic and other developmental artifacts that continuous rather than discontinuous distributions appear. At least, the utility of a clear typology should not be renounced merely because impurities appear on first inspection; this would be like a chemist's throwing away all the ore that is not pure.

This theory of clinical types, especially when supported by reference to the concept of pure elements in chemistry, seems entitled to a careful hearing. It must be conceded that the majority of these types as currently applied in psychology have not as yet been validated in terms of either empirical or rational definitions of points of cleavage. For example, with extroversion-introversion, or ascendance-submission, or superego vs. id orientation, or adjustment vs. mal-adjustment , or aggressiveness vs. shyness, the distribution curves are smooth—indeed, usually normal—with not even that suggestive trace of bimodality which might warrant the belief that a fundamental discontinuity has been smothered by accidental factors. Thus the Kretschmer biotypes studied objectively in normal persons by Kline-berg and his collaborators were replaced by normal curves, and the accompanying psychological characteristics, which were supposed to be associated with these biotypes, also yielded normal distribution curves. Hence, quite aside from our failure to discover functional relations between physical and personality factors, we confront the impossibility of empirically identifying the biotypes originally postulated. It may indeed be true that the normal curve masks a large number of real discontinuities (cf. page 728). But if their number is so large, and if all of them are in fact present simultaneously, it is only by disentangling them and demonstrating their role that the concept of types can be made to serve a useful purpose. The recent quantitative work of Sheldon and his collaborators (cf. page 59), while emphasizing three *components* in physique, demonstrated that each component appears in the individual in some *degree*, not that each person is a full-fledged representation of a "pure type," sharply separated from other "pure types."

DISCONTINUITY IN SELF-ATTITUDES

Nevertheless, a number of clinical types, especially among the neuroses, apparently have a better status because they seem to be based primarily on fundamental attitudes *toward the self*, and because these frequently take the form of discontinuous and mutually exclusive modes of organization they are likely to lead to a true typology. It may be worth while to see whether the normal discontinuities in self-attitude among children may prepare the way for the later discontinuities of normal and neurotic personality structure.

We have considered the likelihood (page 607) that various modes of *coming to terms with oneself* are achieved in early childhood on an all-or-none basis. The classical studies of prestige suggestion in children of school age (page 217) indicate that along with accidental variations there are two fundamental ways of responding to authority. In various test situations most children function at either an essentially infantile or an essentially adult level; mixed or intermediate cases are few. It may be maintained that only among the central traits, not among the peripheral traits, does such discontinuity appear, and there is some truth in this contention. Indeed, while prestige suggestibility, involving a clear-cut attitude toward the self, is bimodally distributed, simple ideomotor suggestibility, involving no such attitude, is normally distributed. Yet we noted (page 609) that centrality and peripherality are largely matters of degree, and sufficiently refined data would probably show bimodality creeping slowly in as we move from peripheral to central traits.

We suggest, then, that the central discontinuity usually appears because of the sharp cleavage between fundamental ways of viewing the self. We suggest the hypothesis that a person can accept and be at peace with himself in terms of a finite number of distinct and well-structured attitudes toward the self. He must accept himself in one way or another because a finite number of ways are offered by the cultural situation; and in order to maintain that attitude he must build up defenses which tend to be discontinuous because they are specific to discontinuous kinds of attitudes. There is no need, however, to insist that attitude toward the self is the *only* attitude that offers a basis for clear typology. For some people in our culture, and for most people in many other cultures (pages 796 ff.), discontinuity may appear in reference to various other *dominant attitudes* prevalent in the group.

The Seat of Discontinuity

As a rule it is only the central attributes that can in this way serve toward discontinuity, because any typology derived from less central characteristics will be broken down almost as fast as it is formulated. The critical point which determines whether a person belongs to one type or another varies constantly with health and with his situation at the moment. Hence if nothing much is at stake, if no life purpose is involved, he will be above the critical point on some occasions, below on others. If, then, a great many individuals are observed, the types will collapse. But a previous means of self-enhancement is likely to be relied upon, and to be stable.

An everyday example is offered by the problem of changing children's habits; everything depends on whether this involves matters of merely momentary convenience, or the fundamental attitude toward the self. During early childhood it is not difficult to make a left-handed child right-handed; if it is done early enough and carefully enough, no bad consequences need follow. The resulting right-handedness is not an all-or-none affair, for in using his hands in all sorts of skilled acts, the child finds certain things that he can do better with his left hand than with his right. In matters of mere convenience, he can add to his left-handed repertory, or subtract from it, with no great strain. But suppose that the child has developed a concept of himself as one who, being left-handed, is at a disadvantage in a right-handed world; or as one who is rare and special; or as one who belongs to a special kind of humanity that is marked off from the common herd and is secretly or overtly considered superior to the rest. Here the shift in attitude accompanying the switching-over process may bear little relation to sheer educability in the right-handed performance. If being left-handed is an attribute that stands rather near the self of selves, it is likely not to be altered by any clinical method short of the heroic process of completely extirpating it by rebuilding the self-attitude. The same rule seems to apply to those instances in which an injury has caused disfigurement of a part of the body regarded as especially beautiful or adequate. One may react to this by shifting the value tendency to another part of the body or to another personal attitude, or he may take it catastrophically; it is an all-or-none matter. However slight the physical impairment may be, the shift in attitude toward the self is likely to be either very profound or very trivial.

In all such instances of the all-or-none principle, we might express what the organism is doing by saying that order is the first rule of living, and that *forced order* is better than *chaos*. If traditional order is lost, a new kind of order based upon a new kind of equilibrium is necessary. No reorganization of components is worth anything unless stability is achieved. For the patient who has suffered disfigurement, there may be no middle ground between the two extremes: thinking of himself as still as lovely or as competent as before, or thinking of himself as wholly valueless because he has lost the one ingredient that made the self lovable. We conclude, then, that type theories, as they relate to personality structure, are useful when they throw light upon modes of *responding to the self*. Throughout the realm of perception there are sudden and complete shifts— "reversible perspectives," etc. The same principle of shifts appears in the way in which a person sees himself. It is likely that the clue to hysteria, compulsion neurosis, etc., lies in distinctive forms of the self-attitude arising from specific factors of conditioning, cathexis, trauma, etc., in individuals with a predisposing constitution.

The Freudian Character Types

A major contribution to typology appears in the Freudian system, especially as developed by Abraham and Erikson. For Freud there is a universal and imperious, yet diffuse and non-specific drive which may be defined in terms of either eros, or pleasure, or tension reduction. It is aroused in the infant by many excitations, notably of the mucous membrane and skin. Much usefulness has been found in this conception (cf. page 485). Through the adience mechanism (page 167) behavior is adjusted to receive more and more of this stimulation. Originally accidental, this stimulation now becomes self-initiated. The process is satisfying in itself and is not merely a means to a satisfying end; thumb-sucking, for example, may be continued for hours as a substitution for or even in the midst of social play.

These self-initiated excitations, though likely to appear at any time—not during visceral stress alone—have greater intensity at some times than at others. In the case of the mouth excitations, the hunger state predisposes to sensitiveness and the thumb or finger may be vehemently sucked and go back to the mouth as fast as the adult can take it out. In other words, these surface sensitivities depend to some degree—though not exclusively—on visceral tensions; this was noted in our discussion of the relation of sensory to visceral drives (page 113). An additional component in such experiences must also be emphasized—the motor and tactual satisfactions in the sucking and rubbing processes. Freud summarizes this rather complicated matter by saying that the mouth is an erogenous zone.

DISCONTINUITY AND TYPOLOGY

While contact with the lips during nursing is arousing vigorous sucking, many associated aspects of the situation, such as the mother's appearance and voice, become involved in the hunger-satisfying experience; and at the same time the oral excitation itself, together with skin warmth and cuddling, fuses into a major wave of satisfaction. Among most primitive peoples the mother gives suck whenever the child cries; among the more civilized the feeding schedule may mean that the child is in a state of acute or, indeed, vociferous need before he is permitted to nurse. In either case the breast is a great consummation; within a few days of birth it has become a regular and attainable if not always controllable good.

Sooner or later the time comes for weaning. Instead of the familiar soft breast and the warm flow, a sticky, pasty, or stringy stuff is stuck into one's mouth and as fast as it is spewed out, more is pushed in. If one is hungry, one has to take it. In time the tongue movements and later the jaw movements of chewing are built up, and replace the sucking pattern.

It would be a cardinal mistake, however, to conclude that the need to suck or the need for the nursing relation is thereby abolished. The weaning experience can force the development of new habits; but a powerful inextinguished canalization upon the breast, and upon the sucking experience itself, remains. The child may find his way to the breast long after chewing and eating habits have been well consolidated; the thumb-suckers and lip-biters are plentiful in the nursery years.

According to the thesis of Freud and Abraham, the forced interruption of nursing leads to true repression, and the energy of the old drive needs thereafter to find its way into other response mechanisms of the oral zone. The more sudden and disturbing the weaning, the more severe the consequences. If thumb-sucking itself is tabu, as it will be sooner or later, the child's craving for reinstatement of the experience may take not only the form of ravenous eating, but many other oral forms such as excessive babbling or, as soon as there are words, excessive talking. He wants to play with and to mouth his father's pipe more than other children do; when his lollipop is gone, he sucks and chews the stick. When numerous toys confront him, he chooses the mouth organ rather than the drum. He becomes a *mouth-centered person*; he lives ever after to recapture the nursing experience. He may become something of a professional baby, or later find a way to keep the mouth central, becoming an oboe player, a lawyer, a college teacher.

The first phase in the Freud-Abraham theory relates therefore to the impact of repression upon local zone satisfaction. The second phase relates not to zones, but to modes or styles of satisfaction. The attitude toward the mother is much more than a nutritive attitude; it is a warmth-cuddle-safety-love attitude. Forcible weaning means both that food is unsatisfactory and that the attendant ministrations are lacking. The result is to generate a personality hungry for the reinstatement of the full mothering experience. The child becomes a nutrient type; he craves to receive, not to give; he needs protection, warmth, sympathy, support. He may be a gentle, friendly soul, eager to be accepted and protected, or a tagger-on to a benefactor or a yes-man devoted to his boss, or a general leaner and a parasite. This is the *oral type* of personality.

The general logic of the oral type applies also to the formation of the anal and genital types. Like other mucous membrane surfaces, the anal surface is very sensitive, the sensitivity varying greatly with the tensions of colon and rectum and with local blood supply. Excitation during bowel-emptying is pleasant, and the little child often discovers that he can get this pleasure by rubbing. But another major ingredient is the power experience (kinesthetic tension and release) in bowel movements; these offer power experiences of another sort in that the child can accomplish all sorts of things—delay a Sunday trip, keep father out of the bathroom, agitate mother, or just show in a general way that he is not to be bossed—by the simple expedient of withholding a bowel movement. According to Freud, however, the critical feature of the situation is the frequent and satisfying erogenous zone excitation by the passing of the semi-fluid bowel contents.

Now appears the inexorable impact of bowel-training rituals.

Unlike the Hopi child, who merely learns where to go when he wants to go, the European or American child is placed on the toilet, solemnly waited for, approved of when he performs. On all other occasions, bowel movements are tabu. The process is hard for the child. It is not like being taught not to touch hot radiators or play with knives; it is a clamping down on internally motivated behavior before he has any inkling of the reasons for it. As a result, the clamping down is felt as a blow, or as violent restraint, that often leads to a powerful wish to continue in the childish state. But this is impossible. The wish must be handled, managed, kept under control. The usual result is reaction formation (page 551) in the form of a drive to limit all his primitive, impulsive, pleasure-seeking activities; he gives up to the environment. *In extreme cases,* being organized around a tabu, one becomes parsimonious, stingy, meticulous, punctual, tied down with petty self-restraints. Everything that is free, uncontrolled, spontaneous is dangerous. Papa will spank. Play safe; put the books back in the right place; rule the note paper neatly; pay your bills on the first of the month; be good. But be sure to take no pleasure in your goodness; be harsh with yourself, with all sinners. The harshness of the over-all picture is taken into account by calling the type anal-sadistic. The genital type, correspondingly, is centered in eros, finds goodness and pleasure compatible.

We have already (page 485) cited an experiment by David M. Levy that is related to this hypothesis. Among a litter of six puppies, two which were fed from rubber-capped bottles with a large aperture, so that in a very short time the milk was gone and the stomach full, got only slight lip-mouth-**jaw** exercise. They continued to suck, throughout the growth period, at practically anything they could find. They had not been active enough in the nursing experience; they had not "worked through" it. This runs closely parallel to the view that frustrated infantile activity can continue to reappear later in new forms. In his most recent experiments, Levy has shown that tics and forced movements regularly follow *restriction of bodily activity*, whether in children, in poultry-yard hens, in horses kept

[747]

in stalls, or in caged animals; impulses which cannot break through into free locomotor activity or postural shift take the form of repetitive tics or "mannerisms."

E. H. Erikson has likewise pointed out the variety of instances in biology in which a function must be exercised *when it is time for it to be*; he has shown that if one function fails to receive adequate expression, other functions that appear later in the organism's time schedule are likely to suffer. In the embryo, each phase of organ development is a necessary precursor of others, so that the full *exploitation of a capacity* made available by a developing organ is necessary if subsequently appearing functions are to be adequate. Each kind of strenuous activity reaches its high point at a different time in the growth process. It would be in keeping with this suggestion to think that the person who as a ten-year-old has had no circuses must, as an adult, have not only circuses but vaudeville and World Fairs, and that he will still be unsatisfied. One is nostalgic for uncompleted experience. This hypothesis of Erikson's is valuable, and suggests further embryological studies.

It may be wiser in the meantime to emphasize a more limited thesis. Levy's experiment with the puppies suggests that a function not used in a completely satisfying way at one period of life may appear later and perhaps become a permanent drive pattern. If used at the right time in the right physiological degree, it disappears. If not, it is never used enough to cause its disappearance; some residual tension remains. An alternative hypothesis regarding the effects of infantile frustration may be useful in many cases. As a child, a person hungered for excitement; circuses were great satisfiers when available. If they were yearned for but were not available, they became values kept active year by year—the child always hoped to go next year. He becomes sorry for himself; other kids have circuses. As a man one looks back on this childhood excitement, the golden age of irresponsibility and sheer fun. He puts himself amid childhood scenes, and he wants those circuses. In such an instance there seems to be no need to accept any principle of growth-stunting. He who has missed the circus excitement as a child may now go to the circus like a child. But so do others who go only "to take the children" but do not find it a burden; and so do still others who do not bother to give explanations. There is, indeed, the nostalgic circus-goer; however, it hardly seems necessary to build about him a hypothesis of growth distortion. At this writing it appears likely that all the many suggestions have some relevance to the problem of persisting infantilism.

But our chief interest in all these hypotheses is their utility as an approach to typology. The Freud and Abraham types may well be true instances of *discontinuity* due to discontinuities in infantile experience; the Levy experiments directly suggest a way in which discontinuities in experience may give rise to sharply contrasting personality types. Freud's character types (cf. page 485) may likewise be based, to some degree, on discontinuity in self-attitudes that arise later in relation to one's own orality, anality, or genitality. Here, however, the cathexes are largely developed before the self is well defined; hence the discontinuities, if they exist, should perhaps be traced to discontinuities which help to *shape* the self.

We have given a rather important place to the concept of clinical types, but have actually found no imperative need for them in the study of normal personality except in respect to the problem of self-attitudes; and even here the empirical evidence is meager. The type approach is highly valuable as a source of useful hypotheses, but as a clue to personality it still lacks solid support.

But here we frequently encounter the objection that the evidence for *empirical* types which represent any degree of continuity or discontinuity in respect to traits has no bearing on *ideal* types, which are conceptually pure like the concepts of geometry, and upon which a clinical psychology must be based. Ideal types are considered valuable as conceptual tools, regardless of the presence of many exceptions, and even if the pure type, the text book case, is rare or nonexistent. They are as useful and as necessary as the concept of absolute zero in temperature—no one expects to achieve it empirically. As a reference point, as a means of studying systematic relations, such types may guide us through a maze of empirical detail. Does not the chemist properly refuse to bother with mud, with unrefined oil, with dirty rust or scum, insisting that chemistry must seek clear and sharply defined elements and compounds which are worth the cost of the purifying and refining processes? And when confronting reagents which are not absolutely pure, does he not insist on building his science in conceptual terms from absolutely pure elements, showing complete indifference as to whether one encounters them often, or rarely, or never in nature? In studying compounds, too, does he not rightly insist that a pure compound, with all its components and all their interrelations, is a prerequisite for the study of less pure or more complex forms of organization? Should we not take our cue from chemistry, abhor purely statistical questions, and struggle to achieve pure, simply defined, logical, manipulable elements and constructs of the ideal type?

The argument is extremely plausible and is in part sound. Simplification, abstraction, is necessary. But the important thing is the *character of the interrelations* which mark the chemical or other compound, the question as to *how* we are to abstract from a world of perceptual confusion, *how* we are to cut through the overrich empirical possibilities. The process of abstraction is a process of noting recurring impressions which appear and reappear in different contexts, and seizing a single property to which we can give a name. We may thus discover both recurrent *objects* and recurrent *patterns*, ordered regularities of spatial arrangement or temporal sequence. We may group together all melodies with a given rhythm, or all sentences which ask a question. We may apply two or more criteria at once, including as continents only those *islands* having a certain *area*, thus excluding Borneo but not Australia. All these elementary principles apply also in personality study. It is possible to group persons on the basis of sharing a single observed characteristic or a given pattern of characteristics. If it helps us to understand, we may regard the *pattern* as a *single criterion* for classification; at the same time we may wish to introduce a second or third criterion, and set up a type meeting all these criteria. If there is a functional relation between extroversion, emotional threshold, and perseverative tendency, we can set up a type in these terms, whether extroversion is a single entity or a syndrome.

But here a danger arises. The fact that we can conceptualize a type does not prove that there is true functional *coherence*, interdependence of the traits. *The whole value of the type lies in the dependable coherence of the characteristics named.* If "types" are made up at will and fall apart again as we turn to new cases, they serve only to mislead. Other types could likewise be made up at will, the only limitation being the mathematical possibilities of combination. The situation is entirely different when traits are genuinely caught up within a unitary functioning system. Here the removal of one means that the system is gone. A new system may be established, but it will not be the system of traits defined to signalize the type.

Most typologists seem therefore to confuse the issue when, through intuitive selection of a group of traits which give a sense of unity, they compare their procedure with that of the chemist seeking a pure element or compound. The chemist can separate the impurities from the coherent structured molecules of the desired compound, because he knows the difference between necessary and fortuitous connections in his material. He has long sought by quantitative methods those ingredients which are not (by his methods) further analyzable; he underwent the discipline of nearly a century of atomic theory before the complexities of the electrical theory of matter appeared. His pure compound satisfies the definition of type, for every atom in it must bear a dynamic structural relation to other atoms. The whole question is whether the Kretschmer types or any purported system of personality types is predicated upon similar *dynamic interrelations and coherences of traits.*

It is not implied that the coherence or non-coherence of a group of traits is inevitably an all-or-none matter. There may well be *degrees* of coherence between traits. These, however, are discoverable by empirical procedures, both experimental and statistical. In any concrete case one could predict the presence of a trait if he knew the actual form and degree of coherence of the traits in the given case;

the concept of ideal type for which a basis is sought would then define as ideal what has in practice been empirically validated. If the type is to be ideal, it must really be ideal—each trait being bound, not fortuitously but of necessity, to others which characterize the type. At this writing it appears probable that only those traits will be found to be necessarily linked which are expressions of the same dynamic relations (like the blushing and blustering of certain Adlerian types; cf. page 579) or of necessary sequences (like the depression following a manic phase in certain patients). But unless we know in advance what the dynamic relations are, we cannot predict in the individual case whether the blustering *will* accompany the blushing, or whether the depression *will* follow the mania.

Socially Defined Types

Instead of stopping with an emphasis upon the individual organism as a structured whole, we may stress the discontinuities that appear in the social order; we may note the ways in which society produces functional cleavages, even among organisms that are essentially alike. Perhaps we shall find that the external situations of life produce kinds of discontinuity which differ from those we have considered heretofore. Perhaps we shall find that these discontinuities are ultimately reconcilable, or even identical, with those we have seen from the more individualistic approach.

The discussion may begin with consideration of the impact of a way of living upon the individual structure. The skeletal and especially the muscular structure, the characteristic postural set of the body, reflect the accustomed work; the vascular system and the skin are almost as eloquent. The man is his work in a physical as much as in a psychological sense. Although there are some selective factors, of course (weaklings seldom become truck drivers, or the tone-deaf musicians), much of the determination is the growth into and through the work itself.

But the structure of life also determines the structure of percepts, attitudes, and thought. What is not relevant to the life of the type is not seen; we move among other types and miss the tenor of their lives. We may move among them, to use James' phrase, as dogs move in our libraries. What is sensed as a threat is feared and hated for its immediate implications; its other aspects are ignored. The dominant autisms of the group define reality in categorical, unambiguous terms —other nations, other classes are good when they can be held at a frictionless distance; they are evil, base, despicable when they encroach. Wealthy men are a pride and emolument of the nation so far as they make business "good"; but they are parasites when their local plant or chain store endangers existing privileges. Labor unions are good when they introduce order into the business process; they may look like gangs of hoodlums, a menace to the nation, when their strikes threaten profits. A person sees it as he *must* see it; it is as easy and natural for the mouse to approve and accept the cat as for the loser in an economic squeeze-play to approve the winner. Autisms engendered in an individual predicament are quickly shared by those who sail in the same boat; it is in general the shared, the uniformly structured attitudes of the group that imprint themselves upon the personality of the child who is growing into social orientation. (Labor organizers, Chinese laundrymen, Germans, bankers, Irishmen, peddlers, are of necessity perceived and valued in terms of stereotypes.) Evidently, then, one's own class being right and its opponents wrong, social thinking that crosses lines is in danger of being limited to inconsequential details.

In view of the simplicity with which a Marxist conception of personality can be written along such lines, each man's economic situation being brought into relation to his individuality, it is remarkable how little the Marxists have done with it. The perceptions, the acts, the thoughts of men can be ordered as well—and indeed, much better as a rule—with reference to their central life tasks as with reference to other interests.

In their first study of Middletown, the Lynds found that people group themselves around fundamental discontinuous centers of activity which constitute nuclei for the life process. Almost everyone in Middletown worked either chiefly with his hands *or* chiefly with symbols. The two groups stood out in rather sharp psychological differentiation, despite the fact that some of the lower paid members of the "symbol" group were on the same economic level as the higher-paid members of the "manual" group. When Middletown was studied later, in 1935, three fundamental constants or types had developed. The dominant clan, the "X" family, stood off from the common run of the business ("symbol") group, just as the latter did from the "manual" group. Other observers have made similar findings. Thus subcultural types, such as the French Canadians of the New England mill town, are sharply separated from the "Anglo-Saxons" on the one hand and the "Portuguese" on the other. Barriers of feeling are such that typing is extremely sharp. Personality studies of school-age children of subcultural groups indicate that the preservation of these socially indoctrinated types is intimately related to the psychology of the self. The individual is identified with the group and accepts its structured pattern of values; hence the type of self-portrait is largely defined by the subcultural system of values.

Much the same thing may occur in vocational grouping. William James stressed the fact that the fluidities characteristic of early adulthood tend to be replaced by hard crystallizations within the first decade of professional life. The specific tasks and values of each professional group, as of each subcultural group, become progressively more rigid. These comments evidently apply to everyone during the first decade of maturity, but much more sharply in the case of the more highly specialized roles which life assigns. To say that professional habits merely overlie a fundamentally stable personality core is an altogether abstract statement whose meaning is doubtful, for professional habits invade the very self and help to form the basis of the inner self-attitude as well as the outer status. All minds are molded to their task. *If the tasks are discontinuous, the minds will be discontinuous*, not only in specific aspects which define distinct areas of life, but in total organization.

On the other hand, there are many people who do not identify with their own economic group. For example, the following personality types among the privileged group identify themselves not with their own group, but with the less privileged: (1) Rebellious members of the dominant group, who protest against the shackles of nobility. Such people are often sturdy defenders of less favored classes and are found among the leaders in evolutionary and revolutionary change. Since their motive is rebelliousness rather than gain, these elite rebels are not easily "bought off" by bribes. (2) The softhearted members of the privileged class, who for reasons of sympathy identify with the oppressed and endeavor to share their burdens. These people have been historically, and are at present, dependable instruments of social change. They do not sell out any more than do the elite rebels. (3) The power-hungry, self-appointed leaders of the under-privileged, who identify with the masses neither because of rebelliousness nor because of sympathy, but for the sake of leading. In nearly every country, such men have shuttled back and forth between political parties as the occasion for power dictated. They *do* sell out, for either pelf or power. Such exceptions to broad economic determinism are extremely important. A large proportion of both the evolutionary and the revolutionary leaders have arisen from groups saturated with an atmosphere impregnated with vested interest, yet have played an individualistic role.

But despite all this, the main lines of class membership are fairly clear. The fact of owning factories or railways vs. the fact of working in them for a wage is too potent to be glossed over. Whether people like it or not, they fall into economic categories. Our real question deals not with the existence of classes but with the discontinuity between them—the psychological cleavage. If we look at the distribution curve of income or examine the more analytical studies of the ways in which people group themselves consciously or unconsciously according to class, our first impression will be in terms of continuity, our more thoughtful conclusion in terms of discontinuity. We shall consider other aspects of class membership in Chapters 33-36. Do we not, then, emerge with types—discontinuities—as sharp and clear as one could ask? We do indeed. Mixed with these discontinuities, however, are the impurities and complications already described. There is some necessary typing that is useful as far as it goes; but it is combined with a number of less central and, to some extent, independent secondary traits which are linked in greater or less degree with the central factors.

The nature of the cleavage between types becomes clear when a person tries to abandon one and assimilate himself in another. A culturally ingrained mode of behaving, and of thinking and feeling about the self and the environment, offers a stable form of organization; but try to adapt the individual to a second culture, and there may be resistance, or an exaggerated effort to give up the old in adapting to the new. Leaving one base, a person is really at ease only when he reaches a completely different base. The laborer "elevated" to the middle class by a legacy must move all the way up, and all of him must move up, before the tensions can disappear. Thus the cultural point of view permits the use of a genuine typology, because of the principle of stable equilibrium; a thing disturbed returns to its base or finds a new base. Gaps between two stable equilibria are found in personality just as they are in the ring systems of atoms; and cultural diversity offers extremely interesting examples. There is often discontinuity between social situations, which, when acting upon more or less similar individuals, necessarily produces sharp typological cleavages. Whenever there are fluid and unstable mechanisms in the individual and he is subjected to two contrary pressures, crystallization and stabilization may occur in either of two directions, depending on inner tendencies; hence if sharp discontinuity appears in the outer world, those subjected to such pressures must display an equally sharp discontinuity. A child caught between two group pressures (parents of different religions, or parents in conflict with the neighborhood) must reach equilibrium in one or another of a variety of discontinuous ways; compromise and fusion usually fail.

A fuller account of the influence of cultural diversity upon personality formation will be attempted in later chapters. At the present point, however, where our interest concerns the general question of types, it seems likely that broad social and cultural factors can be identified as the most important sources of discontinuities in personality. We may summarize our survey of the three chief classes of typology by saying that biotypes (as in some somatic differences) have definite but as a rule limited utility; that clinical types, especially those arising from discontinuities in attitudes toward the self, are of considerable importance, though their validation is still sketchy; and that socio-economic and cultural types give great promise of wide usefulness.

But if this is the conclusion to which we are driven by the sheer weight of evidence and logic, how does it happen that in the arts —literature, portrait-painting, sculpture—typing is common and very effective? The contradiction proves to be more apparent than real. Some typing of personalities has always been found necessary, not because one thing is true in theory and another in practice, but because some of the folds of the garment of life activity have fallen into creases so plain that none can overlook them. No one in the novel or the drama would understand a fine-spun negation of human typology. On the other hand, the dramatist, the painter, the sculptor, the novelist, and the clinical psychologist have found that the core which is defined by the social type is not all there is in the person. The core itself has individual attributes as well as type attributes, so that there is some merit in first using, then dropping, the typology concept as we look at the aspects of individuality which complicate and at the same time give membership character to the type aspects. And as we move out from the core and deal with matters less sharply defined by social roles, we find more and more that must be looked at without reference to types.

We do not imply that a social role is always the core of individuality. It is not uncommon to find a lawyer who cares more about his personal friendships or his country estate than he does about his law practice, or a barber who is far more identified with his musical nephews and nieces than with his status or the tips which mark his own daily round. The core varies in relative size; at times it is a comparatively small part of the total; sometimes it lies outside the professional field. Although typing is valid, many characteristics are always to be found which do not integrate closely with the type;

some of them call for a Gestalt treatment of their own, some are loose and peripheral and lend themselves to no clear interpretation from the point of view of organization. It is permissible to refer to a conglomeration containing type structure and some peripheral items, and these may be true "mixed types," where there are, so to speak, two cores.

The bimodality and multimodality which we have described above (page 735) take on clear meaning in the light of such considerations. Rarely will the constant which marks the different modes be irrelevant to the rest of the personality. Rarely indeed is bimodality or multimodality based on a single peripheral trait. As a rule, multimodality springs from some fundamental aspect of individuality, tightly integrated with much else that is important in the person, so that when we have defined a multimodality with respect to a measured trait we have defined it with respect to Gestalt organization. Multimodality is a direct expression of the social types just described. This is the case in the Minnesota study (page 887), in Hanks' study (page 886), and in Razran's types described on page 200. The discontinuities which are implied are in the first instance discontinuities in ways of viewing the self and are therefore related to the entire personality organization; *but such self-viewing may be engendered by socially discontinuous life situations based on culture, vocation, etc.* These studies have dealt for the most part with young people not yet professionally crystallized; nevertheless, these people—indeed, everyone above the age of infancy—have developed organization. *Consequently the primary factor in human typing is attitude toward self; and the reason why the professional or other social types stand out so clearly is that this attitude follows lines determined in large measure by the tasks and the status assigned to different social roles.* It is true that there may be discontinuity between the self today and the self tomorrow, and therefore between the personality organization as a whole from one occasion to another; but habit generally becomes so crystallized and the external task so clear that the ego structure, once fully attained, permits no temporal break (cf. page 722). The discontinuities existing at a given time in relation to a community are for the most part discontinuities which extend longitudinally through life.

We have urged that ego types and social-role types are real and important; however, we should add that they also play a huge part in the development of pseudo-types or stereotypes, and hence inevitably lead to a wide variety of important artifacts. To hold a given view of the self, whether it is a sound or an unsound view, leads to a particular behavior of enhancement and defense. To believe that others regard us in a particular light requires that we live up to expectations, partly through suggestion, partly through identification with others, but most of all through the fact that status and order require this conformity. Moreover, judging others in a specific way and placing them in a specific category call forth from them behavior which fits logically with our own behavior in the interpersonal context. They surprise and disturb us if they do not behave as we expect, and we find a dozen ways of hounding them until they play their part. The "happy-go-lucky" pattern of the Negro, the "close" behavior of the Scot, have their clear-cut determining factors in remote history; but these patterns are meted out to the Negro and the Scot today in terms of a social constellation which makes their acceptance by society dependent upon their behaving as expected. Types underlie stereotypes, and stereotypes reinforce existing types; when the latter are grossly wide of the mark they build up antithetical types which at times overthrow the types originally present. A profound effect is exerted upon the self by the type to which the individual is assigned; and regardless of sense or justice, the type often becomes less and less of an artifact and more and more of a reality as behavior is forced to conform to it.

The final question we must consider concerns the way in which the concept of the *threshold*, so important in determining all-or-none reactions of single traits, is to be applied to a concept as complex as a type. How does an infinitesimal difference in situations determine the difference between one and another typological organization? The answer seems to be twofold, depending upon the sort of type involved. If the figure-ground relations of personality are extremely clear cut and the figure is highly potent in comparison with every aspect of the ground, the threshold that determines which type will appear is the one that relates to the figure aspect. Let a tiny variation in situation bring the individual from below the threshold to above the threshold with respect to the response that constitutes figure, the type is determined and the whole syndrome of related ground aspects is swung along with the figure to achieve the full pattern. Let the situation fail to elicit this figure, and another figure, with all its associated ground factors, will prevail. Thus under sufficient challenge a man may be a hero; with a little less challenge he may be a mere playboy (war often produces this picture). An infinitesimal inflection may suggest that a remark is made not in fun but is intended to hurt, and the entire syndrome of attitude swings from elated to depressed; if the wound is deep enough, the stable and happy personality becomes traumatized.

If, however, the figure-ground organization is on a more equalitarian basis, so that no one component is very prominent and figure-ground relations consequently are not clear, we shall have to regard the threshold not as a threshold for the figure as such, but as a threshold for the maintenance of the syndrome as a syndrome. The syndrome hangs together if a stimulus is intense enough; not if intensity is slightly less. The two ways of regarding the threshold suggested here may ultimately of course be reconciled, as they are in comparable physical situations; but at the present level of personality analysis it is convenient to distinguish them. We may say, therefore, in conclusion, that what determines an all-or-none shift, or personality readjustment, may be either an alteration in the threshold for a specific prominent ingredient, or an alteration in the threshold for the synergic or integrative tendency as a whole.

Part Six

INDIVIDUAL AND GROUP

32. Group Membership

YOU can tell a Texan by his walk, a Vermonter by his drawl. You can watch the little Texan, the little Vermonter, and see them take on the walk or the drawl. Membership in a social group involves this shaping of personality.

The whole confused "psychology of nations" starts from such facts. As one takes the short, choppy trip from Dover to Calais, he moves almost from one world to another, from stolid, casual, pipe-smoking British tars and longshoremen to the animated and confused bustle of excitable, irritable, nervously intent French sailors, baggagemen, and porters. The life of the whole city of Dover and of the whole city of Calais accentuates the contrast. How can people in our western culture be so different? But one of these, you say, is British, the other is French. It is the nature of the British and Gallic character to be stolid and gay respectively, to be casual and excitable. True enough, if by referring to nature we mean only to describe, not to interpret. The populations of southern England and of northern France are both rather good mixtures of all the elements which make up the white stock, with Nordic, Alpine, and Mediterranean thoroughly scrambled in rather similar proportions, and with some residues of the old Iberian and Mongol stock, some odd remains from the Near and even the Far East complicating the already hopelessly confused picture. The student of culture has a right to make his case for *culturally defined* personality types when heterogeneous stock, subdivided by some barrier (here the English Channel), has been acted upon by equally striking cultural contrasts. The comparison of the people of southern England and the people of northern France fully satisfies the requirement.

We turn in the next few chapters to a study of the meaning of such group membership for human individuality, drawing our data from ethnological and historical studies of widely contrasting human groups. This will mean a primary concern, in these chapters, with cultural problems. But before wrestling with the specific issues which cultural studies present, we shall glance for a moment at the nature of social interaction itself, the problem of social participation and group membership, for this is necessary before the larger problem of personality in relation to culture can be defined.

Primitive Social Responses

Among animals, from the protozoa through to the primates, we find sensitization of individuals to one another, a special preference given to such stimulus objects as the forms, the activities, the sounds emitted by other living individuals, especially those of one's own group. As the sound-receiving apparatus of the locust is sensitized to sounds which locusts make, rather than to those which are made by mankind, so each species has receptor and effector mechanisms that are more or less selectively attuned to the social situations presented by the presence of others. The vital organs and the unstriped and skeletal musculature may respond to either social or non-social stimulation; but here too, the responses are likely to be more massive and to have more significant organic results when the stimulus situation is social. Fear and rage can be aroused by impersonal stimuli, but in animal societies warnings and signs of positive or negative feeling are typically used as signals from one to another member of the group.

As to the relative strength of the social and individualistic impulses in man, we can only point out that the primates, including the anthropoid apes, are typically social, certain gorilla groups marking the only clear exception, and that without any exception all men known either to ethnology or to prehistory have not only participated in but habitually lived in groups. The size of the group and its form are of course determined partly by the problem of self-maintenance. The time is past, however, when it could cogently be argued in the manner of Hobbes that a solitary creature bartered away his freedom solely for the protection of the group against marauders.

At the same time, certain uniformities of behavior appear because of structural and functional similarities between members of a group. Likeness is therefore produced in the behavior patterns; and where there is likeness there is both a tendency to a common response and a tendency to create the same environmental world. Each individual serves to create in some measure the world in which others may live. Certain generic human traits—the capacity to be aroused, the capacity to learn, the capacity to be stimulated by others, as well as all the specific mechanisms of human nature described in the first seven chapters—predispose toward cultural living when once the attitude of adults to children is such that they readily transmit to them the skills they have learned. And children are deeply predisposed through affection, interests, dependence, to learn what parents have to teach. Furthermore, much is learned avidly without formal teaching. It is therefore not true that social participation is imposed upon or used as a mold for human personality. For the nature of human existence has slanted man's response in the social direction; man is deeply ready for society. The little child is called into activity by the sheer presence of others; and the activity, when aroused, tends to take a social direction by virtue of the ordinary mechanisms of social facilitation, by virtue of a selective awareness of this or that activity prominently carried out by the parents, and later, when self-evaluation has become clearcut, by virtue of competition for status within the group and between groups. Moreover, he shows affective spread of response, coming to love more widely and to hate more widely than his first family patterns require; he is canalized and familiarized, and he develops in the group that elementary social response, that primitive sympathy, to which we referred on page 221.

Most important, perhaps, in the early formulation of his sense of his own membership character, is the figure-ground relation which develops between in-group and out-group, the consequent affective anchorage on the activities of parents, and on the parents as values. This cannot, however, be separated from the process of self-realization; for as Cooley and G. H. Mead have well taught us, it is only by constant reciprocity between perception of others and perception of self that individuality can come clearly into existence.

Self-realization is not in opposition to, it is a positive phase of socialization.

In the same way membership in any or all social groups, small or large, involves some balance between defensive and competitive tendencies on the one hand, and tendencies toward participation or even self-immolation on the other. The positive impulse to crowd membership is merely a dramatic manifestation of this impulse to sociality. The group suggestibility so much lamented by writers about mobs involves a positive need of one's fellows. And though it is a full realization of a deep social dependence, it is always mixed in some degree with the countervailing need of the leader, and likewise of the follower, to maintain their individuality. The normal figure in the figure-ground perception of the social group in which one participates is oneself; it is *one's own* group, not just "*a* group of people." If the mob is pathological, it may be because the self has ceased to be the figure.

Indeed, a cardinal concept for the approach to personality through culture is the notion that the individual perceives himself as figure in the figure-ground pattern that is each social group, and that personality develops organically with this perception of the entire figure-ground system. It is for this reason that family membership, specifically in terms of age and sex roles, constitutes the first factor to be emphasized in the shaping of individuality. It likewise follows from this that the structuring of the earliest attitudes—attitudes toward parents, brothers, sisters, and so on—comes to the child in field-structured terms. The complex linkage or interlocking of attitudes which Newcomb has described in young adults (page 892) is no mere late expression of a learning process that appears during adolescence. It is rather a late and complex form of a field-structuring process which has been occurring from the time of birth. The transfer of canalized and conditioned responses and the slow development of verbal symbols to integrate and mediate between them have brought into more articulate form a structuring or even a fusion of dispositions which are there as soon as is the capacity for responding to objects not physically present.

In the same way, social discovery and the capacity for group thinking develop within the contexts of the face-to-face group, usually the family, as big sister tries to thread a needle, or father to hang a picture. The suggestions, the sharing of experience in relation to a new problem, make *individuality* more definite at the same time that one becomes aware of *non-membership*, as we see in Benedict's studies of the deviant (page 812); but even the deviant has his own world, his own deviant group, in which membership is experienced. Most individuals have a wide variety of membership roles.

The Gestalt psychologists have taught us that every aspect of experience reflects the context in which it appears; every color, feeling, or act expresses its place in a system, its "membership character." Just as each aspect of an individual life reflects its context, so each person's role in society reflects the system of group relations. It is, therefore, more than just a play on words when we refer to membership character in the social group. For certain purposes the biologist may treat the cell as if it were a self-contained unit; for certain purposes the physician may consider a single organ, like the stomach, as if it were a self-contained unit; and for certain purposes (cf. page 7) a personality may be treated as if it were a self-contained unit. But for the most vital purposes a cell must be understood as an aspect of the life of an organ and the organ as an aspect of the life of a man. In the same way personality must be understood as an aspect of a social process; it cannot, in most cases, be considered as a self-contained unit. Individually we balk at this fact, for it is very deflating; nevertheless, we are reflections of a broad social process. We should have neither our biological nor our social individuality but for specific cultural processes that have mingled our ancestral strains and our social norms in highly specific ways. Exactly as the Gestalt psychologist shows in the study of perception that the value of a color or a tone depends upon its context, so the individual personality can be understood only if the membership character which it sustains in society at large is made clear. Personalities are not independent building stones of society; they are interdependent. Their interaction makes the social world, and the social world acting on the young makes new personalities.

This does not mean that personalities are the sole components in the development of a form of group life, a culture. On the contrary, there are many events in nature, such as climate, weather, the fertility of the soil, the availability of domesticable animals and of systems of water transport, which act along with personality factors in making the pattern of life what it is. Non-human forces define in large part the nature of the social unit. As the social unit takes shape, the personality of each child introduced into it reflects both these non-human forces and the organized human forces of the group. The group ways are taken over by the child as he perceives the quality and pattern of living, so that he actually becomes an aspect of a social context which is prepared in large measure before he appears on the scene. His personality expresses not only the more obvious personal qualities derived from face-to-face contacts, such as the warmth or rejection of his parents, but the whole mode of social living that characterizes the group. From this point of view, the Gestalt psychology, with its traditional emphasis on the relative self-containedness of individual personality organization, is far from offering a complete full-bodied conception of what personality is. Indeed, as we confront the larger patterns of living, we shall be forced to ask many questions which are in a sense broader and deeper than purely psychological questions; they concern the social matrix from which psychological questions as such arise.

In considering the dependence of the individual upon society, a trap lies ready for us. We have inherited from John Locke and his school the concept that man is molded by society. The word "molded" is ambiguous. Locke's followers, even until Darwin's time, thought of man as being like wax, shaped from the outside by forces alien to his nature. Just as Locke regarded the newborn child as "white paper" written on by experience, so some people, even today, think of him as passively molded and making no response to the process of molding. Darwin, and more particularly Freud, have shown how far from correct this idea is. For the individual reaches out, makes demands; he can love terrifically, fear terrifically, and therefore hate terrifically. With a view to the deep biology of the individual, we have begun to grasp the fact that society does not impose its norms upon individual existence. Man is not passive in relation to these pressures; he reaches out, accepts, rejects, compromises, integrates. So imperious are the individual demands that the organism is injured or stunted if they cannot be met; this holds as much for the purely social demands as for the demand for oxygen, water, or food. Ribble and others suggest the organic damage that mothers can do to children because of inadequate mothering—insufficient cuddling, hugging, caressing. The processes underlying cellular health and growth are affected by softness and warmth, rhythm and activity, emotional release and the sense of security. Much stunting, psychological and physiological, occurs as a result of the cold (misnamed scientific) handling of a child.

The child, then, is not a mass of protoplasm thrown into the midst of society to become the recipient of certain specific cultural molding processes, but rather an organic aspect of an interpersonal pattern of impulsive, demanding existence. From the moment of conception the individual has needs and he has ways of fulfilling them; the child is social to some degree even before he is born. The world of persons is as important as the world of food and drink; and within a few months of birth it is only the very hungry, cold or sick child who is more interested in his physical state than in the people around him. We can make no use, then, of the convenient suggestion that there are *biological* needs and *social* needs; for the social proves to be just as biological a reality as is anything in the world. Society is sustained by biological forces such as the child-mother relationship, and these fundamental biological forces must be understood in any study of personality

A second difficulty with the idea of "taking over the culture" lies in the constitutional differences, visible even at the time of birth, in the way in which the individual responds to any specific aspect of the culture. The child's biological individuality makes it easy for him to take hold here rather than there, or now rather than then. As we have many times emphasized, the individuality of the child cuts across any general stereotype of the learning process. We may combine these two difficulties by saying that individuals differ in the way in which the culture is mediated to them and in the way in which they go to meet the culture. These problems are especially acute in a culture as heterogeneous as ours. We all take over American culture. One of us takes it over with five generations of aristocracy behind him, with a silver spoon in his mouth. Another is born the son of a sharecropper who does not speak "standard English," gets little schooling, and has never seen or heard of motion pictures. Do they both take over American culture? The world is presented to each through membership in his group. If ever he strives to enlarge his world, he finds both obvious and subtle factors holding him back. He must discover with which groups he has status, who will accept him, at the same time that he learns the tasks that he may—or must— do. Linton has given us clear accounts of the roles assigned by a number of primitive peoples in terms of the individual's membership in age and sex groupings, but the pictures of the cultural roles in which most Americans live are still very meager (cf. Chapter 36).

The study of roles is a very literal application of Gestalt psychology. Roles make up a social configuration, and each person who enacts them must make adjustments between his various roles, integrate them in terms of a figure-ground pattern with a high degree of organization. One task stands out for him as figure, and every other task seems subsidiary. Perhaps we shall find that for most people most of the time the self-maintenance role, the getting-a-living role, is the figure. For example, here is a New England village, in which the railroad tracks constitute the fundamental gap for the cleavage of society. The people who live on one side have "Anglo-Saxon names" and are predominantly Republicans, Protestants, and commuters to Boston. The people who live on the other side of the tracks are Irish, Democrats, Roman Catholics, and do not commute to Boston. The roles tend to integrate in the sense that the attitudes befitting a commuter, a Protestant, and a Republican are congruent; in case of doubt, the commuter attitude (self-maintenance attitude) is the anchorage point.

As is so characteristic of things touching closely upon the self, there are almost none of these people whose status is "in between" or uncertain. They all share a common school system; but one stays, as adolescent or adult, on his own side of the tracks. Think of the plight of the boy, who has an Anglo-Saxon, Republican, Protestant background and a grandfather who commutes to Boston, and finds himself interested in a girl from the other side of the tracks. What can he do? Integrate Roman Catholicism with the prevailing commuter attitudes? This is well-nigh impossible. The usual solutions are to marry the girl and repudiate the earlier affiliation, or to give her up for the sake of supposed loyalty to the primary pattern. Which he will take will depend chiefly on the dominance relations of the values (cf. page 281).

Our whole way of looking at these matters has changed greatly in the past ten or fifteen years. In the midst of a social science discussion in the early '30's regarding the nature of *acculturation*, the process by which an individual reared in one culture adapts himself to another, the question arose as to how he assimilates his *first* culture, and it was hoped that this might be clarified before the process of assimilating the second culture was studied. The answer of most of the anthropologists encountered by the writer was that the first culture was "taken over" from the family. But that answer, made over a decade ago, seems today to have been a remarkably naïve and easy solution to the problem. Today it is no longer so easy to reply to that question; at close range the problem of what is "taken over," and how, has proved to be very complex. Different individuals take over different cultures in different ways; a person reacts not to the culture at large, but only to specific aspects by virtue of specific individual dynamic processes. When our attention turns to aspects of the culture that can be directly studied, we find that one child is chiefly dependent on the father; another depends largely on the mother; others learn chiefly from older sisters and brothers; others from uncles and aunts, neighbors, or teacher. Some children find no adequate mediator of the culture and consequently turn to "impersonal" means—the comics or the movies. And in every case we find that the child acquires not only the obvious specific *content*—ideas, norms, skills, etc.—of the culture, but a way of feeling about the relations between persons. The process of acquiring the culture, a process freighted with warmth or anxiety or struggle, profoundly colors the receiving personality.

But though the nature of human personality is to some degree defined by the very fact of social participation, even before any specific human culture has been described, most of the meaning and richness of the social approach can be grasped only when attention has been given to a comparison of various primitive and advanced societies, in order to see the personality pattern characteristic of each set of social arrangements, and, within each such *generic* pattern, the way in which the *individual* copes with the generic problems which the culture defines, the way in which he learns to make use of, adapt to, and bend to his own uses the cultural situation and the roles he is called upon to enact. This will take us into the study of ethnology as we seek an answer to the question: By what specific means can the social group shape the personality of the growing individual?

33. Economic Determinism

IN STUDYING the way in which the raw material of human nature undergoes socialization, we have to begin at some one definite point. There may be a value in looking first at the most obvious feature of a society, namely, its economic base; and we may proceed to define two hypotheses: (1) that the economic problem confronting a society shapes all the phases of its group life, and (2) that individual personality is shaped by this group life. This would give us a simple economic determinism for personality. These hypotheses, we shall find, will need much modification; we begin with them for the sake of their simplicity. But it must be made clear that there is no attempt to define the *origins* of any cultural pattern, or to find, in the course of ceaseless social interaction, something that "comes first" and is uncaused. Rather, the question is whether a radical alteration in economic activities does clearly lead to radical alterations in other aspects of society, and whether, as a result of this, personality is transformed—whether directly, as through new kinds of work, or indirectly, as through alteration of the mother-child relationships. It is emphasized that while we gratefully use, in the next few chapters, a number of studies of primitive peoples, no ethnologist is to be held accountable for the interpretations offered here.

To study the adequacy of these hypotheses and to see where they lead, we shall use a very simple example from Linton. The Tanala and Betsileo of Madagascar speak a common tongue and have much in common. However, there is one striking contrast: their methods of rice cultivation. They once used the same system, but a shift took place in the agricultural arts of the Betsileo, making it possible to proceed from dry-rice to wet-rice cultivation. When this occurred, the individual planter and his family, and the larger clan and chieftainship organization, changed with the new technique. The way in which rice

[773]

is cultivated makes a difference in land tenure, in man's relation to the community, and in the community's relation to the central authority. In the one case, dry-rice cultivation, there is a cooperative society, with a sense of participation in a common enterprise; in the other, wet-rice cultivation, the society is competitive, with one man constantly pressing upon the life of another. In time, democracy yields to a caste system.

These peoples of Madagascar seem to substantiate our first hypothesis. So far as these data go, they suggest that through a change in agricultural technique life has been radically altered. This does not imply that the means of self-maintenance changed automatically, of their own accord; individual attitudes and family and village decisions must have led the way. One individual, or a family, may have leaped in with an eye to the main chance—an individual or family different from the rest, a little less cooperative in feeling, a little more concerned with status. But in general the new method of rice cultivation was adopted because it was economically advantageous, and changing means of self-maintenance drew other institutions in its wake. This is all that the hypotheses require.

One example is only a starter, however; we must proceed to a more cautious analysis of what is involved. In the Madagascar group we saw that the *economic situation* itself—the availability of an area for wet-rice cultivation—seemed to offer an explanation for new *economic institutions;* institutions responded to physical realities. We must examine a broader collection of data to see whether this simple causal relation can be confirmed; we must at the same time consider whether other institutional patterns must perforce yield to the one-way action of economic behavior; and finally, we must determine whether personality can be viewed as the end result of such a causal sequence.

Let us get our terminology clear, and make the distinctions which are imperative if an analysis is to be carried through. By "economic determinism" we mean any system of thought in which the main outlines of social life are derived from the economic organization of the group. A prominent but by no means the only version of the thesis is the conception of Marx and Engels that social life is a reflection of the way in which the dominant social group, at a given stage in the productive arts, maintains its economic status; social change, for example, is forced upon the entire social group as a result of technological changes and inventions which enhance or challenge the power of the ruling class. It is generally conceded, as Marx maintained, that a changing economic pattern causes changes in other aspects of the life pattern; science, the fine arts, philosophy, and religion are transformed as a result of a change in the productive arts. At the same time it is important to emphasize, as did Marx and Engels, that these other "derived" institutions have their own effect upon the productive arts. There is constant interaction (suggested by the Hegelian concept of dialectic), the economic forces being primary but being constantly modified by the influence of the derived institutions.

This defines roughly in what sense economic determinism is valuable as an avenue of approach to personality. Three points must be stressed:

1. The economic situation can limit the possibilities of personality growth in particular directions. If life is a constant struggle against cold and scarcity of food, as it is for the Central Eskimo, the situation is unfavorable for the rise of the philosophies and sciences of a leisure class, or a theology based upon the concept of universal goodness, the "cup runneth over" idea of life. In relation to the subsistence problem which the Eskimo faces, these concepts would be functionally meaningless. Similarly, there can only be certain kinds of personalities when there are such economic limitations.

2. We may go beyond this purely negative statement and say that the economic situation will indicate the likely directions in which the various social patterns will evolve. When, for example, we consider that the Indians of the western part of the Great Plains, such as the Dakota and Sioux, were a buffalo-hunting people, and that during the short period of his adult life the male had great prestige as a buffalo hunter and warrior against other buffalo-hunters, we see why the old man and the boy, the woman and the girl are secondary, why there

is a forced habit of honoring the qualities which only a few of the people can have. We therefore expect to find an aristocratic society based upon the appropriate hunting and war-making arts. Since surplus wealth is possible, there can be a genuine leisure-class philosophy, as witness the beautiful and intricate philosophy and theology developed by the Dakotas.

3. In defining the role of the economic arts, we shall use a principle well described by Margaret Mead: the same geographic problems may take entirely different forms by virtue of different social attitudes, different ways of "phrasing the situation." Suppose, for example, that great schools of fish appear offshore. Among some primitive peoples the right procedure, if a person sees a school of fish, is to run quietly home and tell his closest relatives, who promply make a big catch. Among other tribes with the same food problem, anyone who notices a school of fish noises the fact abroad like a town crier, and the whole community go out with their nets; the fish are corporately caught and corporately devoured. In the first group we are dealing with competitive personalities, and in the second with cooperative personalities; in each generation such personalities result from the pattern of life in childhood. If, then, we look closely at economic determinism, we find that it is not a question of the economic *situation*, but a question of the economic *behavior* of the group. Economic behavior does not result solely from the economic situation, but from a complex which includes non-economic factors. It would consequently be meaningless to say that the economic *situation* alone determines the personality pattern; the economic situation is one of several factors that shape the personalities who express and are expressed in the culture. But we must be clear as to what these other factors are; we shall pursue them through several chapters.

With the above qualifications, we find, then, much value in the concept of economic determinism. But by this phrase is meant determinism not through the economic situation, but through the economic institutions—the social inventions shared by the group in dealing with an economic situation. The economic situation—including climate, soil, forests, fish, game, etc.—constitutes a vital stimulus but does not forecast the response. Social change does not follow directly from changes in the food supply or from disaster or war; it follows from the way in which such a crisis articulates with the prevailing pattern of needs and attitudes.

We may ask how economic institutions originate if they do not derive directly from the economic situation. Their origin is legion. In addition to the economic situation there are many *biological, cultural,* and *personal* factors. An example of a *biological* factor is the fact that a physically diminutive people who can live on a very limited caloric intake (such as African pygmies) will not develop quite the same institutions as a people large in stature who need half again as much food; another biological example is the fact that a people with a long life span will have proportions of old and young differing from those of a people with a shorter span. An example of a *cultural* factor operating to define the role of the economic situation is the fact that when groups with different traditions are brought into a common area and faced with common problems, they understand their economic predicament in the light of their own traditions. Malinowski has emphasized that, under such conditions, there will be a deep unconscious residue of attitude from an earlier period. The *personal* factor is seen in the fact that, within each group, biological variability and the varying impress of different institutions will have yielded differences in personality, and these will lead to various individual ways of coping with each economic problem.

Though we cannot begin with the economic situation and proceed, as through a funnel, to a final description of personality, we shall often have to give the economic situation the place of *figure* in the figure-ground pattern of all situations; it will tend to become the anchorage point in a world of problems. In the same way, economic institutions will often be the *figure* as we confront institutional life as a whole. In consequence, so far as personality is anchored upon a response to social institutions, it will tend to be anchored upon attitudes related to economic goals—goals reached through economic behavior.

The Affective Pull of the Mores

The concept of economic institutions developed so far is cold and impersonal; to be fruitful for the study of persons, there is need to consider the warmth, the vitality, the personal meaning of institutions. A great deal of help to this end is offered by the way of thinking which has come to us from Sumner and Keller. We shall make full use of their suggestions, but shall feel free to offer some modifications.

The life of society is expressed through a group of interrelated social institutions. The institutions have a psychological basis, but it is not enough to say that society has habits. Habit is a convenience, but it has no *necessary* continuity; it can be made or broken. Institutions are a convenience to those who use them. But most social institutions take on a moral hue; one lives by and swears by them. It is right to spend less than one earns, wrong to dress solely with reference to keeping warm. If one has a fancy for idols it is correct to exploit them as works of art, and wrong to prostrate oneself before them. To maintain one's place in society one must do certain things and love to do them; one must not do other things, which are prohibited, and must not want to do them. The *mores*, the affectively toned rules of social living, have become axiomatic among all who pretend to share fully in the life of the group. It is characteristic of social institutions in their moral form (their form as mores) that they cannot be frontally attacked or directly questioned. They are right; that is all there is to it. The rightness of the mores, according to Sumner and Keller, springs from the fact that the prosperity of the group is conceived to depend upon observing them.

Our emphasis here will be upon the interrelations between four fundamental groups of mores. The first are.the *self-maintenance* mores, the mores that sustain and preserve the group and enable it to carry on in the face of obstacles. The term comprises a much broader field than is covered by the word "economic." It includes not only hunting, fishing, mining, forestry, agriculture, manufacturing, and transportation, but also science and the art of war; for these are a primary means of enabling the group to survive against obstacles. The self-maintenance mores likewise constitute a "prosperity policy"; they represent the core of the customs that act as bulwarks against danger. Things like stealing, forgery, and ideological attack upon the group's way of living are therefore all in the same general category, and are responded to affectively in similar fashion. The introduction of new ways of earning a living involves grave moral questions because the prevailing ways are morally right.

The *self-perpetuation* mores comprise courtship, marriage, family, sex relations generally, and the early training of children. These mores, like all the others, have to do with society as a whole, not simply with the biological aspects of self-perpetuation. The self-perpetuation mores take care of the capacity of the social group to perpetuate itself as a social group, not simply as a biological stock; therefore courtship can be morally right or wrong, and the early rearing of children can be right or wrong. The problem of society is whether the early rearing of children does provide continuity in the mores. If it does not, it is immoral. The educator who wishes to give the individual child "freedom" may easily scandalize the group. The self-perpetuation mores, however, agree with our hypothesis about a certain type of "economic determinism," for they tend to change as self-maintenance changes; they must fit with the "prosperity policy." The status of women and the pattern of the family must conform to definite economic meanings.

The *self-gratification mores* have to do with the deriving of satisfaction from all the surpluses of energy and time. This may seem casual and unorganized, but it is not. The use of fire to cook food not only saved energy in digestion; it introduced culinary amenities, substituted postprandial reflection for stupor. In the caves of Spain and France, men painted not only for ulterior purposes but for their own gratification; the stone ornaments and monoliths of Switzerland and Brittany lead us to infer that the people were interested in order and beauty, as well as in utility. The arts and sciences have always been intellectual and emotional satisfiers. But these, too, have their moral value; it would be a grave error to infer that in his leisure time a person may develop the arts and sciences as freely as he wishes. Many a creative artist has been denounced because he used his freedom to rhyme, paint, or compose solely in accordance with a creative impulse that was contrary to the mores of society. It is not only that the arts must not challenge the mores; if the impulse takes a strange form, it is perverse. But the dependence of the arts on the self-maintenance mores is direct and obvious; they use the techniques and the subject matter provided by the economic arts, the ways of the dominant military, religious, or political group, and they must gratify first of all those who sit in high places. The arts have always reflected the way in which society maintains itself. Modern art, for example, moves in the functional direction, rejoicing in its close articulation with the general self-maintenance pattern; in particular, the characteristically modern forms of architecture, interior decorating, and photography take delight in our modern technological culture.

Finally, there are the *self-regulation mores,* for even the rather rigid system of mores based on self-maintenance does not provide complete safety. It has always been necessary to have men-at-arms, policemen, laws, penalties. There is always a system of coercion, and this system naturally expresses what supports it.

Some of the mores do not fit easily into this fourfold scheme. Religion, for example, falls into several categories: it has much to do with marriage and the family, with the arts, and with the self-regulation mores. And of course some of us may prefer to group social institutions in terms of six areas of life, as do the Lynds, or nine, as does Wissler. All these "areas" or "categories" of activity involve abstraction from the flowing interdependence of behavior, and it must be granted that many acts supported by strong moral feelings —like maintaining personal honor—are not objectively classifiable. But the rough crude generalization remains: the mores prescribing how life is *maintained* affect the form of the other mores.

But since the mores are affectively laden, and since we know that perception and thought are anchored in terms of the fundamental values (Chapters 14–16), it may be reasonable to suspect that the *figure* in the figure-ground pattern of life will tend to consist of the self-maintenance mores of the group. Our task is to demonstrate that ultimately the *individual personality* is in a broad way guided and controlled by these mores. Obviously, the only possible validation lies in the study of simple and straightforward examples (Chapters 34–36). First, however, by way of clarifying the hypothesis, let us take a composite example, ridiculously abstract like a composite photograph; we shall use a hypothetical tribe of primitive woodsmen which from time immemorial has used a stone axhead for chopping down trees. Men need wood for barricades, stockades, agricultural instruments, household tools; they sell timber to their neighbors. This group constitutes a relatively simple patriarchal society, for it takes a boy many years to acquire enough of the axman's prowess to achieve power and status in competition with the older males, and women cannot compete at all. We find polygamy, a polytheistic religion, a crude art form—in general, a very primitive society whose life is, in Thomas Hobbes' words, "dull, nasty, brutish, and short." Now into this community come white men with steel axheads. This is a mystery; these instruments are at first nefarious and diabolical. But the white man shows how the steel axhead can in a few minutes bring down a tree that a strong man would require hours to cut down with the stone axhead. Some hearty soul tries the new thing himself. The tree actually comes down without benefit of any further magic, and he who has felled it does not suddenly die, but rejoices in the fact that he has accomplished far more than his fellows in the same amount of time. Before very long it comes about that the people have rationalized or excused the new process; those whose eyes have witnessed such a demonstration will soon be chopping down trees with steel axheads.

The consequences upon the whole institutional pattern are terrific. The first effect is that the energy of the group is enormously extended; a large part of their activity can go into other things than chopping down trees. They have time and energy for other economic exploits; for the beautiful as well as for the practical arts; for the invention of better carpentry, as well as for conversation, the amenities, philosophy; time and opportunity to enlarge their sphere and travel farther into the jungle, making roads and going where they never went before.

With their sharp blades, they have soon made infinitely better instruments of every type than the stone implements they had before. In the course of time their relations with their neighbors change; they have enlarged their power sphere and have become empire builders. Their self-perpetuation mores have been changed too. Woman, who was not strong enough to manipulate the stone axhead, and hence lacked prestige, is now ready to seize upon all sorts of ways of using the new toy—ways of making useful and beautiful things for the house with the steel axhead. She puts this to use when the man goes hunting, and she develops into an artisan. As a result her status soon changes markedly. Moreover, whereas in the earlier era a boy had to be seventeen or eighteen before he could build a boat or a wagon with the stone axhead, he can now build one with the steel axhead when he is 12. This means a change in the internal structure of the family, for the boy becomes a man, and acquires the status of a man, much earlier. More important still, he can earn the bride-price much earlier; and since everyone will marry early in life, polygamy disappears. The old man, too, gains new status, for he can now continue to work past the prime of life. The councils of state now comprise both the old and the young, for all are economically important. The arts and sciences are profoundly influenced, partly because a person can cut more accurately and beautifully, but especially because, having known the wonders of the blade, he strives to understand and to produce it. The gods of field and woodland fade away in place of a craftsman Deity who makes good and beautiful things in six days, more or less, and *rests* (as no neolithic woodsman could) on the seventh.

These are *free associations* on a theme by Sumner and Keller, *not a* picture of any one tribe. Indeed, it is a sort of confabulation, as the Rorschachists would say, based upon the many sorts of things that happen when a transformation in the self-maintenance mores occurs. Our interest in it lies in the hypothesis that as the mores of self-maintenance change, so the personality structure itself must change. This comes partly as a direct result of the self-maintenance changes, with their increasing emphasis upon skill rather than strength, ingenuity rather than endurance, artifice and invention rather than maintenance of a precarious subsistence; and also partly by virtue of the changes in activity and feeling which are appropriate to the changes in the other mores. Female personality, for example, changes even more than the male, and in both sexes gentleness becomes more appropriate than toughness.

Thus far, we have a hypothesis, or a set of hypotheses, only. We have come to the point where empirical research on a variety of human cultures is necessary if we are to sift, validate, improve our formulation. This is the task of the next three chapters.

34. Social Roles

THE hypotheses suggested in the preceding chapter must be tested and developed by reference to case studies of human cultures. But which ones shall we choose? The comparative method yields data both from subcultures within a given cultural area and from distinct cultural wholes. As an example of the former we might compare Virginians with Kansans; as an example of the latter, Hopi Indians with the Ba Thonga of East Africa. Though both methods are feasible, the latter will serve our purpose better. Data already in hand from interviews, questionnaires, clinical records, and historical and sociological descriptions, indicate gross differences in ego and in attitudes in different ethnic and religious groups within the rather uniform culture area of the United States; but these studies have two great limitations in relation to our present problem: (1) They cannot at present accurately trace the diffusion of attitude from one group to another within the larger culture. At any given time the attitudes appearing in a subcultural group may be expressions of its own situation or expressions infiltrating from another subcultural area. Historical methods of a quantitative character would have to be devised to meet this difficulty. (2) They cannot adequately take account of cultural lag. Ego formations or ego attitudes discovered in a given context of cultural events may reflect a situation which existed some time before but has ceased to exist; the persisting expressions of lag may be either stable anachronisms, or moribund vestiges which are doomed to disappear in time. Their true relation to the subcultural situation as it is at present is indeed obscure.

Many ethnological field studies, however, have found it possible to obviate these difficulties. Isolated groups, their culture stable and practically intact, have been described in sufficient number to give at least a conception of the extraordinary diversity of ego patterns and of culturally standardized ways of regarding the self. We shall be interested chiefly in the degree of emphasis given to the experience of awareness of self, and in the self-valuing and disvaluing attitudes. We shall, then, use preliterate peoples as an empirical test of our system of hypotheses.

A suitable example indicating the relation of the self-maintenance mores to personality is found in the culture of the Manus of New Guinea. The Manus tribe consists of about two thousand people. They live as merchants; the life of the group is centered in the processes of trade. They deal in futures; a man calculates that six months hence he will have received payments with which he will meet an obligation due at that time. Not only must he be competent in handling boats and overseeing production, he must be shrewd and remorseless, must allow no one to get the better of him. The physical wear and tear of fulfilling his business responsibilities resembles that experienced by an active member of the New York Stock Exhange. The Manus are as aggressive and as hard in their competitive life as any business leader in our own society.

This tribe is deliberately chosen as an extreme example of what can be "predicted" from knowledge of the self-maintenance mores, from the kind of knowledge just cited. We may predict that marriage will be a matter of cold calculation, that love will mean little; that children will be reared without affection; that because affection is lacking in sexual and maternal relationships, the people will be extreme prudes. We may predict that their arts will be practical, not aimed at esthetic experience; that their politics will be unadulterated power politics, and their religion a straightforward barter with the unseen.

These "predictions" are right on every count. According to Mead, there is no religion except for mediumistic transactions that seek the aid of the dead in health and business affairs. There is little folklore; no poetry or figures of speech mar the practical-minded orientation of the Manus. The marriage institution shows the trend even more severely. The boy's family and the girl's have long since bickered over their children's futures; in early childhood a match, a contract has been made. The girl grows up in the knowledge that marriage is something into which she has been sold and that the boy has been chosen because of his financial future. She marries into her husband's village; laden with finery, she is put into a canoe and shipped to a husband she has never seen. The boy is reared from early childhood without affection for those of the other sex; he plays with other boys and even in his teens remains almost in a bachelor community. When he is about eighteen years old, people suddenly begin to tell him that it is time to marry; it is a shame that he cannot pay for his wife. He is pushed into marriage and into a state of economic dependency, the shamefulness of which is emphasized for years, until he has liquidated the bride price. On top of this, there is instilled the shamefulness of the sex relation.

As the dominant business man, using all his energy, ventures each year greater and greater exchanges of property and climbs to a pinnacle of power, prestige, and self-regard, his younger male relatives work for him, and share more and more in his rewards in accordance with their own energy and skill. By the mid-forties, typically, he reaches his peak and begins to fail in energy; as he fails, his business, his power, his prestige pass into other hands. As an old man he is nothing, not even if he is the father of a successful son.

Thus far, this has seemed to be a very simple, clear example of the way in which self-maintenance mores influence other mores and serve to structure the personalities of those who grow up in a world constituted by these patterns of social relations. Our interest in all this lies not in the Manus' behavior as such, but in the light thrown upon *social roles*, defined by the cultural organization of the group and implemented by the family in such a way as to prepare the individual for enacting the role. Our primary hypothesis has been that the self-maintenance mores serve in large measure to determine the pattern of the mores as a whole; this hypothesis seems to be validated, as far as this analysis has gone, and our second hypothesis is apparently also confirmed, in that such roles genuinely serve to mold personality. This is the writer's view; he does not seek, here or elsewhere, to attribute this interpretation to the ethnologists whom he cites.

But the self-maintenance mores act in different ways on different individuals, according to the role they must play. Among the Manus, almost all adult males share in the commercial system, and almost all adult females participate in a supporting way. Age and sex are therefore the two clear bases for the behavior roles to be assumed by the individual. Personality is congruent with the specific parts which persons of each age and sex must enact. Each role is specified by the number, variety, and quality of the interrelated tasks that the society defines, and each such role depends to a large degree upon the self-maintenance roles. The point applies in detail; e.g., the subroles enacted by merchants at varying levels of power and success reflect their economic status. Thinking more broadly about human society as a whole, we may suspect that only those who are functionally capable of carrying out a role will be admitted to it, and that among those who are capable, only those will be admitted who are acceptable to those who control the society. Moreover, most economic tasks are sex-defined, for both men and women, partly in terms of what each can do, partly in terms of what the men will let the women do. And the day-by-day situation plunges the individual into the role more and more fully; the personality cannot help expressing it more and more profoundly.

As with the Manus, so with other primitive men, and ourselves. The assignment of roles is to a considerable extent incorporated in the child's early education, each family willingly or unwillingly preparing the children for roles analogous to those of the parents. But the roles defined by a person's relation to the whole system of mores are not determined solely by the family; they reflect the total culture. If a child grows up as a member of an Irish policeman's family or a Swiss jeweler's family, there is considerable cultural pressure upon him to play the same role in society as his father, much as his role in other respects depends upon growing up in an ethnic or a religious group, e.g., as a French Canadian or a Russian Jew. Much of the resemblance between children and their parents is due to this carrying forward of specific roles in society.

Sociologists have gone far toward providing a characterology based squarely on these factors of role-playing. They have shown that if a boy is a Portuguese cranberry picker—so that we know his age, sex, subculture, and economic position—we can go a long way rather safely in describing his personality. The compelling force of the socially assigned roles is so tremendous that we can sketch a series of personality interpretations which may be very useful without benefit of any further concepts. The Portuguese cranberry picker, the Maine lobsterman, the Georgia cracker, the fruit vendor from Little Italy—all these and countless others can be defined in a rough general way, not at all because of blood but because of the coercive power of the roles in which their lives are cast.

This is, of course, an example of ideal types (cf. page 749), of types in their ideal simplicity. There is always a reaction of the individual to a central role or to the complex of roles (age, sex, subculture, etc.) which have been assigned. And beyond this we always find that the interpersonal contacts between the individual in his roles and other people in their roles have produced an indefinitely complicated pattern. The social science point of view involves the joint utilization of the concept of the mores and of the individual's role as defined by them, and also his reaction to these various roles and to the interaction of other persons in the various roles which they must fulfill. There are, then, two groups of problems that confront us here: first, the specification of all the roles of a society and their interrelations; second, the relations of role and ego, the ways in which each person regards himself because of the role he is fulfilling. It has frequently been found that primitive people do not understand the rituals they carry out as well as does the ethnologist who studies the whole culture; in the same way we may be able to understand, better than he does himself, why a particular man looks upon himself as he does, because we see his role in society more clearly than he does. This is an instance of the way in which the social science point of view supplies a richer context for the study of individual personality than individual psychology can supply.

SCHISMOGENESIS

An extraordinary study of social roles, particularly as they relate to adult male and female character, appears in Bateson's *Naven*, an

account of the Iatmul of the plains of New Guinea. They were a
martial, head-hunting people until the whites interfered; a strong,
proud, vigorous tribe. Perhaps the figure in the figure-ground
pattern was the waging of almost constant war with their neighbors,
from which they brought back heads. (Since the fighting was not
primarily for loot or conquest, it could not well be subsumed under
"self-maintenance.")

When not fighting, the males spent a good deal of their leisure time
in the ceremonial house to which women could never come, indulging
themselves in perpetual boasting contests. Whenever a few men got
together, one would arise and describe the ancestral glories of his
family, reminding members of other families who were present how
ignoble their own ancestors had been. Life was thus spent in self-
exaltation. It was not enough to be a military hero; the relation of
each individual to the group required that he find constant occasion
for aggression and ego inflation.

This central role, so emphasized by the culture, throws light on
several other roles which appear to serve as complementary or balancing factors. The Iatmul woman's personality pattern is quiet, domestic,
child-rearing; as a rule these women do not compete against one
another, or against men. In certain ceremonials in which a boy appears
in his newly acquired military glory, the women prostrate themselves to show of what little account they are; the boy marches
over their prostrate forms, to show the dominance of the masculine
over the feminine. But in addition to quiet domesticity and submission,
a third pattern is standardized: the procession of the women dressed
in the men's martial regalia. Here the women are as glorious and
magnificent as their men, and they seem to enjoy themselves much
more. They have full respite from obeisance, and exercise another
"set of muscles." Moreover, watching the women's procession gives
the man respite from the exacting role of playing hero that he must
keep up continually; he becomes just a spectator. These roles are
apparently related to the primary role. But there is a further subsidiary feature: masculine clowning. This appears in our own
culture, as when the fourteen-year-old basketball hero, on returning

home, finds that tension can be eased by a take-off on the other players, and makes even his own role ridiculous. Buffoonery is a simple and adequate way of complementing any hero role which calls for tension.

All five roles, then—the two male roles and the three female roles— make sense in terms of the primary martial roles of the group. In particular, the martial role of the man calls for a complementary role in the woman; since he wants to be a hero, she must humiliate herself to magnify his heroic proportions. But both restore their own internal imbalance through buffoonery for the man and magnificent ceremony for the woman.

Bateson has developed a terminology adequate to describe this complex system of personality adjustment. We are confronted with differentiation or cleavage within the social group, of a sort which causes each form of cleavage-producing behavior to become intensified; the chasm is thus progressively widened. *Schismogenesis* is this production of cleavage. When a given kind of behavior, such as physical or verbal aggression, stimulates more of this same kind of behavior in others, there is *symmetrical* schismogenesis. When one kind of behavior arouses qualitatively different behavior, the difference in response increasing reciprocally, there is *complementary* schismogenesis. Some kinds of behavior may arouse, in some societies, both symmetrical and complementary schismogenesis. Although one man's egocentric aggressiveness makes other men more aggressive, the same egocentric aggressiveness may both induce and be induced by the opposite, namely, exaggerated subservience.

This approach to the psychology of social roles in a military society appears to possess the enormous advantage of showing how *roles may be related to other roles, rather than directly to the mores*. A war-centered society must obviously induce heroic roles in the man; but here each of the feminine role patterns is in part a *reaction* to this masculine role, or a reaction, within the woman, to the tensions aroused by the enactment of another of her roles; finally, the clowning behavior of the man seems to be partly a response to the woman but more a let-down in responding to his own high-tension role of hero. We begin to conceive the psychology of role-playing as partly a direct response to the mores, and partly a secondary response to the primary roles; one enacts a part not because of a *task to be done*, but largely because of the strain which has been set up *by enacting another part*.

Though we do not attribute to Bateson the exact formulation which appears here, we believe his work the best introduction to social roles. This way of viewing personality in relation to society is likely to prove the most felicitous of all those which today tempt the student of "personality and culture." It provides full place for the person's fitness for the role, for the influence of role upon personality, for the articulation of personalities in the group, and for fluid, shifting intra-group dynamics. Take as an example the whole vast problem of "sex differences" as they occur in our own or in any other society. Some writers emphasize endocrine differences, others the early training of boy and girl, and both are right. But the problem is much larger; it is centered in the question of the *masculine role*, the *feminine role*.

The roles of course derive in large degree from biology, and some biological core remains in every social redefinition of the tasks to be done. Consequently we soon come to the larger question: What kinds of roles can man, being all that he is, play effectively; what kinds of roles can woman, being all that she is, play effectively? The task of society is to consider all the potentialities of man and woman as personalities and to develop an articulation from which an integrated pattern of compatible roles can be developed. This is not as easy as it sounds. In some reflections as to the general drift of life and in particular as to whether man has good enough stuff in him to survive, W. M. Wheeler refers to "the problem of the male." This is puzzling. A quarter of a species might be a problem, but hardly half of it; any way, it is the female that is usually considered the problem.

But there is profound sense in Wheeler's discussion. Note the father rabbits that kill the young whenever they have a chance; and the tearing and clawing, the fury of combat that kills off so many males in a species that the group as a whole is overwhelmed by its enemies. Females may fight as hard. But they have time and energy for the young. Their constitutional make-up includes a tendency to be interested in, and to have a soft spot for, little samples of the species, and at least a trace of this fondness may persist when the little ones are larger.

Watching junior high-school boys come out of school at three o'clock and crash the subway is an experience. An improvised flying wedge, a few whirling arms, a few sharp shoulders; as the train comes in, there are well-planted socks and casual sideswipes. Through the doors and in shoals into the cars, and they bellow and roar, slap and kick, giggle and guffaw at one another for thirty blocks. These are the young males that "urban civilization" is supposed to have civilized, softened. The "problem" focuses in the delinquent or the hoodlum, the various difficulties occasioned by the ease of picking up anywhere a handful of youths who, for cash or for fun, will beat up members of another class or race. All this is balanced, of course, by the heroism and staying power that the young male shows in an exploring party or on the battlefield. The female shares the heroism and the staying power in the great crises. It is she who cares for the young whom the fury threatens, she who keeps personal life, warmth, humanity alive. In short, though the female can fight when she needs to, she has in her tissues some needs that are seriously interfered with by fighting; in particular, she is interested both in the young and in the character-istic *kinds of feeling* that one has toward the young. The male—drone at times, provider and defender at other times—has more combat energy than he knows what to do with. If you tame him and make him behave, he has periods of running wild, pulling trolleys off the wires, painting the town. Or you must invent for him the "moral equivalent of war."

A mature psychology of roles begins with raw biological problems such as these. But it realizes that not all young males are violent or predatory; the norm is standardized in terms of what *some*, rather than others, tend to do. There is competition between what individuals want, all during the time the norms are developing; and as they take shape they pull all the members of a given group (such as the young males) into the appropriate roles. The consequence is that practically *all* members, whether biologically inclined or not, are drawn into the pattern; in our culture almost all young males are exposed to the aggression-violence pattern. Partly for the reasons described by Bateson, other roles develop in the females, and at the same time secondary male roles develop. In exactly the same way one might, in a society in which females play a more dominant role (Marquesans or Zuñi, perhaps), trace the roles in the other direction.

Bateson's formulation articulates well with several other contemporary approaches, several of which have already been considered. Thus in the discussion of child-parent relations (page 585), we noted the crystallizing of attitudes in each person in consequence of the roles which he enacts, the structuring of personality in terms of an antithesis or a supplementary relation. Again, in discussing the self (page 493), we endeavored to bring out the definition of personality trends through types of interaction which accentuate a specific relation of one person to another; two people are seen to develop their diffuse personal potentialities through the specific canalizations which their relation affords. Similarly, in considering the psychoanalytic method, one encounters the suggestion (Burrow, Fromm) that the infantilism, sexualism, defensiveness of the patient is in part a reflection of the polarity of doctor and patient, that such attitudes develop because of the specific stresses of a one-to-one personal situation. Many of these trends that develop in a polarized situation are carried over to other situations in which a similar role has to be enacted, so that a given person who has a given relation to a group is, when confronting any member of that group, a kind of person he could not otherwise be. When with his students, many a college teacher is the kind of fellow which the years of polarized teaching experience have made him; with his golf foursome he is so different that none would know him. If a group of persons who must frequently enact one phase of a polar situation are studied as a group in relation to another group who must act the other phase of the situation, we may look for the general characteristics of each pole. One of the first things to be discovered by this approach is that the development of the polarity passes through a recognizable series of phases, eventuating in different types of polarization. To Bateson goes the credit of being the first clearly to see and formulate the general dynamics of such trends.

We have attempted an approach according to which the roles which the individual plays by virtue of age, sex, religious group, economic class, etc., constitute not solely an external system of restraints upon him, but a system of relationships which he himself perceives and keeps before him in a world to be fulfilled by his own living. This means that he not only creates an organized Gestalt out of the roles which he must enact, but gives the peculiar quality of his own thinking and feeling to his place in society. As we pursue the economic interpretation, we seem to find that the economic role in most societies tends to become central and determinative, and to have a considerable dynamic influence on other roles; but other roles in turn have some influence upon the economic.

In summary of our thesis regarding roles, we have attempted to show (1) that society, with its system of mores, and with the self-maintenance mores more or less central in the pattern, does not merely "mold" people, but requires from them the enactment of specific roles in accordance with their place in the system; (2) that not all roles are easily accepted, but that many require effort, and indeed frequently put a strain upon the individual; (3) that a given person must enact several different roles (sex, class, etc.) at once, and that their integration is no obvious or mechanical matter; (4) that roles derive not merely from primary obligations, but also in response to the roles of others (there is not only melody but counterpoint); (5) that in consequence of all this the individual develops balancing or complementary roles, so that he is a complement both to others and to himself; and (6) that it is thus a long way from the simplest economic determinism to a realistic role psychology based ultimately upon the recognition of self-maintenance factors.

This way of conceiving the psychology of roles calls for a fuller consideration of the nature of the mores. We noted earlier that the self-maintenance mores cannot "determine" the other mores and the personality. Role psychology helps to show why a one-way interpretation fails. Even if the self-maintenance mores were the only factors acting upon the individual, they would have to set going within him a complex pattern of interdependent role-playing activities, and this pattern within him would then have to spread out to influence the other mores. And since in fact any individual child is acted upon both by self-maintenance mores and by other mores, and since *the unifying factor is the dynamic perceptual and motor response of the individual* by which all the mores arc perceived and used, we must provide for the "return effect" of the other mores upon those of self-maintenance. Do not the marriage institution of the Manus, the pageant of the Iatmul, react upon the self-maintenance mores? Indeed they do. It is not difficult to document the view that in many societies religion (e.g., through severe food taboo or the fear of gods who protect certain trees or animals) greatly influences the self-maintenance mores. In some societies the lawyer and the police overstep the role assigned them and control in large measure the ways of those responsible for self-maintenance; even the artist has at times called the tune for "practical" people. For since human beings play *all* the roles, and since *each member of the group must in some degree perceive the roles and their interrelations*, we should necessarily expect to encounter interacting, interdependent roles. This will lead to an interacting, interdependent system of mores.

35. Ethos

CAN our approach in terms of roles be reconciled with the equally legitimate approach in terms of the individual's *personal outlook*, the unified, central way of thinking and feeling which characterizes him? It is clear that this way of thinking and feeling dominates the interpersonal world, and often constitutes the ingredient in the individual personality around which everything else is organized. The psychology of autism (Chapter 15) will be recalled: If one looks at a tiny patch of fuzzy gray moving slowly in the dusk, it may become a person hurrying home, or a piece of newspaper blown by the wind, or a gray cat, or a ghost; he gives structure to this thing in terms of a dominant feeling, or cluster of ideas charged by such a feeling. In the same way, the whole vast constellation of social experiences may be autistically ordered. The anchorage or fixation point with reference to which people see life most of the time is largely determined by this *feeling tone*, or *ethos*, as Bateson calls it. A number of primitive and advanced societies have been described in terms of their ethos. How, then, is ethos related to a role psychology?

The first answer is apparently found in the fact that the ethos in turn seems to derive in part from the self-maintenance mores. In a buffalo-hunting tribe, for example, the entire way of living which makes a man a successful buffalo hunter—this means taking great chances and winning great rewards—takes on a violent and orgiastic quality, which Benedict finds characteristic of the Plains Indians. Ethos and role are intimately related. To conceive these dynamic relations, we may conceptualize the self-maintenance mores at the bottom of the structure, the ethos above it, and the dominant outlook or autistic perceptual anchorage at the top. We shall find a considerable number of variations and exceptions. The utility of contrasting the Plains Indians with the more placid Indians of the Southwest is the fact that the economic organization and feeling tone throughout the Southwest are in sharp contrast with those found in the Plains; this difference in feeling tone is accompanied by great differences in outlook. The individual personality among the Zuñi Indians of the Southwest, with its communal, non-competitive way of life, is instantly recognized as consonant with this primordial feeling tone or ethos of the Pueblo. So well unified is Plains culture, or Southwest culture, that we may speak of a single focus; the two are "unifocal cultures."

The simpler type of economic determinism (page 773) would find it convenient to view unifocal cultures in terms of a single economic determining force, and to explain more complex personality structures —let us say, those of the Greeks of the Classical Period—in terms of the complexity of a purely economic background. But this doctrine confronts all sorts of psychological difficulties. Thus the Iatmul people have a very simple type of self-maintenance mores, but a very complex personality structure. Personality proves again not to be a passive thing, waiting to be impressed; it is forever reacting. The aspects of personality are not direct reflections of a social pressure; each aspect is drawn out in definite relation to a system of aspects already organized within, and in response to a system of forces acting from without. We cannot at present hope to define all the factors; all we can do is to clarify and emphasize those we can observe, and show certain interrelations between them.

CHILDHOOD EXPERIENCE

Economic factors have, then, an important place in shaping ethos. But let us use a genetic approach. The more we look at early personality formation, the more we confront primitive childish wants which may be satisfied or frustrated in a psychological world that knows nothing at all about self-maintenance. It may be true that self-maintenance as a law of life results in the development of personality in one rather than another direction. But it is likely also that the primitive wants operative in early childhood lay the bases for the later understanding of the problem of self-maintenance; the self-maintenance mores may themselves be determined in part by character just as they in turn help to determine character. This point has been forcibly driven home by the psychoanalysts; their collaboration with ethnologists, as in the recent work of Kardiner and Linton, throws a flood of light on the problem of combining the economic with the psychoanalytic approach. We have already mentioned (page 773) Linton's study of the economic factor in the Madagascar social organization. As we turn to another culture which he describes, that of the Marquesan people of the Southwest Pacific, we find the economic factor appearing in a very different context.

As far back as Marquesan memories go, there has been a great numerical excess of males over females. This may have been due to female infanticide, or perhaps to a religious rite of female sacrifice; no one knows. This sex imbalance gives us a primary clue for psychological study: shortage of any sort in relation to human wants will have far-flung consequences. The Marquesans had another vitally serious shortage, a food shortage; food was stored away in huge pits against a time of famine. Though the Marquesans appeared rugged and hardy, there was insecurity in their hearts. Fortunately, for purposes of analysis, there were these two basic imbalances—not enough women and not enough food—hence the interactions of the two want patterns can be studied.

Let us look first at the shortage of women and what it does to male and female character. In most societies, with the fetishism that prevails regarding masculinity, boys have an advantage. A father is proud to have a son; many mothers openly make a much greater to-do over their boys than over their girls. Relatively few males ever feel inferior because they are males. But in Marquesan society there were so many males that the female child apparently had a queen's position, being specially wanted and specially chosen. At the time of puberty, the males were in a difficult situation. They had no opportunity to look about and choose the "best" girls, nor could their parents choose for them. They had to compete with all the other young men. In our own society, when at a dance there are many girls and relatively few boys, the pretty girls allow themselves to be chosen, the less attractive ones being left out in the cold; there is little "sex solidarity." In the same way, there was no sex solidarity among the Marquesan men. Because the shortage was so great, the women were in a favorable position. Since polyandry was practiced among the Marquesans, the best that most men ever attained was to be a second- or third-order husband.

Because of their favored position, the females in turn attached to their sexual status a degree of importance that is not at all typical of primitive society. They apparently overplayed their sex role, with consequent underplaying of the mother role. This overplaying and underplaying of the two roles took the form of relative rejection of children, with early weaning. The result must have been anxiety in the children, an anxiety that became ever more troublesome for the boys as they looked forward to their position in relation to that of the women.

An ethnologist who studied Marquesan society armed with a theory of economic determinism could easily say that their primary anxiety was due to the food shortage, and that their anxiety about the shortage of females followed from that. But it appears more likely from the Linton-Kardiner analysis that anxiety in the growing child was colored by the sex situation. Indeed, what seemed to be an absolute food shortage, pure and simple, was only a *relative* shortage, such as many primitive peoples constantly experience; it took on a more intense form because of the underlying insecurity of the children, especially of males during their childhood and adolescence. From this point of view, childhood anxiety in relation to the mother colors the subsequent attitude toward the objective fact of food shortage. Thus, though the *men* practice cannibalism, the cannibal in their folklore takes a feminine form. (This is our own simplified—perhaps greatly oversimplified—phrasing of the Linton-Kardiner data. The material is sketched for its theoretical interest; it must not be confused with direct observation of a contemporary living society.)

In keeping with the psychoanalytic approach, the Marquesans did not know why they were anxious. The influence of a factor inducing strain during infancy, with the persisting after-effects, appears in a generalized affect that is partly transferred to other things; the shortage situation has finally been interpreted by the builders of the storage pits as solely a food shortage. But the displacement is easy because the mother is the first source of food and there has been a relative rejection by her. The general feeling of panic may well have been induced by the anxiety state first induced in infancy.

In the light of this study of the Marquesans, we may generalize the relation of certain infantile experiences to the adult personality. It has been known for some time that a severe shock or deprivation in early infancy may have a lasting effect in terms of a sense of danger or of deprivation. We find constantly among nervous people—who do not know why they are nervous any more than the Marquesans do —that the present, apparent sources of anxiety are not the real sources; the real source lies in very early life. We noted (pages 307 ff.) some of the evidence that the period of infancy is especially vulnerable to shock experience, and that specific and enduring effects are wrought into the organism in that period. We mentioned Hunt's studies of food-hoarding in adult rats which had undergone feeding frustration as infants, and Alexander Wolff's report of functional difficulties in adult animals that followed infantile frustration and took a specific form related to the focus of the early interference with function.

As we view the Marquesan people in the light of such studies, we see that something seems to have happened to them in early life in terms of which we can understand the later predominant feeling tone of adulthood. If we were to say that the self-maintenance mores wholly determine the adult feeling tone, a qualification would have to be introduced. The infantile feeling tone apparently has set the stage for later attitudes in the adult personality, including the food attitude and perhaps much else besides. It may be that what actually happens in every human society is that the manner in which the young first come to experience life paves the way to the manner of experiencing adult life. Infantile joys and sorrows, their sequelae and derivatives, can perhaps become central in the personality structure that is to be. This approach is like the contemporary approach in terms of the infant's needs for mothering (cf. page 769). The Marquesans behave like an unmothered people. Much that the adult thinks of as having no permanent significance for the child—in particular, the way in which the child is introduced to the process of living—may make all the difference in the various philosophies of life among which he must ultimately choose.

The world can be filtered through to a child in many different ways. Many peoples whose food supply is very sparse nevertheless have a genial disposition; but in others whose food supply is relatively adequate, anxiety may cut its way through the entire personality. It is not simply the objective situation, nor even the mores for coping with this situation, but the affectively toned way in which the child understands life, the emotionally charged conception of its meaning long before it can be verbalized, that appears to determine the mode and key of the life melody. Similarly, in Cora DuBois' study of the people of Alor (in the Dutch East Indies), one notes that inconsistent chaotic discipline, and the child's inability to count on anyone as a sure source of love and protection, appear to be an important clue to the chaotic and disorganized personality pattern of the typical adult.

In view of the unity and cogency of the emerging picture of the effects of infantile experience, these hypotheses clearly need more direct testing in the field work of the ethnologists. This more direct approach has been made in Mead and Bateson's *Balinese Character*. Having earlier turned their attention to many aspects of childhood and of adolescence as related to the cultural setting, these two ethnologists were determined in their study of Bali to scrutinize more closely the infantile patterns of experience, especially as they appear in mother-child relations, and to bring these observations into line with the predominant Balinese outlook upon life. May not the diverse origins of the components of the culture perhaps mask the psychological unity of their present-day use?

We may begin with a patent and conspicuous fact, the Balinese sensitiveness to ritual—their delight in the dance, in posture, in the use of the body generally. The magnificent public ceremonials of this people, their processions, their portrayal of the struggle between the dragon and the witch, are not only visual but kinesthetic, tactual, visceral experiences. The individual Balinese begin to experience this collective magnificence as little children. Girls seven or eight years old, intently watching the body posturing and the dance, may pass into a state of full or semi-trance. If they carry out the trance role successfully, if they seem to be governed by unseen forces, they may find themselves being prepared to serve as trance mediums. The photographs and motion pictures of these girls and women give the impression of waxy flexibility; they hold a posture for a great length of time. This seems to justify the use of the term *trance*. The dancers seem to have the capacity to take themselves out of the world; they appear to have withdrawn from life.

Proceeding now from this dramatic example, we look at the general temper of ordinary living among the Balinese. We find that there is an excessive amount of withdrawnness; much of the time they seem absent-minded, flaccid, without clear orientation to the world. Yet in public ceremonial, whether pageant or dance or funerary rite, there is an excited display as intense as that of the Plains Indians. The ceremonial in connection with the trance is violent in nature, and certainly the dance itself is the quintessence of hectic excitement; in the exhumation ceremony they plunge their hands frantically into decaying bodies. Life thus alternates between the quiet, the passive, the withdrawn, and the mad, the violent, the orgiastic. Here we have interrelated roles, somewhat reminiscent of the Iatmul (page 789). But there we could throw a good deal of light on the role-structure. Can we do so here?

Bateson and Mead do not use these terms. Rather, they ask us to look directly at infant experience. A very young child is given attention and affection. But before he is a year old, the mother's pattern changes. When he calls for attention and affection, the mother turns away, does not respond. This, however, is not sheer withdrawnness; she begins actively to tease him by leading him on and then frustrating him. Having learned to cry out for warmth and affection, he is now flatly rebuffed. But the teasing does not consist of mere indifference, either; the mother turns to some other child (another mother often contributes one for the purpose) and fondles him. Of course there are temper tantrums. But nothing can be so blissfully ignored as a temper tantrum; the mother smiles as the child carries through his furious protest. In Bali this is the normal, correct way to respond to babies. The father also teases, but not to the same extent.

A primary pattern in personality formation is thus the experience of being led on and then utterly deflated; one discovers that it is dangerous to *give oneself to life;* the only safe thing to do is to develop feelings which cannot be frustrated. We might call this "deflation," but Bateson and Mead prefer "deflection." For there are other means of satisfaction. The child's demand for warmth, attention, and response is converted into other channels (cf. page 799). If your mother won't love you, there is always your own body. Preoccupation with the body expresses itself in posturing, gesturing, and the dance (and also in certain toys which portray the body's form or function). In the gracious curving of limbs or trunk, in the delight in his own person as a supple and ever-changing physical object, the child finds a substitute, and a fairly adequate one, for the original object, the mother who would not respond.

We begin to see the meaning of awayness in the trance and in the whole pattern of Balinese life, and also, in full compensation, the meaning of the almost incredible grace of the Balinese. Personality is built largely around awayness rather than social activity; it is built around the body. So far as personality is organized around awareness of one's physical being (page 484), the "body image," it is a response to the world within, not the world without. What the parents have done is to give the child a definition of himself, his physical person, as the central experience. This does not mean that he himself understands why the dance and the postures are developed to this extraordinary level, and of course he does not know that the violently vivid drama and the orgiastic funeral rites relieve something which is never released by the daily round of reality.

The tendency to turn inward is apparently stimulated by still other activities of the Balinese parents. As the little child wanders a few feet from his mother, wanting to find out what goes on in the big world, she calls out a word that indicates danger. Sudden fear is the means of keeping him on the beaten path. The experience of exploring the unknown becomes a fear experience. He learns to stay strictly on the path; seeks the obvious, the safe, and the sane; takes no chances. In all probability, this has a direct psychological relation to the deflection experience mentioned earlier; the individual learns that if he is to avoid the terrible experiences of fear and frustration, he must limit his demands. There is no more place for the sense of adventure and exploration than there is for full reciprocal social response; the stronger positive demands are mashed flat. In the light of all this, the rather vacant look shown in photographs of Balinese faces becomes understandable. It is not that these people are dissociated; they are not hysterical. Their only way of looking is to look timidly and uncertainly, and not too far into the intense realities of the world. The immediacies are satisfying enough; they ask no more.

But having been frustrated, teased, and cautioned as an infant, the individual as an adult (perhaps because of original identification with the parents) tends to tease, frustrate, and caution his children. Thus the cycle is continued generation after generation. The various aspects of infantile experience, projected on to adulthood, explain the passivity of ordinary living and also the violent release on exceptional occasions. The concept with which we emerge is that the intensities of infantile emotional expression appear in socially sanctioned or socially stylized patterns of a very complicated sort.

It should be admitted flatly that this material, as presented, lends itself poorly to any economic interpretation, whether simple or of the more elaborate type attempted above (page 794). Apparently it would be sounder to say that in Balinese society status does not depend primarily on any kind of self-maintenance activity; that other mores, notably the self-gratification mores, play a huge role in personality formation; and that in this instance relatively less economic and relatively more psychoanalytic emphasis is needed if the resulting personalities are to be understood. Although personality is thus, in a sense, shown to be molded by the mores, it is likewise evident that personality reacts, not always kindly, to the pressure of the molding process.

ETHOS

Though it has seemed feasible to use the self-maintenance mores as a starting point and to derive from them other mores as well as fundamental personality patterns, we have encountered difficulties and complications. These become more serious as we turn to a variety of cultures that face the same economic situation and have essentially similar self-maintenance mores, but very different marriage customs, religion and art forms, and an utterly different feeling tone toward life. Perhaps, instead of being so apologetic about feeling tone, we might experiment by using it as our own anchorage point for a while, and see where it leads.

The overwhelming role of feeling tone and attitude conveyed through the family is evident in another people of the Southwest Pacific, the "sorcerers of Dobu." Dobuan culture is built around black magic. All the weapons of living, all the instruments with which these people confront the dangers of this life, involve magical practices. But the outstanding fact is the malignancy of the magic. Life is organized in terms of hostility and struggle against every living soul who is not a member of the mother unit, the *susu*. This word means the mother's milk, and includes all who have shared the mother's milk. The maternal system provides in-group protection; anyone with whom one has not shared the mother's milk is a potential or actual foe. Since the father comes from an alien village and marries into the wife's village, he does not belong to her susu and is forever an alien to his own family and to the other men of the village. So deep is the suspicion of aliens that when any woman dies, the group assumes that her husband killed her; and he therefore has to do a year's penance of a painful, degrading type. Since suspicion and counter-suspicion are continuous, the Dobuans' existence is an anxiety existence. This anxiety is passed on from generation to generation. The Dobuans are poor, but so are many other peoples; it is not poverty alone, but the malignant feeling tone that seems to serve as a distinctive clue to Dobuan life.

Again emphasizing that the self-maintenance mores do not unilaterally determine the attitude toward life, we see, in the case of the

Zuñi of the American Southwest, that feeling tone serves in large degree to color the self-maintenance mores. These people are group-minded, socially conscious, aware of their dependence upon the cooperative structure of the group as a whole. The priests carry out communal ceremonials at the great seasons of the year, and the harvest is planned on a communal basis. The ritual of worship includes the placing of prayer sticks in the ground by the entire community; if anybody puts his prayer stick in the ground when the others are not doing so, this implies black magic. Religion is not an individual but a shared experience, as is everything else. Yet Goldman has pointed out that there is much backbiting and recrimination; a person may not compete openly but he can "tear others down." Apparently the Zuñi *achieve their outwardly cooperative pattern at a considerable psychological cost;* they experience non-competitive living as a considerable strain. When we say that a person adapts himself to the culture, we are in danger of forgetting at what cost he adapts. The Zuñi pattern suggests that this type of existence has been carried to a point where it is sufficiently far from actual human needs to make trouble. We can only guess that historically there has been a conflict, among the Zuñi, between ego-inflating and rigidly ego-constraining traditions. Apparently the ego needs of the individual have been developed and then brought up sharp against a stone wall.

Similarly, in his study of the neighboring Hopi Indians, Asch noted how consistently the children belittled their own work but were pitifully anxious for any sort of recognition they could get. They resorted to remarks which we would label "fishing"—they had found out that the way to brag is to fish. The child learns early that the self is important; and as his prowess mounts, he learns that his feats need considerable heralding abroad. But there are other egos in the world, and they may object. Hence he learns just what degree of self-advertisement is permissible, and at the same time what degree of self-delusion is appropriate. He learns that "self-respect" is good, "vanity" deplorable, and he fixes approximate limits. All this is evident enough in our own culture, but in Asch's studies of the Hopi child, and in Goldman's observations on the Zuñi adult, these everyday happenings are brought into sharp focus. Self-exaltation is sharply repressed. Not only does a child learn not to boast (and learn it much more thoroughly than our children do); he even learns in many situations not to *excel*. To surpass another in some school competition, or even in clay sculpture, will bring down the ire of his fellows. Each child therefore faces the task of doing well enough to merit the standardized conventional group approval which all can share, but not so well as to attract undue attention. The conflict is apparently even more severe than that arising from the paradox of life in our own culture, with its continual pressure to do well and win approval, and its parallel scorn for those who realize too well the status they have acquired thereby. With them as with us, the individual must not attract attention; he must not even *feel* the importance of his achievements, despite the fact that he has stretched every nerve to secure them. Glory goes to the acquisition of skill; but when success is won, indifference should be cultivated. On the whole, the Zuñi and the Hopi seem to carry the paradox further than we do; they do a "better job" of arousing a need and then stifling it, and perhaps they produce an even more generally neurotic disposition than does western culture.

It is not implied that the men of Zuñi understand the mechanics of these processes any better than we ourselves do. The essential point is that many different attitudes toward the self may coexist, and that these may fuse or conflict; some may be weakened, even overwhelmed by others. But, just as in the other cases of value conflict, so here too it is improbable that any values are ever completely obliterated. Residual tensions remain by virtue of old canalizations, and may cause a sore spot or lower the thresholds for outbursts on petty provocation. In the case of conflict, in which there is continuous prolonged reinforcement of a weaker (non-dominant) tendency, the balance of power may shift. The individual may then undergo a crisis, relegating the previous attitudes to a subordinate position. Though they are hidden away, these attitudes may nevertheless succeed in finding an outlet. Thus the ambitious but restrained man, who inwardly blames and despises himself for his mistakes and is full of a sense of his utter failure, but who still is unconsciously disposed to accept himself as a man of worth, may through unexpected success suddenly become impossibly conceited, far vainer than the same achievement would make a less ambitious man. Similarly, a person whom the world has acclaimed a success but who retains the diffidence of his childhood may, after a petty rebuke, find himself overwhelmed with a sense of utter worthlessness.

It is, moreover, pointed out by Goldfrank that the terrible fear of the supernatural which is instilled in Hopi and Zuñi children, together with their later discovery that the supernatural beings which frightened or punished them were just men in disguise, may plant a deep insecurity in their hearts which lasts for a lifetime; even their parents have deceived them. And Goldfrank stresses that since this disciplinary role of the "supernatural" appears not in infancy but several years later, it is childhood as a whole, and not just infancy, that must be stressed when the cultural sources of adult personality and temperament are considered.

Such conflict, arising from the struggle for perceptual unity, is doubtless reinforced at times by the need to keep the picture reasonably consistent, as in other cases of the need for value focusing (page 639). The result is a loading of the tension with perceptual energies which augment the energies of the simpler conflicting impulsions. This appears to be identical with the psychoanalytic mechanism of reaction formation (page 551), in that the large amount of energy required to keep repressed elements from consciousness serves to maintain a high tension level in the perceptual system; the individual is thus too definite, too sure, of his view.

There can, then, be a feeling tone which not only fails to *reflect* the self-maintenance mores but may be in essential disharmony with them—even in a society of considerable stability. (So, too, in our urban industrial society a man may passionately demand to get away from it all.) The result is of course wear and tear on the individual. We might think that in the case of gross disharmony there would be an automatic adjustment; but people are much less "rational" than that when opposing canalizations are involved. The Zuñi child apparently sees himself as one who "does well" and also as one who makes no claim to do well; and this ambivalence runs through all his life.

Indeed, the Manus type of society has apparently also been produced at a certain cost or strain; there is great wear and tear, both physical and mental, as a result of the harsh competition. Relatively few individuals are really "adjusted" to the cultural norm. In fact, a number of the Manus families have "sidestepped the culture"; they reject the norms and live in their own non-competitive way. In following the naïve idea that personality is a plastic or fluid response to the cultural pattern into which it is poured, we have overlooked most of the devices by which the social inventions of some people put unnatural constraint upon them. The strain engendered by savage competition in a unifocal society is of course different from that entailed in conflicting values; but the simple solution of giving up the mores that cause strain—a theoretical possibility as far as economics is concerned—is seldom adopted. People are canalized on the "successful" self-portrait; and the more "successful" they are, the more dominant they are in the society.

INDIVIDUAL ADAPTATION TO ETHOS

The fact of strain, of wear and tear, however induced, is perhaps sufficient answer to the form of cultural relativism that says that all cultures are equally well adapted to human nature, that human nature can take on any shape with equal ease—theories which ignore the biological bases of human adaptation. Here we can learn a good deal from the Mountain Arapesh of New Guinea. This culture presents an almost perfect antithesis to the Dobu, for this agricultural people has constructed its culture around the ethos of kindliness. No one seems to have much sense of proprietorship. Land boundaries are vague. The pigs at a man's house are on loan from a neighbor; his own household utensils are at a house a couple of miles away. Everyone shares food. When a big job like building a house is to be done, the whole village takes part. Each child growing up in the community is coddled by all. The economic determinist may say that the system of land tenure, with its vague boundaries, is responsible for the entire social pattern; otherwise it would be impossible to develop so fluid, so unconstrained a social system. Here, however, we get the impression that, as the Arapesh views his world, the cooperative way of life is actually the figure, not simply part of the ground.

But just as one ethos involves more strain than another, so *any* group ethos involves a certain degree of strain on each one of the individuals subjected to it. Does the integration achieved by the Arapesh involve such a uniform ethos that *uniformity of personality* results? Does this cooperative culture have a unilateral influence upon the individual? The answer involves two factors: first, the existence of chronic deviants in the group who cannot function as the culture requires; second, the occasional outcropping of deviant behavior in the ordinary normal person. For under pressure, some of the Mountain Arapesh take over certain institutions of less friendly people. Black magic, which is practiced constantly in the valley—and practiced to kill—the Mountain Arapesh will use when very angry; a man may hire one of the magicians from the valley to do damage to his fellow tribesmen. However, it is not habitual with most members of the group, and it passes over quickly as the feeling of rage subsides. Nevertheless it shows that the serenity of this people is not a mold that renders all the members of the group consistently unaggressive; the culture is not hermetically sealed against other cultures with different ideas. Yet in view of the hostility patterns prevalent among the peoples all about them, it is probably fair to say that the ethos of fellow feeling is too well defined to permit hostile ideas to enter often or remain long.

Having learned to look for an explanation of ethos in the experiences of early childhood, we inquire as to child-rearing customs among the Arapesh. We find that they give a welcoming acceptance to the children growing up in the community. Everyone is considered valuable, not for what his parents are or for anything he may accomplish, but because he is a member of the group. Selfhood is unimportant, taken for granted. It is, of course, valued, but apparently as we value the air, non-comparatively and non-competitively. Primitive

affection and mutual aid preclude the development of individual despots. Men regard leadership as a nuisance or burden rather than as
an opportunity for glory and self-enhancement, and they gladly abandon it when they can. To cling to the language we have adopted,
prestige is a commodity of which everyone has the little he wishes to
have, a commodity whose quantity no one is interested in limiting, and
for which there is no market demand.

The Arapesh have taught us three things: (1) Essentially non-
competitive attitudes toward the self can exist and be socially standardized, (2) the result saves an enormous amount of wear and tear,
and (3) even here there is evidence that the culture does not succeed
in molding all its members to a pattern. There are individual temperamental differences in the degree of accepting the ethos. Nor, since
thought reflects temperament, is the prevailing way of thinking in the
group stamped upon each child in standard fashion; it is easily accepted
by some, accepted with difficulty—or not at all—by others.

Like the other variables considered here, ethos is regarded not as a
"first cause" but as an aspect of complex interactions. It may have
its constitutional aspects. We do not know much about inherited
temperamental factors which may vary from one to another inbred
island or mountain community. However, we know more about the
influence of the self-maintenance and other mores, especially mother-
baby practices that produce profoundly satisfying or frustrating
effects. Hence we shall have to deal with the end product of ethos as a
whole.

There is fairly convincing evidence that the feeling tone of a society
may profoundly affect not only its personality types but its mores.
Feeling tone may indeed obscure from the individual the other more
"self-evident economic realities" of his life. Thus among the Ba
Thonga of South Africa, who pursue gain, power, and prestige, life
is arranged in such fashion that each individual feels himself to be
struggling against material obstacles, not against his fellows. It
takes many years to achieve the bride price, thus reaching complete
independence and having all the good things of life in one's possession;
but the achievement of success does not directly block the success of

anyone else, and is not sensed by the successful man or the younger struggling man as *competition*. The result is that though prestige is limited, no one need be humiliated by his lack of it. In other words, there is no "narcissistic wound," no shame; the self grows in importance and also in value as life moves on.

If the role of feeling tone is so huge, it may be possible to *classify culture in terms of ethos*, to look for the manifestation of ethos in every phase of social life. Benedict has taken a brilliant step in this direction. She has borrowed from Nietzsche the terms *Apollonian*—the quality of a Greek divinity, poised, restrained, serene, esthetically appreciative —and *Dionysian*—impulsive, violent, primitive, orgiastic, savage, exotic. She has applied the term Dionysian to the Indians of the Great Plains, such as the Sioux, Crow, Dakota, Blackfoot. Among these tribes, the boy must prove his worth by fasting and going without water in solitary quest of a vision; strenuously pressing upon the gate of the unseen, men dance to the point of exhaustion; or passing wooden skewers through the muscles of the chest and hanging suspended in the sun, they prove that they are the stuff of which heroes are made. Nothing is taken at face value unless a terrible price is given for it; life is lived violently. The Indians of the Southwest, on the other hand, represent the Apollonian. They are gracious and easy, steady workers, lovers of ritual. If one asked which of these groups make exquisite pottery, which give huge prestige rewards for bravery, there would be no doubt as to the answer. When once the feeling tone is given, the rest of the pattern is roughly defined.

Yet Benedict has pointed out that since every human constitution differs from every other one, the process of adapting to the culture in which the individual grows up involves a specific personal type of strain; some cultures are easier for some people, other cultures easier for others. Those who cannot adapt to a given culture—the deviants—might be able to adapt, might be "normal" in other cultures. Suppose that energy output or strenuousness varies widely from culture to culture. Let us imagine three societies, one organized around the most passive values, the second somewhat more active, the third violently strenuous. A person born with a high activity level will be considered violent and manic in the first; in the second he will be thought "rather excitable"; but in the third he will be a "normal person."

Among the Dobu, where black magic is practiced continually, an aggressive child will probably be well adjusted, but among the Mountain Arapesh he will not be able to understand the others and will be completely out of place in the group. The continuum from gentleness to aggressiveness as applied to individuals is also appropriate when applied to cultures; each child will be better or worse adapted to each culture, depending on the discrepancy between his own personal predilection and the characteristic predilection of the culture. The same conceptualization may be made for each characteristic which can be regarded as a continuum. We have in mind here the *constitutional* aspects of temperament (cf. Chapters 3–7), but there will also be discrepancies between the prevailing group tendencies and the individual tendencies on the basis of unique personal experiences.

Those whose deviate behavior is considered pathological in one culture may be highly esteemed in another; we have already noted the Balinese use of dissociative tendencies (page 802). Epilepsy offers another example. One epileptic is born into a society which has medical ideas; it gives him sedative drugs. Another is born into a society which regards epilepsy as possession by a devil; the devil is cast out. But in a third culture the epileptic individual is a channel for divine instruction to human kind. Suppose that instead of becoming unconscious, he displays an "epileptic equivalent," a trance-like or dream-like mental state; he may have a vision revealing the future or the will of God. He becomes a central person in the group. It is easy to see in such an extreme case that any type of deviation may be exploited by the group for its own purposes. Far more important, however, is the use cultures make of deviations "within the normal limits," the manner in which each culture draws upon and exploits the constitutional tendencies which are optimally responsive to it, and pushes toward the norm those who deviate in either direction from this optimal point.

We may summarize the point of view thus far developed in the following hypotheses:

1. The economic situation plays a large part in forcing the development of economic institutions, or self-maintenance mores.

2. Self-maintenance mores are not mere conveniences; they are strongly felt, for they are conceived to be the bedrock of social safety.

3. The self-maintenance mores enjoy two-way relations with other mores, but tend to serve as *figure* in the social figure-ground pattern.

4. In consequence, personality frequently tends to be anchored in the roles which are central in the self-maintenance mores.

5. But in some cultures, and in some persons in every culture, the roles introduced by other mores may serve as a figure.

6. Whenever a number of different roles have to be enacted by the individual, the tasks are not merely summated but are integrated as in an act of perception.

7. Over and above the factor of role-playing, infantile experience exerts a huge influence upon personality development, and serves in some degree to shape all the mores, even those of self-maintenance.

8. Though we have apparently found that ethos depends upon the self-maintenance mores, there are two-way relations; the self-maintenance mores do not completely determine ethos, but ethos exerts an influence on the form of these and other mores.

9. Individuals of different temperaments adapt to any given culture with varying degrees of success, depending on the discrepancy between their own ethos and that of the dominant group. (The term ethos is usually reserved for *group* phenomena; but since it refers simply to predominant feeling tone as this affects outlook, it is used here also to define an *individual* characteristic.)

Better than a verbal summary, perhaps, is a dynamic visual schema, like that shown in the accompanying figure. As we have introduced the complications which beset the economic interpretation of personality, steadily finding ourselves needing to indicate two-way relations, the resulting schema apparently is not unlike those which we have used several times to illustrate a Gestalt approach.

Starting with the economic situation and biological individuality as the two supporting pillars, we have seen the self-maintenance mores as largely derived from the economic situation, and the system of other mores as largely dependent on the self-maintenance mores.

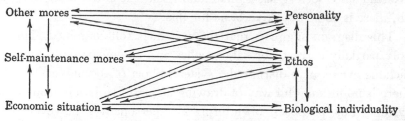

Relations of functional interdependence between six factors are suggested. Each of the six is conceived to stand in a two-way relation with each of the others; but to avoid confusion for the eye, some of the functional arrows are omitted.

But we have seen that the other mores act upon the self-maintenance mores, and the latter, in turn, upon the economic situation. At the right of the chart we have indicated the fundamental outlook or ethos as deriving both from biological individuality, from the economic situation, and from the self-maintenance and other mores. Ethos, involving canalization on existing values (favoring cultural lag), reacts upon the self-maintenance and upon other mores; and indeed, because it affects attitude toward the worth of life, toward health and illness, it influences biological individuality. Finally, it is not difficult to show that the other mores as well as the self-maintenance mores modify the primary economic situation and likewise biological individuality. This book as a whole, we hope, shows that personality has a two-way relation to every one of these interacting components. Consequently we appear to have a complete system of two-way relations, the self-maintenance mores serving as the figure when the social science view is taken. Although the term "figure" is not identical with the term "first cause," it does indicate that motion from this point to others engages our attention more quickly and completely than motion at other points. Sensitized as we are to the problem of individual and group self-maintenance, we find ourselves, like those we study, indicating our roles, anchoring our perception of the social situation at the point of self-maintenance. On the whole, it seems probable that we are here doing what most members of most societies do. And since society has to maintain itself if it is to do anything at all, there is some objective basis for this.

This diagram suggests that the system is self-contained. This is only partially correct, for catastrophes and other completely unpredictable events may disrupt the system. Short of the universe itself, there is no meaningful way of drawing a ring of isolation around the system. For purposes of interpreting personality, however, the system seems to work fairly well, at least well enough to merit criticism and improvement.

36. History as the Proving Ground

AN ATTEMPT has been made to show the interrelation of a group of social factors in the structuring of personality. At best the way of thinking we have followed is tentative, even speculative. But it may be possible to advance our analysis by applying these concepts to more complex societies, to use history as a sort of proving ground for the hypotheses developed, and to see to what extent the personality patterns which have taken shape during European and American history, and the basic character structure of the men and women we know, become intelligible in the light of this way of thinking.

Although a good deal of space is necessary to define, illustrate, qualify, and apply our hypotheses, they can now be condensed: (1) there is a thoroughgoing interdependence between the system of events which we have called economic situation, self-maintenance mores, other mores, biological individuality, ethos, and personality. (2) By and large, the developing individual must define himself first of all in terms of the social roles to be played. (3) The self-maintenance mores tend to be the dominant feature upon which he anchors his perception of his social roles, and they usually serve as figure in the figure-ground pattern of personality. Our problem now is to see whether the history of the culture which we know best—our own— tends to confirm these hypotheses.

EUROPEAN AND AMERICAN PERSONALITY TYPES

Our own cultural antecedents were for the most part a people who had many values; they were multi-focal rather than unifocal. They understood competition, cooperation, and individualism very thoroughly, both verbally and affectively. The social problem of the individual and the many had been solved in all these three phases by the Greco-Roman and also the Hebrew world, for both were at the same time commercial civilizations, as is ours; when Christianity appeared, it preached an integration of these different value systems to people who already knew them. These ways of thinking were thus deeply ingrained in the cultural tradition from which we come.

This makes the problem of economic determinism more complex than in the case of the Manus people, in whose culture may be shown a simple and direct relationship between economic tasks and personality types. We may find, here and there in European culture, little groups that have been split off from the larger world—the Society of Friends or the Swedenborgians—and in whom values are more clearly unifocal; such groups are recruited from among people who reject the chaotic and confusing value pattern of the majority.

Western European character may be introduced by thinking of the medieval man and woman. Draw the picture of man and woman as we find them in the Arthurian cycle. A legendary Celtic king and his court become the theme of a Celtic cycle of romance, carried all over western Europe and endlessly retold. Our question is this: As seen in the Arthurian cycle, *What is a woman? What is a man?* Who is held up as a standard? Who fulfills the listener's heroic hopes? Who fails? What is the basic meaning of masculinity and femininity? It is improbable that Arthur and the Round Table ever existed; the importance of the cycle lies in the revelation of ideals which took shape slowly, made sense, defined a value system. We have chronicles, as well as later literary landmarks (such as Chaucer), which show that the value system of the Arthurian cycle was no artifact of the narrators and troubadours, but an embodiment of the outlook of an age.

The picture that we obtain of an ideal man, an ideal woman, must be put in the baldest, simplest terms. The quintessence of manhood appears in battle. Consider, for example, the tournament. A man heavily encrusted in chain mail and armor, seated on a horse[1] likewise

---

[1] Language offers, as usual, a clue to what was happening. Chivalry is the art of horsemanship; the man who rides dominates those who do not. The test of whether one is a man or not depends on whether or not one is on a horse. The minute the knight came down "off his high horse," the age of chivalry was gone.

heavily encrusted with armor, with an enormous sword in an enormous sheath, and with a huge spear in hand, peered through the visor of his helmet at another man fitted out in the same attire. The two men rode furiously against each other. Both knights might repeatedly splinter their spears against their opponents' shields, which meant that fresh spears were provided by their squires. When, sooner or later, one succeeded in hurling the other from his horse, the man thrown to the ground picked himself up if he could, and shouted to the other to come down and fight. Thereupon the two men slashed at each other with their swords until "whole cantels of armor full of blood" lay on the ground about them. This continued for minutes or for hours until one of them was slain or collapsed and was forced to yield.

What manner of men are these? Men they are who can take and give in such coin as this. The definition of a man in these heroic terms is a result of the specific facts involved in the barbarian invasions. The barbarians had for several centuries forced upon the western world the chaos from which emerged this kind of combat; Charles Martel defeated the Moslems only because men were men such as these; finally the Vikings brought this lesson home to every undefended village. Under the influence of the struggle to survive, the embattled defenders of western civilization took this shape. And as soon as they finished a battle with the heathen, they fought one another. We of the twentieth century are likely to forget that a type of violence was thus crystallized in the European character in the light of which the stories of Samson and Hercules are a bit dull. Tennyson's portrait of the "Great Lord Doorm," a bull for strength and as tough as a Welsh giant, pictures the type of character which stood up against the Moors and the Vikings and saved the society.

The dominant men were thus first of all simple-minded warriors. But we begin to note what always happens when civilized men are driven by circumstance into self-maintenance mores of this type— they feel something missing in themselves. The overplaying of one role calls for the assumption of other roles as counterpoise. The minute that a man developed the security, the power, the prestige of the great lord (as we see him in Scott's Waverley Novels), he realized that he was an incomplete man. He felt about men of learning and of art as a self-made business man today feels; how much better it would be if he had had an education! The medieval man was aware of the other aspects of personality in which he had no share.

What could be done? The first solution lay in the fact that in the medieval church there was an institution offering to a good many of the studiously-minded an asylum from the world. When a man could not find fulfillment in the world, he might find it in the things of the spirit. Here, as a monastic scholar, he reached for the riches of the great Hebrew-Greco-Roman Church tradition, as far as he knew it, in art, in philosophy, in literature. The exquisite rhythm of Gothic art, the utter confidence in the unseen world, the simple and unfailing ardor of St. Francis and St. Bernard, had their wellsprings in the Greco-Roman and Jewish traditions and in the aspiration and humanity of Jesus and Paul; but they arose partly also in response to the terror and chaos of the barbarian invasions.

But a more radical solution was available. The medieval woman helped to seek and find it. She took over many of the functions which men in any period would normally wish to fulfill themselves if they could. Blanche of Castile, Eleanor of Aquitaine, and many lesser lights among the women played a large role not only in statecraft but in the arts. Architecture, sculpture, stained glass, and the ballads and songs which spread over Europe—all these expressed in a thousand ways the civilizing influence of women. Women played an extraordinary part in keeping alive the richness of personality which men as simple warriors had given up.[2] The men were always fighting, drinking, quarreling; chivalry and the cultivation of the amenities, gentleness, esthetic values, were developed largely by the medieval woman. The women who dominated the "courts of love" in this period were consistently pressing civilization to move in a particular

---

[2] G. K. Chesterton in *What's Wrong with the World* points out that man has always tended toward specialization; to provide balance and to preserve the broad range of values he wishes he could keep along with his specialization he looks to the woman. Women are not forced to specialize; they are the keepers of civilization. This is exactly what happened in the age of chivalry.

direction as regards the definition of what it means to be a man and what it means to be a woman, and what the relation of man and woman means. Although the man might in reality be a brute, a picture steadily took shape in which he was a lover, and love a mystery; and in time he responded to what he saw embodied in the woman's exquisite fantasy.

Here, then, we have the response to a compelling situation, a pattern of self-maintenance mores expressed in a primitive form of personal combat; this is the figure for our pattern. The "children of the Roman Empire" stood up to defend what was left of civilization; in the process they were forced through a sieve which made ferocious warriors of them. Vaguely realizing what they were missing, feeling incomplete, they put upon women the tasks which both fulfilled and changed the womanly personality; and the woman in turn formulated an ideal of manhood which tended to change the personality of the man. There is much to remind us here of the Iatmul (page 789).

A curious parallel to this description of the influence of the medieval military situation upon character is offered by medieval Japan, as revealed for example by the Japanese language. When the Chinese tongue was carried into Japan in the sixth century, the spoken language of the Japanese responded only little to it. But the Chinese language, being made up of ideographs, symbols for ideas, lent itself well enough, with modifications, for use in the written language which at first was not particularly well adapted to literary creativeness. In feudal Japan, as in feudal Europe, the men were becoming more and more ferocious, more and more narrow and incomplete as men; and again as in Europe, the court poets were women. These poets made of the rather crude language of the day a gentle, sinuous, melodious tongue. Thus the mellow, gentle form of the Japanese language was created in some measure by the effort of the poetess; the men could not resist it. The same general forces operated in the same general way in throwing upon women the task of developing the roles needed to supplement the central masculine role characteristic of the period.

So far, we have considered only the men and women of the dominant class. Do members of other classes take over the ethos of the dominant class? In medieval European society many certainly did; many of the common people mirrored the value system of the great. They thought of themselves as dependent upon the great, for they were bound to the land and saw the world in terms of the manorial system. In general, we may say that the value system of the dominant economic class seeped down to inundate those beneath. There were exceptions; some spoke out against the current code, and more and more did so as time went on, as witness the bloody revolts of the poor in England during the medieval period and the early Renaissance. But the response to rebel leadership was not massive, for the poor had had no means of developing any ordered outlook except through the eyes of their lords.

We may, then, refer to a well-defined medieval ideal; although never realized, to those identified with its spirit it stands clearly as a peak of aspiration, before the corroding influence of the Commercial Revolution and the Reformation appeared. From our own standpoint, this way of life had to collapse as soon as the dominant role of the knight in armor was successfully challenged. When the barbarians had been assimilated, the only great danger that remained was the Vikings; and when the Vikings were assimilated, there was no basis upon which the heroic model could long be maintained. It is true that men battled among themselves; they were so hardened in the fire that fighting was the only world that was real to them.

But the task of fighting became less and less rational economically; other men began to invent ways of making life more satisfying. Knights did not make inventions; they waited for others to do so. By the thirteenth century there were good roads, banking facilities, gunpowder; the great warriors were soon driven down from their horses, their castles were destroyed or rendered powerless, and within a short time feudalism was done. A new class, the merchants, became dominant. Not that the knight was economically handicapped; as far as economics went, he had more capital, readier access to the market, than the next man. But because of the kind of personality developed in the knight, economic inventions were developed in the hands of other men; personality reacts upon the self-maintenance mores. With the predominance of wool in international trade came a change in the system of land tenure. The wool runs, space for the sheep, encroached more and more upon the village greens and small holdings. Improving transportation brought the possibility of large-scale interarea commerce, wool being the typical British product.

Although land was the property of a few, all could play a part in the trade in wool, and class lines began to blur. The landowner turned his land to wool, the banker dealt in wool futures; the yeoman, even the tenant could invest in wool. The trade permitted vertical mobility (freedom to go up or down); men from city and country, and from every class, could profit from wool in accordance with their astuteness, diligence, and luck. More and more men struggled from the bottom to the top; this reminds us of Manus society (page 785). With the destruction of the manorial system, with the beginning of large-scale exchange between areas specializing in different commodities, there appeared a market open to anyone with the money, and a rapid and continuous process of emancipation of capital, with money and credit more and more displacing fixed goods such as land. This was the Commercial Revolution, the opening of the market to all bidders, the freeing of men from the soil, the development of international trade and of credit systems to facilitate trade.

PERSONALITY SINCE THE COMMERCIAL REVOLUTION

On the influence of the Commercial Revolution upon personality there is an abundance of good material. An integration which appears sound and valuable for our purposes is given by Diamond. In the medieval period a person knew *who* he was by virtue of the class into which he was born, and he had both the privileges and the obligations incurred thereby. The classes were well defined in terms of their relation to their sovereign and to their immediate lord. Not only civil authority, but God in heaven, had ordained that one be a butcher, a baker, a candlestick maker, or a villein or serf. Vertical mobility was slight, and involved great hazards. All this had its advantages and disadvantages in terms of personality. From the earliest days of his life the individual knew where he stood; he had the security of firm group membership. His father and mother, brothers and sisters, would move neither up, nor down, nor away from him, and the bottom could not drop out of his own world. He had many obligations, but his own rights were likewise well defined. People derived a fundamental security from their ability to take the measure of life and apply it to themselves. But with vertical mobility came the opportunity not only to rise but to fall, the dispersion of families to seek new adventures in other parts of the world, the loss of group-membership status, and the uncertain compensation offered by a chance to make an individual name for oneself. When objective goals were no longer taken for granted, attention turned to the self (page 803); it was upon the self that the good things of the world depended. But perhaps the self would fail. How terrifying its inadequacies might prove; how important that the individual self be adequate! Pandora's box is opened for the host of imps to bring insecurities to modern man. Though all society was thrown into confusion, and though the strain upon the individual was of complex origins, it seems fair to say that loss of economic status was feared first of all; the economic role was the *figure* in the new personality ideal.

Much the same view is developed in Erich Fromm's *Escape from Freedom*, and in Karen Horney's *Neurotic Personality of Our Time*. These authors make the point that with the loss of security in the medieval system, the primary problem has become the struggle for status, the struggle to be somebody. Vertical mobility and the dispersion of families are ego threats; whatever the money risks, the situation is much worse from the ego point of view than from the money point of view. A study of business-men's families in 1932 showed in many cases that it was not the loss of high salaries that hurt most; it was the business-man's feeling that he had lost face. Although many could have established themselves as white-collar workers, they belonged to a specific class; and though they had lost the status which this class membership could give them, they could not entirely forego membership in it.

On the other side of the ledger is freedom—freedom not as a gift but as something eternally struggled for. The picture given by the records of the Plymouth and Massachusetts Bay settlements and later by *Poor Richard's Almanac* is not of men exulting in their freedom; it portrays a struggle for a new foothold in a life in which some feudal elements still remain, although they are slowly yielding to a sense of free competition, in which there is much uncertainty and no one is sure where he will come out. Fromm and Horney both suggest that we have paid a terrific price for freedom to come and go, to rise and fall. Not that we should want to give it up. But we live competitively only at great cost (page 568); and in times of grave stress many of us strive to "escape from freedom" through recourse to a pattern of authority.

The problem, however, goes deeper than the loss of security; it involves the development of an impersonal instead of a personal world. In the way life was cast in the medieval period, personal decisions of God or man dictated the course of life. Tragedy was ever at hand, but it was intelligible in personal terms. There might be a great pestilence; but that also was probably God's wise chastisement for the sins of the sovereign or the people. For the most part, things happened for assignable personal reasons. The apprentice worked for and with the master; the thrall knew his lord. The people of the medieval period made sense out of the universe by assigning to the invisible world a constant and continuous expression of loves and hates; there was a purpose behind every good or evil thing. But the Commercial Revolution and the rise of capitalism moved men away from those for whom they worked; a man confronted a task, and ultimately a machine and an impersonal system of production. With the move from country to city, he tended to lose even the sense of community membership. Moreover, the rise of science moved God and the invisible world a great distance away, or dimmed their reality; the "real world" became a mechanical world. Of course thoughtful men hoped that the collapse of dogma, the use of individual reason, would justify the ways of God to man. But instead of making man feel that he knew where he was going and was master of his destiny, science gave him the feeling that abstract natural law was the basis of his experience.

The world has been depersonalized; and lonely man, finding no security in the world, has sought security all the more in other persons. Yet precisely as he seeks directly for those to whom he can cling, he finds the family group disintegrating as a consequence of horizontal and vertical mobility, for people rely upon their individual efforts instead of upon family solidarity.

The loosening of social bonds and the accentuation of individual responsibility were further signalized by the Protestant Reformation, as many historians have shown. There is much in Tawney's *Religion and the Rise of Capitalism* to define the problem. We should expect, Tawney observes, that the Commercial Revolution, which began in northern Europe, notably in England and the Low Countries, and spread thence to France, Italy, Germany, and Switzerland, would prepare the soil for an individualism in man's thinking about his ethical relation to his fellows. During the medieval period Roman Catholic theologians had been able to define moral obligation in the economic sphere in such a way as to give a fairly uniform notion of one's duty to the community. Prices were not conceived to be impersonal adjustments to economic realities alone; they must be "fair." The taking of interest, called usury, was condemned on moral grounds, an attitude that gave way only slowly as business enterprise pressed for thoroughgoing changes. The new religious individualism was congenial to the growth of economic individualism, for individualism meant the right of the individual to use the talents which God had given him. The new vertical mobility had been growing for several centuries before the Protestant Reformation began; but Protestantism, with its ethical individualism and its justification of an individualistic rather than a social outlook in both religious and economic matters, was cordial to the new merchant class. In northern Europe there developed a rather well-unified theological and economic outlook; Englishmen, Scots, Dutchmen adopted a way of thinking that was far more individualistic in economic matters than that which characterized southern Europe.

As we turn to the ideologies and the ethos brought to America from northwestern Europe, we have to consider both the traditional culture

[826]

of the new arrivals and the individualism expressed in the new economic and religious attitudes of the sixteenth and seventeenth centuries. We must, however, be more specific regarding the *regional* character types which developed in the various colonial areas. In the light of the data regarding the Plymouth and Massachusetts Bay settlements, we find that the first American personality type was the Calvinist; many of the settlers were Calvinist "men of the market," and the rest were dependent on the new economy. The relation of the economic to the religious factors in their character has been studied many times, as in Schneider's *The Puritan Mind* and Robinson and Wheeler's *Great Little Watertown*; however, we take responsibility for the interpretation given here. Certain settlers—for example, some of the Covenanters of the *Mayflower*—were men of deep faith; some were adventurers; others had found their economic plight in England so hard that even the wilderness was welcome. But when they found themselves relatively free from the control of the London bankers who had financed the enterprise, the colonists soon came to feel that the risk and the privilege were chiefly their own; they had come over under difficult conditions and were making a new haven where Christians might dwell. For the time being, the economic and religious impulses of the settlers were well integrated.[3] But what was at first glossed over —namely, the conflict between the religious and economic motives— soon broke out into an open row. In their perception of their task, the meaning of their life, the religious motivation was the figure for many people, the making of money the figure for others. Despite the relative unity of the religious outlook of the early settlers, the picture soon begins to agree closely with that for Europe in general, described above (page 824). The chief event that happened to those who came to the northern colonies in the seventeenth and eighteenth centuries was what was happening throughout northern Europe: the Commercial Revolution. In the coastal cities such as Boston, New York,

---

[3] The Puritan character shows great ruggedness and great narrowness; men and women work terribly hard, try terribly hard to be good. The net result is esthetically ambivalent; there is too much tightness and dryness in all their goodness. Yet when they realize that no one will catch them in the act, they prove capable of great sweetness and warmth. A good deal of intensity can appear on such special permissive occasions; the long-smoldering fire can blaze out suddenly.

and Philadelphia, a thriving merchant class was soon established, and by 1700 the urban patterns of life were essentially those of British cities; here too were artisans and laborers of the British type. These were individualists in the same sense as in Britain.

Here, however, a profound difference emerges which soon over-shadows the similarities. The land was limitless, and suitable for the rapid organization of one-family farms. Since the Indians were pre-dominantly either friendly or weak, the land was bought for a song or simply seized. Keller asks, "What is the ratio of mouths to food?" We answer that there were few mouths, and an immense quantity of land which was hilly and rocky, but was arable and suited for small holdings. This was the economic situation. The self-maintenance mores provided amply for small, individually operated farms. The effect upon the colonists was prompt and profound. No one would work for anyone else except at a high wage, for every man could, with an effort, have his own land; no one could set himself up as a landlord except on a brief and precarious basis. The value of a man was high; that of a unit of land, low. Men became more and more individualistic, equalitarian, democratic in character, because both the economic situa-tion and the self-maintenance mores thus defined their tasks, their roles, their interpersonal relations. If a man came, for example, as an indentured servant, he found as soon as he had worked out the pre-scribed period that his bargaining power for wages or land was con-siderable. The situation remained fairly stable for two centuries, for westward migration was not very difficult, and the frontiersman's cutting edge into the wilderness continued to be a steady factor that cheapened land and maintained the value of the individual man in the East, for he could migrate if he wished.

This pattern held only for the northern colonies; the situation was utterly different in the southern colonies. The system by which the southern colonies were established was quite different, for the land lent itself well to extensive holdings and to absentee ownership; the large landowners made the most of an essentially cavalier type of land control. A manorial system was set up by the Virginian and Carolina colonists from the beginning; for the class system inherited from the pre-Commercial Revolution period, with its aristocracy, its servants, its artisans, and its workers on the land, could be adapted without great difficulty to these colonies; moreover, Negro slaves soon made possible a rapid and prosperous development which spread westward as easily as did the northern settlements. Since the land in the South was appropriated by those who could operate on a large scale with slaves, it is clear that character in the South could not be the same as it was in the North.

Two contrasting streams of tradition appeared. Whereas the North developed an urban and urbane merchant class and a class of small farmers, a derivative of the British manorial system took shape in the South, with the graces and amenities of the cavalier, and with hired managers of lower status being responsible for business detail; cities appeared much later and their mercantile activities did but little to alter the essentially rural outlook. The American personality types that came into being were thus European personality types molded by the different economic situations and different self-maintenance mores of North and South.

During the period following the Revolutionary War, the ratio of mouths to food continued to have primary significance. But the frontier remained. This safety valve, which allowed the steam to escape at one point, was very important. Though only a small number of people moved west in any one decade, the fact that one *could* go contributed to the democratic and equalitarian spirit so heavily stressed by De Tocqueville. The Midwest served as an outlet for all those who were restless, all those who needed independence or new land for themselves. Both public opinion and law supported one-family units of land, not absentee landlordism. America was not of course a land of hope to everyone; there was much unrest and often much misery. But the fact that people could go west meant that the frontier set the pace; the pioneer was the type around whom certain American traits gradually crystallized. He was never in the majority, but he was always a symbol; to the restless, there was always this symbol, and a chance to begin anew. Moreover, the top and bottom strata of society participated in the migration much less extensively than did the intervening strata, so that the movement was characterized by a rather homogeneous middle-class ideology; and as the people settled, their memories of class distinctions were dimmed by the new problems in which all must share. A new ethos, a new way of facing life, a new personality type was developed. Although it is proper to pay a certain amount of homage to the rich cultural tradition borne by these men, it is equally important to recognize how rapidly a new economic setting can blur the traditions and redefine human types. Steadily from 1800 onward until the Civil War period, the population, almost exclusively agricultural with very few merchants and professional men, developed a number of characteristics which marked it off sharply both from the southern class types—cavaliers, foremen, artisans, and black and white laborers—and from the two New England types described above (page 828).

The most notable characteristic of these people was an intensification of what the northern colonists had long displayed, namely, individualism. Although this had some historical connection with seventeenth-century English individualism (such as that of John Locke), it rested chiefly on the fact that people were too hard driven by their prime task of conquering the soil to be much concerned with community living. The population increased rapidly and kept always moving west, the one-family farm remaining the social unit. The result was an intensification of the democratic spirit that had already been defined in New England; but here there was no powerful class of bankers, shippers, or slave owners to apply the brakes. The political system created by the Constitution was consequently overhauled in forty years and Jacksonian democracy emerged as a result. This political outcome reacted upon the people from whom it stemmed; they exulted in their power. Their pride in their homespun simplicity and democracy shines through the whole Midwest in the middle of the nineteenth century; for example, it played a large part in the rise of Abraham Lincoln. When, in *Life on the Mississippi*, Mark Twain gives us his picture of plain Americans, he is describing something which had been hammered out very recently, in consequence of a dynamic that is clear cut and inexorable.

It follows that, as Bryce said, the population tended to become "homogeneous." The reasons were simple. (1) It was relatively easy to move whether overland or along the rivers. (2) The fact that the huge midwestern area was almost all arable, with very little of it extremely good or extremely poor, made men feel that it was not all-important where they went; hence people of many origins were soon scrambled. This homogeneity of the land contributed powerfully to the homogeneity of the American character type which emerged.

A final factor calling for more direct study is urbanization. Between the Atlantic seaboard and the Alleghenies a class system of merchants, machinists, and artisans arose. Social change went on rapidly in the cities of the East, both because of commerce and industry and by virtue of new intellectual currents expressed in literature, the arts (e.g., the new use of Greek architectural models before the Civil War), and science, notably Darwinism. Through all this long period (about 1800–1860), however, the Midwest remained almost purely rural;[4] and since books, newspapers, and the theater were essentially luxury items, people maintained their traditional ways long enough to develop a well-defined ideological unity. The midwestern type therefore had a chance to become crystallized, which would not have been possible had there been a single big city to receive and radiate the new ideas of the period.

But the Midwest gave while it received. As the character of its people became defined, in consequence of all these conditions, it began to exert a powerful backward effect upon all the other regions of the country. Mark Twain, leaving his beloved Mississippi for Hartford, was but one of thousands who carried back east a knowledge and love of the Midwest; Lincoln was the most eminent of those whose raw-boned humanity jolted the eastern aristocrats into awareness that they were no longer self-sufficient. The Midwest began slowly to capture the imagination of the East not only as a place where there was land and opportunity, but as the true "center of gravity" of the United States; or to use another figure of speech, this "greatest

---

[4] As Huckleberry Finn drifted down the Mississippi on his raft he said that he had "heard tell" there were 20,000 people in St. Louis, but that wasn't true, for you couldn't get that many people together in one place.

common divisor," including people from every corner of the old East and South, began, by force of numbers and through confidence in itself, to mold the outlook and ethos of other regions.

THE END OF THE FRONTIER

From the Jamestown settlement in 1607 until about 1890, there was always a frontier. Then rather suddenly Americans discovered that the possibility of free homesteading was at an end, that the country was "full," and that pioneering in the strict sense was a thing of the past. The Director of the Census, in his report in 1890 on the density of population in the west, called attention to the fact that the frontier was gone. This may easily be documented by maps which show that the westward wave of migration had spread to the Pacific, and echoing back had met a forward wave in the region of the western Great Plains and the Rockies; there was no more land to be had except in terms of payments expressing its "marginal utility." Almost at one stroke there ceased to be a basis for the indefinite continuance of the personality type which had become dominant during nearly three centuries of American history.

Moreover, in the same decades which witnessed the disappearance of the frontier, the engines of the new industrialism—power-driven machinery, the factory, the railroads, ore refining, etc.—swept like a tidal wave from east to west. Forty years after Tecumseh laid down his arms, Buffalo and Cleveland were belching factory smoke across the Great Lakes. With industrialization came rapid urbanization, which as we saw, means division of labor, and a class system. The resulting change has been rapid in some areas, but in others there has been much cultural lag. Some of the people in Wyoming and Colorado today, for example, make it seem that 1880 and the mining days are just around the corner, a fact attested to by the local-color literature that is placed against this backdrop of a quasi-permanent midwestern character. But *Whirl Is King*, and will have to have his throne.

Our task is to look at American character changes since the passing of the frontier and the rise of individualism. The best material available for studying the changes that have led to the present-day American character is the Lynds' study of a midwestern city as it existed in 1890, in 1923, and in 1935; for here, as the city changed, we can see the character of its typical men and women changing in consequence. The source material for 1890 consisted of diaries, newspapers, letters, and the memories of those still living. The Middletown of 1890 was a homogeneous, rugged, individualistic, democratic community; a one-class community, not in the sense of economic equality, but in the sense that each man was "as good as" another. The most prosperous spoke to the poorest without condescension; a man could sit on the porch in his shirtsleeves on a summer evening, and call out to any passer-by, banker and garbage collector alike, to come up and have a cigar. As the frontier mother declares roundly in *Oklahoma!* "I won't say I'm any better than anybody else, but I'm damned if I ain't just as good." The wealthiest man in Middletown had gone there as a young man in 1887; he had started in with nothing and had had to borrow an overcoat from his neighbor because the winter was so cold. Jacksonian democracy still throve there in 1890; though nearly thirty years of industrialization had gone by since the Civil War, people still breathed an atmosphere of essential equality; there was consequently little tension over status. There was vertical mobility, the Horatio Alger dream of struggling to the top; but since all were potential but none actual plutocrats, people settled for here-and-now equality. There was freedom of enterprise (for not much capital was needed), free speech (especially free name-calling), and free political participation; and much fear (exactly as Jefferson would have expected) of the large city and of large industry. These people believed that, if free from outside interference, natural goodness, talent, and hard work would lead to success; and this belief functioned as an organic aspect of the Protestant attitude toward the individual and toward freedom of competition as defined above (page 830).

There was, then, a sort of standardization of attitudes. The Lynds managed to get at that standard attitude pattern of 1890 by asking 40 business-class and 130 working-class housewives what traits and attitudes their mothers had tried to instill in them as children. The replies indicate that practically all of these women had been subjected to the same general ideology: tremendous emphasis on honesty, hard work, obedience, self-control, will power, persistence, rectitude of life. This was a practically homogeneous picture for wives of both classes.

But now for the change. The year 1890 marked the closing of the frontier, and for Middletown it also marked, approximately, the arrival of the Industrial Revolution. If there was one thing that showed Americans what they were losing as the Industrial Revolution swept them away from individualism into the category of "workers," it was the wave of feeling against trusts and banks, as expressed in Greenbackism and the Sherman Act of 1890. Since the closing of the frontier and the arrival of large industry hit the Midwest in the same period, it would be a very nice problem—one which we cannot consider here—to determine which personality changes were reflections of the one, which reflections of the other. It is clear that most of the men of Middletown made no attempt to answer any such question and that the results were far from uniform. The essential thing, in any event, is that each of these facts, by itself, tended to destroy the one-class system; for if industrialization had been delayed, the closing of the frontier would itself inevitably have led to urbanization, and if the closing of the frontier had been delayed, industrialization alone would similarly have led to urbanization. Middletown men and women knew well enough what a two-class system was, for they were articulate in their hatred of it; nevertheless, it came. The gas boom of the '90's ushered it in, and the glass preserving jars in whose manufacture the town soon excelled hastened its development, as machinery replaced skilled glass blowers.

When the Lynds studied Middletown in 1923–1924 the population had split into two well-defined classes, in about the proportion of one member of the business class to about three of the working class. Are these really *classes*? At this point a statistician might object that there is no sharp cleavage, income shows a perfectly smooth gradation from the poorest to the richest, and a few members of the working class make more money than certain members of the business group. But in terms of social function, social role, and prevailing outlook, there are two classes. In the business group are people who direct the economy by means of symbols, marks on paper; they earn their livelihood by calculating future income and outgo. The worker group deals with material objects; they work with glass-blowing machines, with cylinderheads, with drill presses. There is no organic relation between an owner and his material property except the symbolic system, the agreement of society that he has the right to control; this agreement, however, is deeply ingrained in the self-maintenance mores, and is supported by all the other mores. The classes in Middletown are separated by symbol versus physical action.

The results, for American personality type, may be listed under several heads. (1) As far as the sense of class membership is concerned, we should expect to find a sense of "complacency"—to use Veblen's term—developing among those who own and operate the industrial system; and among those who do not, a sense of insecurity and unresolved frustration, a smoldering hope that they or their children may rise in the scale, this hope vying with a bewildered uncertainty whether there will be a job next week. (2) In accordance with this, we should expect that there would develop among the business group a sense of the amenities, a desire to cultivate esthetic standards and the marks of leisure-class good taste that were lacking in the Middletown of 1890; they must turn to the metropolitan standards of London, Paris, and New York. (3) Educational ideals will slowly shift their emphasis from the straightforward aim of "getting ahead" to assistance in achieving status, a form of "conspicuous consumption"; one must prepare for the role of a college-bred person, with all that that implies.

At this point a natural question arises. Which class is the *new* class? For neither class in 1923–1924 looks exactly like the one class which prevailed in 1890; status has taken on new form, and neither is the equivalent of the older group. Yet analysis shows that the working class is essentially like the plain people of 1890, whereas the business group is saturated with urban ideas at which the earlier Middletown scoffed. The contrast appears in the responses of working-class and business-class mothers to questions about their ways of bringing up children, the qualities they were trying to develop in their children (cf. page 833). While the mothers of 1890 presented a rather well-united front, the replies of the mothers of 1923–1924 show that the business-class mothers—being of course much better informed, much more directly in contact with new ideas in education as in everything else—are endeavoring to inculcate an essentially new pattern, with stress upon originality, independence, flexibility. The working-class mother still emphasizes hard work, thrift, obedience; she has not heard the new doctrines, and she clings to the only security pattern she knows.

Insecurity and disquiet have become characteristic of both groups in 1923. For the business group the old authorities are gone. When people settled in Middletown, the great majority accepted unquestioningly the authority of the Bible; but a hundred years of Biblical criticism and of the historical approach to religion have undermined the old foundations. The scientific attitude toward the world, including Darwinism on the one hand, and an impersonal rather than a personal view of nature on the other, have further weakened the code of life. Calvinist individualism has become much less meaningful in the business life of Middletown than it was to the pioneer. Mothers hesitate to put their children through the cycle of work-thrift-obedience—and no questions answered—that was their own lot, for they remember another ethics, the ethics of reciprocity, which is likewise part of their rich tradition. Moreover, the very rapidity of change and the diversity of modern cultural elements make a stable frame of reference impossible. Education has opened enough books to these people to make them doubtful about what they want their children to believe and live by. The fathers were not interrogated; they were probably less soulful than the mothers, but equally confused.

The working class of Middletown, while continuing to accept the standards of an earlier age, grow vaguely aware, however, that the charm was not effective. Their economic predicament is plainly not removed by traditionally "good" behavior. But it would be a great mistake to say that such continuing beliefs represent pure traditionalism. For one thing, the people identify, Horatio Alger-fashion, with the successful and see through their eyes; for another, they take note of the occasional individual who does "struggle up." Like the child who does not "extinguish" his bedtime crying because once in a hundred times his father relents and picks him up, the Middletowners cannot bring themselves to give up their roseate view of business opportunity because once in a blue moon a man breaks out of the labor ranks and makes good in business. In 1923, for example, the Lynds discovered one very effective labor leader in the town; a few years later he had gone into business. This familiar pattern of identification and emulation of the business class has been called the "bourgeoissification" of the American public. There are, then, two classes, but no clear working-class ideology which can be contrasted with business-class ideology.

It is time to recapitulate the Middletown story of class formation and to make clear the interrelation of factors in the resulting American personality types. We have tried to show that the contributing factors are many and complex, and that even the "economic factor" is a composite; but that in general the self-maintenance mores serve as figure, as our hypothesis requires. But there is room here for a serious misunderstanding. Many have argued as follows: When once the Industrial Revolution appeared in the United States jointly with the closing of the frontier, the old democracy was patently doomed and a class system had to develop; ergo, the personality characteristics of the resulting classes were simply *products of this nineteenth-century situation.* This "obvious" view is, I believe, mistaken. Some effort was made earlier (page 828) to suggest the difference between city and farm people in New England defined as early as 1700. Herbert Schneider and others vividly describe the two-class system in the American colonies in 1700. The two classes in Boston in 1700 correspond well with the two classes in Middletown in 1923—a class of owners, "symbol men," and workers, "machine men." It was urbanization, not industrialization, that produced the class system in the colonies, just as had happened in Greece and Rome. In fact, it could be argued rather convincingly that the insecurity and confusion of the

Bostonians of 1700, at whom the Calvinists preached so thunderously for their "new ideas," greatly resembled the insecurity and confusion of the Middletowners of 1923. In the city there are always classes, and someone is always preaching new and confusing ideas.

The reason why the issue is so important is that the socio-economic base of present-day American personality types lies in the relation of three factors: urbanization, industrialization, and the frontier. According to the thesis developed here, the class system as such is primarily an expression of urbanization; industrialization is a factor reinforcing all the adventuresomeness, frustration, and anxiety which attend vertical mobility; and the frontier still operates (on the basis of a powerful cultural lag) to make American farmers—or garage mechanics—more individualistic, more equalitarian than those of other countries. The individualism and equalitarianism which took shape under the frontier conditions of the midwestern farm have penetrated Midwestern cities and eastern and far-western farms to some extent, and still operate as conspicuous characteristics which differentiate Americans from other industrialized and urbanized peoples. Thus though we can scarcely hope to find any more 1890 one-class Middletowns anywhere, we can perhaps agree that what we ordinarily call an American character type—the breezy, vigorous, self-reliant, "upstanding" individual—is in a sense the product of a cultural lag.

But in another sense he is nothing of the kind. All the America that there has ever been has been a pioneering enterprise; and adventure has taken many other forms than westward migration. Within recent decades scientific discovery, industrial research, and sheer new inventions and appliances have taken the place of geographic pioneering. It is indeed likely that new art forms such as modern photography, and new types of "social discovery" such as "group work," exemplify the same spirit. It may be urged that these adventures involve only a few people. But we must remember that at any given time the pioneers constituted only a small fraction of the total; indeed, our avidity for anything that is new, in education, music, slang, or soap flakes, is at least as intense as any expression of the pioneer spirit in an earlier era. And when we turn to the other prominent aspect of the pioneering spirit, its equalitarianism, we must bear in mind that the farmer has fought against class distinctions (while emphasizing individual distinction with respect to energy, wit, competence) through all the decades of his existence, and has refused to give it up in the face of the extreme difficulties inherent in running a one-man farm. This may indeed be regarded as a case of cultural lag, representing the continuity and stability of an American pattern when everything else has succumbed to urbanization and individualization; but if men stubbornly cling to what they are, and if American government continues to support and encourage the type, there is no certainty that the type will disappear.

This prompts a further word on the confusion of the present American type with the present American *urban* type. We quoted Fromm, Horney, and Diamond on the insecurity of modern man as a result of the loss of his earlier class status, his vertical mobility, the scattering of families, and the growth of impersonality. Now another factor must be added: Urbanization itself is a huge component of the insecurities which these authors describe. Surely any American who goes from a large city to the country and returns to the city notices the harried, anxious faces, the silence, the loneliness of urban man. Urbanization has meant insecurity. And as migration was usually, until the depression, from country to city rather than from city to country, the process has inevitably involved the tearing up of roots and the loss of stability. The insecurity of the new arrivals in a strange world has increased the general level of urban insecurity. Urban psychiatrists have encountered the typical insecurities of the upper and upper-middle urban classes; hence the incomplete but decidedly valuable picture given by *Neurotic Personality of Our Time*.

SOME EFFECTS OF THE DEPRESSION

Middletown was revisited in 1935, and the story retold in terms of the mid-depression picture. What happened after the 1929 crash was that as businesses failed they were bought up and absorbed. Within four or five years the banking system of the town, the department stores, the YMCA, and a large residential section were all directly or indirectly controlled by one large family. The modest and reserved sense of power and leadership which this "X family" showed in 1923 had changed almost to a sense of eminent domain, the right—the duty—to come and go whenever they felt it expedient to do so.

The remainder of the former business class consists of insecure little people who are beholden to the great family, happy when they are invited to a garden party or to tea. We can see the development of an attitude far different from the rather individualistic attitude of 1923. All the people have been through such misery, taken such a beating, that they are glad to be able to keep going, not quite so anxious to assert themselves. There is a loss of that buccaneer spirit which marked the American business-class character in the Gilded Age and kept itself alive until depression times. Sinclair Lewis's pre-depression Babbitt, flabby though he is, is still independent, in his own judgment a man upon whom the world might do well to model itself. But the former business class is now a middle class; it looks not down but up.

Middle-class insecurity, in Middletown and elsewhere, rapidly pervaded the youth in high school and college. In a number of studies of the expectations of college students regarding their own future, the predominant note of the depression years is expressed by the fact that their expectations are no longer in terms of "great killings" but in terms of a hope for security; the majority are glad to "settle for" a safe and modest place in society, rather than taking chances. But at best these students were insecure; the data of Rundquist and Sletto show that the more intelligent were more worried, had a "lower morale," than the less intelligent; they were beginning to feel that perhaps even the decision to play for security was not enough to guarantee it; they felt like the Middletown business man who said flatly, "We are all scared to death."

The pattern of a three-class system had thus taken shape before World War II, and it is universal testimony that larger businesses have gained, smaller ones lost, in consequence of the war. Although this is no place for economic or political prediction, this fact must be recognized because of its relevance in defining present American urban personality types and observing their necessary evolution. All three classes show plain marks of the current wear and tear; all are in a pathological condition. There is anxiety and defeatism on the part of most farmers and workers, even in the midst of momentary dramatic successes in individual struggles; they do not know why they are not "making out," in terms of doing better than their fathers, but most of them are not; they are frustrated and petulant. The middle class, with their confident manner, seem to be secure, but they likewise are confused and frightened. The X family of Middletown and its equivalents everywhere experience great security at the moment of their power, but they fear "politics," i.e., mass expression, which they know holds over them a sword of Damocles. It seems pretty safe to say that all the factors we have tried to stress (page 814) will continue to be interrelated, that personality will reflect them all, and that the roles defined by the self-maintenance mores will continue to serve as figure in the figure-ground pattern wherein personality is expressed. The collective American personality, and our individual personalities as men, women, children, will eventually anchor upon the new self-maintenance roles to be developed.

37. The Family as Mediator
of Culture

IN A Colorado town the Ryersons stood together like a Scottish clan. But Jim Ryerson and his brother Kip had had a falling out and would not speak to each other. One day Kip got into a fight with Lint Corcoran and was being beaten up well. Jim happened by on the other side of the street. He handed his coat to someone in the gaping crowd, challenged Corcoran, thoroughly vanquished him, took back his coat —and never spoke to Kip. It is not enough to say that families serve the cultural process or, as we saw above (page 797), that they may shape infantile personality. Family membership is a primary reality for personality, both because the cultural definition of what a family is, and what it must do, is the starting point in determining personal roles, and, as in the case of the Ryersons, because being a member of a particular family provides a stable and fundamental quality to personal living. It is worth while to look at the give-and-take of feeling between parents and children; and this leads us to a study of the canalization and conditioning of the infant's drives in their constant interaction with the personalities in the family pattern. This will involve a review of many suggestions offered earlier, especially in Chapters 20–23, but a review which takes account of the social science material sketched in Chapters 32–36. The first part of the chapter is a good section to skip if the reader is not especially interested in the family as such.

Sociologists distinguish conveniently between primary and secondary groups. The primary group is the growing individual's face-to-face world, the world of tenderness and immediacy, the world of security. Secondary groups, such as religious or nationality groups, may win deep loyalty from the individual, but he experiences them in the light of his earlier group experiences. The distinction is especially convenient for us because of the probability that, like all other responses, canalized and conditioned responses transfer to persons similar to those with whom the first associations were formed. If this is true, we should expect to find that the deeper and more constantly reinforced responses to parents and to brothers and sisters will become the matrix from which the field of friendships and hostilities, dependent and autonomous social relationships, will grow.

Freud keenly sensed and elaborated this in his *Group Psychology and Analysis of the Ego*, in which he showed that two major social aggregates, the church and the army, derive their primal emotional control from the family structure resident in their very being. Thus when one encounters the male who leads and protects a group, what shall one call him? "Father," of course; and this is what every parish priest is called. In what terms is an assemblage of celibate men devoted to an other-worldly purpose known one to another? As "brothers," of course. How about women similarly consecrated? "Sisters." And who is the protecting and dominant woman? The "Mother Superior." Similarly, the army officer is really a "father to his men"—"Papa" Joffre. The final bond of a soldier's loyalty emerges in such expressions of family experience as "my buddy" (brother).

To use the terminology developed in Chapter 8, these responses are "canalizations upon the family." They are conceived not as mere stepping stones or replaceable timbers in a constantly shifting conditioning and reconditioning process. On the contrary, they are relatively permanent and indissoluble features in character structure wherever the family exists. Despite all the variations in marriage and family patterns, they seem to have the same fundamental emotional loadings wherever dependence, fear, affection, and the security need are predominant in childhood; and this applies to most human societies. Even with the modifications required in the case of the more austere or the more chaotic societies, these features of family solidarity form the chief basis of whatever security and continuity the child experiences. Among the savage sorcerers of Dobu (page 805) it is the *susu*, the mother's milk, that constitutes the protective bond, the region of safety from unknown malevolent forces. Although we may not go so far as Briffault in insisting that *all* tenderness, affection, and protective impulse, and ultimately all cordiality and humanity in living, derive from the halo of sentiment that surrounds the maternal relationship, we can agree that it is the compelling power of the family, expressed in terms of both love and fear, that determines the quest for love and the pattern of escape from fear.

The actual *modus operandi* of parent-child contact, however, proves to be twofold. (1) Through the simplest canalizing processes, the child learns to need certain kinds of persons, certain kinds of experience. He needs, for example, to be with his mother, just as a cub or a foal does; he needs to continue to find in her what he has found in her earlier, to witness the recurrence of her habitual and endearing acts as a mother. (2) The family does more than mold the child in this way; it acts as *buffer*, as a sort of porous barrier that permits some but not all aspects of the broader culture to come through and act upon the child. In the long run, the powerful negative role by which certain parts of the culture are prevented from reaching the child is as important as the positive role. We may conveniently contrast these cultural functions by referring to the family as *sieve* and as *mold*. Neither term is satisfactory; for substances going into sieves and molds are not likely to struggle against them. But perhaps the contrast between the two kinds of process is worth pointing out.

Parents as Standards

Of all the consequences of canalization upon family and upon self—affection, sympathy, loyalty, identification—with which the child develops his system of values, the most encompassing might be termed the sense of basic rightness, the normative character of the immediate world. Just as *I* am right (Piaget's egocentrism) so *father* and *mother* are right; and so, by analogy as well as by daily associative reinforcement, those who stand for the same things and live according to the same plan, are right. The ways in which things are done are the normal, the convenient, the proper, the adequate ways.

Deviation from such patterns is inconvenient and distracting; it "breaks our habit," as Humphrey would phrase it. More than that, he who deviates is one who values what we reasonable people disvalue, and disvalues what we value. His ways are therefore literally *absurd*, since, as we have seen, values are peremptory and absolute through all the childhood period; there is utter absurdity in finding values in persons, objects, and experiences that have been a basis only for disgust or fear. Valuation is usually a matter of an ingrained response to a configuration, a total pattern whose many aspects permit a wide *variety* of responses, depending upon what serves as anchor. The learning process involves emphasis, accent, anchorage, upon one feature of this complex whole. If a positive response to a complex total is encouraged—for example, an English or a Chinese way of behaving—some features are ignored which in different circumstances would become anchors for very different attitudes. The total patterns of Englishmen or Chinese can in time be fractionated so that two or more attitudes can be entertained toward the same person. But the cleavage occurs only when it is absolutely required in practice; and the later it appears, the less profound its consequences.

Parents are complex totalities involving much to be loved, much to be feared, some things to be amused at, and a little to be disgusted or annoyed with; the processes and intensities vary from child to child and from family to family. The canalization process is, however, the affective side of the anchorage process; for the anchorage depends on the dominant drive that is at work. It is, then, not simply the father's affection but the *whole father*, not simply the mother's sustenance but the *whole mother*, that becomes the norm and center of the child's living. The emotional incompatibility between the love aspect and the fear aspect is the reason for the conflict which plays so large a role in Freudian psychology (the Oedipus complex). The fear features of the configuration, dynamically deprived of their control, are the very features which, under altered conditions of dominance, may make the whole father an object of fear (or hate). He may be an object of fear in one mood; in another, an object of affection. The same is true of all the father surrogates, all the grandfathers and uncles, all the policemen and martial heroes, all the kings, presidents, and popes, who derive their first great place in the child's experience as configural duplicates of his first experiences. The policeman is puzzled at the intensity of the child's affection, trust, or fear. The parish priest discovers an intensity of filial response with which sometimes he hardly knows how to cope. The woman teacher in the early grades carries the double brunt of our cultural situation: she must at the same time be mother substitute and wielder of those authority patterns which, in a patriarchal age, a father alone imposed.

But it is not simply the family that is loved and made central; t is the family's *way*, its patterns and rhythms, the spirit and mood of its living. This is the basis for the universal and familiar picture of community loyalties, or *sociocentrism*, as Lerner called it, and the broader process of *ethnocentrism* (page 386) which among all peoples defines the obvious "rightness" of the familiar ways. The tempo and style of conduct, the modulation of voice, the characteristic gesture and locomotion, and perhaps most of all, the ethos, the way of looking at life, become not simply habitual, but the standard for individual living. If the canalization process is irreversible, the individual who assimilates a second culture which is sharply at variance with his childhood culture can do so only under considerable strain and with conscious attention to detail; he never actually outgrows his primary loyalties to the foods and songs of his childhood. Indeed, if our hypothesis is correct, he will frequently manifest "compensation" in the process, repudiating his childhood habits and tastes with a violence suggesting inner conflict, and a shame reflecting his awareness of it; the new member of any group can show his loyalty only through scorn for the ways of the old group. In the meantime, however, he pushes himself into the new culture more rapidly than it can accept him.

From the hypothesis just sketched it follows that regardless of the economic background of the family structure, the structure itself plays a controlling part in determining the character structure of the individual. The children of the same parents will of course be canalized somewhat differently, depending upon their own organic constitution and the changes which have occurred in the parents between the birth of the different children, as well as the parents' responses to each child and their secondary adjustments to broader changes in the cultural whole. Yet children of the same parents share in a family atmosphere; and such an atmosphere can produce, over and over again, a diffuse kindliness, a violent hostility, a lackadaisical vagueness and confusion of affective responses, a petulant or capricious oscillation of moods. It can produce a disciplined rigidity like that of Cato the Censor, or the same rigidity modified by a deep note of sorrow and sentiment, as in the Hebrews of the time of the prophets. Rarely if ever can we trace the ultimate origins of the differences in family atmospheres; but we can say that they are not exclusively determined by geography or economic circumstances, and that as far as the individual child is concerned they operate in a highly specific way, which is for him the first psychological reality. The broader economic background may exert a continuing influence, but it is grasped only dimly and at a much later date. To put it very simply, the basic wants and fears are the results of the particular canalizations encouraged by the relations of the parents to each other and to the children, and for this reason the individual character structure has coherence and tightness instead of the flux and confusion which would result from day-by-day changes in responses to a changing economic pattern. There is thus individual lag in personality structure, and for the same reason cultural lag, so far as the economic changes within a lifetime occur at a pace with which the individual character structure cannot keep up.

All this response to the family as the center of the in-group continues as long as the child is not aware of any conflict between the family and the society in which he lives. If he gradually discovers that the family is in some way rejected by the large group, the shock involves not simply the loss of cherished landmarks of rightness and wrongness; it challenges the central rightness of the self, and leads either to self-disparagement or to embittered protest against society. In the children of European-born Americans, it often results in revolt against the family and powerful identification with the outer group, mingled with considerable inner confusion.

The picture of family membership assumes different forms when boys and girls are considered separately. Complex economic skills, such as the skills of the chase and of combat, of food preparation and the making of clothing, bring out within the latent human nature of the two sexes many characteristics which grow progressively sharper. Such characteristics are partly traceable to different canalizations in boys and girls, such as different types of canalizations upon father and mother. Cultural norms can emphasize the boy's response to his father to such an extent that the mother-son relation is attenuated. The girl's relation to her mother may in the meantime become largely an escape relationship in which she avoids the tension and violence of the culturally emphasized father-son relation, and in which her relation to her father is reduced to the slender personal circumstance of his pride being inflated when he arranges a favorable marriage for her. Whether as compensation for this emotionally frustrating situation or as an independent development, the mother-son cult has had an even greater vogue, many civilizations making it the key to the structure of the universe and the basis not only of human society, but of world order, philosophy, and religion.

Though the relations of parents to children necessarily first engage our attention, the relations of brothers and sisters deserve more than mere discussion in terms of analogy. It is true enough, as the Freudian literature emphasizes, that the big brother is sometimes a father symbol or substitute, the big sister sometimes a mother surrogate. Often, however, the relationships between siblings are direct rather than indirect.

Response to one's own self, as we have seen, is present as early and in as well-defined a form as is response to parents. Attention to self, and concern with self, spreads by transfer or analogy to preoccupation with others like oneself. If others are more or less the same size as oneself, so much the more time can be spent with them. If their locomotion or baby talk is more like one's own, less skillful than that of those formidable older children, all the more opportunity for such analogy or identification. The number of siblings, the period between their birth, and the family constellation as a whole give certain types of canalizations greater scope in some societies than in others. Thus the dominating father, whose many sons are stimulated by him less to compete with one another than to join forces in standing against him, is a familiar feature in Roman history, as well as in the Roman folklore which Sir. J. G. Frazer interpreted in *The Golden Bough.* Thus too, the lonely youngest daughter or the stepdaughter who was dominated by those in the family whose positions were secure, played a considerable part in the old Germanic clan system; familiar repercussions are seen in the numerous fairy tales of the Grimm brothers which tell of despised and rejected younger daughters. These situations led to a "demand" throughout the culture for more and more such tales and, at an advanced level, for more and more stories and plays dealing with isolated and lonely children.

These variations in character structure—which are "dependent," as we may put it, upon the child's "access to" the father or mother—should never be dismissed, however, without recognition of the varying degrees of masculinity within the boys and of femininity within the girls which make any pattern, however normal or extreme, easier for one child to accept than another. The pattern may be expressed in such a rigid form that only a minority of a given sex group can actually achieve it (cf. page 819). Thus in the early medieval period apparently only a minority (chosen from among the most rugged sons of the most rugged fathers) were able to complete the identification process and accept the combined role of patriarch and brigand which was demanded. Two or three of the boys in a family might become underlings of their dominant brothers or might devote themselves to the gentler world of the Unseen. The required "masculinity level," as we might call it, could be reached by, say, only 20 or 30 per cent of the males. It could occasionally be reached by a female too, just as, when six feet is established as the masculine norm of stature, the minority of males and an occasional female will achieve the criterion. In the same way, a minority of females and an occasional male achieved what we might call the troubadour standard of lyric expression in the great Courts of Love during the flowering of chivalry. It is important not to imply that canalizations are easily established around norms by every child. The norms can be located eccentrically; they can demand responses of which only a few boys or only a few girls are really capable. There may be norms toward which all are in some measure drawn, though few can reach them; in response, most members of the group may make compensatory adjustments or, on failure, manifest frustration and displaced aggression.

We saw in Chapter 20 that just as the attitude toward the self serves partly as the basis for the attitude toward parents, especially the parent of the same sex, so the attitudes of child to parent transfer and exert a major force in the development of attitudes toward the self. More and more clearly the picture of the self as a complete person, that is, as a self-reliant and independent adult, develops in the likeness of the parental image. So far as the cultural situation demands reverence for parents, it operates necessarily so as to demand reverence for oneself, to the extent that one can become like them. In consequence, civilizations in which reverence for parents is absolute, as it is in China, inculcate a high degree of self-regard or self-satisfaction in those who have many children. The result, as Veblen saw, is to create among the patriarchal societies a high degree of *status consciousness*. The individual defends himself against both equality and change, not merely because of self-interest in the economic sense, but because he is obviously the heir of all the ages, the incarnation of the eternal values.

Some of the paradoxes of this situation have been glimpsed by the psychoanalysts. From their studies it follows that the mother-son relation, being based in large part upon identification, necessitates the boy's loving himself because this worthy person, his mother, could of course love only a worthy son. When later his affections are powerfully excited, he needs not only an object of affection similar to the mother image but one which maintains toward him the attitudes his mother held. If he is a normal adult, he must be "infantile" in his demand for affection, and also in his demand to see himself as worthy of the specific type of adoring attention to which, as an infant, he was entitled. Were the analysts as much interested in shop and village, church and state, as they are in the conflict phase of infantile experience, they would undoubtedly be able to show that the individual quality of selfhood colors all personal relations, that adult social attitudes depend as much upon the early canalized attitudes toward the self as upon the images of father and mother.

At the same time, such considerations offer a warning against the easy antithesis of self and other—as if the individual's self-regard were in some way a barrier to his achievement of outgoing social relations. Whatever paradox there may be, it follows from all these processes in the individual that it is largely through canalization upon the self that the potentiality for a wide social response can be developed. An especially striking case is a rather neglected family problem, namely, the relations of older to younger children. What a mother and father are to the older children, they in turn tend to become in relation to the younger—in their protection, their affection, their discipline, their punishment. They experience the meaning of parenthood in exercising these habits. To do so, they must inevitably identify with the parents; and because they have been through it all, they must at the same time identify with the smallest child. The same process appears in doll play, in which it is possible not only to be a parent but to identify with the doll's point of view in accepting that quasi-parent, the child in the parental role. Processes of affective transfer are thus constantly in operation. In the same way, children's games permit every child to undertake every role in some measure. It is the nourishment of the complex of attitudes day by day through such processes that constitutes the chief basis for the individual's readiness to become a companion, a leader, an understanding participant in complex groups in which a certain versatility in attitudes is necessary for coordinated action.

David Levy has brought out particularly forcibly the fact that the relation between brothers and sisters inevitably involves competition and potential friction, that there may be an enormous amount of latent or unconscious hostility along with an external pattern of acceptance or affection. With dolls symbolizing the child himself, the little brother or sister, and the mother, Levy allows the child to tell the story of his fears and hates, his ambivalences toward his competitor and toward the mother who gives his competitor too much of the good things of life. Thus from his contact with siblings the child learns how to speak, how to feel toward rivals, how to vent or hide his feelings, how to reconcile or interrelate hostility with affection. In the same way, of course, he learns from them how to love (aside from loving the parent), and how to handle the love responses in the midst of real conflict.

The child develops ambivalent attitudes not only toward father and mother, brother and sister, but toward himself. The fact that he is like his father means that the boy merits both love and hate. The fact that she is like her mother means that the girl is entitled to a variety of marks of endearment and special consideration, and in danger of the same slights, the same supercilious remarks that she has noticed to be the lot of older females in the patriarchal pattern.

The self is a hodgepodge of impressions which in the light of constant and unavoidable experience sooner or later receives a sample of every form of social response. Month by month, year by year, the child struggles to form some picture of himself that will anchor upon the happy, tension-releasing aspects of his existence and at the same time be realistic enough to be workable. He experiments with phrases about himself reflecting every sort of approval and disapproval; he learns what forms of self-approbation are acceptable and what forms prove that he is conceited, what types of self-depreciation are looked upon by the members of the group as modestly normal. The Hopi children of the Southwest (page 806) go through these same exploratory processes with themselves, struggling simultaneously to see themselves in the social mirror and to discover the correct comments to make upon their own capacities. These social usages lead to somewhat different patterns of self-enhancement from those prevalent among ourselves. In both cases, however, the nature of the canalization process—loving the self and discovering the tabus on selflove—insures a high degree of conflict, because of the necessity for arbitrary restriction in the amount and extent of the expression permissible to those attitudes which are given a central anchorage.

Perhaps the most serious of all conflicts is the basic dualism which might be expressed in the words, "Tender person is good, savage person is good." The little boy must be sweet, tractable, affectionate. He develops a picture of himself as a "good boy." He also discovers that the little boy whom he is learning to be is mother's baby, a sissy, whom daddy would like to teach to stand up for his rights and, like a man, to claim no quarter. These are not merely two different habit systems; if they were, they could be indulged conveniently at different times and in different circumstances, just as one behaves differently in church and at a Halloween party. When it comes to attitudes toward the self, however, the picture is more tightly unified, the structure more coherent; one must not be a sissy under *any* circumstances. In the same way the little girl, successfully following through the pattern of mother identification, but also very definitely wanting her own way—wanting things that are integral to her own place in the family and the community—finds that she is being unfemininely aggressive. Here again, she cannot entirely suit the mood to the occasion; nobody likes "girls that act that way." Her picture of herself must be drawn all in the same ink, and in proportion.

Difficult as the problem is in childhood, it is somehow solved more or less effectively for a few years, only to be thrown into a new form, requiring a new solution, with the arrival of puberty. The boy's dominance pattern, so acceptable as a master thread of uniformity in the character structure of the twelve-year-old, must be thoroughly recast if he is not to be an unbearable tease or an absolute clout, and hence unacceptable, among the sixteen-year-olds. He struggles to get a new look at himself, and, as the popular phrase very accurately puts it, becomes "very self-conscious." For the girl, the tension is usually even more severe, because the vitality and positiveness of adolescence make the gentle patterns used in the school grades ineffective both in competition with her peers and in the many situations in which she must compete with boys in terms of energy and endurance. She does not have to excel in basketball, but she needs a picture of herself which will somehow integrate all she has learned about being feminine with all that the boys expect of her in terms of enthusiasm for their own consuming interests in the more savage and predatory world of sports and of jobs.

[853]

This picture of canalization within the family pattern is indeed superficial and incomplete in many ways. It lacks the deep-level approach, and the fine distinctions revealed by a study of the individual's inner patterns of imagery and thought. Even so, it is perhaps of interest to see that the problems of integration and conflict, of continuity and enforced change, arise as soon as the canalizations themselves achieve any complexity. Consideration of the child's bondage to his earliest fixations and of his struggle to achieve unified patterns, despite the divergent stresses, gives clues which the later picture can greatly complicate, but which it will serve for the most part to confirm and enrich, rather than to overthrow.

Early experiences in the family setting are likewise the primary basis for the individual's way of perceiving the society of which he is a part. The little child perceives partly in terms of the physical structure of the situation, partly in terms of the general ethos of the group as determined by "utility" in its mores, and partly in terms of the autisms of the group as assimilated by himself. Thus at any given time, the interlocking pattern of mores will primarily determine what is reasonable and right from the point of view of the economically dominant members of the group.

But autisms also involve the individual's place in the group; the autistic structuring of perception in accordance with his situation as regards the specific outlooks of father and mother and others who are near or dear, or both, is superimposed upon the generic autism of the cultural group. The adults surrounding the child see the world in the light of the way in which they hope to cope with it. They prepare the child to *see* just as they prepare him to *act*. More broadly, since sense perception develops largely as preparation for action, the deep-seated perceptual dispositions, or "sets" to perceive in a certain way, are necessarily closely connected with tendencies to respond in a certain way; i.e., they are clues to *social attitudes*. At the same time, the child learns how to view himself (page 481). To this complex object, which is always with him, there is much positive response, as there is to other complex personal objects which he can see, hear, or touch. This ever-present self-object is gratifying and he loves it; he defends it, enhances it.

Much of this process, over-sharply portrayed here, remains indistinct throughout life. More important, some aspects blend badly with other aspects, like an ambiguous picture that cannot be seen both ways at once. One integration of impressions can be autistically regarded as a pattern that is more satisfying than some other pattern. Disturbing pictures of the self are rejected. The end picture of the self tends, most of the time, to be "good." Even the "bad" pictures are at times caricatures sensed by the individual as "unfair" or not the real self; thus they may actually serve an ego-enhancing purpose (the Adlerian "secondary inferiority feelings"; cf. page 581).

Just as the culturally defined ways of doing things are inherently normal, right, and valuable, so the self as a participant in the world, a "duplicate" of those who act correctly, becomes normal and right. Any picture of the self which shows it out of the cultural focus, or interferes with a high valuation placed upon it, is rejected. Just as one avoids *conduct* which brings punishment, so he autistically avoids *percepts* which mutilate or blur the flattering self-portrait.

It is not only the "desire to be accepted," however, that presses the ego into line. The basic psychology of perception is involved; the individual has learned to see himself as a member of the group, and the self has true "membership character," structurally integrated with the perception of group life. In class societies, a person also sees himself in class-structured terms, experiences his own problem as an aspect of the class problem, etc. If the class lines are not rigid, he may imagine himself a member of a higher class and undergo ego frustration on returning to the level of reality. But in general a person makes the most of his kinship, acquaintance, etc., with the higher-ups.

From this outline, if correct, it follows that there is no reason whatever why social attitudes at a given time should completely express the self-interest of the individual. Self-interest has a place, indeed a cardinal place, in social attitudes, namely, in the initial "rational selection" of self-maintenance patterns by dominant individuals in the group, and its train of subsequent effects upon all the members. But attitudes toward the self-maintenance mores, even on the part of the dominant group, are profoundly colored by identification mechanisms, and by other ego mechanisms. When once they have been adopted and used, they are "our" ways. After long experience with these ways, a person may continue to defend them despite their actual interference with his present self-interest in the economic sense. As far as attitude toward other mores than those of self-maintenance is concerned, it can never be very realistic or rational. We have suggested that people who are not members of the dominant group will tend, even without the influence of propaganda, to structure their attitudes in terms of the major group autisms. To determine the degree to which self-interest in the economic sense controls the behavior of any individual or group is an empirical problem; however, we need never expect it to be one hundred per cent.

Whether or not we adopt the concept of canalization sketched above, the fact remains that the personal values of the individual are defined and consolidated very early in life; experimental studies of early infancy indicate that attachments to persons and things are formed as early as are motor habits, i.e., in the child's first weeks of life. Again, whether or not the theory of the non-extinction of canalized responses described above is correct, the fact remains that these early values apparently enjoy extraordinary tenacity. They seem, in fact, to provide a framework for the multifarious later values in which verbal factors play a large part. Verbally consolidated values and attitudes are, perhaps, less easily extinguished than sheer verbal patterns as such. At any rate, values formed in infancy resist efforts at redirection, even when the compelling demands of the present situation might be expected to change the individual immediately.

These mechanisms probably have a primary role in the essential conservatism of most human societies. In fact, *cultural lag* is grounded in a deep-seated psychological devotion to what is acquired early and in intimate contact with the parent. Self-interest cannot redirect the individual's course the instant that its objective direction is clear to the outside observer. To be sure, these early loyalties are exploited in every possible way by those who are economically or politically dominant at the time; but unless this primitive basis of conservatism were already powerfully at work, it is to be doubted whether such pressures could be effective. Economic and political leaders stand at times almost *in loco parentis*; but even when they do not, they can rely upon a fundamental resistance to any movement which would upset the great landmarks of life.

"AUTHORITARIAN CHARACTER" AS AN EXPRESSION OF FAMILY PRESSURES

As an example of the approach developed in the past few chapters, with special reference to the role of the family in personality formation, we shall briefly sketch one particular kind of personality in which these dynamic principles are easily recognized; this is the pattern known as the *authoritarian character structure*. The broad psychoanalytic, ethnological, and educational foundations of authoritarianism have been rather carefully studied. Our problem is to consider individual syndromes which make, out of rather similar raw material in rather similar social worlds, characters varying from the most authoritarian to the most democratic. Five broad processes can be identified in early childhood, the individual development of which may serve to explain an authoritarian or democratic outcome. These are (1) the identification process; (2) the conception of the self as lawgiver; (3) self-love; (4) attitudes toward rules; and (5) moral realism.

1. The term identification is used approximately in the psychoanalytic sense, to denote the process by which the child's picture of himself is assimilated in some degree to his picture of his parents, so as to lead him to assign to himself qualities which are in fact theirs, to assign to them qualities which are in fact his own, and to act constantly as if in a genuine sense he were one with them (page 543). Since the parents constitute the first seat of authority, a process of identification that is more intense or prolonged than usual may mean for the individual an *overdependence* upon the parental points of view and standards. Even the child of democratic or liberal parents may at times display in his liberalism a rigid devotion which brooks no argument. Childhood adherence to parental norms has been found to be as clear

cut among radicals as among conservatives, the children of independents and socialists holding to the parental norm as do the children of conservatives. We should expect to find in each child a small or large element of immobility or rigidity, deriving from the fact that the parents' ways are central and normative; and individual differences that depend upon parental character in the way the child is reared, as well as upon the child's reaction to the early educative process, should reveal themselves in varying types of immature dependence, a dependence not only upon the original norms but upon what was right at the time when the individual was a little child surrounded by such identification standards.

2. This process of identification leads to a second mechanism. The individual does not identify with the parents in all their roles. The child playing with his dolls may feed and scold them, care for them as parents do, but may be obtuse to many of the central roles which constitute parenthood. The understanding of such roles varies greatly from child to child. The child's conception of the parent may be, as the Gestaltists say, anchored at one or another point. If the anchorage is established in the aspect of parenthood that involves the role of parent as lawgiver, the child will inevitably develop a picture of himself in which the lawgiving disposition is central. Such a child, in order to be a real daddy or mommy, must make rules, must set up taboos. The child's play with little brother and sister, with dolls, and with miniature life toys, shows that the lawgiving role is deeply assimilated by some children, slighted or rejected by others. Whatever makes the lawgiving aspect of parenthood central in the child's conception of the parents' place in society makes the child a potential committeeman, boss, or despot.

3. Behind both processes there lies a third process, self-love or narcissism, which may involve, among other things, a perpetual attempt to see oneself in the most lovable light. Identification, as Freud pointed out, is founded upon love. In order to make the self lovable, the child discovers ways of being right, ways of fulfilling the role assigned by the parents. What is right in one household is wrong in another, and details of conduct may vary; but the general standard

[858]

of being good, the general technique of maintaining a favorable self-portrait, is unfortunately rather uniform throughout a subcultural whole. Those who have trouble in keeping the self-portrait noble and unblemished are the most dependent upon norms, for by definition a deviation from norms is unlovely. We may agree with Erich Fromm that the full-fledged narcissist needs no support from an authoritarian system; it is the people whose narcissism has been wounded, the insecure people, who are pitifully in need of it. Paradoxically, the "weakest" child, the child who is least secure, least able to fend for himself, may become the most authoritarian; for it is by conformity, by the consolidation of the moral law within himself, that he may look upon himself and find himself good. In the analysis of authoritarian character, this constant struggle to maintain self-love is usually found to be at or near the center; and other things being equal, individual differences in narcissism may well determine the faithfulness of one's devotion to the authoritarian pattern which the home and the neighborhood have established.

4. This in turn leads to a pervasive attitude entertained by the individual toward the meaning and the proper place in life of those normative elements which we call rules. Much that is described by society is of course very vague, and much relates to ultimate goals rather than to techniques by which they are to be achieved. We here refer not to the vaguer goals but to the rules which ostensibly make their achievement possible. By a process widely observed at a certain stage in early childhood, rules may become ends in themselves. Rules may be intrinsically good, violations of them intrinsically bad. He who follows them is lovable and worthy of social acclaim; he who violates them is at best a gay dog, a Robin Hood of whom we never know what to expect, and more commonly a troublemaker, a black sheep. While most children gradually develop a more mature functional conception of rules, some members of the group adopt a persistent adoring attitude toward them, all the more adoring if the rule is so arbitrary and its source so obscure that it permits no easy reduction to simple principles which guarantee the good of all. The rules which first enabled the child to achieve status with his parents and

playmates may become a touchstone by which to evaluate his own place in the group. The big boy who knows most about the rules may lord it over the small fry who only dimly understand the rudiments of the game. Thus an annual convention of the Methodist Church a few years ago was thrown into complete impotence for half a day by an ecclesiastical historian who leaped to his feet at every turn to state the precedents, the rules of the church, regarding each new proposal; the whole day's business was held up at the insistence of him who, of all those present, was the most expert regarding the rules applicable in each case. In our studies of the deeper roots of authoritarianism we may have forgotten the tremendous anchorage power of this rule-consciousness, this capacity of some children to make from rules weapons with which to squelch their comrades or to mark off areas immune from adult interference. A parental rule carelessly enunciated six months ago may be effectively played up by the child as self-evident justification for each new venture. This rule-using and rule-abusing technique becomes a central part of all authoritarianism.

Because of their central place in the normative structure, however, rules become a prime device for the seizure of power. The fact that they are blindly followed makes it possible to find in them meanings and sanctions which can be insisted upon, while those who vaguely sense something wrong in the process stand by, paralyzed by confusion. On the one hand, he who knows the rules has a deft and efficient means for making his own kind of order out of an ambivalent situation; on the other hand, he for whom rules have been deeply anchored within the structure of the self has a rigidity which carries him through to his goal successfully against the somewhat flexible or fluid attitudes of his potential competitors. Rules may be a central implement of the power drive.

Unfortunately, the love of rules may be ingrained for all these reasons until the individual demands rules as he does food and drink. In their studies demonstrating the value of democratic as contrasted with authoritarian group leadership, Lewin, Lippitt, and White found that a boy once exposed to authoritarian treatment may prefer it in subsequent situations. "We like him because he is hard. You always know where you're at." It takes real learning first to understand and then to use democracy. The authoritarian system has enough intrinsic satisfactions to constitute a real problem for any who would undertake to melt down and restructure the materials of human nature.

5. The fifth and last point has to do with individual differences in moral realism, as Piaget uses the term (page 498). It will be recalled that for Piaget the rightness and wrongness of things are learned by the little child exactly as he learns the techniques of living that are convenient and practical in his household and community. He accepts his parents' say-so as much when good and bad are involved as when the workings of locomotives or airplanes are being discussed. Instead of moral issues being judged in terms of consequences, the moral flavor of reality is accepted as cognate with the factual flavor. Just as the names of things are *in* the objects themselves, so goodness and badness are *in* the behavior of the individual, regardless of the social consequences.

It seems likely that because of the other mechanisms already described and, in particular, because of the attitudes toward rules, individual children vary greatly in the intensity and duration of their attitudes on moral realism, and that those who remain immature for the longest period, those who cling most blindly to absolutistic standards of right and wrong, tend to combine such attitudes with their rule attitudes and become self-righteous and moralistic at the expense of the world around them. Whatever deviates from the standards once inculcated in us on the basis of moral realism is, in a deep sense, worthy of scorn. The attitude of moral condemnation, formerly assigned by the parent to the wayward little child, is handed on to all who, in later life, break the rigid rules which they ought to follow. From this and all the other principles, it follows that morality is an easy escape, an easy rationalization for petty or major despotisms of all sorts; that moral immaturity in Piaget's sense is a dominant feature in authoritarian character.

In the case of all five of these principles it is assumed that the authoritarian processes are self-perpetuating. He who achieves strength or security in the group by becoming an "authoritarian" forces others weaker or younger than himself into the same pattern, so that a vicious and socially destructive cycle is set up from which no escape is possible except a fundamental and unfortunately very painful reeducation. Authoritarians are inevitably surrounded by other authoritarians, if there is any freedom of movement at all, because they seek one another and find safety in one another's company, building up a formidable pseudo-aristocracy, a pseudo class system of their own; if there is no freedom of movement, those with more flexible or democratic characters enter the battle without weapons and, other things being equal, become easy victims to the weapons of the petty tyrant. It takes only one well-organized authoritarian to disrupt a group process. The advantages of democratic cooperation are paralleled only by the difficulty and complexity of making such a process genuinely pervasive in a group whose culture has allowed authoritarians to appear.

These five principles lead naturally to rough suggestions for a research program to augment our knowledge. The first step, of course, must be to measure authoritarian attitudes, perhaps by means of such devices as Piaget's clinical interview, Maslow's interview and questionnaire schedules, and psychoanalysis. This would be followed by five types of research corresponding to the five problems defined.

1. To ascertain degrees of identification, we should need studies of parent-child resemblance in the more flexible social, esthetic, and moral dispositions, augmented by studies of childhood attitudes toward parental tastes and norms. In addition to the current projective techniques, we might use, with both parents and children, Gladys Deutsch's conformity test indicating the degree of acceptance of the prevailing social patterns. If our hypothesis is correct, those with the most complete identification will, other things being equal, tend toward authoritarianism.

2. To study the attitude to the role of lawgiver, we should need both retrospective studies by adults of their own childhood, as by the Chassell "experience variables," supplemented by direct month-by-month observations of small children, and direct comparisons of parents and their children by means of case histories and such devices

as the Stern cloud pictures and the Murray Thematic Apperception Test. Our hypothesis would be partly validated if we could show that the aspect of parental identification which stands out most sharply in the authoritarian child is the attitude of regarding parents as lawgivers, and that for other children the lawgiving attribute is subordinated to affectionate, comradely, or other personal qualities.

3. To test our hypothesis regarding narcissism in relation to authoritarianism, we should probably require psychoanalytic studies, since the form taken by narcissism in the early years is a deep-level problem; but we may get considerable supplementary aid from case histories of self-conscious and non-self-conscious adults, with special reference to the hurt feelings or other evidences of morbid narcissism which should appear, if our hypothesis is correct, when the authoritarian attitude is well defined. Rosenzweig's frustration-tolerance tests would be useful, and the Thematic Apperception Test would give valuable light as to narcissistic processes.

4. To test the hypothesis relating to rule techniques, the Piaget methods would appear to be most useful, especially in the form developed by Lerner. We should also study the safety and power needs of the individual, as exemplified by Maslow's questionnaire method on the one hand and by the Allport-Vernon study of values on the other. We should expect specifically that the political value would be highly developed among the authoritarians. Here also the direct inspection of group work, as by the Lewin, Lippitt, and White techniques, should quickly reveal whether the rule techniques are actually a center and core in the authoritarian patterns of boys who respond favorably to authoritarian leadership, who turn these techniques to their own uses, and who, when transferred to democratic groups, hanker after the good old days when "you were told what to do and you jolly well did it without asking why."

5. To study our final hypothesis relating to moral realism, the Piaget techniques, again supplemented by Lerner's method, would be useful, and likewise the short-cut Piaget methods used by Wayne Dennis. In fact, there appears to be no greater difficulty in using Dennis' method in studying individual differences in moral realism than

in studying animism, a field in which his quantitative data have already yielded good measures of age and individual differences.

What use may be made of such research as we have, and of that which might follow from the five types of studies suggested here? Many of us speak today as if the only danger were the spread of fascism, as if we must immediately begin frenzied application of all we have learned regarding methods of combating this danger. However, in addition to this negative approach to the patent danger that compulsiveness, exploitation, and general rigidity may stifle our basic scientific and ethical progress, there is a deeper and more comprehensive reason for putting studies of authoritarianism to work. We face today problems of such magnitude that the socialization of our *processes of discovery* affords the only possible way of finding answers before mankind is destroyed. As Harlow Person has shown, every huge social organization, from the federal government or municipality to the manufacturing plant or commercial business, has invented what he calls an institutional mind, a complex process by which division of labor is inaugurated and which permits a hierarchy of specialists to contribute to the effectiveness of one another's thinking. But the democratic process has been the one which works in practice, so far as the internal organization of such structures is concerned. No matter how despotic an industrial organization may be, it must develop *within* its ranks, *within* its hierarchical form, a tendency to listen to points of view, a capacity to use new ideas if they are usable, an ability to forget who one's father was and where one came from. The result has been that in spite of the anti-democratic character of much of our economic evolution, a great deal that is important for the theory of democracy has been learned from such institutional minds. However, we face still more gigantic problems, problems in which democracy of both purpose and organization is the only device thus far discovered by which all the necessary ideas, all the necessary expressions of human wants can be brought into articulate interrelation. Unless we find ways of deflating and removing our traditional authoritarian attitudes, unless we find ways of cultivating genuine spontaneity, genuine comradeship in a quest for a workable social order, it is likely indeed that the crystallized forms of our present authoritarian structures will crack and nothing be ready to replace them.

We may well find, perhaps, that the basic gift, the capacity of men to love one another, about which our machine age is so hesitant to speak, may prove to be dependent, as Moreno has suggested, upon a wooing process and a training process; that we shall have to learn how to respond to and accept one another, not as exemplifications of particular age, sex, race, and economic groups, but as individuals who, as sheer samples of humanity, call forth something primitively resonant within ourselves. This is another way of saying that unless we can move rapidly toward such an understanding of authoritarianism as would make possible its removal, like a cancer, the more naïve, primitive human drives from which a democratic way of living might be constituted may find themselves confronting a wall of pure ignorance. We cannot exorcise authoritarianism, we cannot get rid of it by a pronouncement. If we understand it, we shall in the same moment begin to understand and apply everything we know about the devices that may liberate us for effective group living.

38. Situationism

THE basic difference between the biological approach, with which we began, and the social science approach, as pursued in the last few Chapters, is perhaps the fact that in the former we think simply of the tissues of the body as making their *responses* to outer or inner stimulation, while in the latter we think of all these responses also as enactments of specific *roles* assigned the individual by virtue of age, sex, race, occupational status, religion, or any other category which society emphasizes. The mores specify that people of a certain type are to behave in a certain way; personality then becomes the study of the roles assigned to particular individuals.

We shall try now to see how far we can go in understanding the individual by ignoring all other considerations and defining personality as the locus of intersection of all the roles which he enacts. Roles assigned by society in terms of age, sex, occupation, etc., will clearly tell us a great deal about most personalities in any culture. If, for example, we are drawing a general or composite picture of a young unmarried Chinese coolie, we shall know a great deal about his personality by knowing the role he plays in a particular society; if we specify an elderly Chinese gentleman with many grandchildren, we have already said much that is essential to the personality core.

For example, what can be said about personality characteristics that are defined by age—by infancy, childhood, early maturity, later maturity? Perhaps many attributes of child personality are determined not by sheer biological immaturity, but by the role which society deems appropriate. For instance, a six-year-old girl in Samoa is in many ways like an adult, because she has a heavy responsibility toward the younger children. The role of *substitute mother* is a large component in this child's personality. She can endure fatigue, can wield authority in a way not ordinarily characteristic of little children.

The contrast with the Manus child is striking; here the little girl is protected against the inroads of adult authority, both boys and girls being expected to play in a world of their own until they are ripe for adult tasks. The six-year-old girl of the Manus is still a little child. The considerable literature on the difference between farm and city children and between middle- and lower-class urban children in our own culture makes sense in these same terms; each child is viewed not in relation to the *age of his tissues*, but in relation to the *tasks*, the *roles*, the *social functions* which characterize him.

By following the logic of this psychology of roles a systematic and revolutionary approach has been engendered under the name of *situationism*. This way of thinking was developed by W. I. Thomas but has been given considerable impetus by subsequent research in social psychology. The fundamentals are simple, almost of the nature of axioms; and like other axioms they lead, when rationally pursued, to many paradoxical and revolutionary results.

We begin with the fact that any normal person must discover, in consequence of experience, the requirements necessary to fulfill each role which society expects him to enact. He learns what is standard and acceptable behavior in terms of the age, sex, race, economic status, and other standards that are socially assigned to him. His adaptation to such roles may not be as prompt and unequivocal as is that of the chameleon to a new color, but we may predict just as clearly that those who are required to discover and make use of the attributes of each role will be so deeply colored—stained we might say—by the requirements of the situation that all who have similar roles will be fundamentally alike. Differences between persons will be fundamentally the differences in the roles which different individuals must enact. These differences may of course be quantitative in the sense that response to a situation, e.g., race discrimination, will naturally vary with the stimulus intensity of the situation, or that response according to sex may differ with the sharpness of the male-female differentiation emphasized by various cultures. Situationism maintains simply that human beings respond as situations require them to respond; and that whatever their biological diversities, they will, if capable of learning, take on the attributes which the situations call for. Although some adaptations to situations may be practically instantaneous, the requirements of the situationist theory are met if, after a reasonable opportunity for learning, all human individuals are found to have learned both what is required and how to carry out the required assignment.

Given a changed situation, there is a changed role and consequently a changed personality. For this reason situationism is unlike the current behavoristic systems which emphasize the slow accumulation of habits. Though the situational doctrine may appear at first sight to be rather similar to behavioristic views of social learning, the fact is that situationism is in sharp antithesis to all types of environmentalism which emphasize the fixation of character early in childhood. For the situationist it is not the slow and arduous process of fundamental character formation that is involved; it is not the slow shaping into the pattern required by parents; it is rather the fulfillment, in the adult as in the child, of the *day-dy-day requirements*. In fact, in most instances the situationist has no need for the more elaborate emphasis upon childhood experience that characterizes behaviorism on the one hand and psychoanalysis on the other. Indeed, a child may throw to the winds his entire previous experience and react almost like a chameleon to his new environment. As a matter of fact, most of the literature on individual differences in childhood, in which such differences are related to farm vs. city, or to good vs. poor neighborhood, or to Catholic vs. Protestant vs. Jewish upbringing, or to differences of family pressures, tends to overwork the past and the concept of habit, and to forget that all these pressures dominate the *present moment*. The case history is frequently merely a "history" that makes too much of bygones; it may obscure the fact that we must be concerned with the present experience of the child. The present situation may be far more important than any past experience.

Relevant here is a study of order of birth as related to economic class. Alfred Adler suggested (cf. page 585) that first-born boys are likely to encounter certain difficulties not shared by other boys; emphasis was given the experiences of infancy. Collecting figures on delinquency among first-born as compared with second-born boys in Chicago, and making the proper correction for age and other factors involved, John Levy showed clearly that among underprivileged groups the oldest boys had a much worse record in the eyes of the courts. He was wisely suspicious as to whether this was actually a pure order-of-birth factor as such. Among more privileged children, he found no significant difference between the two groups. To be an oldest boy in a "delinquency area" means an increase in the likelihood of being delinquent. Order of birth, the situation confronting one in the family circle, is not the clue; we need to know the present situation—and it varies specifically with birth order—into which the boy steps when he leaves home for the street.

As we confront the psychology of adolescence we find a good deal of the same sort of thing. We may look at the "biology of adolescence" over a span of a few decades of research. In the '90's Starbuck gathered records on religious conversion among some hundreds of young Americans. He found that it was clearly a phenomenon occurring most frequently in early and mid-adolescence. The experiences leading up to it were stressful and stormy; afterward there was a glow of well-being; the individual felt that God had directly taken him into a relation of personal warmth and affection. Hence adolescence was portrayed as a period in which the individual was stressfully remade with respect to his deepest values. Thirty years later, in a similar study of evangelical groups, E. T. Clark found that less than 7 per cent of the adult church members had experienced conversion; the others had gone through a steady, quiet initiation into the religion of the group. Can we say, then, that the earlier storm and stress is the direct expression of adolescent turmoil as such? No; we must conclude that this, and all other adolescent behavior, is a response to the actual situation which the adolescent confronts.

The danger of confusing biological and social factors in adolescence is great. A comparison of adolescents in many societies indicates that the universal characteristics of this period are apparently limited to those directly expressive of general and sexual growth. We cannot even say that the adolescent personality reflects awareness of approaching adulthood, for in some societies essential adulthood is conferred upon the pre-adolescent. Moreover, biological factors that are significant in their own right may be seized upon by society and assigned great social importance. Thus in the California Adolescence Study, several boys were physically retarded in respect to the onset of puberty changes. There was no biological harm in this; there was time enough for them to catch up. But these children were severely maladjusted simply because they felt themselves to be different from the group. To be emotionally different from the group, to appear immature, to face being an incomplete adolescent, causes psychic strain.

What has been said about the child and the adolescent can also be said about the aged. The process of aging appears to consist, in considerable measure, of a change in the roles to be enacted. At a specified time in life a person is thrust into the role of the superannuated. If society declares that the individual begins to age at forty, he may age conspicuously from that time on; if society puts the age at seventy, one ages at seventy. Almost immediately after he is no longer able to go out with war parties, the Comanche warrior becomes either a "good old man" or a "malevolent sorcerer," depending upon whether he accepts gracefully the fact that he is "old" and out of the running. C. M. Morgan made a study of some 500 recipients of old age pensions in New York State. Under the state law, the sole requirements for receiving pension are that the individual be seventy years old and in need of help. Morgan found that if the aged were still able to do something—run a little store, dig in the garden, sew for their grandchildren—they were in general happy and adequate, but that if all the useful roles were taken away either by impairment of sight or hearing or by the socially induced feeling of being too old to work, they disintegrated quickly. The disintegration of the aged proved to be due in considerable degree to the fact that society defined these people as old.

Similarly in senile dementia, where there is marked brain deterioration, the familiar clinical changes in personality (anxiety, irritability, timidity) are not attributable solely to changes in the brain;

many of them are due to the fact that the individual faces a world which has shoved him into a position that frustrates his wants and deprives him of his usefulness, of his status as an autonomous person, and of the varied companionship he needs.

Let us try the situational approach in the matter of sex differences. Suppose that in Samuel Johnson's circle, which Mrs. Thrale entertained by appraising personality by means of the earliest known rating scale, the learned doctor's friends had expressed complete certainty regarding feminine vs. masculine characteristics. The masculine and feminine roles as defined in Greco-Roman and medieval times, and as known in the eighteenth century, gave the thoughtful the notion of fixity as far as sex characteristics and sex differences were concerned. The continuity of sex differences over two millennia did not actually mean anything as regards inborn sex differences, because for the most part woman was limited throughout that whole period to the world of household economy. But when she left her home to work in a building owned and controlled by someone outside the family, the difference between feminine and masculine traits began to shrink. The women were often transformed almost instantly by a process which was not simply a slow "relearning." The ideological changes in the ideas about what women *should* be—as expressed, for example, by John Stuart Mill or Margaret Fuller a hundred years ago —were not the cause of the change, for they came long after the economic transition was well defined. The characteristics of modern women, as contrasted with men, are thus not greatly clarified by studying their general characteristics over a long period of time; much more is learned by asking what happens when women assume new economic and social roles, and by watching the almost instantaneous effects of the new role patterns. Women behave as any other human being—man or child—would behave in a particular situation, even when this has previously been defined as a masculine way of behaving. Personality may be viewed as an expression of the situation in which the organism is functioning.

This method of approach has a direct application to the predicament of the woman who wants both a family and a professional life. The two roles being defined as they are, as full-time activities, the dilemma presents two antithetical roles for the same person. There is not only insufficient time; the roles trip each other up. As regards sex differences, the problem today does not involve what is mysteriously called feminine psychology. Conflicting roles will hit anyone hard, whether he be man, woman, or child.

Finally, we come to race differences. Much energy has gone into discussing the existence of intrinsic, fixed, and inalienable race differences. As a result of work done during the past twenty-five years, particularly that initiated by Woodworth and by Garth and carried forward and systematized by Klineberg, we can be fairly sure that there are no large and socially important behavior differences between human beings that are based on their racial stock. There are family differences associated with particular groups, large or small, and there are inbred traits in isolated communities, but the individual variability within each racial group is tremendous; and when two of these groups are put together in the *same situation*, the behavior differences attributed to race tend to fade away. There is a cultural psychology of race; we should be able, by means of adequate sociological data, to show that each group which society defines as a race is automatically cast into certain roles and enacts them with consistency. As the roles change, or as society's definition of a race changes, new patterns of behavior characterize these races.

Despite the manifold cultural varieties of the oldest Americans —the Indians—before the white man came, three factors are important if we are to understand their psychology. (1) They are living in a land which is traditionally theirs and with which they identify strongly; (2) they are treated as wards of the state and are given an education which, despite an increasingly enlightened approach, is naturally formulated largely in terms of the white man's conception of schooling; (3) in case of grievances, they have no means of redress as a minority group except to appeal to the support or sympathy of the majority group. Hence we might make bold, on this basis alone, to predict stolidity, reticence, and a lack of humor, and also such undesirable characteristics as the laziness frequently noted in the American

Indian, as reflections of the situation in which he is placed and of the roles which he must enact.

The "childlikeness" of the American Negro is likewise the result of the role into which he is forced. If he escapes this role and through education suddenly achieves maturity, there results a peculiar combination of "inconsistent" roles and therefore of "inconsistent" characteristics. Moreover, when privileges are vaguely promised but not fulfilled, the result is often a combination of aspiration with resentment; hence childlikeness, aspiration, and resentment, which seem to be contradictory, can all be aspects of Negro personality, depending upon which situation it confronts. Which of these will appear depends not chiefly on the past history, but on the situation the Negro faces now. The old-fashioned Uncle Remus Negro had much less bitterness in his soul than the modern Negro intellectual who enjoys a thousand advantages Uncle Remus never heard of. And this is true of all human beings in such situations. Granted that there are definite socially derived Negro traits which differentiate him from the white man as he now is, it makes an enormous amount of difference whether we say that these are due to the Negro's early upbringing or whether we hold that putting any human being *today* into the same situation would bring forth the same characteristics. It is as destructive to insist that Negro traits, in this sense, do not exist as it is to insist that there are innate race differences.

Jewish characteristics can also be studied from this point of view. Here the forms of discrimination are as a rule much less severe, since education and access to privileged occupations are not denied. But resentment against social discrimination is certain to appear; consequently we can predict that the reaction to the mixture of privilege and discrimination will take a form far different from the reaction to a more uniform social barrier, quite independently of the question of Jewish tradition or any other aspect of their institutional or cultural life. We should be able to predict that any group in the United States which is half included in, half excluded from, all the valued things that are theoretically open to every American will manifest considerable open resentment and an aggressive drive to cut away the restrictions.

"Fighting for one's rights" is a possible escape. But the fact that something can be done, the fact that fighting is possible, is likely to increase resentment and, in turn, the reaction against it. We might say also that the humanitarianism of the Jews, their identification with all sorts of liberal and philanthropic interests, is largely understandable without going back to the Old Testament; it springs from their present-day predicament, namely, their need for security in the face of an exclusive if not hostile majority.

This situationist way of thinking may be applied as well to overt behavior as to attitude or outlook. David Efrón has vividly brought out this point in a study of "race differences" in gesture. He compared "traditional" Italians with "assimilated" Italians, and "traditional" Jews with "assimilated" Jews, and discovered, through studying photographs and sketches of free gestures, that the *area in which the person was free to move* was a determining factor. The traditional Italians, who came chiefly from small towns where space was free and status as members of the group was safe, and in "Little Italy" continued to live in the same freedom, used free and sweeping gestures; the traditional Jews, who came from crowded and Ghetto-like quarters where their status was insecure, and continued to live in insecurity in this country, used cramped, withdrawn gestures, with forearms and hands kept close to the body. The second-generation Italians and Jews, photographed and sketched in an environment comparable to that of other Americans, tend to lose these gestural characteristics.

The same logic applies to religious problems. The Roman Catholic group in the United States shows many of the same situational responses. There is a feeling of superiority, because of the antiquity and universality of the Church, balanced by a sense of not being understood and of being relegated to one side as a minority group that continues to accent a value system different from that of the majority. Roman Catholics feel at the same time very superior and very inferior to Protestants, not because of something they learned in parochial school, but because life deals with them in a certain way.

As to individual character, the present approach is championed and extensively supported by the *Character Education Inquiry*, a study by Hartshorne and May and their collaborators which dealt with the basis of moral character in childhood. Some hundreds of children were studied intensively with reference to their honesty, generosity, and self-control. By means of an elaborate testing program, children from the fifth through the eighth grades were confronted with situations in which they might lie, steal, or cheat, or might refuse to do these things; with situations in which they might spend time, effort, or money on themselves or on other children; with situations in which they might resist distractions or yield to them, etc. In general, the predictive power of educational forces in the children's background was found to be low. When some dozens of factors in the past lives of these children were analyzed—the kinds of homes they came from, the camps and Sunday schools they went to, etc.—no item was found to be more important than the one item: what other children around them are doing at the time. For example, one device made it possible, when a child cheated on his arithmetic examination, to detect just how much cheating he did; here the child's honesty score correlated .60 with the mean score of the classroom in which he sat. The general conclusion to be drawn from such studies is that the most important single factor at work in the child's being honest is the situation he confronts. The situationist says that if we could put a person through life by means of "remote control," providing in advance the situations which he will face, we could predict his conduct without bothering about the building up of habits within him.

It may be objected that this is all very well for the little child or for the mental defective, but that mature men and women rise above situations. The issue, however, is not so simple. Situationism is designed to apply to everyday personality changes. Few of these are due to brain changes; many result from situational changes. Thus a man of a very solid, stable, friendly disposition, who thinks carefully before he speaks, never loses his temper, does his work effectively, and is completely at peace with himself and the world, begins to act petulantly; he is disturbed, confused; he says harsh things. Though he has been beloved by everyone around him, some are now estranged by his conduct. To say that the change is superficial is no explanation; bitter-ness permeates his soul. If we know the situation that this man faces today, we know that all he leaned on in life has collapsed. Perhaps we should spend more time in specifying more fully and concretely each man's situation, his circle of friends, his home, his neighborhood, his job.

In a research seminar in social psychology, a student was report-ing on personality studies of middle-class Negro girls, paralleling her earlier studies of underprivileged Negro girls. As it happened, three of the nine students in the seminar were Negroes. When she had outlined the data, one of the Negro men said that this was a good study, but that a control study should have been made in which a Negro did the interviewing, for different attitudes might be released. A Negro woman student remarked that since attitudes depend on the interview situation, there should be not only a male Negro interviewer but also a female Negro interviewer. Another student spoke up to the effect that since the investigator was an unmarried white woman, there should also be an unmarried Negro woman, as well as a married Negro woman. So the conversation went on—until all realized that there is no such thing as the "true" or "real" attitude, independent of the human situation. There are indeed many *potential* attitudes which are real, normal, human, and important, but none can appear and function except in a certain situation.[1] Personality can be defined in terms of situations comprising age, sex, race, occupation, family, friends, etc. We can never know what the personality would be if these roles were not enacted. Situationism suggests that the attempt to define the true personality independently of what can actually be seen in specific situations is a completely unreal quest. Since no two situations are ever alike, no personality is ever twice the same. Such continuity as there is arises largely from the relative continuity of the situations that the person confronts day in and day

---

[1] This is reminiscent of Heisenberg's "uncertainty principle" in physics. The more accurately one specifies where a thing is, the less accurately can one specify its momen-tum, and vice versa. The more exactly one specifies a true inner personality trait, the less certain can one be as to what the personality will do; the more fully one specifies actual conduct, the less can one say about the inner non-situational personality.

out. Personality could almost be defined as the integration of all the roles that a particular person has to enact.

Although situationism runs counter to the ingrained habits of psychologists, it must be recognized that the slighting of situational differences has been a constant source of clinical and experimental errors; the clinical interview and the laboratory have both consistently failed to predict adequately the nature of social behavior that occurs in situations other than those in which the observations are originally made. The laboratory psychologist and the clinician have both conceived the individual as a system of events and tendencies carried around within the skin of the individual subject. They have both assumed that his delinquencies or his triumphs, his interests or his nervous maladjustments, result fully and simply from structured dispositions within him. For example, no volume has yet been written in the English language on the systematic study of the environments in which individual human beings function (a single such book appeared in Germany almost two decades ago but was unnoticed by American observers). It is the American psychologists' bias to make the most of the continuum represented by the stream of heredity and by the span of the individual life history, whereas continuities in the world that press upon the individual are for the most part merely symbolized by a word or two indicating a detail salient for the observer. *The situationist requires that a study of situations that act upon persons should be at least as full and as systematic as is a study of the internal structures which respond to these situations.* For the situationist, personality is the generic human response, the response which any human being has to make to a situation that is fully defined in terms of the role requirements of anyone who must function in that situation.

The Psychodrama

Though differing sharply from pure situationism, the psychological approach of J. L. Moreno is reminiscent of it in many respects. Two of Moreno's contributions, sociometry and the psychodrama, reveal his basic concept that each individual is liberated, made creative, when he is in the situation that is right for him; from this it follows that therapy, instead of getting inside the skin, as in psychoanalysis, should attempt to restructure the situation so as to permit the person to be himself and to grow.

At the New York State Training School for Girls, Moreno found that in self-liberation a great deal depended upon the way in which the girls were grouped. There were more effective ways than grouping them according to I.Q. Using the sociometric method, in which each person chooses his own associates, Moreno had each girl list five girls whom she wished to have in the same cottage with her. The girls were actually placed so that as many wants as possible would be satisfied. Many mutual first choices appeared. Although it was impossible for everyone's demands to be satisfied, the realization of some of her choices meant that almost every girl was more happily placed than if her choices had been ignored. The choice of house mother was also regarded as important. The "parent test" was as follows: As new girls came to the institution, all the house mothers whose cottages had vacancies went to the admission building, and each one talked privately with each new girl. Each girl then made her first and second choice among the house mothers, and each house mother made her own first and second choice among the girls. A further test was used. A "key" girl, representative of each cottage which had a vacancy, privately interviewed each new girl, and here again each new girl chose among the "key" girls, and vice versa—"unless they click, it is no go." In the exceedingly rare instances in which no adequate sociometric placement could be made immediately, the new girl went to the infirmary until new vacancies made such placement possible. The results appear to have been remarkable in terms of both morale and individual adjustment.

Another concept of Moreno's, spontaneity training (page 474), seems on the face of it a contradiction in terms. "Training" is usually conceived to be a way of overcoming the faults due to individual spontaneity; the trained individual is so crystallized into a desired pattern that no spontaneity will mar the process. How can a person be trained to become spontaneous? The paradox disappears as we consider the training technique. Some twenty girls, most of whom hoped to become salesgirls, waitresses, beauticians, or nurses, met together. Moreno assigned a role to each girl; e.g., he made one a visitor to a hospital, another a sick child, a third the nurse on the ward, a fourth a nurse in training. They went up on the stage; the other girls constituted the audience. In this way situations were presented which incorporated the factors the girls would encounter in their vocational roles. The girls quickly responded not in terms of a crystallized habit, not in terms of drill, but in terms of the organic compulsion of the situation itself. From such simple procedures as this, the psychodrama extends to systematic studies of many kinds of role-playing, group structure, and interpersonal relations, with equal attention to diagnosis and therapy. Our interest here lies in the demonstration of the huge influence of experimentally induced roles in bringing out (and therefore really in creating) new personality configurations.

Moreno's system is not a pure example of situationism, for with him both the past and the learning process count. At the training school there proved to be such a thing as learning to be spontaneous. These girls, at first encrusted with mechanized habits, gradually grew capable of spontaneity; it took time to loosen the old shell and get down to a more vital part of the individual. The question was always whether a girl could be brought to the degree of readiness for social participation in which she could do what was most fully responsive to the vital cues about her. In the drama Moreno found that a person given an assignment to respond fully to a certain situation could do spontaneously and creatively what the situation required. If we consider the two aspects of his thought together, sociometry on the one hand and spontaneity training on the other, we come to the conclusion that each personality must be free to select its environment in such fashion as will permit its own unfolding, and will cut through the shell that preserves its past. As we said above, this is in contrast to situationism, for Moreno believes that the past does have a profoundly constraining influence. Nevertheless, his therapy is among the most radically situational of those practiced today.

39. Field Theory

SITUATIONISM leads us to some rather paradoxical conclusions. The situationist maintains that psychology has looked too much inside the skin; it has regarded personality as a system carried around with the individual and full of ready-made responses. We like to believe this, for it inflates the ego. We conquered the soil and the Indians and established our frontier civilization in terms of a sturdy reliance upon individual personality. In spite of the relative uniformity of the outer world, individuality could express itself. We have developed during the last fifty years a positive cult of personality in which we regard the exquisite self-containedness of the individual as a precious and ultimate reality. The situationist believes that a second reason for this emphasis upon internal factors is to be found in our ethical needs; we need to know where responsibility lies, we need to be able to say that this person and no other is responsible. Situationism undertakes, then, to correct a deep-seated cultural bias. It insists that we specify *fully* the situation that is acting upon each human being; perhaps no other person faces that identical situation. Perhaps every person confronting that particular situation must react in that way.

After a moment of shock at this rather novel way of disposing of apparent individual variability, the psychologist prepares a line of defense and offense. He begins to ask questions. His first one is: Are there no differences in personality resulting from the way the individual is made—does it make no difference whether a man is tall rather than short, fat rather than thin, old rather than young, slow rather than quick, that he digests food well rather than poorly? On all these points the situationist agrees; but he adds that all these things are part of the situation.

The psychologist continues. Well, if the person's height, weight, and digestive habits are part of the situation, then why not his fears and hopes? Says the situationist: All that is real at the moment is part of the interaction of organism and environment that makes up the situation. The complexities of the environment are specified at the same time that the complexities of organic response are specified; personality is the going concern which is expressed by the interaction of the living system with the outer world. But this seems to grant a good deal; hence the bewildered psychologist decides next to ask whether perceptual habits as well as emotional habits are part of the situation. When you speak of a situation, he says, do you mean the situation as *you* see it or as *your subject* sees it? Does not each stimulus field have a different stimulus value for each person? Does not each person experience the situation differently, selecting certain aspects of it, remaining blind to the others, and making his own personal organization of its attributes? Is not each situation, as a functionally real thing, determined in part by the individual who confronts it? Will you not admit that just as the outer environment selects from the tissues which are to be active at a particular time—whether by sound, sight, touch, strain, or pressure—selecting certain responses from the individual, so the organism constantly selects from among the outer forces, so that there is a two-way flow? Yes, says the situationist; the situation is an expression of the full organism-environment relation; the individual's own perceptual habits are part of the situation. The situationist has had to grant the importance of much that goes beyond the question of roles played.

Although the psychologist could hardly have wanted more, he asks a final question: Is not the present situation, then, a projection into the present of the structure of past situations; are not individual heredity and past experience relevant to the definition of today's situation? Surely, answers the situationist; all science follows the stream of time and regards the emergent present as an expression of continuing dynamic factors. At this point the psychologist and the situationist have found common ground. Reciprocity of the two aspects of the field is what makes up personality. *The situationist has become a field theorist, and field theory is the point of view which has just been developed.* The situationist has succeeded in making his point that personality cannot be defined without reference to the situation, but in doing so he has capitulated on a series of essential issues.

This way of thinking is rather new in psychology but very familiar in physics. Physicists came upon this way of thinking about 1875, when Clerk-Maxwell developed his celebrated equations for electromagnetic fields. The physicists found that they could no longer explain events by referring to the interaction of particles which push and pull; each event came to be conceived as an aspect of a field of events.

Field theory entered biology with Spemann's work in experimental embryology. It became evident that the individual does not unfold simply by virtue of inner dynamics, nor through response to outer forces alone, but as the result of an intricate interaction of the two sets of forces. Spemann showed that mother and infant are not two independent creatures, but that a single field—in the physical sense—is involved. This concept of a unitary field of organism-environment is important for personality study. The pioneer here is Kurt Lewin; and though our development of the concept takes a form different from his, our great indebtedness to him is obvious. Angyal and Sullivan, too, have developed systems congenial to the present one.

The issue may best be stated by contrasting field theory with the accepted conventional view of the relation of individual to environment. According to this conventional view, there is a clearly defined outer world, or stimulus, and an individual, or organism, upon which the stimulus acts (illustration No. 1); as the stimulus acts, it sets free

No. 1

one of his potential responses. The nature of the stimulus determines which potential response—smiling, jumping, shouting—will be released. Thus the situation can be defined before the individual is defined. But we have just seen that this is not the case, for the individual selects from and consequently defines the situation. Moreover, in line with the conventional view, the individual can be defined before the situation is defined; but here again we have just seen (page 881) that this also is impossible. What the situation will be for this individual, what the individual will be for this situation, will depend not upon properties self-contained within each but upon the properties of the field that constitutes the form of their interaction. This makes a profound practical difference; field theory is not a complicated way of restating the obvious, but a step toward greater realism.

A better schema of what happens is shown in illustration No. 2. Again the circle S represents the situation—the whole of the environment, with all its properties—the circle O represents the organism, the individual. The ellipse represents interaction; the organism is selecting from the situation, and the situation is selecting from the

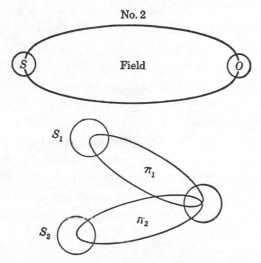

No. 2

organism. Personality, as observed, consists of the portion of the organism that is polarized toward the situation, just as the functional aspects of the situation, the real environment, consists of the aspects of the situation that are polarized toward the organism. Since in this first statement we are concerned with personality not simply as a potentiality but as realized, actualized, an event for science to study, nothing is part of the observed functioning personality π_1 which is not included in the ellipse. Let another situation S_2 act upon the organism, and the manifest personality is π_2.

The portion of the figure relevant to personality varies with the type of situation involved, different aspects being called out by different situations. If all the potentialities could be called forth, the ellipses in the third figure would flow together and a large circle would be produced. In reality however, all the potentialities are never called out. Since all the situations that act on the individual stem as a rule from a single culture, they have much in common; they all draw, so to speak, "from one side of the organism." What is actually realized in personality comes from interaction with many similar S's. If a totally dissimilar stimulus hit the organism "from the other side," there might be no overlap whatever with what was seen heretofore. Cultural uniformities, culturally defined personality types, may be portrayed in this way; for since adult men are essentially alike in respect to the real fundamental things of life, we shall have to grant, with the situationist, that so far as the environmental situations can be matched, the aspects that are realized in personality will often be fairly similar. The same thing holds for women, and more specifically for individuals who belong to subgroups defined in terms of age, sex, economic class, neighborhood. Thus far, there is considerable agreement with the situationist's conception that personality is being made every day, every moment. To the suggestion that somewhere there exists the *true* personality, as contrasted with the visible response to situations in which the personality functions, the reply is simply that no personality is describable as a free unattached "ultimate" which does not confront a situation.

Unlike situationism, field theory asserts that the child achieves (very slowly) an inner organization which is capable of offering considerable resistance to outer pressures. But it calls attention to the difference between taking such resistance for granted and, on the other hand, carefully studying its strength as an expression of all the forces in the field. Education consists largely of an endless adjustment of outer and inner forces. The practical outcome of the process has been shown countless times. For example, this concept was applied literally by Mrs. Morse, when superintendent of the New York State Training School for Girls. Mrs. Morse believed that the girls' personalities were disturbed by factors that lay in the field, and that they were expressions of the field. Many a superintendent of such an institution would have said that these girls should be given liberties only "when they had earned them," only when they had become normal again. But Mrs. Morse doubted whether they could be normal when being treated as convicts; so she eliminated the straight jacket, eased the restrictions, and allowed the girls to decorate their rooms, dress attractively, and receive visitors. In other words, she treated them like normal girls, to see what happened; and in large measure they became what the new environment invited them to become.

In the same vein, it is becoming recognized more and more clearly that what individual therapy can accomplish is limited by the nature of the polarity of the situation between physician and patient. The therapeutic interview is only one kind of situation, and it does not necessarily prevent the patient's subsequent failure when he confronts the other situations of which his life is comprised. For this reason psychiatry is making more and more use of situational therapy, is placing the patient in a world which will bring out what is wanted, a world like the one that he has to face. The psychiatrist who wishes to see the whole personality must see the patient in all the situations of his life; indeed, he must place him in countless new situations to bring out new aspects of his personality. The group therapist often succeeds in shortening this almost infinite process because many of the patient's critical maladjustments appear in group situations, and it is precisely in the group situation that the diagnosis and therapy are carried on. The group situation is likely, moreover, to present, along with people, the symbols and objects of material culture—money, books, houses, etc.—which are part of the day-by-day world of the patient; it is in this full cultural context that his difficulty is observed. None of this is meant to deny the reality of deeper or less accessible aspects of personality (cf. pages 626 and 641); but these, too, so far as we can ever hope to know them, are definable only as they interact with specific life tasks, life situations.

INDIVIDUAL DIFFERENCES

Experiments on individual differences take on a richer meaning when viewed in this way. In one experiment, Marks, using an ergograph, constructed work curves for young adult males. The distribution was not normal, but flattened out. The explanation appeared to be in the form of the instructions: "Work as hard as you can and as fast as you can." About two-thirds of these men apparently heard these instructions with the emphasis on the word "hard," and the other one-third with the emphasis upon "fast." Since it is impossible to give full attention to speed and effort at the same time, some functioned in a "hard"-instruction situation, others in a "fast"-instruction situation. The distribution, however, was normal with reference to each of these two means. The discontinuity between the two probably arose from the fact that the two groups were working in different fields defined by the two ways of perceiving the instructions.

Hanks, administering a paper-and-pencil test for neurotic tendencies, found not a normal curve but a curve with a tendency to three modes. "Too many" cases lay at the extremes—very neurotic and very free of neurosis. Let us see if we can explain this by putting ourselves in the subject's situation as he takes the test. If each test item were a logic-tight compartment responded to without memory of the items which have gone before and without reference to those which may come later, we should expect a normal distribution; for underlying the responses there would be a large number of independent causal factors. There exists within each person a certain number of neurotic tendencies which will be brought out by the various questions. But since there are no such logic-tight compartments, the responses which the subject has already given and his attitude toward the remainder of the test will influence his response at each moment. What is he responding to, an item or a complex field of outer and inner factors? The fact that he has answered certain questions so as to picture his own neuroticism in a certain way is part of the present situation; he perceives the remaining questions in terms of a reference to neuroticism which he might never otherwise have seen, and his replies begin to "snowball" in the direction taken at the beginning of the test. The result is that, having answered the first questions in a healthy-minded way, some people have built up a feeling of assurance about the questionnaire and in consequence fail to see the relevance to themselves of certain items which come later. They would be at point P if they had answered the questions one at a time in different situations, but taking the questionnaire all at once puts them at the left of *P*. Similarly those who have indicated a fair degree of neuroticism find themselves functioning in a neurotic atmosphere. Or perhaps they half-consciously realize what their answers indicate, and determine, as they near the end of the questionnaire, that they will at least be *impressive neurotics*.

A field interpretation may also be illustrated by W. H. Wilke's study of attitude shift in response to propaganda. Three types of propaganda were used: (1) a speaker present in the room, (2) the speaker's voice over the radio, and (3) the printed page. His subjects originally showed a normal distribution in attitude toward the distribution of wealth. Wilke found that the radio propaganda did not shift the group as a whole in the intended direction, as happened when the speaker was physically present, but forced his subjects into marked agreement or disagreement; hence the distribution became flattened out. We are not dealing here with the effects of the summation of single items of the propaganda in the course of a cogent argument. The individual responds to a mounting effort at coercion; he is being "talked into" something. When the speaker is physically present, the listener may identify with him and see through his eyes; hence, though he is being pushed, he may be willing to go along. But in him who listens without such an impulse toward identification, the ego-defensive tendencies are strengthened by the speaker; there is a strong tendency to all-or-none response (page 741) when ego defense is involved.

The case for field interpretation that is implied in such studies as these is notably strengthened by Rundquist and Sletto's *Personality in the Depression*, in which the point is made and well documented that whenever a situation is viewed impersonally, attitudes yield a normal distribution curve, whereas whenever the situation assumes a personal form, forcing one toward a decision, the distribution is bimodal.

THE DISCONTINUITY OF FIELDS

In Chapter 13 evidence was offered to show that cleavage within the organism, functional discontinuity, is as patent and as important as integration, and in Chapter 31 to suggest discontinuity in the distribution of certain traits. Since our attention has been given in the two preceding chapters to discontinuity in the outer situations that act upon the organism, we must now view the three kinds of discontinuity together.

We may best begin with an experimental study, G. L. Freeman's research with the *stress interview*. The individual who is put through a very difficult interview situation—for example, confronted with the brute fact that in a military operation he is one of the "expendables" —either cracks up or holds together; few men fall in between. Discontinuity within the group is clear, and the concept applies just as directly to the social world as to the varying states of the individual organism. Even if the threshold for crack-up could be proved to be a continuum—indeed, even if we could prove that resistance to crack-up is normally distributed—it would remain true that the acid test, the critical situation, breaks the group into two functionally distinct groups. A knife-blade separation in the threshold can make all the difference between two responses, between two subsequent ways of living. If the field theorist is right, social discontinuities must result in definite discontinuous personality types.

For the most part, as we have seen, personality does not lend itself well to typing, the reason being that there are so many organismic traits and so many social situations that an unworkable number of types would have to be dealt with. But there are cases where types appear, cases in which constant massive fundamental differences in situations overwhelm the minor day-by-day situational variations. In particular, life depends, to a large degree, on relatively irreversible *commitments*, and each commitment constitutes a field. Many college men want at the same time to become doctors and to become lawyers. When a man decides at last what he is going to do, much of his personality is rapidly reworked. Old interests and attitudes drop out, and new ones are soon crystallized, and within a few years the regimentation of the professional attitude is practically absolute. Personality may be so deeply invaded by the outer situation that it can see no human problem from a non-professional point of view; we shudder at the very idea of an "unprofessional" outlook.

Field determination goes deep; and when once a commitment has been made, there is usually no possibility of going back to the unformed stage. There are, however, reversible attitudes, which change as freely as the classic outlines of the "reversible staircase." They change because the ego is not committed to either, except as the attitudes are appropriate to specific situations. Thus Schanck made the distinction between "private" and "public" attitudes in a small town; he found that as members of a club or church, people believed so and so, but as private individuals they believed otherwise.

It may properly be argued that what the individual already is at any given time will help to determine which situation he will select. This is a cardinal contention of field theory (as against situationism). But it does not mean that after functioning in a field a person may escape it and go back, scot-free, to an earlier undifferentiated outlook. Of course, until the decision is made he often has no way of finding out what he will become in the new field. The farmer cannot foresee what he will become as a small merchant in town; the twenty-year-old cannot see what marrying one girl, rather than another, will make of him as a person. If social situations are themselves so largely discontinuous and require commitments, decisions, irrevocable choices, then personalities must themselves be discontinuous in considerable measure. And when the social situations are shared by many, as in the case of social classes, discontinuous types may be useful and important in relation to many attributes of personality.

When field theory is viewed in this way, it is sometimes granted at once that animals and small children can be studied in such terms, since internal structure is loose and outer constraining forces are clearly defined, but asserted that the more mature a person, the more complex the inner core of resistance to the outer world which he builds up, the more difficult it becomes to use field principles. Are there not rugged self-reliant people who refuse to change even under the most severe pressure? Is there not plenty of evidence that, as a mature and autonomous individual, man can develop something which is independent of the pressures of the outer world?

This point can be put in such cogent form as apparently to argue that the individual can actually separate himself from the environment, can encapsulate himself from the pressures of the world. In reality, such people are not out of touch with the field; their defiance, their self-assertion, their "independence" are defined in terms of their situation and are relative to it; they reject some aspects of the situation and make the most of other aspects, just as everyone else does. It is important to recognize the personality which can shut off much of the outer world, can overpower others, or can make real to itself aspects of the field that mean little to others. We may call it the "gyroscopic" personality, for it goes on spinning in its own way despite the pitching and rolling of the deck on which it stands.

It may be reasonable to think of a continuum from the plasticity or flaccidity of the newborn child to the martyr mindful only of Paradise, or to the schizophrenic who is completely "inaccessible." This way of looking at the matter recognizes the factor of maturity as very important and compares it with homeostasis (page 32) as a device that prevents the swamping of the inner world by the outer. We become more gyroscopic as we grow up. But such an approach emphasizes also the deep-seated individual factors which define the degree and form of this inner stability. Eugene Lerner used to speak of "beavers" and "chameleons"; the former chew steadily ahead through their tree trunks, the latter constantly change color in response to the outer world. And for every pure beaver or pure chameleon there are many somewhere in between, endowed in some measure with what the psychiatrist calls flexibility, an ability to change direction, but also in some measure with a stubborn constancy. But never—and here is where the emphasis belongs—does anyone completely free himself from either inner or outer pressures. Never does the purest beaver become really self-contained, ignoring the differences between trees; never does the most volatile chameleon lose the inner individuality which distinguishes him from other chameleons.

In the light of this strong emphasis upon individuality, we may ask whether the older formulations cannot be made to serve, whether field theory is necessary. Yes, indeed; the old *can* be "made to serve"; we can stretch Gestalt psychology in the situational direction and stretch situationism in the Gestalt direction, and hold the two, thus stretched, in contact. But what is gained by clinging to the old it is difficult to see. Unless we are forever alert to the oversights made by Gestalt without situationism, or by situationism without Gestalt, we cannot make these two work without constant and crude errors. The stretching process has to be continuous, for an unstretched Gestalt will try to define organization within the organism first, and then look for organization in the situation, whereas in point of fact the organization *within* the organism depends partly on the organization of the situation. Similarly, situationism will try to define the organization of the situation first, before turning to the organism, forgetting that it is partly by virtue of the structure of the organism that the situation achieves structure. *We cannot define the situation operationally except in reference to the specific organism which is involved; we cannot define the organism operationally, in such a way as to obtain predictive power for behavior, except in reference to the situation. Each serves to define the other; they are definable operationally while in the organism-situation field.*

For the writer it was the errors made when personality tests were used without benefit of field theory that first forced a formulation in this direction; for others it will be the clinical sterility of a therapy based on the isolated individual. It may be felt that the geometry has been overdone; however, we are a generation of visualizers, and it would do no harm for everyone, in the routine of his own profession, to get into the habit of drawing circles and ellipses and asking himself constantly whether he is talking about a person as a circle, whether he really knows what sort of person he is talking about, aside from those aspects of his daily life which appear in the ellipse.

The present approach is relevant to the ever-recurring question of *predicting* behavior from the clinical interview or the test profile. The field theorist now considers himself sure enough of his ground to say that the usefulness of the prediction will depend largely upon the care with which the situation pressing upon the individual is studied; for this, considered in relation to the structure of the organic system, will determine the possibilities for transfer. In particular, the interlocking of the outer with the inner system, rather than a piecemeal analysis of isolated trends, will define the specific area of action to which prediction is directed.

Beyond the question of short-range prediction, one of the most pressing problems that confronts the field theorist is continuity through life. If the interdependence of organism and environment is as we have described it, how can a person be recognizably the same when he is constantly acted upon by a new environment? The field theorist believes that the question calls for a quantitative answer; he would expect the nature and degree of continuity to depend upon neither organic factors nor environmental factors nor the sum of the two, but upon continuity of the processes of mutual selection and organization going on between them. To test such a hypothesis we need concrete evidence as to how much continuity there is, and what form it takes; this will carry the story somewhat further than we did in Chapter 30.

A representative study is reported by T. M. Newcomb. Women students at Bennington College were studied through the four years of college, and some of them for a year and a half after graduation, to ascertain the degree of continuity in their social attitudes as related on the one hand to their personalities as freshmen, and on the other to the environment in which they functioned. Through all four years a comprehensive test of social attitudes was administered. The campus atmosphere was liberal, and most girls discovered that liberal views on social issues were in good form; hence the student body as a whole moved in the liberal direction.

But such a situationist statement does not suffice. Certain girls seemed disposed from the beginning to follow the trend of the college as a whole; others seemed disposed to resist it. Each girl responded day by day to a college atmosphere upon which her intellectual and social life depended; she could either accept the trend or shut herself off from it and from her fellows. Relatively few of these girls had the toughness or narrowness to resist these pressures; the majority exposed themselves more and more to the new outlook. But a few who had security in their own little group did not do so; the art students are a clear example of such an autonomous unit. Most of the girls adopted the Bennington outlook so thoroughly that a year and a half after graduation, though back in conservative communities, they still maintained some of their now dissident liberalism.

The continuity of individual response proved to be traceable (1) to individual continuity in the need for social acceptance and social participation in the group atmosphere, (2) to the resulting continuity of exposure to the liberal thought of the faculty, (3) to the mutual reinforcement of attitude among girls who were discovering more and more clearly that the right thing to think, socially speaking, is the liberal thing. This study was made at the time of the Spanish Civil War, and sympathy with the Loyalists was the accepted position. The more socially alert girls were more actively pro-Loyalist. (In the same way, the better-informed girls at a Roman Catholic college were the more actively anti-Loyalist.) Continuity in social attitudes was thus largely continuity in the environment, which went on pressing consistently in one direction; but a factor within the individual played an important part in determining whether and how these continuing pressures would be utilized.

A Science of Biography?

So much for the continuity of a few years; but we find ourselves at a point where the life span must be considered as a whole. The supreme test of field theory is its adequacy to pursue these continuities throughout life in such a way as to develop a sound method for describing and interpreting a life history. Life history studies have become more and more technical, more and more pretentious; but they bog down in prediction because the individual encounters unexpected situations. Perhaps field theory will be able to help at this point. Although new and untried, the concept is worth considering.

Unfortunately the attempt to develop the biographical methods into a sound and sensitive means of revealing personality structure and its trends through time is still characterized by centrifugal forces. The three main factors which influence the taking of case histories in psychotherapy, and likewise the biographical techniques used in laboratory studies, seem to be (1) psychoanalytical theory relative to developmental stages; (2) concepts of wholeness or esthetically conceived structures (with or without benefit of Gestalt theory); and (3) straightforward statistical theories as to cause and effect, which, in the manner of the behaviorists, attempt to relate specific childhood experiences and life history sequences. Most of the efforts to put biography on a sound and systematic empirical basis have been inclined to follow the demands of one of these three factors, to the relative exclusion of the other two; and few indeed appear to indicate any awareness of field problems.

A good beginning, however, has been made. In a study of creative thought as it appears at different points in the life span, Charlotte Bühler proceeded to study the conditions responsible for the differential flowering of such talent. The fact that these studies are expressions of man's life in European culture—their relevance to the Near East or Far East is very uncertain—shows that they deal not with sheer chronology but with man-environment relations.

From the point of view of method, however, our chief concern is with *dynamic sequences* of events within the individual, the tracing of biosocial events from one period in life to sequelae at another period, so that ultimately their lawful trends may be defined. Much of the psychological and psychiatric work reported in this volume, notably that of the psychoanalysts, has proceeded in this way. But the central question is the determination of clear, indisputable, *necessary* sequelae. The pioneer work here is that of Chassell, whose *The Experience Variables* embodies data gathered from men and women by means of a life history schedule of some hundred and fifty questions. Each item was marked in terms of three different periods, early childhood, early teens, and the present. The data were statistically treated on the basis of the prevalence, *among young adults*, of certain types of personality assets or liabilities, as related to various types of early experience. The loneliness, the reserve, the introversion, the insecurity of the young adult were brought into relation to his early experience with the father and mother. (For example, the item of candor vs. harshness in dealing with a child's sex curiosity stood out prominently as of clear-cut significance in relation to the individual's adjustment at the time of answering the questionnaire.) It does not of course follow that the parents' conduct was the sole cause of something that happened to their children fifteen or twenty years later; however, their handling of the child and his response to it is relevant in connection with the social problem with which a young adult has to cope. By extending the method, the biographer could make cross sections of various phases of life, and study what characteristics of the adult in what environment are consistently preceded by certain characteristics of childhood and adolescent development.

A rather similar method was employed by G. V. Hamilton, who, using over three hundred questions, interviewed a hundred men and a hundred women regarding the background of their success or failure in marriage. Certain variables were found rather regularly to precede maladjustment. For example, if the wife had a regular allowance for her own and the family's needs, rather than having to ask for money for each purchase, the marriage had a better chance to succeed; it was not the economic but the ego aspect of the situation that was important. When the data were organized in systematic terms, statistical procedures made it possible to spot the situations in early life which might have led long afterward to strain. These data are meaningful in the context of the world of married couples in our American culture, not otherwise. In connection with method, Hamilton pointed out that the relation of patient to psychiatrist—even the distance between their chairs—was relevant in the patient's attitude.[1]

In life history research, however, there are great advantages in choosing the individuals in advance, first because we can study them continuously from birth (or even from the prenatal period) rather than waiting for a favorable opportunity; second, because by careful planning and the establishment of rapport we can make reasonably sure that these subjects and their parents will give long-range cooperation. J. W. Macfarlane chose the children for her study nearly twenty years ago, before they were born. She began making observa-

---

[1] A somewhat similar approach has been extensively used by Terman and Miles, and a much more elaborate study of sex histories, by means of the interview method, is now being made by the Committee for Research in Studies of Sex.

tions on the mothers during pregnancy, studying their health, attitude toward pregnancy, hopes for the child, and economic and other difficulties; she was present during the hospitalization and watched the children's development after they were brought home. She has maintained close personal contact with every child and his family over the years. Though her main findings can be reported only after her subjects have attained their twentieth year, some data gathered by Macfarlane suggest that the earliest experience patterns, those manifest within the first year or two, are of considerable predictive importance for the growth period as a whole. But she defined her problem and chose her subjects in terms of a reasonably definite and predictable environment, and she has been able to see life histories as expressions not of growth alone, but of interaction sequences. In her case studies it is not physique or health as such, or school or community as such, that gives the key to the developmental pattern, but the way in which each group of factors gives meaning to the other.

The study of juvenile delinquency and crime has likewise witnessed some outstanding efforts at quantitative biography. Sheldon and Eleanor Glueck studied a number of factors in the early life history which proved to be related to subsequent criminal and non-criminal careers. They found six variables in the life histories of 500 young men which had unusual power to predict adjustment as of five years after the expiration of the parole period, if the culture in which these men would be immersed was known in general. Another longitudinal study which should be given special mention because of its concern with the predictive power of *groups* or *syndromes* of experience factors acting jointly, is the Cambridge-Somerville Youth Study, whose subjects are boys and girls in difficulty. In it, an effort has been made to ascertain the meaning of a large number of experience variables in terms of the child's subsequent delinquency history. Is it significant, for instance, that at the age of six the child is a thumb-sucker, that at eight he is severely punished by his father, that at eleven he is failing in school? Primary interest, however, lies not in these factors taken separately, but in their constellations. Despite the limited importance of single factors, it is apparently possible to define a number of syndromes or constellations of factors which seem likely to have predictive value for the child in this urban environment. Having formulated these syndromes and their probable consequences for the life history, the persons who conducted the study made sealed predictions of the adjustment status of the various individuals as of a period after the termination of the study; these are not yet reported.

The term "predictive" may appear overbold. But from the logic of continuity and from the empirical results already achieved, as by the Gluecks, the hope that we shall eventually develop a clear conception of the consistent formal relations between the various phases of the life history appears by no means overoptimistic. In fact, we might say that the trouble is not the overboldness of the method, but the prevalent excessive cautions. This is brought out, for example, by the limited use of the Rorschach method in relation to biography. After over twenty years of Rorschach research, it is surely not too much to ask that the variability of individual Rorschach performance, year by year, be systematically compared with growth and experiential factors. But most of the research has been confined to "limited objectives."

Most such studies, even the Cambridge-Somerville Youth Study which is supposedly to predict the later adjustment of individual boys, attempt to define the relations between a syndrome as of one period and a *simple unitary outcome* as of a later period. No one has as yet undertaken a prediction *from a syndrome or system at one period to a syndrome or system at another*. Although a definite advance is to be noted in the Cambridge-Somerville over the Chassell procedure, the apparent sophistication in the quest for multiple factors evident in looking at data retrospectively is far from being realized when attempts to predict *personality structure* are made.

Yet David M. Levy has demonstrated that the clinical view of the life history can be tested and validated in these very terms. Using the records of children who had been referred for various types of maladjustment, he developed a technique by which life history schedules could be sorted with reference to one factor at a time, such as well-defined maternal overprotection, a suitable control group being automatically provided by the children of the same age, sex, and social status, in whom this factor was not present. From two thousand cases, twenty in which the record clearly defines the problem may thus be chosen. In Levy's approach the qualitative study of the child's life history articulates with the qualitative study of the mother's life history; her biologically and socially determined maternal feelings (cf. page 106) are brought into relation to overprotection. The results are clear; e.g., compensation for a lifetime lack of maternal feeling may lead to a large amount of overprotection. In the same way, any syndrome of family psychology that is desired may be pulled from the files. In the records of any clinic or large office that is research-minded we may, in noting whether the children do well or badly, are happy or unhappy, trace the appearance of syndromes which are sequelae of early personality and upbringing, provided the syndromes are defined in relation to the continuing pressures and problems of the individual's existence. Thus well-defined cases of sibling rivalry or maternal overprotection involve true syndromes of traits not only within the child but within the whole structure of the child-child or mother-child situation respectively; they are field-defined. And they lead back to earlier field-defined patterns and are carried forward in clinical study to determine outcomes. Likewise the Rorschach studies of the after-effects of trauma or of shock therapy, and particularly the studies of the nature of the changes in response during adolescence, give great promise of an emerging picture of field relations. There are obvious limitations, of course, in all this clinical and Rorschach work, for the environmental aspect of the field is even harder to specify than the organismic.

Transcending all such limitations, there seem to be at least four possibilities for a science of biography, four different continuities in terms of which a follow-through, year by year, may be made; all of them involve the use of field theory. First, the biological continuities, in the form of curves of growth and decline in specific function, can be formulated so as to be relative to a biologically defined environment. The individual form of the generic growth curve is now being studied; although all the curves are of one general type, with negative acceleration, their form depends upon the task and upon the individual. The medical history of the family may be used in the same way; certain types of cellular changes, for example, may be predicted far in advance on the basis of genetic considerations. Each adult between the ages of approximately 20 and 50 is growing up with respect to certain functions, aging with respect to others. The time pattern is his own. However, it is defined by the relation between gene patterns and the biological circumstances of living—circumstances of nutrition, health, psychosomatic relationships—and since it is determined by such organism-environment relations, it calls for understanding in terms of field theory.

The second type of continuity, derived from early canalizations (cf. page 719), appears from our present vantage point to depend upon field considerations in two ways. (1) The original canalizations themselves are expressions not of drives alone, but of structural fields comprising both outer and inner components. (2) As the organism's relation to the environment changes, the form of the canalized response pattern changes; it is an aspect of a slowly changing total field.

The third type of continuity demands the most radical and aggressive utilization of field theory. It arises from the daily reinforcement of habits by recurring social stimulation. A large part of the continuity of personality is due to the reiteration of the same old demands, the same old pressures, upon the individual. Many habits owe their life not to canalization but to the fact that the outer world keeps on hammering at them in the same way. Reference might be made to a study of six-year-olds whose nervous habits predicted later delinquency, emphasizing the fact that even for the best-adjusted children at six, fate might provide a tough enough *environment*—violently punishing fathers or frightened and confused mothers—to permit the prediction of trouble at the age of eleven or twelve. The situation inside the child and the situation outside of him are one dynamic whole. In the figure we show the action of the situation by a series of scallops to indicate that whatever happens at the age of six, causing the nervous habits, occurs also at the age of seven, eight, nine, ten, and so on, as the old habits are reinforced. Although the conditioning at six would not by itself provide a residue at sixteen, the events at six years help to determine the field at six years and one month, etc. The value of foster-home placement, advocated by Healy and others, lies in the fact that the vicious pattern is thus cut for a few years, until the child is freed from his habit. It is the day-by-day interaction of the individual and the situation that is important, *not* a habit that remains unaltered from early childhood. Continuity lies in the field, not in the character structure as such.

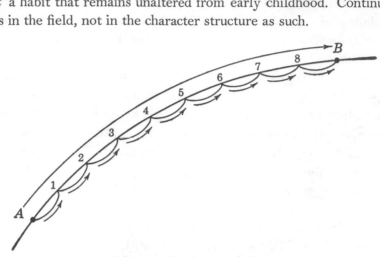

Schematic Developmental Curve

The x-axis represents time; the y-axis, personality growth. According to the usual conditioning hypothesis, A, occurring in early childhood, causes behavior B at a later time. According to the present hypothesis, A can "cause" B only insofar as events 1, 2, 3, etc., follow in dynamic sequence during the intervening period and reinforce or perpetuate the effects of A, the original event.

In particular, the conflict which develops in every normal personality is largely a field conflict. One tries to face a situation without facing it (cf. pages 298 and 302). This seems to be the typical pattern of the neuroses—how to do something without doing it. Such patients are trying to eat their cake and have it too; they wish to maintain a satisfactory picture of themselves and at the same time to do things which will sully it. But since what one wants to do, and the reasons why he cannot do it, have the relation of specific demands and specific obstacles, we offer a field definition of neurosis.

The fourth type of continuity also calls for field formulation; it is the continuity which springs from a tightly organized habit, in which every aspect is dependent upon the rest, so that no one phase can drop out. Professional skills, habits of expression, and every motor disposition deeply organized within the individual involve a complex pattern, each phase of which keeps the others going; each response is conditioned to all the others, and the reinforcement of one of them will maintain the others (page 735). Highly integrated skills as well as values apparently do not fade out or extinguish at all (page 294). We referred above to the gyroscopic type of personality. But every personality has gyroscopic dispositions, in the sense that there is a system that is not broken up by the shifting demands of daily experience. The field theorist stresses gyroscopic continuity. Despite the impersonality of life in this age of industrialization, despite the feeling that it makes little difference what happens to us, stability and even rigidity in the maintenance of the self are common enough. There are great pressures both upon and within individuals to make them stay as they are. When we are told how important, how priceless we are, we take this to mean that we are supremely good as we are. Is not the whole modern American cult of personality conducive to complacency about selfhood in its static aspects? "I owe it to myself," we say, at the same moment that industrialism strives to make us more or less uniform. Today's social environment demands both individuality, independence, and its opposite. The attempt to live this contradiction constitutes part of the illness of modern times. We must enact two roles, the impersonal role and the self-worship role, at the same time; the first requires moment-by-moment adaptation; the second, a hard inner core. To turn to the general problem of the ego, or self-awareness, nothing is more calamitous than to be naïve, unaware of the self; you must be subtle and you must be sophisticated; but you must not think about yourself; nothing is more abhorrent than this. There is, then, as much social pressure to stand pat, or, if you must spin, to spin gyroscopically, as there is to change. The environmental aspects of the field, and likewise the inner aspects, are as important in one instance as in the other.

Though we have been chiefly concerned with *individuality* in the continuities which we can observe, there is an important relation between the method of studying this individuality of pattern and the method of studying the *general* developmental destiny which all human beings share. There is often more continuity of destiny than is evident to one concerned with specific steps observed month by month. Earlier we quoted L. K. Frank's formulation (page 725) of continuity in terms of an essentially common destination for travelers taking many different routes and many different modes of locomotion. In like manner, improvement of techniques for observing and measuring should lead to a generalized study of the dynamics of development, from embryology through to senescence and dissolution. But from the point of view of field theory such a progression can never take the form of a study of the laws of organismic change as such; it is embedded in the sequence of reciprocities with the kinds of environments in which personalities can evolve. Field theory deals, for example, with such progressions in relation to a specified American urban environment. And when it aspires to generalizations which go beyond a specified class of environments, it aspires not to generalized organismic laws that are "beyond all environments" but to laws which relate universally to all the environments, in the broadest sense, which constitute the soil in which personalities may appear and develop. This type of law has already been studied in relation to the life cycles of animals; before it can become an actuality in the study of human life histories, the analytical and quantitative study of social fields will have to progress much further.

40. The Fitness of Culture for Personality

A CURRENT phrase already quoted from social science discussions is that "personality is molded by the social order"; and, as we have seen, this phrase is good, provided it calls up the right image of a mold. Certainly the social science approach has nowhere revealed an easy process by which the individual is assimilated to the cultural norm; the process involves constant struggle. And those who refer to the malleability of human nature are coming to realize that in order to shape it so that it will stay shaped, it is necessary to keep pounding for a long time, with powerful and ever-repeated blows. There is no quarrel between the biological and social science approaches if that fact is kept in mind. Quarrels arise only when the biologically-minded psychologist assumes that the individual successfully resists social pressures, or when the social science psychologist assumes that the molding is done casually and easily. The biological types of psychology, including psychoanalysis, offer proof of the long, arduous, difficult process by which the human being is shaped in the cultural norm; the sociological types offer proof that the task is finally accomplished. It therefore becomes relevant to ask: How well do cultures in general succeed in "fitting" the intrinsic needs of man? And in particular, how well does a complex industrial society "fit" such needs?

Reviewing and condensing much that has been said heretofore, we find four ways in which personality is molded by social pressures. (1) The signals used by society to call forth any given response can be almost indefinitely varied. Signals can secure results in terms of behavior by virtue of a limitless number of words, gestures, flags, pictures; new symbols appear from day to day. Tabus and restrictions depend similarly on an infinite variety of symbols; one society shows disapproval by signals made in one's face, whereas another uses words that threaten corporal punishment. The individual is very effectively molded by being sensitized to a particular system of signals, so much so that he is frequently unaware of these signals, these fleeting and truncated gestures and inflections of approval and disapproval.

(2) The value system of the individual begins in large part with canalizations that are referable to the current modes of satisfaction which society provides for each need. If the child responds positively to the music he hears, society has ways of repeating that experience day in and day out. In the course of time, structured music, with its diatonic or pentatonic scale, its characteristic melodic sequences, its simple or complex harmony, becomes the accepted music and all other music becomes queer. This is accomplished not by arousing in the individual any completely new wants, but by reinforcing and deepening the satisfactions first given to the primitive childhood needs. Every developed art form is the elaboration of responses to socially patterned tone, form, color, rhythm, etc. The curiosity satisfactions, as in scientific thought, can also be traced from child to adult in these terms; society acts not by adding something but by molding something that is already there, giving it characteristic direction.

(3) Somewhat more surprisingly, there is the fact that the impulsive life of the individual can be qualitatively changed to some extent. By emphasizing the legitimacy of one type of satisfaction and the illegitimacy of another within the realm of the accepted drives, society can fuse and pattern the needs and can consequently change their quality. For example, the way in which food is prepared and served involves more than the molding of food preferences by society; it changes the nature of hunger, e.g., emphasis passes from olfactory and gustatory to tactual qualities of food. Food tastes become "coarse," "refined," etc.

(4) Because of this third process, the ethos, the predominant feeling tone, depends upon the cultural process through which the individual goes. Not only are the impulses molded, but the inner core and the flow of feeling into the cognitive outlook are likewise shaped.

Now suppose we say that personality has been molded in these four ways by the cultural pressures, and then stop at that point. Is there not something paradoxical about the fact that profound frustration is characteristic of modern man, woman, and child—so characteristic that the sociologist and psychiatrist take it for granted and attribute to it much of the neurosis and psychosis that characterize society today? Such frustration is certainly evidence that the molding process has not finished its task. Cultural relativists, noting how widely the patterns of human conduct vary over the face of the earth, must still face the fact that in every society there is protest; people do not do and feel what the society says they should do and feel. But as we look at the cultures we have studied, we find nothing more striking than the fact that the amount of frustration varies greatly. Among the Arapesh there seems to be much less than among the Manus.

Our first general objection, then, to the social science view in its naïve form is that no personality is ever completely molded to the will expressed in the social code, even at high temperature and under constant pressure. Even if the external molding is outwardly successful, there is much tension within. Culture meets the needs of man with varying degrees of success. Furthermore, what the culture can do to the individual depends on the stuff he is made of. One child is easily molded with regard to food but fights constantly against socialization of his aggressive impulses; the reverse may be true of another child. The younger the child the more obvious is this individual quality in responding to and fighting against social pressures. The way in which a person grows into the culture is itself an expression of biological individuality. Moreover, from this major point of the social scientist, the malleability of human nature, the conclusion is often drawn that people should simply do the best they can to fit themselves into the scheme of society. This conclusion is ill advised, for it is only by not accepting culture as it is that new cultures are made.

We come then to a rough attempt to show where our own contemporary culture appears well ordered with reference to human needs and where it fits badly. One of the deep general characteristics of our culture which marks its relative success can be expressed in terms of the importance of the individual, the moral and legal conception of individual responsibility, the corresponding pressure upon the individual to strike out for himself, and finally the notion that the individual's welfare is the supreme test of a society. We still gauge things in terms of personal values deeper than any money values. Although we constantly step on the face of the individual, we still cling to that pattern of values; it gives a child the feeling that he counts, that he is a precious thing. It has become obvious that this system of values is self-contradictory, and that it conflicts with the values of a competitive industrial society in which there can be but a few "successful" lives as defined by the competitive task of achieving power and status. It is equally obvious that this older system of values dies hard. Cultural lag based on deeply entrenched demand is powerful, and individualism gives many a sense of personal importance. But wherever individualism fails, especially among the more impoverished, submerged elements of the population, there is clear evidence that the social order has failed, at least relatively. And when many members of the social group are imbued with a chronic sense of failure, the reiteration of the supreme worth of the individual is constructive only when it leads to a definition and a removal of the obstacles to that goal.

A second reason for positive success in our culture is its recognition of individual differences. We place great emphasis upon the richness of individual differences and the desirability of cultivating them; we believe that life is more interesting because we differ. This is a value tendency which is biologically sound. But the way in which it is recognized is poorly adapted to our present social pattern, for most aspects of individuality are subordinated to the few that are of economic importance. Rich personalities have been given meager roles; Aristotle once said that it was not so much that slavery was wrong, but that the wrong people were slaves. The trouble with our society, then, is not that it cherishes the value of individuality, but that it neglects the aspects of individuality which are not directly related to the success pattern of the era.

A third asset of our culture, still talking "biologically," is the conception of freedom, even in its crudest sense—the notion of the right to do, read, talk, think as we wish. One man's freedom is of course always likely to cut across another man's path; nevertheless, the collective demand for freedoms such as these is at the heart of the expansion of the spirit that characterized post-feudal culture. Particularly important, in an age of confusion, is freedom of inquiry. This freedom—the right to ask what makes nature tick, the right to ask what makes mankind itself tick—has been with us only three hundred years. Socrates and Roger Bacon did not enjoy this freedom as we do today. And certainly, whatever the tremendous assets of the Soviet Union, no one can seriously claim that its citizens have freedom of inquiry; it is a "bourgeois democratic" kind of freedom. It inevitably involves the right to challenge the social order itself—yes, the right to challenge the value of freedom, too. And less dramatic, but as pertinent to the role of the free inquirer, is the right to an "outrageous hypothesis," the right to challenge the accepted axioms, the thought forms of the community, the self-evident truths which limit vision and cramp imagination. Scientific inquiry has been made largely by those who were willing to formulate hypotheses and pursue investigations which reasonable people thought ridiculous. This kind of freedom is organically related to the freedom value as a whole.

The freedom value means, of course, a perpetual struggle against uniformity, e.g., against "rationalization" in production, as witness the way we rage at the introduction of efficiency into modern living. We admire and crave it; but we also fear and hate it. When we visit a modern housing project, we recoil at the five hundred houses designed as a unit. Each house has everything imaginable, and far more than we can imagine, in the way of labor-saving devices. But why must all this be the same from one man's house to another? Although we passionately love democracy, we passionately want to be different from everyone else. The freedom value asserts that each person, as a worker in a factory or as a member of a community, needs some form of individualized escape.

A fourth asset of our culture is its unreasoning and ardent belief in the continuity of progress. A World's Fair staged during a depression year may be named a Century of Progress, and no one will blink; for the Fair will be devoted largely to industrial inventions, and belief in man's progress in the fields of science and technology is deep-rooted. We also believe in social progress, but this must be decorous and restrained; we bristle in protest if people talk "radically." For all that, this worship of progress is a great protection against mute acquiescence in a standpat social order.

If now we draw up a brief list of the *liabilities* of western society, there is scarcely any doubt that the most serious frustration of individual personality will be found in the field of security needs. Here are included economic insecurity, and uncertainty as to affection, status, prestige—all that goes with the whirling pattern of change with which we are confronted. The worst phase of insecurity is ego strain. Even if society gives the individual prestige and status, he does not know how long he can retain it. Many people, driven by an insatiable drive to go higher and higher, impose more and more arbitrary and severe strains upon themselves. The individual can bypass this aspect of society, but if he does so, he becomes queer; he cannot, like some who bypass the Manus culture (page 785), simply eke out an existence in his own way. Many, especially in the urban environment, are caught in a network of prestige patterns which cannot be bypassed and which constitute an ego strain both on those who achieve prestige and on those who fail to attain it.

This pathological insecurity is accompanied by the relative loss of group identification. With the dissolution of the large family group and the tendency to wander constantly to new places in search of homes and jobs, the individual's ties with his group have weakened. It may be held that the immediate family is for this reason all the more compact; yet marriage has been one of the institutions most powerfully hit by these centrifugal tendencies. This does not mean only the insecurity of divorced persons. There is usually a long period of injured ego, of frightening insecurity, before the two parties realize that they want to give up. This has been going on long enough in our American culture so that the shadow is thrown in advance over a great many marriages; the marriage is made with the lurking fear that it may not work, and no one dares hope in long-range terms. The pattern also deeply affects the children, who grow up with the painful struggling of irreconcilable loyalties to the two parents; many a child sees the impending separation coming and suffers from the strain.

Finally is to be stressed the general fact that ours is a conflict culture. Not only is there economic conflict of man with man, class with class; there is value conflict. The fundamental conflict of values, resulting from three centuries of anti-authoritarian thought and conduct and capped by the present-day authority of the impersonal business code, means that there are several different *right* ways of behaving in every field of living. Certainly insecurity alone, or ego strain alone, or the lack of group identification alone, or conflict alone, could easily threaten to wreck our society; and any two of them together can unquestionably do so.

By way of comparison, we shall mention briefly some assets and liabilities which are clear in life in the Soviet Union. First among the assets is the conception of identification with the group, a point at which our own culture is dangerously weak. Noting the almost religious sense of unity developed in the collective prosecution of a heroic task, various western observers have asked whether human personality can survive in the face of such complete neglect of the individual. Individualism is so ingrained in our own society that it is impossible for us to imagine that personality might be at its richest where group identification is strongly accented, and where people stress the things they have in common, not their distinctive differences. But, as we saw earlier, there are many attributes of personality which have nothing to do with individuality (page 1). There is, moreover, a place for individuality even in the sharing of a homogeneous task.

Second among the positive attributes of the Soviet way is freedom from the insecurity which goes with joblessness and the attendant sense of personal worthlessness. A personality free of the ordinary economic fears which wrack the souls of men has an enormous head start toward the educational goal, for the individual who has no need to worry as to where he will find his next job and how he can maintain his standard of living is certainly more educable.

Finally, it seems to follow that when these security needs are met, personality becomes enriched in other directions; in Leon Trotsky's words, when the people once have bread, they can have poetry. When once there is real security with regard to elementary things, people begin to demand art, music, and the drama.

If now we look at the liabilities of the Soviet system from the standpoint of personality needs, the most obvious is surely coercion. The opportunity to choose what values a person wishes to satisfy, the experience of exploring nature and himself and making something out of them in his own terms, does not play a large part in a tightly administered plan of life, in which the individual must accept whatever the directing forces require. Furthermore, from this it follows that the individual has to identify with some members of the group rather than with others. One of the great assets of the system, we saw, was group identification; but in a group where there is some conflict—and there is always some—the question with whom to identify becomes a grave source of tension. After the death of Lenin, the problem arose whether to identify with Trotsky or with Stalin; identification with Trotsky soon became a cardinal sin. One cannot have a free and flexible personality (in the usual sense of the terms) if, as child or adult, there are forced upon him the types of identifications which he must develop. Of course the Soviet Union would not have been ready to withstand the Nazi onslaught if it had stopped to think all of this out at a leisurely pace. But the price seems to us to be pretty terrific—one learns unity through fratricide. As Bertrand Russell has said, it was the revolutionists' hope that after men had experienced enough coercion and bloodshed they would discover a new brotherhood; but the question was just how much of the old dream they would remember after the long experience with hate and with the dreaded police system of a resolute authority.

A third negative factor which follows from the others is that an extreme economic definition of personality blinds the student of man to the recognition of factors that are even deeper than the economic. For example, many of the attempts to study individual differences among children in the Soviet Union have been officially sabotaged; the Kremlin determined what could, what could not be inherited, what could, what could not be environmentally controlled. The natural result has been a dogmatic and unproductive study of biological individuality side by side with an extremely productive and valuable study of *medical* genetics, in which official orthodoxy has been much less rigid.

In view of the wide difference between what human nature needs and what it can hope to obtain under these two great social systems, the western and the Soviet, it seems fair to say that despite their considerable assets they are unlikely to continue long as they are. It is no longer possible for any badly functioning system to be held together by sheer force of central control. Our own society cannot long exist with the frustrations and confusions which it involves; nor can the Soviet system, with its coercions, long endure in a world so sensitized to freedom. Our rather hebephrenic outlook is too sick to last; the Soviet tendency to the rigidities of paranoia (both in ideology and in practice) cannot be indefinitely maintained in a world calling so loudly for flexibility. Each may in time learn something; but it is as likely that both will disintegrate within a century or less. If the two do not attempt to destroy each other in fear and fury, a combination of their assets may ultimately occur in a society in which personality has a somewhat better chance to develop its potentialities. The question is whether we have sense enough to develop a workable non-frustrating economy that will maintain our capacity for science, technology, and free inquiry, and the ability to recognize a free personality when we see one.

Although we have been looking at cultures which historically belong to peoples with white skin, there is no reason whatever to believe that cultures remain the exclusive or distinctive property of those among whom they have developed. Western ideas and Soviet ideas are penetrating everywhere, and it is to be expected that the ideas of China, of India, and of countless other nations will be deeply assimilated by our own descendants in a century or less. Perhaps the family unity (and consequent security feelings) so characteristic of China and Japan, the sense of oneness with nature so characteristic of India, and many other sources of strength and satisfaction can be viably grafted into our own make-up.

THE MOLDING OF CULTURE BY PERSONALITY

But have we not again lapsed into the habit of speaking as if the individual were a creature of society and as if the problem of individuality were a question of what society makes of the individual? Is it not a fact that most of the social changes which are important have been brought about by individuals who have defiantly resisted all the ordinary rules, used social forces to defeat social forces, and turned society upside down? Have not societies been blown to bits and reconstituted by individuals too strong for society? We have talked as if we were very sure that, under the industrialism of today, the individual does not count; we have groaned in protest that individuality is being suppressed. But here is a great paradox: the vaster the organizations of power, industrial or political, the greater the power of the individual who knows how to seize the helm. We could, if we wished, build a whole psychology of personality along the opposite lines, taking note that the remainder of this century and the next will not see mere continuations of the present trends; we have every reason to deny that vast impersonal forces are going to make the future. The great individual causes extensive change; the personal factor has become of colossal magnitude.

By what means can the individual possibly exert any such power in the face of the impersonality we have described? A flood of light has been thrown on this point by Sherif's studies. Sherif suggested that when, in a crisis, the perceptual field is disorganized but is capable of being restructured around one of several different anchorage points, the individual who seizes upon one of these anchorage points can induce the group to see things as he does. During a period of successive crises, he who focuses perception in a clear, elemental way upon the means of survival may direct the whole caravan to take one route rather than another. The genius of Lenin was the genius of one who knew what the Russian workers had suffered in the crisis, and who saw how to formulate his own conception of their needs so that they would see them in the same way. Those who understand American personality well enough—the playwright, novelist, newspaperman, statesman, soldier—will show the confused American consciousness of today a way out, will do so over and over again. Fifty ways out are possible; the question is, who will define the situation so that Americans think they see it clearly? Economic determinism here seems as naïve, from the psychological angle, as it did in our study of primitive society. Economic factors will "determine"; they will be like the steam in the boiler. But what they will determine will depend on the design of the engine. Most people will view the economic factor as the figure in the social pattern, but the figure will as usual depend partly on the ground; it will be seen differently and valued differently, in accordance with the structuring tendencies of social leadership.

In a time of crisis the individual likely to become a leader is he who senses the prevalent needs and knows how to structure the solution. Many kinds of leadership, however, are possible. If leadership that will enrich personality and satisfy its many potentialities is what we want, we must begin schooling the leaders early in life; if they are to lead effectively as adults, in competition with leaders who embrace authoritarian methods and appeals, they need democratic experience, and in particular experience in democratic leadership. The more there are of these potential leaders, the more competent they are and the more deeply they love their task, the greater the likelihood that at the points of choice in the coming years they will guide the pent-up energies of a confused people in the direction of genuine self-realization.

41. The Skeptical Psychologist

THREE centuries ago, as chemists exulted in their understanding of nature, Robert Boyle uttered a warning in *The Sceptical Chymist*. He answered their assertion that they had shaken off superstition and found the high road to knowledge; he offered essentially a commentary on the dangers of premature enthusiasm. He saw that the chemists had established no firm basis, not even a method for achieving such a basis, for a new science. True, they had thrown aside some ancient assumptions, but they had replaced them with another system of assumptions. The chemist was too confident; he needed patience and, above all, skepticism. Whereas skepticism is so often regarded as the scientists' weapon against the religionist or the metaphysician, Boyle realized clearly that science needed the tempering influence of a profound doubt, for only when one realizes how little he knows can a sound beginning be made on the task of science.

Psychology is in about the same position today as chemistry was in Boyle's time. It is a hundred and twenty years since Weber's first psychological experiments resulted in a principle—Weber's law—the meaning of which is still obscure. Nearly seventy years have passed since Ebbinghaus made his brilliant studies of memory, the implications of which are still so uncertain that the debate continues today in the psychological journals. The same seventy years have witnessed the rise of psychoanalysis, of psychometric methods, and of cross-cultural studies of personality, all of them full of interest and, to the skeptic, full of untested assumptions. Psychologists find such skepticism irksome; they are like a strong man ready to run his course. Sure of themselves, they are sure they have shaken off, as did the early chemists, the shackles of metaphysics. They have discovered experimental, clinical, and statistical methods. The world is open and free; all that is necessary is to march forward. They are skeptical about everything but psychology; here they radiate confident positivism. So, too, the public, half-aware that the economic and political anguish of the modern world is so largely rooted in the maladjustments of human nature and the psychological contradictions of the culture in which it functions, feels such a need for psychology that it elevates this science, if not to a position of central truth, at least to one of golden promise, and clutches the outlines offered by psychoanalysts, Gestaltists, and behaviorists. To begin asking first questions over again would be so tedious, so wearisome to the flesh.

The growth of these confident "schools of psychology" has been largely due to a series of dialectical protests. It was by denying the assumptions of the earlier psychology that behaviorism and Gestalt psychology established themselves. It was largely by denying the premises of a psychology of consciousness that psychoanalysis had its beginning. Just as Pavlov repudiated psychology in order to establish the physiological principles of learning, so, in general, it has been the repudiation of the laws of association, the oldest and best established of psychological principles, that has resulted in all the main schools of modern psychology. It was the repudiation of the concept of "human nature everywhere the same" which led us to the riches of cultural anthropology. It was the repudiation of the concept of hereditary traits on the one hand, and of the concept that personality derives from learning on the other, that gave us such knowledge as we now have regarding the roots from which personality springs. To the skeptical outsider, psychology might well appear to be a science of negations; its principles are today largely principles that define the narrow limits beyond which generalizations cannot be made. These limits come dangerously near to marking off a pedestrian description of the obvious, without any clear definition of scientific laws.

But the difficulty goes much further. The limitations of our knowledge could be forgiven if we could be sure that our methods were sound. For most of the hundred years during which experimental psychology has existed, experimentation has been the accredited method. However, serious doubt has arisen in recent years as to whether experimentation is adequate—even as adequate as the genetic or the comparative method—with regard to most of the fundamental issues in the psychology of personality. And as has been evident in recent studies—for example, in the present volume—the methodology of genetic and comparative studies is still only fragmentary. We do not know what sorts of genetic observations should be made, or how many and how varied they must be, or how the development of various kinds of human beings or animals should be integrated in a general comparative psychology of general mental development. The most brilliant single contributions dealing with the integration of the genetic and comparative methods are essentially programmatic; they define what we ought to do, rather than offering a convincing demonstration that the methodological problem has been solved.

Neither in content, then, nor in method can we be said to have solved the essential problem of the starting point from which a psychology—any kind of psychology, including a psychology of personality—could be written. These difficulties, however, are dwarfed by a more serious one, uncertainty as to the nature of man and his place in the cosmos. Man is a sample of the stuff of which the cosmos is made. Like other living things, he has evolved by virtue of very complex principles about which the biochemists, the experimental biologists, and the field naturalists are still far from clear. For example, the degree to which Darwin's principles are adequate is still uncertain. We do not know to what extent man's evolution since the dawn of civilization has continued to be guided by the same principles which governed his evolution before that time. We cannot define clearly what human cultures have done to the selective principles upon which evolutionary development depends. We have no clear understanding of the degree to which cultural living has blocked, modified, or redirected the energies that are operative primarily at an animal level. This is one aspect of the fact that we do not know to what extent the principles operating within man are identical with general principles which operate elsewhere in the universe. We do not know whether man exemplifies some principles which are antithetical to others within him, or some which are unrelated to others, as if drawn in a different dimension. It is often assumed, for the purposes of what is called science, that inert and purposeless matter has pushed and pulled until, quite fortuitously, living forms have developed, and that these have reacted in accordance with physical principles until man as we know him appeared. Having started with a purposeless and feelingless universe, we are confronted with a thinking and feeling entity; we have tried either to deny the feelings and the thoughts or to derive them from the inert, non-sentient attributes described by physics. Although it is entirely possible that someone some time will discover a way in which this legerdemain can be accomplished, the relation of mind, feeling, and purpose to the world of physics is almost as obscure as it was in the sixth century B.C. As the intellectual climate changes, man's place in nature changes, and it will become fixed only when intellectual climates cease to change; it seems to be nothing but arrogance to insist that man's place has been discovered with finality. Skepticism of the type expressed by Robert Boyle is the only possible antidote to any of the declarations which would fit man easily into a pigeonhole in the cosmos. Indeed, at the present moment psychologists are still living chiefly in the intellectual climate supplied by nineteenth-century physics. But nineteenth-century physics makes the ultimate physical structure of the world a vast enigma; hence less and less meaning attaches to the statement that man's sentient existence should be attributed to the largely unknowable properties of a largely unknowable material universe. We know neither man, nor the cosmos, nor his relation to the cosmos. Empirical procedure is necessary, an empiricism willing to learn not only regarding the methods of inquiry that will be most fruitful, but regarding the postulates that do least violence to firsthand experience and provide clarity without the arrogance of offering any ultimate classification of man.

Proceeding in this empirical spirit, we see that one of the salient facts of evolution as observable is the *impulsive* nature of the life process, the continuous *effort* at satisfaction and fulfillment of which Bergson never tired writing. The tension or drive of the living individual seems to be one of the first realities; indeed the personality is apparently definable as a system of tensions or impulses, or acts of will. Not until the world of mechanics and of biochemistry is really integrated meaningfully with this world of impulse can the first clear statement about the physical basis of personality be made. In the face of the exquisite order and precision of modern science there is little use in saying that one thing is "explained by" another unless there is an intelligible relation between them. The experience of red is correlated with a region of the spectrum, and appears in conjunction with a specific wave length; but the relation of the two data is not known. Personality tensions are in the same way correlated with, and appear in the context of, physical tensions; but the relations between the two systems are not known. It is perfectly proper to regard man as a biochemical system; in fact, this is one of the dimensions in which he can be observed. He can, however, be empirically observed in terms of many other dimensions; only when these have been grappled with (not merely philosophically but in terms of research) can his cosmic time-space coordinates be defined.

What we do know is that personality tensions are expressive of the instability, the changefulness of biological organization. To follow such a concept to its logical implications would be to regard personality not as a state or form of organization but as a direction of development. Such an approach would lead, by way of the studies of Henry Head and Kurt Goldstein, to a series of questions about the direction of the developmental process, and would prompt a search for factors in the individual life history analogous to the principle of orthogenesis in the derivation of a species (page 35). Personality would thus become not a recognizable cross section but a multi-dimensional trend phase of a complex developmental process. The data for such a psychology of personality are not available and a programmatic discussion of their future role would be presumptuous. It is, however, likely that the concepts in the present volume and other similar material will be regarded, two or three generations hence, as minor fragmentary contributions to an essentially dynamic, temporally oriented view of personality. This approach to personality would cautiously and modestly make the most of the similarities between cosmic evolution and human evolution, with special reference to principles of differentiation and integration; it would take note of the specialized character of human development and the respects in which ontogenetic growth differs from other characteristic types of species development and inorganic development.

While it is natural and proper to give a phenomenon context by stating its relation to a whole, it is equally proper to suggest the nature of a whole by reference to a part, just as a paleontologist deduces the presence of Megatherium from a jawbone. In the same way, the fact that such a thing exists is relevant in trying to decide what the universe may be. Moreover, the *response* of a part to the whole may be important; the response of man to his cosmos is a clue to him and to cosmos alike. In a future psychology of personality there will surely be a place for directly grappling with the question of man's response to the cosmos, his sense of unity with it, the nature of his esthetic demands upon it, and his feelings of loneliness or of consummation in his contemplation of it. There may be a touch of neurotic phobia in the persistence with which the modern study of man has evaded the question of his need in some way to come to terms with the cosmos as a whole. Whenever people have stopped the dizzying round of earning a living or the fascinating task of taking one another to pieces physically or metaphorically—whether they be ancient Hindus or neo-Platonists, or the Whitmans and Sandburgs of an industrial age—they have felt incomplete as human beings except as they have endeavored to understand the filial relations of man to the cosmos which has begotten him, and have tended, in proportion to their degree of seriousness, to recognize the relativity of selfhood and the fundamental unity of that ocean of which the individual personalities are droplets. It would of course be inexcusable dogmatism to insist that this or that is the psychological reason for such experiences, whether they derive from Oedipus complexes, from fear of the "too-bigness" of life, or from a primitive intellectual need for integration of experience. No one knows how adequate these guesses may be or what other factors may be involved. But our study of man must include the study of his response to the cosmos of which he is a reflection.

If, moreover, we are serious about understanding all we can of personality, its integration and disintegration, we must understand the meaning of depersonalization, those experiences in which individual self-awareness is abrogated and the individual melts into an awareness which is no longer anchored upon selfhood. Such experiences are described by Hinduism in terms of the ultimate unification of the individual with the atman, the super-individual cosmic entity which transcends both selfhood and materiality. Western experience too, a few centuries after the hardy period of the swashbuckling Greek warriors of the Aegean and the ruthless colonizers of Rome, found, constantly recurring, an experience of self utterly alien to the principal cultural requirements, a self whose content was the unity of all things. Men of the West, like men of the East, discovered, not by speculation but by experience, a level of awareness at which selfhood disappears.

There is much to suggest, for example, in the depersonalized states described by psychoanalysts and in the "alpha and omega" states of Morton Prince, that the self is attenuated to the point where a blurred impression of body contour is almost all that remains; and we may well conclude by extrapolation that the complete obliteration of such images, and concomitantly the obliteration of those kinesthetic factors emphasized by Rado (page 482), sometimes occurs. Consciousness would then become practically the sensory matrix, the mind stuff, about which James wrote in the essay "Does Consciousness Exist?"

Some men desire such experiences; others dread them. Our problem here is not their desirability, but the light they throw on the relativity of our present-day psychology of personality. It has become probable from research with drugs and with hypnosis that the self is no immutable entity. Not only in Chapter 20, but throughout the present book, the material on personality has been ordered largely in terms of the conception of self, because this is the cardinal frame of reference for personality research in the cultural area in which the experimental method has been used, and clinical method has fully supported this emphasis. For the same reason the data of the physical sciences gathered within the Newtonian time-space frame support that frame. We realize now that Euclidean geometry and Newtonian mechanics are not the universal realities from which electromagnetic phenomena are odd deviations, but that electromagnetic and other field formulations are the general and the Euclidean and the Newtonian merely special cases. In the same way, personality ordered largely with reference to self-awareness has until recently appeared to be the fundamental reality; but it must be seen against the background of a wide variety of cross-cultural conditions, and of developmental, dissociational, and degenerative states in our own culture. Some other mode of personality configuration, in which self-awareness is less emphasized or even lacking, may prove to be the general (or the fundamental). It would of course not be permissible to stress primarily the experience of a segment of the human family living in the Far East, or the number of queer and deviant people among ourselves who have not internalized the western European norm; for these experiences so different from our own *may* be essentially pathological. But when personality without emphasis upon self-awareness has been adequately described in clinical and experimental terms, it may prove to offer a phylogenetic and ontogenetic base through which the specialized psychology of our own acute self-awareness may be understood.

Most curiously, another vast area of human experience, the active, strenuous *participation in group endeavor*, has many of the same results. One literally "loses" oneself in the group—not just in the crowd, but in the disciplined, highly integrated, military, or industrial, or religious, or artistic, or scientific unit. And the enormous importance of "morale" in such group endeavor lies partly in the way in which the preoccupation with petty momentary concerns (and of intrapsychic conflicts) is removed.

Now this relativity of the concept of selfhood suggests that both consciousness and behavior may well take on very different forms of organization if the self can be filtered out. The norms or laws of individual existence relating to a non-self-oriented type of reality may at present be largely masked or obscured by the omnipresent role of figure which the self plays in our figure-ground situation. It is entirely possible, as certain current experimental research suggests, that new dynamic principles of organization, new functional laws, new principles of personal evolution, new forms of interaction between individuals, new types of contact with the cosmos, are released, and new laws formulated, new applications made available, when once the fixation upon the self, with all its masking and screening effects, is removed. It is exactly this, the setting free of new principles, new sources of energy, that the Vedantists and—at the other pole—various socialist writers suggest. It is of course possible that the result of a personality evolution utilizing such principles would be to weaken the personal meanings which are familiar to us. It is, however, just as likely, if not indeed more likely, that the true role of selfhood would be better understood and therefore more effectively used if this deeper non-self context were appreciated. It is quite likely that (as in a dialectical movement) selfhood will be better understood when reference is made to the primordial non-self matrix from which it arises, and that the synthesis, the capacity of human nature to function at self and non-self levels at the same time, or to alternate when it so desires, may prove to be an enrichment of personality far greater than that which the cult of self-contained, self-defined individuality can grant.

The belief in immutable selfhood has, like other beliefs, an intelligible origin; life in our culture requires this emphasis. Another fetish—the one involved in defining individuals by isolating them—is equally imperious. This form of logic, though attacked by Gestaltists and notably by those concerned with semantics, is omnipresent in psychology. We have had to look upon the individual organism as an isolated datum; even in our efforts in relation to field theory we have not found it really feasible, in view of our own thought forms, to define the non-individualistic or perhaps super-individualistic aspects of human experience and conduct. We are so terrified lest we be found using the language of the "group fallacy" that we have forgotten to consider the probability of the individual's being a node, and not a very rigidly defined one, in a vast time-space matrix. Though Lewin's field theory speaks properly of the melting of individual and environment, it fails to bring out with full force the melting of individuals into one another. The doctrine is frightening, for the coercions which men have imposed upon one another in fulfilling evolutionary demands for the good things sought by the individual have led to frantic defensive efforts against the loss of individuality almost like those of the drowning man or the claustrophobic. Hence, when the Marxist on the one hand, the mystic on the other, speak of the merging of individuality in a social goal, we turn at best a cynical and doubting ear. Psychology has studied intensively the aspects of selfhood which are in the area of individual threat against individual and corresponding defense and counter-threat; but it has explored by systematic methods only a few aspects of the deeper interindividual unity that is a phase of the man-cosmos unity mentioned earlier.

But to plead for closer study of less sharply defined individuality would be utterly fatuous. Individuality is there because it is wanted, demanded. The need for it is an integral aspect of the broader need for relative independence, the need for resistance to invasion by the environment. Resistance to physically threatening and disruptive agencies is imperative, but no more so than resistance to those socially overwhelming experiences which might shatter the rigidities of the personal boundaries. In conformity with the general theory of canalization, we would expect all societies, in proportion to their forced induction of this need for individuality, to demand that the rigidities and encapsulations, once achieved, be maintained. For every action, however, there is an equal and opposite reaction; and just as tension systems that become charged with energy in one region are balanced by other regions of tension elsewhere, and just as the military heroics of the Iatmul (page 789) lead to relaxation and the escape from heroics, so a life of frenzied individualism leads to the need for a non-individualized (or super-individual) form of experience.

Another line of thought to which the moralists have given more attention than have the psychologists, namely, the study of the contradiction between the ethics of self-realization and the ethics of unselfishness, supports this approach. Evolutionary principles on the one hand, and the ethical tradition derived from the Hebrew-Greek-Roman world on the other, have made the cultivation of rich and full individuality a primary desideratum. Yet the parallel appreciation of the needs and feelings of others, so central in practically all ethical theory, both western and eastern, characteristically takes the form of belittling the needs of the self. This conflict in ethics goes to the very heart of the problem of defining man. Dissatisfied with the dualism and social escapism which have characterized the resolution of the problem by eastern thought, western moralists have developed an ethics of self-realization that posits a fundamental cleavage between man and his fellows, and at the same time have described an ethical norm in terms of selflessness, immolation of the self in the group. Such contradictions are apparently the consequences of a failure to define man's locus in time and space. If man is adequately defined as an individual organism in competition for the limited goods available, there can be no evasion of the stark reality of competitive selfhood. If, however, following the biological observations of Allee, we stress social participation as being as real and fundamental as the conflict of selves, we may well reach a definition of individuality in terms of social context, the individual being a node or point of relative distinctness in a super-individual context. Such a way of phrasing the problem is, as we saw, alien to our present cultural prejudices; the sharpness of the definition of the individual is regarded as the first step in the sharpness of a logical definition of the problem. This is not a way of saying that the problem of the individual and society can be solved by a renewed verbal assault, for only a better method of observation can indicate where the present frame of reference is adequate and where it falls short. Verbal analysis can, however, do one thing that is urgent in the present connection. It can show that all books such as the present, the contents of which beg the question by presupposing the separateness of individuals and do little toward defining the matrix in which they inhere, are impertinences that are of value chiefly in defining the means by which they are to be superseded.

But this fundamental ethical paradox cannot intelligently be banished by shoulder-shrugging; it points to a psychological muddle of huge proportions. For psychology cannot very well admit, without in some way adjusting the paradox, that human nature is really capable of effective functioning only under conditions of individualistic fulfillment, and at the same time claim that it is the nature of man so to lose himself in others as to care little or nothing about the enhancement of the self. In concrete terms, the more sensitive persons in our own society need to spend time, money, and energy on making themselves educated, thoughtful, richly developed personalities; but when they do this, they take time, money, and energy away from war sufferers and cancer victims, present and future. Christianity extols both ideals but leaves us in confusion. It may also be urged that Marxism is saturated by the same difficulty, since the motives Marxists consider fundamental in revolution and in the leadership of the new society are conceived to be self-fulfilling motives, and Lenin heavily stressed the competitive nature of socialist living; on the other hand, a person pins his hopes on the individual identified with the group and regards the loss of selfhood in the group as an important aspect of the fulfillment of a "scientific socialism." The dilemma appears in outspoken form in Nietzsche, whose superman loves and needs his fellows yet expresses contempt for the selflessness ingrained by Christianity and many other ethical systems.

Perhaps the ethical paradox is capable of resolution only when a deeper exploration is made. For the difficulty really seems to be not with our research or our definitions as to personality, but with plain fogginess as to the nature of man. Man is today understood more or less as a time-and-space-oriented animal, and to a lesser degree as a phase in a process of cultural evolution. Only these two aspects of human nature have been studied with anything that could be called scientific method. It is an open secret that the two methods, the evolutionary and the cultural, are often in conflict, perhaps because neither one is in contact with a large segment of what human nature really is. The abyss of our ignorance cannot be spanned by philosophies of human nature, however profound. The scientific method has begun to take shape and it will be heard. Although not ready today, eventually it will be ready to integrate with older insights of an intuitive or poetic sort, which, though pointing the way, will reach effectively into the unknown only when supported by the methods of a future science. In the meantime it would be sheer impertinence to suggest what this larger integration will find.

The future course of personality research will plainly be governed not so much by the continuation of the methods borrowed from psychoanalysis, Gestalt psychology, physiology, and cultural anthropology, to which emphasis has been given in this book, as by altogether new modes of attack. There is no more reason to believe that the methods of the mid-twentieth century are final, and that their results will stand secure, than to believe that Galileo's methods and results were final. These present approaches will not, however, be outmoded except by their own descendants, the better approaches of which they are the progenitors. Not only the sick, but the healthy, contain within themselves the seeds of their own collapse. The present promising leads will guide us for a few more decades into better physical time-space definitions of man and into more adequate evolutionary and cultural definitions of man. But just as evolutionism and field theory make eighteenth-century rationalism seem rather childlike, so the systematizations achieved in a later century will show the puerile insufficiency of all that present-day science can offer.

Though the skeptical psychologist may dream of the promised land, he cannot enter into it. It will be discovered and entered only by the research investigators of a future period, and only because stubborn facts have shown the insufficiency of present ways of thinking. It was not because the French psychiatry of 1880 was theoretically inadequate that psychoanalysis arose to supersede it; it was because there were facts with which it could not cope. It was not because personality study as conceived by Francis Galton was a poor thing, unworthy of repute, that the personality researches of the cultural anthropologists have superseded it; it was because Galton's simple biological evolutionism came face to face with facts which his psychology was incapable of explaining. The psychology of personality as it exists today will be crushed and pulverized and a new creation made from the debris, not because of the wisdom inherent in criticisms of it but simply because in grappling with the problems of man it will be weighed in the balance and found wanting. Even the increasingly fascinating materials which the present methods are found to produce will leave men dissatisfied. The task of the psychology of personality today is to apply ruthlessly, and to the limit, every promising suggestion of today, but always with the spice of a healthy skepticism which will know how infinite are nature the macrocosm, and man the micro-cosm, how infinitesimal our knowledge of it and of him.

In accordance with the emergence of these baffling and at present rather formless problems, two types of research dominate the scene and will continue to do so for a long time. The first type is that which attempts to systematize and to verify, experimentally or clinically, the major hypotheses which constitute present-day psychology. We may look forward to decades of fruitful research on the experimental testing of psychoanalytic and cross-cultural hypotheses and the improvement of the means of testing personality. The other type of research embodies the effort to grope into the darkness of the fringe surrounding our present-day region of clarity. It involves all the characteristic errors and absurdities of such groping. It makes far more incorrect than correct guesses. It produces much howling nonsense, and much stilted and pretentious reiteration of old platitudes in new words. But here and there it contains a germ of fresh and leavening insight into the larger context which not only our psychology of today but our society as a whole has been afraid to seek. Roger Bacon did not have the context to know what man was; Copernicus put some of his misconceptions to rest. The great enlightenment of the eighteenth century did not have quite the ultimate wisdom it thought it had acquired; Darwinism was necessary. The French rationalistic psychiatry of 1880 did not see quite as far into the darkness as it thought it did; psychoanalysis appeared. Despite all these lessons, we write and speak today as if at last the full context and stature of man were known. But like our predecessors, we shall rectify mistakes not primarily by the minor readjustment of the lines of the argument but by recognition of the fundamental limitations of the whole present system of conceptions. It is preparation for this destruction and rebirth of knowledge to which serious research should be directed.

References

THE method of documentation aims to keep the text as free as possible from footnotes, and to avoid reference numbers in the text. In most cases the name of the investigator in the text permits immediate use of the Bibliography. If, however, the Bibliography lists several pieces of research by one investigator (or if, as happens here and there, research findings are noted in passing without mention of the investigator's name in the text), the following procedure is used:

Reference is given by page, paragraph, and line. The number following each proper name is the number of the item in the Bibliography. The reference is usually "anchored" on the name of the investigator mentioned in the text. When no name is cited, a salient part of the sentence is used as anchor. Paragraph I indicates the opening lines on a page, even when these are the continuation of a paragraph beginning on a preceding page. Weismann, in the third reference, is not given a reference by line because this reference is to the same line as the reference to Morgan.

14	1	7	Lewin, K. (393, p. 25)
15	3	7	Morgan, T. H. (476)
			Weismann, A. (705)
16	3	4	Helmholtz, H. L. F. von (259)
21	3	2	Weiss, P. (706)
22	2	8	Perry, R. B. (521)
			James, H. (302)
25	1	5	James, W. (308)
	2	18	James, W. (309)
		21	James, W. (304)
			James, W. (307)
		21	James, W. (306)
32	1	11	Cannon, W. B. (105)
	2	2	Guthrie, E. R. (236)
		3	Raup, R. B. (552)
	3	3	Wilson, E. B. (727)
			Child, C. M. (118)
33	2	1	Broad, C. D. (78, p. 56)
		2	Goldstein, K. (224)
35	3	3	Scott, W. B., (603, p. 605)
38	1	1	Spemann, H. (637)
			Weiss, P. (706)
	2	10	Child, C. M. (119)

39	2	11	Henderson, L. J. (261)
40	2	14	Miles, W. R. (457)
41	1	11	Morgan, T. H. (475)
42	4	1	Hecht, S. (257)
43	3	3	Allport, G. W. (11)
46	2	16	Tryon, R. C. (689)
		17	Hall, C. S. (239)
			Merton & Hall (453)
47	3	2	Day, C. (137)
50	1	5	Burks, B. S. (91)
51	1	11	Carmichael, L. (109)
53	2	16–23	Weiss, P. (706)
54	1	5	Weiss, P. (706)
	3	4	Shapiro, H. L., (614)
	4	8	Klineberg, O. (349)
57	3	4	Tryon, R. C. (689)
		16	Washburn, R. W. (700)
		21	Shirley, N. (628)
58	1	8	Jost & Sontag (329)
	3	4	Goldstein, K. (224)
59	1	9	Kretschmer, E. (360)
		10	Sheldon, W. H. (619)
			Sheldon, W. H. (618)

REFERENCES

102	1	1	Lashley, K. S. (368, 369)
	2	2	Sherrington, C. S. (624)
103	2	11	Freud, S. (201)
		12	Woodworth, R. S. (737, p. 104)
104	2	12	Anderson, E. E. (19)
			Seward, J. P. (612)
106	2	7	Levy, D. M. (387)
107	1	10	Bourdillon, F. (69a)
		12	Wilder, T. N. (723)
108	1	4	Guthrie, E. (236)
110	1	18	Seitz, C. P. (608)
111	2	11	Jacobson, E. (300, pp. 302 ff.)
	3	5	Gesell, A. (213, p. 197)
112	1	2	Irwin, O. C. (296)
		3	Shirley, M. (628)
	2	1	Schilder, P. (596, pp. 17, 81, 119)
		2	Rado, S. (Unpublished)
113	2	7	Jensen, K. (315)
		8	Lerner & Murphy (379)
		23	Révész, G. (559)
	3	5	Katz, D. (338)
			Bayer, E. (42)
114	1	14	Féré, C. (177)
115	2	2	Diamond, S. (150)
		17	Freud, S. (199, p. 183)
116	3	4	Cannon, W. B. (104)
	4	2	Arnold, M. B. (25)
119	3	entire	Rapaport, D. (Communication to the writer)
	4	3	Landis & Hunt (365)
		8	Goodenough, F. L. (227)
120	1	2	Goodenough, F. L. (226)
	3	8	Goldstein, K. (224)
121	ftn.	1	James, W. (308, II, p. 403)
123	1	6	Stone, C. P. (655)
134	2	5	DuBois, P. H. (158)
		7	Rounds, G. H. (577)
135	1	2	Sherrington, C. S. (624, pp. 106 ff.)
138	ftn.	1	Weiss, P. (706)
139	2	2	Allport, G. W. (11, p. 287)
141	1	26	Tolman, E. C. (682)
143	3	2	Young, P. T. (745)
144	2	10	Allport, G. W. (11, pp. 191 ff.)
145	1	1	Dollard, J , et al. (154)
	2	1	Barker, Dembo & Lewin (83)
148	3	6	Kretschmer, E. (360)
149	1	18	Klineberg, Asch & Block (351)
	2	1	Sheldon, W. H. (619)
			Sheldon, W. H. (618)
151	ftn.	5	Dumas, G. (160, III, p. 136)
153	2	2	Hoskins, R. G. (283, p. 73)
	3	1	Hoskins, R. G. (283, p. 107)
	4	8	Allen, E., et al. (9, p. 877)
154	2	4	Hoskins, R. G. (283, p. 45)
	3	4	Schneider, E. C. (597)
		15	Wolff & Mittelmann (735)
155	1	1	Woodworth, R. S. (738, p. 177)
	2	5	Rich, G. J. (564)
		8	Rich, G. J. (563)
	3	4	Wenger, M. A. (713)
157	1	3	Lynn & Lynn (414)
162	2	6	Janet, P. (311, p. 683)
	4	1	Lukomnik, M. (412)
163	2	3	Maslow, A. H. (434)
	3	5	Beebe-Center, J. G. (48, pp. 123, 149, 229)
164	1	2	Evvard, J. M. (176)
		4	Young, P. T. (744, 745)
	5	2	Sherrington, C. S. (624, pp. 329 ff.)
166	2	3	Whitman, C. (722)
167	2	1	Holt, E. B. (274)
		13	Freud, S. (199, p. 145)
168	1	15	Krugman, H. E. (363)
169	1	13	Mead, M. (Personal communication)
170	1	9	Scheerer, Rothman & Goldstein (595)
171	ftn.	25	Rapaport, D. (Personal communication)
173	2	12	Craig, W. (131)
175	4	1	Krueger & Reckless (362, p. 27)
176	3	9	Woodworth, R. S. (737, p. 104)
178	2	5	Allport, G. W. (11, p. 194)
	3	6	Zeigarnik, B. (748)
179	1	5	Lewis & Franklin (401)
			Rice, Mowrer & Allport, (562)
	2	4	Allport, G. W. (11, pp. 204 ff.)
182	1	16	Murray & Morgan (495)
185	2	4	Freud, S. (193)

263 2 9 Sanford, R. N. (585, 586)
   3 14 Luria, A. R. (413, p. 245)
264 2 9 Allen, C. N. (8)
265 2 5 Wolfe, J. B. (733)
   3 1 Lorimer, F. (410)
266 2 5 Piaget, J. (525)
      McCarthy, D. (439)
    11 Piaget, J. (525)
    14 Werner, H. (714, p. 260)
267 1 23 Chrisman, O. (120)
    28 Werner, H. (714, p. 262)
268 3 4 Veblen, T. (691)
   8 Goldstein, K. (223)
269 2 6 Babcock, H. (32)
270 2 10 Tolstoy, L. N. (684)
271 4 7 Razran, G. H. S. (554, p. 13)
272 2 9 Sanford, R. N. (585, 586)
276 3 13 Hamilton, G. V. (242, 243)
277 1 10 Stone, L. J. (Personal communication)
   2 10 Klopfer & Kelley (352)
281 1 9 Dudycha & Dudycha (159)
282 1 6 Binger, C. A. L., et al. (61)
   2 9 Freud, S. (193)
283 1 1 Marx, K. (425)
   3 6 Spranger, E. (640)
284 2 9 Harris, D. (248)
286 2 11 Murphy, Murphy & Newcomb, (489, p. 786)
    20 Thurstone, L. L. (677)
      Cattell, R. B. (112)
290 2 8 Hudgins, C. V. (286)
293 1 3 Levy & Tulchin (389)
      Reynolds, M. M. (560)
294 1 6 Galton, F. (206, pp. 88 ff.)
   3 7 Cannon, W. B. (105)
295 2 7 Judd, C. H. (330)
297 1 1 Cannon, W. B. (104, p. 13)
   4 Prince, S. H. (543)
   3 13 Muenzinger, K. F. (480)
      Tolman, E. C. (683)
299 1 4 Liddell, H. S. (403)
302 2 1 Guthrie & Horton (237)
303 3 3 Freud, S. (192)
   7 Troland, L. T. (688, p. 418)
305 2 10 Jacobson, E. (300, pp. 309 ff.)
    15 Jacobson, E. (300, pp. 362 ff.)
   3 7 Krout, M. H. (361)
306 1 4 Holt, E. B. (274)
   2 7 Efrón, D. (164)

307 1 3 Hunt, J. McV. (288)
   2 2 Wolf, A. (732)
308 3 1 Lewin, K. (395)
   8 Goldworth, S. (Unpublished)
309 3 3 Pavlov, I. P. (518, pp. 342 ff.)
310 3 2 Maier, N. R. F. (419)
312 2 5 Luria, A. R. (413)
   3 5 Fletcher, J. M. (178)
313 1 1 Travis, L. E. (686)
   5 Starr, H. E. (642)
315 1 1 Chappell, M. N. (113)
   2 3 Mittelmann & Wolff (465, 466)
   3 1 Binger, C. A. L., et al. (61)
316 1 1 Alexander, F. (6)
   2 4 Rosenzweig, S. (573)
    13 Pratt, Nelson & Sun (537)
317 3 1 Mowrer, O. H. (477)
318 1 10 Lazarsfeld & Zeisl (372)
320 1 7 Koffka, K. (358, pp. 27 ff.)
321 2 2 Wolff & Curran (734)
323 2 11 Kempf, E. J. (341)
325 3 2 Girden & Culler (218)
326 2 8 Holt, E. B. (274)
327 3 7 Lewin, K. (396, p. 124)
    11 Enke, W. (168)
332 2 14 Frank, L. K. (183)
    16 Piaget, J. (522, pp. 34, 236)
333 3 8 Werner, H. (714)
334 1 15 Canestrini, S. (103)
    17 Bühler & Hetzer (89)
335 1 10 Mead, M. (Personal communication)
336 1 16 Werner, H. (714, pp. 69 ff.)
   3 3 Piaget, J. (522, p. 236)
337 1 3 Koffka, K. (358, pp. 72 ff.)
   2 2 Piaget, J. (523)
   3 5 Piaget, J. (523)
    18 Freud, S. (202)
338 1 16 Piaget, J. (524)
340 1 9 Piaget, J. (522, pp. 123 ff.)
   2 6 Piaget, J. (523)
    12 Writer's own observation
341 3 4 Holmes, F. B. (272)
342 2 5 Piaget, J. (523)
   7 Piaget, J. (522)
344 2 14 Stern, W. (650, p. 112)
   ftn. 4 Ranson, S. W. (549, p. 302)
346 1 1 Bühler, C. (See 489, photo facing p. 566)

REFERENCES

394	1	8	Jaensch, E. R. (301, p. 9)
	2	9	Galton, F. (206, pp. 105 ff.)
	ftn.	7	Jacobson, E. (300)
395	2	14	Leaning, F. E. (373)
396	1	4	Galton, F. (206, pp. 100 ff.)
		6	Kraepelin, E. (359)
	2	6	Woodworth, R. S. (739, p. 66)
	3	15	Pillsbury, W. B. (527, p. 204)
			Howells, T. H. (284)
		16	Werner, H. (714)
397	1	12	Wells, F. L. (709)
399	3	12	Cameron, N. (101)
		13	Durkin, H. E. (162)
401	2	1	Rasmussen, K. (551)
402	1	1	Buck, R. M. (83)
	2	4	Rosanoff, A. J. (571)
404	3	8	Toksvig, S. (681)
406	2	3	Bleuler, E. (63)
		8	Asch, S. E. (29)
407	2	2	Spearman, C. E. (634)
	4	3	Dimnet, E. (152)
408	1	22	Klopfer & Kelley (352, p. 83)
	2	3	Lombroso, C. (408)
409	2	1	Mill, J. S. (459)
	3	9	Max, L. W. (438)
410	1	2	Santayana, G. (587)
411	2	4	Lasswell, H. D. (370, p. 28)
413	1	2	Sells, S. B. (609)
			Morgan, J. J. B. (474)
414	2	8	Holt, E. B. (275)
418	1	2	DeQuincey, T. (143)
	3	14	Piaget, J. (522, p. 88)
			Kimmins, C. W. (342)
		17	Sarason, S. B. (588)
419	2	6	Welch, L. (708)
420	1	3	Vold, J. M. (693)
		5	Klein, D. B. (345)
		7	Watt, H. J. (703)
			Horton, L. H. (281, 282)
	2	1	Freud, S. (195, p. 101)
			Kimmins, C. W. (342)
421	1	4	Freud, S. (197, p. 417)
	2	1	Freud, S. (198)
		13	Woodworth, R. S. (741)
	3	3	Freud, S. (197, p. 418)
422	3	10	Poetzl, O. (533)
424	2	9	Stekel, W. (647)
		10	Horney, K. (278, p. 31)
	3	4	Klein, D. B. (345)
424	3	12	Jung, C. G. (333)
426	4	7	Stevenson, R. L. (652)
428	1	3	Newbold, W. R. (500, p. 375)
429	2	6	Lowes, J. L. (411)
430	3	2	Mitchell, T. W. (462, p. 12)
		11	Starr, H. E. (643)
432	1	1	Bürklen, K. (90, p. 198)
		3	Keller, H. A. (340)
433	1	1	Mitchill, S. L. (463)
			Taylor & Martin (667)
		17	Stevenson, R. L. (653)
	3	1	James, W. (308, I, p. 391)
434	2	1	Prince, M. (539, p. 269)
	3	10	Mitchell, T. W., (462, p. 30)
435	2	2	Stratton, G. M. (658, p. 45)
436	1	19	Myers, F. W. H. (496)
	2	11	Prince, W. F. (544)
437	2	3	Mühl, A. (481)
	3	1	Binet, A. (60)
		9	Prince, M. (542, pp. 33, 147)
		12	Burnett, C. T. (94)
		18	Messerschmidt, R. (454)
438	1	4	Pattie, F. A. (516)
439	1	4	Janet, P. (312, pp. 73 ff.)
	2	2	Janet, P. (312, pp. 22 ff.)
		4	Janet, P. (312, p. 29)
	3	11	Janet, P. (658, pp. 139 ff.)
440	1	1	Janet, P. (312, p. 44)
		7	Binet, A. (58)
	2	3	Franz, S. I. (184)
441	2	1	Prince, M. (540)
442	2	14	Mühl, A. (481)
444	1	11	Murphy & Ladd (492)
	2	7	Anon. (23)
445	2	2	Prince, W. F. (545)
448	1	9	Hall, G. S. (240)
	2	8	Worcester, E. (742, pp. 82 ff.)
449	3	2	Rowland, L. W. (578)
			Wells, W. R. (711)
			Brenman, M. (72)
			Erickson & Erickson (170)
			Harriman, P. L. (247)
		8	Erickson, M. H. (169)
450	4	2	Goldstein, K. (224)
456	1	4	Jeffries, R. (314)
457	1	7	Bühler, C. (84)
		8	Cox, C. M. (130, p. 115)
459	2	13	Ellis, H. (167, p. 102)

REFERENCES

526 1 11   Leuba, C. J. (380)
   2 10   Leuba, C. J. (381)
     12   Symonds & Chase (665)
527 1 4   Frank, L. K. (182)
   2 13   James, W. (305)
528 1 3   Moreno, J. L. (470, 471)
     11   Moede, W. (467)
529 3 8   James, W. (308, I, p. 291)
531 2 9   Jones, E. (320)
532 2 1   Lecky, P. (375)
   3 3   Freud, S. (195, pp. 288 ff.)
534 1 8   L. B. Murphy's observation
     9   Clark & Clark (124)
   2 11   Newcomb, T. N. (502)
536 1 11   Murphy & Likert (487, pp. 203 ff.)
ftn. 2 2   Mowrer, O. H. (478)
538 2 9   Mead, M. (Personal communication)
539 2 6   Hoppe, F. (276)
   3 1   Gould, R. (230)
540 2 2   Freud, S. (194)
542 2 2   Freud, A. (191)
ftn. 4   Freud, S. (193)
543 1 11   Freud, A. (191, pp. 5 ff.)
   2 23   Piaget, J. (526)
545 ftn. 1   Stearns, A. W. (644)
546 2 5   Freud, A. (191, pp. 46 ff.)
   3 3   Lang, J. B. (367)
     8   Sears, R. R. (604, 606)
547 1 2   Frenkel-Brunswik, E. (190)
   2 1   Jones, E. (320)
   3 1   Freud, S. (195, pp. 294 ff.)
548 2 23   McDougall, W. (441, pp. 281 ff.)
   3 1   Freud, A. (191, pp. 45 ff.)
549 2 3   Kempf, E. J. (341)
550 1 4   Cowper, W. (129)
551 2 13   Freud, A. (191, pp. 46 ff.)
552 2 1   Horney, K. (278, pp. 88 ff.)
      Maslow, A. H. (429, 430, 433)
553 2 3   Howells, T. H. (285)
554 2 18   Thurstone & Thurstone (678)
      Allport, G. W. (12)
      Maslow, A. H. (428, 432)
555 2 4   Bühler, C. (85, pp. 73 ff.)
557 3 5   Veblen, T. (691)
558 1 3   Boas, F. (66)
   2 2   Schreier, F. (600)

559 2 1   Linton, R. (404)
560 2 16   Nietzsche, F. (506, 507)
562 3 16   Rosenzweig & Sarason (575)
563 1 5   Bacon, F. (33)
564 1 8   Adler, A. (4)
   2 11   Wittels, F. (731)
566 4 8   Rivers, W. H. R. (567)
567 2 8   Veblen, T. (691)
      Hocking, W. E. (269)
     14   Kardiner, A. (337, pp. 47 ff.)
568 2 2   Frank, L. K. (182)
     10   Horney, K. (277)
572 2 1   Verry, E. E. (692)
573 2 15   Pressey, Janney & Kuhlen (538)
574 2 5   Perrin, F. A. C. (520)
   3 2   Murchison, C. (486, pp. 20, 21)
575 2 7   Murphy, L. B. (491, pp. 242 ff.)
   3 1   Maslow, A. H. (430)
      Maslow, A. H. (428)
576 1 6   Veblen, T. (691)
578 2 5   Ruggles & Allport (580)
    28   Stone, L. J. (Personal communication)
580 3 10   Jack, L. M. (299)
    14   Jones, H. E. (322)
581 1 4   Adler, A. (3, p. 88)
    11   Maier, N. R. F. (418)
585 2 3   Brill, A. A. (77)
    5   Adler, A. (2, p. 321)
      Wexberg, E. (716, p. 175)
      Weill, B. C. (704)
593 2 3   Mead, M. (450)
      Kardiner, A. (337)
594 1 7   Jung, C. G. (335)
    9   Jung, C. G. (332)
    11   Jung, C. G. (334)
   2 2   Jung, C. G. (331)
596 2 10   Speer, M. C. (636)
597 2 6   Chassell, C. F. (114)
    8   Hartshorne, May & Maller (254)
    10   Terman, L. M. (669)
    13   Berne, E. V. C. (54)
598 1 6   Murphy, L. B. (491, pp. 242-256)
    9   Munroe & Levy (484)

REFERENCES

676 ftn. 1   Gordon, K. (229)
678 3 6   Munroe, R. L. (482)
681 ftn. 8   Harrow-Erickson, M. R. (249)
Harrow-Erickson & Steiner (250)
682 2 3   Klopfer & Kelley (352)
   6   Piotrowski, Z. (529, 530)
   7   Hertzman, Orlansky & Seitz (264)
   11   DuBois, C. (157)
683 2 3   Beck, S. J. (47, p. 336)
   4   Schachtel, A. H. (591)
   6   Piotrowski, Z. (530)
   14   Klopfer & Kelley (352, part 4)
   15   Hertzman & Margulies (263)
684 1 1   Goodenough, F. L. (228)
685 2 1   Elkisch, P. (166)
686 2 3   Waehner, T. S. (695)
689 2 2   Klages, L. (344)
   3 1   Saudek, R. (589, 590)
Pulver, M. (548)
690 2 10   Lewinson & Zubin (399)
691 2 3   Saudek, R. (590)
693 1 12   Munroe, Lewinson & Waehner, (485)
   2 8   Lewinson & Zubin (399)
694 2 3   The conference mentioned was called by Bela Mittelmann on behalf of a committee of the Association for Research in Psychomatic Problems
695 7 1   Munroe, Lewinson & Waehner (485)
702 1 3   Stern, W. (650)
   2 1   Lerner & Murphy (379)
   11   Stern, W. (649)
   14   Despert, J. L. (146)
   17   Lerner & Murphy (379)
704 1 3   Erikson, E. H. (174)
   4 1   Murphy, L. B. (490)
711 2 22   Levy, D. M. (388)
712 2 7   Hurlock & Burstein (292)
715 4 3   Weiss, P. (706, pp. 18 ff.)
   5   Bayley, N. (44)
716 1 5   Driscoll, G. P. (156)
Jones, H. E. (323)
   18   Murray, H. A. (494)

716 1 18   Wolff, W. (736)
717 1 1   Todd, T. W. (680)
Bayley, N. (44)
   4   Rosanoff, Handy & Plesset (572)
   2 1   Jersild, A. T. (317)
   7   Pintner, R. (528, p. 89)
Bayley, N. (43)
   8   Driscoll, G. P. (156)
   3 10   Thorndike, E. L. (675, p.101)
   4 1   Shirley, M. (628)
718 1 11   McKinnon, K. M. (445)
   2 3   Gesell & Thompson (215)
   5   Burks, B. S. (92)
720 1 3   Strong, E. K., Jr. (660)
   3 4   Glueck & Glueck (220)
721 2 5   Cattell, R. B. (112, pp. 62 ff.)
   3 1   Hartshorne & May (253)
Hartshorne, May & Shuttleworth (255)
   10   Horowitz, E. L. (279)
722 1 9   Klimpfinger, S. (347)
Koffka, K. (358)
Beryl, T. (55)
Brunswik, E. (80)
   10   Piaget, J. (522)
   13   Beck, S. J. (47, II)
   2 12   Dearborn & Rothney (138)
   13   Wells & Woods (710)
723 1 1   Cabot, P. S. de Q. (100)
   5   Jones, H. E. (321)
   6   Macfarlane, J. W. (417)
   2 6   Leonard, W. I. (376)
   10   Chassell, J. O. (115)
725 1 14   Frank, L. K. (181)
726 2 5   Greene, E. B. (232, 233)
728 3 5   Shirley, M. (Unpublished)
732 1 1   Holmes, S. J. (273)
   2 5   Bühler, C. (84)
738 1 10   Goldstein, K. (223)
739 2 21   Klüver, H. (354)
740 3 12   Klineberg, Asch & Lewis (351)
741 1 8   Sheldon, W. H. (618)
742 1 1   Aveling & Hargreaves (30)
744 2 2   Abraham, K. (1)
   2   Erikson, E. H. (171)
747 2 10   Levy, D. M. (386)
748 2 1   Erikson, E. H. (172)

REFERENCES

872	2	5	Klineberg, O. (349)
873	2	1	Klineberg, O. (348)
874	2	2	Efrón, D. (164)
875	1	2	Hartshorne & May (253)
876	2	2	Brenman, M. (73)
877	2	15	Busemann, A. (99)
	3	2	Moreno, J. L. (471)
879	2	19	Moreno, J. L. (470)
882	3	1	Spemann, H. (637)
		9	Lewin, K. (393)
			Angyal, A. (22)
		10	Sullivan, H. S. (661)
885	2	23	Kluckhohn & Mowrer (353)
	3	2	Marks, E. S. (420)
886	2	1	Hanks, L. M. (246)
887	2	1	Wilke, W. H. (724)
	3	2	Rundquist & Sletto (581)
888	2	1	Freeman, G. L. (189)
889	1	6	Schanck, R. L. (594)
892	3	1	Newcomb, T. M. (502)
894	2	3	Bühler, C. (84)
	3	8	Chassell, J. O. (115)
895	2	1	Hamilton, G. V. (241)

895	3	7	Macfarlane, J. W. (417)
	ftn.	1	Terman, L. M. (669)
			Terman & Miles (670)
896	2	3	Glueck & Glueck (220)
		11	Cabot, P. S. de Q. (100)
897	4	1	Levy, D. M. (385)
898	1	21	Piotrowski, Z. (530)
		22	Hertzman & Margulies (263)
910	3	20	Russell, B. (583)
911	1	3	Torbek, V. M. (685)
			Zaluzhny, A. S. (747)
912	3	3	Sherif, M. (622)
914	1	2	Boyle, R. (70)
	2	3	Boring, E. G. (69)
		5	Ebbinghaus, H. (163)
915	2	6	Pavlov, I. P. (518, pp. 76 ff.)
917	2	3	Bergson, H. (52)
918	2	6	Head, H. (256)
			Goldstein, K. (224)
920	2	3	Prince, M. (541)
		9	James, W. (303)
924	1	11	Allee, W. C. (7)
926	2	8	Galton, F. (206)

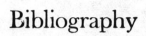

Bibliography

1. Abraham, K., *Selected papers*, ed. by E. Jones, 1927.
2. Adler, A., *The practice and theory of individual psychology*, 1924.
3. Adler, A., *Problems of neurosis*, 1930.
4. Adler, A., *A study of organ inferiority and its psychical compensation*, 1907.
5. Adrian, E. D., in *Factors determining human behavior*, Harvard Tercentenary Publ., 6.
6. Alexander, F., The influence of psychologic factors upon gastro-intestinal disturbances: a symposium, *Psychoanal. Quar.*, 1934, 3, 501–539; also in Tomkins, S. S. (ed.), *Contemporary psychopathology*, 1943, 123 ff.
7. Allee, W. C., *The social life of animals*, 1938.
8. Allen, C. N., Individual differences in delayed reaction of infants: a study of sex differences in early retentiveness, *Arch. Psychol.*, 1931, No. 127.
9. Allen, E., Danforth, C. H., and Doisy, E. A., *Sex and internal secretions: a survey of recent research*, 1939.
10. Allport, F. H., *Social psychology*, 1924.
11. Allport, G. W., *Personality: a psychological interpretation*, 1937.
12. Allport, G. W., A test for ascendance-submission, *J. Abn. & Soc. Psychol.*, 1928, 23, 118–136.
13. Allport, G. W., What is a trait of personality? *J. Abn. & Soc. Psychol.*, 1931, 25, 368–372.
14. Allport, G. W., and Kramer, B. M., Some roots of prejudice, *J. Psychol.*, 1946, 22, 9–39.
15. Allport, G. W., and Vernon, P. E., *Studies in expressive movement*, 1933.
16. Allport, G. W., and Vernon, P. E., *A study of values*, 1931.
17. Alpert, A., The solving of problem situations by pre-school children: an analysis, *Columbia Univ. Contrib. Educ., Teach. Coll. Series*, 1928, No. 323.
18. Alschuler, R. H., and Hattwick, L. W., *Painting and personality: a study of young children*, 2 vols., 1947.
19. Anderson, E. E., The externalization of drive. I. Theoretical considerations, *Psychol. Rev.*, 1941, 48, 204–224.
20. Anderson, J. E., The development of social behavior, *Amer. J. Sociol.*, 1939, 44, 839–857.
20a. Anderson, J. E., Child development and the growth process, *Yearb. Nat. Soc. Stud. Educ.*, 1939, 15-49
21. Anderson, J. E., The dream as a re-conditioning process, *J. Abn. & Soc. Psychol.*, 1927, 22, 21–25.
22. Angyal, A., *Foundations for a science of personality*, 1941.
23. Anon., *I lost my memory! the case as the patient saw it*, 1932.
24. Arnheim, R., Experimentell-psychologische Untersuchungen zum Ausdrucksproblem, *Psychol. Forsch.*, 1928, 11, 1–132.
25. Arnold, M. B., Physiological differentiation of emotional states, *Psychol. Rev.*, 1945, 52, 35–48.
26. Arrington, R. E., Interrelations in the behavior of young children, *Child Developm. Monogr.*, 1932, No. 8.
27. Asch, S. E., Forming impressions of personality, *J. Abn. & Soc. Psychol.*, 1946, 41, 258–290.
28. Asch, S. E., Personality development of Hopi children (see 489, pp. 443 ff.).

29. Asch, S. E., Studies in the principles of judgments and attitudes. II. Determination of judgments by group and by ego standards, *J. Soc. Psychol.*, 1940, 12, 433–465.

30. Aveling, F., and Hargreaves, H. L., Suggestibility with and without prestige in children, *Brit. J. Psychol.*, 1921, 18, 362-388.

31. Avery, G. T., Responses of foetal guinea pigs prematurely delivered, *Genet. Psychol. Monogr.*, 1928, 3, 247–331.

32. Babcock, H., An experiment in the measurement of mental deterioration, *Arch. Psychol.*, 1930, No. 117.

33. Bacon, F., *Essays*, essay on "Deformity."

34. Bagby, E., *The psychology of personality*, 1928.

35. Baker, L. E., The pupillary response conditioned to subliminal auditory stimuli, *Psychol. Monogr.*, 1938, No. 223.

36. Baldwin, J. M., Mental development in the child and the race, 1895.

37. Balken, E. R., and Masserman, J. H., The language of phantasy: III. The language of the phantasies of patients with conversion hysteria, anxiety state, and obsessive-compulsive neuroses, *J. Psychol.*, 1940, 10, 75–86.

38. Barker, R., Dembo, T., and Lewin, K., Frustration and regression: an experiment with children, *Univ. Iowa Stud.: Stud. Child Welfare*, 18, No. 1.

39. Bartlett, F. C., *Remembering*, 1932.

40. Bateson, G., *Naven*, 1936.

41. Bateson, G., and Mead, M., *Balinese character: a photographic analysis*, 1942.

42. Bayer, E., Beiträge zur Zweikomponenten-theorie des Hungers, *Z. f. Psychol.*, 1929, 112, 1–54.

43. Bayley, N., Mental growth in young children, *Yearb. Nat. Soc. Stud. Educ.*, 1940, II, 39, 11–47.

44. Bayley, N., Size and body build of adolescents in relation to rate of skeletal maturing, *Child Developm.*, 1943, 14, 51–89.

45. Bayley, N., and Jones, N. C., Some personality characteristics of boys with retarded skeletal maturity, *Psychol. Bull*, 1941, 38, 603.

46. Beck, S. J., *Introduction to the Rorschach method*, 1937 (Monogr. No. 1 of Amer. Orthopsychiat. Assn.).

47. Beck, S J., *Rorschach's test*, 2 vols., 1944.

48. Beebe-Center, J. G., *The psychology of pleasantness and unpleasantness*, 1932.

49. Bender, M. B., and Siegal, S., Release of autonomic humoral substances in hypoglycemic cats and monkeys, *Amer. J. Physiol.*, 1940, 128, No. 2.

50. Benedict, R., Anthropology and the abnormal, *J. Genet. Psychol.*, 1934, 10, 59–82.

51. Benedict, R., *Patterns of culture*, 1934.

52. Bergson, H., *Creative evolution*, 1907.

53. Bergson, H., *Time and free will*, 2nd ed., 1898.

54. Berne, E. V. C., An experimental investigation of social behavior patterns in young children, 1930, *Univ. Iowa Stud.: Stud. Child Welfare*, 4, No. 3.

55. Beryl, F., Über die grössenauffassung bei Kindern, *Z. f. Psychol.*, 1926, 100, 344–371.

56. Biber, B., Murphy, L. B., Woodcock, L. P., and Black, I. S., *Child life in school*, 1942; with a chapter on the Rorschach test by A. Hartoch and E. Schachtel.

57. Bichat, X., *Anatomie générale*, 1801.

58. Binet, A., *Alterations of personality*, 1892.

59. Binet, A., *La suggestibilité*, 1900.

60. Binet, A., *On double consciousness*, 1890.

61. Binger, C. A. L., Ackerman, N. W., Cohn, A. E., Schroeder, H. A., and Steele, J. M., Personality in arterial hypertension, *Psychosom. Med. Monogr.*, 1945, No. 8.

62. Blatz, W. E., *The five sisters*, 1938.

63. Bleuler, E., *Textbook of psychiatry*, 1924.

64. Blos, P., *The adolescent personality*, 1941.

BIBLIOGRAPHY

65. Boas, F., The central Eskimo, *6th Ann. Rpt. Bur. Ethnol.*, 1884–1885, 399–669.
66. Boas, F., The Kwakiutl of Vancouver Island, *Publ. Jesup North Pacific Expedition*, 1909, 5, Part 2, 301–522.
67. Bogardus, E. S., A social distance scale, *Sociol. & Soc. Res.*, 1933, 17, 265–271.
68. Bolles, M., The basis of pertinence, *Arch. Psychol.*, 1937, No. 212.
69. Boring, E. G., *A history of experimental psychology*, 1929.
69a. Bourdillon, F., "The night has a thousand eyes."
70. Boyle, R., *The sceptical chymist*, 1677.
71. Brandenburg, G. C., Personality and vocational achievement, *J. Appl. Psychol.*, 1925, 9, 281–293.
72. Brenman, M., Experiments in the hypnotic production of anti-social and self-injurious behavior, *Psychiatry*, 1942, 5, 49–61.
73. Brenman, M., The relationship between minority group memberships and group identification in a group of urban middle class Negro girls, *J. Soc. Psychol.*, 1940, 11, 171–197.
74. Brett, G. S., *A history of psychology*, 3 vols., 1914–1921.
75. Brian, C. R., and Goodenough, F. L., The relative potency of color and form perception at various ages, *J. Exp. Psychol.*, 1929, 12, 197–213.
76. Briffault, R., *The mothers: a study of the origin of sentiments and institutions*, 3 vols., 1927.
77. Brill, A. A., *Psychoanalysis*, 2nd ed., 1914.
78. Broad, C. D., *The mind and its place in nature*, 1923.
79. Brogden, W. J., Higher order conditioning, *Amer. J. Psychol.*, 1939, 52, 579–591.
80. Brunswik, E., Zur Entwicklung der Albedowahrnehmung, *Z. f. Psychol.*, 1928, 109, 40–115.
81. Bryan, A. I., Organization of memory in young children, *Arch. Psychol.*, 1934, No. 162.
82. Bryce, J., *The American commonwealth*, 2 vols., new ed., 1914.
83. Bucke, R. M., *Cosmic consciousness*, 1901.
84. Bühler, C., *Der menschliche Lebenslauf*, 1933.
85. Bühler, C., *The first year of life*, 1930.
86. Bühler, C., *From birth to maturity*, 1936.
87. Bühler, C., *Jugendtagebuch und Lebenslauf*, 1932.
88. Bühler, C., *Soziologische Studien über das erste Lebensjahr*, 1927.
89. Bühler, C., and Hetzer, H., Inventar der Verhaltungsweisen des ersten Lebensjahres, *Quell. u. Stud. z. Jugendk.*, 1927, No. 5, 125–250.
90. Bürklen, K., *Blindenpsychologie*, 1924.
91. Burks, B. S., Autosomal linkage in man—the recombination ratio between congenital tooth deficiency and hair color, *Proc. Natl. Acad. Sci.*, 1938, 24, 512–519.
92. Burks, B. S., A study of identical twins reared apart under differing types of family relationships, *in* McNamar, Q., and Merrill, M. A. (eds.), *Studies in personality*, 1942.
93. Burks, B. S., and Jones, M. C., *Personality development in childhood*, 1936.
94. Burnett, C. T., Splitting the mind: an experimental study of normal men, *Psychol. Monogr.*, 1925, No. 155.
95. Burrow, T., *The biology of human conflict*, 1937.
96. Burrow, T., Crime and the social reaction of right and wrong, *J. Crim. Law & Crimin.*, 1933, 24, 685–699.
97. Burtt, H. E., An experimental study of early childhood memory, *J. Genet. Psychol.*, 1932, 40, 287–295.
98. Burtt, H. E., An experimental study of early childhood memory: final report, *J. Genet Psychol.*, 1941, 58, 435–439.
99. Busemann, A., *Pädagogische Milieukunde*, 1932.
100. Cabot, P. S. de Q., A long term study of children: the Cambridge-Somerville Youth Study, *Child Developm.*, 1940, 11, 143–151.

101. Cameron, N., Reasoning, regression and communication in schizophrenics, *Psychol. Monogr.*, 1938, 50, No. 1.
102. Campbell, A. A., and Hilgard, E. R., Individual differences in ease of conditioning, *J. Exp. Psychol.*, 1936, 19, 561–571.
103. Canestrini, S., *Über das Sinnesleben der Neugeborenen*, 1913.
104. Cannon, W. B., *Bodily changes in fear, hunger, rage, and pain*, 2nd ed., 1929.
105. Cannon, W. B., *The wisdom of the body*, 1939.
106. Cantril, H., The prediction of social events, *J. Abn. & Soc. Psychol.*, 1938, 33, 364–389.
107. Cantril, H., and Allport, G. W., *The psychology of radio*, 1935.
108. Carlson, A. J., *The control of hunger in health and disease*, 1916.
109. Carmichael, L., Heredity and environment: are they antithetical? *J. Abn. & Soc. Psychol.*, 1925, 20, 245–260.
110. Cason, H., Sensory conditioning, *J. Exp. Psychol.*, 1936, 19, 572–591.
111. Cass, W. A., An experimental investigation of the dissociation hypothesis utilizing a post-hypnotic technique, *Psychol. Bull.*, 1941, 38, 744.
112. Cattell, R. B., *Description and measurement of personality*, 1946.
113. Chappell, M. N., Blood pressure changes in deception, *Arch. Psychol.*, 1920, No. 105.
114. Chassell, C. F., *The relation between morality and intellect*, 1935.
115. Chassell, J. O., *The experience variables*, 1928.
116. Chein, I., The awareness of self and the structure of the ego, *Psychol. Rev.*, 1944, 51, 304–314.
117. Chesterton, G. K., *What's wrong with the world?* 1910.
118. Child, C. M., Axial development in aggregates of dissociated cells from corymorpha palma, *Physiol. Zool.*, 1928, 1, 419–461.
119. Child, C. M., *Physiological foundations of behavior*, 1924.
120. Chrisman, O., Children's secret language, *Child Study*, 1896, 2, 202–211.
121. Clark, E. T., *The psychology of religious awakening*, 1929.
122. Clark, K. B., Some factors influencing the remembering of prose materials, *Arch. Psychol.*, 1940, No. 253.
123. Clark, K. B., and Clark, M. K., The development of consciousness of self and the emergence of racial identification in Negro pre-school children, *J. Soc. Psychol.*, 1939, 10, 591–599.
124. Clark, K. B., and Clark, M. K., Skin color as a factor in racial identification of Negro pre-school children, *J. Soc. Psychol.*, 1940, 11, 159–169.
125. Clifford, W. K., *On the nature of things in themselves: lectures and essays*, 1879.
126. Coghill, G. E., *Anatomy and the problem of behavior*, 1929.
127. Cooley, C. H., *Human nature and the social order*, 1912.
128. Cooley, C. H., *Social organization*, 1911.
129. Cowper, W., *The solitude of Alexander Selkirk*.
130. Cox, C. M., *Genetic studies of genius*, II. *The early mental traits of three hundred geniuses*, 1926.
131. Craig, W., Male doves reared in isolation, *J. Animal Behav.*, 1914, 4, 121–133.
132. Crozier, W. J., in Murchison, C. (ed.), *The foundations of experimental psychology*, 1929.
133. Cushing, H. M., A perseverative tendency in pre-school children: a study in personality differences, *Arch. Psychol.*, 1929, No. 108.
134. Darrow, C. W., Physiological and clinical tests of autonomic function and autonomic balance, *Physiol. Rev.*, 1943, 23, 1–36.
135. Darwin, C., *The descent of man*, 1871.
136. Dashiell, J. F., *Fundamentals of objective psychology*, 1928.
137. Day, C., *This simian world*, 1920.
138. Dearborn, W. F., and Rothney, J. W. M., *Predicting the child's development*, 1941.

139. Dennis, W., Does culture appreciably affect patterns of infant behavior? *J. Soc. Psychol.*, 1940, 12, 305–317.
140. Dennis, W., *The Hopi child*, 1940.
141. Dennis, W., Infant development under conditions of restricted practice and of minimal social stimulation, *Genet. Psychol. Monogr.*, 1941, 23, 143–189.
142. Dennis, W., On the possibility of advancing and retarding the motor development of infants, *Psychol. Rev.*, 1943, 50, 203–218.
143. DeQuincey, T., *Confessions of an English opium eater*, 1875.
144. DeSanctis, S., *Religious conversion*, 1927.
145. Descartes, R., *Discourse on method*, 1637.
146. Despert, J. L., *Emotional problems in children: technical approaches used to their study and treatment*, 1938.
147. DeTocqueville, A., *Democracy in America*, 1830.
148. Deutsch, G. F., Conformity in human behavior, with a test for its measurement, Master's essay in Columbia Univ. Library, 1933.
149. Dewey, E., *Behavior development in infants: a survey of the literature on prenatal and postnatal activity*, 1935.
150. Diamond, S., A neglected aspect of motivation, *Sociometry*, 1939, 2, 77–85.
151. Diamond, S., A study of the influence of political radicalism on personality development, *Arch. Psychol.*, 1936, No. 203.
152. Dimnet, E., *The art of thinking*, 1928.
153. Diven, K., Certain determinants in the conditioning of anxiety reactions, *J. Psychol.*, 1937, 3, 291–308.
154. Dollard, J., Miller, N. E., Doob, L. W., Mowrer, O. H., and Sears, R. R., *Frustration and aggression*, 1939.
155. Downey, J. E., *Graphology and the psychology of handwriting*, 1919.
156. Driscoll, G. P., The developmental status of the pre-school child as a prognosis of future development, *Child Developm. Monogr.*, 1933, No. 13.
157. DuBois, C., *The people of Alor*, 1944.
158. DuBois, P. H., A speed factor in mental tests, *Arch. Psychol.*, 1932, No. 141.
159. Dudycha, G. J., and Dudycha, M. M., Some factors and characteristics of childhood memories, *Child Developm.*, 1933, 4, 265–278.
160. Dumas, G., *Nouveau traité de psychologie*, 4 vols., 1933.
161. Dunbar, H. F., *Emotions and bodily changes*, 3rd ed., 1945.
162. Durkin, II. E., Trial and error, gradual analysis, and sudden reorganization: an experimental study of problem solving, *Arch. Psychol.*, 1937, No. 210.
163. Ebbinghaus, H., *Memory*, 1885.
164. Efrón, D., *Gesture and environment*, 1941.
165. Eisenberg, P., Expressive movements related to feeling of dominance, *Arch. Psychol.*, 1937, No. 211.
166. Elkisch, P., Children's drawings in a projective technique, *Psychol. Monogr.*, 1945, 58, No. 1.
167. Ellis, H., *A study of British genius*, new ed., 1927.
168. Enke, W., Die Psychomotorik der Konstitutionstype, *Z. f. Angew. Psychol.*, 1930, 36, 237–287.
169. Erickson, M. H., An experimental investigation of the possible anti-social use of hypnosis, *Psychiatry*, 1939, 2, 391–414.
170. Erickson, M. H., and Erickson, E. M., Concerning the nature and character of post-hypnotic behavior, *J. Gen. Psychol.*, 1941, 24, 95–133.
171. Erikson, E. H., Configurations in play: clinical notes, *Psychoanal. Quar.*, 1937, 6, 138–214.
172. Erikson, E. H., Observations on the Yurok: childhood and world image, *Univ. Calif. Publ. Amer. Archaeol. & Ethnol.*, 1943, 35, No. 10.
173. Erikson, E. H., Problems of infancy and early childhood, in *Encyclopedia of Medicine, Surgery, and Specialties*, 1940.

174. Erikson, E. H., Studies in the interpretation of play: I. Clinical observation of play description in young children, *J. Genet. Psychol.*, 1940, 22, 557–671.
175. Estabrooks, G. H., Experimental studies in suggestion, *J. Genet. Psychol.*, 1929, 36, 120–139.
176. Evvard, J. M., Is the appetite of swine a reliable indication of physiological needs? *Proc. Iowa Acad. Sci.*, 1916, 22, 375–414.
177. Féré, C., *Sensation et mouvement: études expérimentales de psychomechanic*, 1887.
178. Fletcher, J. M., *The problem of stuttering*, 1928.
179. Fortune, R. F., *Sorcerers of Dobu*, 1932.
180. Foster, S., Personality deviations and their relation to the home, *Proc. Nat. Conf. Social Work*, 1925.
181. Frank, L. K., Adolescence as a period of transition, *Yearb. Nat. Soc. Stud. Educ.*, 1944, 43, 1–7.
182. Frank, L. K. The cost of competition, *Plan Age*, 1940, 6, 314–324.
183. Frank, L. K., Projective methods for the study of personality, *J. Psychol.*, 1939, 8, 389–413.
184. Franz, S. I., *Persons one and three: a study in multiple personalities*, 1933.
185. Franzblau, R. N., Race differences in mental and physical traits, *Arch. Psychol.*, 1935, No. 177.
186. Frazer, J. G., *The golden bough*, abr. ed., 1922.
187. Freeman, E., *Social psychology*, 1936.
188. Freeman, G. L., Manson, G. E., Katzoff, E. T., and Pathman, J. H., The stress interview, *J. Abn. & Soc. Psychol.*, 1942, 37, 427–447.
189. Freeman, G. L., Suggestions for a standardized "stress" test, *J. Gen. Psychol.*, 1945, 32, 3–11.
190. Frenkel-Brunswik, E., Mechanisms of self-deception, *J. Soc. Psychol.*, 1939, 10, 409–420.
191. Freud, A., *The ego and the mechanisms of defense*, 1946.
192. Freud, S., *Beyond the pleasure principle* (trans. from 2nd German ed.), 1922.
193. Freud, S., *The ego and the id*, 1920.
194. Freud, S., Further remarks on the defense neuro-psychoses (*Neurol. Zentralbl.*, 1896, No. 10), *Collected papers*, 1924, I, 155–182.
195. Freud, S., *A general introduction to psychoanalysis*, 1920.
196. Freud, S., *Group psychology and the analysis of the ego*, 1922.
197. Freud, S., History of the psychoanalytic movement, *Psychoanal. Rev.*, 1916, 3, 406–454.
198. Freud, S., *The interpretation of dreams*, 1900.
199. Freud, S., *New introductory lectures on psychoanalysis*, 1933.
200. Freud, S., Some character-types met with in psychoanalytic work, *Collected papers*, 1925, IV.
201. Freud, S., *Three contributions to the theory of sex* (see for example, Brill, A. A. [ed.], *The basic writings of Sigmund Freud*, 1938, 607 ff.).
202. Freud, S., *Totem and taboo*, 1910.
203. Fromm, E., *Escape from freedom*, 1941.
204. Fromm, E., Individual and social origins of neurosis, *Amer. Sociol. Res.*, 1944, 9, 380–384.
205. Fromme, A., An experimental study of the factors of maturation and practice in the behavioral development of the embryo of the frog, *Rana pipiens*, *Genet. Psychol. Monogr.*, 1941, 24, 219–256.
206. Galton, F., *Inquiries into human faculty*, 1883.
207. Gardner, J. W., Level of aspiration in response to a prearranged sequence of scores, *J. Exp. Psychol.*, 1939, 25, 601–621.
208. Garrett, H. E., A developmental theory of intelligence, *Amer. Psychologist*, 1946, 1, 372–378.

BIBLIOGRAPHY

209. Garrett, H. E., Bryan, A. I., and Perl, R. E., The age factor in mental organization, *Arch. Psychol.*, 1935, No. 176.
210. Garth, T. R., *Race psychology*, 1931.
211. Garvey, C. R., The difficulty of conditioning the Achilles reflex, *Psychol. Bull.*
1932, 29, 555.
212. Gesell, A., *Infancy and human growth*, 1928.
213. Gesell, A., in collaboration with Amatruda, C. S., *The embryology of behavior*, 1945.
214. Gesell, A., and Thompson, H., Learning and growth in identical infant twins:
an experimental study by the method of co-twin control, *Genet. Psychol. Monogr.*,
1929, 6, No. 1.
215. Gesell, A., and Thompson, H., Twins *T* and *C* from infancy to adolescence: a
biogenetic study of individual differences by the method of co-twin control,
Genet. Psychol. Monogr., 1941, 24, 2–121.
216. Gilbert, G. M., Inter-sensory facilitation and inhibition, *J. Gen. Psychol.*, 1941,
24, 381–407.
217. Girden, E., Cerebral mechanisms in conditioning under curare, *Amer. J. Psychol.*,
1940, 53, 397–406.
218. Girden, E., and Culler, E., Conditioned responses in curarized striate muscle in
dogs, *J. Comp. Psychol.*, 1937, 23, 261–274.
219. Givler, R. C., *The ethics of Hercules*, 1924.
220. Glueck, S., and Glueck, E. T., *500 criminal careers*, 1930.
221. Goldfrank, E. S., Socialization, personality, and the structure of Pueblo society,
with particular reference to Hopi and Zuñi, *Amer. Anthropol.*, 1945, 47, 516–539.
222. Goldstein, H., The biochemical variability of the individual in relation to
personality and intelligence, *J. Exper. Psychol.*, 1935, 18, 348–371.
223. Goldstein, K., *Human nature in the light of psychopathology*, 1940.
224. Goldstein, K., *The organism*, 1935.
225. Goldstein, K., The problem of the meaning of words based upon observation of
aphasic patients, *J. Psychol.*, 1936, 2, 301–316.
226. Goodenough, F. L., Expression of the emotions in a blind-deaf child, *J. Abn. &
Soc. Psychol.*, 1932, 27, 328–373.
227. Goodenough, F. L., The expression of the emotions in infancy, *Child Developm.*,
1930, 1, 29–47.
228. Goodenough, F. L., A new approach to the measurement of the intelligence of
young children, *J. Genet. Psychol.*, 1926, 33, 185–211.
229. Gordon, K., Samples of students' originality, *J. Genet. Psychol.*, 1936, 49, 480–494.
230. Gould, R., An experimental analysis of "level of aspiration," *Genet. Psychol.
Monogr.*, 1939, 21, 3–115.
231. Greenberg, P. J., Competition in children: an experimental study, *Amer. J.
Psychol.*, 1932, 44, 221–248.
232. Greene, E. B., *Measurements of human behavior*, 1941.
233. Greene, E. B., *Michigan nonverbal series*, 1931.
234. Guernsey, M., Eine genetische Studie über Nachahmung; summarized in Bühler,
C., *Kindhert und Jugend*, 1928.
235. Guilford, J. P., and Guilford, R. B., An analysis of the factors in a typical test of
introversion-extroversion, *J. Abn. & Soc. Psychol.*, 1934, 28, 377–399.
236. Guthrie, E. R., *The psychology of human conflict*, 1938.
237. Guthrie, E. R., and Horton, G. P., *Cats in a puzzle box*, 1946.
238. Haeckel, E., *Anthropogenie*, 1874.
239. Hall, C. S., The inheritance of emotionality, *Sigma Xi Quart.*, 1938, 26, No. 1,
17–27.
240. Hall, G. S., Some aspects of the early sense of self, *Amer. J. Psychol.*, 1898, 9, 351–
395.
241. Hamilton, G. V., *A research in marriage*, 1929.

242. Hamilton, G. V., A study of perseverance reactions in primates and rodents, *Behav. Monogr.*, 1916, 3, No. 2, Ser. No. 13.
243. Hamilton, G. V., A study of trial and error reactions in mammals, *J. Animal Behav.*, 1911, 1, 33–66.
244. Hammett, F. S., Observations on the relation between emotional and metabolic stability, *Amer. J. Physiol.*, 1921, 53, 307–311.
245. Hanfmann, E., A study of personal patterns in an intellectual performance, *Char. & Pers.*, 1941, 9, 315–325.
246. Hanks, L. M., Prediction from case material to personality test data, *Arch. Psychol.*, 1936, No. 207.
247. Harriman, P. L., The experimental production of some phenomena related to multiple personality, *J. Abn. & Soc. Psychol.*, 1942, 37, 244–255.
248. Harris, D., Group differences in values within a university, *J. Abn. & Soc. Psychol.*, 1935, 30, 95–102.
249. Harrower-Erickson, M. R., Developments of the Rorschach test for large scale application, *Rorschach Res. Exch.*, 1944, 8, 125–140.
250. Harrower-Erickson, M. R., and Steiner, N. E., *Large scale Rorschach techniques: a manual for the group Rorschach and multiple choice test*, 1945.
251. Hartley, D., *Observations on man, his frame, his duty, and his expectations*, 1749.
252. Hartley, E. L., *Problems in prejudice*, 1946.
253. Hartshorne, H., and May, M. A., *Studies in deceit*, 1928.
254. Hartshorne, H., May, M. A., and Maller, J. B., *Studies in service and self-control*, 1929.
255. Hartshorne, H., May, M. A., and Shuttleworth, F. K., *Studies in the organization of character*, 1930.
256. Head, H., *Aphasia and kindred disorders of speech*, 1923.
257. Hecht, S., in Murchison, C. (ed.), *The foundations of experimental psychology*, 1929, 268–269.
258. Heidbreder, E., Measuring introversion and extroversion, *J. Abn. & Soc. Psychol.*, 1927, 21, 120–134.
259. Helmholtz, H. L. F., *On the sensations of tone*, trans. from 4th ed., 1877.
260. Henderson, D. K., and Gillespie, R. D., *A text-book of psychiatry*, 5th ed., 1940.
261. Henderson, L. J., *Blood: a study in general physiology*, 1930.
262. Herbart, J. F., *A text book in psychology*, 1816.
263. Hertzman, M., and Margulies, H., Developmental changes as reflected in Rorschach test responses, *J. Genet. Psychol.*, 1943, 62, 189–215.
264. Hertzman, M., Orlansky, J., and Seitz, C. P., Personality organization and anoxia tolerance, *Psychosom. Med.*, 1944, 6, 317–331.
265. Hilgard, E. R., and Marquis, D. G., *Conditioning and learning*, 1940.
266. Hilgard, E. R., Miller, J., and Ohlson, J. A., Three attempts to secure pupillary conditioning to auditory stimuli near the absolute threshold, *J. Exp. Psychol.*, 1941, 29, 89–103.
267. Hill, A. V., *Living machinery*, 1927.
268. Hobbes, T., *The Leviathan*, 1651.
269. Hocking, W. E., *The meaning of God in human experience*, 1924.
270. Hollingworth, H. L., Correlations of achievement within an individual, *J. Exp. Psychol.*, 1925, 8, 190–208.
271. Hollingworth, H. L., *The psychology of functional neuroses*, 1920.
272. Holmes, F. B., An experimental investigation of a method of overcoming children's fears, *Child Developm.*, 1936, 7, 6–30.
273. Holmes, S. J., The problem of organic form, *Sci. Mo.*, 1944, 59, 226–232, 253–260, 379–383.
274. Holt, E. B., *Animal drive and the learning process*, 1931.
275. Holt, E. B., *The Freudian wish and its place in ethics*, 1915.
276. Hoppe, F., Erfolg und Misserfolg, *Psychol. Forsch.*, 1930, 40, 1–62.

277. Horney, K., *The neurotic personality of our time*, 1937.
278. Horney, K., *New ways in psychoanalysis*, 1939.
279. Horowitz, E. L., The development of attitude toward the Negro, *Arch. Psychol.* 1936, No. 194.
280. Horowitz, E. L., Spatial localization of the self, *J. Soc. Psychol.*, 1935, 6, 379–387.
281. Horton, L. H., Levitation dreams: their physiology, *J. Abn. Psychol.*, 1919, 14: 145–172.
282. Horton, L. H., The mechanistic features in the dream process, *J. Abn. Psychol.*, 1921, 16, 168–196.
283. Hoskins, R. G., *Endocrinology: the glands and their functions*, 1941.
284. Howells, T. H., The experimental development of color-tone synesthesia, *J. Exp. Psychol.*, 34, 87–103.
285. Howells, T. H., An experimental study of persistence, *J. Abn. & Soc. Psychol.*, 1933, 28, 14–29.
286. Hudgins, C. V., Conditioning and the voluntary control of the pupillary light reflex, *J. Gen. Psychol.*, 1933, 8, 3–51.
287. Humphrey, G., The conditioned reflex and the elementary social reaction, *J. Abn. & Soc. Psychol.*, 1922, 17, 113–119.
288. Hunt, J. McV., The effects of infant feeding-frustration upon adult hoarding in the albino rat, *J. Abn. & Soc. Psychol.*, 1941, 36, 338–360.
289. Hunter, W. S., The delayed reaction in animals and children, *Behav. Monogr.*, 1913, 2, No. 1.
290. Hunter, W. S., The delayed reaction in a child, *Psychol. Rev.*, 1917, 24.
291. Hurlock, E. B., *Child development*, 1942.
292. Hurlock, E. B., and Burstein, M., The imaginary playmate: a questionnaire study, *J. Genet. Psychol.*, 1932, 41, 380–392.
293. Hutchinson, E. D., Materials for the study of creative thinking, *Psychol. Bull.*, 1931, 28, 392–409.
294. Hutchinson, E. D., The technique of creative thought, *Psychol. Bull.*, 1929, 26, 139.
295. Hyman, H. H., The psychology of status, *Arch. Psychol.*, 1942, No. 269.
296. Irwin, O. C., The amount and nature of activities of newborn infants under constant external stimulating conditions during the first ten days of life, *Genet. Psychol. Monogr.*, 1930, 8, 1–92.
297. Isaacs, S., *Intellectual growth in young children*, with an appendix on children's "why" questions by N. Isaacs, 1930.
298. Israeli, N., The psychology of prediction: judgments relating to the past and future, *Psychol. Exchange*, 1936, 4, 129–132.
299. Jack, L. M., An experimental study of ascendant behavior in preschool children, *Univ. Iowa Stud.: Stud. Child Welfare*, 1934, 9, No. 3.
300. Jacobson, E., *Progressive relaxation*, 2nd ed., 1938.
301. Jaensch, E. R., *Eidetic imagery and typological methods of investigation*, 1930.
302. James, H. (ed.), *The letters of William James*, 1920.
303. James, W., *Essays in radical empiricism*, 1912.
304. James, W., *The meaning of truth; a sequel to "Pragmatism,"* 1909.
305. James, W., *Memories and studies*, 1912.
306. James, W., *A pluralistic universe*, 1909.
307. James, W., *Pragmatism: a new name for some old ways of thinking*, 1907.
308. James, W., *The principles of psychology*, 2 vols., 1890.
309. James, W., *The varieties of religious experience*, 1902.
310. James, W., *The will to believe, and other essays in popular philosophy*, new impr., 1912.
311. Janet, P., *Psychological healing*, 1925.
312. Janet, P., *The major symptoms of hysteria*, 1907.
313. Jasper, H. H., Electrical activity of the brain, *Annual Rev. Physiol.*, 1941, 3, 377–398.

314. Jeffries, R., *The story of my heart.*
315. Jensen, K., Differential reactions to taste and temperature stimuli in newborn infants, *Genet. Psychol. Monogr.*, 1932, 12, 361–479.
316. Jersild, A. T., *Child psychology*, rev. ed., 1940.
317. Jersild, A. T., Training and growth in the development of children, *Child Developm. Monogr.*, 1932, No. 10.
318. Jervis, G. A., The genetics of phenylpyruvic oligophrenia, *J. Ment. Sci.*, 1939, 85, 719–762.
319. Johnson, D. M., Confidence and speed in the two-category judgment, *Arch. Psychol.*, 1939, No. 241.
320. Jones, E., Rationalization in everyday life, *J. Abn. Psychol.*, 1908, 3, 161–169.
321. Jones, H. E., The California Adolescent Growth Study, *J. Educ. Res.*, 1938, 31, 561–567.
322. Jones, H. E., The case cited is unpublished. The case method is illustrated in: *Development in adolescence: approaches to the study of the individual*, 1943.
323. Jones, H. E., Environmental influences on mental development, in Carmichael, L. (ed.), *Manual of child psychology*, 1946, 582–632.
324. Jones, H. E., The galvanic skin reflex, *Child Developm.*, 1930, 1, 106–110.
325. Jones, M. C., The elimination of children's fears, *J. Exper. Psychol.*, 1924, 7, 382–390.
326. Jones, M. C., A laboratory study of fear: the case of Peter, *Ped. Sem.*, 1924, 31, 308–315.
327. Jones, T. S., Jr., *The rose-jar*, 1906.
328. Jones, T. S., Jr., *Sonnets of the cross*, 1922.
329. Jost, H., and Sontag, L. W., The genetic factor in autonomic nervous system function, *Psychosom. Med.*, 1944, 6, 308–310.
330. Judd, C. H., Movement and consciousness, *Yale Psychol. Stud.*, N. S., 1, 199–226.
331. Jung, C. G., *Psychological types: or the psychology of individuation*, 1923.
332. Jung, C. G., *The psychology of dementia praecox* (German original, 1907), *Nerv. & Ment. Dis. Monogr. Ser.*, 1936, No. 3.
333. Jung, C. G., *Psychology of the unconscious* (trans. by B. M. Hinkle), 1916.
334. Jung, C. G., The theory of psychoanalysis, *Nerv. & Ment. Dis. Monogr. Ser.*, 1915, 19.
335. Jung, C. G. (ed.), *Studies in word-association* (German original, 1904), 1918.
336. Kardiner, A., *The individual and his society: the psychodynamics of primitive social organization*, with a foreword and two ethnological reports by R. Linton, 1939.
337. Kardiner, A., with the collaboration of R. Linton, C. DuBois, and J. West, *The psychological frontiers of society*, 1945.
338. Katz, D., Hunger und Appetit, *Ber. über den XII Kong. der deutschen Ges. f. Psychol.*, 1932, 255–276.
339. Keller, A. G., *Societal evolution*, rev. ed., 1931.
340. Keller, H. A., *The story of my life*, 1908.
341. Kempf, E. J., The social and sexual behavior of infrahuman primates with some comparable facts in human behavior, *Psychoanal. Rev.*, 1917, 4, 127–154.
342. Kimmins, C. W., *Children's dreams*, 1920.
343. Kipling, R., *The jungle book*, 1898.
344. Klages, L., *Handschrift und Charakter*, 15th ed., 1932.
345. Klein, D. B., *The experimental production of dreams during hypnosis*, 1930.
346. Klein, D. B., *General psychology*, 1936.
347. Klimpfinger, S., Die Entwicklung der Gestaltkonstanz vom Kinde zum Erwachsenen, *Arch. Ges. Psychol.*, 1933, 88, 599.
348. Klineberg, O. (ed.), *Characteristics of the American Negro*, 1944.
349. Klineberg, O., *Race differences*, 1935.
350. Klineberg, O., Racial differences in speed and accuracy, *J. Abn. & Soc. Psychol.*, 1927, 22, 273–277.
351. Klineberg, O., Asch, S. E., and Block, H., An experimental study of constitutional types, *Genet. Psychol. Monogr.*, 1934, 16, 145–221.

BIBLIOGRAPHY

352. Klopfer, B., and Kelley, D., *The Rorschach technique*, 1942.
353. Kluckhohn, G., and Mowrer, O. H., "Culture and personality"; a conceptural scheme, *Amer. Anthropol.*, 1944, 46, 1–29.
354. Klüver, H., Do personality types exist? *Amer. J. Psychiat.*, 1931.
355. Klüver, H., Eidetic imagery, in Murchison, C. (ed.), *A handbook of child psychology*, 2nd ed., 1933, 699–722.
356. Klüver, H., An experimental study of the eidetic type, *Genet. Psychol. Monogr.*, 1926, 1, 71–230.
357. Knight, F. B., At the 1923 meeting of the American Psychological Association (abstract of paper appears in *Psychol. Bull.*, 1924, 21, 106).
358. Koffka, K., *Principles of Gestalt psychology*, 1935, 27 ff.
359. Kraepelin, E., *Lectures on clinical psychiatry*, 3rd English ed., 1912.
360. Kretschmer, E., *Physique and character*, 1925.
361. Krout, M. H., Autistic gestures: an experimental study in symbolic movement, *Psychol. Rev. Monogr.*, 1935, No. 208.
362. Krueger, E. T., and Reckless, W. C., *Social psychology*, 1931.
363. Krugman, H. E., Affective response to music as a function of familiarity, *J. Abn. & Soc. Psychol.*, 1943, 38, 388–392.
364. Kuo, Z. Y., Ontogeny of embryonic behavior in Aves. I. The chronology and general nature of the behavior of the chick embryo, *J. Exper. Zool.*, 1932, 61, 395–430.
365. Landis, C., and Hunt, W., *The startle pattern*, 1939.
366. Landis, C., and Hunt, W., The startle pattern (various films).
367. Lang, J. B., Über Assoziationsversuche bei Schizophrenen und den Mitgliedern ihrer Familien, *Jahrb. f. Psychoanal. u. Psychopath.*, 1913, 5, 705–755.
368. Lashley, K. S., Experimental analysis of instinctive behavior, *Psychol. Rev.*, 1938, 45, 445–471.
369. Lashley, K. S., Physiological analysis of the libido, *Psychol. Rev.*, 1924, 31, 192–202.
370. Lasswell, H. D., *Psychopathology and politics*, 1930.
371. Lawton, G., Mental decline and its retardation, *Sci. Mo.*, 1944, 58, 313–317.
372. Lazarsfeld, M., and Zeisl, H., Die Arbeitslosen von Marienthal, *Psychol. Monographen*, 1933, 5.
373. Leaning, F. E., An introductory study of hypnagogic phenomena, *Proc. Soc. Psychical Res.*, 1925, 35, 289–594.
374. Learned, W. S., and Hawkes, A. L. R., *An experiment in responsible learning: a report to the Carnegie Foundation on projects in localization of secondary school progress*, 1929–1938.
375. Lecky, P., *Self-consistency: a theory of personality*, 1945.
376. Leonard, W. E., *The locomotive god*, 1927.
377. Lerner, E., *Constraint areas and the moral judgment of children*, 1937.
378. Lerner, E., The problem of perspective in moral reasoning, *Amer. J. Sociol.*, 1937, 43, 249–269.
379. Lerner, E., and Murphy, L. B. (eds.), Methods for the study of personality in young children, *Monogr. Soc. Res. Child Developm.*, 1941, 6, No. 4.
380. Leuba, C. J., An experimental study of rivalry in young children, *J. Comp. Psychol.*, 1933, 16, 367–378.
381. Leuba, C. J., A preliminary experiment to quantify an incentive and its effects, *J. Abn. & Soc. Psychol.*, 1930, 25, 275–288.
382. Levine, J. M., and Murphy, G., The learning and forgetting of controversial material, *J. Abn. & Soc. Psychol.*, 1943, 38, 507–517.
383. Levine, R., Chein, I., and Murphy, G., The relation of the intensity of a need to the amount of perceptual distortion: a preliminary report, *J. Psychol.*, 1942, 13, 283–293.

384. Levy, D. M., Experiments on the sucking reflex and social behavior of dogs, *Amer. J. Orthopsychiat.*, 1934, 4, 203–224.
385. Levy, D. M., *Maternal overprotection*, 1943.
386. Levy, D. M., On the problem of movement restraint, *Amer. J. Orthopsychiat.*, 1944, 14, 644–671.
387. Levy, D. M., Psychosomatic studies of some aspects of maternal behavior, *Psychosom. Med.*, 1942, 4, 223–227.
388. Levy, D. M., *Studies in sibling rivalry*, 1937.
389. Levy, D. M., and Tulchin, S. H., The resistance of infants and children during mental tests, *J. Exp. Psychol.*, 1923, 6, 304–322.
390. Levy, J., A quantitative study of the relationship between basal metabolic rate and children's behavior problems, *Amer. J. Orthopsychiat.*, 1931, 1, 298–310.
391. Levy, J., A quantitative study of behavior problems in relation to family constellation, *Amer. J. Psychiat.*, 1931, 10, 637–654.
392. Levy, J., in an informal report at the New York Academy of Medicine, 1937.
393. Lewin, K., *A dynamic theory of personality*, 1935.
394. Lewin, K., Forces behind food habits and methods of change, in *The problem of changing food habits*, a report of the Committee on Food Habits, Nat. Res. Council (Bull. No. 108), 35–65.
395. Lewin, K., Intelligence and motivation, in *Yearb. Nat. Soc. Stud. Educ.*, 1940, 39, 297–305.
396. Lewin, K., *Principles of topological psychology*, 1936.
397. Lewin, K., in Murchison, C. (ed.), *Handbook of child psychology*, 1933, 2nd ed., 616.
398. Lewin, K., Lippitt, R., and White, R. K., Patterns of aggressive behavior in experimentally created "social climates," *J. Soc. Psychol.*, 1939, 10, 271–299.
399. Lewinson, T. S., and Zubin, J., *Handwriting analysis: a series of scales for evaluating the dynamic aspects of handwriting*, 1942.
400. Lewis, H. B., Studies in the principles of judgments and attitudes. II. The influence of political attitude on the organization and stability of judgments, *J. Soc. Psychol.*, 1940, 2, 121–146.
401. Lewis, H. B., and Franklin, M., An experimental study of the role of ego in work. II. The significance of task orientation in work, *J. Exp. Psychol.*, 34, No. 3, 195–215.
402. Lewis, S., *Babbitt*, 1922.
403. Liddell, H. S., in Hunt, J. McV., *Personality and the behavior disorders*, 2 vols., 1944.
404. Linton, R., A neglected aspect of social organization, *Amer. J. Sociol.*, 45, 870–886.
405. Lippitt, R., An experimental study of the effect of democratic and authoritarian group atmospheres, *Univ. Iowa Stud.: Stud. Child Welfare*, 1940, 16, No. 3, 43–195.
406. Lippmann, W., *Public opinion*, 1934.
407. Loeb, J., *Forced movements, tropisms, and animal conduct*, 1918.
408. Lombroso, C., *Crime: its causes and remedies*, 1918.
409. Long, L. D., An investigation of the original response to the conditioned stimulus, *Arch. Psychol.*, 1941, No. 259.
410. Lorimer, F., *The growth of reason*, 1929.
411. Lowes, J. L., *The road to Xanadu*, 1927.
412. Lukomnik, M., An experiment to test the canalization hypothesis, Master's essay in Columbia Univ. Library, 1940.
413. Luria, A. R., *The nature of human conflicts*, 1932.
414. Lynn, J. G., and Lynn, D. R., Smile and hand dominance in relation to basic modes of adaptation, *J. Abn. & Soc. Psychol.*, 1943, 38, 250–276.
415. Lynd, R. S., and Lynd, H. M., *Middletown: a study in contemporary American culture*, 1929.
416. Lynd, R. S., and Lynd, H. M., *Middletown in transition: a study in cultural conflicts*, 1937.
417. Macfarlane, J. W., The guidance study, *Sociometry*, 1939, 2, 1–23.

BIBLIOGRAPHY

418. Maier, N. R. F., The role of frustration in social movements, *Psychol. Rev.*, 1942, 49, 586–599.
419. Maier, N. R. F., *Studies of abnormal behavior in the rat*, 1939.
420. Marks, E. S., Individual differences in work curves, *Arch. Psychol.*, 1935, No. 186.
421. Marks, E. S., Skin color judgments of Negro college students, *J. Abn. & Soc. Psychol.*, 1943, 38, 370–376.
422. Marquis, D. P., Can conditioned responses be established in the newborn infant? *J. Genet. Psychol.*, 1931, 39, 479–490.
423. Marston, L. R., The emotions of young children: an experimental study of introversion and extroversion, *Univ. Iowa Stud.: Stud. Child Welfare*, 1925, 3, No. 3.
424. Martin, L. J., *A handbook for old age counsellors: the method of salvaging, rehabilitating and reconditioning old people used in the Old Age Counselling Center in San Francisco, California*, 1944.
425. Marx, K., *Capital*, 1867.
426. Marx, K., and Engels, F., *The communist manifesto*, 1848.
427. Maslow, A. H., The authoritarian character structure, *J. Soc. Psychol.*, 1943, 18, 401–411.
428. Maslow, A. H., Dominance-feeling, behavior, and status, *Psychol. Rev.*, 1937, 44, 404–429.
429. Maslow, A. H., Dynamics of personality organization, I, *Psychol. Rev.*, 1943, 50, 514–539.
430. Maslow, A. H., Dynamics of personality organization, II, *Psychol. Rev.*, 1943, 50, 541–558.
431. Maslow, A. H., Experimentalizing the clinical method, *J. Clin. Psychol.*, 1945, 1, 241–243.
432. Maslow, A. H., *Social personality inventory for college women*, 1942.
433. Maslow, A. H., The dynamics of psychological security-insecurity, *Char. & Pers.*, 1942, 10, 331–344.
434. Maslow, A. H., The influence of familiarization on preference, *J. Exp. Psychol.*, 1937, 21, 162–180.
435. Maslow, A. H., A test for dominance-feeling (self-esteem) in college women, *J. Soc. Psychol.*, 1940, 12, 255–270.
436. Mateer, F., *Child behavior*, 1918.
437. Max, L. W., Experimental study of the motor theory of consciousness. IV. Action-current responses in the deaf during awakening, kinesthetic imagery, and abstract thinking, *J. Comp. Psychol.*, 1937, 24, 301–344.
438. Max, L. W., Myoesthesis and "imageless thought," *Science*, 1932, 76, 235–236.
439. McCarthy, D., in Murchison, C. (ed.), *Handbook of child psychology*, 2nd ed., 1933, 329 ff.
440. McDougall, W., *An introduction to social psychology*, 15th ed., 1923.
441. McDougall, W., *An outline of abnormal psychology*, 1926.
442. McFarland, R. A., and Huddelson, J. H., Neuro-circulatory reactions in the psychoneuroses, studied by the Schneider Method, *Amer. J. Psychiat.*, 1936, 93, 567–599.
443. McGraw, M., *Growth: a study of Johnny and Jimmy*, 1935.
444. McGregor, D., The major determinants of the prediction of social events, *J. Abn. & Soc. Psychol.*, 1938, 33, 179–204.
445. McKinnon, K. M., Consistency and change in behavior manifestations, *Child Developm. Monogr.*, 1942, No. 30.
446. McQueen-Williams, M., Maternal behavior in male rats, *Science*, 1935, 82, 67–68.
447. Mead, G. H., *Mind, self, and society: from the standpoint of a social behaviorist*, 1934.
448. Mead, M., *Coming of age in Samoa: a psychological study of primitive youth for western civilization*, 1928.
449. Mead, M., The concept of culture and the psychosomatic approach, 1945 (mimeographed).

450. Mead, M. (ed.), *Cooperation and competition among primitive peoples*, 1937.
451. Mead, M., *Growing up in New Guinea*, 1929.
452. Meltzer, H., Individual differences in forgetting pleasant and unpleasant experiences, *J. Educ. Psychol.*, 1930, 21, 399–409.
453. Merton, R. F., and Hall, C. S., Emotional behavior in the rat, *J. Comp. Psychol.*, 1941, 32, 191–204.
454. Messerschmidt, R., A quantitative investigation of the alleged independent operation of conscious and subconscious processes, *J. Abn. & Soc. Psychol.*, 1927, 22, 325–340.
455. Metfessel, M., Objective studies of roller canary song, *Psychol. Bull.*, 1935, 32, 716–717.
456. Metfessel, M., Psychological research with roller canaries, *Univ. So. Calif. Alumni Rev.*, 1938, 20, No. 2.
457. Miles, W. R., Age and human ability, *Psychol. Rev.*, 1933, 40, 99–123.
458. Mill, J., *Analysis of the phenomena of the human mind*, 1829.
459. Mill, J., *Autobiography*, 1873.
460. Miller, N. E., and Dollard, J., *Social learning and imitation*, 1941.
461. Minkowski, M., Sur les mouvements, les réflexes, les réactions musculaires du fœtus humain de 2 à 5 mois et leurs relations avec le système nerveux fœtal, *Rev. Neur.*, 1921, 37, 1105–1235.
462. Mitchell, T. W., *The psychology of medicine*, 1921.
463. Mitchill, S. L., *Med. Repository*, 1817, N.S., 3, 185–186.
464. Mittelmann, B., Psychogenic factors and psychotherapy in hyperthyreosis and rapid heart imbalance, *J. Nerv. & Ment. Dis.*, 1933, 77, 465–488.
465. Mittelmann, B., and Wolff, H. G., Affective states and skin temperature: experimental study of subjects with "cold hands" and Raynaud's syndrome, *Psychosom. Med.*, 1939, 1, 271–292.
466. Mittelmann, B., and Wolff, H. G., Emotions and skin temperature: observations on patients during psychotherapeutic (psychoanalytic) interviews, *Psychosom. Med.*, 1943, 5, 211–231.
467. Moede, W., *Experimentelle Massenpsychologie*, 1920.
468. Mohr, G. J., and Gundlach, R. H., The relation between physique and performance, *J. Exp. Psychol.*, 1927, 10, 117–157.
469. Moreno, J. L., Creativity and cultural conserves—with special reference to musical expression, *Sociometry*, 1939, 2, No. 2, 1–36.
470. Moreno, J. L., *Psychodrama*, 1946.
471. Moreno, J. L., *Who shall survive? A new approach to the problem of human interrelations*, 1934.
472. Morgan, C. D., and Murray, H. A., A method for investigating fantasies, *Arch. Neur. & Psychiat.*, 1935, 34, 289–306.
473. Morgan, C. M., The attitudes and adjustments of recipients of old age assistance in upstate and metropolitan New York, *Arch. Psychol.*, 1937, No. 214.
474. Morgan, J. J. B., Effect of non-rational factors on inductive reasoning, *J. Exp. Psychol.*, 1944, 34, 159–168.
475. Morgan, T. H., *Evolution and genetics*, 1925.
476. Morgan, T. H., *The physical basis of heredity*, 1919.
477. Mowrer, O. H., Animal studies in the social modification of organically motivated behavior. Film, Psychological Cinema Register, Lehigh Univ., Bethlehem, Pa., 1940.
478. Mowrer, O. H., Anxiety-reduction and learning, *J. Exp. Psychol.*, 1940, 27, 497–516.
479. Mowrer, O. H., A stimulus-response analysis of anxiety and its role as a reinforcing agent, *Psychol. Rev.*, 1939, 46, 553–566.
480. Muenzinger, K. F., Vicarious trial and error at a point of choice. I. A general survey of its relation to learning efficiency, *J. Genet. Psychol.*, 1938, 53, 75–86.

481. Mühl, A., The use of automatic writing in determining conflicts and early childhood impressions, *J. Abn. & Soc. Psychol.*, 1923, 18, 1–31.

482. Munroe, R. L., Prediction of the adjustment and academic performance of college students by a modification of the Rorschach method, *Appl. Psychol. Monogr.*, 1945, No. 7.

483. Munroe, R. L., (see 488, pp. 131 ff.).

484. Munroe, R. L., and Levy, J. (See 488, pp. 414 ff.).

485. Munroe, R., Lewinson, T. S., and Waehner, T. S., A comparison of three projective methods, *Char. & Pers.*, 1944, 13, 1–21.

486. Murchison, C. (ed.), *A handbook of social psychology*, chaps. 5, 6, 20, 21.

487. Murphy, G., and Likert, R., *Public opinion and the individual*, 1938.

488. Murphy, G., and Murphy, L. B., *Experimental social psychology*, 1931.

489. Murphy, G., Murphy, L. B., and Newcomb, T. M., *Experimental social psychology*, rev. ed., 1937.

490. Murphy, L. B., Personality development of a boy from age two to seven, *Amer. J. Orthopsychiat.*, 1944, 14, 10–20.

491. Murphy, L. B., *Social behavior and child personality*, 1937.

492. Murphy, L. B., and Ladd, H., *Emotional factors in learning*, 1944.

493. Murray, H. A., The effect of fear upon estimates of the maliciousness of other personalities, *J. Soc. Psychol.*, 1933, 4, 310–329.

494. Murray, H. A., *Explorations in personality*, 1938.

495. Murray, H. A., and Morgan, C. D., A clinical study of sentiments: I and II, *Genet. Psychol. Monogr.*, 1945, 32, 3–149.

496. Myers, F. W. H., *Human personality and its survival of bodily death*, 2 vols., 1903, chap. 6.

497. Naumburg, M., The drawings of an adolescent girl suffering from conversion hysteria with amnesia, *Psychiat. Quart.*, 1944, 18, 197–224.

498. Naumburg, M., A study of the psychodynamics of the art work of a nine-year-old behavior problem boy, *J. Nerv. & Ment. Dis.*, 1945, 101, 28–64.

499. Nehru, J., *The discovery of India*, 1946.

500. Newbold, W. R., Subconscious reasoning, *Proc. Soc. Psychical Res.*, 1896, 12, 11–20. The narrative will also be found in Myers, 496, I, 375–379.

501. Newcomb, T. M., The consistency of certain extrovert-introvert behavior patterns in 51 problem boys, *Teach. Coll. Contrib. Educ.*, 1929, No. 382.

502. Newcomb, T. M., *Personality and social change*, 1943.

503. Newman, F. B., The adolescent in social groups, *Appl. Psychol. Monogr.*, 1946, No. 9.

504. Newman, H. H., Freeman, F. N., and Holzinger, K. J., *Twins: a study of heredity and environment*, 1937.

505. Newstetter, W. I., Feldstein, M. J., and Newcomb, T. M., *Group adjustment: a study in experimental sociology*, 1938.

506. Nietzsche, F., *Beyond good and evil*, 1886.

507. Nietzsche, F., *The dawn of day*, 1886.

508. Novikova, A. A., [Conditioned inhibition and conditioned reflexes of "higher order" in children], *Medico-biol. Zhurnal*, 1929, 1, 120–131.

509. Osipova, V. N., [Unextinguished associated reflexes in children], *Voprosy Izucheniya i Vospitaniya Lichnosti*, 1927, 1–2, 33–46.

510. Page, M. L., The modification of ascendant behavior in pre-school children, *Univ. of Iowa Stud.: Stud. Child Welfare*, 1936, 12, No. 3.

511. Pallister, H., The negative or withdrawal attitude: a study in personality organization, *Arch. Psychol.*, 1933, No. 151.

512. Parker, G. H., *The elementary nervous system*, 1919.

513. Parker, G. H., *The origin, plan, and operational modes of the nervous system*, 1934.

514. Patrick, C., Creative thought in artists, *J. Psychol.*, 1937, 4, 35–73.

515. Patrick, C., Creative thought in poets, *Arch. Psychol.*, 1935, No. 178.

516. Pattie, F. A., A report of attempts to produce uni-ocular blindness by hypnotic suggestion, *Brit. J. Med. Psychol.*, 1935, 15, 230–241.
517. Pavlov, I. P., *Conditioned reflexes: an investigation of the physiological activity of the cerebral cortex*, 1927.
518. Pavlov, I. P., *Lectures on conditioned reflexes*, 1928.
519. Peatman, J. G., A study of factors measured by the Thorndike intelligence examination for high school graduates, *Arch. Psychol.*, 1931, No. 128.
520. Perrin, F. A. C., A theoretical and statistical study of alleged compensatory mental mechanisms, *Psychol. Bull.*, 1927, 24, 181–182.
521. Perry, R. B., *The thought and character of William James*, 2 vols., 1935.
522. Piaget, J., *The child's conception of the world*, 1929.
523. Piaget, J., Factors determining human behavior, in Harvard Tercentenary Publ., 1937, 32–48.
524. Piaget, J., *Judgment and reasoning in the child*, 1928.
525. Piaget, J., *The language and thought of the child*, 1926.
526. Piaget, J., *The moral judgment of the child*, 1932.
527. Pillsbury, W. B., *The fundamentals of psychology*, rev. ed., 1922.
528. Pintner, R., *Intelligence testing*, new ed., 1931.
529. Piotrowski, Z. A., The Rorschach method as a prognostic aid in the insulin shock treatment of schizophrenia, *Psychiat. Quart.*, 1941, 15, 807–822.
530. Piotrowski, Z. A., A simple experimental device for the prediction of outcome of insulin treatment in schizophrenia, *Psychiat. Quart.*, 1940, 14, 267–273.
531. Plant, J. S., *Personality and the cultural pattern*, 1937.
532. Podmore, F., *Mesmerism and Christian Science*, 1909.
533. Poetzl, O., Experimentell erregte Traumbilder in ihren Beziehungen zum indirekten Sehen, *Z. f. d. ges. Neurol. u. Psychiat.*, 1917, 37, 278–349.
534. Poffenberger, A. T., *Principles of applied psychology*, 1942.
535. Pope, A., *Essay on criticism*.
536. Postman, L., and Murphy, G., The factor of attitude in associative memory, *J. Exp. Psychol.*, 1943, 33, 228–238.
537. Pratt, K. C., Nelson, A. K., and Sun, K. H., The behavior of the newborn infant, *Ohio State Univ. Contrib. Psychol.*, No. 10, 1930.
538. Pressey, S. L., Janney, J. E., and Kuhlen, R. G., *Life: a psychological survey*, 1939.
539. Prince, M., *Clinical and experimental studies in personality*, rev. ed., 1939.
540. Prince, M., *The dissociation of a personality*, 2nd ed., 1913.
541. Prince, M., Suggestive repersonalization: the psychophysiology of hypnotism, *Arch. Neuro. & Psychiat.*, 1927, 18, 159–180.
542. Prince, M., *The unconscious*, 1914.
543. Prince, S. H., Catastrophe and social change—based upon a sociological study of the Halifax disaster, *Columbia Univ. Stud. in History, Economics, and Public Law*, 1920.
544. Prince, W. F., *The case of Patience Worth*, 2nd ed., 1929.
545. Prince, W. F., The Doris case of multiple personality, *Proc. Amer. Soc. Psychical Res.*, 1915, 9, and 1916, 10.
546. Proshansky, H. M., A projective method for the study of attitudes, *J. Abn. & Soc. Psychol.*, 1943, 38, 393–395.
547. Proshansky, H. M., and Murphy, G., The effects of reward and punishment on perception, *J. Psychol.*, 1942, 13, 295–305.
548. Pulver, M., *Symbolik der Handschrift*, 2nd ed., 1935.
549. Ranson, S. W., *The anatomy of the nervous system*, 1943.
550. Rapaport, D., *Emotions and memory*, 1942.
551. Rasmussen, K., *Across Arctic America*, 1927.
552. Raup, R. B., *Complacency: the foundation of human behavior*, 1925.
553. Razran, G. H. S., Attitudinal control of human conditioning, *J. Psychol.*, 1936, 2, 327-337.

554. Razran, G. H. S., Conditioned responses: an experimental study and a theoretical analysis, *Arch. Psychol.*, 1935, No. 191.

555. Razran, G. H. S., Semantic, synthetic, and phonetographic generalization of verbal conditioning, *Psychol. Bull.*, 1939, 36, 578.

556. Razran, G. H. S., Studies in configural conditioning: III. The factors of similarity, proximity, and continuity in configural conditioning, *J. Exp. Psychol.*, 1939, 24, 202–210.

557. Razran, G. H. S., Studies in configural conditioning: V. Generalization and transposition, *J. Genet. Psychol.*, 1940, 56, 3–11.

558. Rees, W. L., and Eysenck, H. J., A factorial study of some morphological and psychological aspects of human constitution, *J. Ment. Sci.*, 1945, 91, 8–21.

559. Révész, G., *The psychology of a musical prodigy*, 1925.

560. Reynolds, M. M., Negativism of pre-school children, *Teach. Coll. Contrib. Educ.*, 1928, No. 288.

561. Ribble, M. A., *The rights of infants*, 1943.

562. Rice, P. B., Mowrer, O. H., and Allport, G. W., Symposium: the ego and the law of effect, *Psychol. Rev.*, 1946, 53, 307–347.

563. Rich, G. J., A biochemical approach to the study of personality, *J. Abn. & Soc. Psychol.*, 1928, 23, 158–175.

564. Rich, G. J., Some relationships between personality and body chemistry, *J. Neurol. Psychopath.*, 1934, 14, 132–138.

565. Riess, B. F., Genetic changes in semantic conditioning, *J. Exp. Psychol.*, 1946, 36, 143–152.

566. Riess, B. F., Semantic conditioning involving the G.S.R., *J. Exp. Psychol.*, 1940, 26, 238–240.

567. Rivers, W. H. R., *Instinct and the unconscious*, 2nd ed., 1921.

568. Roberts, E., Thumb and finger sucking in relation to feeding in early infancy, *Amer. J. Dis. Children*, 1944, 68, 7–8.

569. Robinson, R. W., and Wheeler, R. R., *Great little Watertown*, 1930.

570. Rorschach, H., *Psychodiagnostics* (trans. by Paul Lemkau), 1942 (German original, 1921).

571. Rosanoff, A. J., *Manual of psychiatry*, 6th ed., 1927.

572. Rosanoff, A. J., Handy, L. M., and Plesset, I. R., The etiology of manic-depressive syndromes with special reference to their occurrence in twins, *Amer. J. Psychiat.*, 1935, 91, 725–762.

573. Rosenzweig, S., An outline of frustration theory, in Hunt, J. McV., *Personality and the behavior disorders*, 2 vols, 1944, I, 379–388.

574. Rosenzweig, S., The picture association method and its application in a study of reactions to frustration, *J. Pers.*, 1945, 14, 3–23.

575. Rosenzweig, S., and Sarason, S., An experimental study of the triadic hypothesis: reaction to frustration, ego-defense and hypnotizability, *Char. & Pers.*, 1942, 11, 1–19.

576. Rossman, J. J., *The psychology of the inventor*, 1931.

577. Rounds, G. H., Is the latent time in the Achilles tendon reflex a criterion of speed in mental reaction? *Arch. Psychol.*, 1928, No. 95.

578. Rowland, L. W., Will hypnotized persons try to harm themselves or others? *J. Abn. & Soc. Psychol.*, 1939, 34, 114–117.

579. Ruger, H. A., The psychology of efficiency, *Arch. Psychol.*, 1910, No. 15.

580. Ruggles, R., and Allport, G. W., Recent applications of the A-S reaction study, *J. Abn. & Soc. Psychol.*, 1939, 34, 518–528.

581. Rundquist, E. A., and Sletto, R. F., *Personality in the depression*, 1936.

582. Russel, R. W., and Dennis, W., Studies in animism: I. A standardized procedure for the investigation of animism, *J. Genet. Psychol.*, 1939, 55, 389–409.

583. Russell, B., *Bolshevism: practice and theory*, 1920.

584. Sanford, F. H., Speech and personality: a comparative case study, *Char. & Pers.*, 1942, 10, 169–198.
585. Sanford, R. N., The effects of abstinence from food upon imaginal processes: a preliminary experiment, *J. Psychol.*, 2, 129–136.
586. Sanford, R. N., The effects of abstinence from food upon imaginal processes: a further experiment, *J. Psychol.*, 1937, 3, 145–159.
587. Santayana, G., *Dialogues in limbo*, 1925.
588. Sarason, S. B., Dreams and thematic apperception test stories, *J. Abn. & Soc. Psychol.*, 1944, 39, 486–492.
589. Saudek, R., *Experiments with handwriting*, 1929.
590. Saudek, R., *The psychology of handwriting*, 1925.
591. Schachtel, A. H., The Rorschach test with young children, *Amer. J. Orthopsychiat.*, 1944, 14, 1–9.
592. Schachtel, E., The dynamic perception and the symbolism of form, *Psychiatry*, 1941, 4, 79–96.
593. Schafer, R., and Murphy, G., The role of autism in a visual figure-ground relationship, *J. Exp. Psychol.*, 1943, 32, 335–343.
594. Schanck, R. L., A study of a community and its groups and institutions conceived of as behaviors of individuals, *Psychol. Monogr.*, 1932, 43, No. 2.
595. Scheerer, M., Rothman, E., and Goldstein, K., A case of "idiot savant": an experimental study of personality organization, *Psychol. Monogr.*, 1945, 58, No. 269.
596. Schilder, P., *The image and appearance of the human body*, 1935.
597. Schneider, E. C., *Physiology of muscular activity*, 1933.
598. Schneider, H., *The Puritan mind*, 1930.
599. Schoenfeld, N., An experimental study of some problems relating to stereotypes, *Arch. Psychol.*, 19, No. 270.
600. Schreier, F., German aggressiveness: its reasons and types, *J. Abn. & Soc. Psychol.*, 1943, 38, 211–224.
601. Schwesinger, G. C., *Heredity and environment: studies in the genesis of psychological characteristics*, 1933.
602. Scott, J. F., Unpublished studies of heredity in dogs. Hamilton Station, Bar Harbor, Me.
603. Scott, W. B., *A history of land mammals in the western hemisphere.*
604. Sears, R. R., Experimental studies of projection, I, *J. Soc. Psychol.*, 1936, 7, 151–163.
605. Sears, R., Motivational factors in aptitude testing, *Amer. J. Orthopsychiat.*, 1943, 13, 468–493.
606. Sears, R. R., Survey of objective studies of psychoanalytic concepts, *Soc. Sci. Res. Council Bull.*, 1943, No. 51.
607. Seeleman, V., The influence of attitude upon the remembering of pictorial material, *Arch. Psychol.*, 1940, No. 258.
608. Seitz, C. P., The effects of anoxia on visual function: a study of critical frequency, *Arch. Psychol.*, 1940, No. 257.
609. Sells, S. B., The atmosphere effect: an experimental study of reasoning, *Arch. Psychol.*, 1936, No. 200.
610. Sender, S., The negative phase in relation to behavior of pubescent girls, Master's essay in Columbia Univ. Library, 1930.
611. Seward, G. H., *Sex and the social order*, 1946.
612. Seward, J. P., Note on the externalization of drive, *Psychol. Rev.*, 1942, 49, 197–199.
613. Shakow, D., and Rosenzweig, S., The use of the tautophone ("verbal summator") as an auditory apperceptive test for the study of personality, *Char. & Pers.*, 1940, 8, 216–226.
614. Shapiro, H. L., *Migration and environment*, 1939.

615. Shaw, F. J., Two determinants of selective forgetting, *J. Abn. & Soc. Psychol.*, 1944, 39, 434–445.
616. Shaw, F. J., and Spooner, A., Selective forgetting when the subject is not "ego-involved," *J. Exp. Psychol.*, 1945, 35, 242–247.
617. Sheehan, M. R., A study of individual consistency in phenomenal constancy, *Arch. Psychol.*, 1938, No. 222.
618. Sheldon, W. H., with the collaboration of S. S. Stevens, *The varieties of temperament*, 1942.
619. Sheldon, W. H., with the collaboration of S. S. Stevens and W. B. Tucker, *The varieties of human physique*, 1940.
620. Shepard, J. F., and Breed, F. S., Maturation and use in the development of an instinct, *J. Animal Behav.*, 1913, 3, 274–285.
621. Sherif, M., An experimental approach to the study of attitudes, *Sociometry*, 1937, 1, 90–98.
622. Sherif, M., *The psychology of social norms*, 1936.
623. Sherif, M., A study of some social factors in perception, *Arch. Psychol.*, 1935, No. 187.
624. Sherrington, C. S., *The integrative action of the nervous system*, 1906.
625. Shevach, B. J., Studies in perseveration: VII. Experimental results of tests for sensory perseveration, *J. Psychol.*, 1937, 3, 403–427.
626. Shinn, M., *The biography of a baby*, 1900.
627. Shirley, M., A behavior syndrome characterizing prematurely born children, *Child Developm.*, 1939, 10, 115–128.
628. Shirley, M., *The first two years: a study of twenty-five babies*, 1931–1933.
629. Shuttleworth, F. K., The physical and mental growth of girls and boys age 6 to 19 in relation to age at maximum growth, *Monogr. Soc. Res. Child Developm.*, 1939, 4, No. 3.
630. Skinner, B. F., The verbal summator as a method for the study of latent speech, *J. Psychol.*, 1936, 2, 71–107.
631. Smith, G. E., Malinowski, B., Spinder, H. J., Goldenweiser, A., *Culture: the diffusion controversy*, 1928.
632. Smith, G. M., Jr., Group factors in mental tests similar in material or in structure, *Arch. Psychol.*, 1933, No. 156.
633. Society for Psychical Research, Report on the census of hallucinations, *Proc. Soc. Psychical Res.*, 1894, 10, 25–422.
634. Spearman, C. E., *The nature of "intelligence" and the principles of cognition*, 1927.
635. Spearman, C. E., Theory of general factor, *Brit. J. Psychol.*, 1946, 36, 117–131.
636. Speer, M. C., Psychological analysis of the fear of death, Master's thesis in Columbia Univ. Library, 1928.
637. Spemann, H., *Embryonic development and induction*, 1938.
638. Spencer, H., *First principles*, 1888.
639. Spencer, H., *The principles of biology*, 2 vols., 1864–1867.
640. Spranger, E., *Types of men* (trans. from 5th German ed.), 1928.
641. Starbuck, E. D., Contributions to the psychology of religion, *Amer. J. Psychol.*, 1897, 8, 268–308, and 9, 70–124.
642. Starr, H. E., The hydrogen ion concentration of the mixed saliva considered as an index of fatigue and of emotional excitation, and applied to a study of the metabolic etiology of stammering, *Amer. J. Psychol.*, 1922, 33, 394–418.
643. Starr, H. E., Promethean constellations, *Psychol. Clin.*, 1933, 22, 1–20.
644. Stearns, A. W., Suicide in Massachusetts, *Ment. Hygiene*, 1921, 5, 752–777.
645. Stefansson, V., *Adventures in error*, 1936.
646. Steinberg, J., Relation between basal metabolic rate and mental speed, *Arch. Psychol.*, 1934, No. 172, 39.
647. Stekel, W., *Die Sprache des Traumes*, 1911.

648. Stern, W., Anfänge der Reifezert: ein Knabentagebuch in psychologischer Bearbeitung, 2nd ed., 1929.
649. Stern, W., Cloud pictures: a new method for testing imagination, *Char. & Pers.*, 1937, 6, 132–146.
650. Stern, W., *General psychology from the personalistic standpoint*, 1938.
651. Stevens, S. S., The operational definition of concepts, *Psychol. Rev.*, 1935, 42, 517–527.
652. Stevenson, R. L., A chapter on dreams, in *Across the plains: with other memories and essays*, 1892.
653. Stevenson, R. L., *Strange case of Dr. Jekyll and Mr. Hyde*, 1888.
654. Stockard, C. R., *The physical basis of personality*, 1931.
655. Stone, C. P., The initial copulatory response of female rats reared in isolation from the age of twenty days to the age of puberty, *J. Comp. Psychol.*, 1926, 6, 73–84.
656. Stone, C. P., and Barker, R. G., The attitudes and interests of pre-menarcheal and post-menarcheal girls, *J. Genet. Psychol.*, 1939, 54, 27–71.
657. Stone, L. J. (*Personal communication*).
658. Stratton, G. M., in *Problems of personality: studies presented to Dr. Morton Prince, pioneer in American psychopathology*, 1925.
659. Stratton, G. M., Some preliminary experiments on vision without inversion of the retinal image, *Psychol. Rev.*, 1896, 3, 611–617.
660. Strong, E. K., Jr., *Change of interests with age*, 1931.
661. Sullivan, H. S., Conceptions of modern psychiatry, *Psychiatry*, 1940, 3, 1–117.
662. Sumner, W. G., *Folkways*, 1907.
663. Sumner, W. G., and Keller, A. G., *The science of society*, 4 vols., 1927.
664. Symonds, P. M., An analysis of tact, *J. Educ. Res.*, 1930, 21, 241–255.
665. Symonds, P. M., and Chase, D. H., Practice vs. motivation, *J. Educ. Psychol.*, 1929, 20, 19–35.
666. Tawney, R. H., *Religion and the rise of capitalism*, 1925.
667. Taylor, W. S., and Martin, M. F., Multiple personality, *J. Abn. & Soc. Psychol.*, 1944, 39, 281–300.
668. Tennyson, A., *The idylls of the king* (Geraint and Enid).
669. Terman, L. M., with the collaboration of B. S. Burks and C. C. Miles, *Genetic studies of genius*, 3 vols., 1925, I.
670. Terman, L. M., and Miles, C. C., *Sex and personality*, 1936.
671. Terman, L. M., assisted by P. Buttenwieser, L. W. Ferguson, W. B. Johnson, and D. P. Wilson, *Psychological factors in marital happiness*, 1938.
672. Theophrastus, *Characters*.
673. Thomas, W. I., The behavior pattern and the situation, *Publ. Amer. Sociol. Soc.*, 1928, 22, 1–13.
674. Thorndike, E. L., *Educational psychology*, 3 vols., II. *The psychology of learning*, 1913.
675. Thorndike, E. L., *The measurement of intelligence*, 1925.
676. Thurstone, L. L., *A factorial study of perception*, 1944.
677. Thurstone, L. L., *The vectors of the mind*, rev. ed., 1944.
678. Thurstone, L. L., and Thurstone, T. G., A neurotic inventory, *J. Soc. Psychol.*, 1930, 1, 3–30.
679. Tinklepaugh, O. L., An experimental study of representative factors in monkeys, *J. Comp. Psychol.*, 1928, 8, 197–236.
680. Todd, T. W., The roentgenographic appraisement of skeletal differentiation, *Child Developm.*, 1930, 1, 298–310.
681. Toksvig, S., *Swedenborg*, 1947.
682. Tolman, E. C., A stimulus-expectancy need-cathexis psychology, *Science*, 1945, 101, 160–166.
683. Tolman, E. C., Prediction of vicarious trial-and-error by means of the schematic sow-bug, *Psychol. Rev.*, 1939, 46, 318–336.

BIBLIOGRAPHY

684. Tolstoy, L. N., *A confession*, 1882.
685. Torbek, V. M., [Errors in my book "Pedology in the pre-school period"], *Pedologia*, 1932, 1–2, 42–45.
686. Travis, L. E., *Speech pathology*, 1931.
687. Tredgold, A. F., *A textbook of mental deficiency* (amentia), 6th ed., 1937.
688. Troland, L. T., *The principles of psychophysiology*, 3 vols., 1929–1932, III.
689. Tryon, R. C., in Moss, F. A. (ed.), *Comparative psychology*, 1934.
690. Varendonck, J., *The psychology of day-dreams*, 1921.
691. Veblen, T., *The theory of the leisure class*, 1899.
692. Verry, E. E., A study of personality in pre-school play groups, *J. Soc. Forces*, 1925, 3, 645.
693. Vold, J. M., *Expériences sur les rêves et en particulier ceux d'origine musculaire et optique*, 1896.
694. Voth, A. C., An experimental study of mental patients through the autokinetic phenomenon, *Amer. J. Psychiat.*, 1947, 103, 793–805.
695. Waehner, T. S., Interpretation of spontaneous drawings and paintings, *Genet. Psychol. Monogr.*, 1946, 33, 3–70.
696. Wallen, R., Ego-involvement as a determinant of selective forgetting, *J. Abn. & Soc. Psychol.*, 1942, 37, 20–39.
697. Ward, J., *Psychological principles*, 1918.
698. Warner, W. L., *Yankee City Series*, 4 vols., 1941–1947.
699. Washburn, M. F., Ejective consciousness as a fundamental factor in social psychology, *Psychol. Rev.*, 1932, 39, 395–402.
700. Washburn, R. W., A study of the smiling and laughing of infants in the first year of life, *Genet. Psychol. Monogr.*, 1929, 6, 397–537.
701. Watson, J. B., *Behaviorism*, 1924.
702. Watson, J. B., *Psychology from the standpoint of a behaviorist*, 3rd ed., 1929.
703. Watt, H. J., *The common sense of dreams*, 1929.
704. Weill, B. C., *The behavior of young children of the same family*, 1928.
705. Weismann, A., *The evolution theory*, 1904.
706. Weiss, P., *Principles of development*, 1939.
707. Welch, L., The development of discrimination of form and area, *J. Psychol.*, 1939, 7, 37–54.
708. Welch, L., The space and time of induced hypnotic dreams, *J. Psychol.*, 1936, 1, 171–178.
709. Wells, F. L., Musical symbolism, *J. Abn. & Soc. Psychol.*, 1929, 24, 74–76.
710. Wells, F. L., and Woods, W. L., Outstanding traits: in a selected college group, with some reference to career interests and war records, *Genet. Psychol. Monogr.*, 1946, 33, 127–249.
711. Wells, W. R., Experiments in the hypnotic production of crime, *J. Psychol.*, 1941, 11, 63–102.
712. Wendt, G. R., An interpretation of inhibition of conditioned reflexes as competition between reaction systems, *Psychol. Rev.*, 19, 43, 258–281.
713. Wenger, M. A., An attempt to appraise individual differences in level of muscular tension, *J. Exp. Psychol.*, 1943, 32, 213–225.
714. Werner, H., *The comparative psychology of mental development*, 1940.
715. Westermarck, E. A., *The origin and development of the moral ideas*, 2 vols., 1906–1908.
716. Wexberg, E., *Individual psychology*, 1929.
717. Wheeler, W. M., Animal societies, *Sci. Mo.*, 1934, 39, 289–301.
718. White, R. W., An analysis of motivation in hypnosis, *J. Gen. Psychol.*, 1941, 24, 145–162.
719. White, R. W., A preface to the theory of hypnotism, *J. Abn. & Soc. Psychol.*, 1942, 37, 309–328.
720. White, R. W., in Hunt, J. McV., *Personality and the behavior disorders*, 2 vols., 1944, I, 214–251.

721. White, R. W., and Shevach, B. J., Hypnosis and the concept of dissociation, *J Abn. & Soc. Psychol.*, 1942, 37, 309–328.
722. Whitman, C., *The behavior of pigeons*, ed. by H. A. Carr, Carnegie Inst. Washington Publ., 1919, 257, 3.
723. Wilder, T. N., *The bridge of San Luis Rey*, 1927.
724. Wilke, W. H., An experimental comparison of the speech, the radio, and the printed page as propaganda devices, *Arch. Psychol.*, 1934, No. 169.
725. Williams, H. M., A factor analysis of Berne's "social behavior patterns in young children," *J. Exper. Educ.*, 1936, 4, 142–146.
726. Willoughby, R. R., Somatic homogamy in man, *Human Biol.*, 1933, 5, 691–705.
727. Wilson, E. B., *The cell in development and heredity*, 1925.
728. Wissler, C., *The American Indian*, 3rd ed., 1938.
729. Wissler, C., *Man and culture*, 6th printing, 1938.
730. Wissler, C., *North American Indians of the plains*, 3rd ed., 1934.
731. Wittels, F., *Sigmund Freud: his personality, his teaching and his school*, 1924.
732. Wolf, A., The dynamics of the selective inhibition of specific functions in neurosis: a preliminary report, *Psychosom. Med.*, 1943, 5.
733. Wolfe, J. B., Effectiveness of token-rewards for chimpanzees, *Comp. Psychol. Monogr.*, 1935, 13., No. 60.
734. Wolff, H. G., and Curran, D., Nature of delirium and allied states, *Arch. Neurol. & Psychiat.*, 1935, 38, 1175–1215.
735. Wolff, H. G., and Mittelmann, B., Experimental observations on changes in skin temperature associated with induced emotional states, *Trans. Amer. Neurol. Assoc.*, 1937, 63, 136–148.
736. Wolff, W., *The expression of personality: experimental depth psychology*, 1943.
737. Woodworth, R. S., *Dynamic psychology*, 1918.
738. Woodworth, R. S., *Experimental psychology*, 1939.
739. Woodworth, R. S., *Psychology*, 4th ed., 1940.
740. Woodworth, R. S., Racial differences in mental traits, *Science*, N.S., 31, 171–186.
741. Woodworth, R. S., Some criticisms of the Freudian psychology, *J. Abn. Psychol.*, 1917, 12, 174–194.
742. Worcester, E., in *Walter Franklin Prince: a tribute to his memory*, Boston Soc. for Psychical Res., 1935.
743. Yerkes, R. M., and Yerkes, A. W., *The great apes*, 1929.
744. Young, P. T., The experimental analysis of appetite, *Psychol. Bull.*, 1941, 38, 129–164.
745. Young, P. T., Studies of food preference, appetite and dietary habit. VI. Habit, palatability and diet as factors regulating the selection of food by the rat, *J. Comp. Psychol.*, 1946, 39, 139–176.
746. Zachry, C. B., *Emotion and conduct in adolescence*, 1940.
747. Zaluzhny, A. S., [Against the theory of two factors in pedology and in theories of children's collectives], *Pedologia*, 1932, 3, 17–22.
748. Zeigarnik, B., Über das Behalten von erledigten und unerledigten Handlungen, *Psychol. Forsch.*, 1927, 9, 1–86.
749. Zener, K., Conditioned response behavior (silent film), Durham, N. C., Duke Univ., 1937.

Name Index

Glossary and Subject Index

DEFINITIONS are adapted from the following sources: A Student's Dictionary of Psychological Terms, *4th ed., by Horace B. English;* Webster's New International Dictionary, *1926 ed.;* The American Illustrated Medical Dictionary, *19th ed., by W. A. Newman Dorland;* A Briefer General Psychology, *by Gardner Murphy; and the present text. The letter in parentheses after the word being indexed indicates the source.*

I have freely adapted all of these to my present purposes and, while deeply grateful to English and the other sources, have resorted to such liberty in modifying definitions that I must assume responsibility rather than holding others responsible for the present form.

Where terms appear dozens of times, as in the case of such terms as self, organic, Freudian, *and* culture, *only the main references are indexed.*

Abulia (E)—*Inability to will effectively:* 301
Acculturation (E)—(*1*) *Transmission of culture or parts of a culture from one social group to another and its fusion with or assimilation into the culture of the latter, e.g., adoption of firearms and horses by the American Indian;* (*2*) *the process by which an individual reared in one culture adapts himself to another:* 771
Acetylcholine (D)—*The acetic acid ester of choline chloride; substance liberated by the parasympathetic nervous system:* 81, 95, 96
Acquisitiveness (E)—*Tendency to crave possessions:* 241
Activity (E)—*Group of responses possessing at least a low degree of organization toward a specific result:* 421, 423
Activity cycles (T)—*Up-and-down swings of activity, usually of the type to which the term "rhythmic" is applied:* 111
Activity drives, 107, 280, 365, 405, 423, 458, 556, 718
See also Drive
Activity needs, 180, 400
See also Need
Adience (T)—*Tendency to immerse oneself ever more deeply in the present situation:* 237, 241, 298, 319, 374 ff.

Adolescence (E)—*Period from the beginning of puberty to the attainment of maturity; transitional stage during which the youth is becoming an adult man or woman. A few authors speak of adolescence as beginning with the close, not the beginning, of puberty. The period is defined in terms of development in many different functions which may be reached at different times, hence only conventional limits may be stated; but these usually are given as ages 12–21 for girls, 13–22 for boys:* 223, 507 ff., 602, 766, 799, 869 ff., 898
Adrenal (glands) (E)—*Endocrine glands lying near and above the kidneys:* 154, 744
Adrenin (BGP)—*The substance secreted by the medulla of the adrenal glands:* 81, 95
Affect (E)—*Any specific kind of feeling or emotion, especially when it is attached to a particular object:* 1, 19, 69, 358, 363
Affective anchorage, 366
See also Anchorage
Afferent—*Leading toward the central nervous system.*
After-discharge (E)—*Neural impulse continued after removal of the stimulus:* 82
Age, 40, 722, 766, 787, 794
Aggressiveness (E)—*Tendency to attack or*

injure, or to push one's own interests or ideas forward, or to carry out one's plans despite opposition: 115, 144, 208, 288 ff., 323, 554 ff., 594 ff., 656, 686, 703 ff., 740, 789 ff., 905

All-or-none (law) (E)—*A single nerve cell reacts with its maximum intensity for a given time if it reacts at all, regardless of the intensity of the stimulus:* 226 ff., 326, 412, 728 ff., 737 ff., 751, 759

Allergy (D)—*A condition of unusual or exaggerated specific susceptibility to a substance which is harmless in similar amounts for the majority of members of the same species:* 79

Ambivalence (E)—*(1) The fact that any object may have both of two opposite affective or feeling values for a person, especially, both love and hate. (2) The fact that two opposed ideas may have the same feeling value. Regarded as a fundamental law in psychoanalysis:* 303, 331, 425, 465, 498, 538, 586

Americans, 454, 817

Amnesia (E)—*Impairment of memory or memories:* 439, 441, 559

Anabolic, 64

See also Metabolism

Anal-sadistic (T)—*Type of personality postulated by Freud-Abraham theory of psychosexual development. Is generally restrained, parsimonious, meticulous, punctual:* 747

Anatomy (E)—*The proportions and spatial relations, especially when these are relatively fixed, of the several parts of a living being; the organism's shape and size. Also the science which studies these:* 147

Anchorage (T)—*Organization of a process about a specific center:* 346 ff., 508, 534 ff., 648, 777, 796, 805 ff.

Anthropology (E)—*Science of man; the comparative study of the chief divisions of man, including somatic characteristics, social habits and customs, linguistics, and prehistory:* 14, 15, 915, 926

Anthropotropic (T)—*Turning toward human beings:* 6

Anxiety (E)—*Emotional state arising when a continuing strong desire seems likely to miss its goal (McDougall). Fear is often used where anxiety is a more appropriate term. As a translation of the German Angst, it means anxious fear, a blend of both emotions:* 264, 536, 615, 636, 677 ff., 706, 805

Apollonian (T)—*Like Apollo; hence serene, gracious, beautiful:* 812

Arapesh, 243, 528, 538, 593, 809 ff., 905

Area factor (T)—*The tendency to use more or less space when making manual, postural, or gestural response:* 624 ff.

Art (T)—*Application of skill and taste to production:* 13, 284, 466, 518, 660, 781, 782

Ascendance-submission (T)—*The characteristic of tending to lead or follow in the group situation:* 554, 575, 604, 611, 626, 740

Aspiration level (T)—*The level to which one aspires:* 488, 539 ff., 609

Association, 321, 398

See also Learning

Associationism (E)—*A theory which starts with supposedly irreducible mental elements and makes development consist mainly in the combination of these elements:* 469 ff.

Assortative mating (T)—*Mating on a selective rather than a random basis:* 598

Atman (T)—*The super-individual cosmic entity which transcends both selfhood and materiality:* 920

Atom (T)—*The smallest particle into which matter or experience can be divided (philosophical):* 34, 59

Attention (E)—*Negatively, attention means a narrowing of the range of objects to which the organism is responding. The positive meaning is differently stated. Behaviorists speak of an increased concentration or integration of the forces of the organism in response to the stimulus attended to. Others speak of increased clearness or vividness of awareness of the content. Probably the same facts are intended by the two descriptions. Occasionally attention is identified with consciousness or awareness:* 347, 350, 354

Attitude (T)—*Readiness to act in one way rather than another. Careful analysis seems to show that it consists, at least in part, of partial and finer symbolic acts:* 279 ff., 442 ff., 489, 596 ff., 632 ff., 742, 784, 854

Attitudinal control, 201, 227, 291, 536

Authoritarian character (T)—*Character type which is rigid, operates in terms of hierarchy and domination, demands unquestioning submission to authority:* 857 ff.

Autism (T)—*Movement of cognitive processes in the direction of need satisfaction:* 341 ff., 406, 419, 473, 529 ff., 577 ff., 607, 753

Frustration tolerance (T)—*Capacity to endure frustration:* 316 ff.

Fugue (E)—*Period during which hysterical patients absent themselves from home. Behavior may not be superficially abnormal but may differ markedly from the patient's usual conduct. Usually a new name is adopted to correspond with the new personality:* 440, 732

Functional autonomy (T)—*The view that a developed action pattern may move forward and evolve in its own right. Adult motives are "self-sustaining contemporary systems, growing out of antecedent systems, but functionally independent of them" (G. W. Allport):* 144, 178

Fusion (E)—*Union of parts into a whole wherein the parts can be discriminated only with difficulty or not at all, or in which the whole functions as a unit:* 144, 178, 245, 397

Gain (W)—*Acquisition; accumulation:* 244, 570, 579

Gait (W)—*Manner of walking, running, or moving on foot:* 633

Galvanic skin reflex (BGP)—*Decrease in skin resistance occurring during upsets of the psychophysiological balance of the organism, as in emotion:* 82, 118, 155, 259

Gametes (E)—*Cells of the two sexes which combine to form a new organism:* 49

Gastrulation (D)—*The passage of the embryo from the blastula to the gastrula stage (the embryonic body takes on a pouch-like form):* 53

General intelligence (T)—*All-round capacity to profit by experience:* 361

Generality and specificity (T)—*The carry-over of a response tendency to a wide or narrow range of situations:* 134, 292, 350, 577, 608 ff., 631, 657 ff.

Generalization (E)—*Process or results of the process whereby one reaches a response applicable to a whole class, often on the basis of experience with a limited number of the class (an extended form of transfer):* 34, 204 ff., 292, 595 ff., 623 ff., 663, 664, 690

Gene (E)—*Factor in the germ plasm which determines that in a certain normal environment the organism will develop a certain specific trait:* 40, 148, 393, 458, 716, 722, 736, 899

Genetic (E)—*(1) Pertaining to heredity;*

(2) concerned with the origin—more broadly the origin, history, and development—of anything. Genetic psychology is the study of acts in terms of their origin and development in the individual (ontogenetic), or in the race (phylogenetic): 15, 911, 916

Genetic method (T)—*Analysis of phenomena in terms of their origin and development:* 15 ff., 333

Genetics (E)—*Science of heredity:* 18, 148, 714, 718

Genital type (T)—*Person who has achieved genital primacy:* 747

Genius (E)—*Ability of the very highest order, especially creative or inventive ability:* 384, 429, 569

Geotropism (E)—*A forced response of an organism, positive or negative, to a gravitational stress:* 6

Germ cells (BGP)—*Specialized cells, the sperm of the male, and the egg or ovum of the female, whose union in the fertilized egg gives rise to a new individual composed of body cells and germ cells:* 29, 49

Germany, 454, 496

Gestalt (BGP)—*A body of doctrine, developed especially by Wertheimer, Köhler, and Koffka, which maintains the necessity of interpreting phenomena as organized wholes rather than as aggregates of distinct and fixed elements. Direct translation from the German is* form: 350 ff., 621 ff., 638 ff., 666 ff., 767 ff., 890 ff., 915, 926

Gestaltungskraft (T)—*Organizing power:* 360, 408

Gesture (T)—*A motion of the body or limbs expressing an idea or attitude:* 265 ff., 314, 652, 655, 684 ff.

Gland (E)—*Organ for secreting into the blood and lymph a substance used in the body. Anatomically of two types: those with and those without outlets or ducts. Two general types of function are also distinguished: internal or endocrine secretion and external secretion through ducts. But it is now known that glands with ducts may also have an endocrine or internal secretion and that some tissues not having a gland-like structure produce a hormone:* 19, 94, 458

Gonad (E)—*Generic name for the sex gland in animals of either sex. It produces the sperm cells or the ova and certain specific sex hormones:* 76

Gradient (E)—*The rate of increase or decrease of a variable:* 38, 122, 600, 622, 641

Grant study, 722

Graphology (E)—*Method depicting the characteristics of a person from his handwriting:* 669, 688

Graves' disease (E)—*Excessive activity of the thyroid. There is excessive and incoordinated energy output, ready fatigue, incapacity for sustained effort:* 97, 98

Greece, 454, 585

Gregariousness (E)—*Tendency of animals to live in groups. By extension, the human tendency, sometimes considered instinctive, to take satisfaction in the company of others:* 240

Ground, 347
See also Figure and ground

Guilt (W)—*Offense; sin; fault:* 672

Gyroscope (T)—*An instrument which through rotation maintains its axis in a constant relation to a plane:* 901

Habit (E)—*An act regularly or customarily repeated:* 121, 453

Habitus (E)—*(1) Characteristic form of an organism, particularly the outward form and as predisposing to disease. (2) Form of an organism as the result of a mode of life:* 148

Hallucination (BGP)—*Extremely vivid image in any sensory field. Usually the term is used only when there is acceptance of the image, by the subject, as a present fact of the environment:* 402, 405

Handwriting (W)—*(1) Writing done with the hand; (2) the cast or form of writing peculiar to each hand or person:* 647, 651, 688, 694, 695

Harvard Growth Study, 722

Hate, 455, 549, 765, 768

Hebephrenia (T)—*Type of schizophrenia characterized by silly behavior; delusions are unsystematized (as contrasted with the systematized delusions of paranoia):* 13, 911

Hedonism (E)—*(1) Psychological doctrine that every act is motivated by the desire for pleasure or the aversion to unpleasure. (2) Ethical doctrine that it is a duty to seek pleasure and to avoid unpleasure or pain:* 303, 375

Heredity (E)—*Fact of transmission of traits through family lines. Within the germ cells of the parents, factors called genes determine that the offspring, if permitted a normal* environment for the species, will develop particular traits similar to those of the stock. Such a trait is said to be due to heredity: 15, 18, 238

Hierarchy (E)—*Graded organization or arrangement from "high" to "low":* 224, 237, 295, 304, 362, 397, 431, 629

Higher-order conditioning, 224 ff., 255
See also Second-order conditioning

Higher units (BGP)—*Group of stimuli reacted to as if they were a unit stimulus:* 472

Hindu, 601

Histology (W)—*Science which treats of the minute structure of tissues:* 39

Holism (T)—*The doctrine that the dynamics of a living whole permits of no differentiation of discrete elements:* 121, 124, 664

Homeostasis (D)—*A tendency to uniformity or stability in the normal body states of an organism:* 32, 40, 91, 107, 124, 489, 636, 739, 890

Homogamy (W)—*The tendency of like to mate with like:* 45

Honesty, 691

Hopi, 222, 747, 784, 806 ff., 852

Hormic principle (E)—*View which denies that behavior is completely explicable in purely mechanistic or physicochemical terms but asserts that it is always chracterized by a striving or urge toward a goal or end:* 125

Hormone (E)—*Chemical substance produced by one organ and carried by the blood or lymph to another where it produces a characteristic physiological effect:* 108

Hostility, 232
See also Aggressiveness

Hyperkinesis (W)—*Abnormally increased muscular movement:* 121

Hypertensions (D)—*Abnormally high tension; especially high blood pressure:* 79, 282

Hyperthyroidism (W)—*Excessive functional activity of the thyroid gland:* 78, 97, 153, 393

Hypnagogic (T)—*Pertaining to the process of falling asleep:* 392, 395

Hypnopompic (T)—*Pertaining to the process of waking up:* 392, 395

Hypnosis (E)—*Artificially induced state of extreme suggestibility. It is usually achieved through bodily relaxation accompanied by concentration upon a narrow range of ideas or objects:* 221, 433 ff., 442 ff., 470, 562 ff., 920 ff.

Hysteria (T)—*Nervous and mental disorder*

with a variety of symptoms: dissociation, suggestibility, somnambulisms, anesthesias, paralyses; when there is a loss of functions (as in anesthesia or paralysis) the psychoanalysts refer to conversion hysteria (repressed processes converted into symptoms): 318, 672, 677, 744, 804

Iatmul, 495, 789, 797, 802, 923

Id (BGP)—In Freudian terminology, the blindly striving, pleasure-seeking impulses that form the original basis of the personality. Later the ego develops out of part of the id: 740

Identification (T)—Tendency to view oneself as one with another person and to act accordingly: 491 ff., 525 ff., 541 ff., 653 ff., 759, 857, 887, 909 ff.

Ideomotor (T)—Pertaining to the process by which an idea leads to an act: 740

Idiosyncrasy (E)—Character, quality, or response peculiar to any individual: 131

Illumination (W)—Enlightenment, inspiration: 460

Image (E)—Experience similar to sensory experience, but arising in the absence of the usual external stimuli: 19, 293, 320 ff., 414, 469, 549 ff., 606, 626

Imageless thought (T)—The result of taking account of the nature of an object without the use of images: 409

Imagery, 19, 414, 469, 606
See also Image

Imaginary companions (T)—Companions created by the child's fantasy: 549, 587, 712 ff.

Imagination (BGP)—Manipulation of images: 19, 391 ff., 668, 674, 696, 702, 704

Imitation (E)—Action which copies, more or less exactly, the action of another: 216, 250, 289, 582

Incentive (E)—Any external stimulus which moves an organism to action: 87, 104

Incubation (T)—The process of subconscious preparation during which the accumulations of knowledge and skill are integrated: 462

India, 246, 911

Indissociation (T)—A term used by Piaget for the stage of undifferentiated blur, when dissociation or differentiation has not occurred: 336, 382

Individual psychology (E)—(1) Descriptive study of all a person's traits and qualities. (2) Theory and practice of the school of A.

Adler, which holds that human behavior is basically conditioned by the struggle for power or superiority: 584

Individualism (E)—Practice of exalting the interests of the individual: 527, 830, 906

Individuation (BGP)—Development of specific functions, replacing mass response: 343

Industrial Revolution (T)—The rapid development of industrialism since about 1750: 527, 613, 834, 837

Industrialism (T)—The high development of productive industries: 559, 616, 726, 901, 903, 906, 912

Infantilism (E)—Manifestation by an adult or adolescent of infantile traits, physical or mental: 850

Inferiority feeling (E)—Feeling that one falls short of one's fellows in some physical or mental trait: 564, 615, 634

Inhibition (E)—The stopping or restraining of a process from starting or continuing: 92, 229, 445, 472, 652

Insecurity (T)—Uneasiness in the face of physical or mental threat: 631, 696, 840, 908

Insight (E)—Realization of the meaning or use of an object or situation: 344, 399, 443, 461, 469, 659

Institution (E)—A social arrangement possessing a high degree of organization so embodied in rules, customs, rituals, or laws as to persist with relative independence of the individual members: 6

Integration (E)—Process of bringing together and unifying parts into a whole: 16, 19, 66 ff., 342 ff., 490, 620, 628

Intellectual (T)—Pertaining to the cognitive processes: 601, 717

Intelligence (T)—Ability to profit by experience: 456 ff., 473, 488, 554, 613, 643, 686, 718

Interest (E)—(1) The attitude with which one attends to anything; the feeling accompanying attention. (2) Especially in the plural, interests are dispositions defined in terms of objects which one easily and freely attends to or which one regards as making a difference to oneself: 144, 283, 611, 719 ff.

Intermediary metabolism (T)—Transition stages in the metabolism of food: 79

Interoceptor (E)—Sense organ inside (in contrast with at, or near the surface of) the body: 500, 596

by its own nature or internal structure: 86 ff., 343, 363, 412, 440 ff.

Motor theory of consciousness (T)—*The theory that consciousness is an expression of motor activity (e.g., that awareness of an object is muscular adjustment to it)*: 354

Multiple personality (E)—*Condition in which the normal organization of mental life is disintegrated or split up into distinct parts or subpersonalities, each with a fairly complicated organization of its own*: 433, 559

Muscle (D)—*An organ which by contraction produces the movements of an animal organism*: 19

Mutation (E)—*Process whereby offspring congenitally differ in some well-marked and considerable way from the stock from which they spring*: 16, 40 ff.

Myograph (W)—*Instrument for making a record of intensity, velocity, etc., of a muscular contraction*: 354

Mysticism (E)—*Doctrine that there is a kind of knowledge independent of perception or reflection*: 402, 520, 584, 599

Myxedema (W)—*A disease due to failure of the thyroid function during the adult period*: 97

Narcissism (E)—*The love of one's own personality, deeds, and qualities*: 492, 499, 536, 553 ff., 602, 609, 635, 699

Need (E)—*The lack of something which if present would tend to give satisfaction*: 631, 635, 670, 704, 710

Need pattern (T)—*Total organization of the needs of the organism*: 395, 397, 401

Negative phase (of puberty) (T)—*Withdrawal from social participation*: 508

Negativism (E)—*Active annulment of tendency to carry out suggested acts*: 217, 292 ff., 348, 505, 587, 602

Negro, 230, 455, 534, 703, 759, 816, 873

Neo-Platonists (T)—*Adherents of a philosophical school which developed Plato's doctrines in a mystical direction*: 919, 922

Neurasthenia (E)—*Ailment characterized by weakness and a general lowering of bodily and mental tone*: 566

Neurobiotaxis (T)—*Tendency of cell bodies during development to migrate in the direction from which they habitually receive their stimuli*: 171

Neurocirculatory instability (T)—*In-*

stability of the circulatory system because of faulty neural control*: 137, 320

Neurosis (E)—*Mental disorder of ill-defined character but generally milder in nature than a psychosis*: 211, 527 ff., 568, 581, 719 ff., 905 ff.

New England, 11, 827 ff.

Node (A)—*A point at which subsidiary parts center; e.g., a point, line, or surface of a vibrating body marked by absolute or relative freedom from vibratory motion; a point of concentrated energy or activity*: 4, 38, 83 ff., 120, 228, 412

Nomogram (D)—*A chart or diagram on which a number of variables are plotted, forming a computation chart for the solution of complex numerical formulae*: 39

Norm (E)—*A standard type or pattern from which continuous departures are possible in opposite directions*: 769

Objectivity (W)—*Freedom from bias; impersonality*: 340, 674

Obsessive-compulsive (neurosis) (T)—*Mental disorder with recurrent obsession accompanied by irresistible impulses to perform apparently unreasonable actions*: 672

Occupational (hierarchy) (E)—*Serial arrangement of occupational groups according to an indefinite combination of criteria; social esteem, financial reward, intelligence required*: 727

Oedipus (complex) (E)—*Repressed desire for incestuous relationships, held by psychoanalysts to be practically universal; especially the male child's desire for the mother, and accompanying fear and hate for the father. In theoretical discussion it includes the Electra complex (an analogous desire of the female child for the father) and all similar formations*: 532 ff., 635, 919

"Omnipotence of thought" (T)—*Belief that thought can unerringly influence the course of events*: 383

Ontogenetic (E)—*Pertaining to origin and development within the life history of the individual*: 919

Operationism (T)—*The definition of processes in terms of the observational steps by which they are known (rejecting all that cannot be specified in terms of such steps)*: 351

Order of birth, 585 ff., 869

Organic (E)—*(1) Pertaining to an organ or organism; that which consists of or has organs.*

motivations which are not open to conscious inspection by the person himself, though these motivations are of the same order as the wishes or desires of actual experience, and in some cases were formed in past experience. These motivations are designated by the term unconscious wishes or desires. They are kept unconscious, according to this view, because of conflict with other more advantageously situated or powerful desires. But through consciousness or behavior certain symbolic representations of themselves and in other ways give evidence of their existence: 186, 323 ff., 404 ff., 540, 584, 656 ff., 793 ff., 903 ff.

Psychodrama (T)—A dramatic technique used for personality study and psychiatric therapy, developed by J. L. Moreno: 877 ff.

Psychogenic (E)—Having an origin in experience as contrasted with an organic origin: 150

Psychognostics (W)—(1) Character analysis through study of body form; (2) any penetrating study of the psyche: 147

Psychoneurosis (E)—Neurosis in which functional or psychogenic factors seem clearly to predominate and for which psychotherapy seems indicated: 738

Psychopathology (E)—The investigation of morbid mental conditions: 13

Psychosis (E)—A relatively severe mental disease, i.e., one in which there is a loss or disorder in mental processes: 365, 550, 727, 905

Psychosomatic (E)—(1) Pertaining to the relations between the visible organic structure and mental phenomena however defined. (2) Being both mental and bodily, having attributes similar to those attributed to both mind and body: 78, 132, 365, 550 ff., 672, 724

Puberty (E)—Period during which the generative organs become capable of functioning and the person takes on the secondary sex characters: 99 ff., 218, 288, 507, 725, 798, 853

Pueblo Indians, 591

Purposivism (E)—Doctrine that purpose rather than simply physical analysis is the clue to behavior: 125 ff.

Quale (T)—The specific and unique quality of a thing: 83

Quantum (W)—An indivisible unit. (In the emission or absorption of energy by atoms or molecules, the process is not continuous but takes place by steps, each step being the emission or absorption of an amount of energy called the quantum): 41, 122, 123

Questionnaire (E)—A prepared set of questions asked of a person: 605, 610, 612, 625, 784

Race (E)—Group of individuals marked off from others by their possession of common inherited biological or psychological traits: 230, 364, 385, 534, 654, 792, 872

Radicalism (T)—Tendency to favor profound changes in the social order: 668

Radix (T)—Root of the personality (Wertheimer): 646

Rage (W)—Strong anger: 120, 556

Rating (E)—Estimate of a person's qualities or character by himself or another. The estimate may be purely qualitative (asserting presence or absence of the trait) or quantitative. In the latter case, the strength of the trait is judged in terms of some conventional numerical scale composed of such divisions as Very Strong, Strong, Average, Weak, Very Weak, or of direct comparison with other persons: 156, 605 ff., 611, 624

Rationalism (E)—Name for various philosophical positions which exalt the value of reason: 926

Rationalization (E)—Process of finding plausible reasons to account for one's practices or beliefs: 230, 531, 540, 547, 781, 861

Reaction formation (E)—Development in behavior of a trend directly opposed to one in the unconscious (psychoanalysis): 360, 551, 634, 747

Realism (T)—Tendency to accept what is experienced as real (Piaget): 340, 365, 387, 539

Reality principle (T)—According to Freud, the regulation of conduct by regard for reality: 340, 389, 416

Recentering (T)—Reorientation toward new points of anchorage: 430

Redintegration (E)—The reestablishment of a whole. Hamilton put forward a principle of redintegration as basic in learning, to the effect that if several experiences—A, B, and C—have formed a whole, the recurrence of any one tends to bring back the others. Hollingworth's redintegration formula holds that a single element of a former event serves to

Movement which patients cannot forego making under certain conditions: 303, 314

Time lag, 80 ff., 124, 235

Trait (E)—*Anything by means of which one person may be distinguished from another:* 506 ff., 516, 604, 621 ff., 641, 676, 749, 751

Trance (E)—*General term for sleep-like states, generally abnormal ones. Sensitivity is reduced, with loss or alteration in knowledge of what is happening. Trances may be hypnotically induced and are frequent in hysteria:* 802

Transfer (BGP)—*Effect of training in one function upon performance in another function or upon performance of the same function in another part of the body:* 204 ff., 549, 575, 620 ff., 653 ff., 691, 711, 766

Transference (E)—*"Displacement of an affect, either positive or negative, from one person on to the psycho-analyst" (E. Jones):* 422, 582

Transvestitism (T)—*Wearing of clothing of the opposite sex (or, in psychoanalysis, the desire to wear it):* 495

Trauma (E)—*Injury or wound, especially "mental injury" or shock:* 224 ff., 254 ff., 549, 606, 723 ff., 738, 760, 898

Triadic hypothesis (T)—*Hypothesis that tendencies to repression, to hypnotizability, and to impunitiveness are interrelated:* 372, 562

Tropism (E)—*Mechanically determined or forced movement of a single cell and analogous movements of groups of cells or whole organisms; movement whose extent is a direct function of the stimulus:* 92, 99

Type (E)—*(1) Central form about which variations center. This is a pre-Darwinian concept but is evidently still the dominant one in most thinking. (2) In a given group, persons having a majority of the characters which are common or peculiar to the group are said to be typical—at least relatively—of that group. Type is thus a matter of averages. It is that which marks off or characterizes a group of persons:* 20, 48, 59, 81 ff., 393, 486, 546, 579 ff., 594, 709, 716, 734

U-curves (T)—*Equivalent to bimodal curves in which the extreme right and left ends are cut off:* 227

Unconscious (BGP)—*In Freudian psychoanalysis, the entire mass of psychic processes which is unable to enter consciousness:* 594

Uniqueness (W)—*The quality of being without a like or equal:* 43

Unstriped muscle, 596
  See also Viscera

Urban (W)—*Belonging to the city or town:* 566, 824 ff., 833 ff., 838, 839, 869 ff.

Valence (W)—*The degree of power which exists between certain bodies or substances, causing them to unite or produce a specific effect upon each other:* 85, 545

Value (E)—*That which makes objects desired or desirable or to be sought after; worth:* 182, 264 ff., 510, 616, 649, 666, 765, 906

Vedantists (T)—*Early philosophers who gave a pantheistic interpretation to the sacred texts of India:* 922

Vegetative (E)—*Those activities of an organism common to plants and animals:* 116 ff.

Viscera (BGP)—*The vital organs of the chest and abdominal cavities; also the glands, arterial walls, and other organs innervated by the autonomic nervous system:* 82, 355 ff., 484 ff., 508 ff., 744

Visceral drives (T)—*Drives which depend directly on varying visceral conditions:* 87, 105 ff., 131, 376

Voice, 633, 647, 649, 745

VTE behavior (T)—*Vicarious trial and error, i.e., trial and error not actually involving overt trials:* 297 ff., 636, 637

Will (T)—*Regulation of behavior by internal symbols:* 290 ff., 316, 340, 363, 394, 400, 429 ff., 443, 592, 668, 917

Yankee City, 524

Zuñi, 793, 806 ff.